STUDIES ON THE CIVILIZATION
AND CULTURE OF
NUZI AND THE HURRIANS

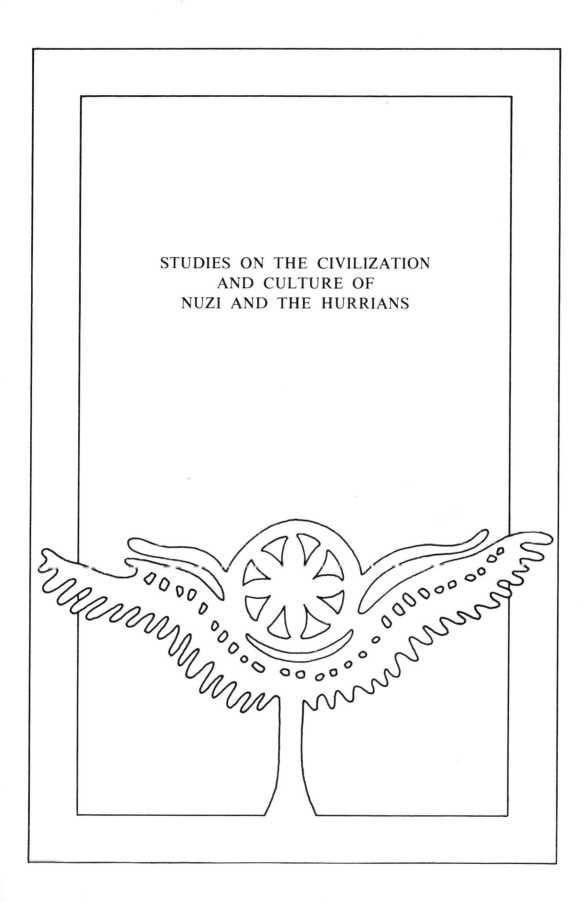

STUDIES ON THE CIVILIZATION AND CULTURE OF NUZI AND THE HURRIANS

In Honor Of

ERNEST R. LACHEMAN

on his
Seventy-Fifth Birthday
April 29, 1981

Edited by

M. A. MORRISON
and
D. I. OWEN

WINONA LAKE, INDIANA
EISENBRAUNS

Library of Congress Cataloging in Publication Data

Studies on the civilization and culture of Nuzi and the Hurrians.

English, French, German, or Italian.
Includes index.
1. Nuzi (Iraq)—Addresses, essays, lectures. 2. Hurrians—Addresses, essays, lectures. 3. Lacheman, Ernest René, 1906- —Addresses, essays, lectures. I. Lacheman, Ernest René, 1906- . II. Morrison, M. A. (Martha A.) III. Owen, D. I. (David I.)
DS70.5.N9S88 935 81-15123
ISBN 0-931464-08-0 AACR2

Eisenbrauns

56.00

63390

Acknowledgments

The Lacheman Anniversary Volume was begun originally by D. I. Owen in 1978. M. A. Morrison joined as co-editor shortly thereafter. The editorial duties were shared and the swift completion of the volume in accordance with the original schedule could not have been accomplished without the complete and cordial cooperation between them. However, their task was greatly facilitated by the publisher, Jim Eisenbraun, and his colleagues at the press, Beverly Turner and Rick Clark. Their care and efficiency in the preparation of the text cannot be overemphasized. Jim's personal interest in and enthusiasm for the volume coupled with his knowledge of the field of Near Eastern Studies allowed him to solve problems on the spot thereby eliminating delays that might otherwise have been necessitated by correspondence with the editors.

The editors wish to express their gratitude to those who offered special assistance. Professor Karlheinz Deller generously shared his exhaustive Nuzi files with us along with numerous observations on the texts published in this volume. Professor Frank R. Jacoby, Professor Leonard Muellner, and Ms. Danielle Chouet carefully read the German, French, and Italian contributions and suggested a number of editorial improvements. Ms. Diana L. Stein prepared the drawing of the seal of Saustattar that appears on the endpieces of this volume. Finally, the editors' respective academic departments, Classical and Oriental Studies (Brandeis University) and Near Eastern Studies (Cornell University) provided the logistic support without which the production of the volume would have been infinitely more difficult.

In closing it should be noted that the diversity of contributions to the Lacheman Anniversary Volume precluded the imposition of a uniform style throughout. Although this was clearly desirable, a much longer production time would have been required. It was assumed that the reader, as well as the contributor, preferred prompt publication over uniformity of style in the footnotes, references and transliterations.

To

Ernest R. Lacheman

on the occasion of his 75th birthday

April 29, 1981

CONTENTS

Ernest René Lacheman, A Tribute

Nuzi studies and the name Ernest R. Lacheman are almost synonymous. From his earliest graduate school days in 1930 at Harvard to the present in his retirement, his direct involvement with Nuzi studies has continued without interruption. As a disciple of R. H. Pfeiffer at Harvard and E. M. Chiera at the Oriental Institute, he was associated closely with those who were the excavators and epigraphers of the site. While Nuzi studies were in their infancy, he worked on the tablets literally as they came out of the shipping crates at both the Harvard Semitic Museum and the Oriental Institute. During this time he amassed a comprehensive collection of Nuzi data and an intimate knowledge of Nuzi civilization. When he assumed the responsibility of publishing the Nuzi tablets, he undertook this task with single-minded devotion. The result of his years of dedicated labor represents a prodigious achievement which has indebted two generations of scholars and students to him.

Prof. Lacheman was born on April 29, 1906, in Geneva, Switzerland. His advanced academic training in the United States was exemplary. He received a B.D. from Yale in 1929 and a Ph.D. from Harvard in 1935. From 1932-35 he was a research assistant at the Oriental Institute. This period was especially important to him, in large part because of the close personal relationship that he enjoyed with E. M. Chiera, whose profound influence on his career Prof. Lacheman gratefully acknowledges.

Even though fate and the Great Depression caused great hardships in the academic world, Prof. Lacheman was resourceful and remained undaunted. During this lean period, he accepted a position as minister to the French Church at Torrington, Connecticut, where he served until 1942. C. H. Gordon recalls this time with admiration for Prof. Lacheman's dedication to his studies. Although there was little hope of any position in Assyriology, Prof. Lacheman continued his active research on the Nuzi texts. It was in this period that they collaborated on "The Nuzu Menology" (*ArOr* 10 [1938]), and Prof. Lacheman perfected the special copying method which has become his hallmark as a copyist.

In 1942 he joined the faculty at Wellesley College where, in 1958, he achieved the rank of Professor of Biblical History. It was at Wellesley that he pursued a distinguished career as a warm and generous teacher to countless young women who benefited from his insights into the Biblical world via his intimate knowledge of Assyriology. In Biblical History classes he would produce a tablet, a sherd, or other small artifact from seemingly bottomless pockets to emphasize a point. Beloved by his students, he was a frequent guest at the Tuesday night faculty dinners where he would fascinate groups with tales of Nuzi and the ancient Near East. At the same time, he pursued his professional activities energetically. On occasion, he ventured into the controversial such as when he joined the fray over the date of the recently discovered Dead Sea Scrolls. However, his first love continued to be Nuzi. In spite of a heavy teaching load he continued to publish volume after volume of texts in copy and/or transliteration. Indeed, Prof. Lacheman singlehandedly maintained Nuzi studies in the post-Second World War years through his regular publications.

Prof. Lacheman's center of activity at Wellesley was a remarkable complex of rooms in the basement of Green Hall. There, in a laboratory housing his photographic equipment, areas for filing and storage, and a classroom filled with books and tablets, he worked, making latex molds and casts of tablets, photographing, processing and even publishing his own volumes. There, too, he conducted seminars and tutored interested students in Akkadian. M. Morrison remembers with deep affection her introduction to Assyriology in the midst of hundreds of Nuzi tablets. The months that Prof. Lacheman generously spent with her reading tablets, providing guidance, and sharing his learning won her to the field of Assyriology. Nor was she alone. Many other Wellesley students pursued graduate studies in Old Testament, Ancient Near East or Classics because of Prof. Lacheman's influence and support.

When Cyrus H. Gordon joined the faculty at nearby Brandeis University in 1956, a new phase began in Prof. Lacheman's career. Gordon had never lost interest in Nuzi, a field which he, too, had pioneered, and the study of Nuzi texts was always a part of his teaching curriculum. Prof. Lacheman's availability and interest was a natural attraction for Gordon's doctoral students and a significant number of these students found their way to that unique basement workshop at Wellesley to work with Prof. Lacheman. D. I. Owen recalls fondly the long hours he spent with Prof. Lacheman during which he learned to photograph, copy, and make casts of texts and cherishes the direct access to the Nuzi material that was afforded him via Prof. Lacheman's familiarity with both published and unpublished sources.

The culmination of Prof. Lacheman's career came in 1969 when he joined his colleague and friend C. H. Gordon in the Department of Mediterranean Studies at Brandeis University as Professor of Assyriology. There, after retiring *Emeritus* from Wellesley in 1971, he was able to teach graduate classes and to supervise a series of doctoral dissertations until his "second" retirement in 1974.

From that time until the present, in spite of serious problems with his health, he has steadfastly continued his Nuzi studies. Aside from publishing the Nuzi tablets in Baghdad and at Yale, he has completed a massive compilation, *The Personal Names from the Kingdom of Arrapha* (= *PNA*), which includes all personal names from published and unpublished texts and collations of many earlier known texts. Nearly ready for press are the remaining Nuzi texts in Chicago, *JEN* 7, and the long-awaited publication of the *SMN* texts at Harvard, *EN* 9. Still energetic and forward-looking, he plans a series of special studies on Nuzi. Few in our field can boast of such a continuity of commitment and productivity.

We the editors take particular pride in presenting this volume to him. As a teacher, friend and collaborator, Ernest René Lacheman, over the long years, has maintained a steadfast relationship with us and has followed with genuine interest the development of our careers and scholarship. It is also he who, with characteristic generosity, supplied the unpublished materials which formed the cores of our respective Brandeis University dissertations. We sincerely hope that this tribute will somehow substitute for an otherwise unrepayable debt.

D. I. Owen
M. A. Morrison
C. H. Gordon

One Hundred and Ninety First Meeting of the
American Oriental Society
Boston, Massachusetts
March 16, 1981

Bibliography of Ernest R. Lacheman

Compiled by

M. A. Morrison and D. I. Owen

BOOKS

Joint Expedition with the Iraq Museum at Nuzi. Miscellaneous Texts. PBST 6, American Schools of Oriental Research, New Haven, 1939.

Excavations at Nuzi. IV. Miscellaneous Texts from Nuzi. Part I. HSS 13, Harvard University Press, Cambridge (Masschusetts), 1942 (with R. H. Pfeiffer).

Excavations at Nuzi. V. HSS 14, Harvard University Press, Cambridge (Massachusetts), 1950.

Excavations at Nuzi. VI. The Administrative Archives. HSS 15, Harvard University Press, Cambridge (Massachusetts), 1955.

Excavations at Nuzi. VII. Economic and Social Documents. HSS 16, Harvard University Press, Cambridge (Massachusetts), 1958.

Excavations at Nuzi. VIII. Family Law Documents. HSS 19. Harvard University Press, Cambridge (Massachusetts), 1962.

Excavations at Nuzi. IX. Real Estate Documents, Loans and Lawsuits. (In preparation).

Joint Expedition with the Iraq Museum at Nuzi. 7. (In preparation).

Personal Names from the Kingdom of Arrapḫa. (In preparation).

ARTICLES AND REVIEWS

"New Nuzi Texts and a New Method of Copying Cuneiform Tablets," *JAOS* 55 (1935) 429-31. Pl. 1-6.

"SU = Šiqlu," *JAOS* 57 (1937) 181-84.

"An Omen Text from Nuzi," *RA* 34 (1937) 1-8.

"Note on Ruth 4:7-8," *JBL* 56 (1937) 53-56.

"Nuzi Royal Seal Impressions," *JBL* 57 (1938) XIX.

"The Nuzu Menology," *ArOr* 10 (1938) 51-64 (with C. H. Gordon).

"Epigraphic Evidence of the Material Culture of the Nuzians," in R. F. S. Starr, *Nuzi. Report on the Excavations at Yorgan Tepa near Kirkuk, Iraq, Conducted by Harvard University in Conjunction with the American Schools of Oriental Research and the University Museum of Philadelphia 1927-31. Volume I. Text*, Harvard University Press, Cambridge (Massachusetts), 1939, 528-44.

"Nuziana I. Tablettes scolaires," *RA* 36 (1939) 81-95.

"Nuziana II. Textes diverse," *RA* 36 (1939) 113-219.

"Nuzi Geographical Names. I. Names of Countries," *BASOR* 78 (1940) 18-23.

"A Matter of Criticism in Assyriology," *BASOR* 80 (1940) 22-27.

"Nuzi Geographical Names. II," *BASOR* 81 (1941) 10-15.

"A propos of Criticism in Assyriology," *BASOR* 81 (1941) 21-22.

"Two Babylonian Parallels to the Prodigal Son Parable," *JBL* 60 (1941) XIII.

"Note on the Word *ḫupšu* at Nuzi," *BASOR* 86 (1942) 36-37.

"The Nuzi Date Formulae," *JAOS* 62 (1942) 221.

"Some Remarks about the City of Nuzi," *JAOS* 62 (1942) 221.

"Nuzi Personal Names," *JNES* 8 (1949) 48-55.

"A Matter of Method in Hebrew Palaeography," *JQR* 40 (1949-50) 15-39.

"The Renaissance of Biblical Theology, A Review Article," *JBR* 19 (1951) 71-75.

"The Authorship of the Book of Zephaniah," *JNES* 9 (1950) 137-42 (with L. P. Smith).

"Can Hebrew Palaeography be called 'Scientific'?" *JQR* 42 (1952) 377-85.

"Hebrew Palaeography Again," *JQR* 44 (1953-54) 116-22.

"The So-Called Bar Kokba Letter," *JQR* 45 (1954) 285-90.

"A propos of Isaiah 7:14," *JBR* 22 (1954) 43.

"The word *šudutu* in the Nuzi Tablets," *Proceedings of the 25th International Congress of Orientalists*, Moscow, 1960, 233-38.

"New Light from Nuzi," *JBL* 82 (1963) 148.

Review of B. L. Goff, "Symbols of Prehistoric Mesopotamia," *Wellesley Alumnae Magazine*, May, 1964.

"Les Tablettes de Kerkouk au Musee d'Art et d'Histoire de Geneve," *Genava* 15 (1967) 5-22.

"The Seraphim of Isaiah 6," *JQR* 59 (1969) 71-72.

Review of *Enuma Eliš. The Babylonian Epic of Creation. JAOS* 89 (1969) 663.

"Le palais et la royauté de la ville de Nuzi," *RAI 19* (1971) 359-71.

"Tablets from Arrapḫe and Nuzi in the Iraq Museum," *Sumer* 32 (1976) 113-48.

"Nuzi Miscellaniana," *Kramer Anniversary Volume* (*AOAT* 25 1976) 311-12.

"Texts from Arrapḫa and from Nuzi in the Yale Babylonian Collection," *Studies on the Civilization and Culture of Nuzi and the Hurrians in Honor of Ernest R. Lacheman on his Seventy-Fifth Birthday*, Eisenbrauns, Winona Lake (Indiana), 1981, 377-432 (with D. I. Owen).

PART ONE
GENERAL STUDIES

Notes on a Pair of Matching Texts: A Shepherd's Bulla and An Owner's Receipt*

TZVI ABUSCH
Brandeis University

The purpose of this note is to share the results of an examination of the inscribed and sealed clay container *SMN* 1854 (*HSS* 16, no. 449) and the related tablet *SMN* 2096 (*HSS* 16, no. 311).[1] The results are given in the form of a transliteration and translation of the documents. In view of the various readings that have been suggested previously[2] and of the constructions that have been built on or supported by one or both of the texts,[3] a new edition hardly needs justification. The present edition is accompanied by two observations—one relating to the writing, the other to the seal impressions and function of the documents. Drawings of the seal impressions and photographs of the tablets are appended (fig. 1 and pls. 1 & 2).[4]

*These notes have benefitted substantially from discussions with Gernot Wilhelm; my warmest thanks to him. I also wish to thank Alan Wachman for drawing the seal impressions, Sharon White for preparing the photographs, and Martha Morrison for sharing her knowledge of Nuzi. My thanks to the officers of the Harvard Semitic Museum: Frank M. Cross, Director; Carney Gavin, Curator; and William L. Moran, Curator of Tablets, for inviting me to work on the Nuzi tablets in 1977; this work was made possible by a grant from the National Endowment for the Humanities. Permission to republish the tablets was granted by William L. Moran.

[1]That the two texts are related was observed by R. F. S. Starr, *Nuzi* I pp. 316-17; see also A. L. Oppenheim, *JNES* 18 (1959) 127.

[2]For previous editions and suggested readings, see, e.g., *HSS* 16; Oppenheim, *JNES* 18 123 and 127; D. O. Edzard, *BiOr* 16 (1959) 136.

[3]See, e.g., Oppenheim, *JNES* 18 121-28; O. Eissfeldt, *Der Beutel der Lebendigen* (*BSGW*, Phil.-hist. Klasse 105/6 [1960]); D. Schmandt-Besserat, *Syro-Mesopotamian Studies* I (1977) 31-70, *Discovery: Research and Scholarship at the University of Texas at Austin*, I/4 (June, 1977) 4-7, *Scientific American* 238/6 (June, 1978) 50-59, etc.

[4]A drawing of the container and copy of its inscription were published by Oppenheim, *JNES* 18 122; a photograph of the container by Schmandt-Besserat, *Sci Am* 238/6 52; translations of the texts by Starr, *Nuzi* I p. 127 and Oppenheim, *JNES* 18 123 and 127.

Texts 311 and 449 record a transaction between a sheepowner Puḫišenni, son of Mušapu, and a shepherd Ziqarru, son of Šalliya. Both documents were found in the same room, S112, a room which was part of an area occupied by five generations of the family to which Puḫišenni belonged.[5]

SMN 1854 = Bulla 449		*SMN* 2096 = Tablet 311
1. NA$_4$.MEŠ *ša* UDU.MEŠ		
2. 21 UDU.MEŠ MUNUS *ša* Ù.TU	obv.	1. 21 UDU.MEŠ MUNUS *ša* Ù.TU
3. 6 *ka$_4$-lu-mu* MUNUS.MEŠ		2. 6 *ka$_4$-lu-mu* MUNUS.MEŠ[6]
4. 8 UDU.MEŠ NITA.GAL		3. 8 UDU.MEŠ NITA.GAL
5. 4 *ka$_4$-lu-mu* MEŠ!NITA![7]		4. 4 *ka$_4$-lu-mu* MEŠ NITA
6. 6 *en-zu* MEŠ.MUNUS *ša* ⸢Ù⸣.[TU]		5. 6 *en-zu* MEŠ MUNUS *ša* Ù.TU
7. 1 M[ÁŠ.GAL] [3] ⸢*la*⸣*-li-ú* MUNUS.ME[Š]		6. ⸢1⸣ MÁŠ.GAL
		7. [3] *la-li-ú* MUNUS.MEŠ
	lo.edge	8. [ŠU.N]ÍGIN 49 UDU.MEŠ *ù en-za*
		9. [*š*]*a* ^{m}*pu-ḫi-še-en-ni*
	rev.	10. [D]UMU *mu-ša-puù* ⸢*ša*⸣
		11. *a+na* ŠU ^{m}*zi-qar-ru*
		12. DUMU *šal-li-ia* LÚ.SIPA
		13. *na-ad-nu*
8. [NA$_4$] ⸢^{m}⸣*zi-qar-ru* ⸢LÚ⸣.[SIPA]		14. NA$_4$ ^{m}*pu-ḫi-še-en-ni* (mistake for: NA$_4$ ^{m}*zi-qar-ru* LÚ.SIPA[8])
	l. edge	15. *i+na* ŠÀ-*šu-nu*
		16. 8 UDU.MEŠ *ṣa-ri-p*[*u*]

1. Counters representing small cattle:	
2. 21 ewes that lamb;	1. 21 ewes that lamb;
3. 6 female lambs;	2. 6 female lambs;
4. 8 full grown male sheep;	3. 8 full grown male sheep;
5. 4 male![9] lambs;	4. 4 male lambs;
6. 6 she-goats that kid;	5. 6 she-goats that kid;
7. 1 he-goat; 3 female kids.	6. 1 he-goat;
	7. 3 female kids:

[5]See Starr, *Nuzi* I pp. 316f. and E. R. Lacheman, *HSS* 16 p. VIII and n. 11. Starr states that the texts were found in Room S112; the room assignment of *SMN* 1854 and 2096 in *HSS* 16 p. X should be corrected accordingly.

[6]MEŠ written over partially erased MUNUS.

[7]Text: ⸢MUNUS.MEŠ⸣

[8]See below observation two.

[9]Text: female.

	8. Total: 49 sheep and goats
	9. belonging to Puḫišenni,
	10. the son of Musapu and which
	13. were given
	11. over to the care of Ziqarru,
	12. the son of Šalliya, the shepherd.
8. The seal of Ziqarru, the shepherd.	14. The seal of Puḫišenni. (mistake for: The seal of Ziqarru, the shepherd.)
	15. Among them are
	16. 8 red colored sheep.

Observation one:

The reading of each document is facilitated by the occurrence of corresponding entries in the other and by the scribe's note that the total number of animals enumerated was 49 (311:8). Thus the numbers in each text should correspond to those in the other and should total 49. Here mention must be made of Oppenheim's emendation of 49 in 311:8 to 48—and his restoration of missing numbers in accordance with this emendation—on the evidence of a slip of paper attached to 449 which stated that 449 "when found contained 48 little stones."[10] However, the explicit testimony of a tablet carries more weight than a modern note.[11] And even if 449 could be shown to have contained only 48 pebbles, one could demonstrate without too much difficulty that the statement ŠU.NÍGIN 49 UDU.MEŠ *ù en-za* (311:8) is still to be reckoned with. Such demonstration is unnecessary in view of Starr's observation that "inside the tablet were forty-nine pebbles."[12]

We begin, therefore, with the evidence of the texts and try to work out the readings accordingly. With the exception of 311:6-7 / /449:7, all numbers are well enough preserved and total 45. Thus 311:6-7 / /449:7 must record four animals. A first examination of 311 is unsatisfactory, for, if anything, traces of too many "heads" seem to be visible in lines 6-7. Fortunately, the number in 449:7a is preserved; accordingly, 311:6 / /449:7a yields: 1 MÁŠ.GAL. Since the difference between the total arrived at thus far (46) and the summary total 49 is three, the number in 311:7 / /449:7b must be three: 3 *la-li-ú*. A reexamination

[10]See *HSS* 16 p. 134 and Oppenheim, *JNES* 18 123 and 127.

[11]The note was written in the early 1930s by an assistant who removed the stones. Ernest Lacheman tells me that when he first saw 449 ca. 1930 it contained pebbles but that these had been removed and the note affixed when he next saw 449 several years later.

[12]*Nuzi* I p. 316. The volume of the container is approximately 19 milliliters (of sand).

Plate 1. *SMN* 2096 = Tablet 311

Seal impression from tablet $16\text{-}311_{2096}$

W. 5.4 cm
H. 1.7 cm

Width of obverse: 6.0 cm
Height of obverse: 5.6 cm
Depth from obv. to rev.: 2.1 cm

Composite drawing of seal impressions taken from seven rollings on the bulla 16-449
(6.0 cm, height; 15.0 cm, circum.)

Figure 1

Plate 2. *SMN* 1854 = Bulla 449

of the traces in 311:6-7 and a comparison with well preserved signs clear up the mystery of the "extra heads" in 311 (and show that the traces can accommodate the readings "1" and "3"), for in the inside of the impress of well preserved signs there is an extra line running through the upper part of the head—a mark comparable to the double line produced by a pencil with a split point—which in a broken sign might create the impression that two or three heads had been inscribed where in actuality no more than one had been. The tablet 311 was written with a stylus with a hair-line crack. A glance at the signs on the bulla 449 confirms what we would have expected from the parallel content of the two texts: the signs in 449 show the same defect as those in 311. Both documents were written with the same split stylus and—we may infer—by the same scribe. This observation accords well with the finding of both texts in the same room but does not account for it. Below we shall consider this archaeological datum and suggest that it explains why only one bulla has thus far been found.

Observation two:

The clay container (449) is covered with multiple rollings of a seal identified as "the seal of Ziqarru, the shepherd" (1.8). This is as expected. There is one seal impression on the tablet (311): on the reverse immediately beneath the identifying notation "the seal of Puḫišenni" (1.14). An examination of the seal impressions (see fig. 1) is most instructive. The impression on the tablet and those on the container are identical: the same seal was used on both documents. We may safely assume that the seal belonged either to Puḫišenni or to Ziqarru.

On the face of it, it would seem that each of the parties sealed one of the records of the transaction and had his name inscribed alongside the sealing: the sheepowner, the tablet recording the receipt of animals by the shepherd; the shepherd, the filled and inscribed clay bulla. Further thought, however, shows this explanation to be fallacious. It is unlikely that two parties to a transaction would use the same seal. This aside, texts such as the tablet serve to document the number and type of animals handed over by a sheepowner to a shepherd and to record the shepherd's acknowledgement of receipt of the animals. The tablet is intended to protect the owner; it is his receipt and, therefore, would be sealed by the shepherd[13] and kept by the owner. This accords with the archaeological findspot of the tablet: a room occupied by the family of Puḫišenni. Accordingly, the notation NA$_4$ ^{m}*pu-ḫi-še-en-ni* in 311:14 may be regarded as a mistake for NA$_4$ ^{m}Zi-qar-ru LÚ.SIPA and the seal treated as the property of the shepherd. This conclusion is not contradicted by other sealings

[13]Cf. J. N. Postgate, *JSS* 20 (1975) 2; regarding Nuzi, Gernot Wilhelm informs me that the tablets of Šilwa-Teššup recording similar transactions are sealed by his shepherds.

of Puḫišenni; to the best of my knowledge, the seal 311 / /449 is elsewhere not ascribed to him.[14]

Having stated that the seal belonged to the shepherd and that he used it to seal both the receipt (311) and the bulla (449), we are required to take account of three related problems: what is the function of the bulla; why is it the only such container found thus far at Nuzi; why was it stored in the same room as the tablet? A. L. Oppenheim proposed answers to the first two questions; he interpreted the bulla as a container used to send counters from one accounting department into another and thought that this "procedure may well represent an exceptional case, which would explain why only one such 'egg-shaped tablet' has been found in Nuzi."[15] I prefer different answers to these questions. Although Oppenheim deemed it unacceptable, he also stated another possible explanation of the bulla, one which I find more convincing: "It seems to be a simple device to control the transfer of animals entrusted to illiterate shepherds, to whom the number of pebbles was meant to suggest tangibly the number of sheep and goats in their care. Such pebbles, inclosed (and sealed) in their container, would serve well to protect the shepherd, no less than the officials who handed out or received the animals, against fraud or error."[16] We need only add that the writing on the bulla itself—a text

[14]I have checked references to Puhišenni *mār* Mušapu and Ziqarru *mār* Šalliya cited in *NPN* and E. Cassin and J.-J. Glassner, *Anthroponymie et anthropologie de Nuzi I: Les anthroponymes*. Seals of Puḫišenni are found on *HSS* 16 322 and *HSS* 19 111; they are different from each other and from 16 311 // 449. *AASOR* 16 no. 62 and *HSS* 15 300 are unsealed. *SMN* 2122 and 2680 are published by D. I. Owen in his dissertation; I have not seen them. The only references to Ziqarru are 16 311 // 449.

[15]*JNES* 18 127.

[16]*JNES* 18 123. Starr, *Nuzi* I 316-17 already suggested what amounts to essentially the same explanation; cf. E. Cassin, *RA* 53 (1959) 164. In view of some of Oppenheim's stated objections (p. 124), I note the following: The bulla served the needs of the shepherd: the pebbles inside gave testimony to the total number of animals given over to his care; the inscription on the outside—writing which was protected from tampering by multiple rollings—attested to the types of animals received and the number of each. The sealed inscription and the sealed contents supplement each other and supply full information. In its own way, the shepherd's bulla provides the same information as the sheepowner's tablet; and just as the tablet did not have to be accompanied by a pouch of pebbles, so the bulla did not have to provide a total on the outside. The bulla and tablet are parallel documents and serve as checks on each other. Furthermore, it is also possible that the writing on the bulla was meant to allow an official to check the document. Such a perusal would be sufficient for certain purposes and would eliminate the necessity of breaking the covering. (The Nuzi bulla may be regarded as having the form of a double document; see S. J. Lieberman, *AJA* 84 [1980] 352.) Finally, the tablet, and not the bulla, protects the owner and prevents the shepherd from substituting less valuable animals. The fact that our bulla is the only one discovered in Nuzi is discussed below. For a

authenticated and protected by multiple rollings of the shepherd's seal in the empty spaces between the lines of text—attested to the number and type of animals in his care. The bulla was intended to serve and protect the shepherd; it was his way of handling the transaction.

The tablet and bulla were intended to fulfill different functions, serve different people, and be kept in different places. Receipts would be placed among the documents of the sheepowners; bullae would be held by the shepherds or stored with their possessions apart from the archives of the sheepowners. Our bulla was the only one found precisely because it was stored together with the tablet of the sheepowner. A possible explanation of this irregular arrangement may even be provided by the earlier observation of the erroneous character of the notation "the seal of Puḫišenni." The bulla may have been kept with the tablet because of the error; perhaps the error was caught and both documents rendered inoperative or the bulla kept to allow redrafting of the tablet or to provide confirmation of the authenticity of the flawed receipt.

The finding of only this bulla is due, then, to an accident of history and of archaeological excavation. Bullae were used by shepherds around Nuzi. This use may be inferred from references to stones in the Nuzi texts.[17] Normally when sheep were handed over by or given to the shepherd, the appropriate number of counters were, respectively, removed from or deposited in the bulla. There was no need to record the withdrawal, deposit, or transfer of counters; the new number of counters in the bulla and, when appropriate, the drafting of a new text were record enough. Only when the procedure deviated from this norm was this fact recorded: hence references to stones almost always mention the fact that stones were not deposited, not removed, not transferred. The small number of references is due to the fact that the texts record exceptions.[18] To be sure, the bulla and receipt tablet were intended to protect, respectively, the shepherd against unfounded claims and the owner against loss. But full protection was not always necessary; the two parties could agree to a transfer without going through the bother of breaking the covering and changing the count and text of the bulla; one simply registered the new situation and the fact that the number of stones had not been altered. Trust based on sustained relationships and common interest may be presumed to have existed between owner and shepherd.

---

different explanation of the bulla, see Edzard, *BiOr* 16 136; as noted above, protection of the owner was provided by the herding contract and not by the bulla.

[17]See Oppenheim, *JNES* 18 125-27 and *CAD* A/I 60.

[18]The exceptional character of the references is noted by Oppenheim, *JNES* 18 125-28; his explanation is different and consonant with the system of recording that he envisioned.

On this note I may draw this discussion to a close. I have perhaps said too much already about a city in which I am only a visitor. But having spent some time working on the Nuzi tablets of the Harvard Semitic Museum, I could not but welcome an opportunity to dedicate a note to Professor E. R. Lacheman; I would thus celebrate a scholar's lifelong devotion to the decipherment and publication of an important corpus of cuneiform tablets.

Toponymic Parallels
Between the Nuzi Area and Northern Syria

with an appendix:

Nuzi Place Names in Egyptian Topographic Lists

MICHAEL C. ASTOUR
Southern Illinois University
Edwardsville

The toponymy of Northern Syria contains several linguistic strata: Amorite-Canaanite, Akkadian, Hurrian, Hittite-Luwian, Aramean, Greek, Arabic, and Turkish.[1] Comparative study of its patterns and individual names with those of other regions of the Near East is of considerable value for both history and linguistics. From the point of view of history, it adds to our perception of ethnic and cultural interpenetration in ancient Western Asia. From the point of view of linguistics, a better understanding of structure and semantics of place names introduced by an ethnic minority can be reached by turning to an area where the same element formed a majority of the population. For toponymy (as well as anthroponymy) of Hurrian origin, the principal source of information is the rich archive of tablets unearthed at Nuzi. Their vast majority belongs to the fifteenth and early fourteenth century B.C. They are approximately contemporaneous with the tablets of Alalaḫ, Level IV, and they end almost exactly at the time of the start of the archives of Ugarit and of the Hittite conquest of Northern Syria. This was the time when Nuzi and its neighbors in the Transtigris area on the one hand, and Alalaḫ and its confederate states in Syria on the other, were peripheral vassals of the Kingdom of Mitanni.

A. Goetze opened the way to comparative structural study of the toponymic material of Nuzi and Alalaḫ in an important paper devoted to one specific type of Hurrian place names.[2] The same year, L. R. Fisher completed a study of Nuzi geographical names which included a comprehensive list of

[1]Cf. my "Continuité et changement dans la toponymie de la Syrie du Nord," in *La toponymie antique: Actes du Colloque de Strasbourg, 12-14 juin 1975* (Leiden 1975) 117-41, map.

[2]"Hurrian Place Names in *-š(š)e*," in *Festschrift Johannes Friedrich* (Heidelberg 1959) 195-206.

them.[3] I am grateful to him for putting it at my disposal when I began my collection and classification of North Syrian toponyms. E. R. Lacheman, one of the most productive publishers of the Nuzi tablets and the author of pioneering articles on Nuzi geographical names,[4] kindly sent me, twelve years ago as of this writing, his own toponymic list, which contained some additional items. I am now happy to dedicate to him this modest contribution to the field of comparative toponymy of ancient Near East.

This paper is not concerned with the general problem of Hurrian place names in Northern Syria. One finds there several beautiful Hurrian toponyms that do not occur at Nuzi, such as *Atanni* ("the fathers"), *Ḫutillurašе* ("the Ḫutellura-gods"), *Šidurašе* ("maiden"), *Šinurḫena* ("twins"), *Turmanni* ("spring"). Nor does it cover the entire region between the Tigris and the Zagros, in which other sources (from Ur III, Mari, Assyria) reveal the presence of several additional homonyms of North Syrian place names. It is limited only to toponyms attested in the tablets of Nuzi, be they of Hurrian or Semitic origin, of which the basic name-forming element (or, in case of composite names, one such element) finds a close parallel in Northern Syria during the age of cuneiform inscriptions. Since anthroponyms and toponyms were often formed of the same lexical elements according to similar patterns, Nuzi names of towns and estates derived from those of their owners have been included if relevant.

In the list below, Nuzi place names are followed by their numbers in L. R. Fisher's catalog; those few that are not found there are provided with direct references. Their N. Syrian parallels are separated by :: and followed by indications of their provenance, *viz.*, +A (Alalaḫ VII), A (Alalaḫ IV), EA (el-Amarna), Eb (Ebla/Tell Mardīḫ),[5] Eg (Egypt), Em (Emar-Meskeneh),[6] H (Hittite), HH (Hieroglyphic Hittite), M (Mari), MA (Middle Assyrian), NA (Neo-Assyrian), OA (Old Assyrian), U (Ugarit); only those of them that cannot be found easily in relevant repertories and indexes of geographical names are supplied with individual references. The determinatives URU and KI

[3] *Nuzi Geographical Names*, Brandeis University Ph.D. dissertation, 1959 (available from University Microfilms, Ann Arbor, Mich.).

[4] "Nuzi Geographical Names," I: *BASOR* No. 78 (Apr. 1940) 18-23; II: ibid. No. 81 (Feb. 1941) 10-15.

[5] So far, the access of the reading public to the reportedly enormous field of Eblaic toponymy is limited to a few articles by G. Pettinato, the most important of which is "L'Atlante Geografico del Vicino Oriente Antico attestato ad Ebla e ad Abū Ṣalābikh (I)," *Or* 47 (1978) 50-73, pl. VII-XII. Toponyms from that source are adduced only when there is a reasonable ground to assume that the places in question were located in N. Syria. Parallel entries in the Abū Ṣalābiḫ list are indicated by AṢ.

[6] The tablets from Meskeneh are to be published by D. Arnaud (Akkadian texts) and E. Laroche (Hurrian texts). I owe my knowledge of the toponyms they contain to the kindness of D. Arnaud.

have been omitted throughout. No special consideration is given to Hurrian omissible and interchangeable suffixes and formatives.

* * *

1. *A-ba-lu-uḫ-ḫé* (11). This toponym has been included under the surmise that, in view of the not unfrequent interchange *l*/*r* in Hurrian in general[7] and in Nuzi place names in particular,[8] it may represent a variant of **Abaruḫḫe*, derived from a common noun with the meaning "chest," which appears at Nuzi as *a-ba-ru-uḫ*/*a-ba-ru-uḫ-ḫu*, in OB as *a-ba-ra-ḫa-am* (acc.), and in NA as *ḫa-ba-ra-ḫu.*[9] A place name *Ḫa-ba-ru-ḫa* is attested indeed in the Transtigris region in a MA text.[10] See Appendix, C:3 :: *A-ba-ru-uḫ-e* (A).

2. A-be-na/*A-be-na-aš* (12) :: *A-be* /*A-be-na*/*A-bi-na* (A).

3. *Ak-ku-ba-wa-ni-wa* (29) :: *A-ku-bi-ia*/*A-ku-bi-a* (A); or *A-qú-bi-ia*, from ᶜQB?

4. *Al-la-i-še* (SMN 2580:9). From Hurr. *allai-*/*alai-*/*alae-* "lady," a very productive onomastic element.[11] :: *Al-li-še* (⁺A), *A-la-ú-wa* (A), *A-la-wa-ri*/[*A*]*l-la-wa-ri*ᴷᴵ (A), *Á-la-wa-'+r-ti* (HH); for *-wari* see No. 68 below.

5. *A-al-li-wa-aḫ-ri*/*Al-*[*li-wa-aḫ*]*-ir*? (38): *alli-* "Lady" + *waḫ(a)r-* "good, beautiful"[12] (cf. Nuzi PN ᶠ*Al-la-i-wa-aḫ-ri*). :: *Za-li-wa-ḫa-ri* (A); for *zal-* see No. 68; for *waḫ(a)r-*/*paḫ(a)r-* see No. 41.[13]

6. *Am-pa* (41). The element *ampa*/*ambe*/*ambi* is common in Nuzi anthroponymy as both the first and the second element; in toponymy, besides this one, see Nos. 7, 52, 54. :: *E-ri-ra-am-bi*ᴷᴵ (⁺A); for *erir-* (*irir-*) see No. 31.[14]

[7]E. I. Speiser, *Introduction to Hurrian* (New Haven 1941) 27, § 37.

[8]H. Lewy, "A Contribution to the Historical Geography of the Nuzi Texts," *JAOS* 88 (1968) 155 and n. 41, with further references. See also Nos. 29 and 52 below.

[9]A. Salonen, *Die Hausgeräte der alten Mesopotamier*, I (Helsinki 1965) 199, and *AHw* and *CAD s.vv.*

[10]Referring to the conquests of Arik-den-ili (1319-1308), see A. K. Grayson, *Assyrian and Babylonian Chronicles* (Locust Valley, N.Y., 1975) 185-87, cf. 66; earlier published in translation: D. D. Luckenbill, *ARAB* I, § 69; A. K. Grayson, *ARI* I, § 361.

[11]It goes without saying that I. J. Gelb, P. M. Purves and A. A. MacRae, *Nuzi Personal Names* (Chicago 1943, 2nd printing 1963) remains an invaluable tool for those dealing with Nuzi anthroponymy and Hurrian onomastica in general. No special references to that work will be given henceforward. Different forms of the word in question are listed in C.-G. von Brandenstein, "Zum Churrischen Lexikon," *ZA* 46 (1940) 109f.

[12]Cf. C.-G. von Brandenstein, "Zur Namenbedeutung der Stadt Paḫarašše," *Or* 8 (1939) 82-86.

[13]An interesting homonym of the N. Syrian town appears in a MA inscription (*ARAB* I, § 114; *ARI* I, § 527) as *Zal-li-pa-aḫ-ri* in Uruaṭri (Urarṭu); the reading of NI as *zal* was proposed by A. K. Grayson, *ARI* I, 81 n. 165.

[14]Cf. also the GN *Ši-ik-ša-am-bi-im*/*Ši-ik-ša-ab-bu-um* in an OB tablet from Tell

7. *A-am-pa-^{d}Sin*: see No. 6.

8. *An-ni-šu* (50)::*A-an-na-še*/*An-na-aš-še*/*An-na-aš-te* ($^{+}$A, A).

9. *Ap-sà-ḫu-ul-lu-uš-še*/*ši* (14): *apsa+ḫul+ušše*, in which the first element is apparently Akk. *apsû* "temple basin" and the second is Hurr. *-ḫuli* (at Nuzi more often *-uḫlu*), suffix of vocation.[15] :: a) *Áp-su* (Eb)/ *Ap-sú-na* (A)/*Ap-su-na*, ethn. *apsny* (U), now Tell Āfes; b) *Za-bu-ḫu-li-e*/ [*Za-b*]*u-ḫul-li-e* (A); *Ḫar-ba-ḫu-li-bi* (H)/*Ḫa-ar-bu-*[*ḫu-li*]/*Ḫrbġlm*(U); *Bi-tu-ḫu-li-bi*/*Bi-tu-ḫu-li-wi* (H)/*Bi-ta-ḫu-li* (U); *Kštġlm* (U);[16] [...]-*ḫu-u-li* (H).

10. *Ar-di-ḫi*/*Ar-ti-ḫi*/*Ar-ti-ḫé* (72), *Ar-ta-ḫu-uš* (73): from Hurr. *ard-* "city."[17] :: *Ar-du-uš-ša* (*ard+ušše*) (H), class. *Ardula* in Commagene, now Ardil.

11. *A-ri-a-wa* (59), *dimti* ^{m}*A-ri-ia-wa* (60) :: *A-ri-an-te*/*A-ri-ia-an-te*/*ti* (A)/*A-ri-ia-an-ta* (H): with Hurr. ending *-ante* instead of *-wa*.

12. *Áš-ḫul-lu-uš-še* (SMN 3357:40): see No. 9 for *-ḫul-*.

13. *A-šu-ḫi-iš*/*A-šu-ḫi-is-ḫé* (95): from Akk. *ašūḫu* "fir." :: *A-ší-ḫi-im* (OA)/*A-ši-ḫi* (H), probably from a dialectal variant of the same noun.

14. *A-šu-nu-uš* (SMN 860:4) :: *A-šu-ni* ($^{+}$A).

15. *A-wa-ra* (6): Hurr. *awar-* "field." :: Perhaps the second element in *A-la-wa-ri*/[*A*]*l-la-wa-ri* (A), if it is to be analyzed *alla+awari* "lady of the field"; but cf. No. 68.

16. *Bi-ir-ša-an-ni*/*Bi-ir-za-ni* (234, 236). The interchange *š*/*z* points to the Hurr. phoneme *ž*. :: ḪUR.SAG *Bir$_{x}$*(or *Bur$_{5}$*)-*zi-ḫé* (U). Cf. No. 17.

17. *Bi-ir-ša-aḫ-ḫé* (235). Same stem as No. 16; ending closer to that of the Ugaritic parallel.

18. *Dūr-Ub-la*/*Du-ru-ub-la*/*Tu-ru-ub-la* (282). A tablet from the Old Akkadian level of Nuzi (then called Gasur) represents a map of the region on which towns are marked with little circles; the only fully extant name reads *maš-gán* BÀD-*Eb-la*, i.e., *maškan* (settlement of) *Dūr-Ebla*, obviously an older form of *Dūr-Ubla*.[18] The Transtigridian Dūr-Ebla, or simply Ebla, is attested in records from the Sargonic,[19] Ur III,[20] OB,[21] and MA[22] periods. It must not

Šemšāra, not far from Nuzi, J. Laessøe, *The Shemshāra Tablets: A Preliminary Report* (Copenhagen 1959), 35.

[15]Common in the terminology of Alalaḫ and Ugarit, cf. M. Dietrich— O. Loretz, "Die soziale Struktur von Alalaḫ und Ugarit (I)," *WO* 3 (1966) 188-205.

[16]All four N. Syrian toponyms in *-ḫuli*/*-ġlm* are hybrid Semitic-Hurrian formations, respectively "barmen," "sword-makers," "house-makers," and "bow-makers."

[17]Different formations from this stem are listed in C.-G. von Brandenstein's article (see n. 11) 112.

[18]Th. J. Meek, "The Akkadian and Cappadocian Texts from Nuzi," *BASOR* No. 48 (Dec. 1932) 2-3; H. Lewy, op. cit. (n. 8) 159 (placed it ca. 28 km south of Nuzi).

[19]Ethnic *Eb-la-ì-t*[*im*] (gen.) used as PN, *MAD* 1 52:4 and p. 232. It is not certain that Ebla mentioned along with Armanum in the famous inscription of Naram-Sin is the now famous Syrian city of that name: it could well have been the Transtigridian

be confused with its N. Syrian homonym.[23] :: *Eb-la* (Eb, Sarg., Gudea, Ur III, Isin, +A, A, H)/ ᵓ*Eb-rə* (Eg)/ *E-eb-la* (Em)/ *E-eb-la-a-pa* (Hurrian text from Boğazköy),[24] now Tell Mardīḫ, 65 km SSW of Aleppo by highway and 3 km by track. The exceptional political and cultural importance of that city as early as the third millennium was revealed by the Italian excavations of the site.

19. *Dūr-Za-an-zi*/ *Du-ur-Za-an-zi* (296). :: *Za-an-zi* (A).[25]

20. *Ḫa-*⌜*ga*⌝*-še* (380). :: *Ḫa-ga* (OA), *Ḫa-qa* (A).

21. *Ḫa-al-ma-ni-wa*/ *Ḫal-ma-ni-wa*/[*Ḫa*]*-al-ma-ni-e* (385). An important town between the Lower Zab and Radanu (ᶜUẓaym).[26] MB *Ḫal-man*, a provincial center of post-Kassite Babylonia.[27] Also called *Ar-ma-an*[28] or *Ar-*

Ebla which a NA copy of an OB geographical treatise (see n. 21) locates in the land of Armanû. At any rate, the only known Arman(um) was located in the Transtigris (see No. 21).

[20] *Dūr-Eb-la* in a ration list from Drehem, C. E. Keiser, *BIN* III 491:32. As for ÍD *Eb-la* in Ur III texts, it is believed to be a canal in the area of Umma, *RGTC* II, 260; P. Fronzaroli, "West Semitic Toponymy in Northern Syria in the Third Millennium B.C.," *JSS* 22 (1977) 155.

[21] Nippur geographical list, appended to S. Levy, "Harmal Geographical List," *Sumer* 3 (1947) 50-83, lists among cities of the Diyala region (105) *Ib-ra-t*[*um*], (106) *Eb-l*[*a*], (107) *Di-ni-*[*ik-tum*], (108) *Ne-ri-ib-tum*. Tablet *KAV* 92, a NA copy of an OB geographical description of Sargon of Akkad's empire, lists in l. 13: *ištu Eb-lá adi* ⌜*Bīt-Na-ni-ib*⌝? KUR *Ar-ma-ni-i*KI among Transtigridian countries; see E. Weidner, "Das Reich Sargons von Akkad," *AfO* 16 (1952-1953) 4, 12-13.

[22] *KAV* 107:8: *mār šipri ša šarri* URU*Eb-li-ta-ia-e* "messenger of the king of the Eblean city." URU*Ki-li-zi* in the next line is not Kiliz (Turk. Kilis) on the Turkish-Syrian border but a city in Assyria east of the Tigris.

[23] But that is exactly what M. Heltzer did in "The inscription from Tell-Mardiḫ and the city Ebla in northern Syria in the III-II millenium [*sic*]," *AION* 35 (1975) 289-317, in which he conflated all three Eblas into one.

[24] Bo 409, which remained a long time unpublished and known only from a quotation in A. Ungnad, *Subartu* (Berlin 1936) 51 n. 2, is now available as *KUB* XLV 84, where the toponym in question appears in l. 15.

[25] Listed as *Šá-an-iš* in the index to D. J. Wiseman, *The Alalakh Tablets* (London 1953) 156; corrected in Wiseman's typewritten revised catalog of Alalaḫ place names, of which he generously sent me a copy. *Dūr-Zanzi* appears in tablets of the Sargonic period; note, however, the MA PN *Za-an-zu-u* (E. Weidner, "Aus den Tagen eines assyrischen Schattenkönigs," *AfO* 10 [1935-1936] 48), which could have been derived from an ethnic.

[26] See H. Lewy, op. cit. (n. 8) 155-56.

[27] J. A. Brinkman, "Provincial Administration in Babylonia Under the Second Dynasty of Isin," *JESHO* 6 (1963) 234.

[28] From Ur III period on, *RGTC* II, 15. Cf. n. 21 above. Also known as *Alman* and *Ḫalwan*. On the question of a second place of that name, high in the Zagros (mod. Ḥolwān), see L. D. Levine, "Geographical Studies in the Neo-Assyrian Zagros," *Iran* 11 (1973) 24-27.

ma-an Ugar-Sa-al-lu/ *Sa-lum*/ *Sa-li.*[29] Shalmaneser II referred to it once as *Arman*, otherwise as *Ḫal-man.*[30] :: Now the same name, *Ḫal-man*, is applied in one version of Shalmaneser III's annals[31] to the North Syrian Aleppo. Hence the bold surmise of Sidney Smith[32] that in view of the interchange *Ḫalman*/ *Arman* in the Transtigris, the same phenomenon must be assumed for Syria and the city of Armanum conquered by Naram-Sin along with Ebla[33] is to be equated with Aleppo.[34] But there is no proof that Aleppo was actually known as Ḫalman to anybody except Shalmaneser III's scribe. In all other sources it appears as *Ḫalab* (M, +A, A, Eg, U, MB, NA, OAram) or *Ḫalba*/ *Ḫalpa* (H). It would seem that the Assyrian scribe, who was much better acquainted with the Transtigris than with Syria, replaced the actual name of the city with a consonant and more familiar one. Similarly, the North Syrian mountain which appears in some editions of the same king's annals under its correct name Atallur, is given in other versions the name Lallar which belonged to a peak in the Zagros range.[35] The Ebla archive, more or less contemporaneous with the time of Naram-Sin, does not mention a city Arman(um) in Syria. The attempt to identify Naram-Sin's Armanum with Eblean Armi[36] needs substantiation; at any rate, it cannot be located at Aleppo because it appears as *A-ar-ma* (A) in the same period as Ḫalab. One must keep the mind open to the possibility that Naram-Sin's Armanum and Ebla were situated not in Syria but rather in the Transtigris.[37]

22. *Ḫa-lu-ul-li-wa*/ *Ḫa-lu-li-wa* (383). Perhaps identical with NA *Ḫa-lu-li-e*/ *Ḫa-lu-li-i*/ *Ḫa-lu-le-na* on the middle Tigris. :: *Ḫa-lu-la-še* (A)/ *Ḫa-ru-rə-śə* (Eg).

23. *Ḫa-ba-te*/ *Ḫa-ba-ti*/ *Ḫa-pa-te* (375). :: *Ḫu-ba-ta*/ *Ḫu-pa-ta*/ *Ḫu-pa-ta-ú*/ *Ḫa-pa-ta-ya*/ *Ḫbt*/ *Ḫpty*, a town; *Ḫu-up-pa-ti*, a district (U).

24. *Ḫa-pu-pa* (374) :: *Ḫa-p*[*a*]-*pí-ia* (A).

[29]Long disputed between Babylonia and Assyria, cf. J. M. Munn-Rankin, *CAH* II^3, 2, 275; J. A. Brinkman, *A Political History of Post-Kassite Babylonia* (Rome 1968) 195 n. 1195; A. K. Grayson, *Assyrian and Babylonian Chronicles* (Locust Valley, N.Y. 1975) 242, 251-52, 264-65.

[30]Cf. S. Parpola, *Neo-Assyrian Toponyms* (*AOAT* 6, 1970) 30, 143.

[31]Monolith Inscr. (*ARAB* I, § 610).

[32]*UET* I, 79-81.

[33]Ibid., 74-79, No. 275; H. Hirsch, "Die Inschriften der Könige von Agade," *AfO* 20 (1963) 73-77.

[34]This identification has had a considerable following, but we cannot list here the authors who shared it or regarded it probable.

[35]See references in Parpola, op. cit., *s.vv. Atallur* and *Lallar*; for the latter also *ARAB* I, § 149 = *ARI* I, §§ 694, 701.

[36]P. Matthiae, "Ébla à l'époque d'Akkad," *CRAI* 1976, 212 and no. 70; 213 n. 71.

[37]Cf. the discussions by H. G. Güterbock, "Die historische Tradition bei Babyloniern und Hethitern, II," *ZA* 44 (1938) 73-75: I. J. Gelb, *Hurrians and Subarians* (Chicago 1944) 103; E. Weidner, op. cit. (n. 21) 12-13.

25. *Ḫa-ar-ma(-a)* (397) :: *Ḫa-ar-ma-na*/ *Ḫa-ar-ma-ni* (U).

26. *Ḫa-ši-ia* (404); KUR *Ḫa-ši* (403); KUR *Ḫa-ši-wa-ri-in* (403a) :: *Ḫa-aš-ši-im*/ *Ḫa-ši-[im]* (M), *Ḫa-aš-šu*/ *Ḫa-aš-šu-wa* (H); for *-wari-* see No. 68 below.

27. *Ḫa-wu-ur-ni*/⸢*Ḫa*⸣*-wu-ur-ni-wa* (373). From Hurr. *ḫawur(ni)*/ *ḫubur(ni)* "earth." :: The same vocable is perhaps present in *Ḫu-bar-mu-u[l]-li*[38] and in *Pa-qar-ḫu-bu-ni* (*et var.*) (NA), which seems to be a transcription of Hurr. **pağar-ḫuburni* "the good earth."

28. *Ḫu-ri-še* (401) :: *Ḫu-ri-ia* (⁺A, A).

29. *Ḫu-uš-ri*/ *Ḫu-uš-li* (411) :: *Ḫu-uš-ri* (A).

30. *I-ri-me*/ *I-ri-mu* (146) :: *I-ri-ma-aš* (U), apparently in the Kingdom of Carchemish. An *Irim* (Eb) also appears in a tablet which describes in great geographical detail a war between Ebla and Mari.[39]

31. *I-ri-ri-til-la* (149), an estate named for its owner. *Irir-* is a frequent element in Hurr. personal names (Nuzi, A, U). :: *E-ri-ra-am-bi* (⁺A), also derived from a Hurr. personal name; for *-ambi*, see No. 6 above.

32. *Ki-ba-ri-wa* (Lach., 1291:7); *Kib-bi-ri* (317) :: Mt. *Ki-bu-ri* (U).

33. *Ki-ki-ia-a-wa* (333) :: *Ki-i-ki* (A).

34. *Ku-be-ia*/ *Ku-be-e-wa* (315) :: *Ku-bi-ia* (⁺A).

35. *Ma-ḫa-zi* (426). According to the quadrilingual (Sumerian-Akkadian-Hurrian-Ugaritic) vocabulary from Ras Shamra,[40] Hurr. *ma-ḫa-[z]i* (from Akk. *maḫāzu* "a market and cult city") is the equivalent of Sum. KAR, Akk. *ka-a-ru* "waterfront, commercial center," and of Ugar. *ma-aḫ-ḫa-[du]*.[41] :: The harbor town of Ugarit, at the bay Minet el-Beiḍa, appears in syllabic texts of Ras Shamra as (ideographically) KAR and (phonetically) *Ma-a-ḫa-di* (gen.)/ *Ma-ḫa-di-ya* (ethn.), and in alphabetic texts as *Miḫd*/ *Maḫd*, which is the Ugaritic cognate of Akk. *maḫāzu.*[42]

36. *Ma-aš-qa-ni*/ *Ma-áš-qa-ni-wa* (438). From Akk. *maškanu*[43] "settlement," "residence," "threshing floor," frequently used as a toponym or as the first element of compound place names. :: *Ma[š?]-kà-na* (U); the

[38]In a tablet published by D. J. Wiseman, "Texts and Fragments," *JCS* 7 (1953) 108, who characterized it as "an unidentified text from Syria" which "has affinities with those from Alalaḫ (Level VII), Ras Shamra, Chagar Bazar, and Mari." Ḫubar-mulli is mentioned there along with Uršu. For *ḫubar*, cf. GN *Ḫalḫubarra* (NA) in the Zagros.

[39]*TM* 75 G 2367, summarized by G. Pettinato, "Relations entre les royaumes d'Ebla et de Mari au troisième millénaire," *Akkadica* 2 (March-April 1977) 20-28. The publication of this tablet in full will perhaps allow to determine the general location of Irim and a few other GN's which closely resemble Transtigridian toponyms.

[40]Published by J. Nougayrol in *Ugaritica V* (Paris 1968), ch. I, 230-51, Nos. 130-42; the Hurrian part is examined by E. Laroche, ibid., ch. II, 448-62.

[41]Nougayrol, op. cit., 242-43, No. 137 II:21′.

[42]Cf. this author's "Maʾḫadu, the Harbor of Ugarit," *JESHO* 13 (1970) 113-27.

[43]At Nuzi, the sign *qa*, because of the simplicity of its shape, was commonly used instead of *ka*.

word also existed in West Semitic languages with the meaning "dwelling, residence."

37. *Na-ma-aḫ-ḫé* (451) :: *Nu-ma-aḫ-ḫé* (A).

38. *Na-na-be-ma* (454) :: *Na-na-ab* (⁺A).

39. *Na-ni-ia-wa* (453) :: *Na-nu-ú*/ *Na-ni-i*/ *Na-a-ni*/ *Nnu*/ *Nni* (U).

40. *Na-ri-ia-wa* (457) :: *Na-ri-e-a* (A); cf. *Na-ra-še* (A).

41. *Pa-aḫ-ḫa-ar-ra-še*/ *Pa-ḫa-ra-aš-we*/ *Pa-ḫar-ra-aš-we*/ *Pa-ḫa-ar-ra-aš-we* (215); *Pa-ḫa-ar-ri-we*/ *Pa-ḫa-ar-we*/ *Pa-ḫa-ar-ḫi* (214) (same place?). From Hurr. *waḫ(a)r-*/ *paḫ(a)r* "good, beautiful,"[44] cf. No. 5. :: *Za-li-wa-ḫa-ri* (A); for *zal-* see No. 69; *Pa-qar-ḫu-bu-ni* (NA), see No. 27: *Pa-ar-ri-e* (⁺A)/ *Fa-ri-wá* (Eg), from *parr-*, a variant of *paḫr-*;[45] but the /ġ/ was retained in class. *Pagrai*/ *Pagrae*, whence Arab. *Baġrās* and Turkish *Bağras*.

42. *Sa-ú-a-wa* (475) :: *Sa-ʾ-[ú?]* (U); Mt. *Sa-ú*/ *Sa-ú-a*/ *Sa-ú-e* (NA), the Bargylus Range.[46]

43. *Ša-a-qa* (or *ša A-qa*?) (519) :: *Ša-ku-e*/ *Ša-ku-we* (A).

44. KUR *Ša-ni-ti*/ *Šá-ni-ti* (548) :: *Ša-an-ni-e* (A).

45. *Ša-an-na-aš-wa*/ *Ša-na-aš-wa* (552): *šanna+š+wa* or *šann+našwe*. :: See Nr. 44.

46. *Ši-la-ḫi-iš* (533): *šila+ḫi+š*? :: *Ši-la-pa-zi-ri* (A).

47. *Ši-lu-⌈un⌉-ta* (335): *šilu+unta* :: *Ši-lu-šu-ma-šu* (A); for *-šumašu* see No. 50; *Ši-lu-ša-*[x x] (A). For the second element, *-unta*, cf. *Ta-du-un-di* (⁺A): *tad+undi*.

48. *Ši-me-ru-un-ni* (539).[47] From Nuzi Akk. *šimeru* "fennel." :: *Ši-me-ri*/ *Ši-mi-i*[*r-ri*?]/ *Ši-mi-ru-ši* (A).

49. *Ši-ni-na*/ *Ši*$_6$*-ni-na* (550) :: *Še-ni-in-na*/ *Še-né-en-na* (A).

50. *Šu-ma-aš-ša-wa-al-li* (541) :: *Ši-lu-šu-ma-šu* (A); for *šilu-* see No. 47.

51. *Šu-ri-ni-wa*/ *Šu-ur-ni-wa*/ *Šur-ni-wa* :: May be compared to (a) *Šu-ru-nu* (⁺A)[48]/ *Šu-ra-an-*[*te*?] (A)/ *Šə̌-wi-rə-ən-tə* (Eg)/ *Šu-ru-un* (H)/ *Su-u-ru-nu* (NA)/ *Sa-ru-na* (NA)/ *Šrn* (OAram) and (b) *Ši-i-ri-na* (H); or, on the other hand, to (c) *Šu-ur-ra-še*/ *Šu-ra-še* (A), analyzed as *šur+na+š+we*.[49]

[44]See n. 12. However, C. Zaccagnini, "The Merchant at Nuzi," in *Trade in the Ancient Near East* (Papers presented to the XXIII R.A.I., Birmingham, 5-9 July, 1976, London 1977) 174, derives *Paḫḫarrašše* from Akk. *paḫḫāru* "potter."

[45]E. Laroche, in *PRU III*, 316.

[46]Cf. this author's "Ancient North Syrian Toponyms Derived from Plant Names," in *The Bible World: Essays in Honor of Cyrus H. Gordon* (New York: Ktav, 1981) 6, Nos. 38, 41, 42 for the derivation of the toponym and oronym from Akk. *sāʾu* "cornel tree."

[47]Probably recurs as *Ši-me-er-ri-ni* in tablet *SH*.867:11, J. Laessøe, *The Shemshāra Tablets: A Preliminary Report* (Copenhagen 1959).

[48]On a seal of unknown provenience, the inscription of which was published and interpreted by M. Dietrich and O. Loretz, "Siegel des Taḫe-Addu," *UF* 1 (1969) 213-15.

[49]A. Goetze, op. cit. (n. 2) 198.

52. *Tam-qa-la-am-bi* (159, 230):[50] *tamqar+ambi*, with Hurr. change *r>l*. For the first element, see No. 53; for the second, No. 6.

53. *Ta-am-qa-ar-ra*/ *Tam-qa-ar-ra*/ *Tam-qar-ra*/ *Tam-qa*[*r-ri-wa*]/ *Ta-am-qa-ri-wa* (271). From Akk. *tamkāru* "merchant."[51] :: *Tam-qá-ri*/ ^{URU}DAM.GÀR (A)/ *Ta-mə́-qu-rə* (Eg.).

54. *Ta-ra-am-bi-ia*/ *dimti ša* ^{m}*Ta-ra-am-bi-ia-wa* (291): *tar+ambi+ia* (+*wa*) :: For *tar*, cf. *Za-la-tar* (A); for *ambi*, see No. 6.

55. *Ta-ar-bi-en* (283) : *tarbi+en(ni)* :: The element *tarbi*/ *tarwe* occurs in *In-tar-we-e*/ *In-ta-ra-we-e* (A), *El-li-ta-ar-bi*/ *El-li-tar-bi* (NA), *Ta-ar-wa-ᵓi* (Eg), perhaps all the same place; and in *Na-aš-tar-bi*/ *Na-aš-tar-we* (⁺A)/ *Nštrbn* (U).[52]

56. *Ta-ri-ba-tú-e* (281). From Akk. *tarībatu*, *tarību* "replacement, substitute, reward," often used as PN's in Babylonia and Nuzi. :: *Ta-ri-bu*/ *Trb* (U).

57. *Te-el-za-ú-un-ni* (268): *til+zāᵓu+unni*, Akk. "mound of resin" with a Hurr. ending. :: *Za-ú-na*/ *Za-ú-ti*/ *Za-i-ti* (A)/ *Za-i-me* (⁺A)/ *Gil-za-ú* (NA), now Zau south of Antakya; *Za-i-ni* (NA) in Gurgum.

58. *Te-te-na* (252) :: *Te-ta-e* (A).[53]

59. *Ti-li-ša*/ *Ti-lu-ša* (269) :: *Ti-li-še*/ *Te-li-še* (A).

60. *Ú-ge* (162), *Ú-ge-en-na* (166)/[*Ú*]*-ge-ni-wa* (165) :: *Ú-gi-te* (U).

61. *Ú-ḫi-na* (169). From Akk. *uḫinu* "a bunch of unripe dates." :: *Ú-ḫé-na-še* (A).

62. *Ú-lam-me*/ *Ú-lam-mi*/ *Ú-la-am-mi*/ *Ú-lam-mi-im-ma* :: *Ul-la-mi*/ *Ul-la-m*[*e*]/ *Ulm* (U).

63. *Ú-ul-lu-a-wa* (172) :: *Ul-la* (A).

64. *Ú-lu-*⌜*li*⌝*-ia-wa* (173) :: *Ull* (U)/ *A-lu-ul-la*/ *A-lu-ul-li* (H). The same two variants of vocalization: *Ù-lu-lum* (Eb)/ *A-lu-lum* (AṢ).

65. *Un-ni-mu-ša*/ *Un-ni-mu-ša-wa*/ *Un-ni-mu-šá-wa* (182): *unni+muša*. The element *muš* (pronounced /*muž*/) is very common in Hurr. onomastica and divine epithets, but its exact meaning is not certain.[54] :: *Mu-zu-un-ni-im* (M)/ *Mu-šu-ni* (A)/ *Mu-šu-un-ni-ba*/ *Mu-šu-ni-pa* (H)/ *Mu-šu-na-ta* (Eg)/ *Mu-s-ní-pa-* (HH).[55]

[50]The first sign, UD, was rendered by L. R. Fisher as *ut*(?) in entry 159, as *pir*(?) in entry 230.

[51]C. Zaccagnini, op. cit. (n. 44) 174 saw in this settlement a special suburb for merchants and compared the similar GN at Alalaḫ. However, the latter place was a normal village whose inhabitants owned vineyards.

[52]In an alphabetical Hurrian ritual text *RS* 24.285, E. Laroche, *Ugaritica V*, ch. II, 511; cf. our note in *UF* 2 (1970) 2, 5.

[53]Thus read, upon collation, by M. Dietrich and O. Loretz, "Die soziale Struktur von Alalaḫ und Ugarit (IV)," *ZA* 60 (1970) 106, No. 26 (= *AT* 185):6 instead of *Te-li-e*.

[54]See P. M. Purves, *NPN* (n. 11 above) 235-36. According to E. Laroche's communication at the XXIVe R.A.I. (Paris, 4-8 July, 1977), *mušunni* means "the just."

[55]See our note in *RA* 67 (1973) 73-75.

66. *Ú-ri* GAL, *Ú-ri* TUR "Great, Little Uri" (186) :: (a) *Ú-ri-e* (+A)/ *Ú-ri*/ *Ú-ur-ri*/ *Ú-ra* (A)/ *Ú-ra-a* (U), now Tell Ūra south of Maᶜarret en-Nuᶜmān; (b) *Ú-ra-a*/ *U-ra-e*/ *Hry* (U), in the area of Ušnatu; (c) *Ú-ri* (Em), perhaps same as (a).

67. *Ú-ri-ḫa-a-a*/ *Ú-ri-ḫa-wa* (185), a suffixed form of the same stem. :: Similar formations are *Ú-ri-iš*/ *Ú-ri-eš-še* (A) and *U-ri-ga* (H).

68. *Wa-ri-i*/ *W*[*a*]*-ri* (194). From Hurr. *wari* "reed, arrow." :: *Wa-ar-ri-e*/ *Wa-ri-ri-i*[56] (+A); and as the second element of *A-la-wa-ri*/ [*A*]l-la-wa-ri (A), *Á-la-wa-'-+r-ti* (HH) "lady of arrows/ reeds" (cf. No. 15); *Za-al-wa-ar* (⁺A), or with assimilation *l>r* *Za-ar-wa-ar* (M)/ *Za-a-ru-ar* (H); river *Sa-lu-a-ra* (NA). For *zal* see No. 69.

69. *Za-al-lu* (488). Only occurrence of *zal* in Nuzi onomastica. :: In Syria, on the contrary, *zal*/ *zall*/ *zala* is found as the first element of several place names: *Za-al-wa-ar* (⁺A) (cf. No. 68), *Za-la-e*, *Za-la-tar*, *Za-al-la-ri-še-na*, *Za-li-wa-ḫa-ri* (A), perhaps *Zlyy* (U, vocalization uncertain.)[57]

70. *Za-mi-te*/ *Za-mi-i-ti* (492) :: *Za-ma-ia* (⁺A).

71. *Zi-il-ia*/ *Zi-il-li*/ *Zi-il-li-wa*, *dimti ša* (486) :: *Zi-la-ia* (A), perhaps *Zlyy* (U) (cf. No. 69).

72. *Zi-ir-zi-ir-ra* (504). From Akk, *zirzirru*, *zizru* "dwarf, minuscule." :: *Zi-zi-ru* (Eb)/ [*Zú*?]-*zú-ur*₄ (AṢ)/ *Zu-uz-zu-ra* (⁺A)/ *Zi-iz-zur*/ *Zi-zur*/ *Zi-zu-ur*/ *Zi-zu-ra*/ *Zi-za-ra* (A), *Zu-un-zu-ur-ḫi* (H).

73. *Zi-za-ar-ri*, a street in the City of Gods.[58] :: (a) *Zi-za-ra* (A), variant of *Zizzira*/ *Zuzzura* (see No. 72); b) *Zi-in-za-ar* (EA)/ *Zi-in-za-ri* (U)/ Śən-*ḏa-rə* / Śə-*ḏa-rə* (Eg)/ *Zi-in-zi-ra* (H), Greek *Sizara*/ *Sinzara*, now Šayzar.

74. *Zu-la-e*, *dimti*/ *Zu-ú-la*, *dimti ša* (485) :: *Zu-lu-te*/ *Zu-lu-ti* (A).

* * *

Taking into account that, as Hildegard Lewy put it,[59] "the Nuzi people usually named towns for their founders and first residents"—and the same may have been true for their congeners in Northern Syria—we add a short list of names which are found in Nuzi texts only as anthroponyms, followed in each case by related North Syrian toponyms:

a) *A-re-en-nu*/ *A-ri-in-nu* :: *A-re-en-na-še* (A).

b) *A-ri-ia* :: *A-ri-ia-an-te*/ *A-ri-an-te* (A)/ *A-ri-ia-an-ta* (H); cf. PN's *A-ri-ia*, *A-ri-ia-an* (A).

c) *A-ta-al-la* :: *A-ta-la-ḫé-na-še*.

[56] Von Brandenstein, op. cit. (n. 11) 104 interpreted *wa-a-ri-ra* in a Bogazköy text as collective plural of *wari*.

[57] But not in *Za-al-ḫé* (A)/ *Za-al-ḫa* (U)/ *Za-al-ḫi* (EA), in which the first sign must be read *sà* in view of the spellings *Slḫ* (U) and *Sa-al-ḫi* (Em).

[58] Lacheman, op. cit. (n. 4) II, 12; he equated the "City of Gods" with Arrapḫa.

[59] Op. cit. (n. 8) 155 n. 34.

d) *Bi-ra-az-zi-na* (*et var.*) :: *Bi-ra-še-na*/ *Be-ra-še-na* (A); this Indo-Aryan PN appears as *Bi-ra-aš-še-n*[*a*] in a fifteenth century tablet from Shechem.[60]

e) ᶠ*Ḫi-in-zu-ri* :: *Ḫe-en-zu-ri-wa* (U). However, this toponym (Akk. *ḫenzūru* "apple, apple-tree") could have been derived directly from the corresponding plant name, which may also have been the case for entries *f* and *n*.

f) ᶠ*Ka-an-za-a*; *Qa-an-zu* :: *Ka-an-za-ta* (U). Since *kanzû* was the Hurrian name of a red-flowering plant,[61] the remark made in entry *e* may apply here as well.

g) *Ku-um-pa* :: *Ku-um-ba* (U).

h) *Ta-du-un-na* :: *Ta-du-un-di* (A).

i) *Ta-e*(*-e*); *Ta-a-a*/ *Ta-a-ia* :: *Ta-ia*/ *Ta-ia-e*/ *Ta-a-ia-e* (A)/ *Ta-e*/ *Ta-ia-a* (NA). Very common PN at Nuzi and Alalaḫ.

j) *Ta-ku*/ *Ta-a-ku*/ *Ta-ak-ku* :: *Ta-ku-wa-aḫ-e*/ *Ta-ku-wa-hé-e* (A). The PN's *Taku*, *Takuwa* were quite common at Alalaḫ and neighboring states.

k) *Tú-ḫe*/ *ḫé-ia*, *Tú-ḫa-a-a* :: *Tu-uḫ-i-ia* (A)/ *Tu-ḫi-i-ia* (U), cf. *Tu-ḫu* (Eb).

l) ᶠ*Ul-me-e*/ *Ul-mi-e*; *Ul-mi-ia* :: *Ul-mu-wa* (U). The PN ᶠ*Ul-mi* was borne by a queen of Amurru in the thirteenth century.[62]

m) *Wa-an-ti-iš-še* :: *Wən-tə*$_x$*-śə* (Eg)/ *Wa*ˀ*-ti*$_4$*-sà-ta-nà-* (HH), a district northwest of Hama. The Hurrian element *want-*, in different spellings, is frequent in North Syrian anthroponymy. The toponym *Ú-wa-an-ta* (A) seems to be a spelling variant of *wanta*.

n) *Zi-ib-be-e*; ᶠ*Zi-be-e*/ *i* :: *Zi-ib-bi* (A)/ *Zi-bi-ḫa* (U). Akk. *zibû* "black cumin"; see remark on plant names in entries *e* and *f*.

o) *Zi-ri-me-ni*/ *Zi-ir-ra-me-ni*, or in correct Akk. spellings, ᵈ*Sin-ra-me-ni*/ ᵈ*Sin-re-me-ni*/ ᵈ*Sin-ir-ra-me-ni* :: *Ṣi-ri-me-ni* (A).[63] The spelling with *ṣi* is singular, but the derivation of the toponym from the same PN as at Nuzi can hardly be doubted. Note also the Nuzi toponym *Za-ri-me-na*/ *Za-ar-*⌜*ri*⌝*-mi-na*/ *Sa-ri-me-e-na* (503), which seems to have a different etymology.

p) *Zu-me*/ *Zu-ú-me* (et var.) :: *Zu-me-ni-e* (A); cf. PN *Zu-mu-an* (A).

APPENDIX

Nuzi Place Names in Egyptian Topographic Lists

In an article dedicated to E. R. Lacheman, it will not be out of place to show how well the Egyptian royal scribes of the New Kingdom were acquainted with the topography of the distant Transtigris region, and in particular with

[60] W. F. Albright, "A Teacher to a Man of Shechem About 1400 B.C.," *BASOR* No. 86 (Apr. 1942) 30 and n. 22; P. F. Dumont, "Indo-Aryan Names From Mitanni, Nuzi, and Syrian Documents," *JAOS* 67 (1947) 251.

[61] See our "Plant Names" (n. 46) No. 23, with references.

[62] *PRU* III, 13 (*RS* 16.111:1).

[63] Mentioned five times in the unpublished tablet 458, kindly provided to the author (in transliteration) by D. J. Wiseman.

numerous localities mentioned in Nuzi tablets. I first called attention to this interesting fact in a paper on the topographic list of Ramesses III,[64] in which I also noted in passing, "It should be stressed that Thutmose III's list, contrary to the prevailing opinion, is not restricted to Syrian localities: it also includes several places located in Cilicia and especially in Transtigris, as we hope to show at another opportunity."[65] I avail myself of the present opportunity to enumerate here those entries in Thutmose III's Naharina List which can be reasonably equated with place names appearing in Nuzi tablets (A), followed by similar excerpts from Ramesses III's Medinet Habu List (B) and from other Egyptian lists and inscriptions (C). The transliteration of Egyptian group writing follows the principles formulated in my 1968 paper.[66]

A. THUTMOSE III'S NAHARINA LIST[67]

1. **142.** *Ru-r-tə-ya* (= *Lultaya*) :: *Nu-ul-ta-aḫ-ḫé* (448), possibly a variant of *Nullu* (*et var.*), Hurrian pronunciation of *Lullu* (cf. C:6 below).

2. **152.** *Ḏə-ən-rə-wi-śu* (= *Zilliwišu*) :: *Zi-il-li-ia-wa*/ *Ṣilli-ia-wa* (489) or *Zi-il-li-wa, dimti ša* (486).

3. **172.** *ᵓA-wi-ru-*⌜*ᵓa*⌝*-na* (=*Awiluᵓana*) :: *A-wi-il-li-ia-wa* (3) or *A-wi-lu-e, dimti ša* (4).

4. **180.** *Wì-ri-*[..] (cf. *Wì-ri-wì* B:6 below) :: *Wi-ir-ra-aḫ-ḫé* (196a).

5. **190.** *Ta-rə-bə́* (cf. A:11 below). This can hardly represent *Ta-ri-bu* (U, see No. 56 above), because no localities of the states of Arwad, Siyannu-Ušnatu, and Ugarit (in its original borders) appear in the Naharina List.[68] :: It may, however, correspond to an unsuffixed variant of *Tar-bi-en* (No. 55 above), *Ta-ri-ba-tú-e* (No. 56 above), or *Tar-ba-aš-ḫé* (B:11 below).

6. **191.** *ᵓA-tu*$_5$*-gə́-n-rə* (= *Atugalla*) (cf. A:9) :: *A-ta-gal*/ *A-ta-kal*/ *A-ta-ag-gal*/ *A-dag-gal*/ *A-tak-kal*/ *A-dag-gal-la*/ *li* (16).

[64]"Mesopotamian and Transtigridian Place Names in the Medinet Habu Lists of Ramses III," *JAOS* 88 (1968) 733-52.

[65]Ibid., 735 n. 20.

[66]Ibid., 749 and chart p. 751 (which is limited to syllabic groups used at Medinet Habu). For the correspondence between Egyptian signs and foreign phonemes see W. F. Albright, *The Vocalization of the Egyptian Syllabic Orthography* (New Haven 1934); J. Vergote, *Phonétique historique de l'égyptien*: *Les consonnes* (Louvain 1945); W. Helck, *Die Beziehungen Ägyptens zu Vorderasien im 3. und 2. Jahrtausend v. Chr.* (Wiesbaden 1962) 589-607.

[67]In the sequence of their appearance, according to the numeration used in J. Simons, *Handbook for the Study of Egyptian Topographical Lists Relating to Western Asia* (Leiden 1937), List I.

[68]Cf. our "Ugarit and the Great Powers," section "Ugarit in the Neutral Zone of Syria," in G. D. Young, ed., *Ugarit in Retrospect*: *Fifty Years of Ugarit and Ugaritic* (Winona Lake: Eisenbrauns 1981) 11-13.

7. **220.** *Ḫu*[!]*-mə₄-rú-rə* (looks like a clumsy rendering of *Ḫu-mellu*) :: *Ḫu-me-el-la*/ *Ḫu-mi-el-la* (389).

8. **221.** *ʾA-tu₅-rə* (= *Aduri*?) :: *A-du-ri* (19).

9. **228.** *ʾA-tə-ka-rə* (= *Atakal*): see A:6 above.

10. **232.** *ʾÙ-bə̀-tə* (= *Ubiti*?) :: *Wa*/ *Wu-bi-ti* (189).

11. **246.** *Ta-rə-bu*: see A:5 above.

12. **248.** *Pá-pá-ʾa* (cf. A:15 below)::URU *ša pa-pa-nu* (202),[69] or *ti-li Pa-pa-an-te* (203, cf. 204).

13. **254.** *Nu-ṯə-na* (= *Nuzina*) :: *Nu-zi*/ *Nu-zu*/ *Nu-zu-e*/ *Nu-zu-ú*/ *Nu-zu-ḫé* (460).

14. **291.** *Tə-kə-ən-wə* (= *Tukiniwa*?) :: *Dug-gi-ni-wa* (255)

15. **296.** *Pá-pa-bə̀*: see A:12 above.

16. **298.** *ʾA-rə-šə-[..]* (= *Arša[wa]*?) :: *Ar-ša-[wa]* (86).

17. **299.** *Má-ri-[..]* (= *Mari[ḫi]*?) :: KUR *Ma-ri-[ḫi]*/ *Ma-ri-ḫi-e* (435): the land of *Marû(m)*/ *Warûm*, Elamite *Mara*, on the Diyala,[70] rather than the more famous Mari of the Euphrates, which no longer existed as a city in the fifteenth century.

18. **312.** *Pər-ʾu-un-ru* (= *Purullu*) :: *Pu-ru-ul-li-wa*/ *Pu-ru-li-wa*/ *Pu-ur-li-wa* (231).[71]

19. **318.** *ʾA-ri-p-nə-ḫa* (probably a distorted writing of *Arrapḫa*) :: *Ar-ra-ap*/ *áp-ḫi*/ *ḫé* (82, 83), historical city, principal center of the area, well known in N. Syria (A) and in Egypt (see B:7 and C:1 below).

20. **320.** *Pu-qí-ya-wə* (Eg. *q* renders Hurr. /ġ/) :: *Pu-ḫi-ya-wa* (213). For the phonetics of the name, cf. PN *Pu-ḫi-še-en-ni* = Ugar. alph. *Pġzn*.

B. RAMESSES III'S MEDINET HABU LIST[72]

1. **15.** *ʾA-⸢ku-⸣šə́-ya* :: *Du-ru-E-kù-še* (289).

2. **23.** *Ka-bu-rə* :: *Kab-ra*/ *Kab-ra* GAL/ *Kab-ra* TUR (323)/ *Qa-ab-ra-a*/ *Qa-ba-ra-a* (M); see B:17 below.

3. **25.** *Tə-śə-ḫa* :: *Ta-šu-uḫ-ḫe*/ *Ta-i-šu-uḫ*/ *Ta-i-šu-uḫ-wa* (303).

4. **26.** *ʾU-ri* :: *Ú-ri* (No. 66 above).

5. **28.** *Mə-tá-na* (cf. C:5 below) :: The Kingdom of Mitanni, Nuzi's overlord, occurs in Nuzi texts only in the title of King Šauššattar, LUGAL *Ma-i-ta-ni*, on his seal (*HSS* IX 1), and perhaps as KUR *Mi-⸢te⸣-en-ni* (439).

6. **30.** *Wì-ru-wì* (cf. A:4 above) :: *Wi-ir-ra-aḫ-ḫé* (196a).

[69] Cf. H. Lewy, op. cit. (n. 8) 152 and n. 14.

[70] Cf. E. Weidner, op. cit. (n. 21) 16; W. König, *Die elamitischen Königsinschriften* (*AfO* Bh. 16, Graz 1965) 82f., No. 28 C I.

[71] Also appears as *Pu-ru-ul-le*/ *Pu-r[u-u]l-li-im* (M) and *Pu-ru-ul-li-we* *SH*[2] 124:2, J. Laessøe, "The Second Shemshāra Archive," *Sumer* 16 (1960) 16, 19.

[72] In the sequence of their appearance in Simons, List XXVII; see the article mentioned in n. 64 for details.

7. **34.** *ᵓA-<rə?>-pa-ḫa* :: Despite the disappearance or omission of *rə*, it is generally agreed that the entry stands for Arrapḫa (see A:19 above and C:1 below).

8. **32.** *Šə-bi* :: *Ši-bi*/ *Ši-bu-e* (511, 512).

9. **40.** *Ka-rə-na* :: *Qa-ra-na*/ *Qa-ra-an-na* (354), also GEŠTIN-*na* (*HSS* XIII 455:11, etc.); not to be confused with the homonymous city in N. Mesopotamia (Tell er-Rimaḥ), which is also listed in the Medinet Habu list (entry 20).

10. **41.** *ᵓA-qə* :: *A-qa-a-a* / *A-ka-a-a* (21)/ *A-qa-áš* / KUR *A-ka-áš* (33).

11. **42.** *Ta-rə-bu-śə* :: *Tar-ba-aš-ḫé*/ *Tar-pa-aš-ḫi*/ *Tar-pa-za-ḫé-na*/ *Tar-ba-az-ḫé-na* (285), recurs as *Tar-bu-si-e*/ *Tar-bu-si-ba*/ *Tar-bu-si-bi* (NA).

12. **44.** ? *ᵓən-ṯə́-ku<-rə??>* :: If thc rcading of the second group as *ṯə́* (rathcr than *tá*) and the restoration of the supposedly omitted *rə* are correct, the entry would correspond to *An-zu-gal*/ *An-zu-gal-li*/ *An-zu-gal-lim*/ *An-zu-qa-al-li*/ *An-zu-qa-al-en* (53, 54).

13. **57.** *Tí-śu-pi* :: A Tešup-holding place name, perhaps abbreviated *dimti ša* ᵐ*Ḫa-i-iš-Te-šup* (407), one of the four known districts of the city of Arrapḫa.[73]

14. **58.** *Ti-śə-ə<n>* (= *Ti-śə-ná *114*) :: *Ti-iš-ša*/ *Ti-ša-e*/ *Ti-iš-ša-e*/ *Di-iš-ša-e* (307). The unequivocal vocalisation of the first group favors this correspondence rather than that with *Ta-še-ni*/ *Ta-še-(en)-ni-wa* (305).

15. **59b+60b.** *Mə-rə-ka-śə-ni-ni* :: KUR *Mur-ku-šá-an-ni-na*/ *Mu-ur-ku-ša-an-ni-it* (434).

16. **50a.** *Tə́-rə* :: *Ti-la*/ *Til-la* (261)?

17. **50b.** *Ka-b-rə* :: *Kab-ra*, see B:2 above.

C. OTHER LISTS AND INSCRIPTIONS

1. *Arrapḫa*, besides the two not quite certain occurrences above (A:19 and B:7), appears as: (a) *ᵓA-rə-p-ḫ<i>* in Amenhotep II's Semneh stele,[74] 1.8, in a fancy enumeration of Syrian and foreign cities and countries; (b) *ᵓA-r-r-pa-ḫá* in Amenhotep III's Soleb list, VIII:A.5.[75] Other occurrences are dubious.

2. *ᵓÁ-rə-tu*$_4$*-gə*/ *ᵓAr-tu*$_4$*-*[*gə*]/ *ᵓÁ-r*[ə]*-tu-*⌜*gə*⌝/ *ᵓÁ-rə-tu-gə*/ *ᵓÁ-rə-tu*$_5$*-gə*;[76] to be

[73]E. R. Lacheman, op. cit. (n. 4) II, 14.

[74]W. Helck, "Eine Stele des Vizekönigs Wśr-Št.t," *JNES* 14 (1955) 22-31, pl. II.

[75]Published (in consonantal transliteration only) by R. Giveon, "Toponymes ouest-asiatiques à Soleb," *VT* 14 (1964) 240-55. The entry in question occurs in a fragment of the list given in hieroglyphic hand copy in Simons, List IXg.

[76]These occurrences are found, respectively, in the following lists: 1) statue inscription from the time of Thutmose III, quoted in E. Edel, *Die Ortsnamenlisten aus dem Totentempel Amenophis III.* (Bonn 1966) 6; 2) funerary temple of Amenhotep III at Kom el-Hetan, List A_N, right side, No. 15, published by E. Edel, op. cit.; 3) Simons, List XI:8 (ascribed to Haremheb but actually of Amenhotep III); 4) Simons, Lists XV:39 (Seti I), XXX:14 (Ramesses III); 5) Simons, Lists XX:6 and XXIIg:8 (Ramesses II).

normalized ᵓ*Artugə*. Identified by E. Edel[77] with the city *Ar-du-uk*[*-ka/qa*?] (H). It must be noted, however, that Arduqqa was located in the far west of Anatolia,[78] and that no names of Anatolian towns north of the Taurus can be found in Egyptian documents of the New Kingdom with the exception of the records of the battle of Qidši and of the list of Hittite gods and their residences in the Egyptian translation of the Hittite-Egyptian peace treaty. Conversely, during their wars with Mitanni the Egyptians collected much geographical information about the territories of the adversary, including the Transtigris region. Since Eg. *g* normally transcribed Hurr. /*ġ*/ (the voiced counterpart of /*ḫ*/),[79] it is preferable to see in ᵓ*Artugə* a Hurr. *ardu+ġi*,[80] probably referring to the town of Ardiḫi near Nuzi (No. 10 above).

3. *Ḫá-bə́-r-ḫə*, Simons List XXIIg:11 (Ramesses II) :: *Ḫa-ba-ru-ḫa* (MA), probably = *A-ba-lu-uḫ-ḫé* (No. 1 above), rather than, as proposed by Edel,[81] *Ḫaburaḫḫi* "Ḫabūr River Land" (unattested).

4. *Ku-rə-ka-nə*, Kom el-Hetan, new fragment[82] of list D_N, left side, No. 1b.[83] Despite the incomplete phonetic correspondence, the only rapprochement that suggests itself is with *Ku-ur-ru-ḫa-an-ni/Gur-ru-ḫa-an-ni* (359) near Nuzi. The interchange *k/ḫ* is attested in Akkadian[84] and in Hurrian.[85]

5. *Mə-ta-ni*: the earliest Eg. mention of Mitanni belongs to the reign of Thutmose I (*ca.* 1520).[86]

[77]"Neue Identifikationen topographischer Namen in den konventionellen Namenszusammenstellungen des Neuen Reiches," in *SAK* 3 (1975) 49-73, §5.

[78]J. Garstang and O. R. Gurney, *The Geography of the Hittite Empire* (London 1959) 106, 108; *RGTC* VI, 40.

[79]E.g. *Ši-nu-ur-ḫé-*⌈*na*⌉ (A) = *Ši-nu₅-rə-gə́-ən-na* Naharina List 211; *Še-et-ḫi-bá-aḫ-e/-bá-ḫé* (A) = *Śə-ta-ḫi-ba-gə*, *ibid.* 155; the correspondence *-ḫuli* = *ġl* in toponyms quoted in No. 9 above; and, in general, E. A. Speiser, *IH*, § 58, and E. Laroche, *Ugaritica V*, ch. II, Hurrian alphabetic texts, *passim*.

[80]A close Hurrian analog to the name in question is the hydronym *Ar-du-ḫi-ni-iš* (H), of unknown location; what is needed, however, is a city name.

[81]Op. cit. (n. 77), § 2.

[82]Kindly communicated to me by E. Edel in 1972.

[83]Second of two names placed in one ring: the first one is *Ma-dú-rə*, probably = *Ma-da-ra-a* (M)/*Ma-da-ra* (NA), now Madar south of Kerh (Kurḫ) on the upper Tigris. One must not be misled by the assonnance *Ku-rə-ka-nə*—Kurḫ: the ancient name of the site was *Tu-uš-ḫi-im* (M)/*Tu-uš-ḫa-an* (NA), and the modern name derives from Aram. *karkā* "city."

[84]Cf. W. von Soden, "Die Spirantisierung von Verschlusslauten im Akkadischen," *JNES* 27 (1968) 214-20.

[85]Cf. C.-G. von Brandenstein, op. cit. (n. 12) 82-83; E. A. Speiser, *IH*, §50d; A. Goetze, op. cit. (n. 2) 200.

[86]Cf. W. Helck, "Überlegungen zur Geschichte der 18. Dynastie," *OrAr* 8 (1969) 301-2, with further references; our "Ḫattušiliš, Ḫalab, and Ḫanigalbat," *JNES* 31 (1972) 104. For other mentions of Mitanni (under that name) in records of the Eighteenth Dynasty, see W. Helck, *Beziehungen* (n. 66) 296 n. 5.

6. *Mə́-r*[ə]*-ku-na*^ROAD^*-š*, Soleb X:B.1, copied *Mə́-rə-ku-*[*nə*]*-š* at ^c^Amārah West, No. 23.[87] :: KUR *Mu-ur-ku-na-aš*/ *Mur-ku-na-aš* (no KUR) (433), a country which exported to Nuzi horses and cloth. Same as B:15 above?[88]

7. *Ru-un-ru* (= *Lullu*), Simons Lists XI:5, XV:43, XX:5, XXI:19, XXII:g:5. :: Long since identified with the people and country *Lullu* (also called at Nuzi *Nullu*) (414, 449) in the Zagros, Akk. *Lulubi* or *Lulume*.

8. *Š-m-š-m*,[89] Soleb VI:B.4b[90] :: *Ša-am-ša-am-mi*/ *Ša-am-ša-am-mu-e* (540), from Akk. *šamšammu* "sesame."

[87]See the article mentioned in n. 64, 739-40, on the spellings and occurrences of this toponym and the possible function of the determinative "road."

[88]If this is so, we are dealing with the nominal stem *murku*, augmented alternatively with the common toponymic formative *-na+š*, or with the rare element *-šan(n)in(a)* which also appears in KUR *Ša-an-har-ra-ša-ni-*[*i*]*n* (for *Šanḫar* = Babylonia) in Tušratta's Hurrian letter *EA* 24:IV:95.

[89]Hieroglyphic copy not available so far; see n. 75.

[90]This ring contains two toponyms; the first one is transliterated *ṯnpìr* by Giveon, which is insufficient for attempting to analyse it.

Hurrians in Babylonia in the Late Second Millennium B.C.

An Unexploited Minority Resource for Socio-Economic and Philological Analysis

J. A. Brinkman
Oriental Institute, Chicago

Four decades ago, in a note on Nuzi geographical names, Professor Lacheman assembled references to Babylonia (Akkad) and to the land of the Kassites occurring in Nuzi texts.[1] On behalf of the Babylonians and Kassites, I should like to reciprocate with a brief discussion of Hurrians in Middle Babylonian and early Neo-Babylonian documents.

The role of the Kassites at Nuzi, recently summarized in *RlA* 5/5-6 (1980) 464-73, has now been placed in new perspective by G. Dosch and K. Deller in an article elsewhere in this volume. Their detailed archival study and genealogical reconstruction trace the presence of one Kassite family in the Nuzi area over a period of seven generations and imply that this family may not have been atypical compared to other families dwelling in the same area: the Kassites may indeed have continued as a distinct and recognizable entity in a Hurrian milieu. The importance of these conclusions for ethnic reconstruction should not be underestimated.

By contrast, the role of the Hurrians in Babylonia during the late second millennium has been passed over in silence by the recent *RlA* article on "Hurriter."[2] This is not difficult to understand because—in contrast to Nuzi—archival studies for late second millennium Babylonia are in an undeveloped state. Whereas two generations of scholars have poured forth monographs and articles on the texts from Nuzi and most of the tablets have now been published (thanks in large measure to the self-sacrificing work of Professor Lacheman), less than one-tenth of the Middle Babylonian economic and

[1] *BASOR* 78 (April 1940) 18-23.

[2] *RlA* 4/6-7 (1975) 507-14. Hurrians in Assyria after 1400 B.C. are also pretermitted. The article focuses on language and written sources almost to the exclusion of history in most conventional senses. This is symptomatic of general lack of interest in the decline of the Hurrians after the loss of their political power base in the middle of the fourteenth century.

administrative archives have been edited; and the majority of texts have never been read. This also means that conclusions drawn from the presently digested material may require substantive revision as research progresses.

I shall attempt in this paper to give only a rough, preliminary sketch of what is currently known about Hurrians in Babylonia between approximately 1350 and 975 B.C. The Hurrians are only one among several ethno-linguistic groups who are present in significant numbers in Babylonia at this time, at least in the well-documented fourteenth and thirteenth centuries.[3] Isolating the Hurrians is not a simple task methodologically, since there is no term corresponding to "Hurrian" in the pertinent Babylonian documents and thus no person is ever labelled specifically as Hurrian. Instead we must detect Hurrians principally through philological analysis of personal names and pinpoint groups and individuals who bear names composed of elements that are commonly accepted as Hurrian.[4]

[3]Others include Assyrians, Elamites, Lullubi, and the Aḫlamû, the precursors of the Arameans.

[4]Other methods of assessing Hurrian presence or influence seem at present less promising or less developed. Archeological finds and analysis have done little as yet to identify material hallmarks of a specifically Hurrian culture. But note that sherds of the distinctive "Nuzi ware" were found in the latest occupational period of level IV of the Middle Babylonian palace at Tell el-ʾAbyaḍ (*Iraq*, Suppl. 1945, p. 11 and pl. XXIV fig. 26); the use of this ware throughout much of the Mitannian realm is detailed in B. Hrouda, *Die bemalte Keramik des zweiten Jahrtausends in Nordmesopotamien und Nordsyrien* (*Istanbuler Forschungen*, 19; Berlin, 1957), esp. pp. 10-21. Further refinements in archeological technique may eventually render evidence from controlled excavations or ceramic surveys more helpful for such problems.

On the textual side, it would help to explore the use of tools other than the analysis of personal names. Institutional or processual influences might be traced from philological evidence. For instance, we might consider the possibility that *ḫurādu*, an Akkadian term for soldier or a military or quasi-military group (often collective in meaning), is a borrowing from Hurrian. The word as Hurrian *ḫuradi*, "soldier" [orthography: *ḫu(-u)-ra(-a)-ti/te/ta(-)*; Laroche, *Glossaire de la langue hourrite*, p. 114] and Urartian *ḫuradi*, "soldier," or "army" [orthography: (LÚ) *ḫu(-ú)-ra(-a)-di (-i)(-e)(-)*; Melikišvili, *Urartskie Klinoobraznye Nadpisi*, p. 396] occurs in the Hurrian-Urartian language family. It first appears in Babylonian and Assyrian around or just after the time of maximum Hurrian contact and across a spectrum reflecting the extent of influence of the Mitannian empire: MA, MB, Amarna, and Boghazkoy. As with certain other foreign occupational loanwords in Akkadian (e.g., *sakrumaš*, *sumaktar*), it has a feminine plural, *ḫurādātu*. In the Neo-Assyrian period, a verb *ḫarādu*, "to keep watch," was derived from it. We do not know the precise character of the *ḫurādu* institution, but it seems to designate men with a particular type of military function. The possibility that it was a borrowing from Hurrian should certainly be considered, though evidence at present is purely circumstantial.

Any techniques complementary to personal-name analysis for detecting cultural influence or cultural interaction are most welcome.

For criteria in distinguishing what belongs to the Hurrian language, I have relied primarily on two works: (1) Pierre M. Purves in *Nuzi Personal Names* (*OIP* 57; Chicago, 1943), pp. 183-279; and (2) Emmanuel Laroche, *Glossaire de la langue hourrite* (*RHA* 34 [1976], 35 (1977]). Only the first of these makes significant reference to Middle Babylonian materials from Babylonia; but the conclusions of each, in matters of lexicon and phonology, will doubtless someday be enriched when thorough study has been made of the Hurrian onomasticon in Babylonia in the late second millennium.

Before proceeding to the discussion proper, I wish to note that the presence of Hurrians, or more accurately of Hurrian names,[5] at Middle Babylonian Nippur is not a new discovery. In 1906, the year in which the first substantial number of Kassite period economic texts from Nippur were published,[6] both A. T. Clay and F. Bork noted the distinctive personal names connected in some way with Hanigalbat or Mitanni.[7] In 1912 Clay followed with a much expanded and more detailed catalogue of Hurrian ("Hittite-Mitannian") name elements and listed more than two hundred Middle Babylonian personal names that he classified as belonging to that group.[8] Clay's basic collection, though now out of date and corrected by later research, remains the last serious study of these names and can still be used with profit. After the discovery of the Nuzi tablets, Purves analyzed many of the Hurrian personal names in them and made occasional brief comparisons with the Nippur material, without however attempting substantially to evaluate the significance of differences in orthography or lexicon between the names attested in the two regions.

Today, undoubtedly, much more can be done. Over the past few months, in the course of my research on another subject, a haphazard and preliminary culling from Middle Babylonian and early Neo-Babylonian texts has yielded

[5]Throughout this paper, the term "Hurrian" will often be used as an abbreviated expression for "person bearing a Hurrian name." The two concepts are not synonymous, as Gelb has noted in similar cases ("Ethnic Reconstruction and Onomastic Evidence," *Names* 10 [1962] 45-52); individuals cannot always be classified as belonging to one or another group simply on the basis of their personal names. Since our primary concern here is with the presence of a substantial group and not so much with the status of this or that individual, the cumulative evidence for Hurrian personal names in relatively large numbers will suffice. It should also be noted that many of the individuals bearing Hurrian personal names are qualified in the texts by gentilics associated with Hurrian regions, e.g., Hanigalbat (*ḫabigalbatû*) or Arrapha (*arrapḫayu*); and such doubly reinforced designations obviously strengthen the identification of an individual as Hurrian.

[6]*BE* 14 and 15.

[7]Clay, *BE* 15 p. 25 n. 4 and Bork, *OLZ* 9 (1906) 588-91.

[8]*Personal Names from Cuneiform Inscriptions of the Cassite Period* (New Haven, 1912), pp. 28-35.

more than three hundred names that are likely to be classified as Hurrian. The following list presents a sample of names that are almost certainly Hurrian.

LIST A.

SAMPLES OF PERSONAL NAMES PROBABLY HURRIAN IN BABYLONIAN TEXTS, 1350-975 B.C.[9]

Babylonian Orthography	*Hurrian Elements*
^{m}*A-gab-še*	*akap*
^{m}*A-gab*(var.: *ga-ab*)*-še-en-ni*	*akap*, *šenni*
^{m}*A-gab-ta-ḫa*, ^{m}*A-ga-ab-taḫ-ḫi*	*akap*, *taḫ(e)*
^{m}*A-gi-ia*	*akiya*
^{m}*A-gi-te-šub*	*aki(p)*, *tešup*
^{m}*Ak-kul-en-ni*	*akkul*, *-enni*
^{m}*Am-me-en-na*	*amm*, *-enna*
^{f}*A-ri-ia-en-ni*	*ari*, *-enni*
^{m}*A-ri-bab-ni*	*ari(p)*, *papni*
^{m}*A-ri-gir-me*	*ari*; *kimre*, var.
^{m}*A-ri-ku-ša*	*ari*, *kuš(a)*
^{m}*A-ri-par*(var.: *pa-ar*)*-ni*	*ari(p)*, *parni*
^{m}*Aš-ta-ra-aš*	*aštar*
^{m}*Aš-tar-til-la*	*aštar*, *tilla*
^{m}*Du-ul-bi-še-en-ni*	*tulpi*, *šenni*
^{m}*Eḫ-li*	*eḫli*
^{m}*Eḫ-li-ku-ša*	*eḫli*, *kuš(a)*
^{m}*El-ḫib*$_{x}$(ḪAB)*-til-la*	*eḫlip*, var.; *tilla*
^{m}*E-zi-ri-en-ni*	*ezira*, *-enni*
^{m}*Ḫa-bi-ir-dil-la*	*ḫapir*, *tilla*
^{m}*Ḫu-di-na-bu*	*ḫutin*, *apu*
^{m}*Ḫu-ut-tir-me*	*ḫut*, *tirwi*
^{m}*I-ri-ri-til-la*	*irir(i)*, *tilla*

[9]The use of voiced and unvoiced consonants is somewhat inconsistent in this chart. The Babylonian column favors more common Babylonian orthographic uses. The Hurrian column tends to follow the transcription system of Purves, *NPN*, and does not usually indicate morpheme boundaries in such cases as *akap* (rather than *ak-ap-*). The evidence in this list is to be regarded as cumulative; individual instances are likely to be open to discussion.

The glide indicated by -IA- in such names as ^{m}*Ṭu-bi-ia-en-na* and ^{f}*A-ri-ia-en-ni* (plus ^{m}*Ba-ri-ia-en-ni* and ^{m}RI*-zi-ia-en-ni* in List B) has been transliterated simply by *-ia-*, although one might make a case in context for *-ie-*. MB glides and their orthography are far from being properly understood or interpreted; compare the name variously written as ^{m}*A-ḫi-ia-a*, ^{m}*A-ḫi-ia-e-a*, and ^{m}*A-ḫi-a-ú-a* in *TuM* NF 5 66:5, 68:10′.41′.

^{m}*Ir-me/mi-ta(-at)-ta*	*erwi, tatta*
^{m}*Ir-ri-gi*	*irrike*
^{m}*Kib-ta-li-li*	*kip, talil*
^{m}*Ki-ra-ri-til-la*	*kerar, tilla*
^{m}*Ma-di-ba-bu*	*matip, apu*
^{m}*Na-e-ma-ra*	*nae/nai, mar(r)a*
^{m}*Na-an-te-šub*	*nan, tešup*
^{m}*Pa-i-da*	*pai, tae*
^{m}*Pa-ap-pa*	*pap*
^{m}*Pu-uḫ-še-en-ni*	*puḫ, šenni*
^{m}*Si-gi*	*zik* (or *šikki*?)
^{m}*Si-il-te-šub*	*zil, tešup*
^{m}*Še-en-da-da*	*šen, tatta*
^{m}*Še-iš-ši*	*šešše*
^{m}*Ši-in-na-nu*	*šennani*
^{m}*Ta-a-a*	*tae*, etc.
^{m}*Ta-di-ba-bu*	*tatip, apu*
^{m}*Ta-e-na*	*taena*
^{m}*Ta-gu-uḫ-li-i*[*a*]	*takuḫle* (poss.: *tak(i), uḫli*)
^{m}*Ta-ḫi*	*taḫ(e)*
^{m}*Ta-ḫib*$_{x}$(ḪAB)-*til-la*[10]	*teḫip, tilla*
^{m}*Tar-ma-ʾ-ḫu-di-in-na-bu*	*tarm(a), ḫutin, apu*
^{m}*Tar-me-te-šub*	*tarmi, tešup*
^{m}*Tu-ra-ri-te-šub*	*turar, tešup*
^{m}*Ṭu-bi-ia-en-na*	*tup, -enna*
^{m}*Un-nu-gi-ia*	*unnuki*
^{m}*Ur-ḫi*	*urḫ(i)*

The next short list presents a few examples of names that may have to be classified as Hurrian and could thus extend our knowledge of the onomasticon.

LIST B.

SAMPLES OF PERSONAL NAMES POSSIBLY HURRIAN IN BABYLONIAN TEXTS, 1350-975 B.C.

Babylonian Orthography	*Hurrian Elements*
^{m}*Al-im-mi-ni*	*al(l), -enni*
^{m}*A-lu-zi-ni*	*al(l)u, zenni* (*šenni?*)
^{m}*Aš-di-qu*	*ašt(e), -ku*
^{m}*Ba-ri-ia-en-ni*	*par(i), -enni*
^{m}*Ḫu-ʾ-a*	*ḫu(i)*
^{m}*Ḫu(-ud)-di-ma-nu*	*ḫut*

[10] Presumably a variant of Nuzi's *Teḫip-tilla*.

^{m}*I-mi-ni-zi-en-ni*, ^{m}*I-me-en-ni-zi-na*	*zenni* (*šenni?*)
^{m}*Ki-ni-ip-pu*	*kin*
^{m}*Ku-up-pa*	*kup(p)*
^{m}*Nap-sa-me(-en)-ni*	*-enni*
^{m}*Ri / Tal-zi-ia-en-ni*	*-enni*
^{m}*Še-en-nu-na*	*šenni*
^{m}*Ta-ik-kir-ḫi*	*tai*, *kir*
^{m}*Ta-ni-il-la*	*tanni*, *lla*
^{m}*Ú-za-an-nu-uḫ-li-ia*	*uza(n)*, *uḫli*

Hurrian names (here abbreviated HPN) occur in one of four formulae:

(a) HPN
(b) *mār* HPN
(c) PN *mār* HPN
(d) HPN *mār* HPN.

The first two forms are reserved for active individuals: one designated by his own name, the second primarily by his patronymic ("son of so-and-so"). The third form indicates only that the father of the active individual bore a Hurrian name. The fourth form shows two successive generations with Hurrian names. Very rough preliminary statistics indicate that approximately 86% of MB references to Hurrian names fall into type (a), about 4% into type (b), about 9% into type (c), about 1% into type (d). Thus Hurrian personal names in the overwhelming majority of cases are borne by living individuals.

The chronological and geographical range of these names is worth noting. In the Middle Babylonian period, the earliest datable examples fall during the reign of Burna-Buriaš II (c. 1359-1333), just after the beginning of the extensive documentation of the Nippur archives. Hurrian names continue through most of the period of the archives, dying out only after the reign of Kaštiliašu IV (c. 1232-1225) when the Nippur texts stop almost completely. Not unexpectedly, the volume of Middle Babylonian material relating to the Hurrians closely parallels the numerical distribution of Middle Babylonian texts as a whole: the overwhelming majority of references come from Nippur in the fourteenth and thirteenth centuries, where there is evidence for a substantial Hurrian population. But evidence for Hurrians is not lacking from other Middle Babylonian sites. Materials pertaining to Dūr-Kurigalzu, Padan, Lubdu, and the as yet undetermined site of the Peiser archives also attest a Hurrian presence in these areas. By contrast, archives from Babylon and Ur have yet to yield a Hurrian name.

In the early Neo-Babylonian period, here taken as 1155-975 B.C., there are only two certain examples of Hurrian names, both occurring in kudurrus concerned with Kassite domains, probably in northeastern Babylonia. The individuals were active in the reign of Nebuchadnezzar I (1125-1104 B.C.) under the Second Isin Dynasty and in the reign of Ninurta-kudurrī-uṣur I

(985-983 B.C.) under the Bazi Dynasty. There are two examples of possibly Hurrian names, both in the early eleventh century, one at Nippur and one at an undetermined site (perhaps Opis).

Turning to a consideration of the roles played by Hurrians in Babylonia, we find a sharp differentiation in their status between the Middle Babylonian and early Neo-Babylonian periods. In Middle Babylonian times, almost all Hurrians were humble workers or of servile status. By contrast, in early Neo-Babylonian times, persons with Hurrian names—probable or possible—held relatively high political or religious office or were related to such officials. This generalization, however, should be treated with considerable caution; the sources, which are heavily concentrated in specific economic archives at Nippur over a period of five generations for the Middle Babylonian period and are extremely sparse for the Neo-Babylonian period, may well be imbalanced and not representative for their eras.

The Middle Babylonian texts, especially from Nippur, show Hurrian names occurring regularly on personnel rosters, especially ration lists. Most of these lists do not explicitly indicate either the status of the personnel or the tasks they were expected to perform. Some of the more detailed lists clearly identify Hurrians as belonging to the guruš class, i.e., servile laborers; but how widely this designation can be extended to other Hurrians remains a matter for conjecture.[11] Hurrians occur as isolated individuals without families.[12] Almost all are adult males, although one female and one youth (GURUŠ.TUR) are attested. Some of them are listed as having occupations: scribes, chariot-builders, leather-workers, farmers (*iššakkū*), fishermen, weavers, and musicians (*nârū*).

In the personnel lists, many of the Hurrians are grouped together by place of origin. When these designations are arranged on a map, we can see that the Hurrians came from places spread out across most of the range of the old Mitannian empire: from Amurru (Syria) in the west through Hanigalbat and Assyria to Lullubi and Arrapha in the east.[13] These people begin to appear in Babylonia just about the time the old Mitannian empire was crumbling. That some of them may have come as refugees or as seasonal workers is possible, but this is not revealed in the sources. In two documented cases in which

[11]Most rosters or ration lists do not contain sufficiently specific information either to prove or to exclude guruš status for the persons listed. The terse documents are utilitarian, fitting silently into a socio-economic context whose character was obvious to contemporaries but can only be surmised today.

[12]Hurrians to date are not attested in those guruš lists that arrange personnel by family units, listing each family member by sex-age classification and by relation to the head of the household.

[13]Hurrians are also sometimes qualified by the gentilic *arunayu* (e.g., *PBS* 2/2 13:41, *BE* 15 198:101), though I am not aware that the place underlying this gentilic has been identified.

members of this group moved into Babylonia or circulated within Babylonia, they were purchased from merchants.[14] In another case, about 1230 B.C., a fugitive leather-worker from Hanigalbat sought asylum with the Babylonian king and was granted a small plot of land in the east in the area of Padan.[15] Hurrian fugitives were also settled in the northeast around Lubdu, but the texts do not specify whether they fled into Babylonia from foreign parts or were fugitives from work-gangs elsewhere in Babylonia. It is unfortunate that we know so little about the mechanisms by which people were displaced at this time, for we might have learned more about the disintegration of the Mitannian empire and about the decline and dispersal of the Hurrian people.

In Middle Babylonian times, the only individual bearing a possibly Hurrian name who seems to have enjoyed demonstrably higher status is Ḫuʾa, a messenger of Burna-Buriaš II who is mentioned in an Amarna letter.[16] It would undoubtedly have been an advantage to employ a messenger who could speak the language of the principal foreign territory through which he would pass en route from Babylonia to Egypt.

After the fall of the Kassite dynasty, in early Neo-Babylonian times, both individuals bearing probably Hurrian names are *ša rēši* officials in Kassite-inhabited tribal areas, most likely in northeastern Babylonia. It is striking that in neither case is a genealogy or patronymic listed—in contrast to most other witnesses in these texts, who usually have the additional designation of either their father's name or a tribal affiliation. Are these men to be viewed as new arrivals, or should this be seen as an indication of a differing Hurrian social structure?[17] Of the two other men who bear possibly Hurrian names, one was a diviner and high temple official (*nišakku* of Enlil) at Nippur; and the other was the father of the *sukkalmaḫ māti*, perhaps to be rendered "grand vizier of the land," in any case a very high official indeed. Humble Hurrians seem conspicuously lacking at this time; but then almost equally lacking are humble economic texts.

[14] An Assyrian merchant sold a Lullubian slave named Šešši, probably to someone in Dūr-Kurigalzu in *Sumer* 9 (1953), plates following p. 34, no. 27; lines 1 and 2 of this text should be read as follows:

(1) 1/3 MA.NA 1 1/2 GÍN KÙ.GI ŠÁM ᵐ*Še-⸢iš⸣-ši lul-lu-⸢ba*?⸣-[*a-a-i*]

(2) *iš-tu* ᵐᵈ⸢UTU⸣-*mu-dam-mi-iq* ⸢DAM.GÀR⸣ *aš-šur-a-a*-[*i*]

Enlil-kidinnī, at one time the governor of Nippur under Burna-Buriaš II, purchased two other Hurrians—also from a merchant (*TuM* NF 5 66).

[15] There is no explicit evidence that some Hurrians came into Babylonia as prisoners-of-war (either directly or through Assyria), although this too cannot be ruled out.

[16] *EA* 11:5.

[17] It should be noted that these men are not the only persons without genealogy in the early NB witness lists and that MB Hurrians on occasion had patronymics listed; so the issue is far from clear.

This has been a preliminary survey, just touching superficially on various facets of our knowledge about Hurrians in Babylonia in Middle Babylonian and early Neo-Babylonian times. It is difficult to draw even a premature synthesis out of the disjointed and perhaps unrepresentative data. In the late second millennium, just about the time when the empire of Mitanni was disintegrating, Hurrians began to appear in substantial numbers in Babylonia.[18] They came from most parts of the former empire, from Syria and Hanigalbat in the west to Assyria and Arrapha in the east. Whether most of them came as immigrants, seasonal workers, fugitives, prisoners, or slaves[19] is not known; but they came for the most part without families and served as workers of relatively low status in Babylonia, sometimes belonging to groups of servile laborers (the guruš class). A substantial percentage of them bore Hurrian names, though many in their common work groups—e.g., from Arrapha—had Babylonian names. For over a century (c. 1350-1225 B.C.), Hurrians formed a notable minority within the population of Babylonia, particularly in the south central area around Nippur. It is unfortunate that there are still insufficient data to make a demographic study of this population: for example its relative size, the process whereby it was replenished over five generations (by new arrivals or by unrecorded families), and its eventual fate (extinction, absorption, or emigration). Later attestations of Hurrians (c. 1125-975) reveal only isolated individuals, but of elevated political or religious rank; it is not known whether these officials were relatively new arrivals or descendants of Hurrian families already settled. At any rate, Hurrians form a distinct, traceable minority group in Babylonia in the late second millennium B.C.; and future research on the subject may throw further light on political history, socio-economic processes, and the various stages of development of the Hurrian language. It may also place what is now an isolated datum in historical context and perspective.*

[18]The Hurrians in Babylonia in earlier periods had already been assimilated (or otherwise disappeared as a distinguishable entity).

[19]I.e., here in the sense of someone sold for money.

*Research for this paper was made possible in part by a grant from the National Endowment for the Humanities, Research Grant program.

Une Querelle de Famille

Elena Cassin
Paris

La famille nuzite dont il sera question ici est connue grâce à un certain nombre de texts dont la plus grande partie a été publiée par celui auquel ces quelques pages sont dédiées.

Il s'agit de la famille de Ḫuia d'après le nom du plux ancien membre auquel j'ai pu remonter. Sur Ḫuia lui-même nous savons très peu de chose à part le fait qu'un *dimtu*[1] portait son nom. Nous connaissons également, grâce à *AASOR* 16 56, quelles sont ses préoccupations en tant que chef de famille lorsque malade et peut-être sentant sa fin prochaine, il essaie de régler la situation de ses fils. A travers les paroles de l'un d'eux, Tarmiia,[2] nous assistons à "une scène très touchante":[3] Ḫuia, alité, prend la main[4] de son fils cadet Tarmiia et lui destine comme épouse une de ses servantes. Il espère par ce biais que le désavantage de Tarmiia qui est encore célibataire, par rapport à ses deux frères aînés Šukriia et Kulaḫupe qui sont déjà mariés, sera comblé.

Ḫuia avait en réalité un nombre d'enfants plus grand que ce texte pourrait le laisser croire. A part les trois nommés, au moins deux ou trois autres apparaissent fréquemment dans des documents juridiques et administratifs. Zilipapu et Šennape figurent souvent dans les procès comme juges.[5] En outre, Tarmiia et Šennape[6] occupent des postes importants dans la vie citadine.

[1] *HSS* 19 30^{10}.

[2] *AASOR* 16, 56 est un procès devant les juges de Nuzi entre Tarmiia et ses deux frères Šukriia et Kulaḫupe au sujet de la servante Ṣululi-Ištar.

[3] A. L. Oppenheim, *Ancient Mesopotamia*, p. 283. Cf. E. A. Speiser, "I know not the day of my death," *Oriental and Biblical Studies*, p. 91-92, donne une excellente analyse de ce texte. En réalité comme Speiser l'a très bien compris il ne s'agit pas seulement d'une scène "vividly described" (p. 92) mais d'une procédure juridique.

[4] Sur le geste de prendre la main et sa valeur juridique, voir Speiser, *loc. cit.*, p. 92, n. 10.

[5] Zilipapu: *JEN* 663^{34}; 669^{75} (sans patronymique), Šennape: *JEN* 663^{32}; 669^{75} (sans patronymique). Ils sont l'un et l'autre juges dans *JEN* $370^{51, 53}$ procès contre leur frère Tarmiia. Leurs sceaux apparaissent sur la tablette avec ceux d'autre juges de Nuzi, entre autres, Akaptukke, fils de Kakki.

[6] Šennaia, contrairement à ce que suggérait *NPN*, p. 130b-131a, s.v., n'est probablement pas la même personne que Šennape.

Tarmiia est *gugallu*, fontainier, et comme tel aura des démêlés avec les autorités de la ville pour des activités illégales dans l'exercice de ses fonctions.[7] Quant à Šennaia, il est *warad bît ḫurizāti*[8] et touche avec son frēre Tarmiia des rations alimentaires du Palais.

C'est autour de Šukriia ou plutôt de ses descendants que va se resserrer mon enquête. Šukriia est un chef de famille nanti d'un patrimoine immobilier assex conséquent. De lui, on sait en outre qu'à un certain moment il parviendra à occuper des terres appartenant aux héritiers du célèbre Teḫiptilla, fils de Puḫišenni, mais ces derniers finiront par récupérer leurs biens.[9]

Le document le plus important que nous avons sur Šukriia est le testament (*ṭuppi šimti*), dans lequel il décide de son vivant le partage de ses biens entre trois de ses fils. Ce texte, *HSS* 19 5, est divisé en plusieurs sections séparées entre elles par une ligne transversale. La première concerne les immeubles que Šukriia destine à son fils aîné Teḫiptilla; la deuxième, ceux de Paitilla et la troisième ceux de Šimikatal. Quant aux autres biens qu'il possède mais qui ne sont pas numérés dans les paragraphes précédents, ils seront partagés entre les trois fils, l'aîné recevant deux parts et les deux cadets une seule part "selon son pied."[10] Quant à Šimikatal, son statut familial est moins favorable que celui des deux autres. Ceci apparaît, entre autres, par l'injonction qui lui est faite de ne vendre à un étranger aucune partie de l'héritage qui lui sera dévolu.[11] Au cas où il passerait outre à cette interdiction, il paiera à ses frères une amende pécuniaire. De plus, il ne participera pas à la division de ce qui aura appartenu à la veuve de Šukriia[12] lorsque celle-ci viendra à disparaître. Ceci nous incline à penser qu'il est probablement fils d'une autre mère que Teḫiptilla et Paitilla. La mère de ces derniers s'appelle Warḫinuzu et Šukriia stipule qu'après sa mort, elle continuera à habiter la maison maritale. Par un autre texte,[13] nous apprenons son patronymique, elle est fille de

[7] *JEN* 370.

[8] *HSS* 16 83[13]. Sur cet édifice officiel on possède plusieures reférences: on sait qu'il était gardé par une troupe de dix hommes (*emantu*) montés sur char (*HSS* 15 82[15]), un *šakin bīti* l'administrait (*HSS* 15 224[4-5]), il avait son propre *ṭupšarru* (E. R. Lacheman, *Sumer* 32, p. 127, 5). Il est fait parfois allusion aux *ḫurizātu* d'autres villes, par exemple, à celui de Tarpašḫe (*HSS* 16 133[4]).

[9] *RA* 23, No. 59 + *JEN* 126 + 105: cf. H. Lewy, *Or*. 11 (1942), p. 212-13.

[10] E. R. Lacheman a été le premier à attirer l'attention sur la signification juridique de cette formule, cf. *JBL* 56 (1937), p. 56. Voir également "Symboles de cession immobilière," *Année Sociologique*, 1952 (1955), p. 129.

[11] Lignes 40-43 Le texte precise que Šimikatal ne vendra à personne d'autre en dehors des ses frères, ligne 41-42: *a-na ši-mi a-na* LÚ *na-ka-ri u*[*š-tu aḫ*]*ḫē*[MEŠ]*-šu-nu la i-na-an-din*.

[12] Tandis que Šimikatal n'approchera pas (*l*[*a*] *i-qè-e*[*r*]*-ri-ib*) des ce que possedait la veuve, Teḫiptilla recevra la maison maritale où elle habitait et, en outre, il partagera avec son frère Paitilla tout ce qu'elle aura laissé.

[13] *HSS* 19 25[3].

Ḫupita. Warḫinuzu apparaît également dans deux autres documents qui ont été certainement écrits après son veuvage.[14] Dans l'un, *HSS* 19 30, qui est d'après son contenu un *ṭuppi zitti,*[15] les deux fils de Šukriia et de Warḫinuzu, Teḫiptilla[16] et Paitilla, livrent à leur oncle paternel Tarmiia deux parcelles de champs situées dans le *dimtu* de leur grand-père Ḫuia[17] et reçoivent de leur oncle de l'orge et des brebis. L'une et l'autre prestations sont appelées également ḪA.LA: *zittu*, part d'héritage, bien qu'il soit évident que l'orge et les brebis constituent le prix des champs, qui ont été octroyés par les deux frères à leur oncle. Ce qui ressort également de la formule consacrée que Teḫiptilla et Paitilla prononcent après avoir été payés: "Nous avons reçu (l'orge et les brebis) et sommes satisfaits" ([19] *ni-il-te-qè ap-la* [-*nu*]). Leur dire est suivi par une déclaration de leur mère, Warḫinuzu: "Je ne suis pas investie de la fonction paternelle" ([19] [*um-ma*] [20] MÍ*Wa-ar-ḫi-nu-zu-ma a-n*[*a-ku*][21] *a-na a-bu-ti la ep-ša-ku-m*[*i*]).[18]

Quel est le sens de cette déclaration? Pourquoi justement au moment de transmettre à un tiers—qui est un parent—une partie des champs de leur héritage—le fait que ces terres se trouvent dans le *dimtu* de Ḫuia et que les deux frères les possèdent ensemble rend la chose très probable—Teḫiptilla et Paitilla font intervenir la veuve de Šukriia pour dire qu'elle n'exerce pas l'*ab*(*b*)*utu*? Ceci, à mon avis, ne peut avoir de sens qu'en rapport avec la libre disponibilité que Teḫiptilla et Paitilla ont de leurs biens d'héritage, la mère qui

[14]*HSS* 19 30[20] et 14 8[7].

[15]D'après son contenu, puisque les premières lignes de la tablettes manquent. On retrouve le scribe de cette tablette Sîn-šadūni, fils de Amur-šarri, dans une autre tablette qui concerne également la famille de Ḫuia, *HSS* 19 67. Il s'agit d'une adoption comme soeur d'une femme, Azunnaia, fille de Ḫašiia, de la part de Tarmiia, fils de Ḫuia qui la donnera en mariage et recevra du futur beau-père ([7]*a-šar ḫa-ta-ni*) un boeuf, tandis que le reste de la *tirḫatu* sera versée à Ḫašip-Tešup, "dont Azunnaia est la soeur" (ligne 10-11). L'originalité de ce scribe se manifeste dans la clause du *šūdūtu* qui est redigée dans *HSS* 19 30[22-25] et 67[17-18] en des termes identiques: *ṭuppi anni ina arki šūdūti ina* URU*Nuzi ina bāb ekalli ina arḫi ḫutalše šaṭir*. Quel est le sens de cette précision temporelle? On retrouve le mois *ḫutalše* dans un contexte similaire dans *JEN* 116 (scribe Adad-rēṣi qui exerce son art à Purulli et à Šurini à l'époque de Kel-Tešup fils de Ḫutiia): "la tablette à été écrite après la nouvelle proclamation à Purulli dans le mois de *ḫutalše* selon l'édit du roi du mois de *kinūnu* de la ville des dieux" (lignes 11-15).

[16]Ligne 10; écrit *It-ḫi-til-la* par erreur, il s'agit certainement de Teḫiptilla.

[17]Ligne 10. La deuxième parcelle de champ est mitoyenne au sud avec un champ de Tarmiia, d'où l'intérêt pour ce dernier d'élargir ce qu'il possède déjà par l'acquisition d'une partie des terres héritées par ses neveux.

[18]La restitution de la ligne 20 est probablement exacte; à moins qu'il ne faille restituer ....*a-n*[*a* DUMU^{MEŠ}-*ia*]: sur mes fils, ce qui serait peut-être possible. Cf. sur l'*ab*(*b*)*utu* conféré par un père à la mère de ses enfants ou de certains parmi eux, mon article dans *RA* 63 (1969), p. 121 sq.

n'a pas été habilitée par son mari à exercer la puissance paternelle, ne peut faire aucune opposition au transfert que Teḫiptilla et Paitilla viennent de conclure avec leur oncle. Par contre, si elle avait été investie par Šukriia de cette fonction, les choses auraient été différentes.[19]

Plus intéressant pour la lumière qu'il projette brusquement sur un aspect insuffisamment connu mais très important de la vie religieuse des habitants de cette région est un petit texte qui met encore en vedette Warḫinuzu.

Il s'agit d'une double déclaration contradictoire que deux adversaires prononcent devant les juges.[20] L'un des adversaires est Paitilla, le fils de Šukriia. C'est lui l'accusateur. Il formule une charge précise contre l'accusé Akiptašenni, fils de Tae. Le premier introduit son affirmation par *šumma..la*, l'autre sa réfutation par *šumma.*[21] Il s'agit en fait d'un double serment conditionnel qui conduit les deux adversaires à prouver la vérité de ce que chacun d'eux avance en se soumettant à l'ordalie par le Fleuve. Le roi prendra une décision à l'égard de celui qui est "pris" par le Fleuve.[22] En quoi consiste l'accusation de Paitilla? Il fait grief à Akiptašenni d'avoir reçu de Warḫinuzu, sa mère, les dieux de sa famille et d'avoir ensuite amené à l'étranger Warḫinuzu et Inipḫatti, la propre soeur de Paitilla, et de les avoir vendues. Akiptašenni nie les deux faits. Voici le texte:

[19]Ceci apparait avec évidence des *ṭuppi šimti* de Nuzi déjà publiés, voir par exemple *HSS* 19 17 où l'*ab*(*b*)*utu* est octroyé à la fille du testateur (ligne 15-16), cf. *RA* 63 (1969), p. 132, n. 7, et également des textes de Kurruḫanni encore inédits. Parmi ces derniers, un contrat d'adoption en filiation présente un intérêt particulier: une femme qui déclare avoir été investie de l'*ab*(*b*)*utu*, adopte un étranger bien qu'ayant déjà un fils. Le fils par le sang partagera avec le fils adoptif les biens que le mari de l'adoptante a laissé. Au cas où le fils par le sang meurt sans enfant, l'adopté héritera de tous ses biens.

[20]Bien que le nom d'aucune des quatre personnes qui ont apposé leur sceau sur la tablette ne soit suivi de la mention juge, il me parait que leur présence ne peut s'expliquer autrement. A noter que l'un des sceaux appartient à Šennape, oncle de l'accusateur, que l'on rencontre dans autres textes comme juge, cf. *supra*, n. 5; quant à un autre sceau, il appartient à Iruia, fils de Zikaia, qui dans *JEN* 662 ^{93}, procès-fleuve des petits-fils de Teḫiptilla au sujet de champs que leur grand -père avait acquis par un contrat de *mārūtu*, appose son sceau sur la tablette à côté de ceux d'autres personnes connues comme juges.

[21]Les termes de l'alternative qui est posée au fleuve sont spécifiés avec clarté afin qu'aucune ambiguité soit possible. Le pouvoir divinatoire du fleuve, et de l'eau, en général, lui permet de déceler entre les deux adversaires, celui qui est coupable. Pour d'autres textes du même type, cf. *JEN* 124, 125, 631; *HSS* 13 422; *AASOR* 16 74, 75 *et pass.*

[22]Contrairement à ce qui a lieu dans d'autres cas (celui qui est "pris," sera tué: *AASOR* 16 74^{25-27}; 75^{30-31}, ou il sera évincé de ses immeubles: *RA* 23, N° 29^{42}) dans *HSS* 19 8, comme dans *HSS* 9 7^{25-26}; 13 422^{37} *et pass.*, c'est le roi qui décidera la peine qui sera infligée à celui que le Fleuve a désigné comme coupable.

HSS 14 8

Face

[*um-*]*ma* ^{I}*Pá-i-til-la-ma mār Šuk-ri-ia*
[*šum-m*]*a* DINGIR^{MEŠ}*-ia* DINGIR.ZAB^{MEŠ} *um-mi-ia*
[*a-n*]*a* ^{I}*A-kip-ta-še-en-ni mār Ta-e*
[*la*] *it-ti-nu-ma ù la ik-ki-ru*
ù šum-ma ki-ma DINGIR^{MEŠ} ^{I}*A-kip-ta-*[*še-en-ni*]
um-mi-ia ù a-ḫa-ti^{MEŠ}*-ia*
^{MÍ}*Wa-ar-ḫi-nu-zu ù* ^{MÍ}*I-n*[*i-ip*]*-ḫa-ti*
a-na māti ša-ni-i a-na šīmi^{MEŠ} *l*[*a it-t*]*a-din*
[*u*]*m-ma* ^{I}*A-kip-ta-še-en-ni-ma mār Ta*[*-e*]
[*šum-*]*ma* DINGIR^{MEŠ} DINGIR.ZAB^{MEŠ} [*š*]*a* ^{I}*Pá-i-til-l*[*a*]
[*š*]*a um-ma-šu a-na ia-ši it-*[*ti-nu*]
[*ù*] *at-ta-ki-ir-šu-mi ù šum-m*[*a*]
[*ki-*]*ma* DINGIR^{MEŠ} *um-ma-šu ù*
[*a-ḫ*]*a-ti*^{MEŠ}*-šu ša* ^{I}*Pá-i-til-la-m*[*a*](?)
[^{MÍ}]*I-ni-ip-ḫa-at-ti i-na māti ša-*[*ni-i*] [*a-na šīmi*^{MEŠ} *at-ta-din*]
[*aš-šum*] *a-wa-ti an-nu-t*[*i*] *i*[*-n*]*a ḫ*[*uršāni*]
[*illakū*]^{ku} *ša ik-kal-lu* [*šarru*]
[*ṭe*]*-e-ma i*[*-ša*]*-ak*[*-ka-an*]

(Le reste est détruit, à part les sceaux de quatre juges)

Traduction

[1]Ainsi (parle) Paitilla, fils de Šukriia:[2] "Si ma mère n'a pas livré mes dieux (et) les dieux ZAB [3]à Akiptašenni, fils de Tae, [4]et si (maintenant) celui-ci ne nie pas (les avoir reçu). [5]Et si, comme (il a eu) les dieux, Akiptašenni [6-8]n'a pas vendu à l'étranger ma mère Warḫinuzu et ma soeur Inipḫatti (sous-entendu: qu'il m'arrive les pires maux)

[9]Ainsi (parle) Akiptašenni, fils de Tae,[10]:" Si les dieux (et) les dieux ZAB de Paitilla [11] sa mère m'a livré [12] et si (maintenant) je le nie. Et si,[13] comme (j'ai eu) les dieux, sa mère [14] et Inipḫatti, la soeur de Paitilla,[15] (j'ai vendu) á l'étranger (sous-entendu: qu'il m'arrive les pires maux)

[16][Au sujet de] cette affaire, à l'or[dalie] [17][ils iron]t. Pour celui qui "est pris," [le roi] prendra une decision.

Ce texte sans présenter de grandes difficultés philologiques pose quand-même deux problèmes. Avant tout, que faut-il entendre par ces DINGIR^{MEŠ} DINGIR.ZAB^{MEŠ} de la ligne 2 et de la ligne 7? La présence d'entités divines désignées par le signe ZAB, précédé du déterminatif DINGIR: dieu,[23] ne se

[23]A. E. Draffkorn, *JBL* 76 (1957), p. 221-22 et 224 lit AN.ZAB. Elle compare leur présence à côté des *ilāni* à celle des *teraphim* par rapport aux *elohim*. Cette étude qui contient des suggestions utiles, n'a pas pu exploiter le texte qui nous occupe ici, le volume *HSS* 19 contenant les textes qui m'ont permis d'intégrer Paitilla, Akiptašenni

rencontre pour l'instant que dans deux seuls passages, dans *HSS* 14 8, et dans *JEN* 478.[5] Or, bien que cela n'ait pas une grande signification à Nuzi, il faut noter que c'est dans *HSS* 14 8, seulement, que la marque distinctive du pluriel suit le signe ZAB, donnant ainsi à penser qu'il s'agirait d'un groupe de dieux plutôt que d'un seul. En outre, et ceci a par contre une certaine importance, dans *JEN* 478,[5] DINGIR.ZAB apparaît comme étant indépendant et séparé des dieux (*ilāni*) et des esprits de la famille (*eṭemmē*) qui sont cités dans un contexte différent ensuite. C'est en effet *ina pāni* DINGIR ZAB: devant le dieu ZAB, que le père au moment de déshériter son fils, brise son *kirbānu*,[24] la motte de terre qui symbolise l'ensemble des relations qui lient le fils à sa famille. J'avais autrefois[25] lu ce passage: *ina pāni* ^{d}*šamaš* ne voyant dans DINGIR.ZAB qu'une variante graphique de DINGIR.UTU, le dieu Soleil. Bien que cette graphie ne soit pas fréquente à Nuzi, on en trouve quelques exemples: dans des noms propres théophores composés avec Šamaš ou UTU[26] et également pour désigner le jour, *ūmu*.[27]

Il faut noter, en outre, que dans un texte du même type que *JEN* 478, *HSS* 19 27, dans lequel il est également question d'un père qui déshérite son fils en brisant son *kirbānu*, on déclare que ce dernier sera privé aussi bien de sa part d'héritage que des dieux de la famille et des esprits des morts,[28] mais la mention DINGIR.ZAB fait ici défaut.

A la suite de ces quelques remarques, on pourrait conclure que les DINGIR ZAB^{MEŠ} dans *HSS* 14 8 sont des objets sacrés en relation avec la famille tout en étant distincts des *ilāni*. Cette conclusion pourrait trouver un appui dans un passage d'un texte dont il a déjà été question plus haut. Dans *HSS* 19 5, qui est le testament de Šukriia, le paragraphe qui concerne les biens immobiliers qui sont destinés à Paitilla se termine par la mention des *ilāni* que Šukriia, contrairement à l'usage plus courant à Nuzi, laisse à son fils cadet[29] plutôt qu'à son fils aîné. Il s'agirait donc de ces mêmes *ilāni* que la mère de Paitilla, Warḫinuzu, enlèvera plus tard de la maison maritale pour les donner à un

---

et Warḫinuzu dans leur contexte familiale, n'ayant pas encore été publié au moment de la parution de son article.

[24]Voir pour le rôle de la motte de terre dans ce contexte familial à Nuzi, "Symboles de cession immobilière," *Année Sociologique* 1952 (1955), p. 115 et. sq. et *JESHO* 5 (1962), p. 133 et sq.

[25]*JESHO* 5 (1962), p. 134.

[26]Quelques exemples: Šamaš-šemī, *JEN* 23$^{2, 10, 11}$*et pass.* (scribe Taia, fils d'Apil-Sîn), Uta-an-dul: *HSS* 19 28^{36} (scribe Muš-Tešup, fils de Ḫupita).

[27]*JEN* 231^{32} (scribe Taia), 554$^{5, 8}$ (scribe Sîn-uballiṭ, fils de Taia).

[28]*HSS* 19 27 ^{8}*uš-tu*$_4$ *u*$_4$*-m*[*i an-ni-i*] ^{9}*ki-ir-bá-an-š*[*u*.....] ^{10}*aḫ-te-pé-m*[*i*] *ù*..... ^{11}*ú-ul i*[*lāni-i*]*a ú*[*-ul e*]*-ṭe-em-me-ia.*

[29]Ligne 21. Les dieux sont cités à la suite des immeubles—en grande partie des maisons et des bâtiments que Šukriia donne à son fils Paitilla.

tiers. Or, dans le testament de Šukriia (ligne 21) les *ilāni* que celui-ci destine à son fils Paitilla sont désignés comme DINGIR^{MEŠ} *ša* SAG.DU-*i*[*a*]: *ilāni*^{MEŠ} *ša qaqqadi-i*[*a*], "les dieux de ma tête,"[30] c'est-à-dire: mes dieux personnels. Avons-nous ici simplement une autre dénomination de ces mêmes dieux que l'on rencontre ailleurs désignés tantôt comme: mes dieux (*HSS* 14 108^{24}: *i-la-nu-ia*; *RA* 23, N° 5^{20}: DINGIR^{MEŠ}-*ia*) tantôt comme les dieux d'un tel (*JEN* 89^{10-11}; 216^{14-16}: DINGIR^{MEŠ} *ša X*)? Ou bien s'agirait-il de dieux personnels au sens propre, distincts des dieux familiaux que l'on se transmet de génération en génération? Plutôt que possédés, ces dieux familiaux devaient constituer un dépôt sacré qui passait du père au fils aîné.[31] On peut supposer que dans cette chaîne où le dépositaire changeait à chaque génération, le seul élément stable était peut-être le lieu où ces dieux étaient remisés.[32] Par contre, dans le cas de dieux personnels, le lien qui les rattachait à un individu particulier était plus indépendant du contexte familial: et c'est peut-être aussi dans ce caractère individuel, dans le fait qu'ils appartiennent à un seul, qu'il faut rechercher la plus grande liberté dans le choix du fils qui allait en hériter.

Ceci dit, qu'on suppose ou non, une relation entre les *ilāni ša qaqqadi*, mentionnés dans le testament de Šukriia (*HSS* 19 5^{21}) et les DINGIR.ZAB^{MEŠ} de *HSS* 14 8, qui appartiennent les uns et les autres à la même personne, Paitilla, il reste que nous avons avec Warḫinuzu le cas—qui n'était peut-être pas insolite[33]—d'une femme qui s'empare des *sacra* de la maison de son mari mort pour les amener dans un autre foyer. Or, nous savons, grâce à un autre texte (*HSS* 19 25) quels liens existent entre la veuve Warḫinuzu et cet Akiptašenni,

[30]Le sumérogramme SAG.DU semble sûr; par contre le début du signe -*i*[*a*] est plus douteux. Il se pourrait que l'on retrouve la même expression dans un autre texte, *HSS* 19 15, un *ṭuppi šimti* également, où aux lignes 22-23, on pourrait peut-être lire: [*um*] -*ma Zi-ga-a-a-ma i*[...*i*-]*na* DINGIR^{MEŠ} *ša*(?) *qa-aq*(?)-*qa-ti*(?)[-*ia*...]. Pour cette expression inusuelle et difficile, voir von Soden, *Akkadisches Handwörterbuch*, p. 974a. Dans deux passages Sîn est appelé, le dieu de ma tête: avant tout dans la lettre de Iarim-lim roi d'Alep à Iašub-iaḫad, roi de Dêr (cf. G. Dossin, *Syria* 33 (1956), p. 67, ligne 28): *ilu re-ši-ia*; en outre dans l'inscription de Šamši-Adad I (*AOB* p. 26, ligne 19) où *il re-ši-ia* pourrait toutefois être une ellipse pour *ilu mulli rēšiia*, cf. A. K. Grayson *ARI* I, p. 21, n. 69.

[31]Cf. *HSS* 14 108^{24}; *RA* 23, N° 5^{20}.

[32]Dans *HSS* 14 107^{1} *I*^{en} É *e-kal-lu ša* DINGIR^{MEŠ}: un grand bâtiment pour les dieux, qu'une femme laisse, avec les dépendences, à son fils. De même dans *HSS* 19 4^{15}, Aršatuia destine à son fils aine une maison dans la campagne autour de Nuzi où il garde ses dieux (I É *i-na ṣe-ri-ti i-na* ^{URU}*Nu-zi* DINGIR^{MEŠ} *ša* ^{I}*Ar-ša-tu-ia*).

[33]Laissant de côté le cas trop connu de *Genesis* XXXI^{19}, Rachel et le vol des *teraphim* de son père Laban, cf. A. E. Draffkorn, citée à la note 22, voir R. Labat, *Un calendrier babylonien, des travaux, des signes et des jours*, p. 104-5: si au mois d'Ulûlu, il ouvre une tombe, une femme de cette maison, voleuse, enlevera la divinité protectrice (DINGIR LAMMA).

fils de Tae, auquel selon l'accusation de Paitilla, elle a remis les *ilāni*. Il est son second mari.[34] En transférant les dieux de son premier mari à Akiptašenni, Warḫinuzu accomplit ainsi une action doublement illégale. D'une part, elle outrepasse le droit qui est le sien d'occuper jusqu' à sa mort la maison maritale puisqu'en s'en allant, elle emporte ce qui ne lui appartient pas. Son rôle se limite à être le gardienne des dieux[35] mais uniquement dans la mesure où elle continue à habiter la maison de Šukriia. D'autre part, en remettant à Akiptašenni ces dieux auxquels il n'a aucun droit, elle commet un vol au dam de Paitilla auquel par la volonté de Šukriia les dieux sont destinés. Quant aux deuxième chef d'accusation de Paitilla, -qu'il fût fondé sur des preuves ou sur de faibles indices-, il pose un problème difficile à résoudre. En effet, suivant la déclaration de Paitilla, il y aurait un lien entre la possession de ses dieux par Akiptašenni et le sort auquel ce dernier accule la mère et la soeur de Paitilla. En deux mots, quel est le sens de cette expression *kīma ilāni* par laquelle débute l'énoncé du deuxième chef d'accusation qui semble subordonner, dans l'esprit de Paitilla, le deuxième chef d'accusation au premier?

La traduction littérale de *kīma ilāni* est: à la place des dieux, au lieu des dieux ou, comme les dieux -ce qui ne présente aucun sens dans ce contexte. Pourquoi en effet Akiptašenni aurait-il vendu à l'étranger les deux femmes "à la place des dieux que l'une d'elles lui avait remis? Les deux opérations, remise des dieux à Akiptašenni et éloignement et vente de Warḫinuzu et de sa fille, ont eu lieu en deux temps successifs, sans que la deuxième opération soit la conséquence de la première. Par contre, le passage acquiert une signification plus plausible si on réfléchit à ce que Paitilla veut exprimer dans une forme très raccourcie. En plaçant en tête de la deuxième partie de son serment ce *kīma ilāni*, Paitilla met l'accent sur ce qui lui tient le plus à coeur, les dieux qui lui étaient destinés et qu'un autre possède. *Kīma ilāni* sert donc à marquer la double forfaiture dont Paitilla accuse Akiptašenni: s'être rendu maître des dieux qu'illégalement Warḫinuzu lui a remis et continuer à les conserver, après avoir vendu à l'étranger sa femme et la fille de celle-ci. On pourrait donc traduire la deuxième partie du serment en interprétant librement *kīma ilāni*: "En outre, tout en gardant les dieux, Akiptašenni a vendu à l'étranger ma mère Warḫinuzu et ma soeur Iniphatti."

[34]*HSS* 19 25 est un *ṭuppi šimti* que Akiptašenni fait en faveur de sa femme Warḫinuzu fille de Hupita (ligne 3). Le texte est malheuresement très abimé. Il semblerait toutefois de ce qui reste de la tablette que les legs d'Akiptašenni consistaient surtout en quantités d'orge, 20 hômer, et dans des objets en bronze dont l'un d'un poids de 6 mines (ligne 5). La tablette est écrite par Muš-Tešup, fils de Ḫupita. S'agit-il d'un frère de Warḫinuzu?

[35]Voir par exemple la clause de *HSS* 19 7: *ṭuppi šimti*: [10] *e-nu-ma* [11] ^{MÍ}*Še-el-tu imât ilāni*^{MEŠ}*-ia a-na* ^{I}*Ḫu-ti-ip-Te-šup* DUMU GAL *na-ad-nu*: "lorsque Šeltu mourra, les *ilāni* seront donnés à Ḫutip-Tešup, (mon) fils aîné." Il est évident que tant que Šeltu, la mère qui a la fonction paternelle, vit, c'est elle qui garde les dieux.

La thème central de ce serment, ce sont les *ilāni*. Il serait imprudent et injustifié de donner à la possession des dieux une valeur trop strictement juridique aux dépens de la bien plus profonde et essentielle signification religieuse. L'association des *ilāni* aux *eṭemmē* dont témoignent certains textes le prouve. Il est certain qu'entre la possession des biens immobiliers reçus en héritage et le fait de conserver par devers soi les dieux de la famille, il y a un lien. Ce lien, j'ai essayé de le mettre en évidence, il y a désormais plus de quarante ans, m'attirant les foudres d'un très grand juriste comme Koschaker et d'une très perspicace décrypteuse de textes comme H. Levy. A tous deux toutefois, malgré leur extraordinaire compétence, a manqué dans des proportions inégales la dimension sociologique. Le rôle central que jouent les *ilāni* dans la société de Nuzi est capital et ses institutions restent incompréhensibles aussi longtemps qu'on néglige leur impact sur les relations qui se nouent entre les hommes et entre les hommes et leurs biens.

Il est vrai d'autre part que malgré le grand nombre de textes qui font allusion au rôle des *ilāni*, on ne sait rien de précis sur eux, ni en quoi ils consistaient, sur leur forme et sur la matière dans laquelle ils étaient faits, ni sur leur culte et non plus sur les gestes dont ils étaient parfois l'objet. Que signifie concrètement par exemple, l'acte de "porter les dieux," *ilāni*^{MEŠ} *našū*,[36] auquel on a très souvent recours comme moyen pour résoudre un conflit judiciaire? A peine quelques indices épars transparaissent parfois sur leur localisation dans la maison.[37]

Par contre, l'importance que l'on attache à leur possession, attestée par de très nombreux témoignages, dont l'un des plus significatifs est justement celui qui nous est offert par les démêlés qui opposent Paitilla à Akiptašenni—prouve que les *ilāni* comme les *eṭemmē* constituent un des éléments-clés de la structure familiale. La position prééminente du fils aîné, déja marquée par l'octroi de la double part d'héritage, se trouve amplifiée et justifiée par la possession des *ilāni* qui lui échoit la plupart du temps après la mort du père. L'association entre dieux et biens familiaux est ainsi affirmée et même lorsque un membre du groupe, ainsi qu'il arrive souvent se trouve obligé d'aliéner une partie de ses biens à un étranger, la déchirure que cela produit dans le tissu familial parvient à se cicatriser en faisant du nouveau venu fictivement par l'adoption

[36]Voir H. Lewy, *Or* 10 (1941) p. 219 selon laquelle deux situations différentes pouvaient se présenter: les deux parties étaient invitées par les juges à porter les dieux, celle qui produisait des témoins et l'autre qui n'en produisait pas, ou alors le defendant seul était invité par les juges à porter les dieux. Pour G. R. Driver et J. C. Miles, *Iraq* 7 (1945), p. 132-38, également il s'agissait d'une ordalie dans laquelle le fait de porter les dieux ou de les soulever était l'élément central. Par contre pour E. A. Speiser, *Or* 25 (1956), p. 15 et sq. il s'agit en réalité d'un serment par les dieux, "*ilāni našū* can be nothing other than the action form that goes with *niš ili.*"

[37]Voir *supra*, n. 32.

un fils ou un frère qu'on empêche toutefois d'avoir accès aux dieux qui restent un bien inaliénable.

Éléments-clés de la structure familiale, les *ilāni* et les *eṭemmē* débordent toutefois largement ce rôle d'intermédiaires entre les hommes d'un même groupe familial et leurs biens, dans lequel ce qui précède n'a aucunement l'intention de les confiner. C'est en définitive à travers leur culte—offrandes et cérémonies religieuses dont ils sont le centre—qu'on pourrait espérer s'il était mieux connu avoir enfin accès à la connaissance de cette religion populaire—par opposition à celle officielle—qui était probablement la seule que pratiquaient les plus larges couches des populations mésopotamiennes au cours de leur longue histoire.

Die Hausgötter der Familie Šukrija S. Ḫuja

Karlheinz Deller
Universität Heidelberg

Unter den von Ernest R. Lacheman veröffentlichten Nuzi-Urkunden familienrechtlichen Inhalts haben jene besonders starke Beachtung gefunden, die von Dispositionen des Erblassers handeln, welche die Hausgötter (*ilānū*) betreffen.[1] Der Ansatz war bereits von Anbeginn an interdisziplinär: die biblischen Teraphim waren bestimmend für das rege Interesse, weniger die Bedeutung, welche diesen Figurinen und dem damit verbundenen Kult in den Familien der arrapḫäischen Gemeinwesen zukam. So fehlt denn immer noch eine monographische Behandlung des Themas, aber auch deren unabdingbare Voraussetzung: verlässliche Umschriften der einschlägigen Texte, gebündelt nach Archiven, Schreibern,[2] Städten, die als philologische Grundlagen für komparative religionshistorische Untersuchungen dienen können. Aber auch in der Nuzologie selbst muss die Aufhellung der individuellen Kasuistik Vorrang haben vor Generalisierungen. Darum erlaube ich mir, dem Jubilar eine Neubearbeitung zusammengehöriger Urkunden zu widmen, die besonders reich an Informationen über die Hausgötter sind: das *ṭuppi šīmti* HSS 19,5; das [*ṭuppi mārūti*] HSS 19,30; die Flussordal-Urkunde HSS 14,8. Sie gehören (zusammen mit dem *ṭuppi titennūti* AASOR 16,63) zu dem Archiv des Šukrija S. Ḫuja. Er war verheiratet mit ᶠWarḫi-nuzu und dieser Ehe entsprangen drei Kinder, die Söhne Teḫip-tilla und Pai-tilla und eine Tochter, ᶠInib-ḫatti. Ein dritter Sohn des Šukrija, Šimika-atal, hatte offenbar eine andere Mutter. Aus der Prozessurkunde AASOR 16,56 erhellt, dass Šukrija zwei Brüder hatte, Kula-ḫupi und Tarmija. Von ersterem besitzen wir keine eigenen Urkunden; der wesentlich jüngere Tarmija wurde von seinem Vater mit der *amtu* ᶠṢulūlī-Ištar verheiratet, stand in Diensten des Palastes und bekleidete das Amt des Kanalinspektors (*gugallu*). Durch seinen Prozess mit Tarmi-tilla S. Šurki-tilla

[1]A. E. Draffkorn, Ilāni/Elohim, JBL 76 (1957), pp. 216-24; M. Greenberg, Another Look at Rachel's Theft of the Teraphim, JBL 81 (1962), pp. 239-48; M. Gevaryahu, A Clarification of the Nature of Biblical Teraphim, Beth Miqra 3 (1963), pp. 81-86.

[2]Den Textcorpora und den individuellen Graphemen der einzelnen Schreiber der Nuzi-Texte widmet sich seit geraumer Zeit Paola Negri Scafa. Sie hat mir auch für diesen Aufsatz wichtige Informationen zur Verfügung gestellt. Dafür gebührt ihr mein aufrichtiger Dank.

(JEN 370) ist er als Zeitgenosse der vierten Generation der Familie Teḫip-tilla relativ datierbar; sein Archiv umfasst wenigstens die Texte AASOR 16,56; EN 9,392 (in Umschrift wiedergegeben bei D. I. Owen, The Loan Documents from Nuzu, Dissertation Brandeis University 1969, University Microfilms 70-12,031, p. 130); HSS 16,321; HSS 19,30 und 67. Die Tafeln des Familienarchivs der Ḫuja-Söhne wurden vorwiegend in Room S 151 gefunden, von wo allerdings auch ein Grossteil des Archivs der Pula-ḫali-Söhne geborgen wurde: ob zwischen beiden Familien Querverbindungen bestehen, konnte bisher nicht ausgemacht werden. Šukrija dürfte der Erstgeborene des Ḫuja gewesen sein und figuriert in der Prozessurkunde JEN 105 als Zeitgenosse der Söhne des Teḫip-tilla, also der dritten Generation dieser Familie. Sein Vater Ḫuja war demnach Zeitgenosse des Teḫip-tilla selbst und begründete in Nuzi die *dimtu ša Ḫuja* (HSS 19,30:10). Auf ihn geht wenigstens ein Teil der Götterfigurinen zurück, die sein Sohn Šukrija weitervererbt. Er tut dies in seinem Testament

HSS 19,5 SMN 2494 Room S 151 147 x 85 x 38 mm

Vs 1 *ṭup-⸢pí⸣ ši-im-ti ša* ^{I}*Šúk-r[i-ja]*
2 DUMU *Ḫ[u$^{!}$-]⸢ú⸣-ja ši-im-ta a-na* [DUMU^{MEŠ}-*šu*]
3 *a-na* ^{I}*[Te]-ḫi-ip-til-la a-na* ^{I}*Pa-⸢i⸣-[til-la]*
4 *ù a-n[a]* ⸢^{f}⸣*Ši-mi-qa-tal i-ši-[m]u*
5 *um-ma* [^{I}*Š]úk-ri-ja-ma* 1[+n] ⸢É⸣$^{ḪI.A.MEŠ}$ *l[i-ib-b]u-ur-šu*
6 ⸢x⸣ *tu₄* [.] *ge en du* ⸢É⸣ *e-kál-lu* [ ]
7 ⸢É⸣ *ar-[pa-n]u* É *bi-[tar-š]u eš-šu* É *a-[bu-us]-sú*^{MEŠ}
8 *tar-bá-ṣú [ša pa]-ni-š[u-nu š]a* É$^{ḪI.A.MEŠ}$ *ša-[a-šu]*
9 *ṣa-bat s[i-ip-pí]* ⸢*ša*⸣$^{!}$ ⸢É⸣ *bi-tar-ši a-du* [ ]
10 *i+n[a]* x[. . . *š]a* ⸢É⸣ *ti-nu-ri* DINGIR$^{ME[Š!}$ *ša*]
11 <S>AG$^{!}$.DU G[AL . . . .]⸢^{m}⸣Q[*ar-r]a-te* PÚ ^{I}*Š[úk-ri-ja]*
12 ⸢*a*⸣*-na* ^{I}*Te-[ḫi-ip-til-la n]a-ad-nu* KASKAL-*ra-šu* [0]
13 ⸢*ša*⸣ É$^{ḪI.A.M[EŠ]}$ *š[a-a-šu na-a]d-nu i+na* ⸢*šu*⸣*-pa-al i[l-la-ak]*

---

14 *[tar-b]á-ṣú ṣa-bat s[i-ip-p]í š[a]* É *bi-tar-ši* [eš-ši]
15 [.]x *tu* ⸢x⸣[. . (.) É *š]a ti-nu-ri* x[ ]
16 ⸢É⸣ *ti-bi-iš-š[u* .] É *a-bu-us-sú*[ ]
17 ⸢É⸣ *li-ib-bu-ur-šu* É *ša ti-nu-*⸢*ri*⸣ [ ]
18 ⸢*qa*⸣*-du sà-aḫ-mi-šu ù mi-nu-um-me-*⸢*e*⸣ [0]
19 ḪA.LA-*ja uš-tu₄* A.ŠÀ *na-aq-qa-d[u pa-i-ḫu]*
20 *ša pa-ni-šu-nu [š]a* É$^{⸢ḪI.A⸣.MEŠ}$ *šu ša š[u*]
21 DINGIR^{MEŠ} *ša* SAG.DU TUR *[an]-nu-tu₄ a-na* [DUMU-*ja*]
22 *a-na* ^{I}*Pa-i-til-la na-*⸢*ad-nu*⸣

---

23 A.ŠÀ *na-aq-qa-du pa-i-[ḫ]u i+na lìb-bi* [0]
24 *tar-bá-ṣí* 37 *i+na am-m[a-t]i mu-ra-*⸢*ak*⸣*-šu*
25 8 *i+n[a a]m-ma-*⸢*ti*⸣ *[ru-pu]-*⸢*us*⸣*-sú*
26 *i+na* ⸢tub⸣-[*bu*]-qa$^{!}$-⸢*ti*⸣ [. . . .]x *an-nu-tú*

27 A.ŠÀ pa-i-ḫu a-na ^{I}[Ši-mi-qa-ta]l n[a-a]d-nu
28 3 i+na am-ma-ti ki-b[i-is .] ⌈i+na⌉ <be>-⌈ri⌉-šu-nu
29 ⌈uš-tu⌉ É-ti a-bu-u[s-sí] ša
30 [^{I}Te-ḫi]-ip-til-la a-na DUMU-ja] a-na
31 [^{I}Ši-mi-qa]-tal n[a-ad-nu] ù mi-nu-um-me-e
Rd 32 [A.ŠÀ^{MEŠ}-ja É]$^{\text{ḪI.A.MEŠ}}$[-ja 1-en NÍG^{MEŠ}]-⌈ja⌉
33 ⌈ù⌉ [mi-i]m!-mu šu-u[n-šu-ja]
34 ri-ḫu-tù ^{I}Te-ḫi-i[p-til-la]
35 [O] ⌈GAL⌉ ⌈2-ni⌉-šu ḪA.<LA> i-⌈leq⌉-[qè]
Rs 36 ^{I}P[a-i-til-l]a te-er-te-e[n-nu]
37 [i+n]a E[GIR]-⌈ki⌉-[šu] ki-i-ma GÌR-šu ḪA.LA i-leq-q[è]
38 [il]-ki-ja il-te-em-ma ù
39 um-ma ^{I}Šúk-ri-ja-ma ^{I}Ši-mi-qa-tal DUMU-ja
40 uš-tu A.ŠÀ^{MEŠ}-ja uš-tu É^{MEŠ}-ja
41 ⌈ù⌉ uš-tu mi-im-mu ⌈šu-un⌉-[šu-j]a
42 a-na ši-mi a-na LÚ na-ka$_{4}$-ri bá-[lu Š]EŠ^{MEŠ}-šu-nu
43 ⌈la i+na-an-din⌉ šum-ma DUMU-ja ^{I}Ši-m[i-qa]-tal
44 ⌈uš-tu⌉ ⌈A⌉.ŠÀ^{MEŠ}-ja uš-tu É[^{MEŠ}-ja a-na ši-mi]
45 a-na LÚ^{MEŠ} na-ka$_{4}$-ri i+na-an-din [O]
46 [^{I}]⌈Ši⌉-mi-qa-tal 1 MA.NA KÙ.BABBAR [1 MA.NA] KÙ.G[I]
47 a-na DUMU^{MEŠ}-ja ú-ma-al-l[a] ⌈É⌉-tu$_{4}$
48 ⌈ša⌉ a-na aš-ša-ti-ja a-na ^{MÍ}[Wa-ar-ḫi-nu]-zu!
49 ⌈ša SUM⌉-nu a-du-ú ^{MÍ}[Wa-ar-ḫ[i-nu-zu]
50 bal-ṭù É ša-a-šu ú-[ka$_{4}$-al]
51 e-nu-ma ^{MÍ}Wa-ar-ḫi-n[u-zu]
52 BA.ÚŠ^{MEŠ} É <<x>> ša-a-šu š[a a-na ^{MÍ}Wa-ar-ḫi-nu-zu]
53 ša [SUM]-nu ù ^{I}Te-ḫi-ip-t[il-la i-leq-qè]
54 ⌈ù⌉ <<1>> mi-nu-um-me-e ši-[mu-ma-ku]
55 ša a-[n]a aš-ša-ti-⌈ja⌉ š[a . . (.)]x
56 ^{I}Te-ḫi-ip-til-la ù ^{I}Pa-i-[til-la]
57 i-leq-q[è] ^{I}Ši-mi-qa-tal ⌈i+na⌉ x[. .]
58 ša ^{MÍ}W[a-a]r-ḫi-nu-zu [la] i-qè-e[r-ri-ib]

---

59 IGI Dub-⌈bi⌉-[ja?] DUMU ⌈A-kap⌉-ta-⌈e⌉
60 IGI Zi-l[i-ja DUMU A]r-nu-zu
61 IGI Šu-ru-[uq-qa DUMU] ⌈A⌉-qa-a+a
62 IGI Ḫu-bi-[ta DUM]U A-kip-še-e[n]-ni
63 IGI Ti-ir-w[i-j]a [DUM]U Ta-a+a-ú-ki
64 IGI Ni-ḫé-er-te-[šup DUM]U Ti-ir-wi-ja
65 IGI A-ri-ip-š[arri D]UB.SAR-rù
66 NA$_{4}$ ^{I}Ḫ[u]-bi-ta NA$_{4}$ ^{I}Du[b-bi-ja?]
67 NA$_{4}$ ^{I}[Z]i-li-ja NA$_{4}$ ^{I}Ni-ḫé-er-[te-šup]
liS 68 NA$_{4}$ ^{I}Ti-ir-wi-ja NA$_{4}$ ^{I}Šúk-ri-ja
69 NA$_{4}$ ^{I}⌈Šu-ru⌉-uq-qa ša EN A.ŠÀ NA$_{4}$ ^{I}DUB.SAR-rù

Kommentar:

Die Urkunde wurde erstmals bearbeitet von R. Beich, Nuzi Wills and Testaments (Dissertation Brandeis University, 1963, University Microfilms 64-3064), pp. 50-53 als No. 22, und nochmals von J. S. Paradise, Nuzi Inheritance Practices (Dissertation University of Pennsylvania, 1972, University Microfilms 72-25, 644), pp. 96-101 als No. C-22. Seit 1973 haben G. Dosch, G. Wilhelm, P. Negri Scafa und Verf. an obiger Umschrift gearbeitet. Der Text ist nicht kollationiert, die ! in den Zeilen 2.10.11.26.33.48 und die < > in Z. 28.35 sind Emendationen des Verf.

Die Oberfläche der Tafel weist besonders auf der Vorderseite zahlreiche Beschädigungen auf, welche die Lesung der Z.6.10.11.15.16.26.28.55.57 stark beeinträchtigen. Am rechten Rand ist wegen des schlechten Erhaltungszustandes vielfach (Z.6.9.11.15.16.17.20) nicht abzuschätzen, wieviele Zeichen weggebrochen sind. Mit 69 Zeilen ist die Urkunde dennoch komplett.

Schreiber von HSS 19,5 ist Arip-šarri (Patronym unbekannt), dessen Corpus mindestens elf Tafeln umfasst:

AASOR 16,58	SMN 2085	S 110	*ṭuppi mārūti*	Utḫap-tae S. Ar-tura	Nuzi
HSS 9,97	SMN 983	A 34	*ṭuppi titennūti*	Ilānu S. Tajjukki	Nuzi
HSS 9,102	SMN 140	A 34	*ṭuppi titennūti*	Ilānu S. Tajjukki	Nuzi
HSS 13,65	SMN 65	C 81	Quittung	Erwi-šarri *šakin bīti*	Nuzi
HSS 14,623	SMN 623	R 76	Ziegelschuld	Tišam-mušni	Nuzi
HSS 19,5	SMN 2494	S 151	*ṭuppi šīmti*	Šukrija S. Ḫuja	Nuzi
HSS 19,12	SMN 2610	P 401	*ṭuppi šīmti*	ᶠJamaštu T. Ninuatal	Nuzi
HSS 19,65	SMN 3758	?	*ṭuppi aḫḫūti*	Zikaja S. Ḫuziri	Nuzi
HSS 19,68	SMN 2244	N 120	*ṭuppi mārtūti*	Utḫap-tae S. Ar-tura	Nuzi
JEN 78	JENu 204	13	*ṭuppi aḫātūti*	Ḫut-arrapḫe S. Tišam-mušni	Nuzi
JENu 627[3]	JENu 627	?	*ṭuppi titennūti*	Paikku	Nuzi

Trotz des Fehlens seines Vaternamens kann nach den Untersuchungen von P. Negri Scafa zur Orthographie und Prosopographie dieser elf Texte als sicher gelten, dass sie alle von ein und demselben Schreiber stammen. Darauf basiert die Lesung der Z. 65 (IGI *A-ri-ip-š*[*arri* D]UB.SAR-*rù*). J. S. Paradise (S. 99) ergänzt hingegen IGI *A-ri-ib*-[*ta*?-*e*] DUB.SAR-*rum*; im Onomastikon der

[For n. 3 see below, p. 55.]

Nuzi-Texte ist jedoch bis jetzt weder ein Schreiber namens *Arip-tae aufgetaucht noch der Name selbst.

Z. 1-4: Formular übereinstimmend mit HSS 19,12:1-5 (Schreiber Arip-šarri).

Z. 5ff.: Der Hausbesitz des Šukrija in der Stadt Nuzi wird unter die beiden Söhne Teḫip-tilla und Pai-tilla sowie seine Ehefrau ^{f}Warḫi-nuzu (Z. 47-53) *explicite* aufgeteilt (Šimika-atal erhält ein Baugrundstück), während der übrige Hausbesitz (Z. 32, z. B. *ina ṣērēti*) und der gesamte Feldbesitz auf die beiden voll erbberechtigten Söhne im Verhältnis 2 : 1 übergeht. Die Beschreibung der einzelnen Gebäude ist sehr exakt und lexikalisch recht aufschlussreich; nicht alle hier belegten Wörter sind in die Wbb. aufgenommen worden.

Z. 5.17: die Gebäudebezeichnung *lippuršu* findet sich nur noch HSS 19, 47:6.16 (vgl. CAD L 176a).

Z. 6: ⸢x⸣ zu Beginn kann ⸢*uš*⸣ (vgl. *uš-tu*$_4$ Z. 19) oder ⸢É⸣ (vgl. É-*tu*$_4$ Z. 47 und HSS 19,12:19) sein; ⸢É⸣-*tu*$_4$ ist wahrscheinlicher. Nach TUM fehlt sicher ein Zeichen und [.]-*ge-en-du* dürfte eine weitere Gebäudebez. sein. Für eine Ableitung von *emēdu* für *en-du* sehe ich keinen Grund. Für É(^{MEŠ}) *e-kál-lu* gibt es aus Nuzi-Texten sechs Belege: É *e-kál-lu* GAL ^{13}*ša* URU *Nu-zi* HSS 19,4:12-13 (SMN 2076; Paradise, p. 94)

⸢É⸣ *e-kál-lu* [ ] HSS 19,5:6 (SMN 2494; Paradise, p. 96) 1 É *e-kál-lu tar*-⸢*bá*⸣-*ṣú* HSS 19,12:15 (SMN 2610; Paradise, p. 180)

1 É *e-kál-lu* [É *a*]*r*-⸢ba⸣$^{?}$-*nu* HSS 19,20:13 (SMN 2656; Paradise, p. 35)

1 É^{MEŠ} *e-kál-lu* HSS 19,47:15 (SMN 3084; Paradise, p. 161, ergänzt Z. 5)

1 É *e-kál-lu ša* DINGIR^{MEŠ} ^{2}*it-ti ap-pa-an-ni-šu eš-šu* HSS 14,107:1-2 (= RA 36, 118; SMN 2603; zitiert Paradise p. 38 ad 13); *iš-tu sí-ip-pí e-kál-lì la-bi-r*[*i*] ^{6}*a-du-ú i-ga*$_5$*-ri ša* ^{7}*ḫu-ri-ze-na* ebd. 5-7.

CAD E 60b listet fünf Belege (HSS 19,4 fehlt), allerdings mit SMN-Nummern; AHw 192b verweist nur auf CAD; die Wbb. übersetzen "main room of a private house" und "ein Gebäudeteil in einem grossen Privathaus" (Z. 1 AHw 59a *appannu* allerdings "1 Göttertempel" und Z. 5 1049a sippu "v. Palasttor" gedeutet). Aus HSS 14,107:1 kann nur geschlossen werden, dass *ekallu* der Gebäudeteil war, in welchem die Götterbilder aufbewahrt wurden, nicht jedoch, dass dieses Gebäude ausschliesslich sakralen Zwecken diente. Eine Ergänzung des Zeilenendes wage ich nicht.

Z. 7: Die Ergänzung ⸢É⸣ *ar*-[*pa-n*]*u* bietet sich auf Grund der Parallele HSS 19,20:13 an; beide Belege sind CAD A/2, 300a arpani nachzutragen. Die zu Z. 6 zitierte Kombination von *ekallu* und *appannu* lässt freilich daran denken, dass **arpannu* durch Geminatendissimilation aus *appannu* entstanden sein könnte und somit das gleiche Lexem unter verschiedenen Lemmata verbucht wäre (*appannu* CAD A/2 178b/179a). Dazu könnte auch *lippuršu* und *pitaršu* (Z. 7.9.14) gestellt werden, falls Bildungen mit dem ḫurritischen Morphem *-šše* (**lippušše*, **pitašše*) vorlägen; dass *tipiššu* (Z. 16) nicht dissimiliert wird, mag an dem *i*-Stamm liegen. Das *pitaršu*-Gebäude ist nur aus diesem Text (Z. 7.9.14) nachzuweisen und fehlt in den Wbb. *abussu* (hier und Z. 16.29) ist aus Nuzi-Texten noch HSS 13, 366:7 (CAD A/1 92b) nachzuweisen; nach AHw 9b war a. eine "Magazin(kammer)" oder "Pferdebox"; letztere Bedeutung ist jedoch erst aus nA Texten erschliessbar.

Z. 8: Die Ergänzungen folgen Z. 20; für das Zeilenende s. dort.

Z. 9: Die Ergänzung *s*[*í-ip-pí*] fusst einerseits auf den Spuren *s*[*í-ip-p*]*í* in Z. 14, andererseits auf dem Ausdruck *iš-tu si-ip-pi e-kál-lì la-bi-r*[*i*] in HSS 14,107:5. Für sippu "Türpfosten, Laibung" vgl. AHw 1049a.

Z. 10: Das auf *i+n*[*a*] folgende Zeichen scheint ZI zu zein. Für das Backofenhaus (AHw 1360b) verwendet der Schreiber *bīt tinūri* (hier) und *bītu ša tinūri* (Z. 15.17). Am Ende der Zeile ist DINGIR^{ME}[$^{\text{Š!}}$ *ša*] parallel zu DINGIR^{MEŠ} *ša* Z. 21. *Arip-šarri* schreibt häufig *ša* am Zeilenende (hier Z. 29; ferner HSS 9,97:1.3 und 102:1.4.27; HSS 14,623:1; HSS 19,12:1.12 und 65:1.16; JEN 78:1).

Z. 11: Die Zeile beginnt mit einer Rasur, es folgt der zweite Teil des Zeichens SAG; <S>AG$^{!}$.DU G[AL ist parallel zu SAG.DU TUR in Z. 21. J. S. Paradise liest zu Beginn *ù du* [, doch das erste Zeichen ist keinesfalls ein komplettes Ù. Die folgenden vier Zeichen kann ich nicht ergänzen; darauf folgt jedenfalls der PN $^{⌈\text{I}⌉}$*Q*[*ar-r*]*a-te*, dessen Beziehung zu Šukrija offenbleiben muss. Die von J. S. Paradise vorgeschlagene Ergänzung *bu*]*-ra-te* ist schon deshalb unzutreffend, weil die Endung des Fem. Plur. in Nuzi nie mit dem Zeichen TE geschrieben wird. Nach PÚ (*būrtu*, "Brunnen") folgt am ehesten der PN ^{I}*Š*[*úk-ri-ja*], falls der Platz reicht, sogar noch [*a-na* DUMU*-ja*]

Z. 12-13: Die hier angenommene Ergänzung beruht auf KASKAL A.ŠÀ *i+na šu-pa-al* É *ša Ku-uš-ši-ja il-la-ak* JEN 255:62 (Schreiber Šimika-atal S. Erwin-niršе, Archiv Kel-tešup S. Ḫutija, Dossier Temtenaš). Für den Stat. abs. *šu-pa-al* vgl. KÁ.GAL *ša šu-pa-al* HSS 5,30:23 (zit. AHw 1278b "unterhalb, westlich von").

Z. 15: Zu Anfang kann nicht ohne weiteres *iš-tu* (Paradise) gelesen werden, weil Arip-šarri—wie P. Negri Scafa ermittelt hat—die Präposition stets *uš-tu* oder *uš-*tu_4, nie aber *iš-tu* schreibt. Der Komplex besteht ferner aus drei Zeichen [.]x-*tu*, dessen zweites *i*]*š*, aber auch *i*]*l* sein kann. Das auf *-tu* folgende Zeichen scheint ZI oder GI zu sein.

Z. 16: *tipiššu* "eine Scheune" (AHw 1360b) ist noch zu belegen aus JEN 342:10-11 (*ša* IN^{MEŠ} *ma-lu-ú* "die voll von Stroh ist") und 28; die vorliegende Stelle ist in AHw nachzutragen.

Z. 17-18: Für *bīt*/*bītu ša tinūri* bietet AHw 1360b keine Nuzi-Belege; auch A. Salonen, Baghdader Mitteilungen 3 (1964) 101-4, führt keine Nuzi-Texte an. Wegen der schwer kalkulierbaren Lücke am Ende der Z. 17 kann nicht als sicher gelten, dass ⌜*qa*⌝-*du sà-aḫ-mi-šu* ein Teil des Backofens sein muss. Es ist auch nicht einsichtig, wie das Wort **saḫmu* mit der Geländebez./dem Flurnamen A.ŠÀ *ša-na-am-ma* [8]*a-šar sà-aḫ-mi* Gadd 43:7-8 (Archiv Akawatil S. Wullu, Dossier Arrapḫa) auf einen Nenner gebracht werden kann (vgl. AHw 1010a).

Z. 19: Ergänzt nach Z. 23; zu *paiḫu* s. dort. Für *nakk*/*qqatu* "eine Art Land" vgl. AHw 722b; die Verbindung *n.* und *paiḫu* findet sich m.W. nur noch in HSS 19,16:12 (*ù* A.ŠÀ *na-aq-qa-du*$_4$ *pa-i-ḫu*).

Z. 20: Ende: Häuser *ša ša š*[*u* könnte natürlich Schreiberversehen für das anaphorische Pronomen sein, das Arip-šarri mit Vorliebe *ša-a-šu* schreibt, doch möchte ich andere Ergänzungen nicht ausschliessen.

Z. 23: *paiḫu* wird AHw 812a (mit Verweis auf P. Koschaker, ZA 48 [1944] 182-84, Anm. 37) als "eine Art Feld" bestimmt, wohl deshalb, weil bei diesem Terminus häufigeres *qaqqaru paiḫu* mit *eqlu* (A.ŠÀ) *paiḫu* wechselt. Dennoch wird die Fläche des *eqlu paiḫu* nie in *imēru* und *awiḫaru* (in JEN 242:4-5 allerdings in *kumānu*) ausgedrückt, sondern in (Quadrat-)Ellen. Der wichtige Beleg JEN 101:3-9 (Archiv Enna-mati S. Teḫip-tilla, Dossier Tentewe, Schreiber Zunzu S. Intija), vgl. CAD A/2 523b, zählt offenbar alle Arten von Grundstücken auf, die es überhaupt gibt: hier sind die Felder *sensu proprio* als A.ŠÀ^{MEŠ} *a-wi-i-ru* (das ḫurritische Wort für "Feld") von den übrigen Grundstücken distinguiert; es folgen [4]*ka-aq-qa-ru pa-i-ḫu* [5]*ù ka-aq-qa-ra ša* É^{MEŠ} *ep-šu*, welche Ausdrücke bereits H. Lewy, Or NS 11 (1942) 310-11, n. 5, richtig als "building plot" und "the ground (on) which the houses have been built" übersetzt hatte. *eqlu paiḫu* verwendet *eqlu* (A.ŠÀ) hingegen *sensu lato* ("Bodenfläche") wie denn auch in JEN 101:16 A.ŠÀ^{MEŠ} *ša pí-i ṭup-pí an-ni-ti* als Oberbegriff für alle Z. 3-8 aufgezählten Bodenflächen verwendet wird. P. Koschaker (S. 184) sieht ein Problem in dem Beleg HSS 5,51:3, den er *eqlu ša qa-qí-ri* liest und das "eine landwirtschaftliche Nutzung (*išpīku*) gestattet." Diese Stelle ist jedoch offensichtlich verlesen, der Text bietet klares A.ŠÀ *ša Qa-di-ri*; er stammt aus dem Archiv des Zike S. Akkuja und Katiri war dessen Grossvater (vgl. G. Dosch, Die Texte aus Room A 34 des Archivs von Nuzi, Magister-Arbeit, Heidelberg 1976, S. 34 Nr. 20). Den Personenkeil hat der Schreiber hier zu setzen vergessen; ferner ist der (assyrische) Genitiv *qaqqiri* in Nuzi-Texten nie bezeugt. Ungeklärt bleibt freilich der Wortsinn von *paiḫu*. Hält man assyrische Grundstücksurkunden und die entsprechenden Nuzi-Texte nebeneinander, wird man leicht feststellen, dass *qaqqirī paṣiʾūti*(*m*) im aA und mA, *qaqqarī puṣāʾe* bei Tukulti-Ninurta I. (ITn S. 9, 2:42) und *qaqqirī puṣê* im nA (Belege AHw 857b *peṣû* 9a und 883b *puṣû* 2) und *eqlu*/*qaqqaru paiḫu* sich ziemlich genau entsprechen; am naheliegendsten wäre darum, *peṣû* mit *paiḫu* (**pai-ḫe*?) zu gleichen. E. Laroche, Glossaire de la langue hourrite, RHA 35 (1977) 193, zweifelt allerdings, ob *paiḫu* überhaupt ein ḫurritisches Wort ist, während W. von Soden, AHw 812a an dem ḫurritischen Ursprung dieses Lexems festhält. Wir wären wahrscheinlich von diesen Zweifeln befreit, wenn nicht R.S. 21.62 Vs 19 (Ugaritica 5,419 nº 135) babbar *pe-eṣ-ṣú* [ ] die ḫurritische Kolumne weggebrochen wäre. (Die ugaritische Kolumne ist durch R.S. 20.426B:4′ [Ugaritica 5, 424, nº 138] *la-ba-nu* vertreten; vgl. dazu R. Borger, RA 63 [1969] 172).

Z. 26: Die gebotene Ergänzung ist ein Versuch. Das auf *i+na* folgende Zeichen ist offenbar DUB. Von *tubqu* "Ecke, Winkel" ist im Mitanni-Akkadischen von Nuzi eine Ableitung *tubuqqatu* (vgl. AHw *tubuqtu* 1365b) wenigstens dreimal nachzuweisen: *ù tù-bu-uq-qa-as-sú* ^{10}*ša* A.ŠÀ KASKAL-*ni ik-ki-is-sú* HSS 5,39:7-10; *ge-er-ru ša* URU ⸢*Tar*⸣-[*ku*]-*ul*-⸢*li*⸣ ^{7}*tù-bu-uq-qa-a*[*s-s*]*ú ik-ki-is* JEN 659:6-7; *ša tù-bu-qa-as-sú* (Rasur) *ge-er-ru* ^{32}*š*[*a* U]RU *Tar-ku-ul-li ik-ki-sú* ebd. 31-32. Eine Schreibung mit *-bb-* ist allerdings bisher nicht bezeugt. Nach der Flächenangabe des Baugrundes kann jedoch eine Information über die Lage desselben innerhalb des *tarbaṣu* füglich erwartet werden.

Z. 28: Hier handelt es sich offenbar um ein Wegerecht: Šimika-atal wird ein drei Ellen (l, 5m) breiter Zugang zu seinem Grundstück eingeräumt. Nach dem Zeichen KI könnte leicht zu *ki-b*[*i-is* ANŠE] "Tritt eines Esels" i.S.v. "Eselspfad" ergänzt werden; auch ein mit Doppelpacksäcken (*zurzu*) beladener Esel kann einen 1,5 m breiten Durchgang noch passieren. Da Arip-šarri auch in Z. 35 ein Zeichen auslässt, könnte ihm der Lapsus auch in <be>-⸢*ri*⸣-*šu-nu* unterlaufen sein.

Z. 31-33: Ergänzt nach HSS 19,65:6-8 (*ṭuppi aḫḫūti*, Arip-šarri).

Z. 32: Ein Teil dieser Felder lag nach HSS 19,30:9-10 in der *dimtu ša Ḫuja*.

Z. 37: Zeilenanfang nach Gadd 5:18 (*i+na* EGIR-*ki* PN) ergänzt; vielleicht ist die Ergänzung -[*šu*] sogar unnötig; vgl. ⸢*i+na*⸣ *šu-pa-al* Z. 13. Die Lesung für *ki-i-ma* GÌR-*šu* bietet *ki-ma še-pí-šu-nu* HSS 19,22:7 (Paradise, p. 45 ad 11; und 125 z. St.; vgl. AHw 1215a *šēpu* 14c). [Korrekturzusatz: Dieselbe Gebrauchsweise von *šēpu* liegt vor in dem spB Ritual RA 71,45 RS 14′:] DINGIR^{MEŠ} *ki-ma* GÌR$^{2?}$-*šú-nu ina* IGI-*šú u* EGIR-*šú il-lak*; vgl. dazu Sylvie Lackenbacher, RA 71,49 n.5].

Z. 38: Zu Beginn fehlt nur ein Zeichen; eine Regelung hinsichtlich des *ilku* ist nach der Teilung des Grundbesitzes, an dem ja das *ilku* hängt, *a priori* zu erwarten, etwa: "meine *ilku*-Verpflichtung (bleibt) eine, d.h. ungeteilt und unberührt durch die vorausgehende Erbteilung. Ähnlich formuliert HSS 19,2:46-47 (vgl. Paradise, p. 134) *i-la-ak*-[*šu-nu*] *ga*$_4$*-bi-šu-nu* ^{47}*il-te-en-nu il-te-il-tu*$_4$. Für die *n*-Assimilation (*iltēm-ma*) vgl. noch *ir-ra-ma-ni-ja* JEN 78:23 (Arip-šarri).

Z. 44: Am Ende ist wegen Z. 42 sicher [*a-na ši-mi*] zu ergänzen; zur Schreibung des Plurals *bītāti* kann man dann auf das kürzere É^{MEŠ} (wie Z. 40) zurückgreifen.

Z. 46-47: Zwischen den Enden dieser beiden Zeilen ist auf dem re.Rd. noch ⌜x⌝^{MEŠ} sichtbar, das ich nicht plazieren kann.

Z. 48: Die Zeichenspuren habe ich gegen die Kopie in -zu! emendiert, weil hier sicher ᶠWarḫi-nuzu stand und alle weiblichen PN, die auf das Element *-nu-zu* enden, stets so und nie **-nu-za* geschrieben werden. In Z. 58 schreibt Arip-šarri denn auch ^{MÍ}*W*[*a-a*]*r-ḫi-nu-zu*.

Z. 55: Das Zeichen am rechten Rand (‚das J. S. Paradise an das Ende von Z. 54 plaziert) ist kein sauberes TUM: es fehlt der die drei Waagerechten kreuzende Senkrechte. Es verläuft, wie viele Zeichen am re. Rd. etwas nach aufwärts, und könnte darum auch MU sein. So ergäbe sich für Z. 55 die Ergänzung *š*[*a a-ši*]-mu! oder *š*[*a i-ši*]-mu!. Der Ausdruck *šimumaku šâmu* liegt vor in HSS 19,11:3-5.

Z. 57: Unsicher bleibt, ob auch am Ende dieser Zeile ⌜*i+na*⌝ *š*[*i-mu-ma-ku*] zu ergänzen ist.

Z. 60: Alle Zeugen Z. 59-64 sind *hapax* ausser Zilija S. Ar-nuzu, der noch einmal in JENu 512:26 (*ṭuppi šupeʾulti*, Archiv Teḫip-tilla, Dossier Unapšewe, dimtu Tupki-tilla, Schreiber Itḫ-apiḫe)[3] als Zeuge figuriert.

Die neue Umschrift von HSS 19,5 weicht nicht nur in zahlreichen Details von der Bearbeitung ab, die J. S. Paradise geboten hat, sondern sie führt auch zu einer abweichenden Interpretation des Testaments des Šukrija. Wem hat er nun wirklich die Hausgötter vererbt?

J. S. Paradise konstatiert (p. 239 unten): "Although the first-born usually receives the gods, text C-22 [d.i. HSS 19,5] provides an example of the second ranking son (*terdennu*) receiving them" und nochmals (p. 241 n. 83): "In two of our texts (C-22 and C-21) it is not the chief heir who receives the gods. This does not exclude the possibility that the heir who received the gods was the first born, though not made chief heir."

Nach meiner Umschrift erhält der Erstgeborene Teḫip-tilla die Hausgötter mit dem grossen Kopf (Z. 10-11) und der Zweitgeborene Pai-tilla die Hausgötter mit dem kleinen Kopf. Beide voll erbberechtigten Söhne des Šukrija und der ᶠWarḫi-nuzu erben also Götterbilder, die bereits nach Zahl und unterschiedlicher

[3]Dieser Text und JENu 512 sind mir in Umschriften E. Chieras bekannt geworden, die mir Frau Prof. Erica Reiner, Oriental Institute, University of Chicago, zur Auswertung in der Dissertation meines Schülers Abdulilah Fadhil freundlicherweise überlassen hat. Herrn Prof. J. A. Brinkman danke ich für die Erlaubnis, diese Texte hier zitieren zu dürfen. [Additional texts of the scribe Arip-šarri include SMN 2711; EN 9 60(SMN 3475); 74(SMN 2314); 170(SMN 3472); 183(SMN 2608); 186(SMN 2112); 244(SMN 2712); 378(SMN 3481). D.I.O.]

Gestalt im Haushalt des Šukrija vorhanden waren und die er selbst wohl von seinem Vater Ḫuja geerbt hat. Sie werden lediglich nach dem Prinzip "grosser Kopf/kleiner Kopf" aufgeteilt, das man sicher nicht generalisieren darf und das ganz individuelle Gründe haben mag. Da in allen Testamenten, in denen Hausgötter *explicite* erwähnt werden, DINGIR^{MEŠ} im Plural steht, ist eine Aufteilung unter die Söhne ohnehin die nächstliegende Regelung.

Wie können aber bei gleicher Ausgangsposition—der Autographie E. R. Lachemans HSS 19,5—so abweichende Interpretationen vorgelegt werden? Die Zeichenspuren in Z. 10-11 sind zugegebenermassen gestört (sowohl durch die Rasur als auch durch Oberflächenschäden), in Z. 21 ist DINGIR^{MEŠ} *ša* SAG.DU TUR deutlich zu lesen, die zweite Hälfte der Zeile, [*an*]-*nu-tu*$_4$ *a-na* [DUMU-*ja*] unschwer zu ergänzen. Das Wortzeichen SAG.DU ist *qaqqadu* "Kopf." Das Zeichen TUR kann natürlich auch DUMU sein, aber wer würde nicht die Übersetzung "die Hausgötter mit dem kleinen Kopf" der Wiedergabe "die Hausgötter mit dem Kopf des/eines Sohnes" vorziehen? Für die Ergänzung *DUMU[^{MEŠ} *an*]-*nu-tu*$_4$ fehlt, wie man leicht ausmessen kann, der Platz. Der Ausdruck **qaqqad mārī* "Kopf der Söhne" = "Haupterbe" ist weder aus Nuzi-Texten noch aus anderen akkadischen Texten zu belegen. Welche sind nun die Argumente, die J. S. Paradise zu der Übersetzung "the gods of the first-ranking son" (p. 99) bzw. "the gods of the chief heir" (p. 100 ad 21) führten? Vier sind aus seiner Dissertation zu eruieren: (a) der Ausdruck **qaqqadumma epēšu* in C-33 = HSS 19,3:10 (p. 100 ad 21; p. 140; p. 143 "shall designate as first-rank(?)"; (b) der biblische Text 1 Chr 26:10 (p. 101); (c) das *ṭuppi šīmti* C-21 = HSS 19,4 (pp. 95-96 und p. 240), die Hausgötter werden dort an eine Person vererbt, die weder Erstgeborener noch *tertennu* ist; (stillschwigend: d) C-46 = JEN 443:4 (p. 173 und 174), wo [DINGIR?] MEŠ [ša?] ⌜SAG⌝.DU ergänzt und "gods of the first rank?" übersetzt wird. Zu (a) ist anzumerken, dass die Lesung qa]-*qa-dú-um*-[ma] DÙ mit der Autographie nicht übereinstimmt; es steht dort -*k*]*a*$_4$ *tu-ka*-[*a*]*l* "du hältst." Der Ausdruck **qaqqadumma epēšu* ist aus Nuzi-Texten also nicht nachzuweisen. (b) Die biblische Stelle ist für HSS 19,5 irrelevant; Aššurbanipal war auch nicht Erstgeborener und wurde dennoch als Thronfolger eingesetzt. Zu beweisen wäre, dass diese Regelungen etwas mit den Hausgöttern zu tun haben. (c) HSS 19,4:15-20 ist teilweise zerstört; die fragliche Z. 15 sagt zwar 1 É *i+na ṣé-re-ti* ⌜*ša*⌝! URU *Nu-zi* DINGIR^{MEŠ} *ša* ^{I}[*A*]*r-ša-du-ja*. Doch ist diese Zeile in Bezug zu setzen zu Z. 7-9: *mi-nu-um-me-e* A.ŠÀ$^{\text{ḪI.A}}$ *ù* É$^{\text{ḪI.A}}$ AN.ZA.KÀR *mar-ši-tù ma-na-ḫa-tù* [*mi-im*]-*ma šu-u*[*n-šu*] ^{8}*ša* ^{I}*Ar-ša-du-ja ša* URU *Nu-zi* ^{9}*ù ša* URU <DINGIR>^{MEŠ}-*ni*. Sollte nicht danach auch Z. 15 in ⌜*ša*⌝ URU *Nu-zi* <*ù ša* URU> DINGIR^{MEŠ} *ša* ^{I}[*A*]*r-ša-du-ja* verbessert werden? (d) In JEN 443:4-5, einem ebenfalls fragmentarischen Text, ist an die Ergänzung É^{MEŠ} *i+na ṣé*-[*re-ti* É]^{MEŠ} [*ku*(-*up*)]-⌜*pá*⌝-*tù* ^{5}*a-na* ^{MÍ}*Ni-si-ir*-[*bi*] SUM-*nu* zu denken.

Nach dem Tod des Šukrija tritt also folgende Regelung in Kraft: Teḫip-tilla und Pai-tilla gründen zwei distinkte Haushalte, in denen sie ihre Hausgötter mit grossem bzw. kleinen Kopf aufstellen. Die Felder ihres Vaters und die restliche Fahrnis teilen sie im Verhältnis 2 : 1. Jeder bewirtschaftet seine Felder für sich, die *ilku*-Verpflichtung tragen sie (bis zu ihrem Tod) jedoch gemeinsam. Diese schliesst *ipso facto* aus, dass sie ihre Felder verkaufen. Ihr Stiefbruder Šimika-atal, der nur ein Hausgrundstück erhält, hat keinen Anteil an dem *ilku*: er könnte legalerweise die Felder und Häuser seiner beiden Halbbrüder verkaufen. Die im Testament festgehaltene Konventionalstrafe wird ihn jedoch davon abhalten. Die Ehefrau des Šukrija erhält ihr eigenes Haus, in dem sie bis zu ihrem Tode unbehelligt leben darf; danach fällt es an Teḫip-tilla. ^{f}Warḫi-nuzu wird jedoch nicht als *ēpišat abbutti* eingesetzt; darum fehlt auch die *ipallaḫ*-Klausel.

Dieser Rechtszustand ist für die zweite Urkunde anzunehmen, die nach dem Tod des Šukrija abgefasst sein muss:

HSS 19,30 SMN 2509 (nach HSS 19, p. vi) Room ? (erschlossen: S 151)
79 x 71 x 34 mm

Für diesen Text werden in der Ausgabe zwei SMN-Nummern angegeben: HSS 19, p. vii trägt er die Nummer SMN 2709; diese Angabe ist auch von der Nuzi-Bibliographie (p. 229b) übernommen worden, während SMN 2509 (p. 227c) als unpubliziert geführt wird. Falls HSS 19,30—wie ich unten nachzuweisen versuchen werde—zum Archiv Tarmija S. Ḫuja gehört, ist als Fundort S 151 so gut wie sicher; zu S 151 passt aber nur SMN 2509, nicht SMN 2709.

Vs Anfang der Vs weggebrochen
0 [*i+na e-le-en* A.ŠÀ *ša* ^{I}]
1 [*i+na il*]-⌜*ta-na*⌝-[*an*] A.⌜ŠÀ⌝ [*ša* ^{I}]
2 [*i+na*] *sú-ta-an* A.ŠÀ *ša* ^{I}[ ]
3 [*ù*] *i+na šu-pá-al a-tap-pí* [*ša* É.G]AL-*lì*
4 ⌜*ù*⌝ *ša-nu-ú aš-lu* 3 ^{GIŠ}AP[IN A.ŠÀ]
5 ⌜*i+*⌝[*na*] ⌜*e*⌝-*le-e*[*n*] A.ŠÀ *ša* ^{I}⌜x⌝[ ]
6 ⌜*i+*⌝[*na i*]*l-ta-*[*n*]*a-an* A.ŠÀ *ša* ^{I}*Ni-iḫ-ri-ja*
7 ⌜*i+*⌝[*na*] *sú-ta-an*! A.ŠÀ ša ^{I}*Tar-mi-ja*
8 *ù i+na šu-pa-al* A.ŠÀ *ša* [^{I}]x-*ni-ja*
9 ŠU.NIGIN 7 ^{GIŠ}APIN A.ŠÀ *an-nu-*[*ú*]
10 [*i+na* AN].ZA.KÀR *ša* ^{I}*Ḫu-ja* ^{I}*It-ḫi-ip-til-la* (Fehler für ^{I}*Te-ḫi-ip-til-la*)
11 [*ù* ^{I}]*Ba-i-til-la ki-ma* ḪA.LA-*šu*
12 [*a-n*]*a* ^{I}*Tar-mi-ja it-ta-ad-nu-uš*
13 *ù* ^{I}*Tar-mi-ja* 3 ANŠE 3 BÁN ŠE
14 *ù* [n] UDU *ki-ma* ḪA.LA-*šu-nu a-na* (Fehler für *ki-ma* NÍG.BA-*šu-nu a-na*)
15 [^{I}*Te-ḫi*]-*ip-til-la ù* ⌜*a*⌝-*n*[*a* ^{I}*Ba-i-til-la*]
16 [*it-ta*]-⌜*din*⌝ [ ]
Rest der Vs weggebrochen
Rs Anfang der Rs weggebrochen
17 [ ]x x[*kī pî*]
18 *ṭup-pí an-ni-i* ⌜x x⌝[ ]

19 *ni-il-te-qè ap-la-*[*nu-mi um-ma*]
20 ^{MÍ}*Wa-ar-ḫi-nu-zu-ma a-n*[*a* DUMU^{MEŠ}-*ja*]
21 *a-na a-bu-ti la ep-ša-ku-m*[*i*]
22 *ma-an-nu i+na be-ri-šu-nu ib-bala-kat*
23 1 MA.NA KÙ.BABBAR 1 MA.NA KÙ.GI *ú-ma-al-la ṭup-pí*
24 *an-ni-i i+na* EGIR-*ki šu-du-ti i+na* URU
25 *Nu-zi i+na ba-ab* É.GAL-*lì ina* ITU *Ḫu-tal-še*
26 *šá-ṭì-ir* IGI *Ut-ḫap-ta-e* DUMU *Ki-ba-a+a*
27 IGI *Du-ra-ri* DUMU *Ta-i-še-en-ni*
28 IGI *Ka-a+a* DUMU *En-na-ma-ti*
29 IGI *Te-eš-ta-e* DUMU *E-ge-ge* 4 LÚ^{MEŠ} *an-nu-tu*$_4$
30 *ša* KÙ.BABBAR *na-dì-na-nu*
31 IGI ^{d}30-KUR-*ni* DUB.SAR DUMU *A-mur-šarri*
32 IGI *Zi-líp-a-pu* DUMU *Ge-el-ša-a-pu*
33 IGI *Še-ḫa-al-te-šup* DUMU *Ḫu-ur-bi-še-e*[*n-ni*]
34 IGI ⸢*A-kip*⸣-[*til-l*]*a* DUMU *Ik-ki-ja*
Rest der Rs weggebrochen
liS 35 [NA$_4$ ^{I}*A-kip-t*]*il-la* NA$_4$ DUB.SAR

Kommentar:

Die Urkunde ist als ganze noch unbearbeitet; G. Dosch hat 1973 eine Umschrift angefertigt, auf welcher (mit kleinen Abweichungen) obige Umschrift basiert. Z. 9-16 hat A. Shaffer, Studies Presented to A. Leo Oppenheim (Chicago 1964), p. 192, n. 33, umschrieben und übersetzt. Z. 10 korrigiert er stillschweigend ^{I}*It-ḫi-ip-til-la* nach ^{I}*Te-ḫi-ip-til-la*; Z. 14 lässt er *ki-ma* ḪA.LA-*šu-nu* unbeanstandet.

Die Tafel ist offenbar wegen zwei querverlaufenden Brüchen in drei Fragmente zerfallen; nur das Mittelstück liegt uns vor. Vor der Zeile 0 der Vs dürften etwa 8 Zeilen fehlen; der Textverlust am unteren Rand ist hingegen geringer. Eine gezielte Suche in den NTF drawers könnte Erfolg haben, zumal man den Texttyp und die Namen der Kontrahenten kennt.

Der in Z.7.12.13 genannte Tarmija ist Tarmija S. Ḫuja und HSS 19,30 gehört zu seinem Archiv. Diese Behauptung stützt sich zunächst auf den Vergleich zwischen dieser Urkunde und dem *ṭuppi aḫātūti* HSS 19,67 (SMN 2104 aus Room S 132). Beide Tafeln sind von demselben Schreiber, Sîn-šadûni S. Amur-šarri geschrieben. Ihre Zeugenlisten (sieben Zeugen in 30, fünf Zeugen in 67) weisen drei Übereinstimmungen auf: Utḫap-tae S. Kipaja, Teš-tae S. Ekeke und Akip-tilla S. Ikkija. Der Kontrahent von HSS 19,67 ist Tarmija S. Ḫuja (Z. 3). In HSS 19,30 ist zwar der Vatername des Tarmija weggebrochen und der Anfang des Namens Teḫip-tilla (Z. 10) als Itḫip-tilla verschrieben, aber allein die Kombination der Z. 11 und 20-21 (wonach ^{f}Warḫi-nuzu die Mutter des Pai-tilla ist) ist ausreichend, um diesen Text prosopographisch mit HSS 19,5 (und HSS 14,8) unwiderlegbar zu verschrauben. Dass die Felder der beiden Brüder in der *dimtu ša Ḫuja* (Z. 10), die nach ihrem Grossvater benannt ist, liegen, kann als weitere Bestätigung verbucht werden, dass

Tarmija eben T. S. Ḫuja ist. Somit ist HSS 19,30 ein Kontrakt zwischen den zwei voll erbberechtigten Söhnen des Šukrija S. Ḫuja—dessen *ilku* sie gemeinsam tragen—mit dem jüngeren Bruder ihres Vaters, also mit ihrem Oheim, Tarmija S. Ḫuja. Welcher Urkundengattung ist dieser Kontrakt nun zuzurechnen? A. Shaffer (Studies Presented to A. Leo Oppenheim [Chicago 1964], 192 n. 33) möchte ihn—auf Grund des zweimaligen *ki-ma* ḪA.LA-*šu* (-*nu*)—HSS 19,30 der Gattung *ṭuppi zitti* (vertreten durch HSS 5,75 und HSS 19,61 sowie, allerdings ohne diese Überschrift, durch das von ihm publizierte Tablet Serota) zurechnen. Ich kann mir allerdings schlecht vorstellen, wie Tarmija auf Grund eines erbrechtlichen Titels seinen Neffen ihnen aus dem *ṭuppi šīmti* ihres Vaters Šukrija zustehende Felder wegnehmen kann, sich gleichsam als Erbe seines Bruders substituierend, und möchte deshalb lieber Z. 14 in NÍG.BA-*šu-nu* emendieren. Damit läge dann ein *ṭuppi mārūti* vor. Nicht auszuschliessen ist auch, dass der Kontrakt als *ṭuppi aḫḫūti* stilisiert war. Endgültig Aufschluss darüber kann freilich nur der Join bringen, auch in der Frage, wie das *ilku* in HSS 19,30 geregelt wurde. Was *e silentio* bereits aus HSS 19,5 zu folgern war, dass nämlich ^{f}Warḫi-nuzu das *abbuttu* über ihre Söhne nicht ausübt, sagt sie HSS 19,30:20-21 *explicite*. Wäre sie *ēpišat abbutti* gewesen, hätte diese Transaktion gar nicht stattfinden können. Von den sieben Zeugen sind drei, wie bereits erwähnt, auch aus HSS 19,67 nachweisbar. Šeḫal-tešup S. Ḫurpi-šenni ist noch Zeuge in HSS 16,321:22 (Room S 151, ebenfalls aus dem Archiv des Tarmija S. Ḫuja). Kaja S. Enna-mati (Z. 28) ist Zeuge in JEN 477:26, einer Urkunde aus dem Archiv des Kel-tešup S. Ḫutija, Dossier Šuriniwe. Turari S. Tai-šenni schliesslich begegnet noch in dem unveröffentlichten Text SMN 2390:42.48 (zitiert bei E. Cassin, AAN I 151b; nach 137a Tai-šenni ist das Patronym allerdings ergänzt). Von dem Schreiber Sîn-šadûni S. Amur-šarri stammen folgende Tafeln: a) mit Patronym: HSS 9,22; HSS 19,30; Jankowska 46; SMN 3103 und SMN 3601 (beide unveröffentlicht; nach R. E. Hayden, Court Procedure at Nuzu, Dissertation Brandeis University 1962, University Microfilms 63-5842 ist SMN 3103 ein *ṭuppi tamgurti* zwischen Šurki-tilla S. Amurrabi und Teḫip-zizza S. Arnuja; SMN 3601 ist NPN 122a zitiert); b) ohne Patronym: Gadd 70; HSS 5,6; HSS 15,144; HSS 19,67.

Durch den Kontrakt HSS 19,30 waren Teḫip-tilla und Pai-tilla S.e Šukrija in Abhängigkeit von Tarmija S. Ḫuja geraten. Welches ist nun das weitere Schicksal der Familie und ihrer Hausgötter? Näheres erfahren wir aus der Ordal-Urkunde

HSS 14,8 = RA 36,116 SMN 2655 Room P 470 99 x 67 x 35 mm

Vs 1 [*um*]-*ma* ^{I}*Ba-i-til-la-ma* DUMU *Šúk-ri-ja*
2 [*šum-m*]*a* DINGIR^{MEŠ}-*ja* AN.ZÁLAG^{MEŠ} *um-mi-ja*
3 [*a-n*]*a* ^{I}*A-kip-ta-še-en-ni* DUMU *Ta-e*
4 [*la*] *id-dì-nu-ma ù la ik-ki*$^{!}$(KU)-*ru-ma*
5 *ù šum-ma ki-ma* DINGIR^{MEŠ} II *A*^{I}-*kip-ta*-<še-en-ni>

6 *um-mi-ja ù a-ḫa-ti*^{MEŠ}-⸢*ja*⸣

7 ^{MÍ}*Wa-ar-ḫi-nu-zu ù* ^{MÍ}*I-n*[*i-ib*]-*ḫa-ti*

8 *i+na* KUR *ša-ni-i a-na* ŠÀM^{MEŠ} *l*[*a it-t*]*a-din*

unbeschrifteter Raum von etwa zwei Zeilen

9 [*u*]*m-ma* ^{I}*A-kip-ta-še-en-ni* DUMU *Ta*-[*e*]

10 [*šum*]-*ma* DINGIR^{MEŠ} AN.ZÁLAG^{MEŠ} [*š*]*a* ^{I}*Ba-i-til*-[*la*]

11 ⸢*ù*⸣ *um-ma-šu a-na ja-ši id-d*[*ì-nu*]

12 ⸢*ù*⸣ *at-ta-ki-ir-šu-mi ù šum-m*[*a*]

13 [*ki-m*]*a* DINGIR^{MEŠ} *um-ma-šu ù* [0]

14 [*a-ḫ*]*a-ti*^{MEŠ}-*šu ša* ^{I}*Ba-i-til-la* x[ ]

15 [*ù* $^{\text{M]Í}}$*Ì-ni-ib-ḫa-at-ti i+na* KUR ⸢*ša*⸣-[*ni-i* (*a-na* ŠÀM^{MEŠ}) *at-ta-din*]

16 [*aš-šu*]*m a-wa-ti an-nu*-⸢*ti*⸣ ⸢*i*⸣[*+n*]*a* ^{Í}[^{D}*ḫur-ša-an*]

17 [*il-l*]*a-ku š*[*a i*]*k-kál-lu* L[UGAL]

18 [*ṭe₄*]-*e-m*[*a i-ša*]-*ak-k*[*a-an*]

u.Rd. unterer Rand zerstört

Rs Anfang der Rs zerstört

Siegelabrollung

19 [NA₄ ^{I}A/Šur]-*kip-šarri* DUMU *Er*-[ ]

Siegelabrollung

20 [NA₄ ^{I}]*I-ru-ja* DUMU *Zi-ka-a+a*

Siegelabrollung

21 [NA₄] ^{I}*A-ta-a+a* DUMU *Mu-uš-te-šup*

22 ⸢NA₄⸣ ^{I}*Še-en-na-til* DUMU *Ḫu-ja*

li.Rd. zerstört

Kommentar:

HSS 14,8 stammt aus Room P 470 (alt C 470) wie die Urkunden AASOR 16,96, HSS 19,20 (Paradise C-3) und 23 (Paradise C-39) und der Brief HSS 14,24. Obwohl aus Z. 16-18 klar hervorgeht, dass es sich um ein Ordalurteil handelt, ist dieser Text nicht in dem Kapitel V. The ḫuršānu at Nuzi der Dissertation von A. I. Liebermann, Studies in the Trial by River Ordeal in the Ancient Near East During the Second Millennium BCE (Brandeis University 1969. University Microfilms 69-20, 729) bearbeitet. Trotz der engen Zusammengehörigkeit mit HSS 19,5 ist HSS 14,8 auch in der Dissertation von J. S. Paradise (vgl. pp. iv, vi und 237-42) nicht erwähnt. Eine Paraphrase des Textes bietet hingegen Ann Draffkorn (Kilmer), JBL 76 (1957) spez. pp. 221-24. Die hier vorgelegte Umschrift geht zurück auf eine Bearbeitung des Textes durch G. Dosch vom 23. März 1973, die Verf. 1980 überarbeitet hat. Leider ist der Name des Schreibers dieser Urkunde weggebrochen; somit können wir aus einem Vergleich mit anderen Urkunden seines Œuvres keine Hilfe für die Interpretation dieses schwierigen Textes beziehen.

Betrachten wir zunächst die Prosopographie des Corpus von HSS 14,8. Pai-tilla S. Šukrija und seine Mutter, ^{f}Warḫi-nuzu, sind bereits aus HSS 9,5 und 30 bekannt. Eine Schwester des Pai-tilla, mit ziemlicher Sicherheit Tochter der ^{f}Warḫi-nuzu, ist jedoch nur aus diesem Text nachweisbar, vgl.

E. Cassin, AAN I 68a. Ihr Name, ^{f}Inib-ḫatti ist ebenfalls hapax. Auch Akiptašenni S. Tae (Z.3.5.9) ist bisher aus anderen Texten nicht belegbar. E. Cassin listet zwar AAN I 19a einen Akip-tašenni "fils de Tae, époux de ^{f}Warḫi-nuzu, fille de Ḫupita HSS XIX 25:1.18." Dieser Text ist von J. S. Paradise als C-45 (pp. 172-73) behandelt. Die ersten drei Zeilen lauten (in einer neuen Umschrift von P. Negri Scafa) wie folgt:

Vs 1 [*ṭup*]-⌈*pí*⌉ [*ši-im-t*]*i ša* ^{I}*A-kip-ta-še-en-ni*
2 [DUMU -r]i *ši-im-ta a-na aš-šá-ti-šu*
3 [*a-na* ^{MÍ}]-*nu-zu* DUMU.MÍ *Ḫu-pí-ta i-ši-im*

Es steht also überhaupt nicht fest, dass die hier in Z.2 genannte Tochter des Ḫupita ^{f}*Warḫi-nuzu heisst, noch kann das Patronym des Akip-tašenni Tae sein; die Spur vor *ši-im-ta* ist am ehesten r]i, a]r oder a]ḫ. Der Fundort von HSS 19,25 (SMN 2783) lässt sich nicht feststellen; die sehr fragmentarisch Zeugenliste weist keinerlei Elemente auf, die auf einen Zusammenhang mit dem Archiv der Söhne und Enkel des Ḫuja schliessen lassen könnten.

Das Corpus von HSS 14,8 zerfällt in zwei Teile: die eidlichen, jedoch kontradiktorischen Aussagen der beiden Parteien (Z.1-8 und 9-15) und die Gerichtsentscheidung, dass sie sich dem Flussordal unterwerfen müssen (Z.16-18). Die grammatische Form der Eide (der erste positiv, der zweite negativ assertorisch) sind Bedingungssätze ohne Nachsatz (GAG § 185 g.h): entsprechend finden sich in Z.4 Verbalformen des Typs *lā* + Präteritum Subjunktiv. Nicht korrekt erscheint jedoch *l*[*a it-t*]*a-din* (Z.8); man würde auch hier *lā iddinu* erwarten. In Z.11 ist *id-d*[*ì-nu*] nach Z.4 ergänzt, dem Sinn entsprechend ohne *lā*. Die Form im Perfekt Indikativ *at-ta-ki-ir-šu*(*-mi*) Z.12 hingegen ist sozusagen uneidlich formuliert. Der folgende *šumma*-Satz müsste in Z.15 als Prädikat *addinu* enthalten; ich habe jedoch—in Anlehnung an Z.8—hier *at-ta-din* ergänzt.

Ein weiteres Indiz für Formulierungsschwächen des Schreibers ist das Ende der Z.14: hier wäre eigentlich der Name ^{f}Warḫi-nuzu zu erwarten; die Spur sieht jedoch eher nach K[U aus.

Die Präposition *ki-ma* Z.5 und 13 dürfte "für, um" (zur Angabe des Kaufpreises, AHw 477a 8b und CAD K 396b) meinen.

AN.ZALÁG^{MEŠ} in Z.2 und 10 (A. Draffkorn liest AN.ZAB^{MEŠ}) lasse ich vorerst unübersetzt, unten versuche ich, mit der gebotenen Reserve, dann eine neue Deutung des Terminus.

Die Z.16-18 ergänzen sich leicht nach HSS 13, 422:35-38 (vgl. Liebermann, pp. 68-69 und CAD K 104a; AHw 429a).

Die vier Richter (Z.19-22) haben eine recht weitgestreute Attestation. In Z.19 würde ich mich nicht auf Akip-šarri (ohne Patronym) festlegen, der aus den Unapšewe-Prozessen JEN 191 und 379 bekannt ist. Iruja S. Zikaja ist Richter in JEN 662:93-94 und (ohne Patronym) AASOR 16,72:31. Ataja S. Muš-tešup ist Richter in HSS 9,12:44; JEN 662:93 (ergänzt) 94; HSS 19,72:46.

Šennatil S. Ḫuja ist Richter in JEN 370:53 und 663:32; SMN 1066:47 (zit. Hayden, p. 252a) und 3053:34 (s. Liebermann, p. 63).
Übersetzung:

Pai-tilla S. Šukrija (machte folgende Aussage):
(Ich schwöre, dass) meine Mutter meine Hausgötter (und) die AN.ZÁLAG^{MEŠ} dem Akip-tašenni S. Tae gegeben hat, er (dies) jedoch bestritten hat. (Ich schwöre ferner, dass) Akip-tašenni für die Hausgötter meine Mutter und meine Schwester, ^{f}Warḫi-nuzu und ^{f}Inib-ḫatti, in das Ausland verkauft hat.

Akip-tašenni S. Tae (machte folgende Aussage):
(Ich schwöre, dass) die Hausgötter (und) die AN.ZÁLAG^{MEŠ} des Pai-tilla seine Mutter mir nicht gegeben hat. Ich habe dies ihm (gegenüber) auch abgestritten. (Ich schwöre ferner, dass) ich für die Hausgötter die Mutter und die Schwester des Pai-tilla, (letztere) Inib-ḫatti (mit Namen) nicht in das Ausland verkauft habe.
Wegen dieser Aussagen werden sie zum Flussordal gehen. Über denjenigen, der sich weigert, wird der König eine Entscheidung treffen.
[Siegel des A/Šur]kip-šarri S. Er[ ]; [Siegel] des Iruja S. Zikaja; [Siegel] des Ataja S. Muš-tešup; Siegel des Šennatil S. Ḫuja.

Der letzte, die Hausgötter des Šukrija betreffende Text—und zwar die Götter mit dem kleinen Kopf, das Erbteil des Pai-tilla—wird zum Zeugnis für die Disintegration dieser Familie. War Pai-tilla aus wirtschaftlichen Gründen gezwungen, seine Mutter und seine Schwester ins Ausland, d.h. in die Sklaverei, zu verkaufen? Und war dieser verzweifelte Schritt nur möglich unter der Voraussetzung, dass seine Mutter dem Händler (als solchen darf man Akip-tašenni S. Tae wohl am ehesten identifizieren) vorher die Familiengötter übergab? Waren demnach die Hausgötter der letzte Schutz der Witwen und Waisen? Auch dann, wenn die Witwe nicht mit dem *abbuttu* betraut und ihre Altersversorgung daher testamentarisch geregelt war? Fragen, die sich beim Studium des Textes HSS 14,8 aufdrängen, von denen wir aber nicht sagen können, ob sie überhaupt richtig gestellt sind. Die Urkunde ist ja nur ein Detail eines Prozesses Šukrija gegen Akip-tašenni: war womöglich dessen Gegenstand die Weigerung des Akip-tašenni, dem Šukrija den für ^{f}Warḫi-nuzu und ^{f}Inib-ḫatti erzielten Preis auszuhändigen? Stand jetzt Šukrija da ohne einen Sekel Silber, von allen guten Göttern verlassen, womöglich sozial wegen des Menschenhandels mit Mutter und Schwester geächtet? Wie kann der König dem Šukrija noch zu seinem Recht verhelfen, da er bestenfalls den Akip-tašenni zur Erstattung des Kaufpreises, vielleicht in mehrfacher Höhe, verurteilen kann?

Wenden wir uns dem Ausdruck DINGIR^{MEŠ} AN.ZÁLAG^{MEŠ} zu, der JBL 76,221 und hier unübersetzt geblieben ist. Ausser HSS 14,8:2.10 ist er noch JEN 478:5 nachzuweisen. In dieser Urkunde enterbt Kurpa-saḫ S. Ḫilpiš-šuḫ seinen Sohn Akip-tilla. Z. 1-12 haben folgenden Wortlaut:

Vs 1 *um-ma* ^{I}*Ku-ur-pa-sà-aḫ-ma*
2 DUMU *Ḫi-il-bi-šu-uḫ*

3 DUMÙ<<šú Rasur>>-*ja* ^{I}*A-kip-la-til* (Fehler für ^{I}*A-kip-til-la*)
4 *ù ki-ir-bá-an-šu i+na pa-ni*
5 (Rasur) AN.ZÁLAG *eḫ-te-pu ù*
6 *i-na* DINGIR^{MEŠ} *ù a-na e-ṭe*$_4$*-em-mi*
7 (Rasur) A.ŠÀ^{MEŠ} *ù* É$^{ḪI.A.MEŠ}$ *la*
8 *i-la-ak-ka*$_4$
9 *ṭup-pu i+na* EGIR-*ki šu-du-ti*
10 *ša* É.GAL-lì *ša-ṭì-ir*
11 *i-na bá-ab a-šar a-bu-ul-li*
12 *ša* URU *Te-em-te-na-aš*

In den beiden letzten Äusserungen zu diesem Text wird AN.ZÁLAG (bzw. AN.ZAB, JBL 76 [1957] 221) jedoch zu ^{d}UTU verändert: "he broke his clod before Šamaš (he will not take the fields and houses)" CAD K 403a, und. "An interesting feature of this text is the fact that the father performs the ceremony of breaking the clump before the god Šamaš. Moreover he states: 'He shall not have rights to gods and (ancestral) spirits. Fields and houses he shall not receive'" (Paradise, p. 311, n. 218).

Vielleicht war diese Emendation von JEN 478:5 doch etwas zu voreilig, besonders wenn man Šurpu III 31-32 dagegenhält, wo wir lesen:

31 [*ma-mit*] *kur-ban-ni* GAZ-*ú* LAG *a-na* A^{MEŠ} ŠUB-*ú* *ú*
32 [*ma-mit* K]I.UD.BA *a-na* IGI LÚ *šá-ka-nu* *ú*

Zwar ist KI.UD.BA (E. Reiner: 'cult lamp(?)') nicht ohne weiteres mit AN.ZÁLAG gleichzusetzen, doch sollte man die Gedankengänge, die Frau Reiner Šurpu, p. 56a ad 32 entwickelt, unbedingt weiterverfolgen (vgl. dazu auch CAD K 477a kizalaqu). Der Ausdruck KI.UD.BA scheint in der Tat verwandt, wenn nicht synonym zu sein mit KI.ZÁLAG.GA, das im Nassouhi-Prisma Aššurbanipals (AfK 2,100-1) belegt ist:

100 I 7' KI.ZÁLAG.GA *šu-bat* ^{d}IZI.GAR 83 GÚ.UN *za-ḫa-lu-ú eb-bu ap-tiq-ma*
8' *a-na nu-um-mur* KI.NE *si-mat* É.ZI.DA
9' *šu-bat* DINGIR-*ti-šú* GAL-*ti nak-liš ú-še-piš*

Dass hier der Umschrift AN.ZÁLAG gegenüber AN.ZAB(^{MEŠ})—dem Vorschlag A. Draffkorns—der Vorzug gegeben wird, hat seinen Grund jedoch nicht nur in dem soeben Gesagten, sondern sie bietet sich auch von der Nuzi-Orthographie her an. Während für den PN Ilu-namer (NPN 69b/70a; keine Belege in AAN I) bisher nur die Grapheme *I-lu-na-mi-ir*, *I-lu-na-me-er*, AN-*na-mi-ir*, AN-*na-wi-ir*, *I-lu-un-na-mi-ir*, AN-*na-me-er* nachzuweisen waren, gibt es jetzt auch die Schreibung AN-ZÁLAG (CT 51, 3 Rs 9: *Ilu-namir tamkāru mār Šummalli*), worauf mich P. Negri Scafa freundlicherweise aufmerksam machte. Mit den drei Stellen HSS 14, 8:2.10; JEN 478:5; CT 51, 3 Rs 9 sind freilich alle Nuzi-Belege für dieses Graphem aufgezählt. Wo findet es sich sonst noch? Die Gebetsbeschwörung KAR 58 Vs 1-24 Parr. (vgl. W. Mayer, Untersuchungen zur Formensprache der babylonischen "Gebetsbeschwörungen," Rome 1976,

p. 406 und 482-84) richtet sich (vom Graphem her gesehen) an AN.ZÁLAG; so Z.1: ÉN AN.ZÁLAG *a-na* ^{d}AMAR.UTU *kur-bu* und könnte deshalb auch als Kultmittelgebet angesehen und gedeutet werden; W. Mayer umschreibt ^{d}*nūru* (Licht, Lampe, p. 433), reiht den Text aber unter die Nusku-Gebete (p. 406) ein. Aus der Ritualzeile (Z. 25: INIM.INIM.MA *ina* IGI AN.ZÁLAG *ša* SAG ^{LÚ}GIG *šak-nu* ŠID-*nu*) geht jedoch hervor, dass etwas Konkretes gemeint sein muss, aus Z. 23-24 sogar, dass es Mund und Lippen hat. Man wird auch AN.ZÁLAG *u* KEŠDA DU_8-*ár* BMS 40:14' (vgl. W. Meyer, p. 407.7) kaum anders als konkret verstehen können. Für die Lesung ^{d}*nūru* wird man zwar auf ^{d}*Nu-ru* ALAM in den Adad-Tempeln von Aššur und Kurba'il verweisen können (3R 66 II 20 // KAV 57:6' und STT 88 II 45 sowie 3R 66 VII 11'), aber es ist klar, dass ^{d}*Nu-ru* ALAM und AN.ZÁLAG nicht dasselbe ist.

Nun ist ZÁLAG ja nicht nur *nūru*, sondern auch *nawrum*/*namru*. Gibt es für AN.ZÁLAG entsprechende syllabische Schreibungen? Aus neuassyrischen Texten notiere ich:

	a]n$^{!}$-*nam-ru*	ABL 483:6
	[a]n$^{!}$-*nam-ru*	ABL 1209:3
	an-nam-ri	ND 1120:3 (Iraq 14, pl.23)
	an-nam-ra-ni	ABL 91:5;
unsicher:	*an-na*]*m-ra-a-*[*ni*	ABL 216 r.1'

AHw listet 52a *annamru* ABL 91:5 und 1209:3, nimmt unbekannte Herkunft an und klassifiziert das Wort als ein Metallgerät. CAD A/2 ***annamru* verweist, mit Bezug auf AHw 52a, auf das Lemma namru. Die Unsicherheit hinsichtlich der Lesung und das ungeklärte Verhältnis von *annamru* zu AN.ZÁLAG dürften Grund genug sein, den jeweiligen Kontext der nA Belege für *annamru* erneut zu überprüfen.

ND 1120 = IM 56880
Autographie: D. J. Wiseman, Iraq 14, pl. 23. Bearbeitung: G. Van Driel, The Cult of Aššur, pp. 198-205. Kollationen: J. N. Postgate, GPA, no. 246, pp. 228-29; S. Parpola (1977; briefl. Mitteilung vom 13.6.1980). Fundort: Kalḫu, c. 10 m east of Burnt Palace, Room viii (Square D 12). Dimensionen: 104 x 99 x 30 mm, ursprünglich etwa 160 x 120 x 30 mm. Datum: 22.X.714, *limmu* Ištar-dūrī, Statthalter von Arrapḫa. Weil seit der letzten Bearbeitung eine ganze Reihe von Korrekturen angebracht wurden, biete ich eine neue Umschrift des ganzen Textes (zu der S. Parpola Wesentliches beigesteuert hat):

Vs
1 [*i-na t*]*ar*$^{!}$*ṣi*$^{!}$ ^{I}LUGAL-GI.NA MAN KUR *Aš+šur*^{KI}
2 [*i-na l*]*i-me* ^{Id}INNIN-BÀD ^{LÚ}*šá-kìn* ^{URU}*Arrap-ḫa*

3 [U$_4$ 20 KÁM K]I.TUŠ *ša* NA$_4$.AD.BAR *ša* KI.TA *an-nam-ri* URUDU *ina* É ^{d}*A-šur ú-se-ri-bu*
4 [ ] KI.TUŠ *i-šá-da-du-ni maš-ki-it-tu i-na* ŠÀ KI-*šu i-da-a'-pu*
5 [*i-na p*]*a-an* LUGAL *ṭè-e-mu ú-ter-ru*
6 [ ] U$_4$ 21 KÁM ^{Id}AG-*šal-lim-šú-nu* ^{LÚ}DUB.SAR LUGAL *a-na* ^{URU}ŠÀ.URU *i-tal-ka*
7 [ ]x *qi-ir-si* KALAG^{MEŠ} TA* É ^{LÚ}GAR.KUR *na-ṣu-ni ina* UGU *maš-ki-it-ti i-taḫ-ṣu*$^{!}$
8 [UDU *dà-ri-*]⌜*ú*⌝ *ina pa-an* ^{d}*A-šur na-si-iḫ* É DINGIR *a-píl*
9 [a]k$^{?}$-*li iq-ṭar-bu*
10 [^{Id}AG-*šal-l*]*im*$^{!}$-*šú-nu* ^{LÚ}DUB.SAR LUGAL$^{!}$ ^{I}Za-za$^{!}$-a ^{LÚ}A.BA URU *i-ti-ti-su*
11 [*dul-lu ša i-n*]*a* UGU *maš-ki-it-ti in*$^{!}$-*né-pa-šu-*⌜*ni*⌝$^{!}$ *e-ta-ap-šu*
12 [K]Ù.BABBAR *ša* É ^{d}*A-šur ú-se-ṣu-né šu-nu-ma maš-ki-it-tu ina lìb-bi up-ta-ṭi*$^{!}$-*ru*
13 ! KAŠ^{M}]$^{EŠ!}$ GEŠTIN^{MEŠ} Ì+GIŠ^{MEŠ} TA* É.GAL *i-ta-an-nu*
14 [ ] *a-na maš-ki-it-te se-a-re* ^{LÚ}ŠEMxA^{MEŠ} *ša* É ^{d}A-šur *ib-tal-lu*$^{!}$
15 [*i*]*na lìb-bi ṭi-id-di ša si-i-ri* TA* ŠÀ *ša* É.GAL *ik-ta-ru*
16 [1-*et* ^{DUG}*nam-z*]*i-tu* KALAG-*tu* 1-*et* QÀL-*su* ^{LÚ}GAL BÁḪAR *i-ti-din*
17 [ ]⌜*i*⌝-*sa-ak-nu i-si-ru* KUR *Ḫu-un-dir-a+a ú-ṣip-pu*
18 [*ki-i dul-lu i-n*]*a* UGU *maš-ki-it-te e-pa-šu-ni* É ^{d}*A-šur pa-su-uk*
19 [ ] É *ubu-sa-a-te ša* ^{d}NIN.URTA *tur-rat*$^{!}$
20 [ ] (blank) *par-sa-at*
21 [ ]⌜É⌝ ^{d}*A*-((AŠ))-*šur i-na* UGU *ki-gal-li i-ti-ti-su*
22 [^{LÚ}]⌜*ḫa*⌝-*za-na-te i-na* KÁ *ša* É *ubu-sa-a-ti ša* ^{d}NIN.URTA *i-ti-ti-su*
23 [KAL]AG^{MEŠ} *i-sa-du-né*
24 [ ] *ki-si-ir-ti* KI.TA É ^{d}*A-šur ú-sa-zi-z*[*u*]
25 [ ] *e-si-*⌜*iḫ*⌝$^{!}$-*ti-šú-nu* UDU^{MEŠ} NINDA^{MEŠ} GEŠTIN^{MEŠ} Ì^{MEŠ} L[ÀL^{MEŠ}]
26 [^{LÚ}]⌜*ú*⌝-*ra-si ša* ŠU^{2} ^{LÚ}GAL *ú-ra-si š*[*a* ^{UR}]^{U}ŠÀ.U[RU]
27 [ ]⌜*ú-sa*⌝-*ar*$^{!}$-*ki-bu* x[ ]
Rest der Vs weggebrochen

Rs Anfang der Rs weggebrochen
1′ [*rik-su i-na*] *pa-an* ^{d}UTU ⌜*i*⌝-[*rak-kas*]
2′ [^{UZU}*síl-q*]*u*$^{!}$ *ḫa-an-ṭu ep-*[*pal*]
3′ [*pa-áš*]-*šú-ri i-na pa-an* <^{d}>UTU *i-rak-*[*kas*]
4′ [*i-na*] *pa-an maš-ki-it-te i-rak-*[*kas*]
5′ [*i-na l*]*ìb-bi i-šak-kan* ^{LÚ}*kar-ka-di-nu nap-ta-an-šu i-šak-*⌜*kan*⌝
6′ [ ]x SA$_5$$^{!}$ ^{GIŠ}LI ^{GIŠ}PÈŠ *ina* UGU NÍG.NA *i-sar-raq*
7′ [BA]L-*qi* Ì+GIŠ^{MEŠ} LÀL^{MEŠ} GA^{MEŠ} KAŠ^{MEŠ} GEŠTIN^{MEŠ}
8′ [*maš-ki-i*]*t-te ina lìb-bi ra-ṭa-a-ti ša pa-an rik-si* BAL-*qí*
9′ [UDU.NÍTA] *i-na UGU maš-ki-it-te i-na-kis* ^{LÚ}GALA *i-za-mur*

10′ [ ] *a-di ḫa-áš-ḫa-la*$^{!}$*-ti-ši-na* UDU.NÍTA *na-ak-su ša* UGU *maš-ki-it-te*

11′ [ ] *a-na* ÍD *e-mi-di i-kar-*⌜*ru*⌝*-ru*

. . . . ———————————

12′ [*ša pa*]*-an* ^{d}UTU *a-di* ^{UZU}*síl-qi-šu* ^{LÚ}DUB.SAR LUGAL *e-kal*

. . . . ———————————

13′ [ ] *ša qaq-qi-ri ša pa-an* $^{\langle d\rangle}$UTU ^{LÚ}DUB.SAR URU *e-kal*

. . . . ———————————

14′ [ ]^{LÚ}GALA *i-na-ši* ^{UZU}*ú-nu-ut lìb-bi* ^{LÚ}MU *e-kal*

. . . . ———————————

15′ [ ] SAG.KI LIBIR.RA ZI-*ḫa*

. . . . ———————————

. . . . ———————————

16′ [ŠU ^{I}*Za-za-a*] ^{LÚ}DUB.SAR URU DUMU ^{Id}*Ba-ú-*ŠEŠ-SUM-*na* KI.MIN DUMU ^{I}U$_{4}$-20-KÁM-*a+a* KI.MIN DUMU ^{I}SUḪUŠ-^{d}PA KI.MIN

17′ [ ] KI.MIN DUMU ^{Id}AG-*be-el-*DINGIR KI.MIN DUMU ^{I}ŠEŠ-*ri-ba* ^{LÚ}DUB.SAR URU KI.MIN

18′ [ ]x-*A-šur* KI.MIN DUMU ^{Id}*A-šur*$_{4}^{!}$*-ki-la*/*na-ni* KI.MIN DUMU ^{Id}30-IBILA-SUM-*na* KI.MIN

19′ [ ]*-šá-kín-šu-me* KI.MIN DUMU ^{Id}MES-*kab*$^{!}$*-tu-*ŠEŠ^{MEŠ}*-šú* KI.MIN. GIR ^{I}*Aš+šur-*EN-DINGIR^{MEŠ} KI.MIN

20′ [*j*]*a* KI.MIN DUMU ^{Id}*A-šur-id-na-ni* ^{LÚ}DUB.SAR URU KI.MIN

21′ [ŠÀ.BAL.B]AL *ša* ^{I}*E-tel-pi-Mar-duk* ^{LÚ}DUB.SAR É *ṭup-pa-a-ti*

22′ [^{ITU}AB.BA].È U$_{4}$ 22 KÁM *li-mu* ^{Id}INNIN-BÀD ^{LÚ}*šá-kìn* ^{URU}*Arrap-ḫa*

23′ [MU(.AN.NA)] 9 *ša* ^{I}LUGAL-GI.NA MAN KUR ^{d}*A-šur*

ABL 91 K.620

Dieser Brief des *šakin māti* Ṭāb-ṣilli-Ešarra an Sargon II. ist unlängst von J. N. Postgate, Taxation and Conscription in the Assyrian Empire, Rome 1974, pp. 250-52, neu bearbeitet worden. Seine Umschrift ist korrekt, weshalb sie hier nicht *in toto* wiederholt zu werden braucht. (Vorbehalte sind jedoch hinsichtlich seiner Deutung des Terminus BE-*qu kaṣāru* anzumelden.) Die für *annamru* relevanten Zeilen lauten: [5]*an-nam-ra-ni* URUDU [6]*ki-la-le ma-za-su-šú-nu* [7]*dam-qa-at a-dan-niš* [8]*dul-la-šú-nu i-ba-ši ša dam-mu-qi* [9]*e-pu-*UŠ *ú-da-mu-qu*.

ABL 483 82-5-22,173 Dimensionen: etwa 68 x 30 mm.

Der Brief stammt aus derselben Korrespondenz. Lesbar ist nur die Vs; der untere Rand ist unbeschriftet; die Rs enthält drei fast gänzlich glasurierte Zeilen, deren letzte auf *-du* endet; der Rest der Rs, ca. 50 mm, ist unbeschriftet. Die folgende Umschrift beruht auf meiner Kollation vom 30. Aug. 1980.

Vs 1 *a-na* ⸢LUGAL⸣ EN-*j*[*a*]

2 ⸢ÌR⸣-*ka* ^{I}D[ÙG.GA-GIS]SU-É.ŠÁR.[RA]

3 *lu* [*šùl*]-*mu a-na* LUGAL EN-*ja*

4 [*Aš+šur* ^{d}NI]N.LÍL *a-na* LUGAL EN-[*ja*]

5 *l*[*ik*]-*ru*-⸢*bu*⸣

6 K[I.TUŠ *a*]*n-nam*-⸢*ru*⸣

7 [*la nu*]-⸢*uš*⸣-*bal-kit i-na muḫ*-[*ḫi*]

8 [*pa*]-*ni-šu ni-ik-ta-ra-ra*

9 [20+n] *ti-ik-pi ina* KI.⸢TA⸣

10 [*i*]-*ta-al-ku* GÌR$^{2.MEŠ}$-[*šu*]

11 [*a-n*]*a pu-tu šub-ti šá*-⸢*an*⸣-*ḫu*-⸢*ra*⸣

12 [n] *ti-ik-pi ša si*-⸢mil⸣$^{?}$-[*t*]*e*

13 *ka-ar-ru*

14 U$_4$ 6 KÁM *ina* UGU ^{GIŠ}MÁ

15 *e-pa-a-še iq-ṭar-bu*

16 *e-pu-šu*

"An meinen Herrn König. Dein Knecht Ṭab-ṣilli-Ešarra. Meinem Herrn König möge es wohlergehen! Aššur (und) Mullissu mögen meinen Herrn König segnen! Wir haben den *annamru*-Leuchter (seinen) Sockel nicht überschreiten lassen (d.h. ihn so plaziert, dass er nicht darüber hinausragt). Wir haben ihn auf seiner Oberseite aufgestellt. 20+n Ziegelschichten sind darunter gegangen. Seine Füsse haben wir der Frontseite des Sockels entsprechend gemacht. [n] Ziegelschichten für die Treppe(?) sind (bereits) gelegt.
Am 6. Tag sind sie zum Schiffbauen angekommen und sie bauen es (jetzt)."

Z.6 ist auch K[I.TUŠ-*šu a*]*n-nam*-⸢*ru*⸣ eine mögliche Ergänzung. Z. 12 ist das Zeichen ⸢mil⸣ nicht ganz sicher; auch die Ergänzung *si*-⸢mil⸣-[*a-t*]*e* ist möglich.

ABL 1209 81-2-4,116 Dimensionen: etwa 58 x 33 mm. Kollation vom 30.Aug.1980.

Vs Anfang weggebrochen

1′ [*be-l*]*í-j*[*a*]

2′ ÌR-*ka* ^{Id}MAŠ/PA-MAN-⸢PAP⸣

3′ [*a*]*n-nam-ru*

4′ [*š*]*a i-na* ZAG *ša* DINGIR

5′ ⸢*az*⸣-[*za*]-*qa-a*[*p*]

6′ *i-na* [U]GU KI.[TUŠ]

7′ *ku-ú-nu* x[ ]

8′ *l*[*ìb-bu š*]*a* LU[GAL EN-*ja*]

9′ *l*[*u*] DÙG.GA[-*šu*]

10′ ⸢*ù*⸣ *pi-x*[ ]

11′ *ú-pa*-⸢*ṭar*⸣ [ ]

12′ *a-na an* x[ ]

13′ [ ]x[ ]

Rest der Vs weggebrochen; Rs unbeschriftet

"[An] meinen Herrn [König]. Dein Knecht Ninurta/Nabû-šarru-uṣur. Den *annamru*-Leuchter, welcher auf die rechte Seite des Götterbildes gehört, habe ich aufgerichtet. Auf (seinem) Sockel steht er fest . . . Mein Herr König darf zufrieden sein." (Rest zu fragmentarisch.)

Z.2′ ist schwer zu entscheiden, ob MAŠ oder PA zu lesen ist; MAŠ erscheint mir wahrscheinlicher. Die Lesung der Ausgabe ^{I}DINGIR-*iq-bi?* ist sicher falsch.

ABL 216 K.1062 Kollation vom 30.Aug.1980.

Vs 1 *a-na* LUGAL *be-lí-iá a-dan-niš*
2 *a-dan-niš lu-u šul-mu*
3 *Aš+šur* ^{d}UTU $^{d+}$EN ^{d}30 ^{d}U+GUR
4 *a-na* LUGAL *be-lí-iá lik-ru-bu*
5 ÌR-*ka* ^{I}*Ḫu-un-ni-i*
6 *ka-ri-ib* LUGAL *be-lí-šú*
7 *šul-mu a-na* É.KUR-*ra-a-te*
8 *a-na* É.GAL^{MEŠ} *ša* KUR *Aš+ šur gab-bu*
9 *šul-mu a-na* ^{Id}30-PAP^{MEŠ}-SU
10 DUMU LUGAL GAL-⸢*e*⸣ [*šu*]*l-mu a-na* DUMU^{MEŠ} MAN
11 x[K]UR *Aš+šur šu-nu-ni*
12 [LUGAL *be-l*]*í-iá*
13 [ ]-*tù*
14 [ ]x
Rest der Vs weggebrochen

"An meinen Herrn König. Es möge (ihm) ganz ausserordentlich wohlergehen! Aššur, Šamaš, Bēl, Nabû, Sîn, Nerigal mögen meinen Herrn König segnen! Dein Knecht Ḫunnî, der für seinen Herrn König betet. Den Tempeln (und) Palästen allensamt in Assyrien geht es gut. Sanherib, dem Kronprinzen, (und) den (übrigen) Prinzen geht es gut. . . ." (Lücke)

Rs Anfang der Rs weggebr.
1′ IGI[$^{2.MEŠ}$-*iá an-na*]*m-ra-a-*[*ni*]
2′ *ša* DINGIR^{MEŠ}-*šú le-e-*⸢*mu*⸣-*r*[*a*]
3′ GÌR$^{2.MEŠ}$-*i*[*á* AN].ZÁLAG^{MEŠ} *lu-u na-pa-ḫu*
4′ *ša* É.KUR-*r*[*a-t*]*i-šú-nu* GIM ⸢*ni-ip*⸣-*ḫi*
5′ ^{d}*Šá-maš* ⸢*i*⸣-*nam-me-*⸢*ru-ni*⸣
6′ *a-na* LUGAL *be-lí-iá* [*lik-ru*]-*bu*
7′ *né-e-nu* ^{LÚ*}ÌR^{MEŠ} [*ša* LUGA]L
8′ GÌR$^{2.MEŠ}$ *ša* LUGAL *be-l*[*í-n*]*i*
9′ *nu-ú-na-áš-*⸢*šiq*⸣
10′ ÌR-*ka* ^{I}*Ḫu-un-ni-i*
11′ *ka-ri-ib* LUGAL *be-lí-šú*
Rd 12′ *ša še-a-re nu-bat-te*

"[Meine] Augen mögen die *annamru*-Leuchter seiner (d.h. des Königs Sargons) Götter sehen! Meine Füsse (mögen mich dorthin tragen, wo) die *annamru*-Leuchter das Erstrahlen ihrer (d.h. der Götter des Königs) Tempel (bewirken) sollen so wie die Sonne bei (ihrem) Aufgang erstrahlt! Sie (die Götter Assyriens oder die *annamru*-Leuchter?) mögen meinen Herrn König segnen. Wir, die Knechte des Königs, wollen die Füsse unseres Herrn Königs küssen. Dein Knecht Ḫunnî, der 'Beter' seines Herrn Königs, der ich (sowohl) am Morgen (wie) am Abend immerdar für meinen Herrn König bete!"

13′ *ka-a<+a>-ma-nu a-na*
LUGAL *be-lí-iá*
14′ [*a-k*]*ar-ra-bu-u-ni*

Die Quellen ND 1120, ABL 91, 483 und 1209 beziehen sich auf ein und dasselbe Ereignis, die erstmalige Aufstellung der *annamru*-Leuchter im Aššur-Tempel von Aššur im Jahre 714 v. Chr. Für die beiden Briefe des Ṭāb-ṣilli-Ešarra ist dies evident, da nach ND 1120:7 der amtierende *šakin māti* selbst mit der Angelegenheit befasst war. ABL 1209 enthält zwar keine Angaben zur Lokalisierung des Vorgangs; in nA Texten kultischen Inhalts meint aber DINGIR ohne weiteren Zusatz stets ^{d}Aššur. ABL 216 setzt offenbar voraus, dass das Ereignis der Aufstellung der *annamru*-Leuchter jüngst stattgefunden hat. Der Brief ist in mancher Hinsicht bedeutsam: Ḫunnî war nach Z.9-10 mit der Erziehung des Kronprinzen Sanherib und der übrigen Prinzen betraut und muss demnach in einem persönlichen Nahverhältnis zu Sargon gestanden haben. Seine Einleitungsformel ist ganz exzeptionell und nur mit den Briefeinleitungen vergleichbar, welche die Kronprinzen Sanherib und vor ihm Ulūlāja (der spätere Salmanassar V.) den Mitteilungen an ihre königlichen Väter voranschicken. Meine Ergänzungen Rs 1′-3′ sind zugegebenermassen gewagt und die Syntax der Rs 3′ ist schwierig; dass jedoch *annamru* vorliegt (einmal in syllabischer und einmal in logographischer Schreibweise), dürfte durch den Vergleich mit dem *namāru* (Aufstrahlen) beim *nipḫi Šamaš* (Sonnenaufgang) hinlänglich gestützt werden.

Welche Bedeutung der Aufstellung der *annamrāni* zukam, wird deutlich aus ND 1120:3 “Am 20. Tag (des Monats Kanūnu, im Eponymat des Ištar-dūrī, Statthalters von Arrapḫa, im neunten Regierungsjahr Sargons, Königs von Assyrien) hat man den Basaltsockel, der als Unterteil für den *annamru*-Leuchter aus Kupfer (dienen soll) in den Aššur-Tempel hineingebracht.” Da diesem Vorgang nur drei Zeilen gewidmet sind, darf man folgern, dass der eigentliche Anlass zur Abfassung dieses umfänglichen Protokolls die Aufstellung der *annamrāni* selbst war, die demnach am 21. oder 22. Kanūnu erfolgt sein müsste; leider sind die Angaben darüber weggebrochen; man darf jedoch vermuten, dass die *annamrāni* Objekt zu]⌈*ú-sa*⌉-*ar*!-*ki-bu* x[(Z.27), “man hat (auf einen Wagen) geladen” waren. Dass das Ganze eine echte “Staatsaktion” war, sieht man schon daran, dass zur Protokollierung Nabû-šallimšunu, der Schreiber des Königs, und Zazâ, der Stadtschreiber von Aššur, aufgeboten waren; letzterer benutzt die Gelegenheit, uns seine lange Genealogie (Rs 16′-21′) mitzuteilen. Der religiöse Charakter der Zeremonie wird unterstrichen durch Opfer und das Singen von Kultliedern (der *kalû* wird Rs 14′ erwähnt). Wie es scheint, hat jedoch die erstmalige Aufstellung der *annamrāni* technisch nicht ganz geklappt, weshalb Ṭāb-ṣilli-Ešarra ABL 91 schreibt: “Der

Standort der beiden kupfernen *annamru* ist sehr gut. An ihnen sind noch einige Nachbesserungen auszuführen; sie werden diese Nachbesserungen (jetzt) vornehmen." Der Bericht über diese Nachbesserungen dürfte ABL 483 sein. Auch ABL 1209, wo berichtet wird, dass das rechte *annamru* jetzt fest auf seinem Sockel steht, dürfte sich auf die Behebung der technischen Pannen beziehen.

Fasst man die gewonnenen Informationen zusammen, gewinnt man folgendes Bild: die *annamru*-Leuchter im Aššur-Tempel waren aus Kupfer (was in diesem Kontext auch Bronze bedeuten kann), hatten ein grosses Gewicht, waren schwer zu transportieren. Sie wurden paarig rechts und links vom Gottesbild aufgestellt, und zwar auf einem Sockel aus Basalt, der möglicherweise in eine Lehmziegelkonstruktion eingebettet war. Über die Etymologie (**nwr*) hinaus lässt sich über die Funktion der *annamru*-Leuchter nichts aussagen.

Vielleicht helfen hier die nA Königsrituale weiter, in denen des öfteren mitgeteilt wird, dass der König "das Antlitz leuchtend sein lässt" (z.B. perfektisch formuliert *zi-mu ú-sa-an-mir* A̦ 125 II 22′ = G. van Driel, The Cult of Aššur, pp. 122-23) und zwar genauer das Antlitz des Gottesbildes, [*z*]*i-mu šá* DINGIR *ú-s*[*a-an*]-*mir*, ebd. V 27′. Es ist m.W. noch nicht geklärt, auf welche Weise der König das *šanmuru ša zīmi* bewirkt. Eine Schülertafel mit Auszügen aus physiognomatischen Omina, STT 324, enthält ein für unser Problem sehr aufschlussreiches Omen, Z.21: DIŠ *zi-im* KÙ.GI *šá* DINGIR *ár-ḫiš* ZÁLAG-*ir ḫa-an-ṭiš* ÚŠ, in zusammenhängender Umschrift *šumma zīm ḫurāṣi ša ili arḫiš ušanmir ḫanṭiš imât*, 'wenn jemand die goldenen Gesichtszüge des Gottesbildes schnell (hastig? übereilt?) leuchtend sein lässt, wird er demnächst sterben." Die Gesichtszüge des Gottesbildes waren also in Gold modelliert, das Bild trug eine goldene Gesichtsmaske, die natürlich aufleuchtete, sobald man eine Lichtquelle auf sie richtete, am wirksamsten in Art eines *spotlight*, wie es auf der Bühne Verwendung findet. Was liegt näher, das AN.ZÁLAG und *annamru* als jene Lichtquelle anzusehen, mittels derer gebündeltes Licht auf die Gesichtsmaske des Gottesbildes ausgestrahlt wurde? Durch die paarige Aufstellung wurde wohl auch die Bildung von Schatten in den Gesichtshöhlungen verringert. STT 324:21 lehrt u.a., dass das *šanmuru ša zīmi* eigentlich jeder *pater familias* vornehmen konnte, es also nicht etwa ein königliches Privileg war. In A 125 agiert der König ja in seiner Eigenschaft als *šangû ša Aššur*; diese Funktion nimmt er nur an bestimmten Tagen des Festzyklus Šabāṭu-Addaru-Nisannu wahr, Funktionen die sonst der *šangû rabi'u ša bīt Aššur* ausübt und in denen ihm der *šangû šani'u* assistiert. Aus der recht fragmentarischen Kolumne I der "Vorschriften für Priester" (PKTA 36-38; vgl. E. Ebeling, SVAT, pp. 23-28) ist denn auch soviel ersichtlich, dass [*ša* GIŠBANŠUR *ra-k*]*a-si* (Z.3), [*ša* UDU.SISKUR MEŠ *na*]-*sa-ḫi* (Z.4) und auch [*ša šá-an-mu-r*]*i šá zi-i-me* zu ihren normalen Pflichten gehörte. Aber es zeigt sich dennoch, dass der Tempelkult und der "Hauskult" in ganz analogen Handlungen seinen Ausdruck fand.

Lässt sich die Bedeutung von AN.ZÁLAG und *annamru* etwa auf "Kultleuchte zum Anstrahlen der goldenen Gesichtsmaske des Gottesbildes" bestimmen, so ist damit noch nichts über die Lesung entschieden. Wenn ich bisher *annamru* umschrieben habe, so deshalb, weil AHw das Lemma unter dieser Form verbucht. Die Argumentation, aufgrund derer CAD die Belege unter *namru* verbuchen will, sind uns noch nicht bekannt. Kultmittel können ja mit dem Gottesdeterminativ geschrieben werden (z.B. *ina* UGU ^{d}*šu-ri-in-ni ša* ^{d}30 ^{5}*ša* ^{URU}KASKAL ABL 489:4-5), die Umschrift ^{d}ZÁLAG und ^{d}*nam-ru* wäre also möglich. Doch ist die Form *namru* bereits für das Adjektiv reserviert und dessen Plural Mask. ist *namrūtu/namrūti*; *an-nam-ra-ni* ABL 91:5 (und den beiden tentativ angeschlossenen Stellen), mit Pluralkongruenz, kann deshalb nicht ohne weiteres *^{d}*nam-ra-ni* umschrieben werden. Andere Nominalformen (wie *pars*, *parrās*, *mapras*, *naprās* und die Möglichkeit eines *ān*-Präfixes) wurden überprüft, aber verworfen. Mein Vorschlag geht deshalb dahin, bis zum Auftauchen weiterer klärender Belege, es bei den Umschriften AN.ZÁLAG und *annamru* zu belassen, freilich im Bewusstsein der hier angesprochenen Problematik. In diesem Zusammenhang ist auch noch das Verhältnis dieser Termini zu *mu-šá-an-mir-a-ti* A 125 II 11′ (G. Van Driel, The Cult of Aššur, pp. 122-23) zu klären, dessen erschlossenen Singular mušanmirtu CAD M/2 258b als "lamp, lighting device"—also ganz ähnlich dem oben vorgelegten Ansatz—bestimmt. Ein Synonym kann es eigentlich nicht gut sein, weil der Text *uq-ṭar-*[*rib*] "er hat herbeigebracht" bietet, was darauf schliessen lässt, dass *mušanmirāti* hin- und hergetragen werden können, was von den schweren, ortsfesten *annamrāni* sicher nicht ausgesagt werden kann.

Die zunächst von G. Van Driel vorgeschlagene Deutung "mirror" für *annamru*, die J. N. Postgate (TCAE, p. 250) und CAD (z.B. K 354b) übernehmen, muss wohl jetzt aufgegeben werden; "Spiegel" ist nA *nāmuru* (*mapras* von *amāru* "sehen"), während bei *annamru* der Bezug zu *nawārum/namāru* "aufleuchten" nicht nur wegen der Schreibung AN.ZÁLAG, sondern auch des Kontexts, in welchen die Belege gehören, unabweislich ist. Damit will ich nicht ausschliessen, dass ein Spiegel—zur Bündelung des Lichtstrahls—ein Bestandteil des *annamru* war.

Kehren wir nach dieser langen Digression wieder zurück zu JEN 478:3-5 (DUMU-*ja* ^{I}*A-kip-til-la* ^{4}*ù ki-ir-bá-an-šu i+na pa-ni* ^{5}AN.ZÁLAG *eḫ-te-pu*), das demnach zu übersetzen ist: "Den Erdklumpen meines Sohnes Akip-tilla habe ich vor der Kultleuchte zerbrochen" (ich setze voraus, dass das Graphem AḪ-*te*-BU Z.5 *eḫtepe* meint; oder steht es verkürzt für **eḫ-te-pu-ú*, Subjunktiv im Eid?). In dieser Formulierung wären dann z w e i symbolische Handlungen (Šurpu III 31-32) in eine zusammengezogen: 'ich habe den Erdklumpen meines Sohnes Akip-tilla zerbrochen; ich habe die Kultleuchte vor ihn hingestellt'. Beide Handlungen sind äussere Zeichen der Enterbung. Ann Draffkorn hatte AN.ZÁLAG JEN 478:5 zu Recht mit AN. ZÁLAG^{MEŠ} HSS 14,8:2.10 verknüpft.

[Korrekturzusatz: G. Wilhelm macht mich freundlicherweise darauf aufmerksam, dass die aB Schreibweise für ^{d}UTU—mit gebrochenem Senkrechten

—für einige Nuzi-Texte epigraphisch gesichert ist; er verweist auf die Belege in seiner rezenten Publikation Das Archiv des Šilwa-Teššup, Heft 2 (Wiesbaden 1980) Nr.11:41, 15:23, 33:136 und 45:11. Es ist darum nicht auszuschliessen, dass JEN 478:5, ungeachtet des oben zitierten Hinweises auf Šurpu III 31-32, doch *ina pānī* ^{d}*Šamaš*, "vor Šamaš" = *sub divo*, gemeint sein könnte].

JEN 478:6-8 wird in der Literatur unterschiedlich interpretiert. CAD E 397b: "(and he swore) by the gods and the spirits of the dead he would not take away the fields and the houses"; J. S. Paradise (p. 311 n. 218): "He shall not have rights to gods and (ancestral) spirits. Fields and houses he shall not receive." Die Verbalform Z.8 ist jedoch von *alāku* (*i-la-ak-ka*$_4$), nicht von *leqû* (**i-la-aq-qa*) abzuleiten. Šimika-atal, der Schreiber von JEN 478, vokalisiert *il-qè* (JEN 87:16 und 204:18) und verdoppelt Auslautkonsonanten (*i-na-an-din-nu* JEN 29:19 und 255:36; *i-na-ak-ki-is-sú* JEN 29:20 und 311:17, *i+na e-le-en-nu* JEN 87:8; *i+na e-le-en-na* JEN 204:10). Neue Übersetzung: "Er soll nicht zu den Hausgöttern und zu den Totengeistern, zu den Häusern und Feldern kommen!" Der enterbte Sohn darf nicht an den häuslichen Kulten teilnehmen und hat sich von dem Territorium seiner Familie fernzuhalten. Die Totengeister werden noch in einer zweiten Enterbungsurkunde erwähnt, HSS 19,27 (J. S. Paradise weist kurz auf den Text hin, p. 311). Soweit die Oberflächenschäden eine Umschrift zulassen, liest man dort[4]:

Vs 1 *um-ma* ^{I}⌜*Ar*⌝-[*-ma*]
2 DUMU *A-ga-pu-ra* ^{I}*N*[*a*?-]
3 *ú-ul ma-ru-ja i+na* [A.ŠÀ^{MEŠ}-*ja*]
4 *ù* É$^{ḪI.A.MEŠ}$-*ja m*[*a-ar-ši*]-⌜*ti*⌝-[*ja*]
5 *ma-na-ḫa-ti-ja* [*mi-im*]-*mu-ja*
6 *ú-ul i-qè-er-r*[*i-ib*]
7 *ù it-ti* DUMU^{MEŠ}[-*ja la i*]-*zu-uz-zu*
8 *ù uš-tu*$_4$ *u*$_4$-*m*[*i an-ni-i*]
9 *ki-ir-bá-an-šu* [*a-bu-ja* ^{I}*A-ga-p*]*u-ra*
10 *iḫ-te-pé* x[ ]x x[ ]
11 *ú-ul* D[INGIR^{MEŠ}]-*ja* ⌜*ú*⌝-[*ul*] ⌜*e*⌝-*ṭe*$_4$-*em-mi-ja*
12 *ù*[ ] *pu-uḫ-šu* x[ ]
13 ⌜É⌝-[*s*]*ú il*$_5$-*te-qè*
folgt Zeugenliste

Wenn nicht alles täuscht, zerbricht hier der Grossvater des zu Enterbenden den Erdklumpen; dass er mit dem Vorgang befasst ist, dürfte auch der Vermerk IGI LÚ^{MEŠ} *ša* ^{I}⌜*A*⌝-[*g*]*a-pu-ra* (Z.27) bestätigen. Trotz der Zerstörungen in Z.10 und 12 ist erkennbar, dass sein Enkel vom Kult der Hausgötter und Totengeister ausgeschlossen bleiben soll und aus seinem Haus

[4]Meiner Schülerin Gudrun Dosch danke ich herzlich. Sie hat mir ihre Umschrift dieses Textes zur Verfügung gestellt und die spezielle Problematik dieser Urkunde mit mir diskutiert.

delogiert wird. Die Prosopographie von HSS 19, 27 erlaubt bisher keinerlei Anschlüsse; es lässt sich nur éine weitere von Wantišše (Z.28) geschriebene Tafel nachweisen, Gadd 44.

Zusammenfassend lässt sich sagen: das Wortpaar DINGIR^{MEŠ} AN.ZÁLAG^{MEŠ} bezeichnet Gegenstände, Götterfigur(in)en mit den dazugehörigen Kultleuchten; das Wortpaar *ilānū eṭemmū* “Hausgötter und Totengeister” (in JEN 478 und HSS 19,27) bezieht sich auf deren Kult. In welchen Quellen ist nun aber explicite von diesem Kult die Rede? Der wichtigste einschlägige Nuzi-Text ist HSS 14,108:23-42 (= RA 36,119). Seine SMN-Nummer kann nicht mit Sicherheit festgestellt werden: HSS 14, p. xi und p. xviii gibt SMN 2676 an, RA 36, 119 hingegen SMN 2673. In der Nuzi-Bibliographie, p. 229a, ist die Urkunde zweimal, d. h. unter SMN 2673 und 2676, aufgelistet, obwohl es sich um ein und denselben Text handelt. Der Fundort ist nicht feststellbar. J. S. Paradise hat Nuzi Inheritance Practices, pp. 90-93, Nr. C-20, eine Bearbeitung des Textes geboten. A. Schaffer behandelte Studies Oppenheim, pp. 187-88, die Z. 13-22 und A. E. Draffkorn (Kilmer) resümiert den Inhalt des Dokuments JBL 76, pp. 220-24. Schreiber der Urkunde ist Balṭu-kašid S. Apil-Sîn, also ein Zeitgenosse des Teḫiptilla S. Puḫi-šenni, für dessen Archiv er hauptsächlich schreibt. [According to Lacheman SMN 2676 is the correct number. D.I.O.]

Für eine Neubearbeitung des gesamten Textes ist hier nicht Raum; die dezisiven Z. 23-42 rufen jedoch nach einer neuen Umschrift, die freilich durch die Textzerstörung am rechten Rand sehr erschwert wird, sowohl hinsichtlich der Lesung einzelner Zeichen als auch der Kalkulation der Zeilenlängen. Sie kann darum nur als vorläufig gelten; eine genaue Inspektion des Originals dürfte ein wenig weiterhelfen.

Vs 23 DUMU^{MEŠ}-*ja ar-ki-ja* DINGIR^{MEŠ} *la i-*⌈*pu*⌉*-šu*
24 *i-la-nu-ja a-šar ma-ri-ja* GAL [ ]
25 *ad-din ù ma-an-nu i+na ma-*[*ri-ja*]
26 1 SISKUR *i-pu-*⌈*uš*⌉ *ù li-*[(*il-*)*li-ka*$_4$]
Rd 27 *šum-ma a-na bi-*⌈*ti-šu*⌉*-nu*
28 *i-le-eq-qú-ma* SISKUR[^{MEŠ}]
29 *i-pu-šu ù* ⌈DINGIR⌉ *i*[*l-la-ku*]
Rs 30 DINGIR^{MEŠ} *ša-nu-ti la i-p*[*u-šu*]
31 *šum-ma* ⌈DUMU GAL ŠEŠ⌉ *a-na ni-ši* [É-ti]
32 *at-*⌈*ta-din*⌉ *šum-ma a-na* ⌈*bi-ti*⌉*-šú-n*[*u*]
33 DINGIR^{MEŠ} *i-leq-qú-ú ù* GAL-*ma* <a-na> ⌈É⌉-[*šu*]
34 *i-leq-qé ù* 1 GÉME ⌈SIG$_5$⌉-[*qú*]
35 *a-na ša iq-q*[*ú*]*-ú ú-ma-a*[*l-l*]*a*

---

36 DUMU^{MEŠ} *it-*[*t*]*a*!-⌈*al-ku*⌉ [ ]
37 ù DINGIR ⌈*la*⌉ *i-zu-u*[*z-zu*]
38 *ma-ru* GAL *ina* KASKAL!(BI)-*ni* [*il-la-ak*]
39 *ù ga*$_5$*-ba-šu-nu-ma* NINDA.KASKAL *ú-*[*ma-al-lu-ú*]

40 *ma-an-nu šu-mi* ḪA.LA
41 *za*$^{!}$(A)-*zi ú-še-il-li q*[*a*-(*as*-)*sú ina* A.ŠÀ^{MEŠ}]
42 *ù* É$^{\text{ḪI.A}}$ ŠEŠ^{MEŠ} *li-še*-⌜*lu*⌝-[*ú*]

Übersetzung:

"Meine Söhne sollen sich nach meinem Ableben keine weiteren Hausgötter machen. Meine Hausgötter gebe ich hiermit meinem erstgeborenen Sohn. Wer von meinen (übrigen) Söhnen ein Opfer darbringen will, möge (zu ihm) kommen.

Wenn sie (die Hausgötter) in ihre Häuser nehmen wollen und Opfer darbringen wollen, werden die Hausgötter (dorthin) gehen, aber andere Hausgötter sollen sie sich nicht machen."

Die Interpretation des zweiten, mittleren Abschnitts ist wesentlich problematischer und daher mit Reserve aufzunehmen:

"Wenn ich meinem erstgeborenen Sohn (und seinen) Brüdern Hauspersonal gebe und wenn sie die Götter in ihre Häuser nehmen wollen, so darf auch der Erstgeborene sie in sein Haus nehmen, aber er übergibt dem, der geopfert hat, eine gute Sklavin."

Der letzte Abschnitt ist von J. S. Paradise missverstanden worden; unter Annahme der beiden Emendationen in Z.38 und 41, (die ich leider nicht kollationieren lassen konnte), scheint mir die nachfolgende Übersetzung aber ziemlich sicher:

"(Wenn die nachgeborenen) Söhne fortziehen, dürfen sie die Götter nicht teilen. Der erstgeborene Sohn wird (mit den Götterbildern) auf die Reise gehen und sie alle werden (seine) Reisespesen bezahlen. Wer das Wort von der Teilung des Erbes aufbringt, den sollen die (anderen) Brüder seines Anteils an Feldern und Häusern verlustig gehen lassen."

Kommentar:

Es ist mir bekannt, dass CAD I/J 103a für Z.23 *la i-li*(!)-*ku* umschreibt und "must not take" übersetzt; in Treue zur Autographie lese ich aber (mit A. Draffkorn, p. 221, und J. S. Paradise, p. 91) *i*-⌜*pu*⌝-*šu*. Die Lesung *a-na bi*-⌜*ti-šu*⌝-*nu* (Z.27) ist *a-na* **bi-ri-šu-nu* (J. S. Paradise) nicht nur wegen *a-na* ⌜*bi-ti*⌝-*šú-n*[*u*] (Z.32) vorzuziehen, sondern vor allem deshalb, weil Balṭu-kašid nur das Graphem *ina be-ri-šu-nu* (JEN 250:4) verwendet (freundliche Mitteilung von P. Negri Scafa). Die Präsentia in den Konditionalsätzen Z.28.29.33 sind nach GAG §161i ("Tun-Wollen") zu interpretieren. Zwischen 1 SISKUR (Z.26) und SISKUR[^{MEŠ}] (Z.28) besteht offensichtlich eine Opposition: wegen nur eines Opfers zahlt sich der Transfer der Hausgötter nicht aus. Z.30 wiederholt inhaltlich Z.23; die beiden Verbotssätze rahmen den ersten Abschnitt ein.

Meine Deutung der Z.31-32 geht davon aus, dass Balṭu-kašid direktes und indirektes Objekt verwechselt hat. Bei der Abfassung des *ṭuppi šīmti* HSS 14,108 (in dem eine Verfügung über Sklavinnen und Sklaven ja nicht getroffen ist), stand offenbar noch nicht fest, ob der Erblasser nicht in einem Zusatztestament noch Hauspersonal an seine Söhne vererben will oder wird. Zwar ist das normale Graphem *ni-iš* É(*-ti*), doch kann wegen 1 GÉME⌜SIG$_5$⌝-[*qú*] (Z.34) hier *ni-ši* kaum anders verstanden werden. Den winzigen Spuren nach könnte die Ergänzung am Ende der Z.31 freilich auch *b*[*i-ti*] lauten. Für die Lesung **ni-qí* (J. S. Paradise, p. 91) besteht überhaupt kein Anlass: *ši* ist ganz klar und Balṭu-kašids Graphem für Opfer ist SISKUR (Z.26.28) Unsicher bin ich selbst hinsichtlich *ù* GAL-*ma* <*a-na*> ⌜É⌝-[*šu*] ^{34}*i-leq-qé*. Z.36 ist entweder nach GAG §160 zu beurteilen oder es ist <*šum-ma*> zu Beginn der Zeile zu interpolieren. Gemeint ist die nicht seltene Emigration der nachgeborenen Brüder, vor allem nach Ḫanigalbat. Z.39 ist *šá* KASKAL (J. S. Paradise) graphematisch unmöglich; es liegt NINDA.KASKAL = *ṣidītu* (AHw 1100a und CAD Ṣ 173a) vor; der Beleg fehlt in beiden Wbb. Um Reisespesen zu kassieren, muss man sich erst einmal auf den Weg gemacht haben: darum erscheint mir die Emendation in Z.38 zwingend. Vielleicht war GIŠ.S[A]R *ša bi-ni* (HSS 14,108:4) nicht ohne Einfluss auf *ina* BI-*ni* in der Autographie Z.38. Die von J. S. Paradise in Vorschlag gebrachte Lesung *ina* **bi-ir*-[*ri-šu-nu*?] hingegen ist aus anderen Nuzi-Texten überhaupt nicht nachweisbar und schon gar nicht in dem Corpus des Balṭu-kašid. Nach ḪA.LA ist die paronomastische Infinitivkonstruktion *šumi zitti zâzi* so naheliegend, dass sie die geringfügige Emendation von A-ZI der Autographie rechtfertigt.

Die Verwendung von *šūlû* (Z.41) anstelle des gebräuchlicheren *qabû* (vgl. *š*[*u-m*]*i* ḪA.LA *la i-qáb-bi* HSS 19,65:12; [*šu-m*]*a* ḪA.LA *la i-qá-ab-bu* ebd. 6:14-15; *šu*-[*mi* ḪA.LA] ^{20}*la i-qáb-bu-ú* ebd. 19:19-20; *šu-mi* ḪA.LA *la i-qáb-bu-ú* ebd. 37:14 und *šu-mi* ḪA.LA ^{19}*la i-qáb-bu-ú* ebd. 37:18-19) ist allerdings singulär und ich frage mich deshalb, ob hier nicht eine Kontamination zwischen *šumi zitti qabû* und *ṭuppi zitti zâzi šūlû* vorliegt; vgl. *ṭup-pí* ḪA.LA HSS 5,75:1 und *ṭup-pí* ḪA.LA^{MEŠ}-*ti* HSS 19,61:1 (dazu A. Shaffer, Studies Oppenheim, p. 192 with nn. 31-32) und nA EN ḪA.LA *zu-a-zi* (Nachweise K. Deller, WZKM 57,33). Am Ende von Z.41 glaube ich den Anfang von QA zu erkennen; dessen Winkelhaken könnte aber auch eine akzidentelle Beschädigung sein: man käme dann auch mit der Ergänzung *in*[*a* A.ŠÀ^{ME}]^{Š} aus; den Raumverhältnissen nach zu urteilen ist sie sogar wahrscheinlicher.

Vergleicht man HSS 14,108 mit dem *ṭuppi šīmti* HSS 19,5—von dem die Untersuchung ihren Ausgang nahm—muss man konstatieren, dass die Erblasser hinsichtlich der Hausgötter diametral entgegengesetzte Dispositionen getroffen haben: in letzterem Testament werden sie ausdrücklich auf den *māru rabû* und den *tertennu* verteilt, in HSS 14,108:37 wird eine solche Teilung ausdrücklich untersagt. Dafür bleibt in HSS 19,5 das *ilku* des Vaters ungeteilt (Z.38), in HSS 14,108 ist hinsichtlich des *ilku* keine Verfügung getroffen. Von der Kasuistik der Enterbung abgesehen, kann aus Nuzi-Texten kein Beleg erbracht werden, dass der Erstgeborene *keine* Hausgötter erhält (vgl. J. S. Paradise, p. 240). Aus HSS 14,108:23.30 kann allerdings inferiert werden, dass—falls der

Erstgeborene *alle* Hausgötter erbt—die nachgeborenen Söhne sich bei Gründung eines Haushalts neue, eigene Hausgötter machen. Da die Dualformen beim Nomen im Akkadischen von Nuzi nicht mehr produktiv sind, kann nicht ausgeschlossen werden, dass DINGIR^{MEŠ} eine Zweizahl von Götterbildern meint. Weil aufgrund des ḫurritischen Substrats die Genusdistinktion wenig entwickelt ist, kann DINGIR^{MEŠ} dann durchaus zur Bezeichnung eines Götterpaares, des Hausgottes und der Hausgöttin, stehen. Ein Ehepaar ist aber noch keine Familie, sie wird dazu erst durch die gemeinsamen Kinder. Rein theoretisch könnte nun auch das Götterpaar bei der Geburt eines Kindes durch eine weitere Figur angereichert werden; doch was geschieht dann beim Tode eines Kindes? Würde dann die das verstorbene Kind repräsentierende Figur vernichtet oder gar zusammen mit dem Kind bestattet werden? Eher möchte man daran denken, dass erst beim Tod eines Kindes ein zusätzlicher *ilu* angefertigt wurde; die Verbindung *ilānū u eṭemmū* (JEN 478 und HSS 19,27) würde uns dadurch begreiflicher. Was aber geschah mit der göttlichen Vaterfigur beim Tode des *pater familias*? Wurde sie umfunktioniert? Fragen, die besonderes Gewicht erhalten, wenn man an die *ilānū u eṭemmū* der Familie des regierenden Königs denkt. Die Thematik mündet jetzt ein in die Problematik des *kispum*. Sie ist Gegenstand einer Tübinger Dissertation (1980), deren Autor Akio Tsukimoto ist; ihrer Veröffentlichung darf man gespannt entgegensehen. Ausgeklammert habe ich auch die Diskussion des Terminus DINGIR^{MEŠ} SAR-*re-na* (HSS 14,186:4; HSS 15,290:9; HSS 16,183:6-7 und 416:9-10, alle Texte aus D 3 bzw. D 6; vgl. AHw 1188b) in Nuzi-Texten und *enna* SAR-*re-na* in ḫurritischen Quellen (KUB XXVII 38 I 1-7; vgl. H. G. Güterbock, ZA 44, 81-83; A. E. Draffkorn, JBL 76,222; G. Wilhelm, mündliche Mitteilung), weil in der Dissertation meiner Schülerin Brigitte Menzel, Neuassyrische Tempel (Heidelberg 1976) der interessante Versuch unternommen worden ist, diese "Puppen" (H. G. Güterbock) mit den Termini ^{d}*sarrānu* bzw. ^{GIŠ}*sarrānu* (Plur. *sarrānāte*) der neuassyrischen Königsrituale (vgl. AHw *saranātu* ? 1028a) zu gleichen und ich ihrer Argumentation nicht vorgreifen möchte. Es sei aber zum Abschluss hervorgehoben, dass gerade die Utilisierung der Nuzi-Texte zur Aufhellung dunkler Punkte im Assyrischen mir ein vielversprechender Erkenntnisweg scheint, den es weiter zu verfolgen gilt. Im Vorwort zu HSS 16, p.v, schreibt der Jubilar: "These 'lowly' documents have a value of their own." Sie haben sich als hochkarätige Juwelen erwiesen. Die Assyriologie ist ihm zu Dank verpflichtet, dass er sie uns zugänglich gemacht hat.

Evidence on the Ethnic Division of the Ḫurrians

I. M. Diakonoff
Institut Vostokovedenija
Leningrad, U.S.S.R

In the literature on the Hurrians[1] it has been repeatedly stated that no proof of any dialectal division in the Hurrian language exists. If that were so, the Hurrians must have been an undivided ethnic unity. Such a unity might have emerged either as the result of inhabiting a particular area under uniform socio-political conditions for a very considerable period of time (hundreds or even thousands of years), or the result of a recent and swift occupation of an area by an ethnic mass having developed as a unity elsewhere. Neither of the hypotheses looks plausible from the historical point of view.

In his Hurrian glossary E. Laroche seems to reject any possibility of identifying dialects in Hurrian.[2] His position is no doubt justified by the present level of our knowledge of the Hurrian vocabulary: what we actually know is a very limited number of specific, mainly cultic word items which by no means necessarily do or can reflect dialectal differences that may have existed in the living language. We must also take into consideration that the degree of the reliability of the translation of nearly all Hurrian words is still very low.

However, there are also other means to establish the existence of ethnic subdivisions (tribes?) among the Hurrians. One of them is by means of morphology. Miss M. L. Khačikyan[3] has plainly shown, that unlike the

[1] I. M. Diakonoff, *Hurrisch und Urartäisch*, München 1971, p. 23 (in the following quoted as *HuU*); E. A. Speiser, "Introduction to Hurrian," *AASOR* 20, New Haven, 1941, and others.

[2] E. Laroche, 'Glossaire de la langue hourrite, Ire partie (A-L)," *RHA* 34 (1976), p. 23. Note that, with all respect to Laroche's masterful and incomparable knowledge of the Hurrian material proper, the Urartian analogies cited in his glossary are insufficient and unreliable, being, e.g., sometimes quoted in an oblique case. Also, Laroche's (and most other Hurritologists') refusal to accept Speiser's reconstruction of a Hurrian **o*-phoneme makes it difficult to understand the structure of Hurrian and Urartian grammatical oppositions.

[3] M. L. Khačikyan, "Iz starokhurritskikh zaklinanij [From Old Hurrian Incantations]," *Hin Aravelk' - Drevnij Vostok* 2, Erevan 1976, pp. 251-64; eadem,

vocabulary, the morphonological inventory of the Hurrian texts and the use of the syntagmatic enclitic conjunctions change very perceptibly from one text group to another. Thus, in the field of grammar the features of a clear-cut dialectal division are readily apparent. Miss Khačikyan has presented these features in tabular form. Without repeating her table, we shall summarize her results in establishing Hurrian dialectal units on morphological and syntactical levels by grouping them according to their typical classifying features (in so far these are known). The features, according to Khačikyan, are as follows:

I. *Urartian language* (9th-6th centuries B.C.) *Noun*: relics of a 1st directive case in **-ta*, replacement of the 2nd directive case **-di* by the postposition **edi*, locative in *-a*. *Pronouns*: possessive 3rd p. *-(i)'ja*, *-ij(ə)*, demonstrative **a(l)le*, subject-of-the-state (=object) pronoun 3 p. *-nə*.[4] *Verb*: 3rd p.Sg. of the subject of action, indicative *-Ø*, *-a*, 3p.Sg. of the subject of state (=object) *-ne* (Pl.*-lə*), plural morphs *-it-*, *-a(š)-*, no negative conjugation, morph of transitivity *-i/-u*, of non-transitivity **-o*, of state *-a*. *Predicative participles*: transitive *-i*, non-transitive **-a-bə*,[5] state *-a*. Non-transitive predicate expressed by verbal form (in distinction from all other dialects which use only predicative participles). No syntagmatic enclitic conjunctions.

II. *Dialect of the inscription from Urkiš*[6] (ca. 22nd century B.C.) *Pronouns*: possessive 3rd p. *-(j)a*, demonstrative *halle*, subject-of-the-state (=object) 3rd p. *-en*, *-m(e)*. *Verb*: 3rd p.Sg. of the subject of action, indicative Ø, 3rd p.Sg. of the subject of state (=object) *-m*, plural morph **-it-*(?), negation morph *-wa-*, morph of transitivity *-i/-u*. *Predicative participle* of action *-i*. No syntagmatic enclitic conjunctions. A number of classifying features not attested.

III. *Dialect of the texts from Mari and North-Eastern Babylonia* (published by F. Thureau-Dangin[7] and J. J. Van Dijk,[8] ca. 18th-16th centuries B.C.). *Noun*: 1st directive case *-da*, 2nd directive case *-di*, locative *-a*. *Pronouns*: possessive 3rd p. *-je*, demonstrative *a(n)na*, subject-of-the-state (=object) pronoun 3rd p. *-n*, *-b*. *Verb*: 3rd p.Sg. of the subject of action, indicative *-a*, plural morphs *-id-*, *-und-*, *-a(z̄)-*, morphs of negation *-wa-*, *-ma*, morph of transitivity *-i*, non-transitivity **-o*, state *-a*. *Predicative participles*: transitive *-i-b*, intransitive *-a-b*, state **-o*. Enclitic conjunctions.

"Dialektnoje členenije khurritskogo jazyka [Dialectal Subdivision of Hurrian]," ibid. 3, Erevan 1978, pp. 39-46.

[4]As part of the doubly-oriented conjugated transitive verbal form.

[5]Actually, in Urartian this is no longer a participle but a conjugated intransitive verbal form, 3rd person of the subject. — Note that the 3rd p. of the verb "to be" is **man-o*.

[6]Last discussion: *HuU*, pp. 110-11, n. 123.

[7]F. Thureau-Dangin, "Tablettes hurrites provenant de Mari," *RA* 36 (1939), 1-28.

[8]J. van Dijk, "Nichtkanonische Beschwörungen und sonstige literarische Texte," *VS NF* 1, 1971, Nos. 5-7, 20, 22, 26.

IV. *Dialect of S.-E. Asia Minor* (Kizzuwadna, Cataonia), attested from Boğazköy (14th-13th centuries B.C.). Coincides with (III), except for the following: *Pronouns*: possessive pronoun 3rd p. *-ja*, demonstrative *anne*, *Verb*: 3rd p. Sg. of the subject of action, indicative *-a*, *-ja*. The plural morph *-und-* is absent, negation in *-ma* doubtful. *Predicative participles -i*, *-a*, **-o*. Developed system of enclitic conjunctions.

V. *Mitannian dialect* (letter of Dušratta, ca. 1400 B.C.) coincides with (IV), except for the following: *Noun*: the 2nd directive case in **-di* is absent, the plural morph *-ža* is typical. *Pronouns*: possessive pronoun 3rd p. *-(i)'ja*, *-(i)je*, subject-of-the-state (=object) pronoun 3rd p. *-(n)na*, *-ma*(?), *-me-*. In the *predicative participles -b* appears only as a relic (in PN). Strong development of enclitic chains of conjunctions.

VI. *Ugaritic Hurrian dialect*[9] (the language of the religious and literary texts and of letters, 14th-13th century B.C.) coincides with (V), except for the following: *Pronouns*: subject-of-the-state (=object) pronoun 3rd p., *-n*, *-ma*, *Verb*: 3rd Sg. of the subject of action *-a*, as in (II), plural morph *-it-* not attested; negative morph *-kk-*; uninterpreted verbal morph *-te*. Weaker development of enclitics.

VII. *Unidentified dialect*[10] (language of the Hurrian text of the variant of ḪAR-ra = *ḫubullu* from Ugarit, date and place of compilation unknown, date of the copy 14th-13th century B.C.) *Noun*: locative in *-e*, plural morph *-až*(ə). *Pronouns*: possessive pronoun 3rd p. *-di*, subject-of-the-state (=object) pronoun 3rd p. *-ne*(?). *Verb*: 3rd p.Sg. of the subject of action *-ja-*, negation morphs *-k*(ə), *-m*(ə), uninterpreted verbal morph *-te*. *Predicative participles*: *-i-ž*(ə), *-a-ž*(ə), **-o-ž*(ə), pl. *-a-ž*(ə)(?). Wide use of quasi-nominal forms in *-ae* ("gerundive" in all the other dialects) instead of the conjugated forms of the verb of action. Syntactic features unknown.

Thus, Miss Khačikyan's data clearly demonstrate that all Hurrian texts (except the glosses from Arrapḫe, Alalaḫ, etc. which she did not study) belong to three clear-cut dialectal groups:

(A), or North-Eastern, includes (II) Urkiš, ca. 22nd century B.C. and (I) Urartian, 9th-6th centuries B.C.;

(B), or Central, includes, as the most archaic, (III), "Babylonian" Hurrian of Thureau-Dangin's and Van Dijk's texts, 18th-16th centuries B.C., and also (IV-VI), the "Cataonian," Mitannian and Ugaritic Hurrian (all from the 14th-13th centuries B.C.), the latter three losing a number of archaic features. They are all very similar but clearly differ in details. The dialects of Arrapḫe and Alalaḫ have been omitted, but it seems to us that Arrapḫean stands nearer to (III), and Alalaḫ probably to (VI). We shall therefore denote these two dialects as (IIIa) and (VIa). — Note that all Indo-Iranian PNs and other "aryanisms"

[9] *Ugaritica* 5, Paris 1968, pp. 519-27 (E. Laroche).

[10] M. L. Khačikjan, "Šumero-khurritskij slovar' iz Ras-Šamry [A Sumero-Hurrian Vocabulary from Ras-Šamra]," *VDI*, 1975, 3, pp. 21-38.

belong exclusively to dialect (VI); this dialect was apparently also used by some dynasts of Palestine and Syria, probably tied by kinship to the Mitannian royal dynasty. Note also that Ugaritic Hurrian has some isoglosses connecting it with group (C), probably the result of territorial contiguity.

(C), or South-Western, includes the unidentified dialect (VII). The text which suggests its existence was found in Ugarit. However, it is improbable that it was actually spoken there because the dialect stands apart from all others and is very archaic. Thus, while A II has a verbal intransitive as well as a verbal transitive predicate, and the B-dialects have verbal transitive though not verbal intransitive predicates (the intransitive ones being virtually participles), C VII seems to have lacked even a developed transitive verb.

Another way to establish whether the Hurrians were ethnically a uniform mass or were subdivided into individual tribes or other ethnic units, may be a comparison of the pantheons. It is well known that from the time of the emergence of the state structure in the Ancient Near East the main organizational unit above the (extended or non-extended) family was the town or "nome" community; each had its own protecting deity and a circle of connected less important gods and goddesses. In the present case, however, we are not interested in the strictly local pantheons. Thus, the community "pantheons" in the different towns and villages of the kingdom of Arrapḫe as established by Deller,[11] were united in one regional pantheon of the entire kingdom. This can be seen from the uniform repertory of the theophorous PNs[12] and from the lists of deities receiving oil offerings.[13] The latter include local gods who have their sanctuaries at Nuzi, the gods of the capital (Āl-ilāni), and deities who were worshipped in other towns of the kingdom. Likewise, the lists of Hurrian deities which have come down to us from Ugarit cannot be regarded as an enumeration of the gods whose places of worship were in the town of Ugarit itself. In this tiny place there was not space enough for so many sanctuaries (note that a number of non-Hurrian gods were also worshipped here). Very telling are the lists of deities involved as witnesses of mutual oaths in the treaties between Hittite and other kings.[14] There was a tendency to enumerate a maximum of gods and goddesses able to safeguard the implementation of the oaths, although certain gods might have been left out for a specific reason (e.g., the "children" and "adolescents," or otherwise deities unimportant or unsuited for this particular task).

An interesting example is the list of deities in the treaty between Suppiluliumas, king of the Hittites, and Šattiwazza, king of Mitanni: from the

[11] K. Deller, "Material zu den Lokalpanthea des Königreiches Arrapḫe," *Summarium (Compte rendu) de la XXI*[ème] *Rencontre Assyriologique Internationale*, pp. 33-45.

[12] See *NPN*.

[13] *SMN* 588, 491, 690, 799, 2153+2154 = *AASOR* 16, Nos. 46-50.

[14] E. F. Weidner, *Politische Documente aus Kleinasien II*, Leipzig, 1923.

Hittite side the gods of the empire are invoked, among them the most revered of the community and "nome" deities. Most of them are Hattic but some are Indo-European (thus, along with the Hattic Sun-goddess of Arinna the Hittito-Luwian Sun-god is also mentioned),[15] or Hurrian (thus, the Thunderer-god has been identified with the Hurrian Teššob, which follows from the fact that he is attended by the Hurrian bull-gods "Sunset and Sunrise" [Šeri and Ḫurri][16] and by the Hurrian mountain-gods "South and North" [Nanni and Ḫazzi]);[17] moreover, included in the list are seventeen Thunderer-gods, differentiated either according to the sphere of life which each of them patronizes, or according to their places of worship (quite a number of them must have been Hurrian Teššobs; their real names are hidden under the sumerogram ᵈIŠKUR); and there are four Ḫebats (the "Lady of Heavens," Ḫebat of Ḫaleb, Ḫebat of the town Uda, and Ḫebat of Kizzuwadna).

From the Mitannian side the deities are divided into three groups: (a) the gods of Kizzuwadna, (b) the gods, presumably, of Ḫarrān (anyway, Semitic gods), (c) Mitannian gods proper. For the purposes of this paper we may exclude the gods whose names are hapax legomena or who are obviously minor deities. Thus, from group (a) we exclude certain chthonic deities, possibly pre-Hurrian; from group (c) the local gods designated by epithets instead of proper names. Group (c) includes also a mention of certain Indo-Iranian gods (probably protectors of the dynasty): there is a Hurrian sentence wedged into the Akkadian text: "the Mithraic gods, the Varunian(?!)[18] gods, Indra, the gods Nāsatya." Further, it includes a number of Akkadian gods firmly rooted in most Hurrian pantheons (they are also mentioned in the mythological texts about the god Kumarwe and other texts of presumably Cataonian origin in the Boğazköy archives, and in the Ugaritic Hurrian lists of deities).

It should be noticed at once that the texts from Boğazköy mention also such gods that are not named among the deities witnessing the oath, either from the Hittite side or from the side of Mitanni (and Kizzuwadna). The

[15] G. Kellerman, "The King and the Sun-god in the Old Hittite period," *Tel-Aviv* 5, 3-4 (1978) pp. 199-207.

[16] *HuU*, p. 165^{10}, 166^{23}.

[17] *Ḫa-zi-*, *Ḫa-az-zi-* (read /Ḫas(s)i-/) is the Hurrian name of Mount *Ṣapānu* which means "North"; presumably that is also the meaning of the Hurrian word. Seeing that *Šeri* and *Ḫurri*, as pointed out in n. 16, ref., means "Sunset and Sunrise," or "West" and East," *Nanni* must mean "South."

[18] The original has "Urwanian (or 'Arunian') gods"; *Urwana-* and *Aruna-* are hard to explain from the Hurrian, and the Indo-Iranian scholars refuse to claim them for their own; the traditional translation "Varunian" has been accepted not on linguistic but on "common sense" grounds, because *Mitra-* and *Varuṇa-* are a constant pair in Old Indian literature (and the same should probably be said of the pre-Zoroastrian Iranian mythology). I am not fully convinced that the "common sense" argument is valid.

opinion which derives all Hurrian influence on Hatti from Kizzuwadna alone and dates it exclusively to the New Kingdom seems to be erroneous. A similar influence must have reached the Hittites from Išuwa, Alzi, etc. But the pantheon of Boğazköy is very syncretic and thus not suitable for the establishment of regional religious peculiarities. Our aim is not a characterization of the Hurrian world of deities.

The inscription from Urkiš is too short; it mentions only two gods who may not be the most important in the pantheon of the region. On the contrary, the incantations from Mari and those from northeastern Babylonia published by van Dijk seem indeed to invoke all the most important deities. Thus the data of the group (III) texts are comparable with the other sources. Among the Urartian texts we have a complete list of the official pantheon.[19]

Characteristic of the Hurri-Urartian cultural world is the inclusion in the pantheon of personifications of divine properties, of lakes, mountains, rivers, winds, clouds, etc.

Selecting only the most important and characteristic gods, we arrive at the following picture of the main regional pantheons:

I. *Urkiš*: The inscription mentions the gods *Ne-gal* (*Nergal*?) and *Lubadaga* (*Nubadig* of the Western Hurrians).

II. *Urarṭu*:[20] the supreme triad consists of the dynastic god *Ḫaldi* (place of worship: Muṣaṣir-Ardine) with his consort *Warubane* (otherwise *Bagbartu*, or *Bagmaštu*); the Thunderer-god *Teišebā* (= Hurr. *Teššob*, place of worship: K/Qumēnu or K/Qumme on the Upper Zab) with his consort *Ḫubā* (=Hurr. *Ḫebā*), and the Sun-god *Šiwine* (possibly of Hittito-Luwian origin, place of worship: Ṭušpā) with his consort *Ṭušpueā* (to his circle may belong the goddesses *Aui* and *Aia*; the latter belongs to the most ancient Near Eastern substratum; in Sippar she had the epithet *kallātum* and was the wife of the local Sun-god Šamaš). *Ḫaldi* seems to be a newcomer to the pantheon, as we hope to show in another paper; the original supreme triad consisted of the Thunderer *Teišebā*, his wife *Ḫubā* and their son, the child-god,[21] *Ṭurā* (=Hurr. *Tilla*). Among important Urartian deities must be counted *Ḫuṭuine* (the name is an epithet; it may have some connection with the Hurrian goddesses of the fates, the *Ḫudena* and the *Ḫudellura*), *Ua* (who may be the Mesopotamian

[19] G. A. Melikišvili, *Urartskie klinoobraznye nadpisi* [*Urartian Cuneiform Inscriptions*], Moscow 1960, No 27 (the inscription Mheridur, or Meher-kapusı, or Taş-kapusı).

[20] B. B. Piotrovskij, *Vanskoe carstvo* [*The Kingdom of Van*], Moscow 1959, p. 224 sq.; G. A. Melikišvili, "Die Götterpaartrias an der Spitze des urartäischen Pantheon," *Orientalia* 34,4 (1965), pp. 441-45.

[21] *Ṭurā* gets a much smaller "food ration" (offering) than his neighbors on the list, although he precedes them.

Ēia?),[22] *Nālaine* (the god of the Nāla Mountains, or the Armenian Taurus), the Moon-god *Šelarde*, the chthonic(?) god *Querā*, the god *Eliwre*; all these are mentioned also in other inscriptions besides the general list of deities, where they, however, are named nearer to the end; the goddess *Sarde* may be a form of Ištar. The considerable difference from the pantheons of the Hurrians proper is obvious. Except *Teišebā* = *Teššob* and his triad, the deities are foreign to the latter.

IIIa. *Arrapḫe*:[23] the goddess Šawuška is not mentioned, either in the documents or in the theophorous names. Therefore the often encountered ideograms ᵈIŠTAR, ᵈU must in most cases denote either the Akkadian Ištar, or else the Hurrian Ḫeba, abundantly attested in the PNs.[24] In Āl-ilāni, the capital of Arrapḫe, there seems to have been four sanctuaries: for Teššob, for "Ištar, the Lady of the Land" (or: "the World")=Ḫeba?, for Ištar Silakku, and possibly for Ištar of Nineveh. Judging from the wall-painting in the palace sanctuary at Nuzi,[25] the three most important deities were imagined in the guise of a bull, a cow and a calf. The bull is certainly identical with Teššob, hence the cow with Ḫeba, the most popular of the goddesses on the evidence of the PN repertory, the calf probably with Tilla, who is second only to Teššob in his popularity in forming theophorous names. The identification of Tilla with the Urartian child-god Ṭurā is linguistically feasible.[26] It is the minority of Tilla which probably explains why he had no sanctuary of his own either in the capital, Āl-ilāni, or in Nuzi; such a sanctuary existed, along with some others, only in the community of Ulamme.

In Nuzi, the second in importance among the communities of Arrapḫe, were worshipped Teššob of Ḫalep (in Syria!), Ištar of Nineveh (=Ḫeba?),

[22]We adopt the form *Ēia* rather than *Ea* on the following grounds: 1) there are Hurrian phonetic transcriptions which directly present the spelling *E-i-a-*; 2) the spelling ᵈ*É-a* is Akkadian, not Sumerian, but it is against all Semitic phonetical rules, and consequently must be read in some other way; 3) in OAkk É is *ḥà*, *hà*, and A (vide A-*a*/*E-a*=A=*nāqu*) is to be read, at least in many cases, as /ăi(a)/. Now *Ḥai* (and even *Ḥāia*, since the pre-OAkk, as well as the Amorite absolute form of the nouns ended in -Ø//-*a*) makes perfect sense from the point of view of Semitic linguistics and mythology. In the later period the reading would be /*Ēia/, as pointed out by the Hurrian phonetic spelling. Whether the Urartian god ᵈ*Ú-a* has anything at all to do with the Akkadian *Ḥāi*/*Ēia* is another matter.

[23]After Deller.

[24]See *NPN*.

[25]R. Starr, *Nuzi, II*, Cambridge, Mass., 1937, pl. 129 D.

[26]The alternation of Hurr. *i*// Urart. *u* is fairly common (v. *HuU*, p. 61), also the alternation of *l*//*r*//*n* (ibid., p. 55). The Common Hurro-Urartian phoneme **ṭ* is preserved in Urartian but >*t* in Hurrian (ibid., pp. 44-45).

probably together with Tilla, and certainly also the Akkadian chthonic(?) goddess Bēlat-ēkalli. The absence of truly local gods is noteworthy.

In Abena, "the Town of the Donkeys," were worshipped the local god Sarie (Sario)[27] with his wife the Tupkilian Ištar (or the Akkubian Ištar), and the Akkadian Nergal with his wife Ḫumella. But in another list Nergal is replaced by a god Zarwa(n), before whom is named Azuiḫḫe, a goddess(?), and after Zarwa(n) comes Zari[...] probably his wife; then are listed the god Tirwi(n) and the Sun-god ᵈUTU (to judge from the theophorous PN, *Šimiga*).

In A(ḫ)zuḫina were worshipped the gods *Kurwe* with his wife *Ištar* of Nineveh (from which probably follows that Kurwe was a kind of Teššob),[28] *Kumurwe* (Kumarwe) with his wife *Aḫulae* (an epithet), *Nergal* with his wife *Ištar Ḫumella*, the Akkubian Ištar, the god Tirwi(n) and the Sun-god.

Apart from these, the PN and other data show that, of the more important gods, the Moon-god *Kužuγ*, the chthonic god ᵈU.GUR, *Ēia*, *Ušum*, etc., were also worshipped in Arrapḫe.

Thus, to the common pantheon of the kingdom Arrapḫe belong the following important deities: the Thunderer-god *Teššob* (*Kurwe*) with the consort *Ḫeba* (=*Ištar* with the different additional characterizations and epithets) and their son *Tilla*, *Kumurwe* (Kumarwe), *Nergal* (Zarwan) with *Ištar Ḫumella*, *Tirwi*(*n*), the Sun-god *Šimiga*, the Moon-god *Kužuγ*, ᵈU.GUR, *Ēia*, etc., but not *Šawuška.

III. *Texts from Mari and North-Eastern Babylonia.*[29] In a text from Mari the goddess *Šaʾuška*, or *Šawuška*, of the militant Ištar type, is named at the head of the other deities. Then follows a triad consisting of the Akkadian wisdom-god *Ēia*, the Thunderer-god *Teššob* of the town Kumme (=K/Qumme, K/Qumēnu on the Upper Zab rather than Kumme/Kummānu/Comana in Cataonia?), and the Sun-god *Šimije*, or Šimige; in another variant the triad consists of the god *Nirae* of Pidena (*nirae* "the swift"; an epithet probably of the same Teššob), of *Kumarwe* (probably another god of Kumme), and of *Šimige*. Also mentioned are the Moon-god Ušum, the god Kubli, etc.

IV. *Kizzuwadna* (*Cataonia*). There is one list which is expressly described as an enumeration of the gods of Kizzuwadna, namely, the one in the treaty between Suppiluliumas and Šattiwazza. (The corresponding lists which must have existed in the treaties of the Hittite kings with those of Kizzuwadna have not, to my knowledge, been preserved.) Unfortunately, the treaty in question lists only certain little known, perhaps pre-Hurrian, apparently chthonic

[27]The alternation of *-i-e*//*-i-u* points probably to the pronunciation /ʹiə/</*io/. Cf. the numerous cases of the suffix *-i-ú*, probably /-io/, in Urartian toponyms, I. M. Diakonoff and S. Kashkay, *Urarṭu, Répertoire geographique cunéiforme* (in print).

[28]The ubiquity of Ištar of Nineveh shows that the sending by Dušratta of her statue to the pharaoh does not prove he ruled over Nineveh (much less over all Assyrian cities).

[29]See nn. 7-8.

deities, then *Alalu* and a group of gods of Akkadian origin, although, according to the myth of Kumarwe, these were connected with Alalu: *Anu* and *Antu*, *Enlil* and *Ninlil*, and, without a pair, *Bēlat-ēkalli*; then come the "mountains, rivers, the Tigris, the Euphrates, Heaven and Earth, winds, clouds." We miss Kumarwe himself, and even Teššob, and many other gods. It seems that from among the gods of Kizzuwadna only those who seemed especially terrible, namely the chthonic gods and the gods of the earlier generation (they may have been felt to be the same thing), were selected to witness the Mitannian oath. Moreover, a number of the gods of Kizzuwadna, among others the *Ḫebat*[30] of Kizzuwadna, had already been mentioned as witnesses on the Hittite side (see above). On the ground of the representations and Luwian Hieroglyphic inscriptions at Yazılı-kaya we may consider the following three groups of deities as gods of Kizzuwadna: (a) the supreme triad *Teššob*, *Ḫebat* and their son *Šarruma* (with two sisters?); (b) the twelve great gods: the Thunderer-god of Kumme(?), *Kumarwe*, *Ēia*(?), *Šawuška* (with her servants Ninatta and Kulitta), the Moon-god *Kužuj*, the Sun-god (=*Šimiga*) and six others (plus *Šeri* and *Ḫurri* who probably were servant-gods); (c) seven(?) goddesses. Also twelve other gods, the Sword-god (cf. the Weapon-gods in Urarṭu), etc., etc. Note that *Šawuška* has a place among the gods, not the goddesses.[30a]

V. *Mitanni*. The list in the Šattiwazza-treaty (after the enumeration of the gods evoked by Š. but foreign to Mitanni proper) gives us probably a rather comprehensive picture of the Mitannian pantheon. It starts with Semitic and therefore probably pre-Mitannian gods of Northern Mesopotamia, beginning with ᵈIŠKUR (meaning Addu? or Teššob?), "the Lord of Heaven and Earth"; then come *Sīn* and *Šamaš* (in Hurrian probably conceived as Šimige and

[30]It is *Ḫeba* in all PN (and therefore this form is the more archaic) but *Ḫebat*, *Ḫebatu* in Boğazköy, in Ugaritic lists, in the Hieroglyphic Luwian texts and elsewhere. E. A. Speiser had pointed out that this *t* does not, contrary to the rules of Hurrian phonetics, develop to **d*, and hence is (a) late, (b) Semitic. He compared West Semitic **Ḥawwatu*, Hebr. *Ḥawwā* "Eve." The name cannot be borrowed from West Semitic because, first, the form *Ḫeba* is earlier than the Semitic addition *-t-* (this is, among other proofs, shown by the existence of *Ḫubā* in Urartian), and second, because intervocalic **b* may develop to West Semitic *ḇ* > /w(w)/, but Semitic **w* cannot be reflected as Hurrian *b*. Of course, cuneiform *b*-signs were frequently enough used for /w/ in Hurrian, but in this case (1) variants with the PI-sign would occur; (2) Urartian *Ḫubā* would be inexplicable. Therefore, although there may have been an identification of Hurr. *Ḫeba*>*Ḫebatu* with West Semitic *Ḥawwā*<*Ḥawwatu*, either the two mythological figures must have originally been quite separate, or it was *Ḫeba* who was the original. The Semitic etymology of *Ḥawwā* is not above some suspicions.

[30a]K. Bittel, "Bildbeschreibung," pp. 125-65; H. G. Güterbock, "Die Inschriften," in: K. Bittel et al., *Das hethitische Felsheiligtum Yazılıkaya*, Berlin 1975. See also V. Haas - M. Wäfler, "Zur Topographie von Hattuša and Umgebung I," *OA* 16 (1977), pp. 227-38 for the history of the controversy and the pertinent bibliography.

Kužuγ), and separately *Sīn of Ḫarrān*, who was to have a long and important history in the Near East. The Mitannian deities proper begin with Teššob "the Lord of (the town) Kaḫat." Then follow *Nergal* of Kurda, *Teššob*, Lord of Uḫašuman, *Ēiašarri*, *Anu* and *Antu*, *Enlil* and *Ninlil*; then come the Indo-Iranian gods, protectors of the dynasty(?), then a few local gods, mostly having epithets instead of proper names; last of all comes *Aššur*. His appearance must be due to the political situation in Mitanni at that particular time.

The goddesses are listed separately (except for Antu and Ninlil who follow their consorts, constituting with them quasi-entities). The list begins with "the Goddess (ᵈ*IŠTAR*) of the Star Dilbat" (i.e., the Morning Star). This is, no doubt, Šawuška, because no other goddess could presume to stand above Ḫebat). Then comes *Šala*, the wife of Iškur, or Addu; this, of course, is Ḫeba masquerading; then *Bēlat-ēkalli* (who here probably is the spouse of Nergal), *Damkina* (the wife of *Ēia*, or *Ēiašarri*), *Išḫara* (a pre-Hurrian goddess), and then the mountains and the rivers, the gods of Heaven and the gods of Earth. (Note that the mountains come before the rivers, possibly a reminiscence of the origin of the Mitannians in the mountains of the North-East.)

The absence of Kumarwe in the list may be fortuitous.

VI. *The Hurrian gods of Ugarit* (lists A, B, C, D and Corpus 166).[31] At the head of all the lists we find the local Western Semitic god ᵓ*El*, preceded only by "father-gods" (or "the father-god") of the first (dormant) divine generation. ᵓ*El* is followed by *Teššob* of Ḫalep and *Kumarwe* (in one of the lists Kumarwe precedes Teššob—probably not by importance but by seniority), and the Moon-god *Kužuγ* (in one case preceding Kumarwe). Then follows *Ēia*, or *Ēia ḫazizi*, [32] and *Aštabi* (in one list the Semitic(?) god Tadmiš and another one whose name is not preserved precede Aštabi), then, in arbitrary order, follow *Ardi* ("town, community"), *Ḫaman*(?), the Sun-god *Šimige*, *Nubadig* and *Pižaežapḫi* (actually an epithet). One list also mentions the West Semitic god Rašp, Hurr. *Iržappa*.

The order in which the goddesses are placed is interesting. The greatest veneration is awarded to *Šawuška*—in most of the lists she is placed directly after Teššob and before Kumarwe. Also among the male deities but lower down in the list are placed the West Semitic ᶜ*Anat* and the Akkadian *Nikkal* (Ningal, wife of the Mesopotamian Moon-god; being a cow-goddess she may have been assimilated to a Hurrian fertility goddess figure) as well as *Pendigalli* (Bēlat ēkalli), and in one list the fate-goddesses *Ḫudena* and *Ḫudellura*. In the

[31]See n. 9.

[32]All the various forms of the last word are spelling variants of **ḫazzizzi*; to read /ḫasisi/ or /ḫassissi/, obviously (in spite of A. Kammenhuber's objections) < Akkad. *ḫasīsu* "wisdom." Note that Hurr. **Ḫazzizzae Madae* is a translation of the Ugaritic Semitic *Kuṯāru wa-Ḫasīsu*. Hence Hurr. **mad-* means "clever, skilful."

lists A and B the other goddesses are enumerated in a batch; in C, D and in Corpus 166 they are left out altogether, except that in the latter *Ḫebat* is added at the bottom of the list. The goddesses in question are *Ḫebat*, *Uzḫara* (=Išḫara), "The Lady" (*Allāne*), the Semitic(?) *Daqqat*, *Ḫudena* and *Ḫudellura*, *Ninatta-Kulitta* and *Adamma-Kubaba*.

Nearly all the Hurrian deities of Ugarit appear in the texts of Boğazköy and in Yazılıkaya, the difference being mainly in their apparent seniority.

To sum up:

1) Common to all groups of Hurrians was the cult of the Thunderer-god *Teššob* (Urart. *Teišebā*) and his spouse *Ḫeba* (Urart. *Ḫubā*, in the West, apparently under Semitic influence, *Ḫebat* or *Ḫebatu*, but only *Ḫeba* in the PN).[33] The sacred animal of Teššob was the bull; his arms were the mace or the battle-ax. The sacred animal of Ḫeba was sometimes, though apparently not always, the cow.

2) In some regional pantheons also their son was worshipped, viz., as a god-child or a calf; he was *Tilla* in Arrapḫe, *Ṭurā* in Urarṭu, *Šarruma* in Cataonia. Already here there is no complete uniformity in the cults of the different Hurrian regions.

3) Significant are the different roles of *Šawuška*. She is absent in the north and in the east (in Urarṭu and in Arrapḫe). But among the Hurrians of Babylonia she is at the head of the pantheon. In Mitanni she heads the goddesses; here, in the guise of the "Goddess of the Morning Star" she precedes Šala (Ḫeba). In Ugarit she is second only to ᵓEl and Teššob. In Kizzuwadna she follows Teššob, Kumarwe and Ēia among the male gods.

4) It is but natural that the cosmic deities of the Sun and Moon should be worshipped everywhere. But, for one thing, they were worshipped under different names (the Sun-god was *Šiwine* in Urarṭu, *Šimiga*, etc., in most other regions; the Moon-god was usually but not universally *Kužuγ*, but *Šelarde* in Urarṭu), and secondly they occupied different ranks in the divine hierarchy: in Urarṭu, in Kizzuwadna and among the Babylonian Hurrians the Sun-god was one of the most important deities, but he was a secondary figure among the Hurrian gods of the other regions. The Moon-god had an important place in Kizzuwadna, Mitanni and Ugarit but an unimportant one in the other regions.

5) The gods ^{d}U.GUR and *Kumarwe* occupy different places in the regional pantheons. However, Kumarwe was apparently known in the whole of the Hurrian area; it is a possibility that he was even known in Urarṭu under some covering epithet. As to ^{d}U.GUR, he was at least known in Arrapḫe and in Kizzuwadna (also, e.g., in Haiasa).

6) In some cases local deities (Hurrian, or belonging to the substratum or adstratum) have been pushed to the head of the pantheon, preceding Teššob (thus *Ḫaldi* in Urarṭu, *ᵓEl* at Ugarit, possibly *Alala/u* in Kizzuwadna).

[33] See n. 30.

7) The Akkadian deities are absent in Urarṭu[34] (*Aia* belongs probably to the substratum, and the identity of *Ua* with *Ēia* is very doubtful).[35] In the other regions they are present, forming a more or less clear-cut group. To it belong *Ēia* (Ea), usually in the form of *Ēia bēl ḫasīsi*, *Ēia Ḫazzizzi*, or *Ēiažarri* (*Ēia šarru*), sometimes worshipped together with his spouse; *Nergal*, married to the native *Ḫumella* (or, presumably, to *Bēlat ēkalli*?); *Nikkal* (Ningal, the cow-spouse of the Moon-god); and in the West, *Anu* and *Antu*, *Enlil* and *Ninlil*, etc. This selection points to an influence from Ur and Uruk and perhaps Nippur, more than to that of the more northerly Babylonian communities. The reason for this is not apparent.

8) Indo-Iranian gods were known only in Mitanni (the Arrapḫean *Zarwa*(*n*) and *Tirwi*(*n*) are hardly Indo-Iranian).

It is immediately apparent that these "isotheoi" do not directly coincide with the grammatical and syntactical isoglosses as established by Khačikyan. However, this is as should be expected, even the different isoglosses rarely coincide fully. Moreover, the above is not a final study of the very complicated material but only a sketch aiming to show that there are means to find out the ethnic infrastructure of the Hurrians. We have only grazed the surface; much more solid investigation should be done with the material which we have but touched upon (or barely even that). Obviously, much known Hurrian material has been entirely left out of our discussion. The conclusions arrived at in this way cannot but be hypothetical in the highest degree, but better results can certainly be achieved by further research, and this is what we have tried to show.

However, if we are allowed to hypothesize, this is the first approach (subject to later correction) to an historical explanation of the data:

The Hurrians, as their name implies, came to the Fertile Crescent from the East or, to be more precise, from the North-East, probably during the 3rd millennium B.C. The earliest wave of the Hurrian tribal migration was (C), leaving its trace in the textual evidence of the Sumero-Hurrian vocabulary of the ḪAR-ra = *ḫubullu* type found at Ras-Šamra. This is the unidentified easternmost dialect (VII), very archaic and differing from the other Hurrian dialects in many respects.[36] The tribes in question may possibly be identified with the bearers of the Kur-Araxes culture (also called Eastern Anatolian

[34]However, note that among the gods worshipped in Urarṭu we most unexpectedly find ᵈAMAR.UTU; whether this means the Babylonian Marduk (which seems improbable), or some other god, cannot be decided. See. N. V. Arutjunjan (Harouthiounian), *Novye urartskie nadpisi Karmir-blura* [*New Urartian Inscriptions of Karmir-blur*], Erevan, 1966, No III, 3, l. 8.

[35]See n. 22 above.

[36]Cf. also the epichoric inscription from Lemnos with its predicative forms in *-ai*, *-aiś*, P. Kretschmer, "Die tyrrhenischen Inschriften der Stele von Lemnos," *Glotto* 29 (1942), pp. 96-98.

Early Bronze) who might have brought it in the form of the Khirbet Kerak culture to southern Syria and Palestine; or the dialect may have been that of the "Eteocypriote" population of Alašia-Cyprus, if we are to assume that the latter were linguistically akin to the Hurrians.

The second wave involved tribes belonging mainly to the (A) group (partly to B). It included the speakers of the Urartian dialect who did not leave the Highland, and of the dialect (I), that of Urkiš, which may have been the first Hurrian dialect to reach not only the Upper Tigris valley but also the territory between Upper Mesopotamia north of the Khabur and the Cilician Taurus. The (A) influence seems to have reached Kizzuwadna in the North-West and Arrapḫe in the East. Both dialects (IIIa and IV) belong to the (B) group but differ from the other (B)-dialect regions by the characteristic (A)-cult of the triad Teššob-Ḫeba-Tilla; the latter received in Kizzuwadna the local name Šarruma.

The third wave consisted of the nucleus of the (B) group tribes. Characteristic of it was the cult of Šawuška, the pre-eminence of the Moon-god over the Sun-god, and the absence of the cult of the child- (or the calf-) god. It included, among others, the dialects of the Babylonian Hurrians (III), of Kizzuwadna (IV), and of the Syrian Hurrians of Ugarit (VI). This wave must have invaded all of Northern Mesopotamia before the Mitannians came, and may have flooded Kizzuwadna and Arrapḫe after the (A) wave, hence their (B) type dialects (IV and IIIa). The Boğazköy material is ambiguous and syncretic because of the plural Hurrian influences from over the Taurus and from beyond the Euphrates (e.g., Hitt. *iwāru* is an early Hurrian borrowing).

The last wave of the (B) migration was the coming of the Mitannians (Matieni) from the Lake Urmia region, bringing along some Indo-Iranian glosses and the Indo-Iranian dynastic gods. Their dialect (V) is the most developed in the (B) group and hence the latest. Its speakers created the new dynasty of Ḫanigalbat (from ca. 1600 also called Mitanni) in Northern Mesopotamia.

A more detailed investigation of the pertinent data is needed, and first of all, monographic treatments of the Hurrian linguistic material from Alalaḫ, Amarna, Qaṭna and especially from Arrapḫe, where such abundant data have been made available by the many years of Professor Lacheman's labor.

Die Familie Kizzuk
Sieben Kassitengenerationen in Temtena und Šuriniwe

Gudrun Dosch - Karlheinz Deller
Universität Heidelberg

Welche Bedeutung kommt den Nuzi-Texten für die Erforschung der Sprache der Kassiten zu? J. A. Brinkman, derzeit der bestausgewiesene Kenner der Kassitenzeit, gab jüngst auf diese Frage folgende Antwort: "The principal present value of the Kassite material from Nuzi is to provide the oldest archival corpus of Kassite personal names for linguistic analysis" (RlA V/5-6, Berlin 1980, p. 470a) und "These names serve chiefly to enrich our knowledge of the Kassite onomasticon" (ebd.).

Da unsere Kenntnis des kassitischen Lexikons (und des Kassitischen überhaupt) wesentlich auf den kassitischen Personennamen beruht, muss natürlich vorab gefragt werden: Woran erkennt man, dass ein gegebener Name kassitisch ist? P. M. Purves gab 1943 dazu diese Auskunft: "Kassite names can be detected with great ease. It is fortunate for present-day knowledge that two relatively short but vital documents have been recovered: a Kassite-Akkadian vocabulary and a Kassite-Akkadian name list" (NPN = OIP LVII, p. 195).

Das Vokabular (82-9-18,5637 = BM 93005) wurde zunächst von Fr. Delitzsch, Die Sprache der Kossäer (Leipzig 1884), p. 25ff. in Umschrift, dann von Th. G. Pinches, JRAS 1917, p. 103ff. in Keilschrift und neuer Bearbeitung bekanntgemacht und liegt jetzt (mit Kollationen von A. Sachs) mustergültig ediert den Kassitenstudien 1. Die Sprache der Kassiten (AOS 37, New Haven 1954) von Kemal Balkan (aus dem Türkischen übersetzt von Fr. R. Kraus) zugrunde.

Die Namenliste (K.4426 + Rm. 617) ist 5R 44 in Autographie publiziert. Umschriften gab Th. G. Pinches, PSBA 3 (1881), p. 37ff., Fr. Delitzsch (1884), p. 19ff. und zuletzt (wiederum mit Kollationen von A. Sachs) K. Balkan (1954), p. 1ff. Die in diesen Quellen enthaltenen Götternamen und prädikativen Elemente waren für A. T. Clay, Personal Names from Cuneiform Inscriptions of the Cassite Period (YOS Res. 1, New Haven 1912), spez. pp. 36-41, für die Autoren von NPN (Chicago 1943), spez. pp. 195ff. und für K. Balkan, Kassitenstudien 1. (1954), pp. 41ff. das entscheidende Kriterium dafür, ob ein Name kassitisch ist oder nicht. Es ist mit dieser Methode zweifellos gelungen, eine recht stattliche Sammlung kassitischer Namen zusammenzutragen und die Nuzologie hat davon anteilmässig (2%) profitiert.

Kann die Nuzologie nun ihrerseits dazu beitragen, die Zahl der kassitischen Personennamen zu vermehren und damit das kassitische Lexikon zu bereichern? Leider sind in Nuzi keine "nuzianisch"-kassitischen Vokabulare gefunden worden, dafür aber Familienarchive von so dichter Attestation, dass daraus Stammbäume rekonstruiert werden können, die bis zu sieben Generationen umfassen. Sollte also der Nachweis gelingen, dass die Masse der nach den obigen philologischen Kriterien ermittelten kassitischen Namen sich auf eine Familie konzentrieren, dürfte man legitimerweise folgern, dass auch jene Namen von Gliedern dieser Familie, die offensichtlich nicht ḫurritischen (oder akkadischen) Ursprungs sind, als kassitisch anzusprechen sind, auch wenn ihre Elemente oder die Namen als ganze bisher nicht für das Kassitische reklamiert worden sind.

Als Vorarbeiten für seine Dissertation "Studien zur Topographie der Provinzstädte des Königreichs Arrapḫe" (Heidelberg 1978) hat Abdulilah Fadhil die Dossiers der einzelnen Städte zusammengestellt.[1] Dabei hat sich herausgestellt, dass die kassitischen Namen eine deutliche topographische Konzentration aufweisen, nämlich auf die Städte Temtena(š), Šuriniwe, Purulliwe und die in ihrem Umkreis liegende *dimtu ša Kizzuk*. Der Eponym ebendieser dimtu lässt sich aus den Urkunden dieser Dossiers als Stammvater einer weitverzweigten Familie nachweisen, die in den genannten Städten tonangebend war. Diese genealogische Kohärenz der Urkunden war, neben den in ihnen enthaltenen topographischen Angaben, für A. Fadhil bestimmend für die Anlage dieser Dossiers. Sie behandeln jedoch nicht nur genealogisch und topographisch Zusammengehörendes, sondern sie haben auch den gleichen Fundort, nämlich das sog. Eastern House der Western Suburban area, N.W. of Yorghan Tepe (vgl. E. R. Lacheman, HSS 16, pp. v-vi, und R. F. S. Starr, Nuzi, vol. II, Plan No. 30), welches unmittelbar angrenzt an das sog. Western House, in dem das Teḫip-tilla-Archiv gefunden wurde.[2]

[1]Wir danken Herrn Dr. A. Fadhil, dessen Dossiers wir benutzen durften, sowie den Mitarbeitern des Seminars für Sprachen und Kulturen des Vorderen Orients (Lehreinheit Assyriologie), Universität Heidelberg, deren Umschriften wir einsehen konnten.

[2]Es handelt sich dabei um folgende Texte:
Room 10: JEN 87, 204, 218, 255, 311, 315, 320, 331, 389, 478, 498, 644 (ist wohl besser Room 12 anzusetzen, da alle genannten Texte aus Temtena stammen, 644 aber aus Kizzukwe).
Room 11: JEN 59, 83, 85, 116, 117, 181, 186, 198, 219, 316, 342, 477, 495, 509, 514, 529, 541, 592, 600, 602, 604, 612, 616, 648?, 666, 671. (Die meisten dieser Texte beziehen sich auf Šuriniwe).
Room 12: JEN 29, 111, 119, 124, 125, 135, 143, 184, 241, 325, 388, 435, 469, 497?, 506, 512, 527, 533, 628?, 646, 672. (Die meisten dieser Texte sind aus Šuriniwe oder Kizzukwe, einige aus Purulliwe und Temtena).
Andere Rooms, aber inhaltlich dazugehörig:
Room 15: JEN 160, 381 (eine Prozesspartei jeweils Temtena).

Das Eastern House besteht aus drei deutlich erkennbaren Bauelementen: einem östlichen Seitenflügel (Rooms 1-5), einem Mittelteil (Rooms 6-9) und einem westlichen Seitenflügel (Rooms 10-12). In den Rooms 1 und 4 wurden die Archive des Ḫašija S. Warḫapi (Waḫrapi), seiner Söhne Mušeja und Itḫapu sowie seines Enkels, Ḫuite S. Mušeja gefunden. Diese Archive sind, wie A. Fadhil überzeugend nachgewiesen hat, nach der Stadt Ḫurazina ṣeḫru zu lokalisieren.

Wie schon E. R. Lacheman (HSS 16, p. vi) erkannt hat, enthielt Room 10 die Urkunden des Ḫilpiš-šuḫ S. Šuḫun-zirira und seines Sohnes Kurpa-saḫ. Nach A. Fadhil sind diese Texte nach der Stadt Temtena(š) zu lokalisieren. Die Rooms 11 and 12 erbrachten die Archive des Ḫutija S. Kuššija und seines Sohnes Kel-tešup. A. Fadhil hat diese mit der Stadt Šuriniwe in Zusammenhang gebracht.

Bisher ist jedoch u.W. in der Literatur noch nicht aufgezeigt worden, dass diese beiden Familien der Rooms 10 und 11/12 miteinander verwandt sind und auf ein und denselben Stammvater, eben Kizzuk, zurückgehen.

Um die Genealogie zurückzuverfolgen, muss zunächst nachgewiesen werden, dass Šuḫun-zirira Sohn des Kirzam-pula ist. Es gibt allerdings keinen Beleg für diese Filiation mit dem vollen Patronym, sondern nur mit dem Hypochoristikon Kirsija: ÌR[!] *Šu-ḫu-⌜un⌝-zi-ri-[ra]* [5]DUMU *Ki-ir-si-ja* JENu 1024a:4-5 (*ṭuppi ardūti*, Fundort unbekannt, wahrscheinlich Room 12 oder 11, da JEN 671 = JENu 1024 aus Room 11 kommt). Dieser Kirsija/ Kirzija hatte noch zwei weitere Söhne, Ḫuti-ḫamanna und Ḫašija: [1]*Ḫu-ti-ḫa-ma-an-na* DUMU *Ki-ir-si-a* HSS 16,331:7 (mit explizitem Bezug Purulliwe) und [[1]]*Ḫu-ti-ḫa-ma-an-na* DUMU *Ki-ir-<si>-ja* HSS 16,332:7; ferner also Zeuge in einer Urkunde des Dossiers Šuriniwe IGI *Ḫu-di-ḫa-ma-an-na* DUMU *Ki-ir-zi-ja* JEN 435:44.49. Von Ḫašija besitzen wir sein *ṭuppi šīmti*, HSS 13,366, zugunsten

---

Room 13: (Möglicherweise Fehler für 10-2, Temtena, Šuriniwe, Kizzuke) JEN 321, 340, 471.

Room 16: (Temtena) JEN 474

D 3: (Purulliwe) HSS 15,41:1-5

A 14: (Šuriniwe) HSS 19,6

Room ?: (Temtena) JEN 645, (Purulliwe) HSS 19,28, (Temtena/Šuriniwe) HSS 19,41

JENu (Umschriften dieser Texte stellte das Oriental Institute, University of Chicago, freundlicherweise dem Seminar für Sprachen und Kulturen des Vorderen Orients, Lehreinheit Assyriologie, Universität Heidelberg, zur Verfügung.) 423, 729, 854, 859, 1024a (Temtena), JENu 448 (Purulliwe), JENu 25a, 620, 629, 703, 730, 991, 1047, 1168 (Šuriniwe). Wir danken Herrn Professor J. A. Brinkman, der die Erlaubnis zur Benutzung dieser Umschriften gab, vielmals.

Die Belege für die einzelnen Personennamen finden sich in NPN (I. J. Gelb, P. M. Purves, A. A. MacRae, Nuzi Personal Names, OIP, Vol. LVII, 1943) oder in E. Cassin, J. J. Glassner, Anthroponymie et Anthropologie de Nuzi, Malibu 1977, Vol. 1 (AAN).

seiner Ehefrau ^{f}Marija: ^{1}*ṭup-pí ši-im-ti ša* ^{2}^{I}*Ḫa-ši-ja* DUMU *Ki-ir-zi-ja*. Im Archiv des Teḫiptilla figuriert er zweimal als Zeuge: JEN 24:14.23 (Turša) und JEN 97:20 (*dimtu ša Pisitta*). Dass Šuḫun-zirira, Ḫuti-ḫamanna und Ḫašija Brüder sind, wird zwar nirgends ausdrücklich gesagt; aufgrund der Archivlage (Dossiers Temtenaš, Šuriniwe und Purulliwe) ist diese Annahme freilich geradezu zwingend. Hinzu kommt, dass Ḫašijas Testament die Siegelungen dreier Personen aufweist, die nicht als Zeugen aufgeführt sind: *Ki-li-ik-še* und *Ar-ḫa-ma-*[*an-na*] (Z.37) sowie *Ša-ti-*⌜x⌝*-ki-tar* (Z.39); in ihnen erkennen wir unschwer Ḫašijas Grossvater Kiliške und dessen Brüder Ariḫ-ḫamanna und Šati-kintar, die zum Zeitpunkt der Protokollierung von HSS 13,366 möglicherweise gar nicht mehr unter den Lebenden weilten. Zum Problem der "heirloom seals" in altbabylonischer Zeit hat J. Renger in Seals and Sealing in the Ancient Near East (Bibliotheca Mesopotamica 6, Malibu 1977), p. 77 und p. 84, n. 42, interessantes Material zusammengetragen. Hier scheint aber doch ein speziell gelagerter Fall vorzuliegen: eine Erbteilung wird posthum von dem Clan sanktioniert. Dass Kirsija/Kirzija das Hypochoristikon von Kirzam-pula ist, lehrt ein Vergleich zwischen ^{I}*Ki-ir-zi-ja* DUMU *Ki-li-iš-ge* HSS 16,24:5 (auf ihn folgt dort sein Neffe Kai-tešup S. Šati-kintar) mit *Ki-ir-za-pu-r*[*a*] DUMU *Ki-le-eš-ki* JENu 679 (nach NPN 88b; Umschrift Chiera liegt in Heidelberg nicht vor); ^{I}*Ge-er-za-pu-ra* DUMU *Ki-li-iš-ki* JENu 730:3 (*ṭuppi šupeʾulti* mit Kel-tešup S. Ḫutija, Dossier Šuriniwe) und IGI *Ki-ir-*⌜*za*⌝*-am-pu-la* [DUMU *Ki-le-eš-ki*] JEN 616:31.37 (Šuriniwe). In der Liste JEN 514 steht ^{I}*Ki-ir-za-am-pu-la* (Z.8) als einziger ohne Patronym, was ihn geradezu heraushebt; prosopographisch gehört dieser Text nach Šuriniwe, er wurde in Room 11 gefunden. Ebenfalls ohne Patronym, ^{I}*Ki-ir-za-am-pu-la*! HSS 14,64:22 (SMN 3081 aus C 23) als Empfänger von Gerste und ^{I}*Ki-*⌜*ir-za-am*⌝*-pu-la* HSS 15,4:4 (SMN 2697 aus N 120) als Empfänger einer Panzerausrüstung. Aus HSS 13,366:37.39 konnte bereits gefolgert werden, dass Ar(iḫ)-ḫamanna und Šati-kintar Brüder des Kiliške sind. Die Filiation IGI *Ki-li-iš-ge* DUMU *Du-ri-ki-in-tar* findet sich nur JEN 486:(34.)36 (Archiv Teḫip-tilla, Room 16, Dossier Zizza) explizit, während sie für seine Brüder u.a. durch ^{24}IGI *Ša-te-ki-in-tar* DUMU *Tu-r*[*i-ki-in-tar*] ^{25}IGI *A-ri-ḫa-ma-an-na* ŠEŠ-*šu š*[*a Ša-te-ki-in-tar*] JEN 232:24-25, einem *ṭuppi šupeʾulti* des Kiliške S. [Turi-kintar] (so Z.2 zu ergänzen) nachgewiesen werden kann. Implizit erscheinen diese Brüder wiederum in HSS 16,366:2, ^{1}DUMU^{MEŠ} *ša* ^{I}*Te-eš-*[*šu*]*-ja* (= *mār šarri*!) ^{2}*it-ti* DUMU^{MEŠ} *ša* [^{I}*Du*]*-ri-ki-in-t*[*ar*] ^{3}DUMU^{MEŠ} *ša* ^{I}*Te-ḫi-ip-til-la* (SMN 1258 aus Room A 34). In den gleichen prosopographischen Zusammenhang gehört ^{I}*Ki-li-iš-ge* HSS 15,228 (SMN 1253 aus Room A 34; vgl. G. Dosch, Die Texte aus Room A 34, Magister-Arbeit, Heidelberg 1976, Nr. 171), das Z.14 noch die Information hinzufügt, dass er *rākib narkabti* war.

Für den vierten, wohl jüngsten Sohn des Turi-kintar vgl. *u*[*m-m*]*a* ^{I}*Du-um-ši-ma-na-ma* DUMU *Du-ri-*[*ki*]*-in-tar* JEN 644:5, wo er neben vier anderen Männern (darunter Tarmija S. Kuššija, Z.1) im Prozess um die *dimtu ša*

Kizzuk auftritt. Ferner begegnet er als Zeuge in dem Teḫip-tilla-Text JEN 79:18 (IGI *Tu-uš-ma-na* DUMU *Tu-ri-ki-tar*[!]).

Die Filiation von Turi-kintar zu Kizzuk ist bislang nicht explizit nachzuweisen. Die Interessen der Söhne des Turi-kintar—wie besonders durch JEN 644 dokumentiert—sind jedoch derart mit der *dimtu ša Kizzuk* verknüpft, dass eigentlich der Schluss unausweichlich ist, dass Kizzuk wenn nicht der Vater so doch ein direkter Vorfahre des Turi-kintar ist. Doch gibt es noch einen weiteren Beleg für diese Annahme.

Aber untersuchen wir zunächst die Linie Turi-kintar - Ar(iḫ)-ḫamanna - Kuššija - Ḫutija - Kel-tešup, also jenen Zweig der Familie, der in Šuriniwe domiziliert ist (oder bleibt) und dessen Archive aus den Rooms 11 and 12 des Eastern House stammen. Die Filiation Kuššija S. Ar(iḫ)-ḫamanna, welche uns zur Verbindung der Archive der Rooms 11/12 mit jenen aus Room 10 noch fehlt, wird geboten von JEN 471 (aus Room 13, Dossier Temtena): [1]*ṭup-pí tá-am-gu*$_5$*-ur-ti ša* [2][I]*Ku*[!]*-us*[!]*-ši-ja* (Kollation NPN 92b) DUMU *Ar-ḫa-ma-an-na* [3]*ù ša* [I]*Ḫe-el-bi-iš-šu-uḫ*$_5$ DUMU *Šu-ḫu-un-zi-ri-ri* [4]*i+na be-ri-šu-nu it-ta-am-ga*$_5$*-ru*. (Sie bietet zugleich einen interessanten Synchronismus mit der 3. Generation Šuriniwe und der 5. Generation Temtenaš). Unter den Urkunden des Ḫutija S. Kuššija ist sicher der Brief JEN 325 (JENu 168 aus Room 12; vgl. H. Lewy, Or NS 11 [1942], pp. 339-41; R. E. Hayden, Court Procedure, pp. 126-27), in welchem drei Richter, Zilija, Šukrija und Ar-tirwi über den Prozess um die *dimtu ša Kizzuk* an den Hof berichten, zu erwähnen. Er enthält folgende Aussage des Ḫutija (Z.7ff.) [URU] *ša Ki-iz-zu-uk* [8]*it-ti* A.ŠÀ[MEŠ]*-šu-ma* [*ša* ([I])*K*]*i-iz-zu-uk* [9]*am-ma-ti-ni ù* LÚ[MEŠ] *an-nu-ti* [10]⸢*a-na*⸣ *aš-ša-bu-ti-ma a-ši-ib* [11]⸢*ù*⸣ *i+na-an-na* A.ŠÀ[MEŠ] *ik-ta-la-šu-nu-ti-ma* [12]⸢*ù*⸣ *i-te-ri-*⸢*iš*⸣*-mi*, aus der hier besonders interessiert, dass Ḫutija den Kizzuk als *ammati* bezeichnet. Dieses ḫurritische Wort wurde bereits von H. Lewy, Or NS 11, p. 340, n. 3. als "grandfather, ancestor" bestimmt (vgl. jetzt auch E. Laroche, RHA 34 [1976] 47). Nach den hier vorgetragenen genealogischen Erkenntnissen war freilich Kizzuk wenigstens der Ururgrossvater des Ḫutija, wenn man die Filiation Turi-kintar S. Kizzuk als erwiesen voraussetzt. Auf jeden Fall ist damit gesichert, dass Ḫutija S. Kuššija ein Nachkomme des Kizzuk ist; die von der vorausgehenden Argumentation aufgezeigte Verbindung der Šuriniwe-Linie mit der Temtenaš-Linie wird dadurch voll bestätigt. In JEN 325 wird auch über die Position der gegnerischen Partei berichtet, die behauptet, dass das strittige URU dem Palast gehört (⸢*ša*⸣ É.GAL*-lim-mi*, Z. 14), gar nicht den Namen URU [17]*ša Ki-iz-zu-uk-we* trage (Z. 16-18), sondern URU *ša Ta-ap*-PAP[!] (Autographie NU; Kollation H. Lewy nach Photo), Z. 18-20, und Turi-kintar sie 'gestohlen' habe (URU [21][I]*Du-ur-ki-in-tar* [22]*iš-ta*[!]*-ri-iq-mi*). Diese Sicht der Besitzverhältnisse kann natürlich gegen die hier verfochtene Genealogie (nach der Turi-kintar das URU von Kizzuk geerbt hat) ins Treffen geführt werden: aber die Richter haben in JEN 325 bereits an die letzte Instanz (*a-na* LUGAL [36]*qí-bá-šu-nu-ti*) appelliert und gegen sie gibt es keine Revision. Indirekt ist

JEN 325:14-22 aber doch eine Bestätigung der Filiation Turi-kintar S. Kizzuk, weil die natürliche Erbfolge bestritten wird.

Ausser zur Bezeichnung von AN.ZA.KÀR/URU *ša Kizzuk* (wozu auch der Strassenname KASKAL [I]*Ki-iz-zu-uk* JEN 106:8 und KASKAL-*nu ša* AN.ZA.KÀR *Ki-iz-zu-uk-we* Gadd 69:7 zu rechnen ist) ist der Name Kizzuk nur noch einmal zu belegen: IGI 30-⌈*i-di*⌉-*en* DUMU *Ki-iz-zu-*⌈*uk*⌉ JEN 435:46, dem *ṭuppi riksi* des Kel-tešup S. Ḫutija, durch das er seine Tochter [f]Jarutte dem Šintip-tešup S. Eḫel-tešup zur Ehe gibt (Room 12, Dossier Šuriniwe). [f]Jarutte gehört der 6. Generation an; sie kann nicht gut kontemporär sein mit einem Mann aus der 1. Generation; so wird niemand ernsthaft behaupten wollen, dieser Sîn iddin sei ein Bruder des Turi-kintar. Wir haben es also mit einem zweiten Träger dieses Namens zu tun. In der Zeugenliste folgt er auf Ḫuti-ḫamanna S. Kirzija (4. Generation) und Nirar-tilla S. Ḫupitaja (6. Generation) und könnte darum ein weiteres Glied dieser weitverzweigten Familie sein, doch wessen Sohn dieser Kizzuk II war, lässt sich leider nicht ausmachen; er wäre in die 3. oder 4. Generation zu plazieren.

Kizzuk I ist innerhalb der Nuzi-Chronologie (die sich an den Generationen der Familie Teḫip-tilla S. Puḫi-šenni orientieren muss) sehr hoch anzusetzen und muss also sehr früh an diesem Ort gesiedelt haben. Ariḫ-ḫamanna und Kiliške (—er hat offenbar sehr lange gelebt—) sind schon in die frühe Teḫip-tilla-Zeit zu datieren; dann wäre Turi-kintar [f]Winnirke-Zeit und der Vorfahre Kizzuk entsprechend früher. Setzt man Turi-šenni, den Vater des Puḫi-šenni, und Kizzuk, den Vater oder Vorfahren des Turi-kintar als Generation Null, kommt man für die erstere Familie auf fünf, für letztere hingegen auf sieben Generationen, also auf über zweihundert Jahre. Die Familie Teḫip-tilla ist damit als chronologischer Orientierungsrahmen der Nuzi-Texte zwar nicht "entthront"—ihr Archiv ist nach der derzeitigen Quellenlage mit Abstand das grösste und zusammenhängendste Familienarchiv des alten Mesopotamiens überhaupt, wie M. P. Maidman, A Socio-Economic Analysis of a Nuzi Family Archive, Philadelphia, Pa., 1976, University Microfilms 77-861, p. 5, mit Recht unterstreicht—, aber die den Nuzi-Texten zugestandenen 150 Jahre (zuletzt J. A. Brinkman, RlA V/5-6, p. 469b, "c. 1550-1400") sind jetzt doch nach oben zu korrigieren: c. 1600-1400 erscheint uns als der realistischere Ansatz. Als Beleg diene der Fig. 1 ausgeführte Stammbaum der Familie Kizzuk.

Zählt man nur die Männer dieses Stammbaums, beträgt die Zahl ihrer Namen 36. Genau die Hälfte, 18 Namen, dürfen, nach dem gegenwärtigen Stand unserer Erkenntnisse, als ḫurritisch angesehen werden, nämlich (in alfabetischer Reihenfolge):

Akip-tilla, Ariḫ-ḫamanna (Ar-ḫamanna), Ḫanatu, Ḫašija, Ḫupitaja, Ḫutiḫamanna, Ḫutija, Ḫutip-ukur, Kai-tešup, Kel-tešup, Mat-tešup, Nirar-tilla, Šummi-šenni, Talluja, Tarmija, Teḫit-tešup, Tupki-tilla und Urḫija.

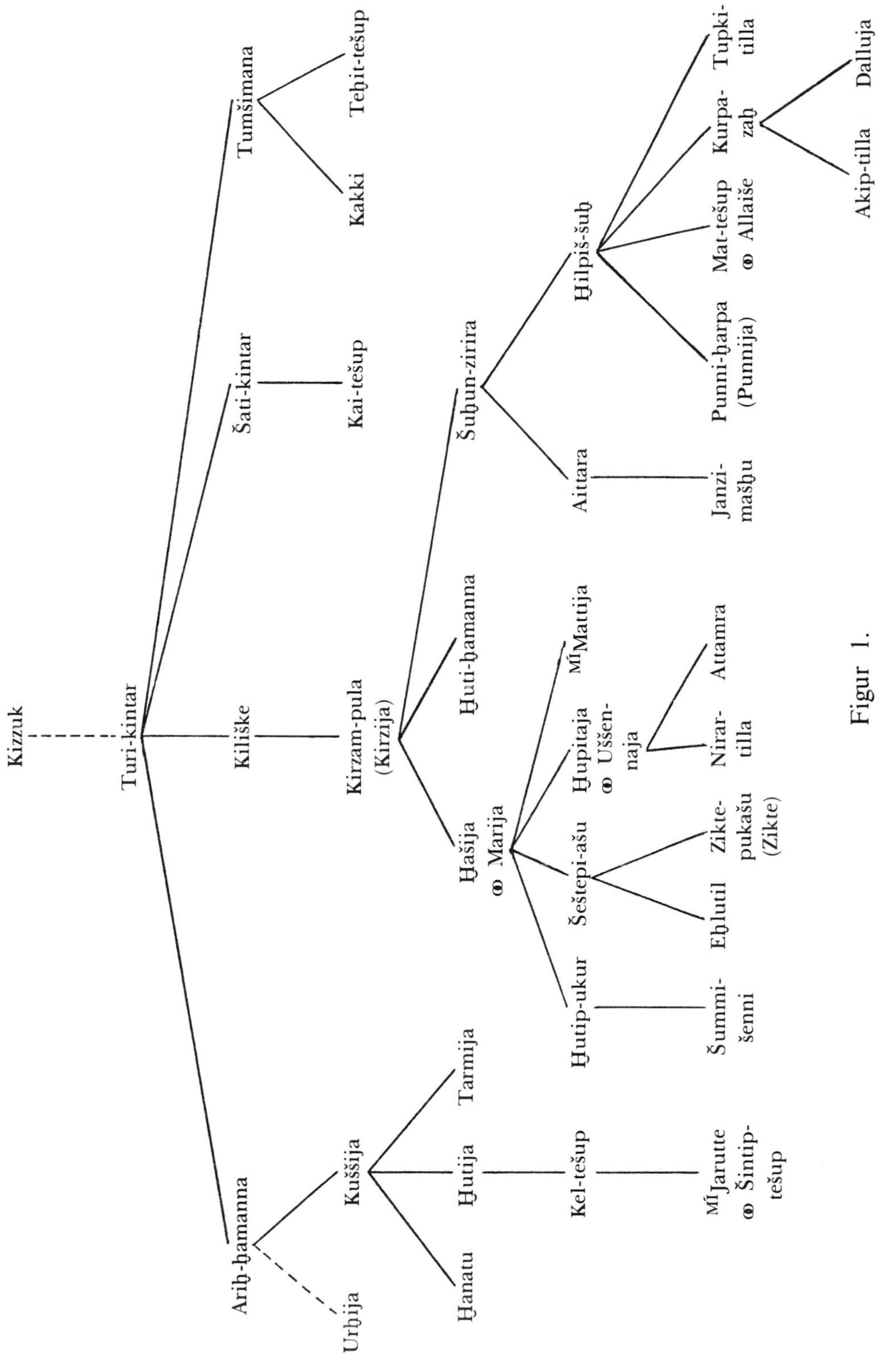
Kizzuk
Turi-kintar
Arih-hamanna
Urhija
Kiliške
Šati-kintar
Tumšimana
Kuššija
Hanatu
Hutija
Tarmija
Kirzam-pula
(Kirzija)
Kai-tešup
Kakki
Tehit-tešup
Kel-tešup
MÍJarutte
∞ Šintip-
tešup
Hašija
∞ Marija
Huti-hamanna
Šuhun-zirira
Hutip-ukur
Šummi-
šenni
Šeštepi-ašu
Ehlutil
Zikte-
pukašu
(Zikte)
Hupitaja
∞ Uššen-
naja
Nirar-
tilla
Attamra
MÍMattija
Aittara
Janzi-
mašhu
Hilpiš-šuh
Punni-harpa
(Punnija)
Mat-tešup
∞ Allaiše
Kurpa-
zah
Akip-tilla
Dalluja
Tupki-
tilla
Figur 1.

Die andere Hälfte der Namen zerfällt in drei Gruppen:

Namen, die bereits K. Balkan, Kassitenstudien 1., pp. 41-90 = Liste 1, als kassitisch deklariert hat (Siglum ^{B} vor dem Namen); sieben Namen;

Namen, die zwar nicht in K. Balkans Liste 1 enthalten sind, aber Elemente aufweisen, die in seiner Liste 6 (Kassitisches Glossar, pp. 142-90) verbucht sind (Siglum + vor dem Namen); vier Namen;

Namen, die offensichtlich nicht ḫurritisch sind, bisher nicht als Kassitennamen anerkannt sind und auch keine Elemente aus Liste 6 enthalten (Siglum ^{o} vor dem Namen); sieben Namen.

Eine methodologische Vorbemerkung sei gestattet: wir massen uns nicht an, im Kassitischen besonders versiert zu sein, sondern stützen uns auf die Resultate K. Balkans. Das Nuzi-Onomastikon setzt sich zusammen aus Namen sehr verschiedenen Ursprungs: sumerisch, babylonisch, assyrisch, ḫurritisch, kassitisch. Einige Namen entstammen sicher uns unbekannten Sprachen (etwa aus dem Lulluäischen). Wenn wir nachstehend uns zugunsten einer kassitischen Etymologie einiger Namen aussprechen, so beruht unsere *vis argumenti* auf der schlichten Einsicht, dass innerhalb einer Kassitenfamilie auch mit einer kassitischen Tradition in der Namengebung zu rechen ist. Dass nur die Hälfte der Männernamen kassitisch sind, die andere Hälfte ḫurritisch, erklärt sich daraus, dass diese Familie in einer ḫurritischen Umwelt lebte und deren Söhne auch Ḫurriterinnen geheiratet haben. Dennoch nimmt der Prozentsatz kassitischer Namen von Generation zu Generation nicht etwa ab, sondern zeigt durchgängig Ausgewogenheit.

Wir bedauern sehr, dass wir uns im Widerspruch befinden zu J. A. Brinkman (RlA V/5-6, 1980, p. 469b—der Artikel wurde uns erst bekannt, nachdem dieser Aufsatz konzipiert war), der zum Problem schreibt: "It may be debated how many of the individuals who bore these names would have identified themselves as Kassite, since they seem to have been immersed in a generally undifferentiated Hurrian population. Where names of their parents or children are known, most of these relatives have Hurrian names (in fact, practically none have Kassite names); and no trace of Kassite clan or tribal structure has been detected in these families."

Im folgenden versuchen wir zu zeigen, dass die Familie Kizzuk ein kassitischer Clan war. Im Anschluss daran wollen wir darlegen, dass dieser Clan nicht ein isoliertes Phänomen war, sondern dass er in seinen Städten Temtena(š) und Šuriniwe zusammen mit anderen Kassiten lebte, die man auch mit diesem Namen bezeichnete (JEN 529:16). So gut es geht, werden wir dabei unterscheiden zwischen Gesichertem und weniger Sicherem. Mit dieser wichtigen Distinktion stellen wir uns, in der Methode und im Ergebnis, der Kritik der Fachkollegen, die einer weiteren Klärung des Kassitenproblems nur dienlich sein kann.

Wegen des zu geringen Anteils an weiblichen Personennamen beschränken wir uns auf die Männernamen. In der Schreibweise derselben folgen wir NPN und AAN I.

1. °Aittara (NPN 11a/b; AAN I 14b): NPN 198a ungedeutet. In JEN 87:32 findet sich das Graphem *I-in-zi-ma-aš-ḫu* DUMU *At-ta-ra* (Schreiber Šimika-atal, Room 10, Temtena). Die mit *A-i-* bzw. *Ai-it-* beginnenden Grapheme lassen sich schwer mit dem Axiom versöhnen, "dass das Kassitische keine Diphtonge kannte" (K. Balkan, p. 205). Ist Attara mit Nr. 2 zu verbinden?
2. °Attamra (AAN 37b), geschr. *At-ta-am-ra*, nur in HSS 19,6. Ist der Name doch in At-tamra zu zerlegen? **tamra* könnte dann Metathesis für *tarma* sein, das als Element in den kass. Namen Taramdi-Saḫ, Tarma-Ḫarbe und Tarwa-Saḫ (K. Balkan, p. 84) erscheint.
3. °Eḫluti(l) (NPN 42b; AAN I 41b), Name nur für den Sohn des Šeštepi-ašu bezeugt. Wird NPN 209a und 266b sowie von E. Laroche, RHA 34,76, ḫurritisch gedeutet. Dagegen lässt sich einwenden, dass *til*(*i*) ein sicheres kassitisches Element ist (K. Balkan, p. 183; vgl. aus Liste 1 Kaštil, Kaštilen-Saḫ, Kaštilyaššu, p. 61f. oder Tiliši-Saḫ, p. 84). Ferner erscheint *eḫl-* in Nuzi nur als *eḫli-*/*eḫel-* (mögliche Ausnahme: ᶠElḫum-alla). Schliesslich ist die Festschreibung der Lesung AḪ = *eḫ* bereits eine *petitio principii.* Die kassitische Filiation könnte die Argumente zugunsten eines ḫurritischen Ursprungs schwächen.
4. °Ḫilpiš-šuḫ (NPN 61a), nur in der Familie Kizzuk bezeugt. Element *ḫilpiš* nach NPN 216b "probably Hurrian," ebenso das Element *šuḫ* (NPN 258b). Wenn aber nicht alles täuscht, liegt ein kassitisches Element *šuḫ* vor in dem Namen ᴵ*Ma-ad-mi-šu-uḫ* HS 155:28′ = TMH NF 5,68:27′ (H. Petschow, Mittelbabylonische Rechts- und Verwaltungsurkunden der Hilprecht-Sammlung Jena, Berlin 1974, p. 48). Es wäre ausserdem noch in den Nuzi-Namen Kari-šuḫ, Šani-šuḫ, Šaten-šuḫ, Tain-šuḫ (s. unten Nr. 49) zu finden.
5. ᴮIanzi-mašḫu (NPN 66b; AAN I 65a), nur in der Familie Kizzuk bezeugt. Kassitischer Ursprung sowohl von NPN (219a/b und 233b) als auch von K. Balkan, p. 58 (*yanzi* + *mašḫu*, "der Gott ist König"), anerkannt.
6. °Kakki (NPN 78a; AAN I 75b), auch mit Geminatendissimilation Kanki, Kange. Der Name ist auch ausserhalb der Familie Kizzuk relativ weitverbreitet. NPN 222a "Hurrian?", zitiert jedoch A. L. Oppenheim, RHA V/33 (1938), p. 20, der **kakk-* für ḫurritisch hält. Bei Durchsicht der *sub kakk* gebuchten Namen gewinnt man den Eindruck, dass hier stärker zu differenzieren ist. So werden z. B. Kakkiše und Kakkuzzi NPN 306b bzw. 322a für eine akkadische Etymologie reklamiert. Dass das Kassitische ein Element *kak* hatte, geht schon aus *ka-ak-ri-me* in

dem Königsnamen Agum *kakrime* (K. Balkan, p. 45) hervor, wie immer auch *kakrime* zu zerlegen und zu deuten ist.

7. +Kiliške (NPN 85a; AAN I 81b), Grapheme *Ki-le-eš-ki*, *Ki-li-iš-ge* und mit Metathesis *Ki-li-ik-še* (HSS 13,366:37); als Anthroponym nur innerhalb der Familie Kizzuk belegt. NPN 227a sondert ein Element *kil* aus und subsumiert darunter die Namen Kilip-šeri, Kilip-tilili und Kiliške. Für *kil* wird ḫurritische Etymologie angenommen: "Perhaps phonetic variant of *kir* . . . See also *kel*." Aber auch K. Balkan listet p. 160f. die Elemente *kil* und *kili* als kassitisch. Das stärkste Argument zugunsten einer kassitischen Etymologie liefert das Frament eines Vertrags(?) des Assyrerkönigs Adad-nirari I. mit dem Kassitenkönig Kadašman-Turgu (geschrieben [I]*Ka-ta-áš-ma-du-ur-gu* LUGAL KUR *Kar-du-ni-aš*), VAT 15420, in Autographie von Fr. Köcher *apud* E. Weidner, ITN, Tf. 12, veröffentlicht, wo Z. 6′ das kassitische Toponym URU *Ki-le-eš-ḫi* (wir verdanken diesen wertvollen Hinweis Kazuko Watanabe) erwähnt wird. Die Varianz *Ki-le-eš-ki* (JENu 679)/*Ki-le-eš-ḫi* erklärt sich leicht nach K. Balkan, p. 208 (k/ḫ). Doch gibt es speziell für die Variante Kilikše Bildungsanalogien:

Ḫar + *a* + *k* + *ši* (p. 124 und 234; kassitischer Pferdename);
Kur + *u* + *k* + *še* + *Bugaš* (p. 125 und 163; Pferdename);
**Kil* + *i* + *k* + *še*

Für die Metathesis Kiliške/Kilikše Sei hier nur auf *Ša-qa-ra-at-ki* HSS 9,126: 9.r.2 gegenüber häufigerem *Ša-ka/qa-ra-ak-ti* (NPN 123a) verwiesen. Kiliške eingebettet in eine kassitische Genealogie, als Toponym gebraucht, durch kassitische Bildungsanalogien abgesichert: dagegen sind die Argumente zugunsten einer ḫurritischen Etymologie zu dünn, um ernstgenommen zu werden.

8. [B]Kirzam-pula (NPN 88b; AAN I 84a), nur innerhalb der Familie Kizzuk bezeugt. Sowohl NPN (228a und 246b) als auch K. Balkan, p. 64, Kirsam-bula, Kirsa(m)-bura: *kirsa* + *m* + *bula*, *kirsa* + (*m*) + *bura*, nehmen kassitischen Ursprung an; vgl. *kirsa/i/u* p. 161 und *pula* (mit l/r-Alternanz pura) p. 173, welche p. 175 als Varianten für *purna* aufgefasst werden.

8a. [B]Kirziia (Kirsii, NPN 88b; AAN I 84a) ist das Hypochoristikon zu Kirzam-pula (vgl. dazu K. Balkan, p. 44f.).

9. [B]Kizzuk (NPN 89b), ausser JEN 435:46 nur als Stammvater der Familie Kizzuk und als *dimtu*-Name bezeugt. NPN 228b *kizzuk* "If H., probably formed on *kizz*." Unter diesem Element (228a/b) liest man: "H.? Perhaps var. of *kezz* . . . though use with *ḫarpa* suggests K. affiliation." K. Balkan listet Kissuk p. 64 als kassitisch: *kissu* + *k*(?). Für das Suffix -(*u*)*k* vgl. p. 223, wo als Parallelen Sambi-ḫaruk, Ula-gisuk und Galduk zitiert werden: "Ein nominales Suffix, vielleicht kassitisch." Durch die genealogische Verknüpfung dieses Namens erhalten die Argumente, die

zugunsten einer kassitischen Etymologie sprechen, neuen Auftrieb. — Für Kizzi-ḫarpa und Kizzii̯a vgl. unten Nr. 21.

10. ^{B}Kurpa-zaḫ (NPN 92a), nur innerhalb der Familie Kizzuk bezeugt. Sowohl NPN (230b und 276a) als auch K. Balkan, p. 68, Kurpa-Saḫ, Gurb/pa-Saḫ: *kur* + *ba* + *Saḫ* (vgl. pp. 114, 146, 163, und 233) nehmen kassitischen Ursprung an. Nach dem kassitisch-akkadischen Vokabular Z. 4 ist *Sa-aḫ* = ^{d}*Šamaš*. Für Kupasa vgl. unten Nr. 45.

11. ^{B}Kuššii̯a (NPN 92b; AAN I 88a/b) wird sowohl von NPN (230b/231a) als auch von K. Balkan, p. 68, Kuššiya: *kuš* + *ši* + *ya* als kassitisch angesetzt. Wohl Hypochoristikon von Kušši-ḫarpe/Ḫušši-ḫarpe; für die k/ḫ-Alternanz vgl. pp. 152, 163.

12. ^{B}Punni-ḫarpa (NPN 118b), nur innerhalb der Familie Kizzuk bezeugt. Kassitisch nach NPN (214a und 246b/247a) und K. Balkan, p. 48, Bunni-Ḫarpa: *bunni* + *Ḫarba*, "Schützling des Ḫarba"; in der kassitischen Namenliste findet sich IV 1 die Gleichung ^{m}*Ú-lam-Ḫar-be* = ^{m}*Li-dan-*^{d}EN.LÍL, "Junges des Enlil"; vgl. CAD L 182a. (Die von K. Balkan, p. 3f., vorgebrachte Lesung und Gleichung Ḫarbu = ^{d}Anum nach Z.[1].49, lässt sich nach Kollation E. Sollberger, *apud* J. A. Brinkman, Materials and Studies for Kassite History, vol. I, Chicago 1976, p.151, n.11, nicht aufrechterhalten.)

12a. ^{B}Punnii̯a (NPN 118a/b; AAN I 112a) ist das Hypochoristikon zu Punni-ḫarpa, vgl. K. Balkan, p. 48, Bun(n)iya: *bunni* + *ya*.

13. $^{+}$Šati-kintar PN 126b; AAN I 121a), nur innerhalb der Familie Kizzuk bezeugt (Beleg HSS 19,96:2 fraglich). Das Element kintar ist in Nuzi mit den Elementen *šati-*, *turi-*, *wantar-* und *ziwir-* belegbar (NPN 227a). Davon sind *šadi-* und *ziwir-* eindeutig kassitisch (K. Balkan, p. 179 und p. 190). Im kassitischen Vokabular steht Z. 9 die Gleichung *Gi-dar* = ^{d}*Ninurta*. Dazu K. Balkan, p. 106: "Gidar kommt in Personennamen nicht vor. Jedenfalls kassitisch, darf vielleicht Identität mit dem Element kintar . . . der Nuzi-Namen vorgeschlagen werden." Ob man aber nicht den von K. Balkan, p. 78, zitierten Namen *Šad-in-da-ar* (E. Dhorme, Revue biblique 20 [1911], p. 277, Z. 3) in KUR-<*ki*>-*in-da-ar* emendieren sollte? Aus Šuriniwe selbst stammt der zweite Nuzi-Name mit eindeutig kassitischem Element *šadi-*: ^{14}*i+na šu-pa-al* GIŠ.SAR *ša* ^{15}[^{I}]*Ša-ti-gal-du* JEN 83:14-15 (Room 11, Archiv Kel-tešup S. Ḫutija). (Es ist uns nicht ganz einsichtig, warum NPN 126b—trotz des klaren kassitischen Kontexts—angezweifelt wird, ob Šadi-galdu überhaupt ein Personenname ist; vgl. dazu unten Nr. 46). Weitere kassitische Šati-Namen sind ^{m}KUR-*me-zi*, [^{m}KU]R-*me-zi-Bu-ga-aš (p. 78)*, ^{m}KUR-*dag-me*/*mi* (p. 77f.), wohl auch ^{m}*Ša-ad-maš-ḫu* (p. 78).

14. $^{+}$Šeštepi-ašu (NPN 132b; AAN I 126b), nur innerhalb der Familie Kizzuk bezeugt (auch JENu 620:23 liegt sicher Eḫluti(1) S.Šeštepi-ašu vor). Beruft man sich auf das Graphem *Še-iš-te-bi-ja-šu* (JEN 638:37), kann der Name ebenso gut in Šešteb-i̯ašu zerlegt werden. Nach dem

kassitisch-akkadischen Vokabular, Z. 34, ist *ya-šu* = *ma-a-tum*. Dieses Element zahlreicher Kassitennamen (K. Balkan, p. 155f.), *yašu*, hat die jüngeren Varianten *yaši* und *yaš*. — Das erste Element *šešteb* (mit den Varianten *šeštab* und *šištib*) wird von K. Balkan nicht registriert, ist aber—rein formal—zu dem Element *šintab* in *Ši-in-tab-ši-ni* AASOR 16,44:17.32 (Temtena) und HSS 14,64:22 sowie in *Ši-in-ta-Bu-ri-aš* HSS 19,129:4.9.16 zu stellen. In Analogie zu der Vokabularangabe *šim-di* = *na-da-nu* "geben" (K. Balkan, p. 4, Z. 46)—dessen Wurzel freilich, wie p. 180 gezeigt, *ši* oder *šim*/*šin* ist—müsste denn auch für **šešti* am ehesten eine Verbalwurzel **šeš* postuliert werden. Vielleicht liegt sie auch *šeššimur* (K. Balkan, p. 141) zugrunde.

15. °Šuḫun-zirira (NPN 135b), nur innerhalb der Familie Kizzuk bezeugt. Die Grapheme dieses Namens sind *Šu-ḫu-un-zi-ri-ri*, *Šu-ḫu-zi-ri-ru*, *Šu-ḫu-un-si-ri*, *Šu-ḫu-zi-ir-ra*, *Šu-uḫ-ni-zi-ru* und [*Šu-ḫu*]-*un*-[*z*]*i-ri-ra*. NPN 258a subsumiert diesen Namen unter das Element *šuḫ* und nimmt ḫurritischen Ursprung an. Wie oben Nr. 4 gezeigt, muss man hier doch stärker differenzieren: so kann für das Endelement *-šuḫ* eine kassitische Etymologie zumindest wahrscheinlich gemacht werden. Freilich darf man *šuḫ-* am Anfang und *-šuḫ* am Ende nicht einfach gleichsetzen. Die von E. Laroche, RHA 35,240, unter dem ḫurritischen Lemma *šuḫunni* zitierten drei Belege *šu-ḫu-u-un-ni-eš-š*[*a*] (—diese Stelle auch schon NPN 258b-), *šu-ḫu-un-na* und *šu-u-ḫu-un-na-ši* darf man sicher nicht ignorieren. Andererseits sucht man das Element *zirira*/*i*/*u* bzw. *zirra*/*i*/*u* im ḫurritischen Lexikon vergeblich. — Vielleicht lässt sich doch ein neuer Ansatz finden, wenn man das Graphem *Šu-uḫ-ni-zi-ru* (AASOR 16,37:36) mit dem Graphem [I]*Šu-uḫ-ni-ki-pa* in JENu 9 (vgl. NPN 135b) vergleicht. Das Element *-kipa* jedoch muss kassitisch sein, vgl. Alli-kipa, Awiš-kipa, Kuš-kipa, Tampuš-kipa. Ohne hier eine grosse Dokumentation auszubreiten, sei in Kürze vermerkt, dass Awiš-kipa aus Temtena stammt (HSS 16, 31:7.10) und der Name Kuš-kipa u.a. von dem berühmten Händler Kuš-kipa S. Kušše aus Kikkija/Kinkijawe (Texte: HSS 13,377; HSS 9,2; SMN 1435 = EN 9,319 = D. I. Owen, Loan Documents from Nuzu, pp. 106-7) getragen wird, der ähnlich wie sein ebenfalls kassitischer Kollege Pula-ḫali in Tupšarriniwe im Metallgeschäft tätig ist und deutliche kassitische Affiliationen aufweist (für Einzelheiten vgl. A. Fadhil, Studien zur Topographie der Provinzstädte des Königreichs Arrapḫe, Heidelberg 1978, Kikkijawe 2). Für das zweite Element (*zirira*/*zirra*) geben die Kassitennamen [m]*Ši-ri-ya* und eventuell [m]*Ši-ri-ša-áš* (K. Balkan, p. 77) sowie die Lexeme *sirpi* (p. 26 und 126), *sirnaḫ* (p. 138), vielleicht sogar *siriam* (AHw 1029b) gewisse Anhaltspunkte. Das noch problematische Element *-zir* in Minimzir, Mirizir und *minzir* (K. Balkan, pp. 111-14) muss zur Klärung von Šuḫun-zirira ebenfalls ins Spiel gebracht werden. Abschliessend sei wiederholt, dass der Name Š. in eine kassitische Genealogie verwoben ist.

16. °Tumšimana (NPN 157b), nur in der Familie Kizzuk bezeugt. Grapheme: *Du-um-ši-ma-na, Du-uš-ma-na, Tu-uš-ma-na*. Dieser Name wurde 1943 von den Professoren Paul Émile Dumont, Johns Hopkins University, und Julian H. Bonfante, Princeton University, für "Indo-Aryan" erklärt (NPN 194, 233a, 269a). Er hat alle "Ent-Arisierungen" der Zeit nach dem zweiten Weltkrieg überstanden (vgl. A. Kammenhuber, Die Arier im Vorderen Orient, p. 117f., wo der "arische" Rest an Nuzi-Namen zusammengestellt ist). Für eine ḫurritische Etymologie gibt es keinerlei Anhaltspunkte, wie eine Durchsicht des Glossaire de la langue hourrite (1976/77) zeigt. Aber wie wäre es mit *dušman*, Varianz (K. Balkan, p. 203, Wechsel von a und u) zu **dašman*? Das Element **dašman* gewinnen wir aus Kadašman, dem prädikativen Bestandteil vieler kassitischer Königsnamen (K. Balkan, pp. 58-60). Das Vokabular (Z. 39) bietet die Gleichung *ka-dáš-man* = *tu-kul-tum*; die Namenliste (Z. 9-10) scheint sie zu bestätigen. Über das Wort kadašman ist bereits viel geschrieben worden (vgl. K. Balkan, p. 156f.); festzustehen scheint jedenfalls, dass es wenigstens aus zwei Elementen besteht. Die Zerlegung *ka-dašman* und die Kombination mit *dušman* aus obigem Namen ist u.W. noch nicht vorgeschlagen worden. Belässt man Tumšimana/Dušmana in seinem angestammten Familienverband mit einer Tradition kassitischer Namengebung, wird man (erkenntnispsychologisch) eher geneigt sein, sich mit der Separation *ka-dašman* näher zu beschäftigen, als wenn man der herkömmlichen Methode anhängt und aus NPN *ad libitum*, ohne Rückgriff auf die Texte und deren Archivzusammenhänge, Namen herauspickt und sie in den Zettelkasten "Indo-Arisch" einordnet.

17. +Turi-kintar (NPN 160a; AAN I 152b), nur innerhalb der Familie Kizzuk bezeugt. Zum Element *kintar* vgl. bereits oben Nr. 13 (im Namen seines Sohnes Šati-kintar). Das Element *turi-* findet sich sowohl im Ḫurritischen als auch im Kassitischen. Es dient u.a. zur Bildung des Namens Turi-šenni, des Vaters des Puḫi-šenni, des Stammvaters der grossen ḫurritischen "Dynastie" (NPN 269b). Ob dieses *turi* identisch ist mit ḫurr. *turi* "unterer" (s. E. Laroche, RHA 35, 273), muss erst noch bewiesen werden. K. Balkan listet p. 148 ein Element duri mit Verweis auf *turi*; leider fehlt aber dieses Lemma p. 184f. Da Turi-kintar einmal (JEN 325:21) auch *Du-ur-ki-in-tar* geschrieben ist, kann eine formal-graphematische Übereinstimmung mit *Du-ur-mar-ti* (AASOR 16, 37:3.13.18.21, Temtena) nicht übersehen werden. Tur-marti hat aber eine saubere kassitische Etymologie (s. unten Nr. 47 und 51). Frau Kammenhuber nimmt (Die Arier im Vorderen Orient, Heidelberg 1968, p. 117f.) zwar noch eine ḫurritische Etymologie, NPN folgend, für Turi-kintar an; wir sind aber überzeugt, dass unsere Argumentation bei ihr ein offenes Ohr finden wird.

18. BZikte (NPN 177a), nur in der Familie Kizzuk bezeugt, Kurzform von 18a.

18a. ^{B}Zikte-pukašu (NPN 177a), nur in der Familie Kizzuk bezeugt, Vollform von Nr. 18. Der kassitische Ursprung dieses Namens ist bereits NPN 246b angedeutet. Sowohl Sikte (<*sik* + *te*) als auch Sikte/i-Bugašu (<*sik* + *te*/*i* + *Bugaš*) werden von K. Balkan, p. 76f. als kassitische Namen geführt. Für eine (weitausholende) Diskussion des Theonyms oder numinosen Begriffs Bugaš vgl. K. Balkan, pp. 102-4.

Fassen wir zusammen: Der ersten, gesicherten, Gruppe (^{B}) sind die Namen 5, 8, 8a, 9, 10, 11, 12, 12a, 18 und 18a zuzuordnen; der zweiten Gruppe ($^{+}$) die Namen 7, 13, 14, 16; der dritten Gruppe (^{o})—die besonders kontrovers ist—die Namen 1, 2, 3, 4, 6, 15 und 17. Für 3, 4, 6, 15 und 17 konnten Anhaltspunkte zugunsten einer kassitischen Etymologie ermittelt werden. Für alle achtzehn Namen gilt: sie stammen aus einer nachweislich kassitischen Familie.

Leben die Nachkommen des Kizzuk nun in den Städten Temtena(š), Šuriniwe und Purulliwe "immersed in a generally undifferentiated Hurrian population" (RlA V 469b)? Gibt es irgendwelche Hinweise darauf, dass sie sich als Kassiten "fühlten"? Aufschluss darüber gibt JEN 529 (aus Room 11, Dossier Šuriniwe):

Vs	1	12 ANŠE ŠE^{MEŠ} *ša* ⌜*A*⌝-[*ri-i*]*p-e-en-ni*
	2	*a-na* ^{Id}IM-LUGAL *i*[+*n*]*a-an-din*
	3	12 ANŠE ŠE *ša* KI.MIN *a*+*n*[*a*]
	4	^{I}*Ka-an-ge i*+*na-an-din*
	5	12 ANŠE ŠE *ša* KI.MIN *a*+*na*
	6	^{I}*Ut-ta-zi-na i*+*na-an-din*
	7	12 ANŠE ŠE *ša* KI.MIN *a*+*n*[*a*]
	8	^{I}*Zi*-⌜*il*⌝-*te-šup i*[+*na-an-din*]
	9	12 ANŠE ŠE *ša* KI.M[IN *a*+*n*]*a*
	10	^{I}*A-bi-lu i-na-an*-[*din*]
	11	12 ANŠE ŠE *ša* KI.M[IN] ⌜*a*+*na*⌝
Rd	12	^{I}*Ḫé-ša-al-li i-na-an-din*
Rs	13	*ma-ḫi-iṣ pu-ti* ŠE^{MEŠ} [ ]
	14	^{I}*Ge-el-te-šup ù* ^{I}*Še-ka-a*[*r-te-šup*]
	15	*ù* ^{I}*Ḫé-ša-al-li*
	16	*an-nu-tu*$_4$ ŠE^{MEŠ} *i*+*na* KUR *Ku-u*[*š-š*]*u*-[*uḫ*]-*ḫa-ú*
	17	*i*+*na-an-din*
	18	NA$_4$ ^{I}*Ge-el-te-šup* NA$_4$ ^{I}*Ḫe-ša-al-li*
	19	NA$_4$ ^{I}*Še-ka-ar-te-šup*

Kel-tešup, Ḫešalli und Šekar-tešup fungieren als *māḫiṣ pūti*, "Bürgen," für sechs Personen, denen sie je 12 Imēru Gerste des Arip-enni ausgeben. Z. 16-17 kann nur dahin verstanden werden, dass mit *annûtu* die drei Bürgen und Verteiler, mit *māt Kuššuḫḫājū* die sechs Empfänger der Gerste gemeint sind.

Vier der in JEN 529 genannten Personen finden wir wieder in der Liste JEN 514 (ebenfalls aus Room 11, Šuriniwe):

Vs 1 [^{1}*Qar-ti*]-*ja* [DU]MU *E-ni-ja*
2 [^{1}*Ku-pa-ar-ša*] DUMU *Ur-ku-ti*
3 [^{1}*Túl*]-*bi-še-ni* DUMU DINGIR-*ma*-ŠEŠ-*ḫi*
4 ^{1}*Ú-an-tar-ki-in-tar* DUMU *Pal-te-šup*
5 ^{1}*Ḫé-šal-li* DUMU *Pal-te-šup*
6 ^{1}*Pu-ḫi-še-ni* DUMU *Te-ḫi-ja*
7 ^{1}*Ta-ku-ja* DUMU *Dub-bi-na-bi*
8 ^{1}*Ki-ir-za-am-pu-la*
9 ^{1}*A-kip-til-la* DUMU *A-ri*!-*pu-um-bi*
10 ^{1}*Ú-na-a+a* DUMU *E-ge-ge*
11 ^{1}*Aḫ-wa-qar* DUMU *Ši-mi-qa-tal*
12 ^{1}*Ur-ḫi-ja* DUMU ^{d}IM-*ni-šu*
13 ^{1}*Ar-te-e-a* DUMU *Šu-pu-ki-ja*
14 ^{1}*A-bi*-DINGIR DUMU *A-ri*!-*pu-um-bi*
Rd 15 ^{1}*Še-eš-wi-ja* DUMU *Ta-a+a*
Rs 16 ^{1}*Ma-at-te-e-a* DUMU *Ur-ku-ti*
17 ^{1}*Te-eš-šu-ja* DUMU *Ṣíl-lí-mar-ta*!
18 ^{1}*Qa-an-ge* DUMU *Du-um-ši-ma-na*
19 ^{1}*Ku-a-ri* DUMU *A-ki-ja*
20 ^{1}*Ši-ri-in-ta* DUMU *Šúk-ri-ja*
21 ^{1}*Pu-ru-sa* DUMU DINGIR-*ni-šu*
22 ^{1}*Eḫ-lu-ti* DUMU *Še-eš-te-bi-a-šu*
23 ^{1}*Še-qar-te-šup* DUMU *Wa-an-tar-ki-tar*

(Kollationen: Z. 9 NPN 29b; Z. 14 ebd.; Z. 17 NPN 178a.)

Konkordanz zwischen JEN 529 und JEN 514: JEN 529:4 = JEN 514:18; JEN 529:10 = JEN 514:14 (vgl. 9); JEN 529:12 (wohl = 15.18) = JEN 514:5; JEN 529:14-19 = JEN 514:23. Mitglieder der Familie Kizzuk (vgl. Stammbaum Fig. 1) sind: Kel-tešup JEN 529:14; Kirzam-pula JEN 514:8; Kange JEN 514:18; Eḫluti JEN 514:22.

Von Puḫi-šenni S. Teḫija (JEN 514:6), der u.a. die Zeugenliste von JEN 477:22 (Archiv Kel-tešup, Room 11, Dossier Šuriniwe) anführt, wissen wir aus HSS 5,53 (SMN 1353, Room A 34; vgl. G. Dosch, Die Texte aus Room A 34 des Archivs von Nuzi, Nr. 63, S. 94f.), dass er ein Kassitenmädchen geheiratet hat. Er. tritt in einem Prozess zwischen Akaja (=Akawatil) S. Elli und dessen Schwager Kinni S. Izuzaja als Zeuge auf und erklärt: "Ja, ich habe ^{f}Ḫaluja dem Akaja als *kallatu* gegeben. ^{f}Azena, die Mutter der Ḫaluja, ist mir Ehefrau und meine Ehefrau ^{f}Azena hat mir (die Tochter) ^{f}Ḫaluja geboren. Ich habe ^{f}Azena aus dem Kassitenlande herausgeführt und ihr Bruder Kinni hat sie mir überdies zur Ehe gegeben" (Z. 15b-26). Auf Grund der Information aus HSS 5,53 sind wir darum auch berechtigt, HSS 16,391:8-9 ^{1}*Pu-ḫi-še-en-ni-ša* UR.[U

Šu-ri-ni-we] 9 1 DAM-*sú* *Ku-uš-š*[*u-uḫ-ḫa-ú*] zu ergänzen. Aus Z. 6 ebendieses Textes geht hervor, dass es kein Einzelfall war.

Wie ein Blick auf JEN 514 zeigt, koexistierten im Šuriniwe zur Zeit des Kel-tešup S. Ḫutija Babylonier (Aḫ(u)-waqar, Abī-ilu sowie die Patronyme Ilum-ma-aḫī, Adad-nīšu und Ila-nīšu) neben Ḫurritern (Puḫi-šenni, Akip-tilla, Urḫija, Mat-teja, Teššuja) und Kassiten. Das Auffällige ist nur, dass—im Gegensatz zu anderen Gemeinwesen des Königreichs Arrapḫe—sich in den Städte Temtena(š), Šuriniwe und Purulliwe ein auffallend hoher Prozentsatz von Kassiten aufhält. Ohne den Untersuchungen Abdulilah Fadhils über die genannten Orte vorgreifen zu wollen, seien im folgenden weitere Anthroponyme (in Auswahl) behandelt, die aus Texten der Rooms 10, 11, 12 stammen.

Beschränken wir uns zunächst auf jene männlichen Personennamen der Rooms 10-12, die auch von K. Balkan als kassitisch anerkannt sind. Wo angängig, werden auch kurz die Tätigkeitsbereiche dieser Personen angegeben:

19. ᴮḪašuar, Vater des Teḫip-tilla (JEN 321:64, Zeugenliste). K. Balkan, p. 55, fasst Ḫašuar als lautliche Variante zu *ḫaš-mar* = *ka-su-su* "Falke" im Vokabular (Z. 43; vgl. CAD Ḫ 142b; K 257a) auf. (*Obiter* sei verwiesen auf Ḫašuar, den Ehemann der ᶠTulpunnaja aus Temtenaš, und auf Ḫašuar, S. Šimika-atal, aus der dimtu Arikkani, die zu Lubdi gehört. Lubdi aber ist Grenzstadt zwischen Arrapḫa und *māt* Kuššuḫḫe, das Tor nach dem kassitischen Babylonien.)

20a. ᴮIpša-ḫalu S. Ḫutiia (JEN 541:3.6.12.19; Schuldner des Kel-tešup S. Ḫutija). K. Balkan deutet (p. 56) Ibs/ša-Ḫalu als Metathesis von *iš* + *i* + *b* + *Ḫalu* (vgl. Išib-Ḫalu, p. 57). Für die Göttin Ḫala/i/u, die im Vokabular Z. 10 mit ᵈGula geglichen wird, vgl. K. Balkan, p. 106. Die Namenliste bietet IV 2 (p. 2) ferner die Gleichung ᵐ*Me-li-Ḫa-li* = ᵐ*Amēl-*ᵈ*Gu-la* (NPN 213a und 220a wird für Ipša-ḫalu noch eine ḫurritische Etymologie angenommen.)

20b. ᴮIpša-ḫalu S. Akip-tura (JEN 320:8.10; *titennūtu*-Gläubiger von Mat-tešup und Kurpa-zaḫ S.e Ḫilpiš-šuḫ).

21. ᴮKizzi-ḫarpa, Vater des Tai-tešup und des Alippija (passim, s.NPN 89a/b). Nach K. Balkan, p. 64, kassitisch *kissi* + *Ḫarpa*/*Ḫarbe*; vgl. oben Nr. 9 zu Kizzuk und Nr. 12 zu Punni-ḫarpa. Der Kurzname *Ki-iz-zi-ja* begegnet als Vater des Zeugen Ḫašip-tilla in dem *ṭuppi šīmti* des Ḫupitaja S. Ḫašija HSS 19, 6:34 (Room A 14; Dossier Šuriniwe).

22. ᴮNinkirap-zaḫ S. Partasua (JEN 666:[26] und 671:6, jeweils Zeuge im Prozess für Tarmija und Ḫutija, S.e Kuššija). K. Balkan, p. 74, zerlegt *nimgir* + *a* + *b* + *Saḫ*; vgl. Namenliste IV 7 ᵐ*Nim-gi-ra-bi-Saḫ* = ᵐ*E-ṭé-ru-*[ᵈ*Šamaš*] (p. 3) sowie Vokabular Z. 41 (p. 4), *nim-gi-ra-ab* = *e-ṭé-rum* "retten." Für seinen Vater Partasua nahm NPN 243b, unter

Berufung auf E. A. Speiser, eine indogermanische Etymologie an, welche A. Kammenhuber (Die Arier im Vorderen Orient, S. 116) als “wertlos” erklärt.

23a. ^{B}Purei̯a (NA$_4$ ^{I}⸢*Pu-re*⸣*-e* : DI.KU$_5$ JEN 666:25:26, Richter in Šuriniwe). K. Balkan, p. 48, fasst diesen Kurznamen als *bure* + *e*(*y*)*a*; p. 174 wird *pure* als Nuzi-Variante zu *pura* + *purra* < *purna* erklärt. (Der Name Purra ist für Purulliwe bezeugt: ^{I}*Pur-ra* [O] ^{I}*Dup-ku-ra-aš-še* ^{I}Zi$^{?}$-⸢x⸣-ti$^{?}$ 2 DUMU^{MEŠ}-*šu* ^{2} ^{MÍ}*Ḫa-lu-*[*j*]*a* 4 NAM.LÚ.⸢LÚ⸣ *ša* ^{I}*Pur-ra* . . . ^{4}. . . *š*[*a* URU *P*]*u-ru-ul-l*[*i-we*] HSS 15,41:1-4, D 3).

23b. ^{B}Purei̯a (ŠU *Pu-re-e-a* [DUB.SAR] HSS 19,6:37). Schreiber des oben Nr. 21 erwähnten *ṭuppi šīmti*, das die einzige von ihm auf uns gekommene Tafel ist (mündliche Mitteilung von Paola Negri Scafa).

24. ^{B}Purnapai̯a, Vater des Ḫanatu (JEN 255:45) wird von K. Balkan, p. 49, als hybride Bildung *burna* + *paya* (hurrisch) erklärt. Zur Diskussion von *purna* vgl. p. 175; für *pai̯a* vgl. NPN 242a.

25. ^{B}Purni-mašḫu (NPN 119a), S. Tain-šuḫ (Belege s. unten Nr. 49). Von K. Balkan, p. 50, als *burni* + *mašḫu* bzw., p. 51, als *burra* + *mašḫu*, “Schützling des Gottes” kassitisch erklärt.

26. ^{B}Širinta S. Šukrii̯a (JEN 514:20; vgl. JEN 340:17.19) ist nach K. Balkan, p. 82, Kurzname *šir* + *i* + *n* + *da* (s. auch pp. 147, 152, 169, 181, 232) und von dem Pferdenamen *Ši-ri-in-du* (p. 126) nicht zu trennen.

27. ^{B}Šuta-ḫali, Vater des Tarwa-zaḫ (Nr. 28) besteht nach K. Balkan, p. 83, aus *šu* + *da* + *Ḫali* (s. dazu oben Nr. 20), vgl. p. 182.

28. ^{B}Tarwa-zaḫ S. Šuta-ḫali (JEN 56:21.32 und 241:24.30, Zeuge in Landtauschurkunden des Kiliške und des Kuššija) wird von K. Balkan, p. 84, zu dem BE 14, 41:3 bezeugten Namen ^{m}*Tar-ma-Ḫar-be* gestellt und p. 183 in dic Elcmcntc *tar* + *ma*/*wa* zerlegt; zu *Saḫ* s. oben Nr. 10.

29. ^{B}Uttaz-zina S. Pui-tae (JEN 529:6 Empfänger von 12 *Imēru* Gerste und explicite als Kassit, Z. 16, bezeichnet; oft als Zeuge, s. NPN 168a) wird von K. Balkan, p. 83, Tamta-zina gelesen und in *tam* + *da* + *zina* aufgelöst; parallele Bildung zu ^{m}*Tam-da*/*di-Saḫ* aus mB Texten. Für die Elemente vgl. pp. 183, 187f., 213, 231. NPN 273b und 276b wird für diesen Namen eine indo-arische Etymologie vorgelegt (vgl. A. Kammenhuber, Die Arier im Vorderen Orient, S. 118). Auffälligerweise hält auch B. Landsberger, JCS 8 (1954) 129b, sowohl an der Lesung *Uta-* als auch an der “indoarischen” Etymologie fest (vgl. A. Kammenhuber, S. 173). Durch JEN 529:6.16 als auch durch die Einbindung des Namens in die Kassitenpopulation der Stadt Šuriniwe ist jedoch eine ganz neue Basis für die Deutung dieses Namens geschaffen.

30. ^{B}Ukin-zaḫ (JEN 143:6). Dieser Name ist in den Archiven Rooms 10-12 als Anthroponym nicht bezeugt, kommt jedoch in dem Brief JEN 143 als Toponym vor: ^{1}*um-ma* ^{I}*Ḫu-ta-an-ni-a-pu-ma* (vgl. JEN 321:63)

[2]DUMU *Tar-mi-til-la* [3]10 SU KÙ.BABBAR[MEŠ] *ši-im-šu* [4]*ša* ANŠE.KUR.RA [5]*ša ḫu-ub-ti* [6]*ša* URU *Ú-ki-in-za-aḫ-we* [7]*a-šar* [1]*Ge-el-te-šup* [8]DUMU *Ḫu-ti-ja* [9]*el-qè-mi* [Rs 10]NA4 [1]*Ḫu-ta-an-ni-a-pu.* K. Balkan listet diesen Namen, p. 85, als kassitisch Ukin-Saḫ: *ug* + *i* + *n* + *Saḫ* (für die Elemente vgl. pp. 152, 169, 185, 232 sowie NPN 271a und 276b).—Ob URU Ukin-zaḫ-we identisch ist mit der *dimtu ša Ukim-zaḫ*/*Ukin-zaḫ*, lässt sich nicht mit Sicherheit ausmachen; für letztere (bezeugt in JEN 243:6-8, JEN 247:2-3 und JENu 390:5-6, Dossier Unapšewe) und ihren Eponym *Ú-ki-in-za-aḫ* JEN 528:13 bzw. *Ú-ki-za-aḫ* JEN 52:33, vgl. A. Fadhil, Studien zu den Provinzstädten des Königsreichs Arrapḫe (Diss. Heidelberg 1978) Unapšewe 3.2 Nr. 13. Die Ergänzung der Z. 6 des *ṭuppi mārūti* JENu 390 geht auf eine Ergänzung A. Fadhils vom 26.12.1974 zurück, die, verbunden mit einer prosopographischen Analyse der Zeugenliste, die Zuweisung von JENu 390 an das Dossier Unapšewe erst ermöglichte.

31. [B]Zanunu, Vater des Akkul-enni und des Ekeke (JEN 666:32; 671:14 — JEN 140:21; 602:28) ist zwar von K. Balkan nicht in die Liste der Personennamen aufgenommen worden, kann aber kaum von dem kass. Pferdenamen *Sa-nu-na* bzw. *Sa-nu-na-aš* (p. 126) getrennt werden.

Ausser diesen dreizehn kassitischen Namen (Nr. 19-31), die alle aus den Archiven der Rooms 10-12 erhoben sind und demnach mit Sicherheit nach Temtena(š), Šuriniwe und Purulliwe zu lokalisieren sind, die drei Städte, in denen die Kassitenfamilie des Kizzuk sesshaft war, es zu Ansehen und Wohlstand gebracht hat, finden sich in diesen Archiven noch eine Reihe ungedeuteter Personennamen, deren Herkunft überprüft werden sollte. Die folgende Liste erhebt selbstverständlich keinen Anspruch auf Vollständigkeit. Die Aufnahme eines Namens will nicht besagen, dass damit dessen kassitische Etymologie behauptet wird.

32. °Alippiia S. Kizzi-ḫarpa (NPN 19a; für das Patronym s. oben Nr. 22).
33. °Ḫalippa (NPN 50b). Aus methodologischen Gründen sei hier das Graphem *Ḫa-li-pa-a*/ *Ḫa-li-ib-ba* von dem Graphem *Ḫa-li-pa-a* getrennt, da nur letzteres aus Rooms 10-12 bezeugt ist, und zwar AN.ZA.KÀR ša [1]*Ḫa-li-pa-a* JEN 85:11 zur Bezeichnung einer *dimtu* von Šuriniwe.
34. °Ḫašipu (JEN 512:7.18): Name eines Zeugen im Prozess um die *dimtu* Kizzukwe. Da er innerhalb des Nuzi-Onomastikons hapax ist, steht nichts im Wege, JEN 512:7 [1]*Ḫa-lim-pu ša* URU *Ḫa-aš-lu-ni-a* (und nicht [1]*Ḫa-ši-pu*, wie NPN 58b) zu lesen. Der Name könnte so mit Nr. 33 verbunden werden.
35. °Ḫamtiše (JEN 512:5.22), Zeuge wie Nr. 34, stammt aus URU Eteš-šenniwe. Der Name könnte das Element *ḫamat* (K. Balkan, p. 149f.) enthalten.
36. °Karrutti (JEN 29:43.45), in Zeugenliste, Room 12, Dossier Temtenaš.

37. °Kip-iššuḫri, Vater des Akkul-enni und des Šukrija (JEN 255:51.52, Room 10, Temtena; AASOR 16, 30:27, C 120, Archiv der ^{f}Tulpunnaja, Temtena). AAN I 83b ist dieser Name noch als Patronym eines Pazazi zitiert; der Beleg MAH 15.867:2 ist uns unzugänglich und daher nicht lokalisierbar. NPN 221a hält den Namen für "Hurrian in view of the elements used with it." Vgl. aber oben Nr. 4 Ḫilpiššuḫ.
38. °Kuparša (vgl. NPN 91a mit den Graphemen *Ku-pa-ar-ša*, *Ḫu-pa-ar-ša*, *Ku-bar-ša* und *Ku-ba-ar-ša*), jeweils als Zeuge in Urkunden des Dossiers Šuriniwe aus Room 11 (JEN 644, Room 10 Fehler für 11?). NPN 230a konstatiert: "Interchange of initįal k and ḫ suggests non-Hurrian origin": vgl. oben Nr. 11 Kuššija/Ḫuššija und K. Balkan, p. 208 (Wechsel von k und ḫ).
39. +Nazija (JEN 218:18 und 255:46.58, S. Šešwaja), in Zeugenliste, Room 10, Dossier Temtena. Sicherlich Hypochoristikon eines kassitischen Namens Nazi + GN; vgl. K. Balkan, pp. 72-74; Namenliste I 53 und IV 11.12; Vokabular Z. 38: *na-zi* = *ṣil-lum* "Schatten"; dazu K. Balkan: "Wir haben keinen Grund, der Erklärung nazi als *ṣillu* . . . und dem echt kassitischen Ursprung dieses Wortes zu misstrauen" (p. 169).
40. +Pakka (NPN 110a) Vater von Enna-mati, Unnuka und Zilija; alle NPN 110a zitierten Texte aus Temtena. Zu vergleichen ist der kassitische Name ^{m}*Pa-ak-ki-Saḫ*, den K. Balkan, p. 76, in *pakki* + *Saḫ*, p. 172, in *pak-ki-Saḫ* fraktioniert.
41. +Parpi S. Zike(JEN 600:24), Zeugenliste Room 11, Šuriniwe. Vgl. auch URU *Bar-bi* HSS 14, 190:3; 204:10-11; 207:10; URU *Bar-bi-we* HSS 14, 192:2. Dieses Toponym ist in der Nähe von URU Eteššenniwe (HSS 14, 204:7) zu lokalisieren, das nach JEN 135:8; 184:3; 321:29 in der Nachbarschaft der *dimtu* Kizzukwe lag.
42. +Pinkeia (NPN 114b) in ^{I}*En-šúk-rù* DUMU *Bi-in-ge-e* JENu 729:2 und *E-na-šúk-ru* DUMU <*Bi*>*-in-ge-ja* JENu 859 (beide Texte aus Temtena); vgl. die kassitischen Pferdenamen *Pi-kan-di* und *Pi-ik-ka-an-du* (K. Balkan, p. 125 und 172).
43. +Pununni JEN 315:9 (Feld) *i+na* KASKAL *ša* AN.ZA.KÀR *Pu-nu-un-ni* (Room 10, Temtena); da ohne Personenkeil geschrieben, nicht sicher, ob Personenname; vgl. aber die kassitischen Elemente *pun*(*n*)*a*/*pun*(*n*)*i* (K. Balkan, p. 173) und *nuna* in Finalposition (p. 171).
44. +Pur-purutta (NPN 119a): ^{I}*Ši-il-wa-a+a* DUMU *Pu-ur-pu-ru-ut-ta* JEN 592:2 (Room 11, Purulliwe, *šaṭir* Šuriniwe), danach ergänzt [IGI *Ši-il-wa-a+a* DUMU] *Pu-ur-pu-ru-ut-ta* JENu 620:26 (Šuriniwe). Die Namensform des Patronyms lautet jedoch nach JEN 644:27.33 (Šuriniwe) *Pu-ur-šu-ru-ut-t*[*a*] bzw. *Pu-*⸢*ur*⸣*-*⸢*šu*⸣*-ru-u*[*t-ta*], vgl. NPN 119b. Zu denken ist an das Toponym Burrattaš (K. Balkan, p. 93) und natürlich an den Gottesnamen Marut(t)aš (p. 110f.). Die beiden (durch Personenidentität!) unlösbar miteinander verbundenen Grapheme lassen sich u.E. nur durch eine Emendation in JEN 644:27 auf einen Nenner bringen. Wir schlagen

darum die Lesung *Pu-ur-*Ma[!]*-ru-ut-t*[*a*] vor (in Z. 33 ist das Zeichen halb zerstört).

45. +Purusa (NPN 119b; AAN I 112b): [I]*Pu-ru-sa* DUMU DINGIR*-ni-šu* JEN 514:21 (Šuriniwe); [I]*Pu-ra-sa* AASOR 16,38:37 (C 120, Temtena). Für diesen Namen wurde von J. H. Bonfante, NPN 247b, eine "indo-arische" Etymologie vorgeschlagen. Wie bei A. Kammenhuber, Die Arier im Vorderen Orient, S. 117, Anm. 370, zu erfahren, wurde die Ableitung von altindisch *púruṣa-* "Mann" sogar von M. Mayrhofer, IIJ 4 (1960) 147[76] und 7 (1964) 210[14], abgelehnt. Für die Etymologisierung dieses Wortes darf man jedoch nicht irgendeines der sieben bisher belegten Grapheme auswählen, sondern muss sie im Ensemble evaluieren. Auffällig ist die nuzologisch seltene Vertretung des Lautes /*sa*/ durch das Zeichen *sa*, und die Parallele zu dem PN Kupasa (NPN 91a, AAN I 87a) springt sofort in die Augen:

(a) *Pu-ra-sa*	(b) *Pu-ra-a-sa*	(c) *Pu-ú-ra-a-sa*
Ku-ba-sa	*Ku-ba-a-sa*	*Ku-ú-ba-a-sa*
Ku-pa-sa		

Die Grapheme (d) *Ku-ú-ba-sa* (e) *Ku-pa-sa-a* (f) *Ku-up-pa-sa* sind vielleicht nur zufällig ohne Entsprechung bei Purasa. Die Vokalisierung mit *-u-* in der mittleren Silbe findet sich nur in (g) *Pu-ru-sa*, auch "gebrochen" (h) *Pu-ru-a-sa* und (i) *Pu-ru-ú-za*. Letzteres Graphem stimmt in der Schreibung der letzten Silbe überein mit (j) *Ku-pa-za*. Von diesem Graphem ist es nur noch ein kleiner Schritt nach (k) *Ku-ba-za-aḫ* HSS 13,349:92 = G. Wilhelm, Das Archiv des Šilwa-Teššup, Heft 2, Nr. 6, Z. 104 (nach Manuskript zitiert, das der Verf. K. Deller überlassen hat). Beurteilt man die verschiedenen Grapheme beider offensichtlich parallel gebauter Namen ohne ideologische Apriorismen, wird man in ihnen unschwer nuzianisch deformierte Lautformen der bekannten kassitischen Namen Burna-Saḫ und Kurpa-Saḫ (die allerdings in ihren 'Plene'-Schreibungen ebenfalls nur aus Nuzi-Texten bezeugt sind, vgl. K. Balkan, p. 50 und 68) erkennen.

46. [B]Šati-kaltu (NPN 126b; vgl. oben Nr. 13). Die irrige Position, die NPN 225a bezogen wurde, hat bereits A. L. Oppenheim, AfO 12, S. 32, Anm. 13, berichtigt. Da /*galdu*/ in diesem Namen der einzige Beleg für die Selbstbezeichnung der Kassiten (vgl. K. Balkan, pp. 131-32) aus Šuriniwe ist, soll die Wichtigkeit dieser Attestation hier besonders hervorgehoben werden.

47. +Šattu-marti (NPN 127a; AAN I 121b): [I]*Ša-ad-du-mar-ti* DUMU *E-ni-iš-ta-e* JEN 124:25 (Room 12, Temtena); [I]*Ša*[!]*-at-tu-mar-di* DUMU *E-*[*ni-iš-ta-e*] AASOR 16,25:27 und *Ša-ad-du-mar-ti* DUMU *E-ni-iš-ta-e* AASOR 16,32:21 (beide Texte C 120, Temtena), identisch mit dem Vater von *Dub-bi-ja* DUMU *Ša-ad-du-mar-ti* JEN 255:43 (Room 10,

Temtena). *Marti* ist nach K. Balkan, p. 165, Nuzi-Variante des kassitischen Götternamens Maruttaš, p. 110f., und begegnet noch in dem Namen Tur-marti (Nr. 51). Für das Element *šattu* vgl. die Diskussion oben Nr. 13.

48. +Šeršiia (NPN 132a; AAN I 126a/b), Schreiber des Grossteils des Dossiers Temtena(š) (AASOR 16,23.26.31.45; JEN 124.198.218.315. 600.604; JENu 854; freundliche Mitteilung von Paola Negri Scafa). Der Name scheint ein Hypochoristikon von der Basis *širiš* (K. Balkan, p. 181) zu sein, die Namen des Typs ᵐ*Ši-ri-iš-ti-Ši-ḫu* (p. 82) zugrundliegt. Die von NPN 256 versuchte ḫurritische Etymologie könnte sich auf *še-er-še* und *še-er-šu-un-(pal-la)*, RHA 35, 228 stützen; da aber Šeršija Schreiber in der Kassitenstadt Temtena ist, scheint die kassitische Ableitung nicht ganz ohne Chance zu sein.

49. +Tain-šuḫ (NPN 144a; AAN I 137a), *Pur-ni-ma-aš-ḫu* DUMU *Ta*!*-in-šu-uḫ* JEN 85:30; *Pur-ni-ma-aš-ḫu* [DUMU *T*]*a-i-in-šu-uḫ* JEN 219:23; *Pu-ur-ra-ma-aš-ḫu* [D]UMU ⌜*Ta*⌝*-i-in-*⌜*šu-uḫ*⌝ JEN 616:31; [ᴵ*Pu-ur-ra-ma-aš-ḫu* D]UMU *Ta-i-in-šu-uḫ* JEN 666:23; ᴵ*Pu-ur-ra-ma-aš-ḫu* DUMU *Ta-i-in-šu-uḫ* JEN 671:3 (alle Texte Room 11, Šuriniwe). Zu Burra-mašḫu/Burni-mašḫu (K. Balkan, p. 50 und 51); s. oben Nr. 25; für das Patronym ist eine kassitische Etymologie noch nicht vorgeschlagen worden. Wie aber oben Nr. 4 gezeigt, wird man doch mit einem kassitischen Element *šuḫ* zu rechnen haben. Konsequenzen für die frühe Siedlungsgeschichte der Stadt URU Tainšuḫwe müssten daraus gezogen werden.

50. +Takuški (NPN 145b): *El-ḫi-ip-til-la* DUMU *Ta-gu-uš-ki* JEN 218:17 und 315:21 (beide Texte Room 10, Temtena). Mit diesem Graphem ist zu vergleichen *Ta-gu-ḫi-iš* ⁹DUMU *Tu-ur-ma-ar-di* HSS 16, 458:9-10 in klarer kassitischer Filiation. Man könnte Anschluss an das Element *takuša* (K. Balkan, p. 183) versuchen, wie es in dem Namen ᵐ*Ta-ku-ša-Ḫar-be* (p. 83) vorliegt. Strukturell ist eine Analogie zu der Bildung des Namens Kiliške (s. oben Nr. 7) augenfällig.

51. +Tur-marti (NPN 160b; AAN I 152b): ᴵ*E-zu-ú-a* DUMU *Dur-mar-ti* JEN 342:45 (Room 11, Šuriniwe, *dimtu* Kizzukwe). Für das Element *marti* s. oben Nr. 46, für tur Nr. 16; für eine kassitische Filiation Nr. 50.

52. +Ulu-niki (NPN 163a): *A-ta-a+a* DUMU *Ú-lu-ni-ki* JEN 204:37 (Room 10, Temtena). Die Trennung der Elemente wird NPN 163a und 271a als "Div. uncert." angegeben. K. Balkan, p. 85f., zählt eine Reihe von Namen auf, die mit den Elementen *Ula-*, *Ulam-* und *Ulan-* beginnen; dort könnte auch ein Element **ulun* angeschlossen werden.

53. +Wantar-kinta (Belege s. NPN 170b; AAN I 164b): der Name begegnete bereits oben JEN 514:23 als Patronym des Šekar-tilla. Das Element *kintar*, *kitar*, wurde oben Nr. 13 und 16 bereits mit dem kassitischen Theonym *Gi-dar* = ᵈ*Ninurta* in Verbindung gebracht. Schwierigkeiten

bereitet in der Tat das Element wantar, ob man dessen Anlaut nun mit *w-* oder mit *u-* ansetzt, weil "die Belege <*für*> den Nachweis des Halbvokales *w* im Kassitischen nicht ausreichen" (K. Balkan, p. 205) und auch die Vokalfolgen *u-a, u-i, u-e* am Wortanfang sich nicht nachweisen lassen (ebd.). Spirantisierung (**pantar* < **fantar*) lässt sich ebenfalls nicht nachweisen. So muss also, aus rein phonetischen Gründen, die Ableitung von *wantar-* offengelassen werden. Dennoch kann nicht ausgeschlossen werden, dass wegen ḫurritisch *wandi-* "droit" (RHA 35, 293f.) hier ein ḫurritisch-kassitisches Hybrid vorliegt.

54. +Zilli-marta (NPN 178a; AAN I 174b) in [I]*Te-eš-šu-ja* DUMU *Ṣíl-lí-mar-ta*[!] JEN 514:17 und *Te-eš-šu-ja* DUMU *Ṣí-il-li-mu-ur-ta* JEN 616:30 (beide Room 11, Šuriniwe). Sowohl *Marta* als auch *Murta* werden von K. Balkan als Nuzi-Varianten des kassitischen Gottesnamen Maruttaš verbucht (p. 165). Die Verbindung mit akkadischem *ṣilli* "Schatten, Schutz von" zeigt, dass auch Hybride dieser Art möglich sind.

Die Darstellung des kassitischen Onomastikons, soweit es sich aus den Archiven der Rooms 10, 11, 12 für die Städte Temtena, Šuriniwe, Purulliwe erheben lässt, sei hiermit abgeschlossen. Nicht unerwähnt darf bleiben, dass in Nuzi noch ein zweites, auf die Stadt Temtena(š) bezügliches Archiv geborgen wurde, und zwar in C 120. Es handelt sich um die Urkunden der *entu*-Priesterin [f]Tulpunnaja T. [f]Šeltunnaja und umfasst wenigstens dreissig Tafeln (AASOR 16,15-45). In ihren Zeugenlisten figuriert häufig Janzi-mašḫu S. Aittara, aber auch dessen Vater Aittara S. Šuḫun-zirira und Onkel Ḫilpiš-šuḫ S. Šuḫun-zirira. Ein Teil der Tafeln ist von dem Schreiber Šeršija geschrieben (s. oben Nr. 47). So kann das Archiv der [f]Tulpunnaja mit der 5. und 6. Generation der Familie Kizzuk (relativ) synchronisiert werden. Die Prosopographie dieser Tafeln unterscheidet sich nicht von jener der Rooms 10, 11, 12; der Anteil kassitischer Namen ist hier wie dort relativ hoch. [f]Tulpunnaja war verheiratet mit Ḫašuar, also einem Kassiten oder Träger eines kassitischen Namens (s. oben Nr. 19). Aber auch andere Namen wie *Ar-ta-mu-zi* (28:3), *A-wi-iš-ki-pa* (31:7), *Ḫa-ap-zi-la-ak-ku* (34:36), *I-la-ab-ri-ja-aš* (39:2.3), *Ši-in-tab-ši-ni* (44:17) lassen zumindest kassitischen Ursprung vermuten.

Doch zeigt nicht nur das cluster Temtena(š), Šuriniwe, Purulliwe eine Konzentration kassitischer Namen. Das in Room S 132 gefundene Archiv des Pula-ḫali und seiner Söhne, das A. Fadhil nach der Stadt Tupšarri(ni)we lokalisiert hat, weist deutlich kassitische (vgl. K. Balkan, p. 47, Bula-Ḫali) Deszendenz auf. Da sich das Haus Pula-ḫali auf den Metallhandel spezialisiert hatte (vgl. D. I. Owen, The Loan Documents from Nuzu, Dissertation, Brandeis University 1969, University Microfilms 70-12, 031, p. 44), könnten daraus bestimmte Schlüsse für die Handelsbeziehungen zwischen Arrapḫäern und Kassiten gezogen werden, zumal wenn man sich vergegenwärtigt, dass in der singulären Schenkungsurkunde TF_1 426 (IM 70985), gefunden in dem

Tupšarri(ni)we benachbarten Kurruḫanni, einem [LÚ]*ḫa-bi-ru* ⌜DAM.GÀR-*ri*⌝ *Ku-zu-uḫ-ḫe*, einem Zuwanderer, einem kassitischen Händler, vom Stadtrat, bestehend aus vierzehn Personen (darunter auch Pašši-tilla S. Pula-ḫali) die Riesenfläche von 30 *Imēru* Feld samt Häusern und Tennen überschrieben werden (Freundliche Mitteilung von A. Fadhil).

Seit einem Jahrzehnt versucht die Heidelberger Assyriologie das Phänomen Nuzi dadurch besser zu begreifen, dass die von Stadt zu Stadt variierenden gesellschaftlichen und ökonomischen Komponenten schärfer herausgearbeitet werden. Die Resultate dieser Methode lassen sich am ehesten als "Mikrohistorie" kleinster Einheiten, der Familien und Clans, der *dimātu* und der (Klein)städte charakterisieren, die sich nicht so ohne weiteres für die Universalgeschichte des Zweistromlandes in der Mitte des 2. vorchristlichen Jahrtausends nutzbar machen lässt. Punktuell ergeben sich aber bisweilen doch Anhaltspunkte für ein differenzierteres Bild des Spiels der Kräfte, in das Ḫurriter und Assyrer, Babylonier und Kassiten im Osttigrisland verwickelt waren. Herkunft und Aufstieg der Kassiten ist immer noch in undurchdringliches Dunkel gehüllt. Die dürftigen Informationen aus altbabylonischer Zeit (vgl. J. A. Brinkman, RlA V 466 und B. Groneberg, RGTC 3, 135-36, beide Arbeiten 1980) und die recht ungesicherte Quellenlage über die Anfänge der Kassitenherrschaft über Babylonien (vgl. RlA V 467) sollte eigentlich Anlass sein, die im Vergleich damit doch ergiebigeren Texte aus Nuzi, Arrapḫa und Kurruḫanni ganz systematisch zu untersuchen und historisch auszuwerten. Es wird sich dabei zeigen, dass dieses Quellenmaterial weit mehr an Informationen hergibt als eine blosse Bereicherung unserer Kenntnis des kassitischen Onomastikons. Wir hoffen, mit diesem Aufsatz einen neuen methodischen Ansatz gefunden zu haben, bitten um die Kritik der Fachkollegen und wünschen, dass Berufenere den Weg weitergehen. Dem Manne, dessen Autographien uns täglich vor Augen sind, sei dieser Beitrag in Dankbarkeit gewidmet.

Suprarational Legal Procedures in Elam and Nuzi

Tikva Frymer-Kensky
Ann Arbor, Michigan

The most important suprarational trial in the Ancient Near East was without question the river ordeal. It was not, however, the only such trial, and its very prominence has obscured the existence or interpretation of other procedures which also used divine means to settle legal disputes, but which should not be confused with the river ordeal. Three such institutions are drinking in Elam and Israel, and "lifting the gods" at Nuzi.

Drinking Trials

The existence of a water procedure in Elam has long been known, but the procedure itself has not been understood. The widely held view, most recently pronounced by Hirsch[1] and Klima[2], is that the Elamite texts show evidence of a river ordeal similar to that in Mesopotamia. However, a close examination of the texts does not support this view.[3] There are two distinct corpora of texts, which may in fact represent two distinct legal procedures. One might possibly be a river procedure, but is certainly not an ordeal. The second may be a type of ordeal, but cannot possibly be a river trial.

The first corpus is a set of twenty Elamite contracts which contain the sanction-imprecation clause *ana mê illakma ina mê lu-li-i* ^{d}*Šazi qaqqassu/ muḫḫašu limḫaṣ*.[4] This clause is placed right after the main body of the text

[1]Hirsch, "Zum Fluss-ordal in Elam," *RA* 67 (1973) 75-77.

[2]Klima, "Das Wasserordal in Elam," *Ar. Or.* 39 (1971) 401-25, "L'ordalie par le fleuve en Elam," *RA* 66 (1972) 39-59.

[3]For an edition of the relevant texts and a fuller discussion of the question, see my forthcoming *The Judicial Ordeal in the Ancient Near East*, and my Ph.D. dissertation of the same name, Yale 1977.

[4]The clause appears in its full form in *MDP* 1, 16, 166, 285, 381, 382, and restored in *MDP* 6, 137, 138; and with *illakma* instead of *ana mê illakma* in *MDP* 374. The phrase *ana mê illakma* is omitted in 377, 382bis; *ina mê lulī* in *MDP* 341 and ^{d}*Šazi qaqqassu limḫaṣ* in *MDP* 287. *Ina mê lulI* appears alone in *MDP* 404 and ^{d}*Šazi muḫḫašu limḫaṣ* in *MDP* 376. Other variants are in *MDP* 2 *mê il*[*lak*] *mê lulI* ^{d}*Šazi* [ ] *i-na-ap-pi*[ ], *MDP* 131 *ana mê lillikma ina pī Wardi Šazi muḫḫašu limḫaṣi*, and perhaps *MDP* 405 *i-da-li-ik ana A i-da-li-ik*.

(before the witnesses) and immediately following the mention of the person to whom it applies, i.e. whoever disputes the adoption, division or grant. It may appear alone, as in *MDP* 2, 6, 138 (?), 382 and 382^{b}, or it may appear together with other sanctioning clauses known from these contracts, *ina awāt ili u šarri liṣi*[5], *ḫaṭṭu ša ili u šarri ina qaqqadišu liššakin*[6], ^{na4}*sumetam ša ili u šarri liba*[7], and *kiden* ^{d}*Šušinak ilput*[8]. These sanctioning clauses are used in the contracts whenever it is expected that a third party might have a vested interest in denying that the transaction took place, i.e. in divisions of property, adoptions and grants. They have a dual purpose, to reinforce the transaction in which they are used, and to prevent the potential chaos that could result if interested parties could freely claim that any transaction that diminished their fortunes never took place. The water clause is the most frequently used sanction clause. It is not common in contracts of division (only in *MDP* 22 6 and 16, 23 166 and 24 341), for in cases of division the party likely to contest the division has also sworn the contractual oath to the original transaction; the texts therefore use only the *ša ibbalakatu* "whoever overturns (this transaction)" clause.[9] The two adoption texts in which the water clause is found (*MDP* 22 1 and 2) and the fourteen deeds of grant (*MDP* 22 131, 137, 138; 23 285, 287; 24 374, 375, 376, 377, 381, 382, 382bis; 28 404, 405), on the other hand, are a very high proportion of the extant documents of this type.[10]

[5]For the initial discussion of all these clauses see Koschaker *OLZ* 35 (1932) 318f. This clause appears together with the water clause in *MDP* 1, 16, 287, 376, 384, and 404. For discussion see Frymer-Kensky, *The Judicial Ordeal*; Hinz, *CAH*^{3}II/1 282; de Meyer, *L'Accadien des contrats de Suse* (1962) p. 160; and Salonen, *St. Or.* 36 (1962) 16f.

[6]This appears together with the water clause in *MDP* 1, 16, 374, 377, 381 and probably 166. For discussion see Frymer-Kensky, op. cit., and Landsberger, *WO* 3 (1964) 58 n. 48.

[7]Appears with the water clause in *MDP* 131. For discussion, Frymer-Kensky op. cit., Landsberger and Balkan, *Belleten* 14 (1950) 210, 26; Brinkman, *JNES* 28 126.

[8]Appears with the water clause in *MDP* 341 and 381. For discussion see Frymer-Kensky, op. cit., and Leeman, *Fest. van Oeven* (1946) 36f.

[9]There are forty-six published documents of division. Of these, eleven contain no sanctions at all, and twelve are broken, six being too broken for us to know whether any sanction is involved. Of the remaining texts, ten use the standard *ša ibbalakatu* clause at the end, and five insert it into the body of the text. In the few texts that remain, the *kiden* formula appears five times, mutilation of hand and tongue three times, *ina awāt* three times, *ḫaṭṭu* twice, *sumitu* four times, and the water procedure four times.

[10]Of the thirty-two grants and charters, seven are totally broken and eight do not deal with third-party intervention. Of the remaining seventeen, one is from Malamir (Haft-Tepe), which does not use the phrase, one (*MDP* 286) is really an *aḫḫūtu*-adoption and at least two are clear royal charters rather than family grants. The water clause is found in twelve of the remaining thirteen texts.

When the water clause is used together with the other sanctioning clauses it almost invariably precedes them, and is placed right after mention of the party who raises the claim and against whom the sanctions are intended.[11] The water clause also has a more complex structure than these other sanctions. It is composed of three distinct phrases. The final phrase ^{d}*Šazi qaqqassu limḫaṣ* is a precative like the sanctioning clause and is a wish that Šazi intervene in the case.[12] Šazi does not appear in Elamite texts. He is, however, known from the Mesopotamian god lists as the son of ^{d}Íd, the divine river, and it is this association that suggests that we may have a river procedure here. The second phrase, *ina mê lu-li-i*, presents considerably more difficulties. *Lulī* is almost certainly not a noun (as von Soden, *AHw* 562b), but the derivation may be either from *elû* or *le'û*, and it is not known whether the form is third person (when we would expect *lilli*)[13] or first person[14], which has the difficulty that in some cases the speaker is certain to be dead by the time the transaction is contested.

The legal function of the water procedure is indicated by the first phrase, *ana mê illakma*, which is unique among the sanctioning phrases. It is not a precative, and should not be understood as an imprecation. It is not a preterite, and should not be understood as a generally ominous statement like *kiden* ^{d}*Šušinak ilput. Ana mê illak* always comes immediately after the mention of a future contest, and is connected to this introduction by the almost invariable *-ma* and the use of the present-future tense. It cannot appear alone, and is always followed by other parts of the water clause. It should therefore be understood as the continuation of the protasis rather than as the beginning of the sanctions "should someone arise and should he go to the water," then *ina mê luli* ^{d}*Šazi qaqqassu limhaṣ*. The phrase *ana mê illakma* is a reflection of an accepted legal procedure in which the plaintiff initiates or substantiates his claim by going to the water. Since sales could not be contested by such a procedure, the water clause is not found in sale contracts. Royal grants also seem to have been beyond the reach of such a procedure, and therefore the water clause is not found in contracts of royal grants even though these contracts do use sanctioning clauses. Non-royal grants, adoptions and divisions could be contested by "going to the water," and the contracts attempt to forestall such an eventuality by calling down dire implications on whoever would use this procedure.

[11]The only exceptions are *MDP* 341, where the *kiden* sanction appears first, and 376, where, however, only the phrase ^{d}*Šazi muḫḫašu limḫaṣ* appears.

[12]The only question with this phrase is whether the clause is meant literally, "may Šazi smite his skull" or in the idiomatic sense of "May Šazi indict him." For the idiomatic use of *qaqqadam mahāṣu* in the sense of "accuse, indict" see the Mari letter of Iatar-Ami to Zimri-Lim *SD* 2 112f 22-23.

[13]So Klima, *RA* 66 51 "Qu'il monte à l'eau."

[14]Hirsch, *RA* 67 75 and *CAD* L 243 "May I come up from the water."

The water procedure indicated by these Elamite contract clauses should not be considered an ordeal. Ordeals are always trials: they are always invoked to settle legal cases which cannot be resolved by other means.[15] This distinguishes them from divinatory procedures which may have marked similarities in form. It also distinguishes them from a procedure such as that reflected in these contracts, which is used by the claimant to substantiate the claim that he is initiating. Although there are similarities between these procedures, it is best to recognize the analytic differences, and therefore to refrain from drawing inferences from one to the other.

The second Elamite corpus of "water" texts, four Susa court memoranda (*MDP* 22 162, 23 242, 24 373 and 394), refer to a procedure called *mê leqû*, "taking the waters." The Susa texts begin with the statement that the plaintiff "freely and voluntarily ... took the waters," *ina ṭūbātišu ina naramatišu ... mê ilqi*, from which it is clear that the procedure is at the option of the litigant who undergoes it, rather than at the command of a judge. The texts record the alternative results of "taking the waters" by the terms *mê ušellima* and *ina mê illima*. This listing of alternative (future) results from a procedure already undergone indicates that this trial is not a river ordeal: you cannot throw someone in a river and not know whether he has floated or sunk.

The terminology of this procedure is difficult. One term, *ina mê illima* "he comes up from the waters" (from *elû*) or "he wins in the waters" (from *le'û*) seems clear. It could even refer to a river ordeal except that the result is not immediately apparent when the person "takes the waters." The other term, *mê ušellima*, also seems straightforward: it is the preterite of the Š stem of *elû* "to cause to go up," and it varies with the present *mê ušellam*. Under the common assumption that all suprarational trials must be river ordeals this term has commonly been explained as "making the waters rise above him, i.e. drowning." One must, however, torture Akkadian syntax to get such a meaning, and the only clear lexical evidence for *mê šūlû* is *ša mê šūli* which is, as we should expect, a dipper.

The texts do not even permit us to be certain whether *ina mê illima* or *mê ušellima* is a more favorable result for the litigant who takes the waters. In the Susa texts, *mê ušellima* seems to be the better result, for in *MDP* 23 242 Taribatum will get the field if *mê ušellama*, whereas the status quo remains in effect if *ina mê illima*; and in *MDP* 24 373 Elmešum will get seven oxen if *mê ušellima* and one ox if *ina mê illima*. The problem arises because of another Elamite text *MDP* 22 162 from "Malamir" (Haft Tepe), which is connected to these texts by the use of the verb *mê šūlû*. In this text, the two

[15] For a theoretical discussion of oaths, ordeals and divination procedures see Frymer-Kensky, op. cit., part one.

parties agree to go and take an oath.[16] The result is (lines 28-29) *Ainlungu me-e šu-la-at, Attaḫatet li-i.* Here *mê šulat* appears to be the unfavorable result. It is possible that the text of *MDP* 22 162 is corrupt and should be read *Attahatet* [*il*]-*li-i*, from *elû* in the sense of "to lose." This would fit the sense and would resolve the discrepancy between Haft Tepe and Susa, but it assumes a radical mistake in the text, an error on the order of the "Adultery Bible," in which the word "not" was left out of the seventh commandment. There seems, therefore, to be a real difference between the Haft Tepe and Susa texts.

Partially in order to resolve this discrepancy, and under the assumption that the Susa procedure was a river ordeal, and therefore that *mê šūlû* meant "to make the water rise, i.e. to sink," and on the further assumption (again on analogy with the Mesopotamian river ordeal) that sinking could not be a favorable result, the results in the Susa texts have been understood to be the reverse of what they seem, with *mê ušellima* being the unfavorable result. This has been done by positing a change of subject between the protases and apodoses. *MDP* 24 373 would then read "if (A) *mê ušellima*, then (B) takes seven oxen; if (A) *ina mê illima*, then (B) takes one ox" (So e.g. *CAD* E 130 *elû*). It is hard to imagine, however, that legal texts would be written with such chaotic syntax and ambiguous subjects. The Susa and Haft Tepe texts may in fact record different procedures, for in *MDP* 22 162 both parties participate, at Susa only one party (the claimant) is recorded as "taking the waters." If they record the same procedure, the differing results may be related to an active/passive distinction between *mê ušellima* and *mê šūlat*, with the active being favorable and the passive unfavorable. Yet another possibility is that the same physical result of the water procedure may also have had different legal consequences in different places.

Although much still remains obscure about the Elamite procedures, the most likely explanation for the Susa texts is that they represent a drinking trial in which the litigant drinks a potion while avowing the legitimacy of his claim. This fits the form of *MDP* 23 242 and 24 373, in which the procedure has already been undergone and the alternative possible results are stated, for one can conceive of a situation in which the litigant has already drunk the potion and in which the drinker is expected to manifest signs of guilt or innocence within a certain set time. This explanation also fits the terminology of the trials. *Mê leqû* "to take the waters" is self-evident; *mê ušellima* would indicate regurgitation, one of the possible results known elsewhere for drinking trials. If *mê ušellima* is indeed the favorable result, then *ina mê illima* would

[16]Reading *MDP* 162:22-23 [*ni-*]*il-la-ak ni-tam-ma-mi* [*il-*]*la-ku i-ta-am-mu-ma* "let us go and take an oath; they went and took an oath," with Hirsch, *RA* 67 77 and earlier Alvin Lieberman, *Studies in the Trial By River Ordeal in the Ancient Near East in the Second Millenium* B.C.E., Brandeis Ph.D. 1969.

mean something like "come away empty-handed," somewhat similar to other idiomatic uses of *elû*. If regurgitation is an unfavorable result, *ina mê illima* would mean "he wins in the water (trial)," from *le'û*.

Drinking procedures are known elsewhere in the Near East. Among the Hittites we hear of drinking the rhyton of the life of the god (*KUB* 13 4), but the details are not known. At Mari we have a fealty oath (*ARM* 10 9) in which minor deities drink a potion of water with dust from the gate of Mari. And in Israel we have the trial of the suspected adulteress (Numbers 5). This is not the place for an elaborate treatment of this trial but, again, comparison with the river ordeal in Mesopotamia, and with the potion ordeals of Africa has led to a distortion of our view of this trial. It is in fact not an ordeal, but a classic solemn oath in which great emphasis is placed on the solemn adjuration by the priest and the self-curse of the woman as she drinks the "bitter curse-bearing waters." As in all oaths (unlike ordeals), jurisdiction over the accused is thereby transferred to the divine, and the human court will let the case rest, in effect acquitting the accused on the assumption that no one would submit themselves voluntarily to the punishment of the divine. In the bitter waters trial the woman is adjured by a legal curse that she will become barren if she drinks while guilty. If she drinks and affirms her innocence after agreeing to this adjuration she convinces human eyes of her innocence (and the final proof may be delivered by pregnancy).[16a]

našû ilāni

The *našû ilāni* procedure from Nuzi is generally understood to be an ordeal-like oath procedure, and translated "oath of the gods" or "ordeal by oath."[17] However, these translations do not reflect the legal nature of the procedure, which is best understood as a trial in which one litigant "lifts (or carries) the gods" in an attempt to discredit the testimony of the opposing litigant and his witnesses.

When the first major collection of Nuzi texts was published by Gadd (*RA* 23 [1926]), he immediately understood the phrase *našû ilāni* as an oath procedure, explaining the term as related to the common *niš ilim*, "oath," and thereupon explaining the term *niš ilim* as itself coming from *našû*, "signifying the gesture of holding up the band(!) in the act of taking an oath" (*RA* 23 106 apud 28:29). *Niš ilim*, however, does not come from *našû* but from *nêšu*, "life." The early interpretations therefore understood *našû* in its normal sense of "to

[16a]See J. M. Sasson, "Numbers 5 and the 'Waters of Judgement,'" *BZ* 19 (1972) 249-51, eds.

[17]For studies of this procedure see Driver and Miles, "Ordeal by Oath at Nuzi," *Iraq* 7 (1940) 131-38; Liebesny, "Evidence in Nuzi Legal Procedure," *JAOS* 61 (1941) 130-42; Speiser, "Nuzi Marginalia," *Or.* 25 (1956) 1-23, esp. 15-23; and Roy Hayden, *Court Procedure at Nuzu*, Brandeis dissertation (1962) 34-39.

raise, etc." Driver and Miles translated *našû* as "to bring," and reconstructed a procedure in which people were either sent to the gods or the gods (i.e. their emblems) were brought to them. The defendant was ordered to bring the gods to the plaintiff's witness or to him and his witnesses, or vice versa; or to take them to the gods. If the party told to do so refused to bring the gods or escort the other party to the gods he forfeited the case. Driver and Miles assumed that the party brought to the gods or to whom the gods were brought was thereupon compelled to take an oath (*Iraq* 7 [1940] 132-38).

It was generally assumed that *našû ilāni* referred to an oath, with the only dissenting opinion that of H. Lewy, who also took the terms *našû* and *ana* literally, and understood the procedure to be one in which the litigants carried the gods and the one who broke down under the weight of the gods lost the case. The party who had witnesses to help him carry the gods was at a tremendous advantage, and therefore usually he and his witnesses carried, but the other party refused to do so, thus losing the case (*Or.* 10 [1941] 218). Speiser, however, demonstrated that if Lewy's interpretation were correct, the syntax of *HSS* 5 47 *u B qadu šībūtišu ittašiš* would have to indicate that the defendant carried the plaintiff as well as the plaintiff's witnesses (*Or.* 25 [1956] 18). He therefore took *našû* as an action verb corresponding to *niš ilim*, which he claimed was misanalyzed by the Nuzi dialect as coming from *našû*. Speiser's interpretation has been generally accepted.

However, the reconstruction of *našû ilāni* as an oath will not fit the evidence, for in two texts (no. 8, *HSS* 5 47, and no. 18, *JEN* 347) we are explicitly told that the defendant performed the *našû ilāni*. Both these cases are "criminal" suits in which the defendant is charged with theft and was allegedly caught with the stolen items. In no. 8, *HSS* 5 47, the witnesses testify that they saw the defendant steal these items even though he claimed to have been given them; in no. 18, *JEN* 347, the witnesses themselves claim to have caught the defendant. The judges order the defendants to lift the gods and they do so, *ittašiš*, *ittaši*. Despite this, the texts state that the plaintiffs won the cases, and the judge impose fines upon the defendants. The *našû ilāni* in these texts cannot refer to an oath procedure. In an oath the party swearing the oath places himself under the jurisdiction of the gods, who are expected to punish him if he swears falsely. There is therefore a presumption that anyone who would dare face the gods must be telling the truth. The human court therefore accepts a defendant's purgatory oath as evidence of innocence, acquitting him of the charge. If *našû ilāni* were an oath, it would be incomprehensible to award the case to the plaintiffs after the defendant has sworn the oath.

Našû ilāni is not a rare procedure, and there are thirty texts discussed here:

1. *RA* 23 27
2. *RA* 23 28
3. *RA* 23 35
4. *AASOR* 16 33
5. *AASOR* 16 56
6. *AASOR* 16 73

7. *HSS* 5 43
8. *HSS* 5 47
9. *HSS* 5 52
10. *HSS* 9 12
11. *HSS* 9 108
12. *HSS* 9 141
13. *HSS* 14 592
14. *JEN* 324
15. *JEN* 326
16. *JEN* 331
17. *JEN* 332
18. *JEN* 347
19. *JEN* 352
20. *JEN* 353
21. *JEN* 360
22. *JEN* 366
23. *JEN* 372
24. *JEN* 383
25. *JEN* 385
26. *JEN* 386
27. *JEN* 666
28. *JEN* 669
29. *SMN* 672[18]
30. *SMN* 974[19]

These represent a large variety of cases. The biggest group is what we would consider "criminal" offenses. There are various cases of theft: simple theft of barley (no. 23) and sheep (no. 18); theft of Prince Šilwa-tešup's trees (no. 10 and no. 12); theft of deposited grain (no. 26) and of articles from an adopted father's house (no. 8), and theft with battery (no. 9). Further offenses are slander (no. 2) and libel (no. 17); unlawful distraint (no. 6); battery (no. 16) and injury (no. 7); unauthorized flaying of oxen (no. 15 and no. 20) and butchering and eating a horse (no. 21); unjustified taking of the oath of the king (no. 14); trespass (no. 13) and refusal to release stored items (no. 11). *Našû ilāni* is also used in property disputes, both in disputes over the disposition of persons (no. 3 and no. 4, about women taking in daughtership; no. 22, about a son "given" in adoption, and no. 5, about a slave-girl given as a wife in a death-bed testament) and in field/grain disputes (no. 19, no. 24, no. 25, no. 28, no. 29 and no. 30).

Našu ilāni coexists with another suprarational trial at Nuzi, the *ḫuršan* trial, or river ordeal, known also from elsewhere in the Near East.[20] Like *našû ilāni*, the *ḫuršan* trial can be used for both personal offenses and property disputes. However, the two trials are not used interchangeably. There are eleven Nuzi texts in which cases involving personal offenses are sent to the *ḫuršan* (*AASOR* 16 74, *AASOR* 16 75, *HSS* 9 7, *HSS* 13 310, *HSS* 13 422, *HSS* 14 8, *JEN* 124, *JEN* 125, *JEN* 631, *SMN* 855, *SMN* 3557).[21]The range of these cases is more restricted than that of *našû ilāni*, for in all the cases in which the condition of the texts permits us to see the nature of the dispute, it has to do with some form of theft, whether straight theft (*AASOR*

[18]Text is unpublished, a synopsis is given in Hayden, *Court Procedure at Nuzu*, p. 114.

[19]Text is unpublished. Translation and transliteration in Hayden, *Court Procedure at Nuzu*, 150-52.

[20]For edition and discussion of the Nuzi *ḫuršan* texts see Frymer-Kensky, op. cit.

[21]*SMN* 855 and *SMN* 3557 are unpublished. Translation and transliteration in Hayden, *Court Procedure at Nuzu*, 176-77 (855) and 41 (3557).

16 74), theft and resale of religious objects (*HSS* 14 8), the theft of royal trees (*HSS* 9 7, *HSS* 13 422), burglary (*JEN* 125) or the theft of sheep (*HSS* 13 422, *JEN* 124, *SMN* 855).[22]

A comparison of one of these *huršan* texts, *HSS* 13 422, with a *našû ilāni* text, *HSS* 9 12, clarifies the occasions for the use of each procedure. These cases both involve the theft of the royal trees of Šilwa-tešup. As such, they are similar to *HSS* 9 7 (also a *ḫuršan* text), *HSS* 9 141 (also a *našû ilāni* text), *HSS* 9 8 (decided by the discovery of concrete evidence in the accused's house) and *SMN* 736 (trees of Ḫišmi-tešup, apparently decided by the testimony of witnesses).[23] In *HSS* 13 422 and *HSS* 9 12, the defendant is the same, Pa'a son of Ḫanatu. Furthermore, the same judges affix their names to both documents; the differing choice of procedure can therefore not be due to any different status of the defendant, nor to differing predilections of different judges, but to a difference in the nature of the cases. In *HSS* 13 422 Pa'a is charged with having first stolen and then burnt Šilwa-tešup's wood. Not only is there no evidence, but no evidence can be forthcoming, since he was not caught *in flagrante* and the wood is no longer in existence. Both litigants (Pa'a and the agent of Šilwa-tešup) back up their claim by taking an oath, and the text records their testimony in the *šumma . . .* (*lā*) formula of the self-curse. Faced with this impasse, the judges send the case to the *ḫuršan*-river. *HSS* 9 7 (also about Šilwa-tešup's trees) is similar, as are all of the court depositions that result in a *ḫuršan*:[24] there is no evidence presented, the nature of the charge and defense is such that no evidence could turn up upon further investigation, and the parties are willing to affirm their positions under oath. The texts record the conflicting oaths, and refer the case to the *ḫuršan* with the formula *aš-šum a-wa-ti an-na-ti*/*an-nu-ti ina*/*ana* ÍD *hur-ša-an illakū*. No decision is reached pending the results of this *ḫuršan* trial, but the texts may include a statement that the king will decide the fate of the loser (*HSS* 9 7, *HSS* 13 422, and *HSS* 14 8) or that the loser will be executed (*AASOR* 16 74 and *AASOR* 16 75). In *HSS* 9 12 (*našû ilāni*, Case no. 10), on the other hand, Pa'a has been found with a wooden object which allegedly came

[22]This pattern is so consistent that it leads one to suspect that in the two court depositions in which the nature of the dispute is not clear, *JEN* 651 and *AASOR* 16 75, the charge also concerns thefts. *JEN* 631 might be concerned with the price paid for the land, or with possible illegal possession by Šukr-apu, and *AASOR* 16 75 with misappropriation (?) of the *ilku* of the king that is mentioned in the fragmentary lines.

[23]*SMN* 736 is unpublished. A synopsis is given in Hayden, *Court Procedure at Nuzu*, 160-61.

[24]The only text enumerated here that is not in the form of these court depositions is *HSS* 13 310. In this text, which also deals with theft, the form is more like that of standard Nuzi trial records. The text begins with a statement that A and Y came before the judges, and the deposition is not made under oath. The text then continues with the statement [DI.KURU$_5$.MEŠ *i-na*] ÍD *ḫur-ša-an a-na iš-tap-ru*, but the text is broken as one of the litigants begins to speak again.

from Šilwa-tešup's stolen wood. This is a specific charge, which Pa'a refutes by claiming that he was given the object by a third party, bringing witnesses to confirm this. This third party is then sent to a *našû ilāni*, after which this third party is fined. Although most of the *našû ilāni* cases do not involve a third party, this case is typical of the others in its essential feature: the claim of one litigant (here that of Pa'a against the third party, who becomes the new defendant) is substantiated by witnesses, and the opposing litigant can only deny the substantiated claim.

There are three "criminal" cases in which the judges invoke a *našû ilāni* despite the fact that there are no witnesses. In no. 16, discussed below, no witnesses are mentioned. Here the *našu ilāni* may be used because of the identity of the litigants. In no. 6 the defendant (B)'s defense to the charge of unlawful distraint of the plaintiff (A)'s son is that A owed him money. He calls a witness, who, however, denies any knowledge of the affair, and the judges tell B to lift the gods. And in no. 20 B claims that the cattle overseer flayed the oxen; when the cattle overseer denies it, B is told to lift the gods. In all the other "criminal" *našû ilāni* cases, however, one of the party has brought witnesses to substantiate his claim, and the other party is to lift the gods.

The distinction between the *ḫuršan* and *našû ilāni* cases in the property disputes is similar. Again, the *našû ilāni* cases have a wider range than the *ḫuršan* texts, for they include disputes over persons as well as grain and field disputes, whereas the *ḫuršan* texts are all land controversies. Again the prominent feature in the *našû ilāni* texts is the presence of witnesses for one party, the only exception being no. 28, discussed below. In the *ḫuršan* texts there are no witnesses. When witnesses are requested (of B in *RA* 23 29 and *JEN* 662), the party cannot produce them. Similarly, in *JEN* 467 a renunciation document, the speaker recalls that he had no witnesses when he laid claim to the field. The parties then make their depositions under oath in *RA* 23 29 and *JEN* 393. The only case in which the litigants do not give their testimony under oath is *JEN* 662. This case, an involved land dispute concerning an exchange field, is very similar to no. 28, a *našû ilāni* text also concerning an exchange field, and the only one in which there are no witnesses. Both have the same format, that of a case record, standard for most Nuzi lawsuit texts, including the *našû ilāni* cases, but not for the *ḫuršan*-texts. The texts begin with a statement that A and B appeared before the judges in the matter of the case, and both proceed to depositions not given under oath. Furthermore, in both cases the judges ask one of the litigants for witnesses, but they do not have them. In no. 28 the plaintiff is asked, and when he cannot produce witnesses he is told to lift the gods. In *JEN* 662 the defendants are asked for expert witnesses. When they do not have them, the judges send investigators to measure the field and thereupon award the case to the plaintiff, providing for a *ḫuršan* option. Possibly when the plaintiff could not produce witnesses he lifted the gods, while when the defendants could not, the judges decided the case. In all of these *ḫuršan* cases dealing with property, unlike those dealing with "criminal" offenses, the judges decide the case, awarding the field to the plaintiff in *JEN* 393 and *JEN* 662, and dividing the field between the litigants in *RA* 23 29. The *ḫuršan* is mentioned in these texts as an optional alternative to accepting the decision of the judges. Similarly, in *JEN* 467 the speaker is renouncing his claim to the field: he had lost his claim in court and was given the option of going to the *ḫuršan*, an option he has chosen not to take.

With these few exceptions, the presence of witnesses seems to be the determining factor in the choice of procedure. In their absence the parties may corroborate their testimony by oaths, and the judges thereupon send the cases to the *ḫuršan* (in felony cases, possibly restricted to theft) or decide the issue and provide for the *ḫuršan* as an option (in land cases). When, however, there are witnesses, the judges may invoke a *našû ilāni* before making their decision.

It is normally the plaintiff who brings the witnesses. This is not, however, invariable. In some of the cases the plaintiff (A) is not asked for witnesses because the facts of his claim are not disputed; the defendant (B), who has offered a counterclaim, must corroborate his statement. In no. 6, B admits that he distrained A's son: the question is whether B's action was justified because A owed him money. In no. 11, everyone admits that A stored items with B, who now refuses to release them; the question in dispute is B's claim that A had already taken all the stored items and had indicated this by "loosening his hem," *qanni imtašar*. B therefore brings witnesses who saw the ceremony. In no. 22 there is no doubt that B is holding A's son; witnesses attest to B's claim that A's son was given to their father in perpetuity. B's witnesses are also mentioned in no. 25. The text is fragmentary, and the claims of both parties are broken. Ḫubita, apparently the plaintiff, has brought a tablet in support of his claim. He also seems to have brought witnesses, who are mentioned but not named. Four witnesses for B, however, are named, and give their (broken) testimony.

In three cases B's counterclaim involves a third party. In no. 10 B claims that C gave him the wood that he is accused of stealing, and brings witnesses to that effect. In no. 20 B claims that C (the cattle overseer) flayed the oxen B is accused of flaying; when C denies it, B cannot produce witnesses. In no. 21 B claims that C gave him the already butchered horse. The text is fragmentary, but there are witnesses, apparently for C. B is then asked for witnesses, but cannot provide them.

The testimony of the witnesses in these cases would seem to be decisive, and we would expect the decision to be made on the basis of this testimony. In the "criminal" cases there are seven instances in which the defendant was caught *in flagrante*: no. 7, no. 8, no. 9, no. 12, no. 13, no. 15, no. 18. In these cases the witnesses testified that they saw the theft (no. 8 and no. 9), the trespass (no. 13) or the injury (no. 7); that they saw the defendant caught (no. 12, fragmentary); or even that they saw and caught the defendants themselves (no. 15, no. 18). Similarly, witnesses testify that they heard the slanderous statement (no. 2), libelous charge (no. 17) or the oath of the king (no. 14), and in no. 23 the witnesses testify to the theft, although in this case they do not indicate the source of their knowledge. Only in two cases is any defense to these charges mentioned: in no. 2 the defendant simply denies having said the slanderous words and is thereupon confronted by witnesses who heard him say them; in no. 8 the defendant claims that he was given the articles he is accused of stealing, and is then confronted with witnesses who saw him take them. In all these cases we would expect the case to be awarded to the plaintiff on the strength of the witnesses' testimony; instead, the judges tell the defendant to "lift the gods."

The testimony of the witnesses would also seem to be decisive in the property disputes. In no. 3 the witnesses testify that they heard the disputed woman's father give her to A in daughtership; in no. 22 they heard A give his son to the father of B in perpetuity.[25] Similarly, in the two field disputes resulting from adoptions, the witnesses state that the field in question was given to another party rather than to B (no. 19) or that when they heard the adoption procedure they did not hear anything about a payment B alleges was promised him (no. 24). In no. 30, a dispute over the yield of a field, the witnesses testify that B had planted despite the oath of the king pronounced against him and that the produce should therefore belong to A.

In both the "criminal" and property disputes the testimony of the witnesses would seem to be decisive and we would expect the judges to be able to decide the issue on the basis of the testimony. Similarly, in the four cases in which there are no witnesses, we would expect their absence to be a decisive factor. Yet, in no. 16 and no. 20 the accusers (A in no. 16, B against C in no. 20) lift the gods when they have made an unsubstantiated charge; and similarly in no. 6 B lifts the gods having made an unsubstantiated counter-charge. In the property case no. 28, A lifts the gods while making an unsubstantiated claim to a field. In all of these cases and in all the cases in which the testimony of the witnesses seemed so compelling, the judges decide to send the case to a *našû ilāni* for reasons that are unstated.[26] There are several formulae by which the texts record this, one using the verb *šapāru*, one *šapāru*/ *qabû ana našê*, and one using imperatives of the verb *našû*. The use of these formulae make it clear that the *našû ilāni* normally involves the witnesses who testified in the case.

[25]In the other two cases involving the disposition of persons, no. 4 and no. 5, there is only a notation that witnesses were examined, but their testimony is not recorded. Presumably they testified to the effect that the girl had been given in daughter- and daughter-in-lawship in no. 4 and that the slavegirl had been given to the plaintiff on his father's deathbed in no. 5, and that they had witnessed these grants.

[26]The texts do not indicate why the judges decide to send one case to a *našû ilāni* and not another, why, for example in *SMN* 736, a royal trees case, the defendant is convicted on the testimony of witnesses whereas in the similar cases discussed above there is a *našû ilāni*.

In the *šapāru* formula the witnesses are sent to the gods, IGI.MEŠ *ša* A *ana* DINGIR.MEŠ *ištaprūšunuti* (no. 1, similarly no. 3); A may be sent with his witnesses (no. 27, no. 30): in no. 4 it is the husband of A who is sent with the witnesses.[27] There is only one case, no. 12, *HSS* 9 141 in which the party mentioned as "sent" is the party who is usually considered to be the one who undergoes the procedure, i.e. the party without the witnesses, the one who is said to have refused the procedure or "returned" from it and who ultimately loses the case. This text is too fragmentary to tell why in this one case it is B who was "sent" to the gods. In all the other cases it is the witnesses, who must therefore be involved in some direct way.

The *šapāru*/*qabû* formula makes it clear that the lifting of the gods was done before the witnesses. The judges may tell B to lift the gods before A and his witnesses, *ù* DI.KURU5.MEŠ DINGIR.MEŠ-*e a-na na-še-e a-na pa-ni* A *ù* IGI.[MEŠ-*š*]*u iq-ta-bu-ú* (no. 19), or before the witnesses of A, *ù* DI.KURU5.MEŠ *a-na* B DINGIR.MEŠ *a-na* IGI.MEŠ-*ti a-na na-a-še-e iš-tap-ru-uš* (no. 24). In three cases officials called *manzaduḫle* are to lift as well as B: in no. 2 the *manzaduḫle it-ti* B *a-na* DINGIR.MEŠ *a-na na-še-e iš-tap-ru-šu-nu-ti*; in no. 14 and no. 17, B is commanded to carry and a separate statement indicates that *manzaduḫle* have been sent *ana našê*. Similarly, in no. 6, B is commanded to carry and the judges send three men *ana ma-an-za-ad-duḫ-lu-ti a-na* DINGIR.MEŠ. The *manzaduḫle* are normally considered to have been designated to witness the procedure and bring back a report.[28] These texts, however, may indicate that the *manzaduḫle* actually took part in the lifting of the gods.[29] This would clearly indicate that the focus of the procedure is on the witnesses before whom the gods are raised rather than on the person doing the raising, a fact that seems clear in any case.

By far the most common formula is the *išimi* form, in which the judges address the party without the witnesses and tell him to lift the gods in respect to the witnesses and/or the opposing party, (*ana*) *šībūtī* DINGIR.MEŠ *išimi*. In many of these cases (no. 5, no. 6, no. 11, no. 13, no. 14, no. 15, no. 16, no. 17, no. 21, no. 26, no. 28) the command of the judges begins with the word *alik*, "go," perhaps an indication that the lifting of the gods was not done in "court," but in some appropriate spot, perhaps the temple. The relationship between the *išimi* and *šapāru* formulas is indicated by no. 28, *JEN* 669. Here the judges say to A, who has told them that he does not have witnesses (lines

[27]It is unclear why the husband of A is sent with the witnesses in no. 4. In no. 7 the defendant is female, and she is told to lift the gods. Possibly women could perform the lifting of the gods, but could not undergo it. There may also have been other reasons that the husband of A is involved in no. 4.

[28]Thus Hayden, *Court Procedure at Nuzu*, 13.

[29]It may or may not be relevant that in all three of these cases the defendant is accused of a felonious statement: slander, libel and unjustified pronouncing of the oath of the king.

56f) [*alikmami* (*ana*)] B. DINGIR. MEŠ i-ši[-*mi*] "go and lift the gods before/in regard to B." The text continues *ki-me-e* DI.KURU$_5$.MEŠ B [*a-na* DINGIR.]MEŠ *iš-tap-ru-uš ù* [A] *a-šar* ⸢DINGIR.MEŠ⸣ *it-tu-ur* "because the judges sent B to [to the god]s and [A] returned from the gods . . ." and later we hear that B won the case. The party who is "sent" is the party before whom, or in regard to whom the gods are lifted.

The judges address the party who is to lift the gods with various forms of the imperative of *našû*: *i-ši-mi* (no. 9, no. 10, no. 13, no. 18, no. 20, no. 22, no. 22, no. 25), *i-ši-šu-mi* (no. 7, no. 8, no. 26, no. 28), *i-ši-šu-nu-ti-ma* (no. 21), *i-ši-iš-mi* (no. 16); *i-ši-iš-šu-mi* (no. 14), *iš-šu-mi* (no. 11), *iš-šu-uš* (no. 17), *i-ša-šu-mi* (no. 6), *iš-šu-uš-šu-nu-ti ma* (no. 15). There is only one case in which the verb is not in the imperative, no. 5. Here the judges say to B *a-li-ik-ma-mi* LÚ.MEŠ *ši-bu-tum ša* A DINGIR.MEŠ *li-iš-ši-šu-nu-mi*. The use of the precative plural here seems to indicate that in this case it is the witnesses rather than B who are doing the lifting. This would be an exceptional case, and in fact the text then continues with the notation that B returned unsuccessful, so possibly the use of the precative here is in error.

The verb *našû* governs two objects, the gods who are lifted, and the other party, usually the witnesses. The syntax is usually a double accusative, the party being ordered to lift the gods before or simply in respect to the witnesses. In six cases (no. 9, no. 15, no. 18, no. 20, no. 22, and no. 25) the preposition *ana* is used. Although this may simply mean "in regard to" (so Speiser *Or*. 25 18), it may also indicate "before" in the physical sense. This is certainly the meaning of *ana pani* ^{LÚ}*Zilikuḫle*, "in front of the witnesses," in no. 13.

Most commonly, the persons in respect to whom the gods are lifted are the witnesses of A, either alone (no. 5, no. 7, no. 9, no. 13, no. 14, and no. 18) or together with A (no. 8, no. 17, no. 26). In three cases A is addressed and told to lift the gods in regard to B's witnesses: no. 11, in regard to B and his witnesses; no. 22 and no. 25, in respect to the witnesses alone. In two texts (no. 16 and no. 28) A carries in respect to B. In those cases in which B's defense indicts a third party, A is not involved in the *našû ilāni*, and the issue is resolved between B and C. In no. 10 Pa'a and his witnesses are the new accusers, and C must lift in respect to them. In no. 20 B lifts in respect to C,[30] and in no. 21 in respect to C and his witnesses.

In eight cases the person told or sent to lift the gods does not agree to do so: DINGIR.MEŠ *a-na na-še-e la im-gur* (no. 13, no. 19), DINGIR.MEŠ B/A *la*

[30] In this case C is the cattle overseer whom B has accused of doing the flaying. The overseer is important also in no. 15. In this case Bēliya is accused of flaying three oxen without the overseer's permission. He must carry against the witnesses, who caught him red-handed, and the overseer, who presumably stated that he had not authorized the flaying.

im-gu₅-ur a-na na-še-e (no. 20, no. 22), *a-na* DINGIR.MEŠ *na-še-e la im-gur* (no. 15), *la i-ma-an-gur-ru a-na na-še-e* (no. 21), or just *ul im-gu₅-ur* (no. 24) or *ul-li-im-g*[*ur*] (no. 3). In these cases the other party thereupon wins the case, *ina dīni iltēma*.

The more common statement is that the party sent to carry the gods "turned" from the gods, *ašar* DINGIR.MEŠ *ittūr*, with variations *ištu* DINGIR.MEŠ *ittūr* (no. 1, no. 3, no. 30), *uštu* DINGIR.MEŠ *ittūr* (no. 4, no. 15), DINGIR.MEŠ *ittūra* (no. 10, no. 27), and the fullest form *a-šar* DINGIR.MEŠ *a-na ši-bu-ti na-še-e it-tu-ur* (no. 25). It is important to remember that in those texts which use the *šapāru* formula to indicate that the witnesses of A were "sent" to the gods, it is nonetheless B who "returns," and A who wins. In those texts that use the other formulas, the party who is told or sent to lift the gods is the one who "returns" and the other party wins the case.

The verb *ittūr* was read by Gadd as *id-du-ur*, which he translated "he shrank," apparently taking the form from *adāru*. On the basis of the writings *it-tu-ra* and *it-tu-ú-ra* in the Middle Assyrian Laws (22 and 24), it became clear that the underlying root was *târu*, "to return"; nevertheless the sense was understood as if it were *adāru*, and Speiser suggested the possibility that the Nuzi scribes had confused the two preterites (*AASOR* 16 [1936] 91-92). The verb has been universally taken to mean "to turn back from taking, to return before the trial, i.e. to refuse to take the test"; in other words, to mean fundamentally the same thing as *lā imgur*, forfeiture of the case by declining the procedure. In two texts, however, no. 15 and no. 21, both the *lā imgur* and *ittur* formulas are used together, and this apparent superfluity prompted Roy Hayden to suggest that the verb *târu* might mean that the person failed to vindicate himself (*Court Procedure at Nuzu* [1961] p. 201 no. 117).

The legal use of the verb *târu* is not confined to the Nuzi *našâ ilāni* texts, but is used in the *ḫuršan*-ordeal texts *MAL* 22 and 24, *UET* 7 9 (Middle Babylonian) and *ABL* 965 (Neo-Assyrian). In *UET* 7 9 and *ABL* 965 *târu* is used as the contrastive term to *zakû* which is a technical term for victory in the ordeal in these periods. Thus in *UET* 7 9 we read that the judges sent the litigants to the *ḫuršan*, then (1.12f) *it-⌜bu?⌝-ma* ᵐ*Man-nu-ú-kal-me-ša iz-kam-ma ù* ᵐᵈ*Marduk-eriš*ⁱˢ *i-tu-ra-am* "they w[ent down into? the] waters. Mannu-ukalmeša won and Marduk-eriš lost the case." In *ABL* 965 we hear (rev. 14f) *ḫur-šá-an ki-i il-lik-ú* ᵐ*Bul-lu-ṭu i*[*z-kam-ma*] *ù* ᵐ*Ḫi-in-nu-mu it-tu-ru* "when they went to the *ḫuršan*, Bullutu w[on] and Ḫinnumu lost." The presence of the statements *itbûma* (if read correctly) "they went into the waters" and *ḫuršan kī illikū* "when they went to the *ḫuršan*" would indicate that the implication of the verb *târu* is not that the individual refused to undertake the ordeal, but rather than he was unsuccessful. This is further confirmed by the presence of the pair *zakû*/ *târu* in *UET* 7 11. In this case the issue is an ox that A had entrusted to B and that had died in B's house. The *šakkanaku* Adad-šum-uṣur decided that A's messenger should bring out the carcass of the ox from B's house. If it then turns out that it had been dragged down by a dog, then (lines 12-15) B *li-iz-kam-mu* LÚ *ša* A *li-tu-ra*. If, on the other hand, he cannot get the corpse from B's house, then LÚ *ša* A *li-iz-kam-ma* B *li-tu-ra*. Here there is no question of ordeals, oaths, adjurations or refusal to undergo various procedures. The contrast of *zakû* / / *tāru* makes it clear that *tāru* is used as a technical term for defeat. The semantic development of "to return" into "to lose" is obscure: perhaps the bridge is "to return empty-handed" or to return to the court to face the penalties. The sense, however, seems clearly indicated by the contexts in which it is used.

The *našû ilāni* texts thus present several different possibilities. If the party refuses to undergo the procedure (*ul imgur*), the other party wins the case. If the party returns unsuccessful (*ittūr*), the other party wins the case. If the texts simply note that the party "lifted/carried the gods" (*ittašiš*, *ittaši*) the other party still wins the case. The party who is told to carry thus seems to have no chance of winning the suit. This is not really surprising if we remember that the testimony of the witnesses was so crucial to the cases and so decisive that it seemed odd for the judges to send anyone to the *našû ilāni* rather than simply deciding the case in favor of the party with the witnesses.

There is one case, no. 16, in which the party who is told to lift the gods ultimately wins the case. Kurpa-zaḫ has accused his brother Mat-tešup of striking his (Kurpa-zaḫ's) wife and injuring (?) her (!) hand. There are no witnesses, but possibly because of the identity of the litigants,[31] the judges tell Kurpa-zaḫ to go and lift the gods *a-lik-⌜ma⌝ [a-na]* ^{m}*Ma-at-te-šup* DINGIR.MEŠ *i-ši-iš-mi*. When Kurpa-zaḫ went to the gods (*i-na-ak-mi*, possibly *i-la!-ak-mi*)[32] Mat-tešup grabbed him and did something to the hem of his garment, *ḫe-ez-mu-ma i-pu-uš*. Kurpa-zaḫ thereby won the case. Although this text has been called a "belt-wrestling" case (Gordon, *HUCA* 23 [1950-51] 131-35), there is no hint of this in the text, and the terminology makes it clear that this is a *našû ilāni* text. Mat-tešup apparently attempted to prevent Kurpa-zaḫ from carrying out the procedure and so he grabbed him. The belt either tore

[31]These sons of Ḫilpi-iššuḫ are known from a fair number of Nuzi texts. For the archive of the family, see H. Lewy, "A Contribution to the Historical Geography of the Nuzi texts," *Speiser AV JAOS* 88 (1968) 159 no. 73. Kurpa-zaḫ in particular had complex dealings with the rest of his family. In *JEN* 204 he is adopted into brothership by his own brother Tupki-tilla, who gives him an orchard and three sheep as his share. In *JEN* 87 he is also adopted into brothership by one of his own brothers, Punni-ḫarpa (Punniya), who gives him pasture land. He also takes large fields from Punniya *ana tidennūtu* (*JEN* 315, 311, the latter text witnessed by Tupki-tilla and Mat-tešup). The relations of Mat-tešup and Kurpa-zaḫ seem to have been somewhat bitter. Although they appear as partners in *JEN* 320, they are at odds here and in *JEN* 124. There Mat-tešup claims that Kurpa-zaḫ took 8 sheep belonging to Tamar-Tae from the grove of Tupki-tilla into his own. As in *JEN* 331, the judges do not want to decide between Mat-tešup and Kurpa-zaḫ in that case, but send it to a divine procedure. Here they invoke a *našû ilāni*, there they send the case to the *ḫuršan*.

[32]According to Speiser, *Or* 25 (1956) 19 n. 1 *in(n)ak* is an attested local phonetic variant for *illak*.

or something similar as a result of his grabbing him, or grabbing and tearing the hem of his garment may have been a symbolic act for "giving up" (as loosening the hem was a symbol for quitclaim in no. 11, *HSS* 9 106).

The *našû ilāni* trials thus seems to be a procedure in which an individual is given an opportunity to win a case which he would otherwise be certain to lose. Normally the situation is such that the opposing party has witnesses to support his claim, and the party without the witnesses is to lift the gods before or in respect to these witnesses and sometimes the opposing party. In those cases in which there are no witnesses the person who makes the charge may lift in respect to the party who denies it. The object of the procedure seems to be to allow the party who is about to lose the case to shake the testimony that seems decisive against him, the testimony of the witnesses or the denial of the party against whom he has made an unsubstantiated charge. The *našû ilāni* is not really "imposed" upon the losing party, but rather offered as a privilege. We do not know whether this privilege was always offered, but only recorded in these texts, or rather (as seems more likely) the *našû ilāni* could be offered at the discretion of the judges.

The party offered the *našû ilāni* is to lift the gods, or most probably their emblems, perhaps inclining them in the direction of the witnesses, or possibly carrying them toward him, and possibly uttering an adjuration as he does so. This invokes the divine, involving the power of the gods in the case, with the understanding that the gods will punish the witnesses if they persist in unjustified testimony. The expectation is, of course, that lying parties will fear to be at the risk of the gods and will therefore withdraw their testimony. For the legal system, *našû ilāni* has the same effect as a legal curse or a witness-oath, and if the witnesses or litigants persist in their testimony, it can be accepted by the court as true. The *našû ilāni* is at the same time not without risk to the litigant who lifts the gods, for he has entered the divine realm and thus put himself in their power. He may therefore refuse to lift the gods (*lā imgur*): the testimony of the witnesses and opposing litigant thereby stand unchallenged, and the opposing litigant wins the case. Lifting the gods, however, is no guarantee that the witnesses will withdraw their testimony. On the contrary, we would expect that in most cases witnesses are honest. The party may therefore lift the gods, as in no. 8 and no. 18, and the opposing litigant still win the case, and thus most people return unsuccessful from the gods (*târu*) having failed the procedure by not having caused the other side to withdraw its testimony. If, however, the opposing party is disconcerted at the procedure, and either backs down or physically tries to prevent it by grabbing the lifting party or perhaps doing something to his hem, then the lifting party has won his case.

Alalaḫian Miscellanies II*

ERNÖ GAÁL
Budapest

5. ^{KUR}*Ḫurri on an Alalaḫ VII document (*119:3)?*

It is possible that the very fragmentary condition of the tablet *Al.T.**119 gives cause for neglecting its datum referring to ^{KUR}*Ḫurri.*[1] Originally the text was published in D. J. Wiseman's catalogue without asterisk which denotes that the tablet belongs to level VII, but later this omission was corrected.[2] The two persons, the witness Talm-ammu in line 14 and ^{f}Sumunnabi in line 4, place the text unambiguously among the level VII tablets.[3]

The beginning of the tablet is lost. The name of the protagonist also is broken, but we know that he is living in the Ḫurri-land (11. 2-3, *i-na* ^{KUR}*Ḫu-r*[*i*^{KI}]/ *wa-ši-ib*). This man was sent up (1. 5, *uš-te-li-šu*) by ^{f}Sumunnabi, and he was given 40 *parīsu* of barley, and the balance of the barley of *ḫandūtu* they entrusted to him.[4] During the night he opened and stole (the barley). The rest of the tablet is broken.

Although the end of line 2 is broken, the completion suggested by D. J. Wiseman is plausible, traces of the *ri* sign are visible on the autograph. Among the level VII place names there are only two, in addition to ^{KUR}*Ḫurri*, which begin with the *ḫu* sign. These are *Ḫurzanu*[5] and *Ḫutamma*,[6] both of them with

* "Alalaḫian Miscellanies I" is in press, *Annales Universitates Scientiarum Budapestinensis de Rolando Eötvös Nominatae - Sectio Classica* 7 (1981); 1. TAR, 2. *sarrupabinni*, 3. What is the size of an Alalaḫian *pīsannu*-box?, 4. How many times did king Ammitakum II get married?

[1]D. J. Wiseman, *The Alalakh Tablets. Occasional Publications of the British Institute of Archaeology at Ankara*, No. 2; London, 1953, p. 61; D. J. Wiseman, "Supplementary Copies of Alalakh Tablets," *JCS* 8 (1954) 10.

[2]D. J. Wiseman, *JCS* 8 (1954) 3.

[3]N. Na'aman, "A New Look at the Chronology of Alalakh Level VII," *AnSt* 26 (1976) 132, 140.

[4]*CAD* Ḫ 79b; may be it is connected with *ḫimtu*/*ḫindu*/*ḫintu* meaning "a leather bag," *CAD* Ḫ 192b f.; D. J. Wiseman interpreted as "spiced? barley."

[5]*Ḫurzanu*, *RlA* 4/6-7 (1975) 552b.

[6]*Ḫutamma*(*na*), *RlA* 4/6-7 (1975) 524b.

URU determinative. (On level IV tablets there are *Ḫulaḫḫan*, *Ḫurri*, *Ḫušri*, *Ḫutamma*, *Ḫutilluraše* and *Ḫuturu* place names which begin with *ḫu* sign.[7])

If [f]Sumunnabi really was in contact with a man of Ḫurri-land, this datum offers support to the theory of M. C. Astour, namely, as early as under Ḫattušiliš I there existed a Ḫurrian state with a strong military power, which was able to invade the Hittite Kingdom when Ḫattušiliš I campaigned in the west Anatolian land of Arzawa.[8] On the basis of tablet *Al.T.**119 we can assume that a Ḫurrian state with the name KURḪur(r)i[9] existed before the destruction of Alalaḫ by Ḫattušiliš I and before the attack of Ḫurrians/Ḫanigalbatians on Hittite territories.[10]

M. C. Astour's theory was criticized by N. Na'aman saying that the *Res Gestae* of Ḫattušiliš I was written during the period of the Hittite Empire, and the early name Ḫurri cannot in any circumstances be regarded as indicating the early existence of the kingdom of Mīttani.[11]

6. *Arrapḫians in Alalaḫ*

Among the tablets of the Alalaḫ IV archive there are only three references to Arrapḫa. Also there are very few materials through which it is possible to outline the nature of the connections which combined the Mītanni[12] controlled territories from Alalaḫ to Arrapḫa.[13]

In *Al.T.* 416:3, 3 TÚG*ú-su(?)-zi-a-šu-nu* KUR*Ar-ra-ap-ḫé*, "three garments[14] from Arrapḫa," are mentioned as part of the legacy of a certain [f]Piriašše and her mother.[15] This datum refers to the trade connections that existed between the two vassal states of Mīttani.

[7] *Ḫulaḫḫan*: *Idr.* 67; Ḫurri: *Idr.* 44, 46, 49; *Al.T.* 2:73, 74; *Ḫušri*: *Al.T.* 141:6; 163: 16; 185: 20; 196: 24; 223: 23; 224: 3; 228: 2; 231: 6; 287: 5; 329: 11; 338: 4; 355: 6; 422: 11; *Ḫutamma*: *Al.T.* 152: 2, 3, 5; 165: 4; 180: 21; 186: 3; 307: 32; 308: 1, r. 1; 343: 18; *Ḫutilluraše*: *Al.T.* 146: 25; 342: 1; *Ḫuturu*: *Al.T.* 181: 3.

[8] M. C. Astour, "Ḫattušiliš, Ḫalab, and Ḫanigalbat," *JNES* 31 (1972) 104f.

[9] I. M. Diakonoff, *Hurrisch und Urartäisch*, München, 1971, p. 11, note 11: "Der von der früheren Forschung angenommene Staat (oder eine Stadt) 'Ḫurri' existierte anscheinend nicht."

[10] *KBo.* 10, 1-3; *RlA* 4/2-3 (1973) 106b.

[11] N. Na'aman, "Syria at the Transition from the Old Babylonian Period to the Middle Babylonian Period," *UF* 6 (1974) 267f., n. 12.

[12] G. Wilhelm, "Parrattarna, Sauštatar und die absolute Datierung der Nuzi-Tafeln," *Acta Antiqua Hung.* 24 (1976 [1979]) 149, n. 2.

[13] N. Na'aman, *UF* 6 (1974) 265ff.

[14] A. Draffkorn, *Hurrians and Hurrian at Alalah: An Ethno-Linguistic Analysis*, 1959 (unp. diss. of the University of Pennsylvania), p. 243, "part of a garment?".

[15] D. J. Wiseman, *The Alalakh Tablets*, p. 108, Pl. XLI.

It is more interesting that Eǵli-Tešub,[16] a citizen of Arrapḫa—according to *Al.T.* 82—extended his scope of activity into Alalaḫ.[17] ᶠPaban-ella ran to help the Arrapḫian businessman in financial difficulties. Before Niqmepa, king of Mukiš/Alalaḫ, Eǵli-Tešub had rights and possibilities similar to those of the citizens of Alalaḫ.

The third text, *Al.T.* 216,[18] mentions ᵐ*A-na-ni.* ᴸᵁ́*Ar-ra-ap-ḫe*. The beginning of the text is broken, thus it is impossible to define the locality where the Arrapḫian Anani possessed a vineyard of 6 GÌR.[19]

It is true that this vineyard isn't a considerable landed property, but this datum enables us to presume that in Mukiš/Alalaḫ it was possible for a foreigner to buy some fields, too. As I earlier demonstrated, in Alalaḫ the system of the common household land of extended families of Nuzi type[20] did not exist.[21] The village where Anani possessed vineyard—in my opinion —was a territorial community of land (civic community).

[16] A. Draffkorn, *Hurrians and Hurrian at Alalah*, pp. 28f.; without his patronymic it is impossible to look for him among the Nuzi personal names.

[17] D. J. Wiseman, *The Alalakh Tablets*, p. 53, Pl. XXI.

[18] D. J. Wiseman, *The Alalakh Tablets*, p. 77; M. Dietrich - O. Loretz, "Die Weingärten des Gebietes von Alalaḫ im 15. Jahrhundert (Die soziale Struktur von Alalaḫ und Ugarit (V)," *UF* 1 (1969) 55f., No. 23.

[19] M. Dietrich - O. Loretz, *UF* 1 (1969) 62, 1 GÌR = 60 m^2, thus the measure of Anani's vineyard was 360 m^2.

[20] N. B. Jankowska, "Communal Self-Government and the King of the State of Arrapḫa," *JESHO* 12 (1969) 235 ("joint ownership").

[21] E. Gaál, "The 'eperum' in Alalaḫ," *Annales Universitatis Scientiarum Budapestinensis de Rolando Eötvös Nominatae - Sectio Historica* 17 (1976) 3ff. with literature.

The Nuzi Collections in the Harvard Semitic Museum

CARNEY E. S. GAVIN
Harvard Semitic Museum

Among the many achievements of Professor Ernest Lacheman perhaps least generally acknowledged has been his invaluable contribution—over half a century—to the work and spirit of the Harvard Semitic Museum (*HSM*). When Professor Ernest Lacheman first came to the Harvard Semitic Museum in 1930, he was taken by the second Curator of the *HSM*, the late Professor Robert Pfeiffer, to an immense wooden box ("four feet by four feet by four feet") full of Nuzi cuneiform tablets. "Little did I realize what a wealth of information was in them," recollects Professor Lacheman about this "treasure chest" from which he has been dispensing riches for five decades. From those days of his first investigations, Professor Lacheman has continued his research through the time during which the museum was inactive to recent years that have witnessed substantial reorganization of the collections. During extraordinarily difficult periods when an attempt was made to close the Museum, Professor Lacheman physically saved many *HSM* artifacts and, as a unique human link between the days of our first Curator and tomorrow, Professor Lacheman has proved a constant encouragement to all who have toiled over the last decade for the Museum's re-emergence.

Both to report on the present status of the *HSM* Nuzi collections and the efforts of recent years to put those collections in order as well as to express formally the Museum's gratitude for five decades of Professor Lacheman's labor here and for the inspiration his devotion has given to us, the following pages are submitted as a much abbreviated summary of the results of new work in organizing and preserving various components of those collections, especially: the tablets, the seal impressions, the artifacts, and the field photographs.

Recent Projects at the Harvard Semitic Museum

In 1974, two grants from the Museums Program of the National Endowment for the Arts (*NEA*) enormously assisted our work: in a *Cataloguing Project*, most *HSM* collections were inventoried, given new numbers (based upon a modification of the Library of Congress' code), and photographed. A triple filing system (by accession, provenance, and object type) was prepared by teams which included students of Professor Lacheman. A *Visiting Specialist Project* enabled the *HSM* to draw upon the expertise of Professor Lacheman himself to begin putting the Nuzi tablet collection in proper order—with particular regard to the return to the Iraq Museum of published tablets. Part of this project involved the preparation of macrophotographic studies of seal impressions upon those Nuzi tablets scheduled to return to Baghdad.

During these *NEA* projects, it became clear that the artifacts as well as the tablets from Nuzi required urgent attention and correlated cataloguing. The vast extent, potentially invaluable coherence, and special problems of the many types of evidence excavated at Nuzi—as well as the prodigious opportunities which the various Nuzi materials promised to yield to newly developing methods of analysis—combined to necessitate a multi-dimensional approach to put these long-neglected collections in order. Systematic inventories, physical preservation measures, and safe-storage were the essential first steps for any re-evaluation of the Nuzi discoveries.

In 1976, the Research Division of the National Endowment for the Humanities (*NEH*) provided funds for a 3-year project to put in order the Nuzi research collections, including the tablets, the seal-impressions, and the artifacts. As the project proceeded, several modifications in work-patterns developed organically: thus, the ordering of the Nuzi tablets became ever more integrally associated with the tablet-by-tablet investigation required by the process of recording the seal impressions on the tablets. So, too, the collating of original field records developed into a major effort as the rarity, fragility, and potential danger of the nitro-cellulose ("non-safety") photographic records from Nuzi became evident. Beyond long-neglected inventories and typological studies, various materials-analyses-experiments and special conservation needs were integrated into the cataloguing of the Nuzi artifacts.

The following pages are not intended to serve as substitutes either for new *HSM* Nuzi collection *control-documents* which specialists will have to consult before working directly with Nuzi objects, or for the detailed *reports of the methods followed* in the project. Instead, these brief summaries of the reorganization of the *HSM* Nuzi collections (tablets, glyptic, artifacts, photographs) outline what has been started through *NEH* support and are presented as an invitation to the scholarly world to join in following trails blazed by Professor Lacheman.

The HSM *Nuzi Tablet Collections*

Preliminary attempts to arrange the Nuzi tablets in the *HSM* were hindered by a number of obstacles: Many tablets were unlabelled. Some were incorrectly labelled. Others had become associated with small boxes (or plastic bags) with numbers different from those inked on the tablets or on the various scraps of paper found inside the containers for individual tablets.

At least four diverse systems of numeration were found on or with the tablets: *field numbers* (*SMN*) assigned to the tablets as they had been unearthed or after they had been hardened by preliminary baking in the expedition's improvised oven; *room numbers* written on scraps of tissue or 50-year-old newspaper fragments kept with the tablets; *registry numbers* reflecting the expedition's object-entry-ledger; and *publication numbers*.

In particular, confusions occurred because of the simultaneously variant volume numbers given within both the *HSS* and the *EN* sequences to each individual published book of Nuzi texts. To assist future tablet-consultations which may yet encounter individual discrepancies in *HSM* Nuzi tablet order, the principle sorting and mislabelling difficulties resulted from confusion among:

- *HSS* 9/*EN* 2 and *EN* 9 (not yet published)
- *HSS* 13/*EN* 4 and *HSS* 15/*EN* 6 and *HSS* 16/*EN* 7
- *HSS* 14/*EN* 5 and *HSS* 5/*EN* 1
- *HSS* 16/*EN* 7 and *AASOR* 16

For puzzling instances, the accuracy of Professor Lacheman's original tablet listings in each (*HSS*/*EN*) Nuzi text volume has been *consistently confirmed* as individual tablets have been examined for correlation with numberings published elsewhere or erroneously ascribed to the tablets themselves.

A vast quantity of tablet-fragments was returned to the *HSM* by Professor Lacheman in 1973. The original order of these fragments has been retained with whatever scraps of field annotations could be found. Potential usefulness of these fragments (from which uninscribed clay labels or "*bullae*" have been removed for glyptic analysis) is indicated by Professor Gernot Wilhelm's success in making 16 significant joins (to published tablets belonging to the archives of Prince Šilwe-Tešup) from among these fragments now stored coherently adjacent to the cabinets containing whole tablets.

The physical preservation of the *HSM* Nuzi tablet collections has presented highly technical conservation problems which arise mainly from the chemical action of salts and other minerals within the tablets combined with deleterious attempts to use animal glues as preservative 50 years ago.

The major work that has been accomplished in the area of conservation includes: a comprehensive survey of Nuzi tablet preservation problems; systematic tablet de-salination in distilled water to permit the next steps for those tablets needing various treatments; carefully graduated re-baking of tablets; re-gluing of incorrectly mended tablets; surface-hardening of flaking or otherwise decomposing texts; latex-mould fabrication of tablets to be returned to Iraq; moulage-fabrication from latex moulds to provide both accurate copies of returned tablets for consultation in the *HSM* as well as educational tools for schools studying ancient Mesopotamia; consultations with the conservation laboratories of the Iraq Museum on treatments to prepare the tablets for their homeward journey; detailed reports on each tablet's treatment; and guidelines for any conservation work which future research may require.

Despite many arduous months of work and at times imaginative solutions to urgent problems of physical preservation, *HSM* Nuzi project conservation measures have from their outset been deliberately "minimalistic." Only truly necessary steps for tablet preservation have been implemented so as not to destroy material that might lend itself to scientific analysis in the future. For instance, although the original baking in the field may have irretrievably destroyed the validity of some investigative techniques, it is possible that analysis of trace elements in the clay of individual tablets might someday indicate their provenance.

An important part of the work relating to the Nuzi tablets has involved the return of the tablets promised to the Iraq Museum by the conditions of the original excavation permit. All tablets requested by the Iraq Museum have now been segregated from the rest of the Nuzi tablet collections for special attention (such as priority in glyptic analyses and study for any possible joins to be made with surviving tablet fragments). Symbolic of *HSM* good faith, a small number of tablets were returned to Iraq in 1975, 1977 and 1978. In 1978 a team from the Iraq Museum visited the *HSM* to observe the process and progress of the Nuzi research collections project and report on our efforts.

As an indication of the international good will generated by the *NEH* Nuzi research collections project as well as, we all sincerely hope, in anticipation of a new era of close scientific collaboration among American and Iraqi scholars, such Nuzi tablet returns have produced cooperation on other levels: a *HSM/ASOR* team represented the U.S., as guests of the Ministry of Culture, at the first International Conference for the Restoration of Babylon and Aššur convened in Baghdad in December 1978. Subsequent consultations in Baghdad in Spring 1979 and 1980 have coordinated joint *HSM*/Iraq Museum efforts to preserve early photographic documentation and preliminary discussions have begun to explore possibilities of a joint international traveling exhibition of Nuzi antiquities to celebrate the final homeward journey of the Nuzi tablets.

The Seal Impressions on the HSM *Nuzi Tablets*

By far the largest coherent assemblage of ancient Near Eastern art which can be associated with a specific region, period, and set of people, Nuzi seal impressions in the *HSM* have required the most effort of any part of the Nuzi research collections project. Because of the inherent difficulties of discerning faint designs, extreme patience as well as skill have been required to find and record these personal signatures which visually reflect mysteriously fantastic visions both of cosmic order and the nightmare powers of the praeternatural.

By early 1980, careful preliminary line drawings (twice natural size) had been made by artists from analyses of almost all the seal impressions on the Nuzi tablets, and a photographic record of most of the seals had been

Scale 2:1 Composite of *HSS* 13 161:A NA$_4$ ^{m}du-ra-ri amēli ḫa-za-an-ni ša āl ilāni
HSS 13 114:H NA$_4$ ^{m}du-ra-ri amēli ḫa-za-an-ni
KEL 89522 NA$_4$ ^{m}du-ra-ri mār šur-ku-ma-tal

FIG. 1

assembled. The identification of seal owner's names is progressing in anticipation of the editing of the comprehensive Nuzi glyptic corpus scheduled to begin in the summer of 1982.

In the course of the glyptic project, various possibilities of using computers to sort glyptic motifs have been explored. Pilot clusterings of seal designs (on the basis of such objective criteria as the quantity and types of figures and ornamental patterns) proved so successful that coherent stylistic and chronological groupings emerged with totally unanticipated consistency. Eventually, the designs of many partial rollings may be reconstructed through such computerized sortings. Despite the glimpse of efficient research possibilities ahead which these experiments have afforded, arduous precision in accurately drawing each impression remains the indispensible first step for all subsequent analyses.

Plans are now being formulated for the editing of a comprehensive *Corpus of Nuzi Glyptic* which, with proper support, should be published within two years. To illustrate this summary, examples of the designs to be shared throughout this *Corpus* appear in Figures 1-3.[1] The drawings are described briefly with regard to their iconographic components and other significant aspects.

FIGURE 1

The design here reconstructed from fragmentary components discovered on *HSM* Nuzi tablet *HSS* 13 114 shows: a solar disc surmounting a foliated knobbed standard from which sprout two pairs of antithetic volutes and which rises from a mountain-like base (comprised of five drillings, two above three). The standard is held and flanked by two bullmen who face each other as they

[1]Drawings prepared by Ms. Diana L. Stein.

Scale 2:1

Composite of *HSS* 14 6:B
HSS 15 171:A
HSS 15 334:A

Fig. 2

each grasp the standard shaft beneath its knob in one hand and touch the upper volute on each side with the other hand. Behind the torso of the bullman on the left, a vertical ballstaff separates him from a winged seated sphinx wearing a plumed helmet beneath a horizontal scorpion. Behind the torso of the bullman on the right, a seven-globed rosette separates him from a winged seated bull held by leash grasped in one hand by a striding helmeted figure who wears a long robe open-in-the-front and who grasps the plume of the sphinx's helmet in his other hand.

This composition's continuously rolled design can be considered as having two central motifs: As primary motif, the "tree of life" linking celestial and terrestrial symbols is symmetrically flanked and faced by the inner and outer pairs of monsters interspersed with geometric astral devices. A secondarily central motif (not "respected" by the monsters who all face the tree) evokes very ancient heroic themes. The so-called "*potnios theron*" compositions descend from prehistoric stamp seal patterns which show a powerful humanoid figure grasping bestial figures in each hand in a manner which reveals that he has subdued them (often by holding both upside down by one of their rear legs, as though they were hunting tropies, in the manner of the central figure in the Great Seal of Sauštattar on the cover and endpapers of this volume). In this case, the "Master of Beasts" can be clearly identified as a storm-god type by reason of his leashed winged bull and the nearby rosette. The weapon which the storm-god usually holds (in the hand which does not grasp the leash of his *ušumgallu* or bull) has been replaced here by the sphinx' plume. Iconographic coherence has, however, been visually preserved here because the plume's form evokes the outline of the curved knife, scimitar, or sickle-sword which such storm gods carry on Nuzi seals at least as frequently as the "Lightening-Fork" they wield more usually on designs from other regions.

The seal which rolled this design belonged to a certain Turari who on the *HSM* Nuzi tablet (*HSS* 13 114) is entitled "Mayor of the city of Ilāni." The similarly named gentleman whose father's name is given as Šurkum-atal on *KEL* 89522 (published in this volume by Professor David Owen) which does not mention any civic office, can be proven to be the same Turari because the impressions on the tablet show that he employed the identical seal to sign both tablets.[2] Thus, beyond revealing visions of preaeternatural powers which were invoked to protect seal owners' interests, Nuzi seals can establish the identity of such owners on scattered documents today just as they did 35 centuries ago.

FIGURE 2

From very fragmentary rollings on many *HSM* tablets, a most unusual design has been reconstructed which, apart from its tantalizing juxtaposition of "the lamb and the lion" known as a paradigm of peace from so much Near Eastern wisdom literature, reveals an artistic *tour de force* unparalleled in antiquity: "a bird's-eye-view" of a recumbant antelope beneath a similar animal shown in profile!

A full-bearded regal figure in a long robe open-in-the-front holds a sickle sword behind him in one hand as he clutches his robes in the other hand while striding towards a scene horizontally divided by a guilloche:

Beneath a winged sun-disc (rimmed by 16 globular petals) positioned above the horizontal (eight-knot, dotted) guilloche, a male sheep and a lion walk towards a six-locked nude hero whose head and torso are shown full-face and who clasps his hands together above his three-stranded belt. To the right of the ringleted hero, a vertical interlaced pattern is saluted by the figure of an Intercessionary Goddess in a divine helmet and *kaunakes* who raises both forearms in adoration. Behind her head and that of the regal figure sits an antelope above the form of a similar antelope rendered as though seen from on top (with its head bent forward as though grazing).

Among many peculiarities of this design (cut with muscular modelling characteristic of the "Isin Larsa" period some four centuries before most of the Nuzi seals) are the non-heraldic gentle pace and relative positions of the sheep and the lion who are rendered with unusual anatomical fidelity and realism. The bird's-eye-view of the antelope, shown with its haunches uppermost, resembles the outlines of insect-like forms and mysterious space-fillers (sometimes identified as goat-fish and lion-fish because of their similarity to indubitably clear renderings of those monsters on seals cut by experts in

[2]The same impression is found on tablet *AO* 6031 in The Louvre, published by Contenau, G., "Les tablettes de Kerkouk et les origines de la civilisation Assyrienne" in: *Babyloniaca* 9, fasc. 2-4 (1926); p. 78, Fig. 130.

a. *HSS* 13 435:B NA_4 KIŠIB ᵐpa-i-til-la

b. *HSS* 13 352:C NA_4 KIŠIB ᵐpa-i-til-la

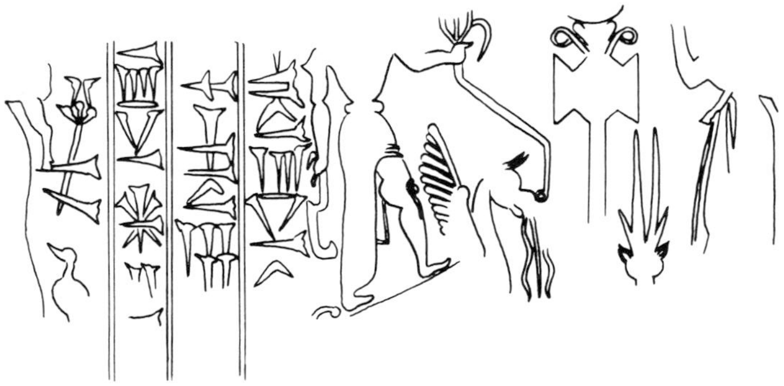

c. *HSS* 14 232:A NA_4 KIŠIB ᵐpa-i-til-la

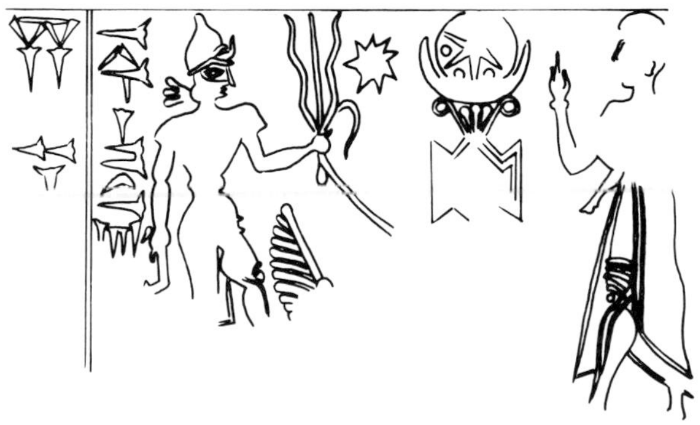

d. *HSS* 15 134:A Seal owner's name not preserved.

e. *HSS* 13 Pl.9B:C NA4 KIŠIB [m]ku-lu-ḫu-pi

f. Composite of the above impressions a-e

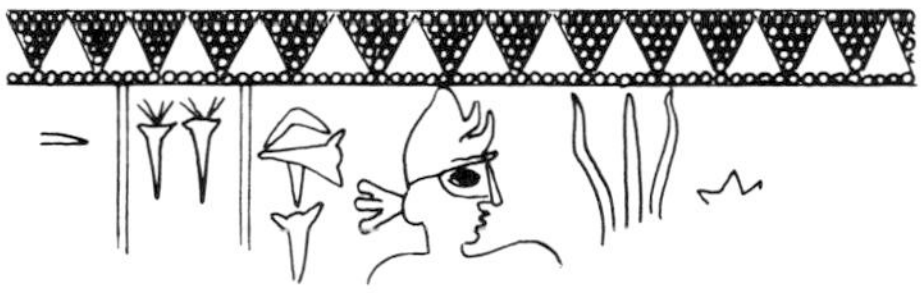

g. *HSS* 15 129:A NA4 KIŠIB [m]ar-ša-li(m)

Scale 2:1

FIG. 3

detail). Thus, this unprecedented form suggests caution in identifying strange shapes solely on the basis of analogical outlines.

Most unusually, the central scene of this design seems by reason of size, its compositional importance, and its framing (by the regal figure on the left, the winged sun-disc above, and the ringleted hero on the right) to be the two animals. These animals walk so placidly and with such relative proportions that the cutter—undoubtedly aware that most lions are bigger than most sheep and *a fortiori* conscious that glyptic convention stressed such size differences in the normal rendering of those animals as prey and predator—seems to be attempting to show them walking side by side. Thus, a rudimentary effort at perspective distinguishes this seal as much as does the rendering of an antelope from two directions at once, almost as though the artist anticipated the attempts of Muybridge's photo-records.

A secondarily central motif seems to be the vertical interlacement—a geometric device which, in simpler form, is sometimes employed on Nuzi seals as a space-divider to mark the end of a "non-continuous" rolled design. The "tree of life" at Nuzi is often rendered by a vertical geometric pattern (of discs or interlacements) but only in this instance do we find a simple guilloche—without any solar disc above it or mountainous or altar-like base below—saluted by an adjacent goddess. The ringleted hero (a form antedating the Akkad period and long erroneously identified with Gilgamesh) is frequently used as a flanking device for two scenes at once. Although his frontally rendered head and torso permit his form to be considered as ancillary to the sheep and lion scene, the direction in which his feet point confirm the compositional importance of the vertical guilloche.

Figure 3

Of all the remarkable designs recoverable through re-assembling fragmentary rollings on Nuzi tablets, this seal is surely one of the most startling: the "Tree of Life" seems to incorporate a double axe motif-evocative of the Cretan *labrys*!

In this case we present various fragmentary components from which (with others) the entire design has been reconstituted. The seal's basic composition is simple: The elegantly-cut, finely-detailed design shows an intricately composite "Tree of Life" flanked on the left by a storm-god and, on the right, by a kid-bearing worshipper. The details of the design deserve careful attention: Upon the back of a winged seated lion (with a triple-tufted tail evocative of the feathered tail of the *ušumgallu*) who vomits lightening, the storm-god is clad in a long robe open-in-front to reveal a kilt and he wears on his head a helmet with a horn in front. Behind him the storm-god holds a sickle sword while in front he grasps with uplifted hand both a lightening-fork and a leash attached to his lion's nose by a ring.

Between a star (actually an eight-rayed disc) on the upper left and an antelope's head (shown frontally!) on the lower right, a standard rises from the back of a small recumbent antelope, to culminate in a double-axe-shaped top from which sprout two antithetic volutes, with three fronds between them. Above the standard, a horizontal crescent encloses the lower half of a sundisc containing a six-pointed-star with tiny globes between each ray.

The kid-bearing worshipper is clad in a cap and a long robe open-in-front to reveal a kilt and raises his free arm in salute to the disc and crescent. To the right behind him is seated an "eagle."

The inscription cut on this seal is a rarity at Nuzi for non-royal seals (other than for numerous semi-illiterate renderings of the signs for the gods ^{d}Utu and ^{d}Aia) and suggests that this seal had a pre-Nuzi history elsewhere.

This seal is used by four different individuals: Pai-tilla (*HSS* 13 17:B; 352:C; 435:B; 14 232:A); Kula-ḫupi (*HSS* 13 Pl.9B:C; 14 636:A); Ar-šalim (*HSS* 15 129; probably 14 240:B); and Ḫeltip-apu (*HSS* 14 587:A). It also appears on *HSS* 15 134 with no inscription. There is the possibility that this was an "office seal."[3]

The way in which seals are rolled on tablets has not yet received sufficient attention. Sometimes Pai-tilla seems to have looked first at his cylinder seal before placing it against the clay to roll it so that the inscribed panel would be reproduced centrally in the impression. Such accent upon the legibility of the seal-legend's words was typical of the Ur III period. Then, for several types of ration documents, one side of each tablet was first prepared by continuously stamping the cylinder's legend on the clay before the stylus was used to write the cuneiform message. On the other side of such Ur III tablets the cylinder would actually be rolled out as a signature but in such a way that the legend was centrally impressed and the "presentation-scene" design would normally be visible only in fragmentary details flanking the legend (the back of the seated god's throne and his head on the left of the text panel and on the right bits of worshippers or an intercessory goddess, all facing away from the text panel).

Because of the vast numbers of surviving seal impressions and the need for far more precise study of the evolution of traditional cutting methods and motifs, we should be cautious in suggesting that the same hand had produced two different seals. However beyond extraordinarily skillful techniques of anatomical rendering (especially of muscular knees and calves) and the unconventional renderings of the geometry of sacral symbols occurring in both Pai-tilla's seal and in the sheep and lion seal, a proclivity for unusual views of antelopes (from on top and from the front) may indicate that both seals are the work of one artist with a *verve* for experimentation rarely encountered in glyptic.

[3]Along the top edge of the two examples where this seal was used by ^{m}*ar-ša-li(m)* (*HSS* 14 240:B, *HSS* 15 129:A), there is an impression of a cap decorated with a geometric design which is not visible on impressions of the same seal associated with other palace officials where the upper edge is preserved (*HSS* 13 17:B, *HSS* 13 Pl. 9B:C, *HSS* 15 134). The geometric design consists of triangles filled alternately with the small circular impressions characteristic of granulation which indicates that part, if not all of the seal cap was made of gold. It is interesting to note that the attachment of the cap reduces the height of the seal proper and, in this case, obliterates the first cuneiform signs of the legend which are clearly visible on the other impressions of this same seal without caps. The golden cap is undoubtedly a later addition to the seal and, thus, serves as a useful chronological indicator. (D.L.S.)

HSM *Collections of Artifacts Excavated at Nuzi*

The Nuzi artifacts had been stored in very rough groupings of pottery, stone, metal, and organic materials as well as beads. During initial inventory, several joins were made from parts-of-objects long separated in the former inadequate storage conditions.

For an object-registration-system, a modification of the Library of Congress Cataloguing system was introduced to permit correlation with other *HSM* collections as well as to preserve the integrity of Nuzi object assemblages: "930" was chosen as the code for Nuzi artifacts (primarily because during 1930 no objects had been formally accessioned by the *HSM*). To "930" have been appended codes for *artifact classification* (wherein the numerals signify *object type* and the letters refer to typological, decorative, or stylistic *distinctions* within each category) and sequential *item-numbers* for each classified object. Thus, 930.4A.2 refers to a Nuzi (930) whole zoomorphic vessel (4A) recorded as the second item (2) in the series of similar objects. A full table of the new object-type-codes is appended below (Chart I) to illustrate the variety of artifacts sorted as well as the designations assigned to their groupings.

In making registry cards for each artifact, the following categories of information were recorded as fully as possible:

1) Site provenance (including soundings near the main mound at Nuzi).
2) Field provenance (including "room numbers" whenever attainable).
3) Artifact classification (of code designations enumerated below).
4) Registry number (including new modified L.C. system and original designations).
5) Physical data (measurements, weight, description of decoration, etc.).
6) Research-to-date (where applicable).
7) *HSM* location (storage cabinet and drawer).

The registry cards themselves were typed in triplicate to provide three systems for access to the artifacts through:

1) *Location* in the *HSM* (so materials can be studied drawer-by-drawer).
2) Artifact *classification* (to facilitate typological and statistical studies).
3) Field *provenance* (to permit stratigraphical, demographic, and building-use analyses as far as possible).

Chart I

Nuzi Artifact Classifications—Spring 1980

(NB: The following codes for *object-types* form the central part of the *HSM*'s new Nuzi object numbers—preceded by the code 930 (for Nuzi) and followed by the item-number accorded each individual object within the classified type.)

930.1	Wall Nails
1A	Whole Wall Nails (without glaze)
1B	Wall Nail Fragments (without glaze)
1C	Whole Wall Nails (glazed)
1D	Wall Nail Fragments (glazed)
930.2	Model Chariots
2A	Model Chariot Bodies
2B	Model Chariot Body Fragments
2C	Model Chariot Wheels
2D	Model Chariot Wheel Fragments
930.3	Duck Weights
930.4	Zoomorphic Vessels
4A	Whole Zoomorphic Vessels
4B	Zoomorphic Vessel Fragments
930.5	Zoomorphic Objects
5A	Whole Zoomorphic Objects
5B	Zoomorphic Object Fragments
930.6	Animal Figurines
6A	Whole Animal Figurines
6B	Animal Figurine Fragments
930.7	Human and Deity Figurines
7A	Whole Figurines
7B	Figurine Fragments
7C	Stylized Figurines and Fragments
930.8	Anthropomorphic Fragments (ceramic/stone)
930.9	Weaponry and Implements (non-metallic)
9A	Sling Stones and Fragments
9B	Mace Heads and Fragments
9C	Flints and Fragments
9D	Weapon Mold
9E	Mortars
9F	Pestles and Pounding Stones
9G	Indented Stones
9H	Miscellaneous Implements
930.10	Loom Weights and Spindle Whorls
10A	Whole Loom Weights
10B	Loom Weight Fragments
10C	Whole Spindle Whorls
10D	Spindle Whorl Fragments
930.11	Needles
11A	Whole Needles
11B	Needle Fragments
930.12	Strainers
12A	Whole Strainers
12B	Strainer Fragments
930.13	Miscellaneous Clay Objects
13A	Braziers and Fragments
13B	Building Bricks (inscribed and plain)
930.14	Glazed-Objects and Fragments
930.15	Glazed Whole Vessels
930.16	Glazed Sherds
930.17	Covers
930.18	Stands
930.19	Partitioned Vessels
930.20	Goblets
930.21	Cups and Small Goblets
21A	Flat Base
21B	Developing Foot
21C	Footed Cups
21D	Ring Base
21E	String-cut
21F	Misc. Cups, Small Goblets & Fragments
930.22	Small & Medium Bowls (width of 30 cm. and less)
22A1	Footed Bowls and Fragments - Pronounced Carination (PC)
22A2	Footed Bowls and Fragments - Moderate Carination (MC)
22A3	Footed Bowls and Fragments - No Carination (NC)
22B1	Ring Base Bowls PC
22B2	Ring Base Bowls MC
22B3	Ring Base Bowls NC
22C1	Tripod Bowls and Fragments PC
22C2	Tripod Bowls and Fragments MC
22C3	Tripod Bowls and Fragments NC

22D1 Round Base Bowls PC
22D2 Round Base Bowls MC
22D3 Round Base Bowls NC

22E Bowl with Hole in Bottom

22F String-cut

22G Miscellaneous

930.23 Large Bowls (width of 20 cm. and more)
23A Shallow Bowls and Plates (depth of 5 cm. and less)
23B Deep Bowls
23C Large Footed Bowls
23D Large Coarse Ware Bowls

930.24 Plates

930.25 Small Jars
25A Round Bottom
25B Ring Base (string-cut)
25C Button Base
25D Flat Base
25E Footed Base
25F Pointed Base
25G Ring Base
25H Round Bottom with Hole in Side
25I Miscellaneous

930.26 Medium Jars
26A Round Bottom
26B Ring Base and Wide Mouth
26C Button Base
26D Ring Base and Narrow Mouth
26E Flat Base

930.27 Pitchers
27A Handled

930.28 Coarse Wares

930.29 Lamps

930.30 Burial Jars

930.31 Large Jars
31A Ring Base Jars
31B Ring Base Handles Pitchers
31C Round Bottom
31D Trumpet Base
31E Painted Jar
31F Flat Base

930.32 Oversize Vessels

930.33 Miscellaneous Pottery Categories
33A Spherical Vessels with Hole
33B Triangular Vessels
33C Spouted Jar
33D Stamped Sherd
33E Chalice Base
33F Footed Base Incised Jar
33G Cylindrical Jar
33H Open-ended Jar
33I Coil Made Jar Fragment

930.34 Plain Indicator Sherds
Plain Body

930.35 Incised Indicator
Incised Body

930.36 Painted Indicator
Painted Body

930.37 Relief Sherds

930.38 Osteological Remains

930.39 Botanical Materials

930.40 Miscellaneous Ceramic Objects
40A Sling Stones
40B Discs
40C Beds
40D Pillar
40E Small (Votive) Bowls
40F Painted Ceramic Fragments
40G Perforated Plaques
40H Cylindrical Objects

930.41 Unidentified Ceramic Objects

930.42 Miscellaneous Stone Objects
42B Pierced Stones of Various Shapes
42B Stone Vessels and Fragments
42C Worked Stone Objects

930.43 Unidentifiable Stone Objects

930.44 Beads

930.45 Miscellaneous Artifacts

Identifying photographs were made for each Nuzi artifact. A small print of each photograph has been attached to each registry card and negatives are on file for enlarged study-prints as will be required for future research.

Now that the Nuzi artifact collections have been organized, the work still to be done emerges more clearly. In the course of the 3-year project, related investigations have yielded results which should be correlated with analyses of the Nuzi artifacts now sorted. Professor Giorgio Bucellatti has encountered closely related material at his excavations at Terqa on the Euphrates—including storage jars daubed with bitumen "signs" identical to markings on Nuzi jars. Iraqi archaeologists have excavated a nearby site at Tell al-Faḫḫār—possibly ancient Kurruḫanni. Materials analyses experiments at Rochester Institute of Technology, Massachusetts Institute of Technology, and the U.S. Army's Metals Laboratories at the Watertown Arsenal have begun to yield significant insights into the technology of ancient Nuzi. Indeed, it has been shown that the beads at Nuzi reveal that every major form of ancient glassmaking technology (including sophisticated uses of glass rods) was known there a thousand years earlier than had previously been supposed.

Because at Nuzi, more than has been so far possible at any ancient site, at least in Mesopotamia, detailed records provide us with unimpeachable evidence of the daily affairs of families over six generations, prosopographic analyses required by the glyptic research may be able to attach names of some individuals and their families to some structures and the object assemblages found in those structures.

Actually to be able to study articles of an individual's everyday use together with original accounts of their acquisition and tallying—presents historians with an unprecedented opportunity. Except for grave-deposits and royal-palace-finds, archaeology can only connect objects inscribed with personal names with individuals. Only very rarely have such inscribed artifacts been found in coherent contexts, and even then one must always suspect that the inscribed artifact could be an heirloom from an earlier period or a different place. For this reason, the *HSM* has decided to postpone further work on the Nuzi artifact collections as a whole until the prosopographic tallies of the glyptic corpus are completed. Individual experiments in materials analyses and the study of specific object-types will be encouraged during this period, but we see as part of our responsibility to the Nuzi collections the protection of this invaluable repository of solid evidence from erroneously premature analyses.

For such multi-disciplinary artifact analyses as will be possible once this prosopography of the seal impressions on the tablets has been clearly established, a team approach will be necessary—so that Assyriologists, cultural anthropologists, materials specialists, and historians can reinforce one another's investigations as is both required and uniquely facilitated by reason of the inter-related character of the Nuzi evidence.

HSM *Field Photograph Collections from Nuzi (1928-31)*

Although a 3-year *NEH* project was intended to produce a thorough inventory of all surviving field records, including photographs, several factors combined to intensify the photo-archival aspects of the Nuzi project far beyond what had originally been anticipated. In the first place, Nuzi film-negatives of nitro-cellulose "non-safety" material posed grave danger because their explosive character could be detonated by even slight shock waves, or they could spontaneously combust through unpredictable chemical deterioration. Thus, measures were taken to copy carefully original negatives and to make final prints from them before segregating dangerous material elsewhere. Secondly, various *HSM* projects (at first unrelated to Nuzi) began to direct efforts of our colleagues throughout the world towards finding and preserving endangered visual documentation for the study of the cultural heritage of the Middle East. Apart from the record of the archaeological excavations at Nuzi, the Nuzi field-photographs came to be recognized as a unique source for many disciplines.

Tarkhalan, the village nearest the site of Nuzi, was populated by Arabs, Kurds, and Turkomen as well as recently sedentary Beduin. Fortunately, photographs were made not only of the expedition's work at the site of Nuzi but of daily life in the village and of celebrations ranging from workers' informal line-dances to remarkable performances by a visiting gypsy troupe. Mrs. Mathilde Pfeiffer recorded such scenes on motion picture film in 1928. In addition, she filmed other events, including a deluge which destroyed the houses of Tarkhalan, the playful insouciance of the villagers in the face of this adversity, and the group-work of swiftly and efficiently rebuilding the houses with clay bricks without any straw. With the exception of the films made at Nuzi, the earliest motion picture record of life in Iraq was the film of a 1935 Boy Scout Jamboree in Baghdad—scarcely to be considered a typical indigenous celebration.

The present overview of the *HSM* Nuzi collections is not the place to list the thousands of Nuzi photographs discovered and catalogued—for future investigators to check for *in-situ* relationships of the objects excavated from individual rooms or to study "baulks" photographed while still moist for stratigraphic clues in an excavation where methods of the time did not deliberately record variations in layers of fill. Moreover, the *NEH* project has generated new photographs, including color transparencies for use in public educational efforts. Also, special xero-radiographic techniques have been developed to investigate the interior of closed ceramic objects (such as whole vessels, tablets still sealed in envelopes, and moulded figurines).

A manual for cataloguing archaeological photographs has been developed for sorting Nuzi field photographs. This manual is being tested for adaptability for other expedition records by *HSM* colleagues overseas within the International F.O.C.U.S Project (to *F*ind, *O*rganize, *C*opy, *U*se and *S*hare endangered photographic collections for the preservation of Middle Eastern cultural heritage). With adaptations suggested by our colleagues, the Manual will be available for use by archivists throughout the world through UNESCO's Sector for Culture and Communications.

Besides microfilming Nuzi records, the *HSM* has recorded the recollections of those present at the excavations, especially of Professor Lacheman himself. Such recordings, the 1928 cinematographic records, original field photographs, and project color transparencies as well as pictures taken at the site today have been edited in video-tape form as *Nuzi - 1500* B.C. as a demonstration of the educational possibilities of archaeological sleuthwork-sharing.

Through the gracious invitation of the Foreign Ministry of the Federal Republic of Germany, the present status of the *HSM* Nuzi collections was reported to many of the principle European Nuzi scholars during the summer of 1980. Thus, plans for the next phases of investigation and publication of the Nuzi discoveries are being formulated in consultation with scholars throughout the world and Iraqi officials.

Nuzi's discoveries, as proven by Professor Lacheman's research, provide a key to understanding "Antiquity's Dark Age." Inspired by the example of Professor Lacheman, the *HSM* hopes by ordering the Nuzi collections, to be able to share that key and thereby open new dimensions for understanding—in scientific investigation, international cooperation and the appreciation of perennial human values.

Erēbu Marriage

Cyrus H. Gordon
New York University

It would be hard to name another scholar who has been as dedicated to a specific field for as long as Ernest Lacheman has been to Nuzi Studies. He has labored quietly without fanfare on each of his Nuzi volumes. Now, after half a century of steady productivity, his accomplishment is massive and enduring. Lacheman is not a "committee man." He stands alone and has made his outstanding contribution single-handed. I feel privileged to know him, to have worked with him, and to have been his colleague.

The Nuzi tablets confront us with some illustrations of marriage whereby the husband is to live with his wife in her father's domain. The plainest reference to this kind of marriage appears in the Assyrian Laws. Normally, in the Near East (ancient and modern), including the Assyrian Laws, the wife leaves her own family to join the house of her husband. However, Assyrian Law A:27[1] reads: "If a woman is residing in her father's house, (and) her husband pays visits[2] to her, any settled property[3] which her husband has given to her, he may take back; (but) he shall not touch[4] what belongs to her father's house." The Akkadian verb *erēbu*, as used here, has given rise to the terminology whereby such marriages are called "*erēbu* marriages." Yet this is illogical because in normal marital arrangements, where the wife enters the husband's house, the same verb (*erēbu*) is employed (as in A:28[5] and A:29[6]).

"*Erēbu* marriage" is not necessarily a permanent arrangement obliging the couple to reside in the house of the bride's father as long as the couple remains wed to each other. A marriage that starts out with the groom entering the

[1]G. R. Driver and J. C. Miles, *The Assyrian Laws*, Scientia Verlag Aalen (Germany), 1975 (reprint of the Oxford edition of 1935), p. 399.

[2]The frequentative *-tan-* infix in *e-ta-na-ra-ab* (literally, "he keeps entering") suggests that the husband does not reside steadily in her father's house, but instead visits his wife there regularly.

[3]*Nu-dun-na-a.*

[4]The verb (*i-qa-ar-ri-ib*) is literally "he shall draw near" (i.e., to claim).

[5]Gt *te-ta-ra-ab* "she has entered."

[6]Again Gt, this time spelled *te-ta-rab* "she has entered."

bride's house, may be altered into a more "normal" relationship with the bride leaving her father's house to depart permanently with her husband.[7]

There are Nuzi adoption tablets[8] that deal with a father who has daughters but no sons. The father adopts a man as an heir, simultaneously marrying off a daughter to him.[9] The newlywed couple becomes part of the father's household. The tablet will go on to specify that if a real son is subsequently born to her father, that real son becomes an heir, usually the chief heir, with the adopted son-in-law relegated to subsidiary heir.[10] One text[11] adds that if no real son is born to the father-in-law, the adopted son-in-law takes the household gods, which are tangible symbols of family leadership, conveying control of the family cult.

C. J. Gadd's pioneering publication of the Nuzi tablets[12] includes the contract of Našwi, who adopted Wullu, simultaneously giving him his daughter as wife. Wullu is to be Našwi's heir and inheritor of Našwi's household gods, unless a real son is subsequently born to Našwi. In that event, the real son gets the gods and divides the rest of the estate with Wullu. The text runs thus:

> The adoption tablet of Našwi son of Aršenni. He adopted Wullu son of Puḫišenni. As long as Našwi lives, Wullu shall give (him) food and clothing. When Našwi dies, Wullu shall inherit. Should Našwi beget a son, (the latter) shall divide equally with Wullu but (only) Našwi's son shall take Našwi's gods. But if there be no son of Našwi's, then Wullu shall take Našwi's gods. And (Našwi) has given his daughter Nuhuya as wife to Wullu. And if Wullu takes another wife, he forfeits[13] Našwi's land and buildings. Whoever breaks the contract shall pay one mina of silver (and) one mina of gold.

It was Sidney Smith[14] who perceived that this text explains Rachel's theft of her father's teraphim (or household gods) in Genesis 31. This discovery

[7]The accounts of the marriages of Jacob and of Moses, discussed below, illustrate this.

[8]Called *ṭuppi mārūti*, but not in the usual Nuzi sense of a "sale adoption" to mask the sale of land. The cases under discussion are "real adoptions" calling for filial service and care on the part of the adoptee toward the adoptor.

[9]In *HSS* 5 67, the bride given to the adoptee may not be the adoptor's daughter, for her father's name is not stated.

[10]The term for "subsidiary or secondary heir" is *te-ir-te-en-nu* (e.g., *HSS* 5 67:10). The distinctive Nuzi word for "heir" is *ewuru*; the verbal expression made from it is *ewurumma epēšu* "to inherit" (*CAD* E, 415; *AHw*, 267).

[11]Gadd's tablet #51, translated below.

[12]C. J. Gadd, "Tablets from Kirkuk," *RA* 23 (1926) 49-161. The text in question is #51 (126-27, 155).

[13]This clause reflects the fact that *erēbu* marriage tends to protect the woman's favored status.

[14]Sidney Smith, "What were the Teraphim?," *Journal of Theological Studies* 33 (1932) 33-36.

foreshadowed the spate of Nuzi parallels to the Patriarchal Narratives.[15] The theft of the teraphim and the adoption aspects of Jacob's marrying Laban's daughters, and much else, were put into perspective by the Nuzi parallels. Since then, other parallels from other periods have been brought into the discussion. Accordingly, one should not insist that, since the date of the Nuzi tablets is fixed (± 1400 B.C.), the Patriarchal Narratives stem from precisely the same date. Customs are often quite durable. Marriage, adoptions, religion and funerary customs may persist with little change for millennia. But to say that the Nuzi parallels to the Patriarchal Narratives have little or no significance in biblical studies would be incorrect.[16] Many hitherto strange phenomena in the Patriarchal Narratives (and elsewhere in the Bible) were removed from isolated mystery and put into ancient Near East perspective by the Nuzi tablets.

HSS 5 67[17] is an adoption tablet from Nuzi whereby Šennima is given by his father to Šuriḫil as an adopted son. Šennima is to be the heir of Šuriḫil, and take care of Šuriḫil as long as Šuriḫil lives. If a real son is born to Šuriḫil, that son is to be the chief heir, with Šennima next in line.[18] This adoption goes hand in hand with Šennima's marriage to a girl named Gilimninu (whose parentage is not specified). The motive of the adoption is to provide continuity of the family even if the adopting father does not beget a son of his own.

The closest parallels to such Nuzi marriages are provided by the Genesis narratives about Jacob's marrying the daughters of Laban. Laban states that he prefers Jacob as a son-in-law to anyone else (Genesis 29:19) possibly because of their blood relationship (Genesis 29:14-15). No sons of Laban are mentioned until two decades later (Genesis 31:1, 4, 41), long after Jacob has married Leah and Rachel. Genesis 31:26 shows that Laban was master of the entire household including Jacob's wives, Jacob's children and possessions (Genesis 31:43). It is also clear that Rachel had no right to take the household gods (Genesis 31:19, 30, 32), which were to remain with Laban and presumably to be passed on to his own son(s), probably the eldest. The text repeatedly states that Rachel stole the gods. Note that Jacob could have left honorably with his wives, children and possessions merely by asking and receiving

[15]Cyrus H. Gordon, "Biblical Customs and the Nuzu Tablets," *The Biblical Archaeologist Reader* 2, Garden City (N.Y.): Doubleday (Anchor), 1964, pp. 21-33.

[16]Such downgrading has been expressed in print as a result of recent attempts to ascribe a very late date to the Patriarchal Narratives. Cf., for example, J. Van Seters, *Abraham in History and Tradition*, New Haven: Yale University Press, 1975; T. L. Thompson, *The Historicity of the Patriarchal Narratives* (*BZAW* 133), Berlin: de Gruyter, 1974; and idem, "A New Attempt to Date the Patriarchal Narratives," *JAOS* 98 (1978) 76-84.

[17]Restored, transliterated and translated with notes by E. A. Speiser, *New Kirkuk Documents Relating to Family Laws* (*AASOR* 10, for 1928-29, appeared in 1930), pp. 126-27.

[18]The real son is termed the *rabū* and received a double share, while Šennima is called the *te-ir-te-en-nu* (as noted above).

Laban's permission (Genesis 31:27, 30). Indeed, Laban and Jacob finally decide to make a peace treaty and part company, with Jacob permanently leaving Laban's domain and journeying to his homeland with his wives, children and flocks. This shows that *erēbu* marriage could develop into the usual type of marriage in a patriarchal society. It is also interesting to note that a promise is imposed on Jacob not to mistreat Laban's daughters nor to marry other women (Genesis 31:5).[19]

There is an aspect of Jacob's marriages that is not inherent in the Nuzi documents. Jacob is a refugee, far from home, when he seeks asylum with Laban, marries his daughters and becomes part of Laban's menage. Jacob had wronged Esau and fled for fear of violent vengeance at Esau's hands. Fugitives who made a good impression, or were for one reason or another desirable, were acceptable as sons-in-law. But such a son-in-law could not legally force his wife to leave her father's house. She and their children and property belonged to her father for life. This follows, as we have noted, from Laban's complaint to Jacob in Genesis 31:43.

Erēbu marriage with a desirable fugitive in a foreign land is also illustrated by Moses and Zipporah. Moses had committed murder in Egypt and feared punishment there (Exodus 2:11-15). Accordingly he fled to Midian where he met Jethro's[20] daughters. The girls were favorably impressed by the gallant behavior (Exodus 2:17) of the Egyptian (Exodus 2:19) Moses. So Jethro invited Moses to dinner and eventually gave his daughter Zipporah in marriage to Moses (Exodus 2:21). Moses not only joins Jethro's household but takes care of Jethro's flocks (Exodus 3:1), as Jacob had taken care of Laban's. When it comes time for Moses to return to Egypt to fulfill his mission there, Jethro hands over to Moses Zipporah and the sons she had born Moses (Exodus 18:2-6).[21] So again we note an *erēbu* marriage modified into the more normal arrangement (with the husband in direct control and away from the domain of the wife's father) through the permission of the father-in-law (Exodus 4:18) while the latter is still living.

Samson's marriage is also of the *erēbu* type. As a Hebrew outsider, though not a fugitive, among the Philistines, he weds a Philistine girl. Angered because the Philistines had pressured his bride to find out and reveal the answer to his riddle, Samson leaves her in the house of her father. On the assumption that Samson no longer loved her (Judges 15:2), the father gives her to another man (Judges 14:20). When Samson returned to claim conjugal

[19]Cf. the penalty for taking another wife in the Našwi and Wullu tablet, above. In *HSS* 5 67:18, Šennima is forbidden to marry another wife.

[20]The father-in-law of Moses is called by different names, of which "Jethro" and "Reuel" are the most familiar. I have used "Jethro" consistently to avoid confusion.

[21]The separation of this statement in chapter 18, far from the earlier narratives in chapters 2, 3 and 4, obscures the sequence of events.

rights with his wife, only to discover that she had been given to another, the "wrath of Samson"[22] took a dire toll of Philistine property and life (Judges 15:4-8).

Homer (Odyssey 6:244-45) describes the desire of a native princess for an *erēbu* marriage with a fascinating foreigner. Nausicaa (the princess in the land of the Phaeacians) wants to wed Odysseus but remain in her own land. Her words are: "Would that such a man as he might be called my husband, dwelling here and that it might please him to remain."

In the Middle Egyptian Romance of Sinuhe[23] the apprehensive courtier Sinuhe, flees from Egypt to Syria-Palestine during the period of uncertainty that followed the death of Amenemhet I, when his son Senusret I hastened to Thebes to secure the reins of government in the capital. As a fugitive, Sinuhe roamed through "Retenu" (= Syria-Palestine) until he reached the land of Yaa where the king took a liking to him, and married him to his eldest daughter.[24] During a successful career in Yaa, Sinuhe established rapport with the Egyptian court. Senusret finally welcomes Sinuhe back to his native land with all the happy features of a homecoming[25] including the guarantee of an honorific burial in his own home town. The text never even raises the possibility of taking his wife and children with him to Egypt. It is tacitly assumed that when the foreign husband returns to his native land, his local wife and their children remain in her father's domain. Sinuhe, being a responsible administrator, left his house in order, with his sons carrying on after him. His wife's status as a princess in her own land was protected; in Egypt she would have been reduced to the status of a foreign woman.

In general it may be said that *erēbu* marriage provided economic opportunities to the man but upheld the social status of the bride. The husband was the outsider who benefited from the marriage only as long as he respected his wife's privileges, accepted the jurisdiction of her father, and resided in her domain.

It is of more than passing interest to note that the prototype of marriage in the Bible is *erēbu*. "A man shall forsake his father and mother, and cleave unto his wife and they shall become one flesh" (Genesis 2:24).

[22]Cf. "the wrath of Achilles" which caused many to perish on account of the anger of a hero whose woman had been taken away from him (Iliad 1:1-4).

[23]The hieroglyphic transcription of the text is in Aylward M. Blackman, *Middle Egyptian Stories*, Brussels: Fondation Egyptologique Reine Elizabeth, 1932, pp. 1-41. For an annotated translation, see Miriam Lichtheim, *Ancient Egyptian Literature* I, Berkeley: U. of Cal. Press, 1973, pp. 222-35.

[24]The oldest daughter would normally be favored as regards status and inheritance.

[25]As in the Odyssey, the happy ending is the *nostos* "homecoming." This is also featured in the Gilgamesh Epic, the Egyptian Tale of the Shipwrecked Sailor, and other works of literature. The theme is so natural and widespread that it cannot be used as hard evidence for diffusion.

The variant forms of *erēbu* marriage surveyed above, place the Nuzi adoptions of sons-in-law in a broad Near East and Mediterranean framework, for the examples come from Assyria and Egypt, and from the Bible and Homer.

Dowry and Brideprice in Nuzi

Katarzyna Grosz
University of Copenhagen

The marriage prestations of dowry and brideprice have long been of particular interest to social anthropologists working in societies ranging from China to Africa.[1] These societies are often quite different from that of Mesopotamia. However, certain similarities can be traced. In this article, the Nuzi system of dowry (*mulūgu*) and brideprice (*terḫatu*) will be examined, and features that it shares with other such systems will be discussed.

Presentation of terms

Dowry

Dowry is the property received by the bride from her father at the time of her marriage. It may be considered an advance on inheritance or a kind of "pre-mortem inheritance to the bride."[2] While sons are generally expected to wait for their inheritance until the death of their father, daughters receive their share when they are married. At the core of the dowry system lies the notion of female property right, and the dower property usually remains a separate unit throughout the marriage. Although dowry is female property, it is considered a trust held for the couple's children and its alienation, if at all possible, is considered at least reprehensible.

The contents of the dowry vary from culture to culture; household utensils, blankets and textiles, jewelry, cash, cattle, and sometimes land can all be given to the bride as her share. The fact that women can inherit land or receive it as their dowry has far-reaching effects. Greater flexibility can be achieved because the new couple, besides choosing to reside with the groom's parents (virilocal residence) or taking a quite new residence (neolocal residence), can also reside with the wife's family (uxorilocal residence). Because children inherit from both parents, "the shift and transmission to bilateral kinship and

[1]I should like to express my gratitude to Dr. Susan Whyte of the Institute of Ethnology and Anthropology of Copenhagen and to Dr. Mogens Trolle Larsen of the Institute of Assyriology, Copenhagen, for all their interest and help.

[2]J. Goody and S. J. Tambiah, *Bridewealth and Dowry*, Cambridge Papers in Social Anthropology, 7. Cambridge, 1973, p. 1.

ambilocal residence"[3] are made possible. If a couple resides virilocally, arrangements for working the dower land situated in the wife's native village would have to be made between the villages. In this way a network of various affinal relationships develop across the whole countryside. These relationships are very important, because they are employed in situations when help is needed and thus constitute a considerable factor in the economy.

J. Goody wrote about female rights of inheritance of immovables:

> It must be clear that the question whether or not land was a woman's portion, either as dowry or as inheritance, is of fundamental importance for other aspects of the social system. The splitting up of holding can be prevented only by complex exchange or by close marriage, and it is not surprising that close connubium prevails where land devolves on women.[4]

An example of a society where women have inheritance rights to land is Vasilika, a village in Boeotia in Greece.[5] In Vasilika, men and women have equal inheritance rights to their patrimony. The patrimony consists of lands inherited in paternal line, mother's dower property and acquisitions made by the father (these categories are sharply distinguished, although there is no tendency towards homoparental inheritance, i.e. males inheriting from males and females from females). Girls receive their share of inheritance in the form of dowry. It is considered an important duty for men to provide dowries for their women. A girl's dowry consists of land and cash. The more cash the father is able to put away for his daughter's betrothal, the less land he will have to part with. The amount of dowry would be expected to equal roughly the patrimony which the groom will inherit from his father. The bride will move to her husband's village and some arrangements will be made for the tilling of her dower land. In cases where there are no sons, the daughter would be the sole heiress and a son-in-law will be "imported" to live with his wife's family.

The husband administers his wife's dower property but will not dispose of it without his wife's consent. Selling dower property for everyday expenses is considered reprehensible. The dower property will be inherited by the couple's children. If the wife outlives her husband, she will inherit a little plot of land, which will be offered as an addition to the plot of the son with whom she chooses to live.

The Vasilika inheritance system has been defined as a "mechanism by which property is transmitted from the woman to her children with a period of

[3] S. J. Tambiah, ibid., p. 68.

[4] J. Goody, ibid., p. 21.

[5] E. Friedl, *Vasilika. A Village in Modern Greece.* Case Studies in Cultural Anthropology, New York, 1962.

intermediate administration by her husband."[6] Thus the dowry forms a part of a conjugal fund and it moves from generation to generation.

Brideprice

It must be stressed that brideprice is not the opposite of dowry. While dowry is a form of inheritance and thus a transaction between the father and his daughter, brideprice is a transaction between the groom's kin and the bride's kin. While the bride and her dowry move in the same direction, the brideprice travels in the direction opposite to the bride and her dowry. The brideprice is used by the bride's male kin (typically brothers) to acquire wives for themselves. A daughter's brideprice would be used to acquire a wife for her brother. The dowry coming in with a daughter-in-law, however, would not be used to equip a daughter. It is from the start destined as the new couple's "nest egg," forming the beginning of their conjugal fund.

The dowry is always paid at the moment of marriage and the whole amount is transferred at once. The brideprice, on the other hand, is often paid in installments over a period of time and consists of movables (food supplied by the groom's kin before and during the marriage feast cannot be considered brideprice as it is not used later by the bride's brothers or her father). In some societies the brideprice can be paid in objects which are inherently valueless and are used only for brideprice payments.

A part of the brideprice can be given to the bride to constitute her dowry. This type of transaction is called "indirect dowry" by Goody.[7] In the case of dissolution of marriage the brideprice is sometimes returned to the groom's kin, but the dowry is always returned to the bride herself. Thus, while the dowry forms a conjugal fund that moves vertically through generations,[8] the brideprice, circulating with the society, forms a societal one that moves on a collateral plane.

Examination of problems related to the main subject

Sources

The present study is based on the following groups of texts: testaments;[9] marriage contracts; documents of transfer of property employing the terms

[6]E. Friedl, "Dowry and Inheritance in Modern Greece," in *Peasant Society. A Reader*. ed. by J. M. Potter, Boston, 1967, p. 59.

[7]Goody, op. cit., p. 2.

[8]Cf. Tambiah, op. cit., p. 62.

[9]The testaments from Nuzi and texts related to problems of inheritance have been treated by J. S. Paradise, *Nuzi Inheritance Practices*, unpublished Ph.D. diss., Pennsylvania, 1972.

mulūgu and *terḫatu*; and receipts of goods, livestock and silver termed "*kaspu ša FN*" (silver for FN), considered here equivalent to *terḫatu*-texts. Also included are some special cases of adoption, in which the adoptee marries the adoptant's daughter.[10] It is of course impossible to discuss all texts, but the tables appearing on the following pages contain all the relevant information from these documents. Excluded from this study are the documents of transfer of rights to marry off women (*ṭuppi kallātūti*), because they require a separate study.

The household in Nuzi

Before turning to particulars of women's economic and social situation and the problems of dowry and brideprice, a general description of the Nuzi household would be appropriate.[11] The inheritance system plays a very important role here.

There can be no doubt that agriculture was the main source of income of the people appearing in these texts. They possessed fields, orchards and gardens, houses and cattle sheds, wells and pastures; immovables constituted the largest and most important part of their property. They also owned animals, tools, as well as various other implements and installations necessary on a farm.

A typical Nuzi household consisted of quite a few family members.[12] Nuzi testaments contain several proofs of this. First, a man and his adult sons often lived together. Sometimes the sons would be married and have children of their own. There would also be a wife, unmarried daughters, and unmarried sisters (widowed sisters would live with their deceased husband's kin, at least when they had children). The man's mother could also be alive and live in the same household (*HSS* 19 18 is a will styled in favour of the testator's mother

[10]For the problems of adoption in Nuzi cf. for instance, E. Cassin, *L'Adoption à Nuzi*, Paris, 1938. Limited space does not allow a full list of studies concerned with this subject.

[11]A full bibliography of studies dealing with Nuzi social structure cannot be given here. Studies representing different approaches to this subject include: P. Koschaker, "Fratriarchat, Hausgemeinschaft und Mutterrecht in Keilschriftlichen," *ZA* 41; the same author "Neue Keilschriftlische Rechtsurkunden aus der El-Amarna Zeit," *ASAW*, Leipzig, 1928; H. Lewy, "The Nuzian Feudal System," *Orientalia* 11 (1940); N. B. Jankovska, "Extended Family Commune and Civil Self Government in Arrapha," in I. M. Diakonoff (ed.), *Ancient Mesopotamia*, Moscow, 1969; and "Communal Self-Government and the King of the State of Arrapha" in *JESHO* 12 (1969).

[12]At least some families owned slaves and perhaps also had a number of dependent persons in the house. At the present stage of study we know next to nothing about the position and number of slaves and "clients" in the private sector.

and investing her with authority over his children).[13] The advantages of a large household are apparent; pooling of labour and resources is more efficient than individual farming on small parcels of land.

Divison of patrimony

The division of patrimony took place after the death of the father.[14] Usually, but not always, there was a chief heir who received a double share of property, while other sons each received a single share. Sometimes a specified item of property could be given as an additional, "outright gift" (*kitru*) to one of the heirs. An unmarried daughter also received her share (see Table 1). If a girl was married in her father's lifetime, she was equipped with a dowry and thus counted as "paid off." In a majority of Nuzi testaments no provisions are made for daughters. In some cases one could assume that the testators had no daughters at all, but the probability is that in at least fifty percent of all cases the daughters were already provided for, i.e. married at the moment when the will was written. If this was not the case, i.e. if the testator still had an unmarried daughter at the moment of the writing of the will, she was treated as an heir and received her share.

A testament always reflects an unusual situation. If no problems of inheritance were envisaged, a testament was not needed. If there was a single male heir and one, perhaps two, daughters who had already been provided for, the transition of property from father to son would take place automatically. The problems arose when there were too many sons, and the father was unable to provide for them all, when there were no sons but only daughters, or when the children (or, rather, sons) were differentiated by descent (i.e. when they had different mothers, or if some sons were adopted). If there were too many sons, some of them could be excluded from the patrimony. This could happen in different ways: some sons could simply be excluded from inheritance;[15] sons who did not live in their father's village could be excluded;[16] or a son could be given in adoption and sometimes even married to his adoptive father's

[13]More than 50 percent of Nuzi testaments make provisions for wives. This could indicate that women lived longer than men or that they married at an earlier stage of their lives than the men did. Many women certainly died in childbirth and men remarried younger wives.

[14]Sometimes the division was further postponed. In *HSS* 19 6 the testator forbids his sons to divide the property before the death of their mother. *HSS* 14 108 states that the son who demands the division will forfeit his share.

[15]For instance *HSS* 19 17 and *HSS* 19 9.

[16]*HSS* 19 7 contains the following stipulation: "Zike and Tamar-tae, my sons, live in another country, so, should they return, I have disinherited (them) from my fields and my houses and they will not divide nor come near anything which is mine" (1.35-39).

daughter. *HSS* 5 67 describes the agreement whereby Zike, son of Akkuya, a wealthy man, gave one of his sons in adoption[17] to an adoptant who had only a daughter (who was his heiress) and no sons:

> Adoption tablet (according to which) Zike, son of Akkuya, gave his son Šennima in adoption to Šuriḫa-ilu, and Šuriḫa-ilu gave Šennima all these fields, his installations, everything belonging to him, to the last thing. Should there be a son of Šuriḫa-ilu, he will be the chief heir (and) take (his) share (accordingly) and Šennima will be a secondary heir and take his share accordingly. As long as Šuriḫa-ilu lives, Šennima will respect him. When Šuriḫa-ilu dies, Šennima will become *ewuru*.[18] Also he (i.e. Šuriḫa-ilu) gave Kelim-ninu as wife to Šennima. If Kelim-ninu bears children, Šennima will not take any other wife, but if Kelim-ninu does not bear children, Kelim-ninu will take a slave-girl from the land of Nullu as wife for Šennima and Kelim-ninu herself will have authority over the child (of the slave girl). Whichever sons Kelim-ninu bears to Šennima—[all] fields, houses, [everything], [....] will be given to the sons. But if she bears no son, Kelim-ninu's daughter will take all fields and houses; and Šuriḫa-ilu will not adopt (any) other son over Šennima. Whoever of them violates (the agreement) will pay one mina of silver and one mina of gold. And Yalampa is given as slave girl to Kelim-ninu and Šatim-ninu is given a father's authority. As long as she lives he (i.e. Šennima) will respect her. Šatim-ninu may not break his clump.[19] Should Kelim-ninu bear children and Šennima take another wife, he will tear off his hem[20] and leave. (Names of witnesses.) Other sons of Zike will not come near any fields or houses (of Šuriḫa-ilu).

This text illustrates well the institution of an uxorilocally residing son-in-law. However, importing of a son-in-law is not enough to supply a man with an heir, because the son-in-law's children would automatically belong to their father's lineage. The property which they would inherit will in time pass from their mother's to their father's lineage. This is why the son-in-law had to be adopted as son. The mere fact of the uxorilocal residence was not enough for his children to belong to their mother's lineage. It is difficult to say whether the young man thus adopted was considered as belonging to his new lineage or to his original one. He continued to use his original patronymic. This was the case with Šennima although he was explicitly excluded from inheritance in his

[17]As a matter of fact, Zike adopted away two of his sons—Šennima and Šelluni. He was a wealthy man so the adoptions can be explained only as an effort to keep the property undivided.

[18]For a discussion of the term *ewuru* cf. Paradise, op. cit., pp. 242-48.

[19]Breaking of a clump is to be understood as rendering unvalid the adoption. Cf. also note 23.

[20]Tearing off a hem signified a complete abandonment of any claim or privilege to the matter in question.

father's testament. Also Zike, his father, was "real-adopted,"[21] although he himself was a wealthy man. It seems generally that the purpose of the "real adoption" in Nuzi was primarily to secure the adoptant in his/her old age and to provide somebody who could perform burial rites.[22] The question or continuation of one's lineage was perhaps not so important. The adoptee continued to use his original patronymic, identifying him as belonging to his original kin. Moreover, a wealthy man like Zike could become an adoptive son of a man obviously poorer and less important than himself and continue in his role as the head of the Akkuya line.

The outcome of *HSS* 5 67 is known. *HSS* 5 48 is the declaration of witnesses before judges that Šuriḫa-ilu has officially declared Šennima his only son and heir. The document contains also a declaration of Šuriḫa-ilu's wife, confirming her husband's declaration.[23] The document further includes the phrase "Šennima won the case," which indicates that there was a claim to Šuriḫa-ilu's property. *HSS* 5 59 is a real adoption; Šennima adopts his own brother, Ar-zizza. Ar-zizza, whom we know to be the chief heir of Zike, receives Šuriḫa-ilu's whole property, with the exception of one *imēr* of land given to Šennima's daughter for lifelong use. After her death the field is to be transferred to Ar-zizza. Here there is a clear violation of the terms of Šennima's adoption. The last clause of *HSS* 5 67 explicitly forbids other sons of Zike to participate in the inheritance of Šuriḫa-ilu's property. *HSS* 19 18 is the testament of Ar-zizza. Among other property he wills Šuriḫa-ilu's estate to this sons who are to divide it equally. No mention is made of Šennima or his daughter and it may be assumed that they were both dead at that time.

This group of tablets sheds an interesting light on principles of descent and inheritance in Nuzi. Nuzi was a patrilineal society, that is, children belonged to their father's lineage. Daughters belonged to the same lineage as their brothers, but while brothers' children would belong to the same lineage, the sister's children would belong to that of their father. The only way to circumvent this was by adopting the sister's husband. The fact that the adopted son-in-law continued to use his old patronymic could signify that through adoption of the son-in-law a mirror situation to that of a woman at

[21]There are two kinds of adoption in Nuzi: real adoption for the purpose of providing an heir, and sale adoption which is a camouflaged sale of land.

[22]A thorough investigation of the "real adoption" in Nuzi and its exact scope is still lacking.

[23]The wife's name was Umpaya and she is known from other documents. Her marriage with Šuriḫa-ilu must have been difficult, judging from the fact that she ran away from him to her father's house (*HSS* 5 49) and that the matters were settled by the king himself (*HSS* 5 103). The woman Šatim-ninu, mentioned in *HSS* 5 67 was either Šuriḫa-ilu's first wife or his sister.

Table 1. Daughter's share on the basis of testaments from Nuzi

Text nr.	Male inheritance	Female inheritance	Remarks
HSS 19 1	Equal division between three S and two D		Size of property not stated, but probably very small, therefore equal division.
HSS 19 7	All immovables (quantity unknown) given to 2 S.	D given authority over herself; her silver is tied in her hem; she is perhaps given some movables.	The silver tied in her hem means probably that she is to keep her own future brideprice.
HSS 19 12	One S receives 10 *imēr* of land and 10 sh. of silver.	Two D are given a cattle shed each.	Will made by the mother.
HSS 19 17	Three S receive all property.	A D is given father's authority over her brothers as long as she lives.	
HSS 19 20	If a S is born, he will inherit 2 *imēr*, 2 *awēharū* of land, houses, movables.	A D will be given 1 *awēharū* of land and a house in Nuzi.	If there is no S, the D will inherit everything.
HSS 19 21		Two D receive a *paiḫu* field as an "outright gift" (*kitru*).	This will constitutes the title to the property mentioned in it, therefore no sons are mentioned although they are known to have existed.
HSS 5 59	Adoptive S receives whole property.	A D is given 1 *imēr* of land for lifelong use.	This adoption document is discussed above, p. 167.
JEN 443		A D receives a house and perhaps products of her own labour, like oil and silver.	No S mentioned. This tablet was probably the title to the property mentioned in it.
RA 23 5	Four S receive all property.	A D will be given a house measuring 7×5 cubits,[24] adjoining the paternal house.	The house will be built by the testator's S.

Abbreviations: D-daughter, S-son, F-father, Z-sister, sh.-shekel

[24] A cubit was roughly equivalent to 50 cm. The "house" would thus measure 8.75m^2.

the moment of marriage was achieved. Although the son-in-law belonged to his father's lineage, his children belonged to that of his father-in-law. He also resided in his father-in-law's household. But what happened if the adopted son-in-law failed to produce heirs? In Rome, the solution would be to adopt a new heir. But this was obviously not the case in Nuzi. Šennima's daughter was an heiress to the property of her mother and the last link in her lineage (we assume that Šuriḫa-ilu had no brothers). When she did not produce offspring, the lineage of her mother was finished and the property passed to the family of her father.[24] It might be concluded that in Nuzi a blood link was necessary to continue the lineage, and that it was impossible to be adopted to lineage in the same way as to property.[25]

Dowry and inheritance in Nuzi

Table 1 shows that a daughter's share was much smaller than that of a son. This is understandable because the son's share was supposed to provide means of independent economic existence for him and his family, whereas the daughter's share was a token of her inheritance rights. Only in combination with property belonging to her provider (brother or husband) would it constitute an independent and sufficient economic unit.

The dowry tablets complete the picture of female inheritance rights in Nuzi. Six tablets (Table 2) deal with the transfer of the dower property. These documents have the form of a declaration made by the equipping party (the bride's father or brother). He states what kind of property he is transferring to the bride; there is no mention of the groom or of his family. This proves the personal character of the dowry, a transaction between the bride and a male of her kin. Each tablet mentions explicitly that the property transferred is a dowry of a female. The term used is *mulūgu*, and the property is transferred "*ana mulūgi/mulūgūti.*"

It is interesting to see that out of six cases the brother appears twice as a giver of the dowry. Once he refers to the fact that his father had decided beforehand which items his sister was to receive. We can also see that, with the exception of the princess's dowry, daughters were given only a small amount of property, which corresponds well with the information concerning female inheritance in the testaments. Another important fact is that all the *mulūgu*-texts deal with transfer of immovable property.

[25]Although this did not happen automatically—Šennima had to adopt his brother, perhaps to circumvent the original stipulation of the adoption, that no other sons of Zike were allowed to receive any property of Šuriḫa-ilu.

[26]Problems of descent and kinship need a thorough study before anything definite can be said about the subject. The fact that there are some mentions of gods (perhaps family gods) in the texts from Nuzi seems to indicate that notions of descent were known in Nuzi.

Table 2. Dowry payments

Text nr.	Payer	Amount paid	Remarks
HSS 19 79	B	2 houses	The B states that the houses were marked off for his Z by their F—he is only accomplishing the transfer
RA 23 31	B	*qaqqaru paiḫu* measuring 90 cubits	
HSS 5 11	F	1 *imēr* of land	Woman's declaration concerning her dower land[27]
HSS 5 76	F	1 *imēr* of land	
HSS 19 76	F	unknown quantity	
HSS 13 93	?	32 *imēr* + *qaqqaru piaḫu*	Princess's dowry. Atypical with respect to the amount and absence of the counter-dowry[28]

One more group of documents (Table 3) deals with dowry payments. These texts are quite different in character from the *mulūgu*-texts and contain the so-called indirect dowry transaction. The institution of indirect dowry is well-known to social anthropologists. It can be found in a wide variety of cultures, for instance in India or in China. The indirect dowry is closely linked with the brideprice in that it is a part of the brideprice turned over to the bride to constitute her dowry. In India, the indirect dowry masked the fact that the brideprice was being paid, for receiving money for a daughter was considered a contemptible practice. In China, the indirect dowry would be used among the poor, where a girl would be equipped with a dowry bought with the help of the money received as her brideprice.

The institution of indirect dowry is represented by four cases at Nuzi, but the status of this institution is not known. The existence of the indirect dowry is conditioned by the existence of the brideprice. Stipulations concerning this transaction are found in marriage contracts and in texts dealing with brideprice payments. The bridegiver declares that he has received a part of the brideprice and that the rest is to be tied in the bride's hem, i.e. is to be her legal possession.

The indirect dowry could either be paid at once or at a later time. The person receiving the brideprice either transferred a part of it to the bride immediately, or having received only a part of the brideprice, declared that the rest was to be paid to the bride. Payment in installments is connected with the

[27]For a short description of *HSS* 5 11 and *HSS* 5 76 see the conclusion of this article.

[28]For the institution of counter dowry cf. Table 4.

Table 3. Indirect dowry payments

Text nr.	Amount of brideprice	Amount of indirect dowry	Payer of indirect dowry
AASOR 16 55	20 sh. of silver	20 sh. of silver	MB
HSS 13 263	?	whole brideprice	M
HSS 5 80	1 ox, 10 sh. of silver	rest (amount unknown)	B
HSS 19 144	5 sh. of silver in cash and 10 in installments	rest (amount unknown)	B and Z (?)

Abbreviations: MB-mother's brother; Z-sister

payment of the bride price which could extend over a number of years (see Table 5).

In *HSS* 13 263 the mother states that her daughter has born a child to her husband and that the *terḫatu* is tied in the daughter's hem. It was not unusual to postpone the payment of the brideprice until the marriage was consummated or, as seems to be the case here, until the bride has proven her fertility. If the brideprice was not paid until a child was born the transfer of the indirect dowry also had to be postponed.

It should also be noted that the indirect dowry was usually not given by the bride's father. Fathers seem to have equipped their daughters with dowries or provided for them in testaments.

Returning to *HSS* 13 263, it is interesting that the mother plays the role of an indirect dowry giver. The brideprice was perhaps the only asset of which the mother could freely dispose in this case.[29] Even if she had immovable property of her own (i.e. her dower property) she would not be allowed to alienate any of it unless a stipulation to such effect had been made by her (presumably) deceased husband. The testament *HSS* 19 10 contains such a stipulation—the testator declares that his five daughters are to be given to his wife, together with some other property and various household implements from her father's house.[30] This can mean only that the wife was made responsible for marrying off the daughters and that she was given the right to arrange their brideprices.

Women could not alienate property, even after the death of their husbands. All testaments providing for wives are explicit on this point.[31] It is not

[29]The fact that the mother is given right to dispose of her daughter's brideprice is contrary to the spirit of this institution. The brideprice should be turned over to the bride's male kin. The only explanation in this case is that no male members of the family were alive at this moment.

[30]*Unūtu ša abīša* consisted in this case of furniture, oil, wine and copper.

[31]Cf. Paradise, op. cit., p. 288f.

known exactly what happened to the woman's dower property during the marriage. The absence of stipulations concerning women's dower property in testaments could be explained by the fact that the dowry was considered women's private property and that there was no reason to mention it in the husband's will. If this were the case, however, there should be testaments made by women concerning their dower property.[32] However, the three women's testaments that deal with transfer of immovables are clearly concerned with the property left in their trust by their husbands. *HSS* 5 74 and *HSS* 19 34 state that the property in question belonged to the husbands of the respective testators. *HSS* 19 12 has no such stipulation, but the amount of land involved (10 *imēr*) is too large to be a woman's dowry.

It is possible that sometime during the marriage, most probably when the children were born, the dower property of the wife was merged with the property of her husband to constitute the familial fund for their children. From that time the woman enjoyed a lifelong right to support and perhaps some limited right to the products of her own labour in her husband's household. Thus, women in Nuzi enjoyed limited inheritance rights (at least to immovables). Married women could not sell their shares, because they were predestined to their children. Single women could not sell their shares, and after their deaths, they would pass to their brothers.[33]

In two of the texts from Table 3 (*HSS* 5 80 and *HSS* 19 144), a brother gives the indirect dowry. This can be understood in light of the fact that the indirect dowry was a part of the brideprice which was ultimately to be used by the bride's brother to acquire a wife. In these cases it is possible that the brother was already married at the time of his sister's marriage. Obliged to supply his sister with a dowry, the brother preferred to part with some of the brideprice to both equip his sister with an indirect dowry and to keep the property undivided.[34]

Even though the sources are of an incidental nature, the paucity of documents dealing with the dowry is surprising. It is possible that some marriages were unaccompanied by any marriage prestations. Alternatively, marriage with a dowry consisting of immovables may not have been very common, in part because this practice could lead to an excessive division of land. To avoid this problem and still equip a woman with some land, marriages in all societies where immovable property devolves on women

[32] *HSS* 5 11 apparently is the only document in which a woman openly disposed of her dower property, transferring it to her granddaughter.

[33] Cf. *RA* 23 5 and *HSS* 5 59.

[34] In the absence of the father, it was the brother's obligation to equip his sister. *HSS* 19 19 is explicit on this point: "My daughters, grown and small, I hereby give to my sons born by Tieš-naya (the second wife), for marrying off, and they will keep their silver." This can mean only that the sons from an earlier marriage have the obligation to find husbands for their half-sisters and they have the right to keep the brideprices.

Table 4. Counter-dowry payments

Text nr.	Value of dowry	Counter-dowry payment
HSS 5 76	1 *imēr* of field	1 textile, 1 sheep, 1 pig with 10 piglets
HSS 19 79	A house measuring 20×25×8×9 cubits	1 good donkey, 1 blanket of middle quality, 10 mina of lead
RA 23 31	*qaqqaru paiḫu*, 90 cubits in circumference	[x] new textiles of good quality, 1 good new blanket—representing together the value of 25 sh. of silver
HSS 19 71	2 houses, 16×10 cubits	20 sh. of *ḫašaḫušennu* silver

usually take place within the kin group (endogamy). Otherwise, women marry with a dowry that did not consist of land. Contemporary Near Eastern peasants often equip their daughters with dowries composed of blankets, rugs and animals, in the production of which the bride participated. In exceptional cases, a particularly generous father may give his daughter some land as her dowry.

If this form of dowry existed in Nuzi, it need not have appeared on written documents. The transfer of the dowry is a strictly personal transaction involving only the dowry giver and the dowry recipient, both belonging to the same family. If the dowry were composed of typically "female" property like blankets, household utensils and animals, there would be no need to write a document of ownership. When the dowry consists of land, however, a document recording the transfer of the dowry is necessary because it is the title to the plot in question and must be produced should claims be raised to this field. Should the field be sold, the document of the dowry would be demonstrated to prove that the land in question belonged to the family. The document would then probably be transferred to the buyer. Thus it seems clear that a valid tablet would be written whenever the dowry was composed of land, but that there was no reason to write a document when the dowry was of a more "orthodox" character.

There may be one indication that the dowry in Nuzi could consist of livestock and textiles.[35] The tablets dealing with the transfer of the dower property all contain a stipulation which may be called a "counter-dowry payment." The bride receiving a plot of land as her dowry presents the dowry-giver with a gift.

[35]The document mentioned in note 30 also proves that a woman received various movables from the paternal house. They could perhaps be considered her dowry. *TCL* 9 1 is an inventory of objects of bronze, household implements and furniture transferred by a man to a woman. We do not know the relationship between the two parties and can therefore only very tentatively assume that the objects transferred constituted the woman's dowry.

These presents (for so are they called—NÍG.BA) represent considerable value and cannot be considered token gifts of gratitude (see Table 4). With the exception of the last document, all gifts could be products of the girl's own labour. The 20 shekels of silver in *HSS* 19 71 are more difficult to explain. The term *ḫašaḫušennu* is sometimes employed for brideprice when it seems to be an equivalent of *terḫatu*, or for payments made in connection with sale of slave girls. Thus *ḫašaḫušennu* seems to be connected with a transfer of rights of women. However, it is difficult to explain how the bride from *HSS* 19 71 acquired this large amount of silver and whether the term *ḫašaḫušennu* was connected in this case with the transfer of rights to herself (her brideprice?) or to somebody else (her slave girl?).

A possible explanation of the counter-dowry payment, or gift, is that upon receiving her dowry in land the girl officially gave up the claim to a part of (her own?) produce, which would normally constitute her dowry. She received land, and renounced her claim to livestock and textiles. Another similar but not identical explanation is that the livestock and textiles which she officially presented to her father or brother (whichever of them supplied her with a dowry) represented her produce in their common household, which she was not entitled to transfer to her future husband's household. It is very difficult to say how much property the individual family members owned within the household. Although the sons lived together with their father, they must have acquired some possessions which were their own.[36] Animals would also multiply, increasing the value of domestic herds. The sons' wives certainly spun and wove, perhaps deriving some income from this (although a greater part of their production would be for the household use). It is not known whether this individual production was pooled or was strictly private. There are some indications in testaments that all property and production of a household, although earned privately, was nominally the property of the father of the family. In *HSS* 19 2 the testator states: "Whichever are the private accumulations of my sons, I am hereby releasing them to them." In *HSS* 19 37 the father says: "There will be no private accumulations."[37] These two examples indicate that it was customary for household members to acquire private property and that this property remained under the nominal authority of the father of the household. A man's private accumulation remained in the household because he himself remained in it, but a woman's private property would leave the household permanently at the moment of her marriage. Therefore, upon leaving her family, the daughter would be obliged to leave her individual possessions, if she was to receive the dowry in land. She

[36]Carpentry, house building, making pottery and perhaps work for the palace could perhaps be considered as potential sources of private income.

[37]The word for private accumulations is *sikiltu*. For the discussion of this term cf. Paradise, op. cit., pp. 253-58.

would acquire new private property in her husband's household (through her work or as presents) and these would again be to some extent her own.[38]

Brideprice

The Akkadian term for brideprice, *terḫatu*, is well attested in Nuzi—much better than *mulūgu*. There are various documents dealing with brideprice payments: 1) receipts of goods constituting *terḫatu*; 2) marriage contracts (*ṭuppi rikṣi*) containing stipulations about payment of the brideprice; 3) short receipts of various goods or silver, termed "*ina kaspi ša* FN" ("out of money for FN") and not using the term *terḫatu* at all. Table 5 shows brideprice payments in Nuzi. Code numbers refer to these three types of texts.[39]

A brief examination of table 5 shows that the recipient of the brideprice was the bride's brother in a vast majority of cases. This is consistent with the nature of the brideprice institution. The declaration *AASOR* 16 54 illustrates well how closely the institution of brideprice was linked to the person of the brother:

> Declaration with Kuni-ašu, daughter of Ḫut-tešup, made in front of these witnesses: "In the past, Akam-mušni married (me) off and took 40 shekels of silver for me from my husband, but now Akam-mušni and my husband are (both) dead, and now (as to) myself, Akkiya, son of Ḫut-tešup, seized me in the street as his sister and took the authority (of brother) over a sister over me. He will marry me off and take 10 shekels of *šurampašḫu* silver from my (future) husband." Whoever among them breaks the agreement will pay 1 mina of gold. Tablet written at the entrance of the great gate of Nuzi.

There are several interesting points in this declaration. The difference between the amount of brideprice paid at the first marriage and expected at the second marriage is large indeed. The low brideprice in the second marriage may be due to the fact that Kuni-ašu was no longer a virgin or because she had already proved herself barren with one man. The form of the document, a

[38]The testaments contain some indications that women could own some private property within the household. *HSS* 19 2 states: "Whichever are the products of Šuḫur-naya's labour (*minummē mānāḫāti ša Šuḫur-naya*) (be it) grain, oxen, sheep, wool, oil, textiles are given to her. Šuḫur-naya will give them to whichever son she prefers, but she will not give them to a stranger." A thorough investigation of the women's rights to private property during the marriage is outside the limit of this study.

[39]Excluded from this table are five instances of the *terḫatu* consisting of immovables. These are: *JEN* 438, a difficult and damaged text seemingly concerning a marriage of a slave girl who is given her freedom. The immovables consist of 1 *imēr* 5 *awēḫarū* of land; *JEN* 436 and *HSS* 19 98 specifies the property transferred as various houses; *HSS* 19 93 deals with transfer of 3 *imēr* of land; and *HSS* 19 97 transfers 5 *imēr* of land.

Table 5. Brideprice payments

Text nr.	Code	Recipient	Amount to be paid as first installment	Total amount of the brideprice	Terms of payment
AASOR 16 54a	*	B	40 sh. of silver ?	40 sh. of silver	?
AASOR 16 54b	*	B	?	10 sh. of silver	?
AASOR 16 55a	(2)	B	?	30 sh. of silver	50 sh. to be paid in yearly installments of 5 sh.; 20 sh. to be bound in the bride's hem
AASOR 16 55b	(2)	MB	20 sh. of silver	40 sh. of silver	
HSS 5 13	(3)	B	36 m. of lead instead of 1 ox and 5 m. of bronze	?	Installments
HSS 5 16	(3)	B,Z (+1 more man)	5 sheep, 9 m. of copper, 1 m. 40 sh. of wool, 5 m. of lead	?	?
HSS 5 25	(2)	B	40 sh. of silver	40 sh. of silver	Cash
HSS 5 80a	(2)	B	1 ox, 10 sh. of silver	?	Rest to be the indirect dowry
HSS 5 80b	**		0	?	20 sh. of silver to be paid after the bride has slept with her husband
HSS 9 111	(3)	B	5 sh. of silver, 6 m. of lead	?	Installments
HSS 19 80	(2)	B?	[ ] sh. of silver	Broken	1 ox to be paid when the bride has borne a child (rest too fragmentary)

HSS 19 84	(2)	B	45 sh. of silver	45 sh. of silver	Cash ***
HSS 19 75	(2)	F?	1 donkey, 2 sheep, 3 m. of lead, all this to the value of 15 sh.	30 sh. of silver	15 sh. to be paid after the bride has satisfied the husband (? - *ana* LÚ *ka₄-ši-id*)
HSS 19 83	(2)	F	1 she-donkey, 10 sheep (value of 10 sh. of silver)	40 sh. of silver	Installments
HSS 19 96	(1)	F	?	?	Probably cash
HSS 19 99	(1)	F	35 sh. of silver	Broken	Broken
HSS 19 134	(1)	Broken	[x]+5 m. of bronze - value of 5 sh. of silver	Broken	Broken
RA 23 12	(2)	F	?	40 sh. of silver	?
HSS 19 144	(2)	F and M (?)	5 sh. of silver	15 sh. of silver	10 sh. to be paid in yearly installments of [x] sh. to the bride
JEN 186	(1)	F	3 sh. of silver, 13 sheep, 1 ox	30 sh. of silver	Cash
HSS 19 82	Broken	M?	1 ox	Broken	Broken

* *AASOR* 16 54 is a declaration, see below, p. 175, ** the husband from the transaction a) adopts his wife's daughter; *** the present form of *nadānu* is used, and it is difficult to say whether this implies a payment by installments or by cash

Abbreviations: m. - mina (equal to 60 sh.)

declaration of Kuni-ašu, indicates that the woman's consent was necessary if her brother was to assume authority over her. This could also signify that after her husband's death she was legally free, provided there were no children. Although the circumstances that led to *AASOR* 16 54 may never be known, the role played by the brother in the institution of brideprice and his responsibility to provide for his unmarried sister are particularly clear from this text.

Conclusion

The aim of this article was to examine the two marriage prestations, *terḫatu* and *mulūgu* and to set them in a wider context of present social anthropological research on the marriage prestations called brideprice and dowry.

The brideprice, defined as a transaction between the kin of the bride and that of the groom, is paid to the bride's kin and serves the purpose of equipping the bride's brothers with wives. The brideprice is a transaction linking together the two families. The use of the term *terḫatu* in Nuzi is consistent with the above definition. The *terḫatu* is indeed paid by the groom's family (or by himself) to the bride's family. The mere fact that the terms of payment or at least the amount of the *terḫatu* are stated in the documents of marriage involving the two families proves this. The recipient of the *terḫatu* in Nuzi is in over 50 percent of cases the bride's brother. The dowry, which is a personal transaction within a single family was not recorded in the *ṭuppi rikṣi*, unless it was to consist of a part of the brideprice. Another characteristic feature of the brideprice, the fact that it is often paid in installments over a period of time, is also attested in Nuzi. The contents of the brideprice may vary, but it is always composed of movable property. Nuzi furnishes some notable exceptions here. Although the *terḫatu* is usually composed of movables and livestock, grain or silver, there are five instances of the *terḫatu* consisting of land[40] and in at least two cases (*HSS* 19 93 and *HSS* 19 97) the amount of land transferred is surprisingly large (3 *imēr* and 5 *imēr* respectively). These transactions are contrary to the spirit of the brideprice institution, which should constitute a circulating societal fund. However, it is possible that the brideprice transactions involving land either concern endogamous marriages, where the land given as brideprice would stay within the same family, or mask some manipulations with land which at the present are impossible to discern.

The dowry was defined as a pre-mortem inheritance to the bride. The dowry in Nuzi corresponded to the share which an unmarried daughter could expect to inherit through her father's testament, and a daughter's share was smaller than that of a son. A daughter's share could be considered a token of female inheritance rights, because it clearly could not form the basis for an

[40] Cf. note 39.

economically independent existence. In order to keep her social status, a Nuzian woman would have to marry a man whose inheritance share was much more valuable than her own dowry, that is, she would have to marry within the same social group. As female and male inheritance shares were unequal within the same social group, marriages within the same group could not be organized along principles of match which require that the dowry and the groom's inheritance share equal each other.

The Nuzi system of marriage prestations included, not unusually, both the brideprice and the dowry, marriage prestations reflecting two different institutions. The dowry is an expression of female inheritance rights and the brideprice is a transaction linking two families. The dowry forms a part of the conjugal fund and serves to establish the young couple, whereas the brideprice is a circulating societal fund and, with the exception of the indirect dowry payment, does not serve the young couple at all.

It is very interesting to note that in Nuzi the brideprice and the dowry can occur together within the same marriage. Two documents transferring marrying rights to women mention such a situation. Although this type of document (*ṭuppi kallātūti*) is excluded from the present study, the specific situation of the dowry and the brideprice occurring together should be mentioned. In *HSS* 19 76, a declaration before witnesses, a man states that he is transferring the marrying rights to his daughter to a certain woman. The young girl is transferred together with a field,[41] and the woman who is taking her over will find her a husband and keep the brideprice. In *HSS* 5 11, also a declaration, a woman transfers marrying rights to her granddaughter to another woman. The girl receives a field which her grandmother had received as her own dowry. The girl will be married to a free man and the woman who provides the husband will keep the brideprice for herself.

The fact that the brideprice and the dowry can occur together within the same marriage is by no means astonishing in Nuzi. §§163 and 164 of the Code of Hammurapi suggest that it was the usual practice in Mesopotamia. In many societies of the world, however, marriages are concluded *either* with the brideprice *or* with the dowry.

At the present stage of study it is impossible to say what happened to the dower property during the marriage. An investigation of this topic is beyond the limits of this article. If the wife's property was merged with that of her husband at some stage of the marriage, as suggested above, the husband can be considered only an administrator of the dower property of his wife. The ultimate recipients of this property were the couple's children and even the wife could not alienate any of it. *HSS* 19 2 is a testament made in favour of three real sons and one adoptive son who is also married to the testator's daughter. The testator states: "Whichever are my fields and my houses, which I have given to Akip-tašenni, and whichever are the fields and houses he has

[41] *It-ti ṭup-pí-šu-ma ù it-ti* A.ŠÀ *ša pí-i ṭup-pí.*

taken from his father's house, they (all) are to be given to Azuya's (the daughter of the testator's) children." *HSS* 19 14 is badly broken, but it seems to have been a real adoption with the adoptee marrying the adoptant's daughter. The adoptant/testator states that all his possessions are to be given to the children which his daughter bears to her husband and concludes: "And should there even be ten sons born to Tarmiya by another wife—they will not approach my fields, my houses, nor anything which is mine." Also *HSS* 5 11, mentioned above, proves that the dowry was destined for the bride's children. The fact that the sons-in-law in *HSS* 19 12 and *HSS* 19 14 are adopted by their father-in-law is irrelevant in this context.

The lack of women's testaments disposing explicitly of their dower property suggests that after the birth of children the wife did not have any right to dispose of her dower property. After the birth of the children a wife acquired the right to lifelong support by her husband, or, if he died before her, by her son(s). This is amply attested by the wills, for more than 50 percent of all testaments contain stipulations concerning the wife. Although provided for for the rest of her life, the wife had no right to dispose of any property apart from rare cases when her private accumulations were released to her.[42] The couple's joint property was ultimately destined for their children.

* * *

The research of the institutions of brideprice and dowry has gone much further than the mere establishing of terms. The most interesting theories about these two prestations and the women's general role in pre-industrial societies are those of Ester Boserup and Jack Goody.

Ester Boserup is an economist, whose book *Woman's Role in Economic Development*,[43] considered today a classic on this topic, gives data about the methods of production in various societies of Asia and Africa today and the division of labour between the sexes. Jack Goody's book *Production and Reproduction*[44] deals partly with the same subjects from the social anthropological viewpoint.

E. Boserup established the interdependence between the kind of agriculture practised and the division of labour between men and women. The two kinds of agriculture are shifting farming and plough farming. Shifting farming exists today in Africa, south of the Sahara. Fields are tilled with the help of hoes and women do most of, or all the work in the fields, thus being real producers of the means of sustenance. The surplus of their production can be sold on the market, the profit often considered as strictly private property of the women.

[42] Cf. note 38.

[43] E. Boserup, *Woman's Role in Economic Development*, New York, 1970.

[44] J. Goody, *Production and Reproduction*, Cambridge Studies in Social Anthropology, vol. 17, Cambridge, 1976.

The women thus have some economic independence and they also enjoy considerable private liberty necessary for them to work in the fields and sell their products. The women in shifting farming societies are valued not only as mates but also as workers. There is a strong tendency towards polygyny in shifting farming societies, because the fields are plentiful while the yield is small, and a man must have many wives to till as large an area as possible for him. Wives are acquired by means of paying brideprice. If a wife does not produce children she will usually not be divorced, for the children can be produced with another wife, while the barren one still has her value as a worker. This also means that all wives enjoy the full status of wife, although they can be differentiated by order of marriage. The women in shifting farming cultures usually have no inheritance rights.

Plough farming is characteristic for Asia. E. Boserup observed that some shifting farming societies of Africa change to plough agriculture. This change occurs because the increase of population makes more intensive exploitation of land absolutely necessary. Boserup writes:

> In very sparsely populated regions where shifting cultivation is used, men do little work, the women doing most. In somewhat more densely populated regions where the agricultural system is that of extensive plough cultivation, women do little farm work and men do much more. Finally, in the regions of intensive cultivation of irrigated land, both men and women must put hard work into agriculture.[45]

Boserup observed also that the African societies tended to employ polygyny and have the brideprice as the most common form of marriage prestation. The Asian cultures, on the other hand, were usually monogamous and employed dowry. In his book *Production and Reproduction* J. Goody provided an explanation for these basic differences.

According to Goody, the scarcity of land and the intensity of its use produces a large demand for it and creates in advanced agricultural societies the basis for social differentiation. This social differentiation based on the size of land holdings will be sought and maintained, the persons belonging to the same social stratum tending to intermarry. Another way to keep one's social status is by leaving one's possessions to one's children. Thus, an elaborate system of inheritance emerges, including female inheritance and dowry as a form of it.[46] It is especially important for members of advanced agricultural societies to produce heirs, so in such societies marriage is primarily an heir-producing device. Whenever women are married with dowry only their children will be entitled to inherit it. This limits the possibility of polygyny. If a wife fails to produce heirs other measures will be sought to provide the

[45] E. Boserup, op. cit., p. 35.
[46] J. Goody, op. cit., p. 20.

family with them. An heir can be adopted or produced with another woman. This woman, however, will not enjoy the full status of wife. She will either be a wife of lesser rank or a concubine. As the last resource, the barren wife may be divorced while the husband marries another wife, thus giving rise to serial monogamy. The Asian societies employing intensive farming are characterised by inheritance rights. This is why Asiatic marriages use dowry rather than brideprice as the usual marriage prestation.

A comparison of the Nuzi material to these broad definitions finds a society bearing characteristic features of both systems. Nuzi was undoubtedly an advanced agricultural society with very pronounced inheritance rights of both men and women. In the marriages the stress is laid upon the bride's fertility (almost all documents contain clauses concerned with the possibility of childlessness and the groom's right to acquire a new wife in case the first proves herself barren). On the other hand, we have the institution of brideprice much better attested than that of dowry (although the absence of dowry documents does not prove that the dowry composed of movables did not exist). It is also clear that the brideprice was a feature characteristic for all of Mesopotamia and cannot be considered a transitional phenomenon.

The Nuzian *terḫatu* does not conform completely to the definition of brideprice. In some instances women can obtain a part of the *terḫatu* as their dowry, or the whole *terḫatu* can be turned over to the mother of the bride. In some cases the *terḫatu* was composed of land. These circumstances are clearly in contrast with the usual notion of brideprice. In the effort to explain this situation, it must be remembered that models encompassing whole continents have limited value for the study of single cultures, unless an allowance is made for a wide range of variation. It is possible that the Nuzian society represents the third stage of agriculture according to Boserup's model, i.e. the situation in which both men and women have to put hard work into agriculture. In this case women's value as workers is appreciated in the institution of brideprice, while their inheritance rights are expressed by the institution of dowry.

The Nuzi system of inheritance and brideprice appears to be characteristic for all of Mesopotamia and cannot be attributed to the Hurrian population prevalent in that city. The subject of marriage and its social implications in Mesopotamia urgently needs the close attention of Assyriologists, as it is of crucial importance for our understanding of Mesopotamian society.[47]

[47] The most complete study of the institution of marriage in Mesopotamia published until now is van Praag's *Droit Matrimonial Assyro-Babylonien*, Amsterdam, 1945, but it focuses on the legal aspects of marriage and not on the social ones.

Betrachtungen zum Gotte Tilla

VOLKERT HAAS
Freie Universität Berlin

Im Pantheon des Königreichs von Arraphe ist unter den dort vertretenen osthurritischen Gottheiten die Gottheit Tilla von hoher Bedeutung. Sie, nach der auch eine Ortschaft benannt ist,[1] besaß—wie es ein Brief aus Tell al-Faḫḫār, der antiken Ortschaft Kurruhani, bezeugt—sogar eine entu-Priesterin.[2] Nach der Häufigkeit des Elements *-til(l)a* in den Personennamen aus Nuzi zu schließen, scheint Tilla eine beinahe ebenso bekannte Gottheit wie der Wettergott Teššub gewesen zu sein.[3]

Über das Wesen der Gottheit jedoch ist den Texten aus Nuzi nur wenig zu entnehmen: In HSS 13 pl. VIII, 799:1-15 (=AASOR 16 49) werden Ölrationen für eine Reihe von Gottheiten, darunter auch Tilla, aufgeführt:

1 2 *uš-bi* Ì^{MEŠ} DÙG.GA
2 2 *uš-bi* Ì *el-lu*
3 *a-na* ^{D}*til-la*
4 2 *uš-bi* Ì^{MEŠ} DÙG.GA
5 2 *uš-bi* Ì *el-lu*
6 *a-na* ^{D}IŠTAR [*b*]*e-la-at du-ri*
7 3 *uš-bi* Ì DÙG.GA
8 3 *uš-bi* Ì *el-lu*
9 *a-na* ^{D}IŠTAR *pu-ta-aḫ-ḫé*
10 1 *uš-bi* Ì DÙG.GA

[1]AASOR 16 47:23, 48:34; hier werden als die zu beopfernden Gottheiten der Stadt die beiden Paare Wettergott und Ištar von Ninive sowie Nergal und Ištar *ḫumella*, nicht aber Tilla selbst, aufgeführt, vgl. auch 50:26.

Zur Unterscheidung eines ost- und westhurritischen Götterkreises s. V. Haas, Substratgottheiten des westhurritischen Pantheons, RHA 36, 1978.

Zur Verbreitung des Namens Tilla über den osthurritischen Raum hinaus—zur kassitischen Zeit in Nippur und vereinzelt in Elam—s. NPN 266 mit Literatur.

[2]K. Deller, Materialien zu den Lokalpanthea des Königreiches Arrapḫe, CRRA, Rom, 1976, 33-45, p. 34 c.n. 8.

[3]Von den in NPN 266 unter *-til(l)a* aufgeführten 61 Namen sind in 38 derselben die Namenselemente *-til(l)a* und *-teššub* mit den gleichen Elementen gebildet (nicht gezählt sind die Varianten mit und ohne *-p-*).

11 1 *uš-bi* Ì *el-lu*
12 *a-na* ^{D}IM
13 1 *uš-bi* Ì DÙG.GA
14 1 *uš-bi* Ì *el-lu*
15 *a-na* ^{D}IŠTAR *ni-nu-a-wa*

Der Text ist nach Götterpaaren angeordnet (vgl. auch 18-19). Unser Abschnitt unterscheidet zwei Götterkreise—zum einen die Gottheit Tilla, der die Ištar *bēlat dūri* verbunden ist, während die Ištar *putaḫḫe* wahrscheinlich ebenso alleinstehend ist wie die Ištar *allaiwašwe*; zum anderen Teššub (^{D}IM), der ja bekanntermaßen mit der Šawuška (^{D}IŠTAR) von Ninive ein enges Paar bildet.[4] Demnach steht Tilla durch die Verbindung mit einer Ištar-Gestalt auf einer Ebene mit Teššub.

In dem westhurritischen, von Nordsyrien aus beeinflussten und geprägten Pantheon von Hattusa der Großreichszeit,[5] ist Tilla nicht vertreten. Als selbständige Gottheit erscheint Tilla lediglich in der zweiten Tafel des "Ullikummi-Lieds"[6] als einer der beiden Stiere des Teššub. Der folgende Absatz berichtet von den Vorbereitungen der ersten Kampfhandlungen des Teššub gegen den Steindämon Ullikummi; Teššub befiehlt seinem Vezir Tašmišu:

3′ Das Futter soll man mischen und das Feinö[l soll man herbeibring]en;
4′ man soll die Hörner des Stieres Šerišu (damit) salben!
5′ Den Schwanz des Stieres Tilla soll man mit Gold(stücken) verzieren![7]
6′ Die Schulter(n) aber soll man 'wenden' und ihnen Stärke
7′ im Innern bringen;[8] außen soll man von den Rädern
8′ die starken Steine entfernen! Die Unwetter

[4]Zur Šawuška von Ninive als Schwester des Teššub s. zuletzt I. Wegner, Gestalt und Kult der Ištar-Šawuška in Kleinasien, AOAT 36, HurrStud. III (1981), 44.

[5]V. Haas, l.c.

[6]Bearbeitet von H. G. Güterbock, The Song of Ullikummi. Revised Text of the Hittite Version of a Hurrian Myth (first Part), JCS 5 (1951), 135-61, The Song of Ullikummi (continued), JCS 6 (1952), 8-42.

[7]In Bo 5005 Vs. 1′-7′ wird während der Zeremonien des EZEN KI.LAM die Statue des Wettergottes aus dem Tempel gebracht und in einen Wagen gesetzt, vor der zwei Stierfiguren gespannt sind. Nach KBo X 24 Vs. II 19″-21″, einem anderen Textstück dieses Festrituals, sind die Hörner der beiden Stierfiguren—[Šeri] und Hurri—aus Gold oder mit Gold überzogen. Zu der Sitte die Hörner heiliger Stiere mit Gold zu überziehen, vgl. T. von Margwelaschwili, Der Kaukasus und der alte Orient, ZE 69 (1937), 309.

[8]Dieser Satz ist mir unklar, scheint sich aber doch eher auf die beiden Stiere als etwa auf den Wagen zu beziehen.

9′ soll man herausrufen; die Regengüsse und die Stürme, die sich auf 90 mal 3600 qm auf die Fels[en]
10′ niederhocken und 800 mal 3600 qm bedecken,
11′ soll man rufen! Den Blitz, der furchtbar
12′ aufzuckt, den soll man aus dem Schlafgemach
13′ herausholen und auch die Wagen soll man herausstellen!
14′ Dies alles bereite vor, bewirke es und bringe mir danach Bericht!

15′ Und als Tašmišu die Worte hörte, da eilte er,
16′ sputete er sich und [trieb] den Stier Šerišu von der Weide,
17′ den Tilla aber [trieb er] vom Berge Imga[?]rra -
18′ [ja,] in den äußeren Torbau
19′ [trieb er sie] hinein. Er brachte das Feinöl, und des Stieres Šeriš[u]
20′ [Hörner salbte er; des Stier]es Tilla Schwanz aber
21′ [schmückt]e er [mit den Gold(stücken)]...[9]

Dieser Absatz ist insofern bemerkenswert, als im hethitischen Schrifttum als Stiere des Wettergottes sonst stets Šeri(š) und Hurri(š) genannt werden,[10] nie aber die osthurritische Gottheit Tilla.[11] Ungewöhnlich ist darüberhinaus die hurritische, wohl aus einer Ergativ-Form **šeriš-uš* verkürzte Form *šerišu.* Da zudem *hurri(š)* in Nuzi unbekannt ist, scheint die anzunehmende hurritische Vorlage dieses Textstückes dem osthurritischen Raum zu entstammen, in dem der Mythos vom Steindämon Ullikummi seinem Kern nach ja auch beheimatet ist.[12]

War Tilla in der Ölrationenliste aus Nuzi eine dem Teššub gleichgestellte Gottheit, so ist er im "Ullikummi-Lied" zu einem Stiertrabanten des Teššub geworden.

[9]KUB XXXIII 87+113+MGK 12+14+KBo XXVI 64, vgl. H. G. Güterbock, JCS 6 (1952), 32ff.

[10]In der Form *šeriš* und *hurmeš(i)* sind die beiden Stiere auch im "Götteradreßbuch" von Assur aufgeführt, während in der assyrischen Götterliste An : Anum III 257-59 *šeriš* und *māgiru* "der Willfährige" als "die zwei Stiere des IM/Adad" genannt sind, zuletzt V. Haas, RlA 4 (1975), 506.

[11]An osthurritischen Gottheiten im Pantheon von Hattusa erscheinen neben den großen Göttern Teššub, Šawuška (von Ninive), Šimige, Kušuh (und Ugur) vereinzelt noch Argapa, der in Nuzi durch den Monatsnamen *arkabinnu* belegt ist (vgl. V. Haas-H. J. Thiel, Ein Beitrag zum hurritischen Wörterbuch, UF 11 [1979]) sowie Šukri (*šukr-* "protect, bless," vgl. F. W. Bush, *A Grammar of the Hurrian Language*, Ann Arbor, Michigan, 1965, 68) NPN 259, eine Gottheit, die sich in den Texten aus Boğazköy bezeichnenderweise nur in den sogenannten Išuwa-Festritualen findet (KUB XII 12 Vs. I, 24′ [ ], KUB XL 102 Vs. II 9 und VBoT 116:4′).

[12]Vgl. V. Haas, Betrachtungen zum ursprünglichen Schauplatz der Kumarbi-Mythen, SMEA 22 (1980).

Das Element *-tilla* findet sich auch im Namen eines Berges, der in zwei hethitischen Berglisten der sogenannten Festrituale von Išuwa—einer hethitischen Provinz und einstigem Königreich, das sich in einem Gebiet am oberen Euphrat mit dem Kernland um Elaziğ bis fast zum Tigris hin erstreckt hat[13]—genannt ist.[14] Der Name dieses Berges ist *še-e-nu-ti-el-la* mit der Variante *ši-na-ti-el-la*, der in der Liste auf den Berg *še-e-ra* folgt.[15] Zugrunde liegt dem Bergnamen das hurritische Zahlwort *šin-/šina* "zwei." Da der Berg wohl kaum "die zwei Tilla-Götter" benannt worden sein wird, Tilla aber durch den Passus des "Ullikummi-Liedes" als Stier ausgewiesen ist, liegt der Schluß nahe, in Tilla das hurritische Wort für Stier zu sehen.[16] Ein Bergname in der Bedeutung "die zwei Stiere" findet in dem Namen HUR.SAG*taruš*[17] eine Parallele und entspricht den religiösen Vorstellungen des nordsyrisch-südostanatolischen Raums durchaus: Als die Hethiter erstmals unter ihrem König Hattusili einen Beutezug nach Syrien unternahmen, raubten sie in Hassuwa (nach G. Wilhelm mündl.) am Ostufer des Orontes (= Puran), neben anderen Kultgegenständen auch "zwei silberne Rinder," die sie in dem Tempel der Sonnengöttin von Arinna deponierten.[18] Zwei gleichgearbeitete rote Stierfiguren aus Ton, die in das 16. Jahrhundert datiert werden, wurden in Hattusa gefunden.[19]

Wir halten fest, daß Tilla, der Stiergott, in Nuzi ein dem Teššub eng verwandter, nicht jedoch wie im "Ullikummi-Lied" ein ihm untergeordneter Gott ist.

Der Stier, der im westhurritischen Kreis zum Begleittier des anthropomorph gedachten Wettergottes wurde, war ursprünglich selbst derjenige Gott, der Regen und Fruchtbarkeit gewährt.[20]

[13]Vgl. H. Klengel, Išuwa, RlA 5 (1977), 214ff.

[14]KBo XV 52 Vs. I 43′ *pa-ab-bi-en-na ši-na-ti-el-la*, KBo XV 61 Rs. 5′ HUR.SAG *še-e-nu-ti-el-la*.

[15]Der Name *šeri(š)* liegt auch dem Berge *še-e-ra* (*pa-ab-bi-en-na še-e-ra*, var. HUR.SAG *še-e-ra*) zugrunde.

[16]Vgl. auch V. Haas-H. J. Thiel, *l.c.*

[17]2012/u (unpubl.). Der zentralanatolische, bzw. hattische Name des Wettergottes *taru* ist wohl zu dem mediterranen Wort tauros "Stier" zu stellen.

[18]KBo X 1 (akkadische Fassung) Vs. 37ff. und 2-3 (hethitische Version); zu zusäzlichen Fragmenten s. E. Laroche, OLZ 57 (1962), Sp. 27f. Zur Übersetzung dieses Dokuments Hattusilis I in späterer Abschrift s. H. Otten, MDOG 91 (1958), 78ff. Zur Problematik des Textes zuletzt A. Kammenhuber, Die Arier im Vorderen Orient, Heidelberg 1968, 30 c.n. 68, 32f., 123 c.n. 390, 189 c.n. 562.

[19]Zuletzt K. Bittel, Die Hethiter, München 1976, 156, 131 Abb. 156.

[20]Dies zeigt vielleicht auch das zu hurri(š) zu stellende urartäische Nomen hurišḫi "Bewässerer(?)," G. A. Melikišvili, Die urartäische Sprache. Aus dem Russischen übersetzt von Karl Sdrembek. Mit einem Anhang von Mirjo Salvini. Herausgegeben von A. Kammenhuber und M. Salvini. Studia Pohl 7 (1971), 82.

Eine alte, von Teššub verdrängte Stiergottheit, ist auch der "Bergkönig" genannte kilikische Gott Šarruma, der im Zuge der Schaffung eines hethitischen Reichspantheons zum Stierkalb, hurritisch *hubiti*, des Teššub geworden ist. Am eindrucksvollsten aber tritt uns die Vorstellung vom Gottstier in dem aus der hethitischen Großreichszeit stammenden Felsrelief von Hanyeri am Paß Gezbel im Antitaurus entgegen, das statt des Wettergottes einen auf einem Berge stehenden Stier zeigt,[21] sowie auch in jener Halluzination Hattusilis I., in der ihm bei der Überquerung dieses Gebirges der Gottstier erschien.[22]

Die kultische Verehrung des Stieres, die uns bereits in den Kulträumen der Terrassensiedlung Çatal Hüyük begegnet, tritt auch im althethitischen Anatolien,[23] so z.B. im lokalen Kult der Stadt Nerik noch deutlich hervor;[24] sie ist aber auch im nordsyrischen Raum, bzw. im westhurritischen Kreis erkennbar, so wird z.B. in einer hurritischen Hymne der Teššub von Halab—ebenso wie Adad—als Sohn (und) Rind des Anu bezeichnet: *wu*$_{u}$*-ú-ut-ki bi-ta-a-ri a-nu-ni-we*$_{e}$ (KUB XLVII 78 Vs. I 10). Eine Verehrung des Hurri(s) unabhängig von der des Teššub belegen Opferlisten, die den Stier zusammen mit den Gebirgen Hazzi und Namni aufführen.[25] In Opfer- und Schwurgötterlisten sind Šeri(š) und Hurri(š) ohne in unmittelbarer Nähe zu Teššub zu stehen, zusammen mit Himmel und Erde aufgeführt.[26] Und falls sich die auf kaukasisch-hurritischen Sprachvergleichen gewonnenen Namensbedeutungen *hurri* "Tag" und *šeri* "Nacht"[27] bestätigen sollten, so könnte— ähnlich wie in der Theogonie des Hesiod—die kosmologische Vorstellung zugrunde liegen, daß Tag und Nacht aus der Paarung von Dunkel und Chaos hervorgegangen sind.[28] Für eine solche urzeitliche Entstehung der Zwillingsstiere spräche schließlich auch, daß beide in einer Opferliste vor den Vorfahrengöttern des Teššub, d.h. den "Vatergöttern des Teššub" genannt sind—sie wären also älter als der Wettergott, der der Generation nach Kumarbi angehört. Zudem

[21]H. Th. Bossert, Das hethitische Felsrelief bei Hanyeri (Gebeli) (tab. XXIV-XXIX), OrNS 23 (1954), 129-47.

[22]H. Otten, Aitiologische Erzählung von der Überquerung des Taurus, ZA 55 (1962), 156-57.

[23]Personennamen aus den altassyrischen Urkunden wie ^{D}GUD oder *al-pì-li/lí* "der Stier ist mein Gott," H. Hirsch, Untersuchungen zur altassyrischen Religion, AfO, Beiheft 13/14 (1961), 24f., belegen ebenso wie die auf den Rollsiegeln jener Zeit abgebildeten, auf einem Postament stehenden Stiere—zu vergleichen ist auch eine entsprechende Szene auf der althethitischen Inandik—Vase—die Vorstellung vom Gottstier.

[24]Vgl. V. Haas, KN 63f.

[25]KBo XX 119 Vs. I 15f. // KBo XVII 86 Vs. I 4′ und KBo XX 122 3f.

[26]Z.B. KBo XIV 143 Vs. I 9′.

[27]I. M. Diakonoff, Hurrisch und Urartäisch. MSS Bh. 6 NF (1971), 165.

[28]V. Haas, Ḫurri und Šeri, RlA 4 (1975), 506.

entspringt der Typus der Zwillingsgottheit einer höchst altertümlichen religiösen Vorstellungen, da er einem Denken in Dualformen entspringt. Interessanterweise trägt nun auch der Doppelstier—wie Zwillingsgottheiten in anderen Religionen auch—den Charakter eines Nothelfers und Fürbitters.[29]

[29]Vgl. V. Haas, Nordsyrische und kleinasiatische Doppelgottheiten im 2. Jahrtausend, WZKM 73 (1981), im Druck.

The Hurrian Story of the Sungod, the Cow and the Fisherman

HARRY A. HOFFNER, JR.
Oriental Institute
Chicago

Among the literary texts in the Hittite language found at Boğazköy there is a small group of Hurrian tales, which are of great interest. This group was first edited by J. Friedrich in 1949.[1] Since Friedrich's edition one of these, the Appu story, has been re-edited, using new fragments which have enlarged the basis for reconstituting the text.[2] But the other two stories, one concerning a hunter named Keššì, and another about the Sungod, a cow, and a fisherman and his wife, have remained unaugmented by more recently published fragments. For this reason no new edition of these texts has been attempted.

The stories themselves, or what remains of them, are quite charming and well worth scholarly attention. Since I have devoted considerable study to them in my classroom teaching over the years, I would like to share with a wider audience certain evidence, not generally known, which bears on the proper interpretation of one of these tales, namely, that of the Sungod, the cow and the fisherman.

Friedrich's edition was based on the cuneiform copy of *KUB* 24.7 made by Arnold Walther, who was a careful copyist. In the summer of 1979 I was permitted to collate and photograph this tablet (Bo 2024) in the collection of the Istanbul Archaeological Museum.[3] I found Walther's copy to be, in almost all points, quite faithful.[4] I would like, however, to communicate certain

[1] "Churritische Märchen und Sagen in hethitischer Sprache," *ZA* 49 (1949-50) 213-55.

[2] J. Siegelová, "Appu-Märchen und Hedammu-Mythus," *StBoT* 14 (1971) 1-34.

[3] I would like to express my thanks here to Veysel Donbaz and Fatma Yıldız, curators of the Istanbul tablet collection, who permitted me to examine and photograph Bo 2024, and to the Chicago Hittite Dictionary Project, through whose funding I was enabled to make the trip.

[4] The following are admittedly very minor criticisms, but should be made in the context of a general collation of this tablet. The spacing and vertical alignment of the signs as copied in *KUB* 24.7 does not reflect the actual situation on the tablet. Thus if one selects the signs which lie on a hypothetical vertical line bisecting each column, one finds them in the copy sometimes to the left and sometimes to the

information at the outset to supplement his copy. Bo 2024 measures 26 x 20 cm in overall dimensions. The lefthand column on both obverse and reverse measures 10 cm from the left extreme of the inscribed surface to the left edge of the intercolumnium. The intercolumnium itself is 1 cm wide. The righthand column on each side measures 9 cm from intercolumnium to beginning of the tablet edge. In most lines the scribe has continued his line out onto that right edge. The arrangement of the writing on the tablet is quite neat. The lines run almost at a precise 90° angle from the vertical margins. There is not, therefore, that noticeable upward slant which one finds on some Hittite tablets, but which is generally not represented in the hand copies. The scribe was usually quite careful to indicate divisions between words by spacing. He wrote in a medium-sized script. The average number of signs in a line of the lefthand columns is 20, while that in the righthand columns is 17 (not including overruns onto the edge). Thus the average sign was 5 mm wide. Walther estimated that the columns on the obverse contained about 65 lines, while on the reverse 70 lines. The reverse, being more convex, naturally accommodated more lines. Each line of script required a vertical space of about 4 mm.

The Cow and Fisherman story occupied only the last part of this tablet, which was a *Sammeltafel*. The first column and much of the second contained a poetic composition which celebrated the activities of the goddess Ishtar.[5]

Of the opening part of the story preserved in ii 46ff. not much can be learned from the badly broken lines. *Šarkuš* (ii 47), which Friedrich translates "hervorragend," modifies gods and kings. Perhaps the Sungod is intended. The plural verb *nannieškir* "they were accustomed to drive (livestock)" suggests that shepherds are the subject. *arḫa piddalait* (ii 49) is a singular; who is the subject? This verb was well treated by Friedrich in *JCS* 1 (1947) 285f. There he posited the meaning "unbeachtet (unangerührt) lassen; laufen lassen" which he later incorporated in *HW* 171. The other occurrence of this verb which most closely resembles the situation here is *KUB* 9.32 i 25-27 with duplicates HT 1 iii 38-42 and *KUB* 9.31 iii 44-46, the ritual of Ašḫela. According to that passage sheep are driven into the fields to graze, and *ANA* ZAG [LÚ]KÚR *anda*

---

right of the same hypothetical bisecting vertical. Thus in the rare case when the pertinence of wedges lying between lines is questioned, one cannot always be sure what sign lies above or below the line under consideration. Table one shows the forms of certain signs which are typical for this tablet. Walther did not always correctly draw certain signs. The following asterisks are samples of those which are incorrectly drawn in *KUB* 24.7: i 14 *-ra*-zu-un*-na*-an . . . ku*-it*; i 16 *-wa-u-wa*-an-zi . . . nu** KIN-*an ku*-it* . . . ; i 19 SAL.MEŠ É.GE$_4$.A-*uš**; i 38 DAM*; i 42 *ar-nu*-uz-zi*; i 47 *ku-it-ki**; i 56]x-*iš-ki*-mi*; ii 5 *ḫu-el*-pí*.

[5]*CTH* 717 with earlier literature. Most recently treated by A. Archi, *OrAnt* 16 (1977) 305ff.

[6]On this usage of *-pat* to refer to an object or a condition mentioned just previously see Hoffner in *Fs Otten* 107-9, section B.

arḫa pittalanzi "they let them run (i.e., graze) in(to) enemy territory." In the *KUB* 24.7 story, too, grazing stock are in view. Two occurrences (*KUB* 21.27 i 16-18 treated by Friedrich and *KUB* 19.12 ii 4a not treated by Friedrich) concern the military-political actions of rulers or generals, who "neglect" territories. A final occurrence from the poem about Ishtar's powers and activities (*KUB* 24.7 ii 10) poses unique problems. The verb is only here construed with the particle *-za*, which was not noted by either Friedrich (*JCS* 1:286) or Archi (*OrAnt* 16:309) in their translations. Archi has detected the essential meaning of the lines, which I would translate: "You don them (i.e., men) like clean clothes. One you soil, and the other you allow to remain clean (*parkun* to be understood as *parkuin*) as before (*-pat*)[6] for yourself (*-za*)." Thus here *arḫa piddalai-* must be translated "allow to remain," which is not far removed from the translation "unangerührt lassen" offered by Friedrich, and somewhat better than Archi's "e chi puro lasci andare."

Friedrich's transliteration of the first preserved part of this tale (II 46-65) was marred by his failure to observe Walther's note in his hand copy, which cautioned users that for economy of printing he had compressed his drawing of the space to the left margin by 3 cm. Friedrich did not allow for that and thus gives the impression that there is space in the break at the left for about four fewer signs that what actually exists.

51 [o o o o o o o *ḫu*]*-el-pí* ⌜*ḫa*⌝[*-ap-pu-r*]*i*[*-i*]*a-an-na nu* ⌜GI?⌝*-an*
52 [o o *az-zi-ik*]*-ki*[*-i*]*t nu* GUD*-uš m*[*e-ek-k*]*i mar-r*[*i*] SIG$_5$*-t*[*a-at*?]
53 [o o *mi-iš-r*]*i*!*-u-e-eš-ta* ^{d}UTU*-uš-kán* AN*-za* GAM *a-u*[*š-ta*]
54 [*nu* SIG$_5$?*-an*?*-ti*? *A-*]*NA* GUD ZI*-aš pa-ra-a wa-at-k*[*u-u*]*t*

". . . and tender grass. And [the cow at]e reeds(?).[7] And the cow became exceedingly fat;[8] [the cow] became [bea]utiful.[9] The Sungod looked down from heaven. His sexual desire leaped upon [the fat[8]] cow."

[7]Walther's copy shows Z[I] or G[I] in ii 51, the decisive righthand part of the sign is broken. GI*-an* would be Hittite *natan*, where the singular is probably collective. Friedrich transliterated ZI*-an* with no indication of the broken condition of the sign.

[8]Middle form SIG$_5$*-t*[*a-at*] (contra Friedrich: SIG$_4$*-t*[*a*]) seems called for by the sense required. See now *CHD* sub *lazziya-* 3b. The translation "fat," not employed in *CHD*, is suggested here as conveying the physical appearance of a healthy, thriving cow.

[9]Friedrich, overlooking Walther's note about the size of the break on the left, allowed only [*nu*? PI]Š?*-e-eš-ta*, which would be a hapax. Since more space is clearly available, I read the traces [o o *mi-iš-r*]*i*!*-u-e-eš-ta*, a known and appropriate verb. In the Hittite translation of Akkadian lunar omens *KUB* 8.13:13 *mi-iš-ri-u-e-eš-zi* describes the moon as being full, as opposed to *tepawešzi* "is partial" (line 14). I do not believe that the fundamental idea underlying *mišriwant-*, *mišriwatar*, *mišriweš-*, etc., is splendor or brilliance, as assumed by HW and other colleagues. It seems rather to me

Friedrich's transliteration through III 24a can only be improved upon in small details. But I offer a different translation of III 18ff.: "[The first month passed,] the second month, the third month, [the fourth month, . . .], the ninth month. And the tenth month arrived.[10] [And the cow gave birth.] The cow [called(?)] back up to heaven, she looked . . . and she began to say [to the Sungod(?)]: "I call for mercy.[11] [My calf] (should have) four legs. Why have I given birth to this two-legged one?"

24 . . . GUD-*uš* UR.MAḪ-*aš* GIM-*an* KAxU-*iš* *ar-ḫa*
25 *ki-nu-ut na-aš* DUMU-*li a-da-an-na pa-iš-ki-it-ta* GUD-*uš-za šar-ḫu*[*-wa-an-da-še-et*]
26 *ḫu-u-wa-an-ḫu-e-šar ma-a-an ḫal-lu-wa-nu-ut n*[*a-a*]*š* DU[MU-*l*]*i* [. . .]
27 *i-ia-an-ni-i*[*š*]

"The cow opened her mouth like a lion and goes to the child to eat (the attached fetal membranes). Like a wave she released her aft[erbirth], and went to the child [to suckle it]." The interpretation of Friedrich that the cow went to harm the child was based on the interpretation of *tarkuwa* as "angrily" and the metaphor of the lion. It seems to me that these two facts need not so be understood. *Tarkuwa* is a hapax. The cow's words "I call for mercy"[11] and her

---

that the words express perfection in the sense of that which has no essential part lacking. This notion is as appropriate to a beautiful woman, to a sacrificial animal, as it is to temples and lands. I would suggest that the basic idea is "full, whole, entire, perfect" and an extended meaning "(visually) perfect, beautiful." Supporting the restoration here of *mišriweš-* is the pairing of SIG_5-*ant-* and *mišriwant-* elsewhere (*KUB* 15.34 ii 7, 15, 38, 46; *KBo* 15.10 i 17). Someone or something which is *mišriwant-* is further described as *ḫumandaz aššanuwanza* "endowed with everything" in two different texts (*KBo* 4.6 i 13-14; *KUB* 33.121 ii 5-6).

[10] The ten-month gestation formula is, of course, common enough in describing human pregnancies (H. Hoffner, *JNES* 27:199). It happens, however, that it is not inappropriate here for a cow, since the bovine gestation period is 283 days on the average (G. P. West, ed., *Encyclopedia of Animal Care*, 1977, p. 629).

[11] *duddu*/*duwaddu* as an interjection is similar in meaning to Akkadian *aḫulap* (*CAD* 213ff.), which is used to express or seek compassion. *aḫulap* is similar in meaning to Akkad. *maṣi* "enough" and *adi mati* "for how long?". In a ritual to heal a sick man (*KUB* 17.12 iii 16-21) they bind the sick man's hands with woolen cords and whip (*zaḫ-* "strike") him with the same woolen cords, while he cries out *duddu* ("Mercy! Enough!"). Oettinger (*Die Stammbildung des hethitischen Verbums*, 230ff.) has shown that *duddu*/*duwaddu* is a 2nd sg. imperative of the verb *duddu-*, for which he puts forward the translation "gnädig behandeln, gnädig beherrschen." The OH examples of this imperative show the fuller form *tuwattu*. For the imperative Oettinger suggests "sei gnädig." The imperative form is regularly used in prayers as a plea for

question may actually reflect concern for the strange, two-legged offspring. The cow opened her mouth wide to eat the fetal membrane.[12] Through the use of metaphor to indicate how wide, the story-teller has alluded to an animal whose wide open mouth is nearly proverbial, the lion. This is a myth, of course. But one sees in the context no other evidence that the cow wanted to kill her offspring. And that being the case, one might expect her to do the following: (1) eat or lick away whatever fluids of fetal membranes adhere to her "calf," (2) expel her afterbirth, and (3) begin to suckle the new "calf." The GAM *paššūna* "to swallow down" of lines 31 in broken context might refer to the cow's swallowing the fetal membranes or the afterbirth, or to the offspring's swallowing milk from the cow's udder. In line 35 read *ḫa-aḫ-re-*⌜*es*⌝[*-ki-iz-zi*] instead of Friedrich's *ḫa-pu-ri-*x[. . .]. In iii 57 restore perhaps: [. . . *ḫa-le-e*]*n-zu*^ḪI.A^ *arrauwanzi ḫarnamnieškant*[*a*] "[The . . . -s] are stirred up to wash away the [water pl]ants." For iii 65ff. see now the *CHD* sub *liliwant-*. In iii 69 read: [*IŠ-T*]*U* KAK.ḪI.A-*ŠU-NU*, and in iii 70: [*nu a*]*n-da dammenkandušman*. Lines iv 49ff. should be translated: "The woman's wits were sharp. She had ignored commands, and . . . . But she had attained the (proper) subjection of woman and no (longer) alters (i.e., disobeys) the man's word."

The preceding remarks, while not directly concerned with the plot of the story, are essential for the interpretation of certain passages which affect our reconstruction of the plot.

While the body of texts written in the Hurrian language grows steadily, we should not underestimate the importance of the study of Hurrian compositions in Hittite translations. The most important of these are surely the myths which form what is called the Kumarbi cycle. But the smaller corpus of tales, the initial studies of which we owe to J. Friedrich, hold a position of great

---

divine pity (*KUB* 30.62+:12; *KBo* 17.4:4; *KBo* 17.1 ii 41; *KBo* 11.72+ iii 22). Note also: *nu wašduli duddu ḫalzai* "He cries 'Mercy' for (his) offence" *KUB* 4.47 i 8.

[12]KAxU-*iš arḫa kinut* iii 24-25. Were this agonistic behaviour, it would certainly involve horns and hooves, not "eating." For bovine partuition behaviour see G. P. West (ed.), *Encyclopedia of Animal Care*, 581f. And note in particular: "The cow licks the foetal membranes and fluids from the calf and usually eats the placenta, and sometimes the bedding contaminated by foetal and placental fluids as well. The normally herbivorous animal suddenly and briefly exhibits a carnivorous appetite. . . . During this time the mother and calf stay close together, and the calf feeds for the first time." (E. S. E. Hafez [ed.], *The Behaviour of Domestic Animals*, 1962, p. 278). I translated *šarḫu*[*wandaššet*] "her afterbirth" because *šarḫuwanda* has the meaning "placenta, fetus" in the laws (numbers 17-18, 77a-77b) and in Tunnawi I 4-5. In law 77a the Old Script version A has the Akkadian *ŠA* ŠÀ-*BI-ŠA* (*ša libbiša*) in its place. The afterbirth is also referred to by the Akkadogram ^UZU^*ŠALĪTU*, which is offered to deities at the time of birth of calves, lambs and kids (*CAD* Ḫ sub *ḫakurratu*, and add KBo 22.222 iii 1, 5).

importance as well. This attempt to enlarge upon the understanding of one such Hurrian story in Hittite translation is offered as a tribute to E. R. Lacheman, who, through his long labors on the texts from Nuzi, has made a major contribution to our understanding of the history and culture of the Hurrians.

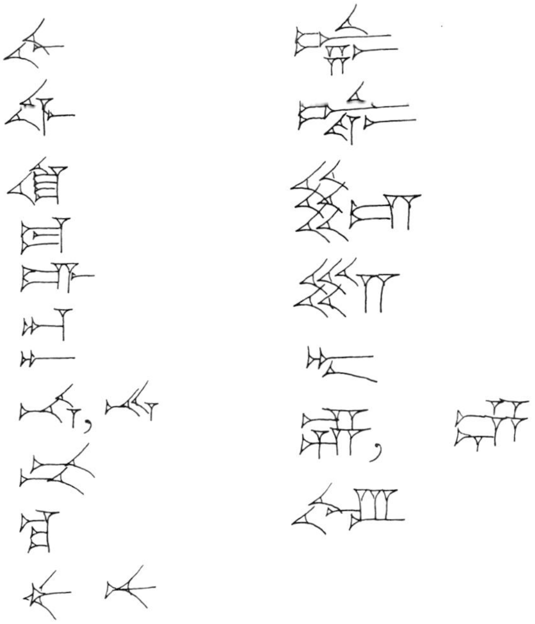

Table One: A selection of sign forms typical for Bo 2024, which are usually not drawn correctly in *KUB* 24.7. Other signs, correctly drawn in *KUB* 24.7 and therefore not shown here, combine with these to indicate a date for the copy during the Empire Period.

Life of the Military Élite in Arrapḫe

NINEL JANKOWSKA
The Hermitage
Leningrad, U.S.S.R.

In the following paper we have collected the data on the life of the military elite of Arrapḫe, namely the charioteers. The data, to our knowledge, have never been brought together. Most of the documents were published by Professor Lacheman. A short letter, *JEN* 498, says:

> 1) *a-na* ^I^*Šu-ur-Te-šub* 2) *qí-bi*$_4$*-ma* 3) *um-ma* ^I^*Šer*$_9$*-ši-*j[a] 4) ^I^*Kur(!)-pa-za-aḫ i-na* 5) *āli el-qí a-ši-im-mi* 6) *ù aḫḫū*^MEŠ^*-šu a-na* 7) ^GIŠ^*narkabāti*^MEŠ^ *aš-bu-mi* 8) *ù bal-ṭe*$_4$*-mi* 9) *kunuk* ^I^*Šer*$_9$*-ši-ja*
>
> Say to Šur-Tešub, thus (says) Šeršiya: "I caught Kurpazaḫ in the city. He dwells (there, he says), and his brothers on account of the chariots dwell (there, he says). And he is alive (he says)." Seal of Šeršiya.

Although all of the persons mentioned in this letter are named without their patronymics, the provenience of the text makes it possible to differentiate them from possible namesakes. The letter was found together with more than a dozen documents that comprise the archive of Kurpazaḫ and his brothers.[1] From these other documents we learn that they were all the sons of Ḫelpišuḫ.

Before turning to the documents, let us study their archaeological context. They derive from Room 10 on mound T, named after Teḫib-Tilla, whose archive was found there. A detailed study of the buildings under this mound shows that only a portion of Teḫib-Tilla's own house has been preserved, while two other houses are more or less complete. The middle building consisted of six rooms on the ground floor with a total area of about 150 m^2. This was certainly a residence: in the back room (18) there was a bath-tub that used the drain pipes of Teḫib-Tilla's house; adjoining it was a large store room (16). When the house was rebuilt, a second wall was erected dividing it from

[1] *JEN* 87, 204, 255, 311, 315, 320, 331, 478, 604, 645; *JENu* 423, 629, 859. The following documents were either registered erroneously or found their way into other rooms by accident: *JEN* 214 (Room 12), *JEN* 198 (Room 11), 471 (Room 13). The last document belongs to Ḫelpišuh, son of Šuḫun-ziriri, father of Kurpazaḫ and his brothers. Thus the name of his grandfather is also known.

that of Teḫib-Tilla. Judging from the archive found in Room 13,[2] the rebuilding must have taken place under Tarmi-Tilla, the grandson of Teḫib-Tilla. Like his grandfather, he was the chief of the military district (*ḫalṣuḫlu*). This is attested by the following letter, apparently addressed to him by the king (*JEN* 551):

1) *ki-na-an-na a-na* ^{I}*Tar-mi-Til-la* 2) *ṭe₄-ma iš-ta-ka-nu* 3) *mi-nu-um-me-e bītātu*$^{\text{MEŠ.tum}}$ *ša e-kal-lim* 4) *ša ḫal-ṣi-ka₄ aš-bu* 5) *a-na 10 sinnišāti*^{MEŠ} 1 šīra eššа(!) *ša alpi* 6) *ù 3 šīrāni*^{MEŠ} *eššūtī*(!) *ša immeri i-na-an-*[*di-nu*] 7) *eṣ-mi-tum* [*ša*] *šīri ešši*(!) *ša* ⌜*alpi*⌝ 8) *i-na āl-ilāni*^{MEŠ} [*ú*]*-ub-bá-lu-ni* 9) *šum-ma kar-ṣú ša* [*alpi*] *bur-ru-mu* 10) *i-ba-uš-ši-m*[*a*] [*ú-na-a*]*k-*<*ki*>*-is-su-ú* 11) *ù i-na-ūmi*^{mi} *ša* [*alpī ù ṣēnī*^{M}]^{EŠ} 12) *i-ṭa-ab-ba-ḫu a-na e-kal-lim* 13) *ú-ub-bá-lu-ni* 14) *maškī*^{MEŠ} *ù še-er-a-ni*^{MEŠ} 15) *ša na-ag-la-bá-ti* 16) *ša alpi a-lik il-ki* 17) *ù ša aš-šá-be-e* 18) *a-na ši-mi i-leq-qì-ma* 19) *ù a-na e-kal-lim* 20) *ú-ub-bá-lu-ni*

This order is issued to Tarmi-Tilla: "all those who dwell in the houses of the palace of your district shall give for (the) 10 women one fresh ox's carcass and three fresh rams' carcasses, (and) the bones of the fresh ox's carcass they must bring to Āl-ilāni. If a piece of the [ox's] carcass is spotted, [c]ut it [off], and on the day they slaughter the [cattle and the sheep] they shall bring (the rest of the meat) to the palace; the skins and the carcasses, (those) of the shaved ones <and> (that) of the ox, the people liable to the *ilku* and those of the settlers may take for a price, and bring (it, i.e. the price) to the palace!"

What does all this meat "for the ten women" mean? And why should the meat, except the "spotted" or "variegated," and the bones be sent to the religious center of the country? It is hardly food, but more probably an expiatory offering. The quality of the meat may have had a portentous significance, hence the cutting off(?) of the "spotted" pieces. In any event, the letter provides a picture of the living standard of the palace inhabitants and those liable for state service in the communities. It is interesting that the head of the military district is responsible for the operation. [However, see the article of Maidman, below in this volume. eds.]

The house adjoining the dwelling of Tarmi-Tilla, the one farthest to the right on Mound T, is the biggest of the buildings. On the side where Starr supposed the main entrance to be, the rooms are destroyed; the others are grouped around a central court of ca. 80 m^2. On three sides of the court twelve rooms are preserved with a total area of ca. 300 m^2., or double the size of

[2] *JEN* 9, 27, 61, 102, 103, 108, 147, 151, 294, 296, 314, 402, 403, 492, 535, 536, 538, 542, 547, 548, 550, 557, 558, 573, 624, 642. The documents of Tarmi-Tilla *JEN* 115 (Room 11), 443, 496, 551 (Room 12) were erroneously registered or moved accidentally into other rooms.

Tarmi-Tilla's house. Here *three* archives, none of which belongs to the family of Teḫib-Tilla,[3] were found.

There is no doubt that the house had an upper storey. In the right outer corner of the house there is a room (1) which has no entrance from the other rooms on the same floor. This is typical of tower-type buildings, where such rooms were entered by a ladder from the upper storey. If this was a tower, it may have protected the entrance. Room 2 yielded plates of armour, an arrowhead, and a considerable number of fragments of different military equipment. Therefore Starr suggested that this was the house's armoury.[4] In this part of the house the *first* archive was found. It belonged to the brothers Waḫr-Abi and Ḫuite, to Ḫašia, son of Waḫr-Abi, and to Mušeia his grandson.[5] The archive must have been kept in the upper storey, and some of the documents fell through the floor into Room 1 and others into Room 4. The room contained a little basin for water which ran in from the court through an open drain. It seems that when the tower collapsed, its top tumbled into the court, and the tablets were carried with the water along the drain. The family that lived in this part of the house may have been the guards responsible for its protection.

On the other side of the court through Room 12 there is a side entrance which Starr thought to be secondary to the main one which has disappeared. In this passage and in the adjoining Room 11 the *second* archive belonging to one Kel-Tešub and his father[6] was found. He may have been connected with this house by his service. He was a *rab ḫanšē*, the head of fifty chariots (*JEN* 612). As we will see below, each ten chariots had a following of twenty riders and two hundred infantrymen. Thus, Kel-Tešub was the head of about a thousand warriors. This constituted a whole military district (cf. *HSS* 15 44).

Through the above-mentioned side passage we enter the biggest room of the house, Room 10, where the *third* archive, that belonging to Kurpazaḫ and his brothers, was found. From this room there is an entrance to the central

[3]Three documents appear there accidentally: one belonging to Teḫib-Tilla, the grandfather of Tarmi-Tilla (*JEN* 75), one to Wur-Tešub, cousin-german to Tarmi-Tilla (*JEN* 290), and one to Ennamadi, uncle of Tarmi-Tilla (*JEN* 625).

[4]R. Starr, *Nuzi I*, Cambridge, Mass. (1939), p. 335.

[5]*JEN* 39, 47, 88, 89, 150, 189, 216, 221, 291, 292, 298, 300, 301, 318, 396, 444, 475, 485, 491, 537, 568, 606, 629, 664; *JENu* 775, 797, 972, 974, 979, 1002, 1008.

[6]*JEN* 59, 83, 85, 116, 117, 125, 135, 143, 181, 186, 219, 316, 325, 342, 435, 489, 477, 495, 512, 527, 529, 533, 541, 592, 600, 612, 616, 646, 666, 672. Erroneously registered or accidentally moved into the adjoining room (13) are two documnts of Kel-Tešub, *JEN* 321 and 340. This may mean that the entire archive was kept in rooms of the upper storey in both wings of the house, so that when it collapsed it fell into different rooms of the ground floor.

court of the house. The doorways are broad, as if designed for the passage of crowds.

The room that produced the archive of Kurpazaḫ was no less than 100 m^2. in area. In the preceding building period it had two hearths, which suggests that it was designed as a residence. After Tarmi-Tilla occupied the middle house, this room may have become the quarters of the guard on duty.

Having described the provenience of the archive, we may turn now to the problem of the identities of Šeršiya and Šur-Tešub the sender and recipient, respectively, of the letter *JEN* 498.

The name Šeršiya is a rare one. A scribe Šeršiya wrote two documents (*JEN* 198 and 124) in the same archive. Both documents contain legal claims of Mad-Tešub, brother of Kurpazaḫ. The first was a suit against the prince Šugriya (son of Teššuya, cf. *JEN* 311), a nephew of Itḫi-Tešub, king of Arrapḫe. Thus, the defendant belonged to generation III of the Arrapḫites. The prince had borrowed a horse from Mad-Tešub for five days, but returned it after six. Hence, the prince became liable to the penalty clause, according to which he had to pay the price of the horse if he kept it instead of returning it as agreed. The second document was drawn up in connection with a suit againt Kurpazaḫ who was accused of driving eight sheep into the garden of a third brother, Tupki-Tilla. We shall return to this text below.

The sons of Šeršiya appear as witnesses in the deeds of women belonging to the house of Teḫib-Tilla: of Uzna, the wife of Ennamadi, the elder son of Teḫib-Tilla (*HSS* 13 418), and of Tarminaia, a MÍ.LUGAL and daughter of Teḫib-Tilla.[7]

Thus, the sender of the letter *JEN* 498 was a scribe and perhaps a contemporary of Teḫib-Tilla, since their children were contemporaries.

The Šur-Tešub in question was probably the son of Akkuya, a head of twenty riders, according to the list *HSS* 15 31. Twenty riders was the usual number following ten chariots, so that Šur-Tešub, son of Akkuya, may well have been the same as Šur-Tešub the *emanduḫlu* "head of ten (chariots)" in the list *HSS* 14 40. This list was found in the archive of certain high officers. It included some eighty documnts (Sector C, Room 28 and the adjoining ones). In these Šur-Tešub is named three times: 1) One of his men receives some armour belonging to the palace (*HSS* 15 6). 2) Šur-Tešub, himself, and five of his men are named in the list of more than two hundred warriors, for all of whom he is responsible (*HSS* 16 405). These may be the two hundred

[7]The document was found in the palace (Room K-32), the dwelling of Tarminaia. According to M. P. Maidman, the kinship between Tarminaia and Teḫib-Tilla, son of Puḫi-šenni, is not proved and her father might have been a namesake of the well-known owner of the archive. However, the document cited may argue in favor of Tarminaia's relationship to the house of the heirs of Puḫi-šenni, as originally suggested by E. A. Speiser. Incidentally, a scribe Šeršiya held a responsible position in the estate of Teḫib-Tilla (*HSS* 13 492).

infantrymen who followed his ten chariots (twenty men for each). 3) Šur-Tešub is mentioned among eleven officers of the left flank; in the same list Tešurḫe, great-grandson of Teḫib-Tilla, is mentioned among the fifteen officers of the right flank (*HSS* 16 109). Among the officers of the left flank Šur-Tešub is also mentioned in a document (*HSS* 15 121) found in the archive of external relations (D-6). He is named immediately before the prince Ḫudib-Urašše, the grandson of Agib-Tešub, a brother of Itḫi-Tešub, king of Arrapḫe (see Jankowska, *Carskie brat'ja...*, "Kul'tura Vostoka," L. 1978).

Thus, Šur-Tešub appears at least twice among the Arrapḫites of generations IV or V. This might well happen in a society where very early marriages were the rule. We pointed out in the paper cited above that representatives of three and even four generations may actually be encountered in the same document (cf. *HSS* 13 410). Anyway, Šur-Tešub was in a position to require information on the whereabouts of Kurpazaḫ, a man perhaps of the same age as the scribe of the letter and thus considerably older than the young recipient.

What do we know about Kurpazaḫ, himself, except that he and his brothers were apparently charioteers (see the letter quoted at the beginning of the paper)? The tower (*dimtu*) of Kurpazaḫ is mentioned among the thirty rural communities from every one of which the palace requisitioned a plot of 1 *imēru* of land in compensation for supplying water (*HSS* 15 128:29; for a revised interpretation of the text, see Jankowska, *JESHO* 12/13 [1969], p. 268). The same list mentions the settlements of Ennamadi, elder son of Teḫib-Tilla, and of Šuwar-Ḫeba, sister of Šilwi-Tešub, both of whom belong to generation III-IV of the Arrapḫites. Owning a tower was a matter of prestige for a family or clan, and Kurpazaḫ was the head of the family.

It seems that Kurpazaḫ was somewhat older than the average member of the third generation. *JEN* 320 is an agreement between the brothers Mad-Tešub and Kurpazaḫ and the still active Teḫib-Tilla, the main figure in generation II. Teḫib-Tilla paid 5 *imēru* (ca. 375 liters) of barley to the brothers' creditor and in return received their field in mortgage (this was the third time it was mortgaged). The plot was situated on the land of the village Zalmānu (Zalmu) and thus lay in the neighborhood of the estate belonging to the family of Niḫri-Tilla, prince Ḫudib-Urašše's father (*RA* 28, 6).

The debt which the two brothers incurred may have been related to Kurpazaḫ's transactions with his brothers. 1) He lent to his brother Punni-Ḫarbe one ram, 1,5 kg. of copper and 14 *imēru* (ca. 1050 liters) of barley for the right to use three plots belonging to P. (*JEN* 315). 2) He transferred to the same Punni-Ḫarbe a plot of pasture-land for 115 liters of barley. The deed is cast in the form of Kurpazaḫ's being "adopted as brother" by Punni-Ḫarbe, though they were brothers already; this meant that he was included in the undivided fraternal economy. Among the witnesses a son of Mad-Tešub, Kurpazaḫ's brother, appears (*JEN* 87). 3) A garden was transferred to Kurpazaḫ by another brother, Tupki-Tilla, also in the form of "adoption as brother" (*JEN* 204). 4) Kurpazaḫ exchanged his own garden for the plot near the house of a neighbor (*JEN* 255). 5) Finally, we have a prolongation of the mortgage deed for two hectares of the land of Punni-Ḫarbe (*JEN* 311). The first of the witnesses is Kainni, son of Kurpazaḫ, the crier (*nāgiru*). He is followed by the two full brothers of Kurpazaḫ, Tupku-Tilla and Mad-Tešub. The last of the witnesses is prince Šugriya, son of Teššuya, who went to court with Mad-Tešub because of a horse.

Kurpazaḫ quarreled with his elder son, Agib-Tilla, disinheriting him from fields and houses and prohibiting him from going near the family gods (*JEN* 478). The document was drawn up before Šamaš, and Mad-Tešub was one of the witnesses.

Though the brothers appear united for the most part, occasionally, serious conflicts arose. Thus, according to *JEN* 331, Kurpazaḫ sued Mad-Tešub for assault on his wife. Mad-Tešub denied the accusation under oath and was sent by the judges to the ordeal. During the latter, Kurpazaḫ accused Mad-Tešub of using a charm while taking the oath. For misleading the judges Mad-Tešub was fined and had to give Kurpazaḫ an ox.

The reader will remember that the sender of the letter *JEN* 498 was Šeršiya. He was also the scribe of the court proceedings document *JEN* 124, recording a suit between Kurpazaḫ and Mad-Tešub about sheep that were driven into a garden. This time Mad-Tešub was the plaintiff, and Kurpazaḫ was the one who swore under oath that the accusation was false and was sent to the River by the judges. The "City" of the text is probably the "City of the Gods" (*Āl-ilāni*), the religious center of the country. It is possible that the information in the letter *JEN* 498 that Kurpazaḫ was alive means that the ordeal ended favorably.

The cited documents show that the families of the charioteers belonged to a social stratum of medium opulence. It also seems that the service of Kurpazaḫ and his brothers was for life and was more of an honorary than of an active nature, at least in times of peace. The house where Kurpazaḫ's archive was found may have gone along with the office of the head of the military district and may have changed hands with the change of the officers.

Note that the charioteers of Arrapḫe, from the commanders of the military district (as Teḫib-Tilla, Tarmi-Tilla and Kel-Tešub) to the senior officers, like the flank commanders (Šur-Tešub, Tesurḫe, etc.) and down to such men as Kurpazaḫ, standing close to the élite, were all native Hurrians. Not a single one of them was Aryan.

gurpisu ša awēli: The Helmets of the Warriors at Nuzi

TIMOTHY KENDALL
Museum of Fine Arts
Boston, Mass.

By far the most important written evidence for the types of armor in use in the Ancient Near East during the Late Bronze Age is found in the Nuzi archive of the late fifteenth and early fourteenth centuries B.C. Of the more than four thousand cuneiform tablets recovered from Nuzi, at least eighty are known that describe the armor, weapons, and chariots of the local militia.[1] Being largely inventories itemizing the military equipment flowing to and from the palace arsenal, these documents are extraordinarily detailed, distinguishing no less than fifteen different types or styles of armor,[2] and providing very full data on the armor and harness of the chariot horse as well as on the construction and armament of the chariot. Despite the evident richness of these texts, they can be made to reveal their secrets only if the numerous specialized terms that occur within them are correctly interpreted. Since the first of the documents were published in 1939 by E. R. Lacheman,[3] they have been studied and discussed by many Assyriologists and frequently mentioned

[1]For a full, albeit preliminary, discussion of these and the many other texts relating to the military establishment at Nuzi, see Timothy Kendall, *Warfare and Military Matters in the Nuzi Tablets* (unpublished doctoral dissertation, Brandeis University, 1974). Specifically, the texts mentioning suits of armor or their parts are as follows: *JEN* 527, 533; *HSS* 5 93, 106; *HSS* 13 195; *HSS* 14 616, 236, 258; *HSS* 15 2a-12, 14-16, 20, 23, 24, 39, 142, 167, 212, 215, 305; *HSS* 16 441. Those mentioning swords: *HSS* 14 263b; *HSS* 15 2a, 4, 38; bows and quivers: *JEN* 196; *HSS* 5 93; *HSS* 9 55; *HSS* 13 354; *HSS* 15 2, 17, 18, 21, 37, 50; arrows: *AASOR* 16 90; *JEN* 519; *HSS* 5 44; *HSS* 13 60, 71, 85, 99, 100, 103, 116, 175, 206; *HSS* 14 586, 626, 11, 224-28; and chariot equipment and parts: *HSS* 13 198, 276, 283, 326, 439; *HSS* 15 46, 59, 78, 82, 92, 95, 146, 167, 195, 196, 202, 208.

[2]A brief listing of all the known types of body armor in use at Nuzi appears in the text below. Specific references to each type are given in nn. 10-18.

[3]E. R. Lacheman, "Nuziana II," *RA* 36 (1939), 113ff. (copies of selected texts) and in R. F. S. Starr, *Nuzi* v. I (Cambridge, 1939), pp. 540ff. (summaries).

by historians of ancient armor,[4] yet to date, they still have not been fully translated or explained, and many of their terms remain problematical. One of the most common terms to appear in them, but still one of the most frequently mistranslated, is the word *gurpisu*, whose meaning I hope to be able to establish once and for all in this present paper. It is my extreme pleasure to be able to offer this study to Dr. Lacheman, who not only brought these remarkable texts to light and first discussed them over forty years ago, but who also brought them to my attention and encouraged me to make these and other related Nuzi texts and subject of my Brandeis University doctoral dissertation.[5]

The word *gurpisu* (*gurpissu*, *gurpizu*, *gursipu*, *gursippu*) in Akkadian has long been recognized as the name of a particular element of armor, which together with the *sariam* (*siriam*, *širiannu*, *šir'anu*) comprised the basic body armor of the warrior. Even the chariot horse was said to have been clad in *sariam* and *gurpisu*. At Nuzi the *sariam ša awēli* ("*s*. of a man") is frequently described as *ša ramāni* ("of the body") or *ša irti* ("of the breast"), leaving no doubt that it was an armored tunic or "corselet."[6] The *sariam ša sīsi* ("*s*. of a horse,"), therefore, would have been an armored back pad. Occasionally the *sariam* "of a man" is further described as having *aḫū* ("sleeves,"), a *ṣēru* ("back"), and a *tikku* ("collar"),[7] and sometimes it was issued with *kalkū* ("flaps") hanging "from the waist,"[8] or with "pairs of *tutiwa*," perhaps wide straps or "bandoleers" crossing at the chest, which gave further protection to the midriff.[9] The *sariam* of the warrior came in a variety of styles and

[4]For Assyriological commentaries on these texts, see references throughout and nn. 19-22 and 44. See also B. Thordeman, *Armour from the Battle of Wisby, 1361*, v. I (Stockholm, 1939), p. 447; Y. Yadin, *The Art of Warfare in Biblical Lands* (New York, 1963), pp. 85, 196; H. R. Robinson, *Oriental Armour* (London, 1967), pp. 1ff.

[5]See n. 1.

[6]D. Cross, *Movable Property in the Nuzi Documents* (New Haven, 1937), p. 57; Lacheman in Starr, v. I, p. 541; Starr, v. I, pp. 479ff.; E. Speiser, "On Some Articles of Armor and Their Names," *JAOS* 70 (1950), 47ff. I read NÍ (IM) as *ramānu* rather than *zumru* because it is spelled phonetically in *HSS* 14 616:11, 12.

[7]For *sariam* with *aḫū*, see *JEN* 527:2, 4, 6, 7, *HSS* 13 195:18, *HSS* 15 3: 5, 13, 19, 30; 5:2, 6, 11, 16; 11:5; with *ṣēru*, see *HSS* 15 4:15, 46; with *tikku*, see *HSS* 15 12:16, 19, 25, passim; 45:5; 280a:13. On the armored neckpiece and its use, see P. Greenhalgh, "The Dendra Charioteer," *Antiquity* 54 (1980), 201ff. For illustrations of the *tikku*, see figure 8 and reference in n. 56.

[8]See text below and n. 33.

[9]The Nuzi word *d/tutiwa* is almost certainly derived from Akkadian *d/tutittu* (or *d/tutinatu*), generally translated "pectoral" or "breast ornament" (*AHw*, p. 1365). Although Asiatic troops of the fifteenth century are often shown wearing disk-shaped pectorals, they are even more frequently shown wearing pairs of wide shoulder straps or "bandoleers" over their armor (ref. nn. 23, 61). That these straps were the *tutiwa*, rather than the former, is suggested by *HSS* 13 431: 43f. and *HSS* 14 246:27f. which

materials: it was "of leather" (*ša maški*),[10] "of leathers" (perhaps "of leather scales") (*ša maškē*),[11] "of leather with bronze sleeves" (*ša maški . . . ša aḫišunu ša siparri*),[12] "of leather with a back of bronze" (*ša maški ašar ṣērišu sippari*),[13] of bronze, for the breast" (*ša irtišu ša siparri*),[14] "of bronze, for the body" (*ša ramānišu ša siparri*),[15] of bronze scales and leather scales,[16] or of bronze scales, the known types of suits having from 400 to 560 "large scales of the body" with both short and long sleeves covered with "small scales."[17] (There even seems to be some evidence for a fully lamellar breastplate.[18])

---

mentions "pairs of *tutiwa*" (*ṣí-mi-it-tu ša tu-ti-wa*). The *tutiwa* for horses are also listed with *ašatu* ("reins") further suggesting that they were straps (*HSS* 15 17:27ff.). Crossing straps or sashes, sometimes studded, appear as armor for the common troops from Sumerian and Akkadian times on. Their primary purpose, it seems, was to lend protection to the chest while leaving the arms free and unencumbered for close combat. (See, for example, the "Stele of the Vultures," in André Parrot, *Sumer* [London, 1960], p. 134; and the several Akkadian stelae discussed by J. F. X. McKeon, "An Akkadian Victory Stele," *Bulletin of the Museum of Fine Arts* 68 [1970], 226ff.). By the Old Babylonian Period a pectoral seems to have been worn at the juncture of the crossing straps, so that straps and pectoral actually comprised the same element of armor. (See M. T. Barrelet, *Figurines et reliefs en terre cuite de la Mésopotamie antique*, v. I [Paris, 1968], pl. LIII, 562.) This would seem to explain how the word *tutiwa* (*tutittu*, *tutinatu*) could under certain conditions have been used to indicate either a pair of straps or a pectoral or both.

[10]*JEN* 527:14, 533:10; *HSS* 14 236:9; *HSS* 15 3:33, 4:5, 22.

[11]*JEN* 533:1, 8; *HSS* 5 93:1; *HSS* 13 195:17; *HSS* 15 7:6. The occasional description of leather armor as "*sariam* of leathers" perhaps suggests, if not a scribal inconsistency, a slightly more elaborate body defense than the "*sariam* of leather." The use of the plural KUŠ.MEŠ = *maškē* = leathers" may indicate a type of corselet consisting either of more than one layer of leather or of a number of overlapping leather scales of the type described in *HSS* 15 11:6f. (see n. 16). In *JEN* 533, simple "leather armor" (*sariam maški*) (l. 10) seems to be distinguished from "armor of leathers" (*sariam maškē*) (ll. 1, 8), suggesting that the two were indeed different.

[12]*JEN* 527:3, 5, 7; *HSS* 13 195:17; *HSS* 15 7:6.

[13]*HSS* 15 4:15, 40.

[14]*HSS* 13 195:15f.

[15]*JEN* 533:6; *HSS* 13 195:14; *HSS* 14 616:9, 12; *HSS* 15 3:2f., 18f., 27f., 4:33, 38, 44; 142:10.

[16]*HSS* 15 11: [*x ma*]-*ti 79* [*kur*]-*zi-mi-tu ša* ZABAR GAL.MEŠ *ša* NÍ.MEŠ [*x*] *ma-ti kur-zi-mi-tu ša* ZABAR TUR.MEŠ *ša a-ḫi-šu-nu 2 ma-ti 46 kur-zi-mi-tu* GAL.MEŠ sa KUŠ.MEŠ *a-na* ŠU ^{m}*A-ḫi-il-li-ka*$_4$ *na-ad-nu ù sa-ri-am* DÙ-*uš* ("[x] hundred and seventy-nine large bronze scales for the body, [x] hundred small bronze scales for the sleeves, two hundred and forty-six large leather scales are given to Aḫī-illika and he shall make a corselet"). On the etymology of *kurṣimtu* ("scale"), see Speiser, p. 48.

[17]*HSS* 15 3:2f., 10f., 18f., 27f.; 5:1f., 5f., 10f., 13f.

[18]Lamellar armor is armor in which the scales are sewn together to form the corselet rather than sewn to a leather or fabric tunic. Note that in *HSS* 15 8:13 there

In nearly every text where the *sariam* is listed, the *gurpisu* appears with it, obviously as an item without which the warrior's battle garb was considered incomplete. The *gurpisu* "of a man," like the *sariam*, came in several distinct styles and materials: it was made "of wool," "of leather," or "of bronze" (i.e., beaten sheet bronze?), or else it was covered with from 140 to 200 bronze scales. It too possessed *kalkū* ("flaps") and was sometimes said to be *ṣuppuru*, literally "trimmed, tasselled." The difficulty with identifying the *gurpisu*, however, has been largely due to the fact that the texts speak of it both as "of the body of a man" (*ša ramān* [*awēli*], *JEN* 527:15) and "of the head" (*ša qaqqadi*, *HSS* 15 9b:2f and 208:9f), at once suggesting that it was some kind of armored mantle, perhaps covering the helmet or attached to its rim, that hung down over the shoulders, or indeed "the body," and fully protected the neck, cheeks, and throat.

In an early article on Nuzi armor terminology, Speiser noted a reference to a "*gurpisu* of the head" and also the fact that the scaled *gurpisu* never bore more than a fraction of the number of scales said to be attached to its accompanying *sariam*. He thus conjectured that the *gurpisu* was "a visor, a beaver, or perhaps even the helmet itself."[19] Subsequently, Oppenheim proposed viewing the *gurpisu* as "a designation of the protective leather apron (densely covered with metal scales), which was directly attached to the helmet and covered the neck, ear, chin, and throat of the soldier, leaving exposed only the eye and nose."[20] Armas Salonen, citing a possible etymology for *gurpisu* in Sanskrit or Middle Iranian meaning "neck . . ." or "body protection" saw the word as referring both to "eine Art 'Helm' für Pferde und Soldaten" and to "einen mit Metallplättchen überzogenen ledernen Brustschutz . . . wie ihn Pferde trugen (bei soldaten Brustkoller, ein kurzes Panzerhemd)."[21] Thus *CAD* G (139) interpreted the *gurpisu* as a "leather hauberk covered with metal scales (as part of armor for soldiers and horses)," and *AHw* (p. 929) followed with "ein Panzerüberwurf mit Nackenschutz für Menschen und Pferde." The meaning of *gurpisu* was no further clarified by Erkki Salonen, who after reviewing the data, still saw it either as a kind of body armor or helmet, and translated the word merely as "eine Art Panzer."[22] Later volumes of *CAD* (A/1 208; S 250), however, translated *gurpisu* as "helmet."

Although texts mentioning the *gurpisu* occur from the Old Babylonian period on, it is the Nuzi tablets that provide the best clues to the meaning of

---

is listed "a set of armor scales for the body of a man, for his chest, of bronze' (*1-nu-*[*tù kur-zi*]*-ma-tu ša* NÍ LÚ *a-šar i-ir-ti-*[*šu*] ZABAR).

[19]Speiser, p. 48.

[20]A. L. Oppenheim, *JCS* 4 (1950), 192f.

[21]A. Salonen, *Hippologica Accadica* (Helsinki, 1955), pp. 141ff.

[22]E. Salonen, *Die Waffen der Alten Mesopotamier* (*Studia Orientalia 33*) (Helsinki, 1965), pp. 101ff.

the word. Proof of its meaning, though, can only be established when the written documentation is compared with contemporary illustrations of Asiatic armor from Egypt, which can show us clearly what the armor of the period looked like.[23] This comparison indicates, first, that the *gurpisu* of the warrior could not have been the "neck protector" or "apron of scales" envisioned by Oppenheim, because such pieces of armor evidently did not exist during the Late Bronze Age—or if they did exist they were very rare. The Nuzi texts suggest that the *gurpisu* was worn by every soldier. If, on the other hand, the *gurpisu* was a "hauberk" or "coat of mail," it would seem only to have duplicated the purpose of the *sariam*. Furthermore, such heavy double layers of armor do not appear in the pictorial sources. Finally, if the *gurpisu* was something other than the helmet itself, there would be no word in the texts that could have designated the helmet, and we would have to imagine that helmets were either not used at Nuzi or never mentioned, which would, of course, be unthinkable. The only possible conclusion one can reach, therefore, is that the *gurpisu* was indeed the helmet itself.

As for the single reference to a *gurpisu* "of the body of a man," this seems to be no more than a scribal error. The text *JEN* 527 begins by listing four *sariam ša ramān awēli* ("suits of armor for the body of a man"). It then lists four accompanying *gurpisu*, each described only as *ša awēli* ("of a man"). Then (11. 14-16) the text continues: (14) *6 ta-pa-l[u sà]-ri-am* KUŠ *sa* NÍ [LÚ] (15) *1 gur-pí-sú* ZABAR [*ša*] NÍ [LÚ] (16) *1 gur-pí-sú* ZABAR *ša* LÚ ("[14] Six suits of leather armor for the body of a man, [15] one bronze *gurpisu* for the body of a man, [16] one bronze *gurpisu* of a man"). This, in turn, is followed by a list of horse armor including a *gurpisu ša sīsi*. It is most likely, therefore, that the *gurpisu* in l. 15 was intended to be described only as *ša awēli* to correspond with that in l. 16. This fact, when coupled with the clear references in *HSS* 15 9b:2f and 208:9f to *gurpisū ša qaqqadi* ("*gurpisū* of the head") indicates that this object can only have been a helmet.[24] Of helmets, of course,

[23]See W. Wreszinski, *Atlas zur altaegyptischen Kultursgeschichte*, v. II (Leipzig, 1935), pls. I-II (reprinted in Yadin, v. I, pp. 192-93).

[24]In *CAD* G 139, many occurrences of the word *gurpisu* are cited, although in every case it has been incorrectly translated as "hauberk." Possible alternative interpretations of some of these texts are as follows: OB Ishchali, *IM* 31309: *4 šu-ši kur-bi-su ša šar-ki-im 7 šu-ši 38 kur-bi-su sa aš-li-im* "240 helmets of. . . . 458 corded helmets." (A view of a *gurpisu ša ašlim* [lit. "helmet of rope"] may be that in Barrelet, pl. LXXVI, 782); Mari, *ARM* 7 255:2: *2* ^{GI}*gur-si-pu* UŠ "two helmets of (woven) reed, ordinary quality" or perhaps "two codpieces of (woven) reed" (*CAD* translation: "two hauberks (reaching to) the genitals"). But note the parallel text *ARM* 240 i:3f. *x kur-bi-si* SAG [....] *4 kur-bi-si* UŠ = "x helmets of the he[ad]. . . . four codpieces [?]."). (For a revised translation of *EA* 22 iii 37ff., cited by *CAD*, see n. 25.) In NA, Tell Halaf 49:1: *2 gur-pis-si ša parzilli 1 gur-pis-si ša* URUDU.MEŠ "two iron helmets, one bronze helmet" (*CAD* translation: "two hauberks with iron scales, one hauberk with bronze [scales]"); NB, *YOS* 3 190:28: *šir'ani gur-sip-pi u arâta* "corselets, helmets, and shields"

the contemporary Egyptian representations of Asiatic troops are full. The standard body defense, by these illustrations, would seem to have been the corselet, the helmet, and the shield, which are evidently the very items listed as comprising the armor sent to Amenhotep III by Tušratta as part of his daughter's dowry.[25] As for the *gurpisu ša sīsi*, this would seem to have been the type of "horse helmet" that appears in the nearly contemporary representations of the horses of Tutankhamun and Ramesses II.[26]

Having established with a virtual certainty that the word *gurpisu* means nothing more nor less than "helmet," we may now proceed to examine the Nuzi data to discover (a) what kinds of helmets were in use at Nuzi, (b) what kinds of helmets were worn with particular types of armor, (c) what kinds of troops wore particular types of helmets, (d) how the helmets were made, and (e) how much certain helmets weighed. Finally, to amplify the written material from Nuzi, we shall review the contemporary pictorial evidence from Egypt and elsewhere to establish what the Nuzi helmets may actually have looked like.

gurpisu maški ("helmet of leather")

A "helmet of leather" appears as part of a soldier's panoply only once in the Nuzi texts, in *HSS* 15 4:38. This particular document, one of a series of at

(*CAD* "coats of mail, hauberks, and shields"). The references to *gurpisu* URUDU and *gurpisu kaspi* in *TCL* 3:392, 358, 378 among the booty taken by Sargon during the sack of the Urartian cult-center at Musasir undoubtedly refer to "bronze..." and "silver helmets" rather than "hauberks," In *TCL* 3:392, in fact, *gurpisi* URUDU is followed by *gulgullat* URUDU ("skullcaps of bronze"). Votive helmets are now known by excavation to have been deposited in great numbers in Urartian temples. (B. B. Piotrovskii, *Urartu: The Kingdom of Van and Its Art* [New York, 1967], pp. 45ff., pls. 16-20.)

[25] Compare illustrations cited in n. 23 with *EA* 22 iii 37-43: (37) *1* ŠU *sa-ri-am* ZA[BA]R *1 gur-z[i-i]p* Z[AB]AR *sa* LÚ(!) (38) *1* ŠU *sa-ri-am ša* K[U]Š *1 gur-z[i-i]p* ZABAR (39) *ša* LÚ(!) *za-ar-gu-ti 1-nu-tum sa-[r]i-[a]m ša* KUŠ (40) *ša* ANŠE.KUR.RA.MEŠ *k[u]-l[a]-a-na ša* ZA[BA]R *m[u-u]ḫ-ḫu-zu* (41) *2 gur-si-ip ša* ZABAR *ša* ANŠE.KUR.RA.MEŠ (42) *1* KUŠ *a-ri-tu*$_4$ *ú-ru-uk-ma-a-a[n-nu-š]u* KÙ.BABBAR *uḫḫuz* (43) *10* GÍN KÙ.BABBAR *ša i-na* ŠÀ-*š[u!]* (44) *9* KUŠ *a-ri-tu*$_4$ *ša u-ru-uk-ma-an-ni-šu-nu* ZABAR "One corselet of bronze, one helmet of bronze for a man; one corselet of leather, one helmet of bronze for a *sargutu* warrior; one armored back-pad of leather for horses, overlaid with plates of bronze, two 'helmets' of bronze for horses; one leather shield to which is affixed a silver *urukmannu*; ten shekels of silver are employed thereon; nine leather shields to which bronze *urukmannu* are affixed." (J. A. Knudtzon, *Die El-Amarna-Tafeln* [Leipzig, 1907], p. 172.)

[26] See Nina M. Davies, *Ancient Egyptian Paintings*, v. II (Chicago, 1936), pl. 78; Yadin, v. I, pp. 240-41.

least twenty-nine enumerating the suits of armor, weapons, and horse equipment of certain named warriors,[27] describes the military apparel assigned to twelve militiamen. Eleven of the men are said to have been issued a *gurpisu siparri* ("helmet of bronze") with their corselets, which were either "of leather" or "of bronze," but only one among them is said to have received a *gurpisu maški* ("helmet of leather") with his corselet, which was "of bronze."[28] Since each of the recipients of this equipment was also issued components of horse armor, there can be little doubt that all of the men listed in the text were charioteers.

Because the *gurpisu maški* is only once mentioned in this text and not at all in the other texts of this type (which also seem to be describing only the equipment of charioteers), one would conclude that leather helmets were not regularly worn by the charioteers at Nuzi. Being the lightest-weight form of head defense, as well no doubt as the cheapest to produce, the *gurpisu maški* is most likely to have been the standard helmet type of the infantryman, about whose armor the Nuzi texts apparently have little to say.

We can know rather precisely how much leather was needed to produce one of these casques, for in *HSS* 15 196:12f Ḫutip-tilla the *aškapu* ("leather-worker") is said to have been given "seven goatskins to make three leather helmets" (*7* KUŠ.MEŠ *ša en-zi a-na 3 gur-pi-is-su* MEŠ KUŠ *sa* DU); which would seem to indicate that approximately 2⅓ goatskins were required for the production of each helmet. We may speculate, therefore, that the armorer covered each helmet with as many layers of leather as two goatskins would permit—three or four?—and that from the extra third of a hide he cut the thongs by which the whole was laced together.

[27]These texts may be categorized as follows: (a) those listing the armor and weapons issued to the troops from the arsenal to complete their own outfits, those of their chariots, their horses and their support personnel: *JEN* 527, 533; *HSS* 14 616; *HSS* 15 2a, 2b, 4, 15, 23, 93, 142, 167, (b) those listing the suits of armor and weapons of certain individuals that are either lost, damaged, or in need of repair: *HSS* 13 195; *HSS* 15 3, 6, 12, 39, 50, 145, (c) those listing the personnel and material that "did . . ." or "did not go (to Zizza)": *HSS* 15 10, 14-16, 20, 305, (d) those listing the men lacking certain elements of armor and equipment: *HSS* 15 46, 49, 106, (e) and those listing the chariots of certain individuals and the number of suits of armor stored with each vehicle: *HSS* 15 13, 82.

[28](38) [*x sà-ri-am*] *ša* NÍ-*šu* [*ša* ZABAR *gur*]-*pi-is-su ša* KUŠ (39) [*x sà-ri-am ša*] ANŠE.KUR.RA [*mi*]-*iš-la ta-ḫa-ab-ši* (40) [x] *kùr*-[*pi*]-*sú* [*ša*] ZABAR (41) [x x x] *k*[*a*]-*ri-ni-ta* ZABAR (42) [*x*]+*4* GI.MEŠ *ša* ZABAR *2* GIŠ.BAN (43) [*a-na* ŠU ^{m}*x-x-til*]-*la na-ad-nu* "[a corselet] for his body [of bronze], his helmet of leather, [an armored back pad for] a horse, which is half of felt, [and] a 'helmet' of bronze . . . a bronze *karinita*, [x]+4 bronze-tipped arrows, and two bows are given to (personal name)." For an explanation of the meaning of *taḫabšu* ("felt,"), see Kendall, p. 314.

gurpisu siparri ("helmet of bronze")

The most common form of head defense mentioned in the Nuzi armor inventories—and thus probably the standard helmet type of the charioteers—was the "helmet of bronze," which seems to have been issued to the troops with all forms of armor except the heaviest metal-scaled types.[29] Like their prototypes from Ur and Tello, these helmets would have been wrought from sheet bronze, beaten skillfully to a conical or near hemispherical shape.[30] Occasionally such a helmet is described by the adjective *tegipu*, which seems to have had the meaning "finely wrought," "ornamented," or perhaps "crested."[31] Some others are said to have been *ṣuppuru*: "trimmed," "tasselled," "plumed," or also possibly "crested."

One *gurpisu siparri tegipu* is listed in *HSS* 15 3:35, with a "leather corselet for the body" and a "bronze shield for the right (arm)," as the armor issued to "Erwi-ḫuta, the baker," who from the context of the document would seem to have been a chariot's shield bearer. *HSS* 15 8, which records the chariots, weapons, and armor returned to the palace arsenal by "the men of Aril-lumti's command," lists as one warrior's charge (l. 15) "a chariot, a set of scales for a man's chest, and a bronze helmet with plume" (*1* GIŠ.GIGIR *1-nu-*[*tù kur-zi*]-*ma-tù ša* NÍ LÚ *a-šar i-ir-ti-*[*šu ša*] ZABAR *1 gur-pi-su* ZAB[AR *ṣu*]-*up-pu-ru*).[32] Again in *JEN* 527:9 four *gurpisu siparri ṣuppuru* ("plumed bronze helmets"), accompanying four "suits of leather armor with bronze sleeves" are totalled as

[29]Bronze helmets are issued with leather armor in *JEN* 527:9, *HSS* 15 3:35, 4:5, 34, 36, 38, 44; with leather armor having bronze sleeves in *JEN* 527:16; with bronze armor in *HSS* 14 616:14; *HSS* 15 8:5, 15; and with "a set of bronze scales for the chest" in *HSS* 15 8:15 (see text below and n. 18).

[30]Helmets from Ur: C. L. Woolley, *Ur Excavations v. II: The Royal Cemetery* (Philadelphia, 1934), pp. 63; 66, no. 18, 303; from Tello: A. Parrot, *Tello* (Paris, 1948), pp. 106 and 109, fig. 26d.

[31]*Tegipu* occurs several times in *HSS* 15 3 describing helmets for both men and horses (l. 16: *gur-pi-is-su ša* ZABAR *te-gi-pu*, l. 35: *gur-pi-is* ZABAR *te-gi-pu*, and l. 23f.: *gur-pi-is-su ša* ZABAR *2 ma-ti 42 kur-zi-me-tu*$_4$*-šu-nu ka-ka*$_4$*-ni-aš-wa-na ša* ZABAR-*ri te-gi-pu* ["a bronze (horse) helmet with 242 bronze scales of the *kakaniašwa* type, *tegipu*"]. Again in *HSS* 14 589:12, it appears as a plural noun: *ka-sá-tu*$_4$ *ša* ZABAR *ṣa-ar-pi te-gi-pe-na ša ti-iš-nu-uḫ-ḫe-na* "a cup with a silver edge, having *tegipena* of *t*." The key to the meaning of the word, however, is provided by *HSS* 13 498:9 and *HSS* 14 502:8, which list a woman named Tegipe. Since the latter text (l. 9) describes her as a "singing girl of Ḫanigalbat" (*nu-a-ra-tu ša* KUR *Ḫa-ni-gal-bat*), one would expect that her name was a favorable epithet and one that would describe both feminine charms and the qualities of worked metal. In each of these texts (*HSS* 13 498:12 and *HSS* 14 502:4) one of her companions is named Damqinaja, "beautiful-eyes"; thus *tegipu* as an adjective would seem to have meant something like "bright, gleaming, polished; finely wrought, decorated," or as a noun probably "design, ornament, embellishment."

[32]See n. 18.

"equipment which they distributed to the charioteers" (*an-nu-tu*$_4$ *<ú>-nu-tu*$_4$ *a-na* LÚ.MEŠ *ra-kib* GIŠ.GIGIR.MEŠ *i-zu-u*[*z-zu-š*]*u-nu*). One of these four helmets, however, is more completely described as a "helmet of bronze, with a leather tassel (or perhaps 'crested with leather'), having three bronze *kalkū* (hanging?) from it" (*1 gur-pí-su* ZABAR *ša* LÚ KUŠ *ṣu-up-pu-ru 3 ka*$_4$*-al-ku iš-tu pa-ni-šu ša* ZABAR). Here the word *kalkū* almost certainly has the meaning "appendages" or "flaps." The three *kalkū* here would seem to have been the helmet's two cheek pieces and neck guard, which would have been separately made and hinged or riveted to the rim.[33]

gurpisu siparri kurṣimētu ("bronze, scale-covered helmet")

The most elaborate helmets in use at Nuzi were those covered with large numbers of bronze scales called *kurṣimētu* (*kurṣimtu*).[34] In the texts these are listed only with suits of heavy scale armor, which would appear to have been the special battle garb only of the elite charioteers. In *HSS* 15 3, three of five named warriors are listed as having taken both scale-covered helmets and corselets from the palace arsenal to replace the armor that they had "lost on campaign" (*i-na ṣēri ḫal-qu*). Each of the helmets was said to have borne 190 scales (ll. 6, 20, 31), while each of the corselets were said to have contained between 400 and 435 "large scales" (*kur-ṣí-me-tu-šu-nu* GAL.MEŠ) and between 280 and 360 "small scales" (*kur-ṣí-me-tu-šu-nu* TUR.TUR). Although the scales attached to the helmets are described as neither "large" nor "small," it perhaps went without saying that they were small. Again, the fact that certain individuals named in this text were also the recipients of various components of horse armor would seem to indicate that all were charioteers.

Helmets bearing 140, 170, and even 200 scales are described in *HSS* 15 5, which records the armor assigned to four men "of the *emanti* ('chariot squadron') of Kurmi-šenni."[35] Here the first two individuals are said to have received identical suits of armor made up of "500 scales on the body, 500

[33] Suits of armor, as well as helmets, are said to have had *kalkū*. In *JEN* 527:1 a leather *sariam* is said to have had "7 *kalkū* as its girth" (or "around its waist"?) (*7 ka*$_4$*-al-ku* [*k*]*i-i li-mi-is-su-nu-ma*). Another (l. 3) is said to have had "3 *kalkū*," while a third (l. 5) is said to have had "4 *kalkū*." *JEN* 533:6 notes another with "8 *kalkū* as its girth." We suppose these, too, to have been armored flaps attached to the corselet at the waist, forming a kind of skirt which lent protection to the thighs. In my dissertation (Kendall, pp. 214, 269ff.) I suggested that the word might have meant "band of armor scales," but I now believe this is an incorrect assumption. Armored kilts made of multiple vertical bands actually appear worn by Asiatic troops in contemporary Egyptian art (see refs. in n. 23).

[34] See n. 16.

[35] For a thorough discussion of the terms *emanti* and *emantuhlu*, see Kendall, pp. 68ff., 99ff.

scales on the sleeves, and 200 scales on the helmet" (*5 ma-ti kur-ṣí-im-tù ša* NÍ-*šu 5 ma-ti* [*kur-ṣ*]*í-im-tù ša a-ḫi-šu 2 ma-ti* [KI.MI]N *ša gur-pí-su*). The third was given a suit consisting of "560 scales on the body, 160 scales on the sleeves, and 140 on the helmet" (*5 ma-ti 1 šu-ši* KI.MIN *ša* NÍ-*šu 1*[*ma-t*]*i 1 šu-ši* KI.MIN *ša a-ḫi-šu* [*1*] *ma-ti 40* KI.MIN *ša gur-pí-su-ma*), and the fourth received a suit consisting of "420 scales on the body, 130 scales on the sleeves, and 170 on the helmet" ([*4*] *ma-ti 20* KI.MIN *ša* NÍ-*šu* [*1*] *ma-ti 30* KI.MIN *ša a-ḫi-šu 1 ma-ti 7*[*0*] KI.MIN *ša gur-pí-su*).[36] The first two of these outfits are totalled in the colophon (l. 20) as "two suits of armor of the land of Ḫanigalbat" (*2 ta-pa-lu sà-ri-am ša mât Ḫa-ni-in-gal-bat*), while the latter two are described (l. 21) as "two suits of armor of the land of Arrapḫa" (*2 ta-pa-lu* KI.MIN *ša mât Ar-ar-ap-ḫi*). The implication here is that these four ponderous costumes with their equally ponderous helmets represented two distinctive styles of armor, perhaps even specific "uniforms." The first two were probably suits of armor of the type typically worn by the men of the crack chariot units known variously in the texts as the "*martiannu* of Ḫanigalbat" or the "chariots of Ḫanigalbat."[37] The second two were probably suits of armor of the type worn by the ranking charioteers of the local levy.

Heavy scaled helmets of these same types may also have been called "great helmets" (*gurpisu arābu*), since one so called is mentioned in *HSS* 15 167:21 apparently as part of the outfit of a chariot.[38]

Some surprising data relating to the construction of these elaborate headpieces is provided by three documents again describing the work of the armorer Ḫutip-tilla. In *HSS* 15 9b, he is said to have been given a total of "580 scales for three helmets of the head" (*5 ma-ti 80 kur-ṣi-ma-tu* MEŠ *ša 3-ti gur-pi-*[*su*] *sa* SAG-*du*), which indicates that he was preparing to make three helmets of the two types listed in *HSS* 15 3:6, 20f, 31 and *HSS* 15 5:3, 7: namely, helmets covered with either 190 or 200 scales (190 + 190 + 200 = 580 scales). Then in *HSS* 15 208:9f, he is said to have been given "three minas of wool for two helmets of the head" (*3* MA.NA SÍG.MEŠ *a-na 2 gur-pí-su-ú ša* SAG-*du*), which apparently tells us the exact amount of wool required by the craftsman for their felt liners: 1.5 minas per helmet. (Whether this was a

[36]The numbers of scales here have been restored from the total given in the text: *7 ma-ti 20* KI.MIN *ša* ZABAR ^{m}*Ḫa-na-a-a il-qi* ("720 bronze scales Hanaja took").

[37]*HSS* 14 171:8f., 523:17f.; *HSS* 15 32:25f. Kendall, pp. 62ff., 128ff. and C. Zaccagnini, "Les rapports entre Nuzi et Ḫanigalbat," *Assur* 2 (1979), 4ff., 20ff.

[38](15) *il-te-en-nu-tu*$_4$ *ma-gar-ru* (16) *še-ša-tu*$_4$ *ḫal-wa-at-ru* (17) *il-te-en-nu-tu*$_4$ *ma-gar-ru wa-su-uḫ-ri* (18) *1 šu-ki-tu*$_4$ *ù 1* ANŠE.KUR.RA (19) *2* <GIŠ>.BAN.MEŠ *30* KAK.Ú.TAG.GA *ša* ZABAR (20) *50* KAK.Ú.TAG.GA *ša* URUDU.MEŠ (21) *1(?) gur-pi-su a-ra-bu* (22) *1 a-ri-tu*$_4$ *sa* GIŠ.GIGIR . . . "one set of six-spoked (?) wheels of *ḫalwatru* wood, one set of *wasuḫru* wheels, one lance (?), one horse, two bows, thirty bronze-tipped arrows, fifty copper-tipped arrows, one (?) 'great helmet,' one chariot shield. . . ."

standard amount of wool used for the liners of all types of helmets, or whether it was an overly generous portion used only in the best helmets cannot be known, although one would suspect the latter.) Even the very weight of a helmet is given in *HSS* 15 24, which states that Ḫutip-tilla was given "a helmet (weighing) 3 minas 40 shekels" apparently so as to make six others just like it.[39]

Evidence for the Weights of Metal-scaled Helmets at Nuzi

It is doubtful that a helmet weighing "3 minas 40 shekels" could have been a leather helmet, for it would have been far too heavy. If the weight of a shekel at Nuzi has been correctly estimated at 8.4 grams,[40] then the weight of this helmet would have been about 1.85 kg. (or just over 4 lbs.). Nor is it likely that this weight described a helmet of beaten bronze, first, because even a helmet of sheet metal is unlikely to have weighed so much[41] and second, because Ḫutip-tilla's title was *aškapu* or "leatherworker"; and bronze helmets would probably have been produced by the guild of *nappaḫu* ("smiths"). As the texts quoted above indicate, Ḫutip-tilla's tasks were (a) the manufacture of leather helmets (or the leather forms for metal-scaled helmets) from goatskins (*HSS* 15 196:12f), (b) the preparation of felt helmet liners (*HSS* 15 208:9f), and (c) the production of scale-covered helmets by lacing on to their leather forms the great numbers of small bronze scales that were supplied to him. Taking these points into consideration, as well as the fact that a metal-scaled helmet would have had a greater thickness and hence greater weight or metal on it, it is most likely that the weight provided by *HSS* 15 24 was that of a helmet entirely covered with metal scales.

Assuming for a moment that the given weight of 3 minas 40 shekels (or 220 shekels) was its total weight, then we may calculate, based on *HSS* 15 208:9f, that about 1 mina 30 shekels (or 90 shekels) was the weight of its felt liner. The remaining 2 minas 10 shekels (or 130 shekels) would thus have been the weight of its leather base, its lacing, and its metal scales combined. If, as suggested above, the total weight of the helmet was roughly 1.85 kg. (or about 4 lbs.), then the weight of its metal would have been about 1.09 kg. (or about 2 lbs. 7 oz.). Were this helmet one of the types that bore 140, 170, 190, or 200 scales on its surface, therefore, the average weights of the scales attached to it would have been somewhat less than 7.8, 6.4, 5.7, and 5.4 grams, respectively.

39(1) *1 gur-pi-is-*⌊*su*⌋ (2)*ša 3 ma-na 40* G[ÍN] (3) *ša 6* TA.A.AM (4) *a-na iš-qa(!)-*[*ri-šu*] (5) *a-na* ŠU [^{m}*Ḫu-ti-ip-til-la*] (6) *na-ad-nu* (7) *NA₄*.KIŠIB ^{m}*Ḫu-ti*[*ip-til-la*] "One helmet weighing 3 minas 40 shekels, for duplicating six times as his work assignment is given to Ḫutip-tilla. Seal of Ḫutip-tilla."

40Cross, p. 11.

41See n. 45.

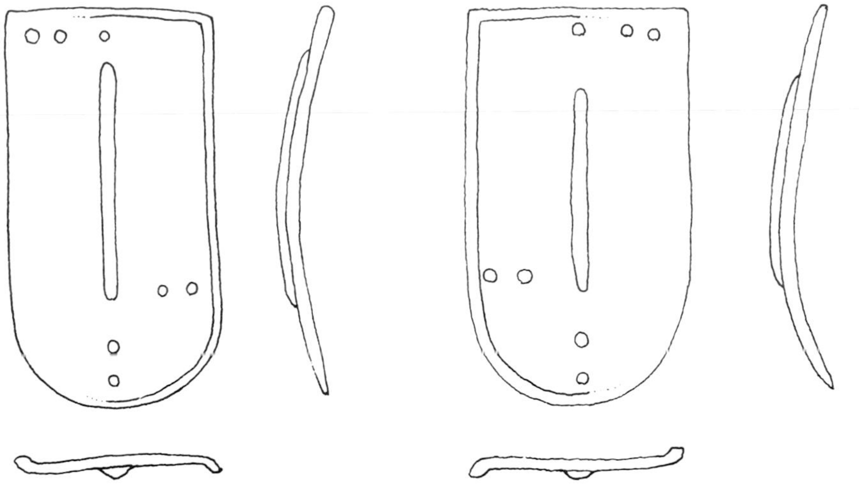

Figure 1. Bronze scales from Nuzi, possibly used in helmet construction. Harvard Semitic Museum. Left: no. 1012. Right: no. 1282 (similar to 1006).

If we assume, on the other hand, that the 200 shekels given as the weight of the helmet was not its total weight but only that of its bronze,[42] then its total weight, now adding the 90 shekels of its felt liner, would have been about 310 shekels or 2.6 kg. (approximately 5 lbs. 12 oz.). Again, if this casque was one of those bearing 140, 170, 190, or 200 scales, then the possible average weights of the scales would have been 13.2, 10.9, 9.7, and 9.2 grams, respectively.

It is of great interest in this regard that of the many original armor scales excavated at Nuzi,[43] the weights of the two smallest known types are perfectly compatible with these last estimated weights. Through the kindness of the curator of the Harvard Semitic Museum, Dr. Carney Gavin, I was permitted

[42]This would seem the most likely interpretation, based on a comparison with other similar texts. For example, in *HSS* 13 195:15f. there is mention of a "suit of armor of the body, of the breast, (weighing) one mina of bronze" (*1-nu-tu*$_4$ *sà-ri-am* [*ša*] NÍ *ša* GAB *1* MA.NA *sa* ZABAR). Again, in *JEN* 527:5f. there is listed "a suit of armor of leather for the body of a man, with four flaps (to protect the thighs?) and sleeves of bronze, weighing one mina eighty-five shekels" (*1-en-nu-tu*$_4$ *sà*-[*ri-am*] KUŠ *ša* NÍ LÚ *4 ka*$_4$*-al-ku-ù ša a-ḫi-šu-nu ša* ZABAR *1* MA.NA *85* [GÍN]). Using the weight of 8.4 grs. to the shekel, these corselets would seem to have weighed .504 kg. (about 1 lb. 2 oz.) and 1.218 kg. (about 2 lbs. 10 oz.), respectively. Either these were extremely lightweight corselets, or else, as seems probable, the given weights refer only to the amount of bronze employed in their construction.

[43]See Starr, v. I, pp. 475ff.; v. II, pl. 126; Kendall, pp. 266ff. Cf. also Y. Mahmoud, "Tell al-Fakhar," *Sumer* 26 (1970), 122 and pl. 124.

to measure and weigh all the Nuzi scales preserved at that institution.[44] The scales numbered HSM 1006, 1282, and 1012, representing two different sizes (fig. 1), weighed 14, 12, and 9.4 grams, respectively. Each of these is rounded at its lower end and pierced with holes for lacing, and each possesses a longitudinal medial ridge for strength. In vertical profile, each is markedly convex—ideally suited for covering a helmet— and each, too, is wrought so that one edge curls slightly outward and the other inward. This feature indicates, of course, that such scales were probably intended to overlap one another when attached to their base.

Were the metal-scaled helmets of Nuzi actually covered with platelets identical to these, then an estimated minimum and maximum weight may be established for each type of scaled helmet described in the texts simply by multiplying the given scale weights by the number of scales stated to have been used per helmet and adding to this figure the roughly .76 kg. (8.4 grams × 90 shekels = .76 kg.) said to have been used in the felt padding. Thus:

140-scale helmet (*HSS* 15 5:12):
min. 2.08 kg. (4 lbs. 9 oz.) max. 2.72 kg. (6 lbs.)
170-scale helmet (*HSS* 15 5:17):
min. 2.36 kg. (5 lbs. 3 oz.) max. 3.14 kg. (6 lbs. 15 oz.)
190-scale helmet (*HSS* 15 3:6, 21, 31)
min. 2.55 kg. (5 lbs. 10 oz.) max. 3.42 kg. (7 lbs. 8 oz.)
200-scale helmet (*HSS* 15 5:3, 7):
min. 2.64 kg. (5 lbs. 12 oz.) max. 3.56 kg. (7 lbs. 12 oz.)

Although these weights seem to be substantially greater than those of the typical bronze helmets of antiquity,[45] they are comparable to those of many

[44]The well-preserved examples of the Nuzi armor scales at Harvard belong to seven of ten known sizes. The weights and numbers of the three smallest types are given above, while those of the several larger types are as follows: (a) rounded at bottom, pierced only on left side of central ridge, flat profile: 6.4 × 3.7 cm., .2 cm. thick (Starr, v. I, pp. 335, 346, 476ff.; v. II, pl. 126 H). Example: 1075 = 14.8 gms.; (b) rectangular, unpierced, with knob-like projection at one corner, slightly convex profile: 7.4 × 4.1 cm., .4 cm. thick (ibid., v. I, pp. 346, 476, 480; v. II, pl. 126 D, J). Examples: 1201, 1213, 1229 = 25 gms., 1230 = 27 gms., 1202 = 27.3 gms., 1221, 1226 = 28 gms.; (c) similar to scales in figure 1, flat profile: 5.8 × 3.8 cm., .2-.25 cm. thick (ibid., v. I, pp. 335, 346, 476; v. II, pl. 126 F). Example: 1021 = 31 gms.; (d) rectangular, large bronze plates probably for horse armor: 10.9 × 6.4 cm., .2-.25 cm. thick (ibid., v. I, pp. 342, 475; v. II, pl. 126 L). Example: 1081 (three scales fused together) = about 52 gms. each.

[45]I make this assertion based on the weights of several bronze helmets examined by me in the Museum of Fine Arts, Boston. Although these are not helmets of the period under discussion, their weights may be thought to form an interesting comparison: (a) Urartian helmet, ninth century B.C. (1981.25) = .767 kg. (1 lb. 10 oz.), (b) South Italian

helmets of the late Middle Ages and Renaissance.[46] There can be no doubt, at any rate, that the metal-scaled helmet was the heaviest in use during the Late Bronze Age, for it encased the skull in a much greater thickness of metal than was possible with the ordinary helmet wrought from sheet bronze. Due to the difficulties inherent in annealing and forming the latter, it is probable that the typical bronze casque of the day averaged no more than 2 mm. in thickness.[47] Metal scales, on the other hand, which required less skilled smithing due to their small size, could be easily cut from sheet metal of even heavier gauge. These, when laced together, not only overlapped themselves within each row, but also overlapped those in the rows above and below, thus providing as much as double the thickness of metal as the former. Furthermore, since each scale was ribbed and slightly convex, a surface of such scales presented a much stronger defense against a sharp blow to the head than a broad expanse of sheet metal, which could be dented easily or even punctured. So laborious and expensive to produce must these metal-scaled helmets have been, however, that it is unlikely that they were worn by any but the most privileged troops.

---

pot helmet, fifth century B.C. (1970.35) = 1.30 kg. (2 lbs. 14 oz.), (c) Etruscan helm with crest holders, fifth century B.C. (1969.1075) = .933 kg. (2 lbs.), (d) Corinthian helmet, fifth century B.C. (61.375) = 1.103 kg. (2 lbs. 7 oz.), (e) Corinthian helmet, fifth century B.C. (98.664) = 1.180 kg. (2 lbs. 9 oz.), (f) Thracian helmet, fourth-third century B.C. (69.1077) = 1.103 kg. (2 lbs. 7 oz.). Because in no case is the liner preserved, the original weight of each helmet must have been somewhat greater. (For illustrations of all but the first of these helmets, see M. Comstock and C. Vermeule, *Greek Etruscan and Roman Bronzes in the Museum of Fine Arts, Boston* [Boston, 1971], nos. 581, 582, 586, supp. 589a-c.)

[46] I am grateful to Dr. Stuart W. Pyhrr, Assistant Curator, Department of Arms and Armor of the Metropolitan Museum of Art for very kindly supplying me with the weights of typical examples of helmets of the fifteenth and sixteenth centuries in the Metropolitan Museum's collection. (It should be kept in mind that the linings of these helmets, too, are all missing and that the weights given below represent only the weight of the metal): (a) cabasset, Italian, ca. 1585 (04.3.204) = 3 lbs. 2 oz., (b) kettle hat, Italian, ca. 1450-75 (04.3.236) = 3 lbs. 12 oz., (c) barbute, Italian, ca. 1450-75 (14.25.581) = 5 lbs. 3 oz., (d) close helmet, Austrian, ca. 1500 (29.158.35) = 5 lbs. 8 oz., (e) bascinet, W. European, ca. 1450 (29.156.65) = 6 lbs., (f) kettle hat, Burgundian, ca. 1475 (04.3.228) = 6 lbs. 7 oz., (g) barbute, Italian, ca. 1450-75 (42.50.15) = 7 lbs. 4 oz., (h) armet, Italian, ca. 1440 (42.50.2) = 8 lbs., (i) sallet, German, ca. 1475-1480 (29.150.8a) = 9 lbs. 4 oz. (j) armet, English or Flemish, ca. 1500 (14.25.584) = 9 lbs. 10 oz., (k) tilt helm, German, ca. 1500 (29.156.67a) = 18 lbs. 10 oz.

[47] This is the average thickness of the bronze in the helmets described in n. 44. Were the helmets thinner, they would have been of little use in battle. Were they much thicker, they would probably have been very difficult to form according to technology of the day.

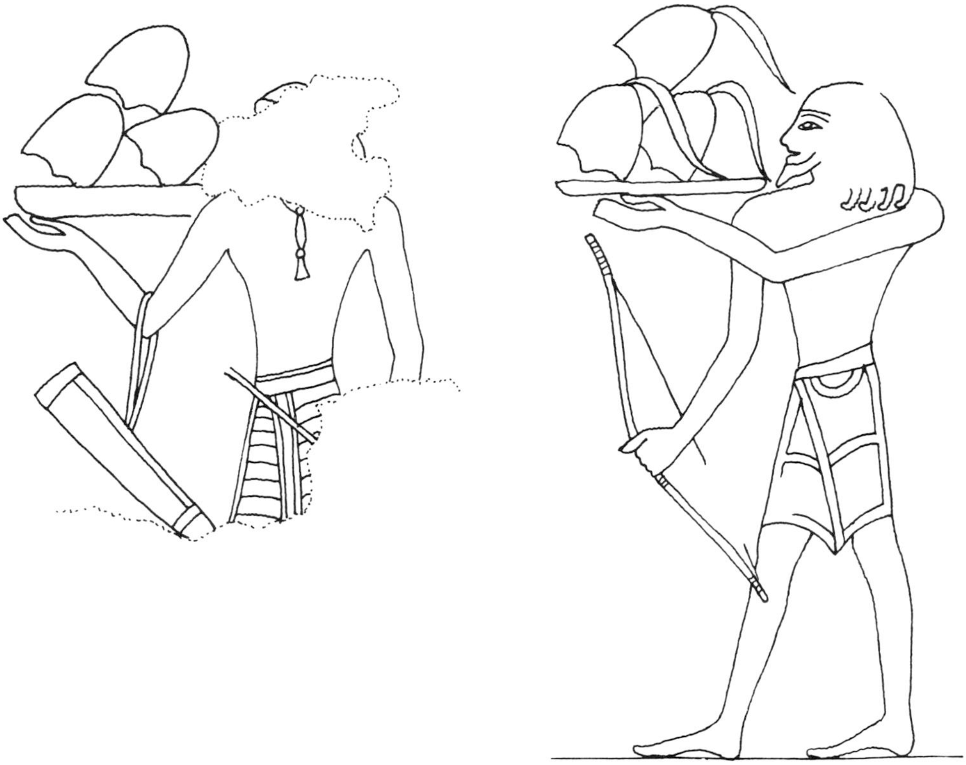

a. b.

Figure 2. Asiatics bearing helmets as gifts. Tomb of Menkheperre-Seneb (TT 86), Thebes. Reign of Thutmose III.

Evidence for the Appearance of the Helmets at Nuzi

Of all the various headdresses, caps, and crowns manifested in the published glyptic art from Nuzi,[48] probably none can be considered a reliable indicator of the true appearance of any of the types of helmets discussed above. Direct pictorial evidence for the helmets of Nuzi would thus seem to be nonexistent. However, since the Nuzi militia was a levy of the king of Arrapḫa, who was himself an eastern confederate of the king of Mitanni, it stands to reason that the armor described in the Nuzi texts would not have been significantly different from that worn anywhere else in Mesopotamia or on its periphery at the same time. Consequently, probably any representations of Ancient Near Eastern armor from a time contemporary with the Nuzi tablets could be considered to portray equipment similar to that in use at Nuzi. The primary pictorial evidence for the armor of Asia during this period,

[48]Cf. Edith Porada, "Seal Impressions of Nuzi," *AASOR* 24 (1944-45)

a. b.

Figure 3. Asiatics bearing helmets as gifts. Tomb of Amenmose (TT 112), Thebes. Reign of Amenhotep II.

of course, derives from Egypt, and this, it will be seen, parallels the Nuzi data to a remarkable degree.[49]

In the Theban Tomb of Menkheperre-Seneb, which dates to the reign of Thutmose III, two Asiatics are presented carrying trays of helmets in processions of foreigners bearing gifts to Pharaoh during the New Year's festival.[50]

[49]For a full discussion of the evidence for the political situation at Nuzi immediately prior to its destruction, see Kendall, pp. 13-51. On Mitannian-Arrapḫian relations, see ibid., pp. 15ff., Zaccagnini, pp. 1ff. On Egyptian knowledge of "the land of Arrapḫa," see Wolfgang Helck, *Urkunden der 18. Dynastie*, Heft 17, p. 1344, l. 7 (letter from Amenhotep II to his viceroy Usersatet on a stele from Semneh, Museum of Fine Arts, Boston 25.632), and J. J. Simons, *Handbook for the Study of Egyptian Topographical Lists Relating to Western Asia* (Leiden, 1937), p. 132 (from a list of Amenhotep II in the Amun temple at Soleb).

[50]N. and N. de G. Davies, *The Tomb of Menkheperrasonb, Amenmose, and Another (Nos. 86, 112, 42, 226) (Theban Tomb Series, Fifth Memoir)* (London, 1933), pp. 8-9, pls. V, VII.

One of them, walking between a man carrying a chariot yoke and another leading a team of horses hitched to an empty chariot, is unfortunately too damaged to identify as to possible national origin (fig. 2a). The other, however, who stands amid bearers of quite unrelated goods, is depicted with a hairstyle that the Egyptians sometimes identified with the men of "Sangar" (Babylonia)[51] (fig. 2b). The three helmets borne by each of these individuals are painted yellow, probably so as to indicate polished bronze. They are also ovoid in shape and suggest that the originals were so wrought that the rims arched over the brow ridges, extended wholly or partly over the ears, and passed low around the back of the skull. The helmets carried by the first figure are quite plain, but each of those carried by the second has a ribbon-like plume, colored either red or blue, affixed to its summit. It is not clear, though, whether such ornamental attachments were actually feathers or braided leather tassels. Both types of helmets would seem to have had their counterparts at Nuzi in the *gurpisu siparri* ("bronze helmet") and the *gurpisu ša siparri ṣuppuru* ("tasseled bronze helmet"). Furthermore, because the first helmet-bearer is here closely associated with horses and chariots, one is left with the feeling, only reinforced by the Nuzi data, that bronze helmets of this type were considered primarily the equipment of the charioteers.

More casques of Asiatic origin appear in the tomb of the "Captain of Troops, the Eyes of the King in the Two Lands of Re<u>t</u>enu" Amenmose, which is dated to the reign of Amenhotep II.[52] Here again two foreign tribute bearers are shown carrying trays of helmets to be laid at the feet of the Egyptian king during the New Year's ceremony. One figure, whose head has not been preserved, stands as before amid horses and chariots, holding aloft a tray on which there are three helmets (fig. 3a). On another register the second figure carries a tray on which seven helmets are stacked (fig. 3b). Although damaged, this figure appears to have had the shaven head and long beard often associated with citizens of "Naharin"—or Mitanni itself.[53] These helmets differ from those portrayed in the previous tomb in that they are much more conical in shape, even coming to a point, and that they are colored white, suggesting that they might have been made of silver or were themselves painted white. The rims of these helmets, furthermore, would seem to have extended lower over the ears and around the back of the head than the former. While several are drawn without plumes, the majority have at their peaks distinct pointed crests, colored blue, to which the plumes, now uniformly red, have been affixed.

The helmets in figure 3 seem to have a definite affinity to that worn by the warrior carved in relief at the "King's Gate" at Boğazköy, which is probably

[51]H. Carter and P. E. Newberry, *The Tomb of Thutmosis IV* (Westminster, 1904), p. 32; A. H. Gardiner, *Ancient Egyptian Onomastica*, v. I (Oxford, 1947), pp. 209ff.

[52]Davies and Davies, p. 29, pls. XXXIV, XXXV.

[53]Carter and Newberry, p. 32.

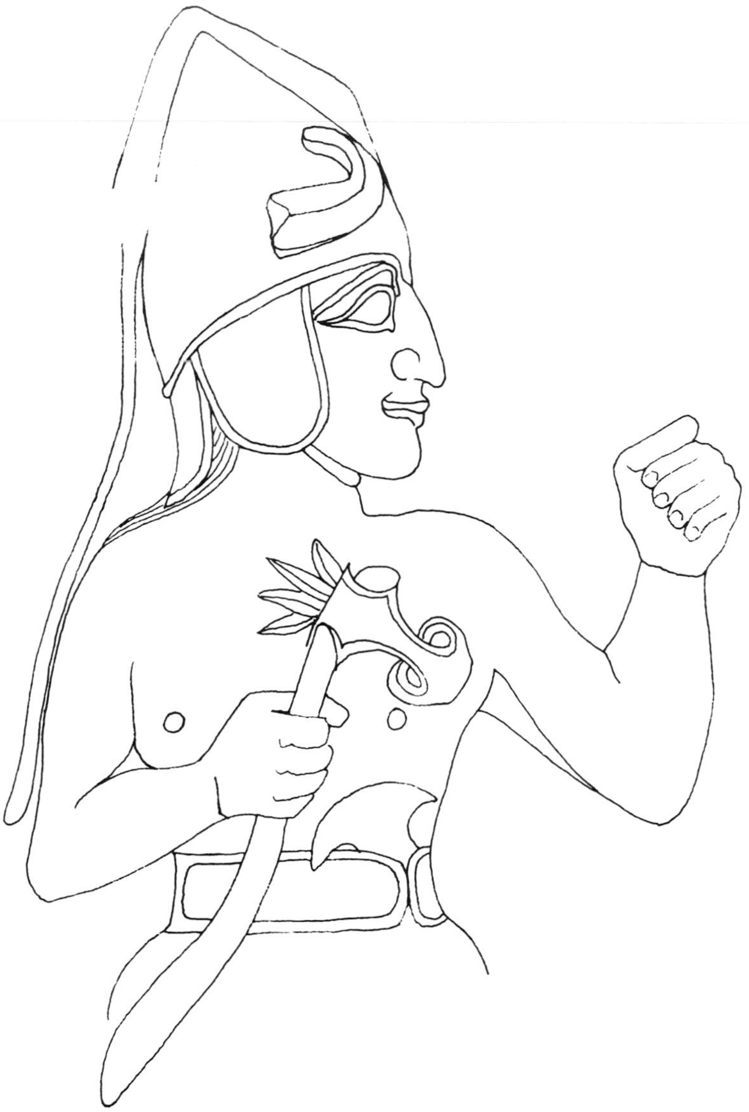

Figure 4. Warrior relief from the "King's Gate" at Boğazköy. Hittite, early 14th century B.C. (?).

very nearly contemporary both with them as well as with the Nuzi archive (fig. 4).[54] Both this helmet and the helmets in the tomb of Amenmose are conical, but the Hittite version seems to have had a pair of side-mounted horns for decoration, and its rim was cut straight, to encircle the cranium above the

[54]E. Akurgal, *The Art of the Hittites* (New York, 1962), p. 98, pls. 64-65.

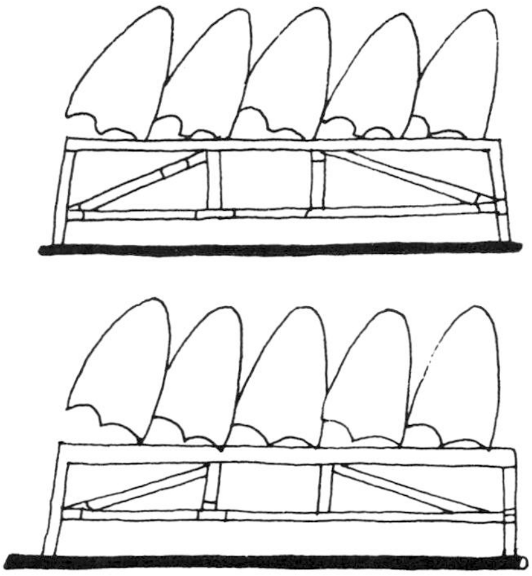

Figure 5. Helmets arrayed on tables. Tomb of Rekhmire (TT 100), Thebes. Reign of Amenhotep II.

ears. Protection for the sides of the head and neck was afforded by three separately made flaps, attached to the rim: two ear flaps and a neck guard. The two ear flaps were fastened under the chin by means of a strap or thong. On the top of the helmet extending fore and aft and coming to a point at the apex was a crest of unknown material to which a long plume was attached so as to hang down the wearer's back. This arrangement is especially similar to the helmets in figure 3. A helmet nearly identical to these may well have been that described at Nuzi in *JEN* 527:9f as a "helmet of bronze, plumed (or 'crested') with leather, having three bronze *kalkū* (hanging?) from it" (transliterated above). If we imagine that the ornament on this helmet looked at all like that of the helmets in figures 3 and 4, it may well have consisted of a low dorsal-fin-like structure of stiffened leather, to which a long, leather tassel or plume was attached. The crested helmets in the tomb of Amenmose actually distinguish these two crest elements by color: the pointed "fin" being blue, and the "plume" red, indicating that the originals were probably painted or dyed. As for the "three bronze *kalkū*," these, as suggested above, were almost certainly the three "flaps," attached to the rim, as on the Boğazköy helm.

Still more helmets may be seen in other Egyptian tombs dated to the reign of Amenhotep II. These helmets are all quite similar to the foregoing, except that none of them have plumes or crests. However, in these particular contexts, the helmets do not appear as Asian products but as the handiwork of Egyptian armorers, who at this time had evidently begun to produce helmets modeled after Asiatic originals for the Egyptian army, specifically for use in the Asian campaigns.

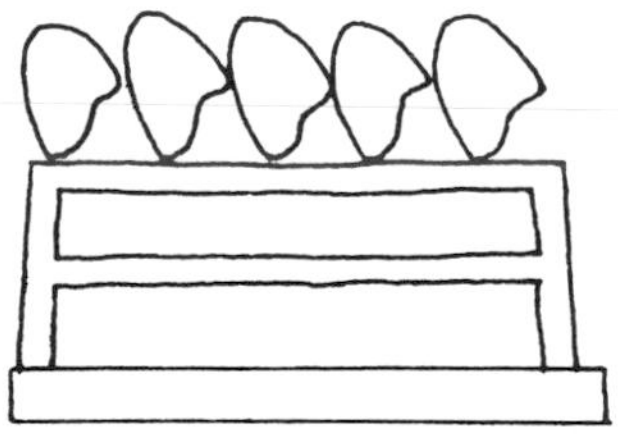

Figure 6. Helmets arrayed on a table. Tomb of Sennufer (TT 96), Thebes. Reign of Amenhote II.

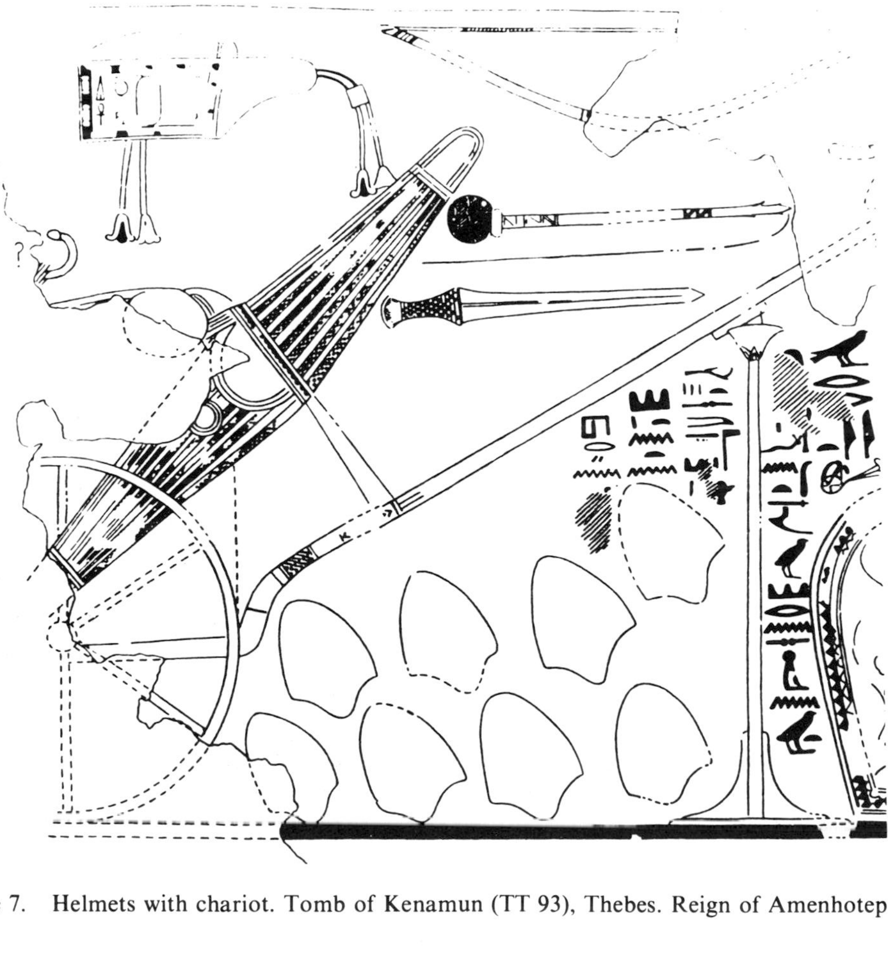

Figure 7. Helmets with chariot. Tomb of Kenamun (TT 93), Thebes. Reign of Amenhotep II.

In the tombs of the Vizier Rekhmire and Sennufer at Thebes, helmets in rows of five are depicted resting on tables.[55] In the first tomb, amid stacks of weapons, two such tables are drawn (fig. 5), each bearing high-peaked casques of ovoid shape with fixed earpieces, much like those in the tomb of Menkheperre-Seneb (fig. 2). A similar arrangement of helmets is also found in the tomb of Sennufer, although the helmets depicted are markedly lower (fig. 6). In the tomb of Kenamun, within a register of military supplies (including two suits of heavy scale armor of the very type described in the Nuzi tablets),[56] a group of eight helmets are drawn beneath the yoke of an unharnessed chariot (fig. 7).[57] These are painted white, like those in Amenmose's tomb, but they are less conical, and their fixed earpieces are rounded and more elongated than any of the previous. That these were helmets in "Asiatic style" rather than direct Asiatic imports may be suggested by the text inscribed beside the chariot, which states: "This is the chariot of His Majesty. Its name is 'The Syrian (Ten-net-'Amu). Its wood was brought from Ta-Neṯer, a mountain in the hills of Naharin."[58]

The Egyptian representations of Asiatic helmets most striking in their correlation to the Nuzi data are those that appear in the battle scenes carved on the sides of the wooden chariot body from the tomb of Thutmose IV.[59] Each of these minutely detailed reliefs presents the king in his battle chariot putting to rout two enemy chariot corps, which by their distinctive physical features can confidently be identified as North Syrian and/or Mitannian.[60] Although a variety of different armor types can be observed within the ranks, each of these armies seems to be outfitted very similarly, and moreover, outfitted in just the same way that the Nuzi charioteers would seem to have been, judging from the texts.[61] The Nuzi documents, in fact, seem to verify

[55]N. de G. Davies, *The Tomb of Rekh-mi-re at Thebes* (New York, 1953), v. I, p. 38; v. II, pl. XXXVII, and in *Metropolitan Museum Bulletin*, pt. II (Dec., 1928), fig. 6, cf. p. 46.

[56]N. de G. Davies, *The Tomb of Ken-Amun at Thebes* (New York, 1930), p. 27, pls. XVI, XXIV. It is of particular interest that these long coats of mail are drawn showing approximately 223 scales on the front. This would indicate that overall, if the drawings are accurate, the originals would have borne about 450 to 500 scales, well within the range of scales said to have been attached to the heavier suits of armor at Nuzi. Note also in these suits of armor the prominent neck pieces.

[57]Ibid., p. 31, pl. XXII.

[58]Ibid. (my translation).

[59]Carter and Newberry, pp. 24ff., and refer to n. 23.

[60]Ibid., p. 32.

[61]Of the troops shown here, only a relative few are clad in scale armor, which is just the situation implied in the Nuzi tablets (see also n. 62). Most of the men appear to be wearing leather tunics with long sleeves, over which one or two wide straps hang from the shoulders diagonally across the chest like bandoleers. These straps are sometimes rendered as though they were covered with scales. The Nuzi texts frequently

most of the details of military dress represented here and suggest strongly that the Egyptian artist actually used as his models genuine articles of Asiatic armor, either those received by the court as gifts[62] or those taken by the army as war booty.[63]

Ten helmets can be seen on the two panels; three appear on the heads of warriors, the others are lying about loose on the field of battle. The surfaces of each have been given slightly different textures and details, obviously so as to suggest the different materials from which they were made. Furthermore, all of them bear plumes at their peaks, which, by the hatching or herringbone

---

mention corselets with sleeves (see n. 7) as well as *tutiwa*, which I have suggested (n. 9) may be the name of these straps. *Tutiwa* are said to have been woven (*HSS* 13 431:43f.), made of dyed leather (*HSS* 14 246:27f., 253; *HSS* 16 441), or covered with scales (*HSS* 15 3:3f., 11f., 18f.). For protection of the legs, most of the troops wear knee-length skirts or kilts, while others, possibly the elite charioteers, wear long-length skirts. A few men wear leggings. These skirts, I have proposed (n. 33), may have been the items called *kalkū* at Nuzi. The relative scarcity of helmets in these scenes may suggest that many men did not wear them at all into battle. At Nuzi, to be sure, there are occasional references to men being issued armor "without helmets" (*HSS* 15 4:22). As for the weapons depicted, one sees only the bow, the sword, and the axe, which is uncommon. The shields represented are all rectangular. The Nuzi texts inform us that chariots were each provided with two quivers (*išpatu*) each filled with thirty to forty arrows (*qanû*), a shield (*arītu*), a whip (*iltuḫḫu*), and possibly a lance (*šukitu*) (Kendall, pp. 175ff., 210ff., 215ff., 250ff.). The charioteers themselves are normally said to have been issued bows (*qaštū*) and swords (*paṭrū*) (*JEN* 527; *HSS* 13 195; 15 4, 12, 21), but the battle-axe (*ḫaṣinnu*) is mentioned only once (*HSS* 15 17:1).

62 Such as those listed as part of the "tribute of Reṯenu" in year 42 of Thutmose II (Kurt Sethe, *Urkunden der 18. Dynastie*, pt. III [Leipzig, 1907], IV.732), or those featured as New Year's gifts in the tombs of Menkheperre-Seneb and Amenmose (see nn. 50, 52) or those sent to Amenhotep III by Tušratta (see n. 25).

63 Note that at the Battle of Megiddo Thutmose III is said to have seized 200 suits of scale armor from his enemy (Sethe, *Urkunden* . . . IV, 664). This text is of particular interest in containing the earliest reference to scale-armor in Egyptian literature; it is clear from the context that the Egyptians at this time regarded it as a novel item. Whereas in later times they knew it as *ṯryn* (probably from the Hittite pronunciation *šaryanni*), here these garments are described by the Egyptian word *mss* "tunic," which, though given the leather determinative, is preceded by the word *ḥsmn* "bronze": ". . . a fine bronze (-covered) leather tunic of a warrior of that enemy, a fine bronze (-covered) leather tunic of the Prince of Megiddo, and 200 [bronze (-covered)] leather tunics of the warrior(s) of his wretched army." It is important to note that at Megiddo Thutmose also claims to have captured 924 chariots, which, if we assume two men to a vehicle, implies a chariot force of over 1800 men. If from these 1800 men the Egyptians were able to seize only 200 scale-covered corselets, then it would appear that of the total number of charioteers at Megiddo only about 10% wore scale armor. This would suggest, like the Nuzi data, that such elaborate armor was worn only by the elite and was not necessarily a decisive factor in the warfare of the day.

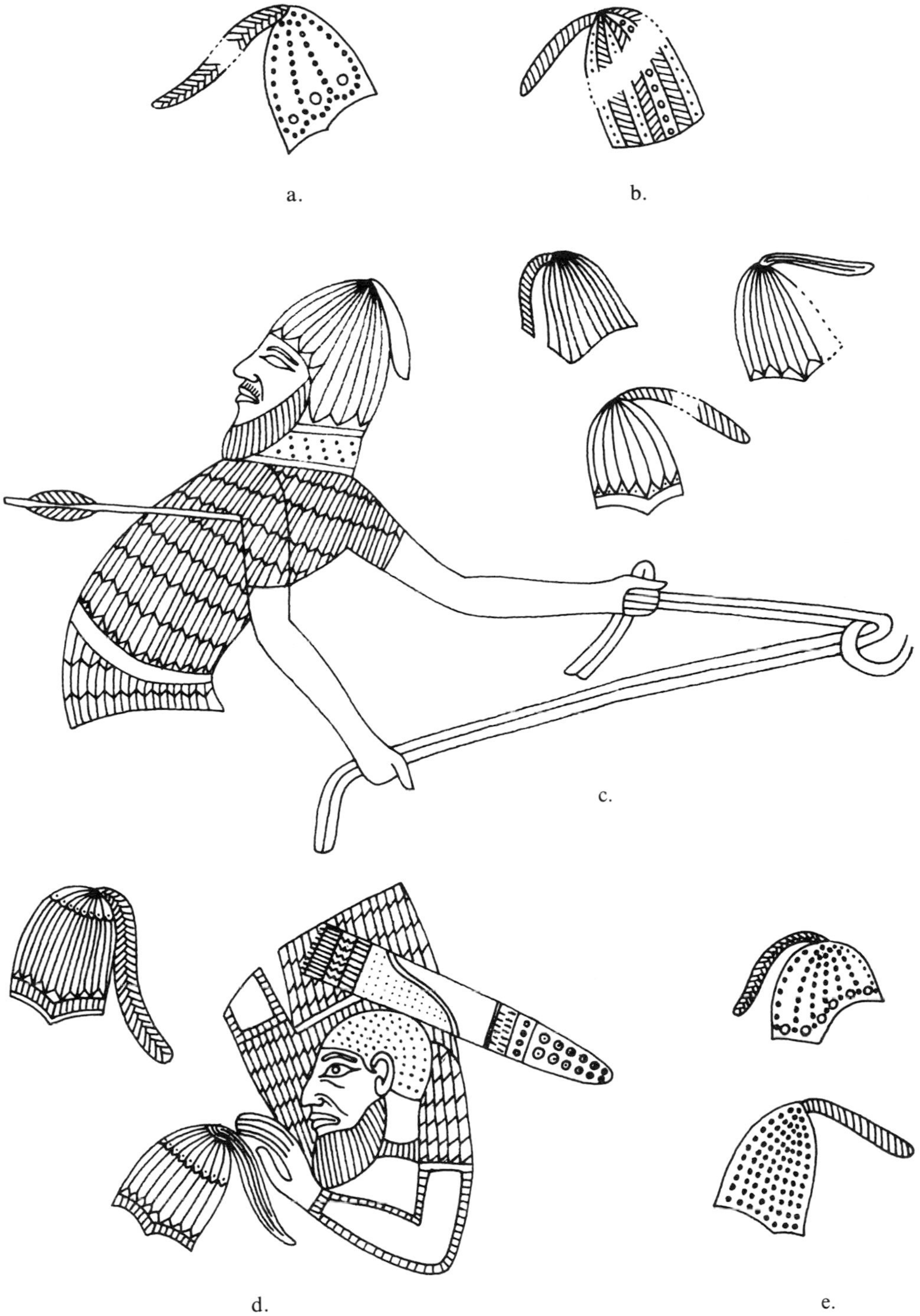

Figure 8. Asiatic helmets (and charioteers) depicted in the battle scenes carved on the sides of the state chariot found in the tomb of Thutmose IV. (Drawings by Lynn Holden).

patterns they bear, suggest that they may have been braided leather bands or even long thin feathers.

One of these helmets (fig. 8a) displays a surface divided by evenly spaced vertical rows of tiny dots, extending from the apex to just above the rim, where they join a perpendicular scalloped line of similar dots. Single large circular points appear between each scallop. Perhaps this was intended to represent a leather helmet composed of several long triangular leather sections sewn together. The rows of dots may have suggested the stitched seams, while the large points may have suggested metal studs.

Another helmet, adorned with vertical panels of dots alternating with vertical panels of hatchwork (fig. 8b), is harder to classify. Possibly it, too, represented a leather helmet, but one with a heavily laced exterior reinforced with metal bands and studs. On the other hand, such patterning may have been intended to evoke a decorative chased and *repoussé* design applied to the surface of a metal helmet (see fig. 10).

More easily identifiable in these compositions are the helmets covered with metal scales, which, as in the Nuzi texts, are most conspicuously identified with the troops that also wore the heavy scale armor. One type of helmet featured here appears to have been covered by a single row of very long pointed scales, which extended the full height of the helmet from peak to rim (fig. 8c). Another type seems to have been covered by two overlapping rows of similar, but less elongated scales (fig. 8d). Each of these helmet types, however, if accurately represented, would seem to have borne a relatively small number of large scales, which stands in sharp contrast to the scaled helmets at Nuzi, which are said to have borne from 140 to 200 scales. While such a discrepancy may be due only to the Egyptian artist's need to abbreviate the details of his drawing while working at such small scale, helmets of such a type may actually have existed—even at Nuzi. A single example of an elongated scale of what would seem to be the very same type appearing in figure 8c and d was actually found at Nuzi in one room of Prince Shilwa-tešub's house (fig. 9).[64] Its sides are not quite parallel; its lower end is pointed, and it is curved and ribbed for strength.

Only the last two helmets depicted on the chariot panels (fig. 8e) could have represented metal-scaled originals like those described in the Nuzi texts. The artist has covered each completely with a chased pattern of dots, which may well have indicated a surface of small scales. A more precise rendering of such a helmet at this scale would have been exceedingly difficult, even for an Egyptian artist.

Substantially corroborating the helmet data from Nuzi is that deriving from the Aegean and Mycenaean milieu, where many detailed representations

[64]Starr, v. I, p. 477; v. II, pl. 126 o.

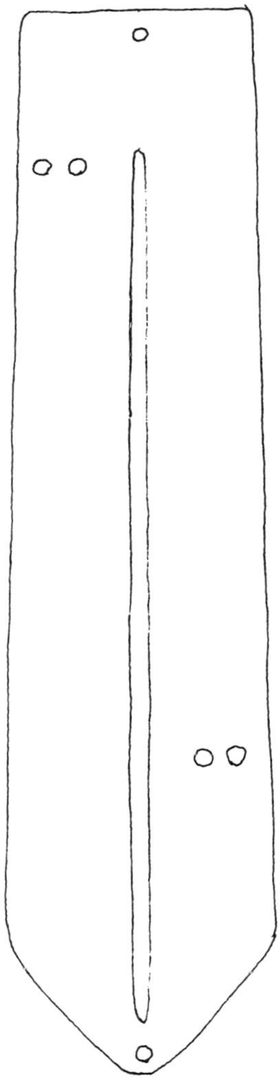

Figure 9. Bronze scale from Nuzi, possibly used in helmet construction. Baghdad Museum. (Actual size. No profile published.)

and even original examples of helmets have been preserved.[65] The *Iliad* itself is a particularly rich source of information on the helmet types of the Late Bronze Age and also confirms the Nuzi material in many important ways. As at Nuzi, the Homeric tradition recalls helmets of three basic types: those of leather, those of bronze, and those covered with rows of scales (except that here the scales are not of bronze but of boar's tusk sections).

[65] H. L. Lorimer, *Homer and the Monuments* (London, 1950), pp. 211ff.; J. Borchhardt, *Homerische Helme* (Mainz, 1972).

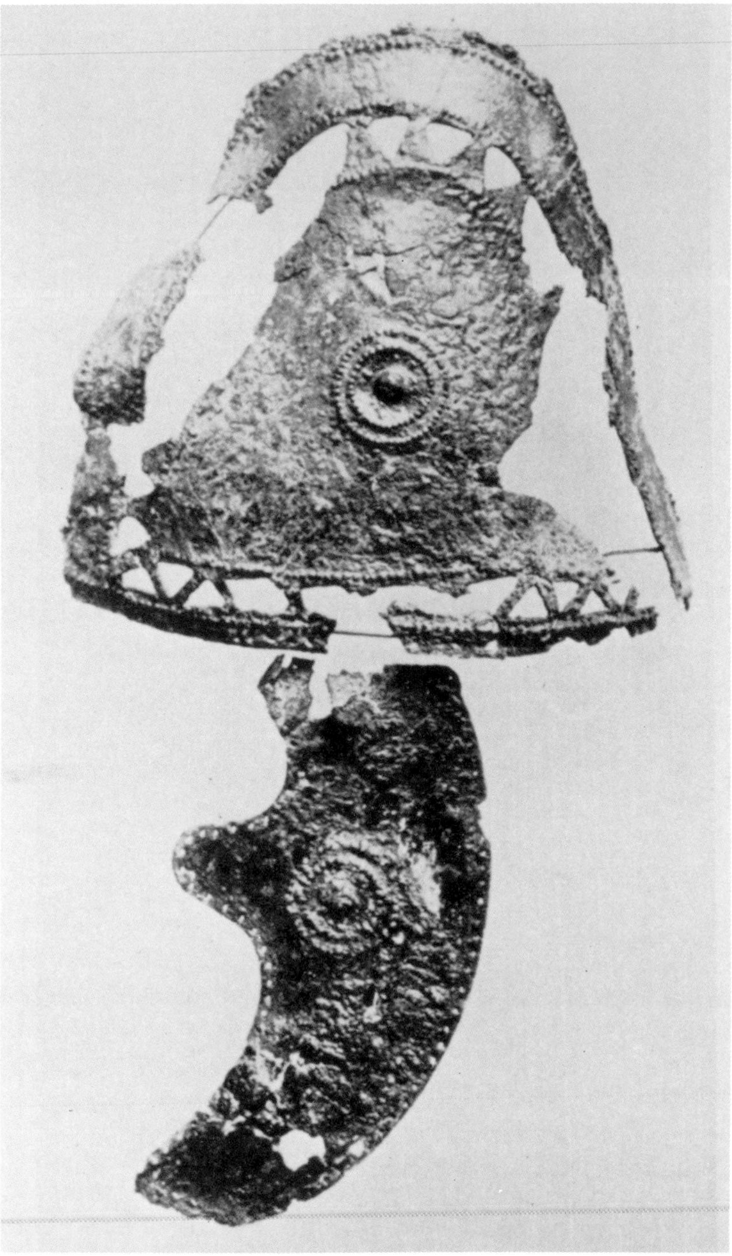

Figure 10. Fragmentary bronze helmet from Tiryns. Late Helladic IIIc or Sub-Mycenaean, 12th-11th century B.C. (After Borchardt, *Homerische Helme*, pl. 8:4.

In *Iliad* X 258 Diomedes is said to have worn a "helm of bull's hide, without horn and without crest, a helm that is called a skull-cap (κατᾶιτυξ) and that guards the heads of lusty youths."[66] As at Nuzi, the implication remains that the simple leather casque was a head defense normally worn only by the lowest-ranking or most junior warriors.

The most common form of helmet described in the *Iliad*, as at Nuzi, is the bronze helmet, which is sometimes described as having cheek pieces of bronze (XII 184, XX 398), a crest (XVIII 611) or a socket at the peak (XV 535), from which a thick horsehair plume sometimes emerged (III 337, XIII 714, XV 535). The plume was also said to have been dyed red (XV 535). Such descriptions are, of course, reminiscent of the Nuzi helmet described in *JEN* 527:10ff, with its bronze "flaps" and its "crest of leather." The existence in Mesopotamia of helmet plumes dyed red is proven by their appearance in the wall paintings of the tomb of Amenmose (fig. 3).

Two original bronze helmets of the Mycenaean age have actually been excavated. One, deriving from a warrior's grave at Hagios Johannis near Knossos and dated to Late Minoan II (ca. 1450-1425 B.C.), is conical, lacking decoration but for a knob at the peak, and fitted with two cheek pieces.[67] Holes were pierced around the rim and the flaps, indicating also that a liner of leather or felt had been attached. Another helmet, from a grave at Tiryns generally believed to be of the eleventh century,[68] shows a more ovoid form reminiscent of the Egyptian paintings except that this casque, too, had movable cheek pieces (fig. 10), What is notable about this object is its ornamental surface, with bands of hollow-work and raised beading, proving that some early bronze helmets were given chased and *repoussé* designs as suggested perhaps by that in figure 8b.

Perhaps the most extraordinary account of a helmet in the *Iliad* is that given the headpiece of Odysseus in X 261, which was described as "a helm wrought of hide; . . . with many a tight-stretched thong was it made stiff within, while without the white teeth of a boar of gleaming tusks were set thick on this side and that, well and cunningly, and within was fixed a lining of felt."[69] The text goes on to say that the helmet was a curiosity and an antique even then.

Boars' tusk helmets of this sort appear commonly in Mycenaean and Minoan art during Late Helladic and Late Minoan I and II times (ca. 1500-1350 B.C.); they appear to have been status symbols and objects of great value. Depicted either by themselves or as worn, they may be seen engraved on seals

[66] A. T. Murray, trans., *Homer: The Iliad* (Loeb Classical Library), v. I (Cambridge, 1952), p. 455.

[67] Borchhardt, p. 60, pl. 67.

[68] Ibid., pp. 43ff., pl. 8, 4-5.

[69] *Iliad* (Loeb ed.), v. I, p. 455.

Figure 11. Ivory carving of a Mycenaean warrior wearing a boar's tusk helmet. From a chamber tomb at Mycenae. Late Helladic IIIa-b, ca. 1500-1350 B.C. Nat. Mus. Athens.

Figure 12. Ivory carving of a Mycenaean warrior wearing a boar's tusk helmet. From a chamber tomb at Spata. Late Helladic IIIb, 14th century B.C. Nat. Mus. Athens.

and gems and painted on pottery or in frescoes. Several fragmentary examples have even been excavated. Of these helmets, much has been written already,[70] and it would be needless here to discuss them at great length. What is of particular interest to this study, however, is that the most detailed representations of boar's tusk helmets serve to reinforce and verify the Nuzi data on the metal-scaled helmet, especially in illustrating how the latter could have been covered with up to 200 scales.

One of the finest depictions of a boar's tusk helmet derives from a chamber tomb at Mycenae.[71] Forming part of the lid of an ivory box, this is a carving of a warrior's head in high relief (fig. 11). The elaborate helmet represented is conical and has six rows of tusk sections. The apex terminates in a knob-like projection, to which a horsehair plume would doubtless have been shown attached. Below the rim, cheek flaps extend to the chin, where, as in the Boğazköy helm (fig. 4), they are tied together. If we count the visible tusk "scales," we will see that were the head carved in the round rather than only in half-section, the helmet above the rim would have borne approximately 180 "scales." With some thirty-five tusk sections on each cheek piece, the total number of scales would have been about 250.

A less fine example of an object of the same genre, from a grave at Spata in eastern Attica, depicts a helmet of similar type, which seems to have possessed no less than 150 scales on its cone, and about 190 if the cheek flaps are included (fig. 12).[72] The unusually bulky appearance of this helm upon the head is perhaps due to the thickness of the felt liner, over which, according to the *Iliad*, such helmets were constructed.

The apparent similarities between the Mycenaean helmets, particularly the latter, and those described in the Nuzi tablets may be a result of more than mere chance. The peoples of the Aegean, in frequent contact with those of Syria,[73] would have developed armor not unlike that of their Asiatic contemporaries. They certainly experimented with armor made from metal scales, for bronze scales much like those found at Nuzi have been found at Troy and Mycenae and in Bronze Age Cypriote sites.[74] The very word for "helmet" in

[70]See n. 64 for refs. giving full bibliography.

[71]Borchhardt, pl. 2, 1.

[72]Ibid., pls. 2-3, cf. also 4-6, pls. 3-6.

[73]M. C. Astour, *Hellenosemitica* (Leiden, 1965), pp. 323ff.; V. Hankey, "Mycenaean Pottery in the Middle East: Notes on Finds since 1951," *Annual of the British School at Athens* 62 (1967), 107ff.; Acts of the International Symposium "The Mycenaeans in the Eastern Mediterranean," Nicosia: March 27-April 2, 1972 (Cyprus, 1973).

[74]H. W. Catling, "A Bronze Plate from a Scale-Corselet found at Mycenae," *Archäologischer Anzeiger* 85 (1970), 441ff.; V. Karageorghis and E. Masson, "A

the Linear B tablets is *ko-ru*, which may indeed reflect a relationship with *gurpisu*.[75]

---

propos de la découverte d'écailles d'armure en bronze à Gastria-Alaas (Chypre)," *Archäologischer Anzeiger* 90 (1975), 209ff.

[75]Borchhardt, pp. 3ff. See also F. Vandenabeele and J.-P. Olivier, *Les idéogrammes archéologiques du Linéaire B* (*Études Crétoises* XXIV) (Paris, 1979), pp. 40ff.

The Office of *ḫalṣuḫlu* in the Nuzi Texts

M. P. Maidman
York University
Toronto, Canada

No Assyriologist has devoted his efforts so tirelessly to the texts from a single site as has E. R. Lacheman in his dedication to the tablets from Nuzi. His work at text publication, edition, and elucidation represents the very sizable core of the Nuzi material available to the scholarly world. As a student of Nuzi society—and, therefore, as a student of Lacheman—I am happy to express my appreciation by dedicating this paper to him.[1]

The Nuzi official called *ḫalṣuḫlu* has been an object of sporadic scholarly interest for over fifty years.[2] In that time, no consensus as to the function of

[1]A summary version of this paper was delivered 16 April 1980 at the 190th annual meeting of the American Oriental Society in San Francisco, California.

[2]To my knowledge, the first to have discussed this term was Paul Koschaker, *NRUA* (ASAW Philologisch-historische Klasse 39; Leipzig, 1928), p. 15, n. He resumed his discussion in his review of Chiera, *HSS* 5 in *OLZ*, 34 (1931), 226; in his review of Chiera, *JEN* II in *OLZ*, 35 (1932), 402f.; and in "Drei Rechtsurkunden aus Arrapḫa," *ZA*, 48 (1944), 202.

Subsequent examinations of the Nuzi *ḫalṣuḫlu* include, aside from the dictionaries, Cyrus H. Gordon, "Nouns in the Nuzi Tablets," *Babyloniaca*, 16 (1936), 68; E. A. Speiser in Robert H. Pfeiffer and E. A. Speiser, *One Hundred New Selected Nuzi Texts* (*AASOR* 16; New Haven, 1936), p. 82; E.-M. Cassin, *L'Adoption à Nuzi* (Paris: Adrien Maisonneuve, 1938), p. 32; Hildegard Lewy, "The Nuzian Feudal System," *Or.*, 11 (1942), 7ff., 12 with n. 1; Herbert Liebesny, "The Administration of Justice in Nuzi," *JAOS*, 63 (1943), 129ff.; Pierre M. Purves, "Commentary on Nuzi Real Property in the Light of Recent Studies," *JNES*, 4 (1945), 71, n. 18; Jacob J. Finkelstein, "Cuneiform Texts from Tell Billa," *JCS*, 7 (1953), 116, n. 30; Roy Edmund Hayden, "Court Procedure at Nuzu" (Diss. Brandeis, 1962), 11f.; Frederic William Bush, "A Grammar of the Hurrian Language" (Diss. Brandeis, 1964), 112; V. Korošec, "Keilschriftrecht" in *Handbuch der Orientalistik* ed. B. Spuler, Erste Abteilung: Der Nahe und der Mittlere Osten, Ergänzungsband III: Orientalisches Recht (Leiden: Brill, 1964), p. 167; N. B. Jankowska, "Communal Self-Government and the King of the State of Arrapḫa," *JESHO*, 12 (1969), 237; "Extended Family Commune and Civil Self-Government in Arrapḫa in the Fifteenth-Fourteenth Century B.C." (trans. G. M. Sergheyev) in *Ancient Mesopotamia*, ed. I. M. Diakonoff (Moscow: "Nauka," 1969), pp. 237f.; Noel Kenneth Weeks, "The Real Estate Interests of a Nuzi

this official has been reached. Indeed, in recent studies, we find this personage variously defined as a "head of [a] military district,"[3] an officer only two rungs below the king on the bureaucratic ladder,[4] a petty official concerned with local real estate records,[5] and any private citizen living in a fortified town.[6] Such wide disparity in perceptions of this official's functions, as well as the important role accorded the *ḫalṣuḫlu* in different models of Nuzi society,[7] suggest that a re-examination of the function of the Nuzi *ḫalṣuḫlu* is in order.

Previous students of this problem, implicitly or explicitly, have exploited the etymology of the term in attempting to determine its functional definition. The etymology of *ḫalṣuḫlu* is quite transparent: Akkadian *ḫalṣu* to which is added the Hurrian occupational suffix, *-uḫlu*. These data, however, have led to opposing conclusions. The *ḫalṣuḫlu* is thus the commander of a fortified district or merely someone who happens to live in one. To argue a definition of a term from its etymology, clear though it may be, is, in any case, a doubtful means of determining the word's functional weight. Such a procedure is especially dubious for the Nuzi *ḫalṣuḫlu* since, as is shown below, the definition of *ḫalṣu* is far from clear.[8] Thus, to argue *ḫalṣuḫlu* from *ḫalṣu* is to argue an unknown from an unknown. The procedure adopted here is to survey the Nuzi contexts in which the *ḫalṣuḫlu* appears and preliminarily to define his functions according to these contexts. Secondarily, and in more abbreviated fashion, the same procedure will be applied to the term *ḫalṣu*. Finally, it will be determined whether the term *ḫalṣu* in the Nuzi texts sheds additional light on the functions of the *ḫalṣuḫlu*.

Family" (Diss. Brandeis, 1971), 313; Abdulillah Fadhil, "Rechtsurkunden und Administrative Texte aus Kurruḫanni" (M.A. thesis Heidelberg, 1972), 109; Jonathan S. Paradise, "Nuzi Inheritance Practices" (Diss. Pennsylvania, 1972), 316, n. 225; Maynard Paul Maidman, "A Socio-economic Analysis of a Nuzi Family Archive" (Diss. Pennsylvania, 1976), 129f., 329f., n. 165; E. M. Cassin, "Le Palais de Nuzi et la royauté d'Arrapḫa," in *Le Palais et la Royauté*, ed. P. Garelli (Paris: Guethner, 1974), p. 376; E. Lacheman, "Le Palais et la royauté de la ville de Nuzi: Les Rapports entre les données archéologiques et les données épigraphiques," in *Le Palais et la Royauté*, p. 369; Walter Mayer, *Nuzi-Studien I* (*AOAT* 205/1; Kevelaer: Butzon and Bercker, 1978), p. 126.

[3]Jankowska, *JESHO*, 12 (1969), 237. [See also the article of Jankowska, above p. 195ff. eds.] Cf. Mayer, *Nuzi-Studien I*, p. 126.

[4]Fadhil, "Kurruḫanni," 109. Cf. Korošec, *Handbuch*, p. 167.

[5]Weeks, "Real Estate Interests," 313; Cassin, *Le Palais*, p. 376. Purves, *JNES*, 4 (1945), 71, n. 18, considers it a minor office whose precise significance is obscure.

[6]Lacheman, *Le Palais*, pp. 360, 369.

[7]See, for example, H. Lewy, *Or.*, 11 (1942), 7ff.; and Jankowska, *JESHO*, 12 (1969), 237, 246, 251, and elsewhere. See also below, n. 45.

[8]Any connection of Nuzi *ḫalṣu* or *ḫalṣuḫlu* with anything military is particularly doubtful as has already been noted, for example, by Finkelstein, *JCS*, 7 (1953), 116, n. 30; and Mayer, *Nuzi-studien I*, p. 126.

ḫalṣuḫlu

The term *ḫalṣuḫlu* is found in 53 Nuzi texts. Of these 53, 46 are so-called *lišānu*, or "declaration," texts, three are records of litigation, two are memoranda, one is a letter, and one a contract.[9] For our purposes, the texts may be divided into three categories. First, two texts, a trial text and the letter, describe the activities of a *ḫalṣuḫlu* in his capacity as *ḫalṣuḫlu*. Next come contexts in which the operation of this official is reflected or in which his function is assumed as part of the context. These include two trial texts, all the *lišānu* texts, and the two memoranda. The third category, represented by the sole contract, mentions the *ḫalṣuḫlu* in other than his capacity as functionary. The first two categories describe and allude to the *ḫalṣuḫlu's* official activities; the last category may inform us regarding his social status.

Starting with texts describing the official activities of the *ḫalṣuḫlu*, here, as in so many other cases, a trial text affords us our clearest glimpse into the function of the object of our study. According to this particular record, *JEN* 336,[10] "A" and "B" dispute a piece of real estate before a court composed of judges. "A" asserts his ownership, noting (ll. 7-9) that the crown dispatched one Arteya, a *ḫalṣuḫlu*, who circled the disputed field to survey it,[11] and awarded it to him (i.e. "A"). (The size of the plot was, it seems, decisive evidence in this case.) "B" confirms "A" 's account but asserts, nonetheless,

[9]The *lišānu* texts include: *JEN* 104, 106, 109, 114, 122, 129, 132, 136, 137, 141, 142, 144, [145], 146, 148, 149, 152, 153, 156, 157, 160, 165, [167], 168, 169, 170, 171, 172, 173, 176, 180, 185, 187, 188, 193, 194, 197, [200], 480, 481, *JENu* 734, 822, 985, [1097], *AASOR* 16 17, 19.

The records of litigation are: *JEN* 336, 352, 382. The memoranda include *HSS* 13 261, 265; the letter is *HSS* 9 1 and the contract, *HSS* 16 452.

[10]The text has been examined by Weeks, "Real Estate Interests," 277f., 313. Cf. H. Lewy, *Or.*, 11 (1942), 8.

[11]The form, *ultelw*[*iš*]*u* (1.8), derives from *šulwû*. In the Nuzi texts, this verb has the technical meaning, "to circumambulate in order to determine before the law the dimensions of real estate." For references, see *CAD*, L, p. 76. *JEN* 336:8 should be added to the passages there cited. Cf., on the implications of this term, Carlo Zaccagnini, *The Rural Landscape of the Land of Arrapḫe* (Rome, 1979), p. 123.

The act of "encircling" is one which the *ḫalṣuḫlu* undertakes in specific conditions. It may be germane that in other accounts of real estate litigation where the surveying of fields is called for, this act is performed by a litigant together with (court appointed?) "envoys" (*JEN* 365:34-42) and by "surveyors" (*JEN* 662:73-78). Also, it is common that individuals designated simply as "witnesses" or "surveyors" measure real estate prior to its lawful alienation (see, for example, *JEN* 89:18-20; *CAD*, M/2, p. 264). Cf. *JEN* 390:14-15 where *manzatuḫlu* officials are charged by the court to measure fields.

In sum, "*šulwû*" is an important legal act concerning real estate and, at the same time, an act of sufficient simplicitly so that members of the community at large may perform it satisfactorily.

that the field is his. The judges then call for expert witnesses. The case continues and a decision is reached but, at this point, the tablet becomes fragmentary.

We learn from this text that the crown (LUGAL [1. 7]) may dispatch the *ḫalṣuḫlu* to determine the area of real estate and that this official may, at least under these circumstances, award the disputed land. Such a decision, be it noted, may be challenged by a claimant and, it is implicit, be overthrown by a court composed of judges.

The impression given by *JEN* 336 is buttressed by a royal letter, *HSS* 9 1.[12] The text indicates that the crown, in this case perhaps the king of Mittanni himself, wishes real estate transferred from one individual to another. To this end, one Sauš-satti, a *ḫalṣuḫlu* "of" or "from" (i.e. *ša*) the town of Atilu (11. 7-8) is sent to shift a border marker and to define the new limits of ownership so as to ensure that illegal encroachment by either party not take place. Once again, the *ḫalṣuḫlu* is dispatched by the crown. He determines limits of real estate and confirms title to real estate.

Turning now to texts where the function of the *ḫalṣuḫlu* is more or less assumed, the resulting picture complements the one already perceived. Two trial texts, *JEN* 352 and 382, describe real estate disputes.[13] Though such documents typically record that the dispute was heard by judges, these two texts specify courts composed of judges and a *ḫalṣuḫlu*.[14] There is nothing otherwise peculiar about these real estate trials when compared to other such accounts. One gets the impression that the judge and the *ḫalṣuḫlu* are here all but interchangeable officials. Indeed, the case described in *JEN* 382 finds expression in another, parallel text, *JEN* 392. The case is *there* described as tried before judges only.[15] In the other of our cases, *JEN* 352, a court order is

[12]Discussion of this text, in addition to references cited in Borger, *HKL* I and II, include E. A. Speiser, "A Letter of Saushshatar and the Date of the Kirkuk Tablets," *JAOS*, 49 (1929), 269-75; Martha A. Morrison, "The Family of Šilwa-tešub *mâr šarri*," *JCS*, 31 (1979), 15; and Carlo Zaccagnini, "Les Rapports entre Nuzi et Ḫanigalbat," *Assur*, 2/1 (1979), 18, n. 73.

[13]Apart from the references in Borger, *HKL* I and II, *JEN* 352 has been treated by H. Lewy, *Or.*, 11 (1942), 218f., 239f.; Hayden "Court Procedure," 79-81; Paradise, "Inheritance," 319-21; and Weeks, "Real Estate Interests," 279f., 312f. while *JEN* 382 is discussed by Jankowska, *JESHO*, 12 (1969), 250f.; Paradise, "Inheritance," 315f.; and Weeks "Real Estate Interests," 72f., 127f.

[14]*JEN* 352:4-6; 382:4-6.

[15]*JEN* 392:7. This is not to say that the *ḫalṣuḫlu* is a class of judge or vice versa in the sense that the same individual could bear either the title of *dayyānu* or that of *ḫalṣuḫlu* indiscriminately. (However, as noted below, since the functions of both at times overlapped, the *ḫalṣuḫlu* could be classed as *dayyānu* when involved with other judges. See *JEN* 352:4-5, 26.) *JEN* 382, where judges and a *ḫalṣuḫlu* sit, is sealed (11. 34-36) by Tarmiya son of Unap-tae, Teḫip-tilla son of Puḫi-šenni, and Tarmi-tešup son of Eḫli-tešup. *JEN* 392, where judges alone sit, is sealed (11. 38-40) by Teššuya

described (l. 26) as emanating simply from the judges, though the bench includes judges and a *ḫalṣuḫlu*. Apparently, in these instances of real estate litigation and title determination, the *ḫalṣuḫlu* functioned virtually as a judge.

The 46 *lišānu* texts mentioning *ḫalṣuḫlu* are remarkably homogeneous and may be described as a unit. All but two record declarations before judges in addition to the *ḫalṣuḫlu* and all confirm the transfer of real estate title.[16] Like the two aforementioned trial texts, these declarations describe proceedings before a bench or board composed of judges and a *ḫalṣuḫlu*[17] and deal with

---

mār šarri, Tarmiya son of Unap-tae, and Tarmi-tešup son of Eḫli-tešup. Thus the shift in designation involves a shift in personnel: Teḫip-tilla is the *ḫalṣuḫlu* and the others are judges.

The rationale for parallel trials (and parallel texts) *may* be found in this difference in court personnel. This particular *ḫalṣuḫlu*, Teḫip-tilla, was also a litigant in this case. Note, however, *JEN* 352, where Teḫip-tilla also sits on the bench as a *ḫalṣuḫlu* and is also a litigant.

[16]These 46 texts are listed above, n. 9. The two texts claiming to involve *ḫalṣuḫlu*'s alone are *AASOR* 16 17 and 19. Even there, however, judges are likely involved. See further below, n. 17.

The homogeneity of these 46 texts is due in part, of course, to their archaeological provenience: all but *AASOR* 16 17 and 19 come from the house of Teḫip-tilla. It is, therefore, no surprise that in all but these same two texts, Teḫip-tilla is a principal party. Beyond this, however, several (doubtless interrelated) features— from the possibly minor to the significant—unite these texts even in contrast to other tablets of declaration from the Teḫip-tilla family archives. The first features, as stated above, are the mention of the *ḫalṣuḫlu* and the subject matter of real estate transfer. Furthermore, of the 44 texts from the house of Teḫip-tilla, 38 were excavated from room T15 and only 5 from room T16 (*JEN* 137, 141, 144, 149, *JENu* 985 [the provenience of *JENu* 1097 is unknown]). At least 43 of these texts (excluding the probable *JENu* 1097) involve Teḫip-tilla himself rather than other members of his family. From the group of 46 texts, 41 (from the hands of at least five different scribes: Taya, Itḫ-apiḫe, Balṭu-kašid, [d]AK.DINGIR.RA, and Šumu-libšī son of Kiannipu) preserve or allow for the restoration of the first line. And of *those* 41, 37 begin *li-ša-an-šu*(*-nu*), not EME-*šu* (*-nu*). (The others are *JEN* 173, 187, 194, *JENu* 985.) In this, as in other cited instances of text patterning, in declarations not involving *ḫalṣuḫlu*'s the distribution is far different. Cf. EME in *JEN* 102, 105, 107, 108, 117, etc., as opposed to *li-ša-an-šu* in *JEN* 119, 123, 131, 161, 166, etc. Further patterning regarding the location of the real estate involved is also discernable but cannot be discussed here. See also below, n. 17.

It is nevertheless clear, as asserted below, that this class of declaration is substantially identical to other such texts where the *ḫalṣuḫlu* is not mentioned. See, for example, *JEN* 105, 107, 166, etc.

The declaration texts, in general, deserve careful, detailed study.

[17]Furthermore, it appears likely that, with the exceptions of *JEN* 160 and 176, all these declarations were undertaken before a bench composed of the same individuals: Tarmiya son of Unap-tae, Tarmi-tešup son of Eḫli-tešup and Teḫip-tilla son of Puḫi-šenni—the court which presided at the trial recorded in *JEN* 382. As already noted

confirmation of the alienation of real estate. Furthermore, these declarations, like their trial record counterparts, are virtually indistinguishable from similar texts in which judges alone are involved.[18]

The contents of two administrative memoranda muddy somewhat the clear picture thus far obtained for the Nuzi *ḫalṣuḫlu*. *HSS* 13 261 names six envoys (otherwise unattested) of one Šu-[ ], a *ḫalṣuḫlu*. To this point in the present discussion, the *ḫalṣuḫlu* is always linked to real estate matters. Now the Nuzi official called "envoy," *mār šipri*, elsewhere *does* perform the function of field surveying and, thus, may be so linked to the *ḫalṣuḫlu*.[19] However, the present context, though laconic and unclear, nonetheless seems to deal with barley transport. The bearing of this text, involving a *ḫalṣuḫlu*, envoys, and grain, on the problem under discussion seems unclear.[20] The

---

above, n. 15, Teḫip-tilla is the *ḫalṣuḫlu* and the others are judges. In *AASOR* 16 17 and 19, these individuals are called simply *ḫalṣuḫlu*'s! In *JEN* 176, the bench is composed of individuals known from *JEN* 392 (see above n. 15) as judges: Tarmiya (son of Unap-tae), Teššuya *mār šarri*, and Tarmi-tešup son of Eḫli-tešup. Yet in *JEN* 176:2-3 they are classified as judges and *ḫalṣuḫlu*! *AASOR* 16 17, 19 and *JEN* 176 reveal, I believe, a certain scribal confusion or carelessness in the face of a sitting *ḫalṣuḫlu* acting virtually as judge. This problem was first (and successfully) attacked by H. Lewy, *Or.*, 11 (1942), 5-7. She also proposed, ibid., 7, to identify Tarmi-tešup as both judge and *ḫalṣuḫlu*. That identification remains questionable.

Teḫip-tilla's presence in the declaration corpus from his house is a double one: he is both a principal party and a presiding official. In theory, though not perhaps in reality, these capacities must be kept separate. Teḫip-tilla could, and did, seal real estate declarations as *ḫalṣuḫlu* even where he was *not* a principal party: *AASOR* 16 17, 19.

For further on the *lišānu* text type and for Teḫip-tilla's exploitation of the genre as principal party and *ḫalṣuḫlu*, see, for the moment, Maidman, "Socio-economic Analysis," 124-30 and the notes thereto.

JEN 160, a declaration before judges and a *ḫalṣuḫlu*, was sealed by [Teš]šuya *mār šarri*, [Tarmi-t]ešup son of Eḫli-tešup, and [ ] son of Puitae (11. 25-27). The last must be another *ḫalṣuḫlu*.

[18]Except for the instances noted above, n. 17, the personnel occupying these different positions *are* discretely identifiable. Thus, the functions of the positions may overlap, but the holders of those positions do not.

[19]"Envoys" survey real estate (much the same as the *ḫalṣuḫlu* does sometimes) in *JEN* 365. See already above, n. 11. Cf. *JEN* 662:73-78 where six men (the same number as appears in *HSS* 13 261) perform this act. There (1. 77), however, they are identified as "surveyors," *mušelwû*.

[20]The functions of the *mār šipri* at Nuzi are several. C. Zaccagnini, "The Merchant at Nuzi," *Iraq*, 39 (1977), 171f., discusses the role of this functionary as a transporter of goods within the sphere of the internal palace administration. Furthermore, in my review of *Trade in the Ancient Near East* (=XXIII Rencontre volume= *Iraq*, 39 [1977], 1-231) *BiOr* 37 (1980) 185-89, I note that the activities of the Nuzi

second memorandum, *HSS* 13 265, names five members of the *aššabu* class of a certain town, ultimately to be delivered to a certain *ḫalṣuḫlu*.[21] Why these individuals, who are somehow dependent on Šilwa-tešup, are to be delivered to someone else, and why that someone else is a *ḫalṣuḫlu*, are questions still awaiting solution.[22]

Finally, a contract, *HSS* 16 452, involves a *ḫalṣuḫlu*, one Enna-mati, —seemingly in his private capacity—in partnership with a shepherd in a contract involving livestock. He and the others are equally subject to penalties for non-fulfillment of terms.

No further data regarding *ḫalṣuḫlu*'s are gleaned by comparing the personal and geographical names in these texts with other texts containing these PN's and GN's but *no* mention of *ḫalṣuḫlu*.[23]

Thus, our conclusions may be summarized briefly. The *ḫalṣuḫlu* is a crown official whose major, if not only, functions are the determination of the dimensions of real estate and the assignment or confirmation of title to real estate to new owners or to those whose ownership is challenged. In the realm

---

mār šipri are not confined to the palace economy and involve the transport of words as well as goods. In short, the *mār šipri* really is a "messenger."

In the present context, the *mār šipri* could, theoretically, be either a distributor of palace goods (following Zaccagnini's lead) or some other functionary, general deliverer or even *ad hoc* errand runner. The former notion *might* argue for the *ḫalṣuḫlu* as high bureaucrat but that is not a legitimate argument. Given the elasticity of the functions of the *mār šipri* (and the obscurity of *HSS* 13 261) we must, rather, look to the function of the *ḫalṣuḫlu first* in establishing semantic ranges. And this leads us to the tentative conclusion that *ḫalṣuḫlu* and real estate represents a vital linkage.

[21]The identity of the *ḫalṣuḫlu* is, perhaps, Ḫa-[ ], who seals this text (l. 15).

[22]Cf. the translation of this text in *CAD*, A/2, p. 461b.

[23]To note the single most important instance examined, the *lišānu* texts and the trial records *JEN* 352, 382 all but prove, as shown above, n. 15, that Teḫip-tilla son of Puḫi-šenni once held the post of *ḫalṣuḫlu*. Of the seven *ḫalṣuḫlu*'s of whom we are aware—Tehip-tilla himself; [ ] son of Pui-tae (*JEN* 160:6, 27); Arteya (*JEN* 336:7-8); Sauš-satti of Atilu (*HSS* 9 1:7-8); Šu-[ ] (*HSS* 13, 261:15-16); possibly Ḫa-[ ] (*HSS* 13, 265:12, 15); and Enna-mati (*HSS* 16 452:5-6)—for only one, Teḫip-tilla son of Puḫi-šenni, is the personal name and patronymic known.

Altogether, approximately 500 texts mention this individual, real estate and commercial texts, public as well as private records, accounts of his duties to, and relations with, the state as well as tablets of his personal business affairs. For no other individual at Nuzi are there as many and as informative tablets of record. Yet, except for the tablets already noted, in none of these records is Teḫip-tilla linked with any function which could be identified with that of *ḫalṣuḫlu*. But for his service as *ḫalṣuḫlu* in real estate contexts, his links to the apparatus of government seem to have been limited to military service as an infantryman (*HSS* 13 410:17) or, perhaps, as a charioteer (*HSS* 13 6:21); and to his several close links with local so-called "sons of the king" (see Maidman, "Socio-economic Analysis," 541-43).

of real estate, his function seems to overlap that of the judge, though a court composed of judges at times may overturn a *ḫalṣuḫlu*'s determination.[24] The *ḫalṣuḫlu* uses envoys and perhaps others in his activities. The nature of that use is not altogether clear. The *ḫalṣuḫlu* appears to be, in short, a minor real estate official. Incidentally, *if* one wishes to correlate this description with the etymology of the term, then one must conclude that, at Nuzi, *ḫalṣu* is simply "territory" or "land."

ḫalṣu

Turning to the attested usages of the term *ḫalṣu* at Nuzi, the evidence is both slight and ambiguous. Twelve texts mention *ḫalṣu*, most often in combination with a town name.[25] Persons and commodities come from *ḫalṣu*'s. Carlo Zaccagnini recently devoted attention to this term[26] and concluded that, at Nuzi, the *ḫalṣu* is a district, larger than an *ālu*, indeed, often including several towns. The name of a *ḫalṣu* often is taken from that of the largest town in the district, that is, the district's seat or capital. The most effective support for this proposition is *HSS* 16 397.[27] There, persons are identified as being from the towns of Ulamme, Tīl-duri, and Tarkulli. These people are, perhaps, further identified as hailing from the *ḫalṣu* of Ulamme (11. 8-9). Such a context easily permits of a definition of *ḫalṣu* such as that suggested by Zaccagnini. His interpretation is indeed attractive but is beset by several nagging (and, cumulatively, serious) problems.

Beginning with general issues and then turning to specific data, the following points regarding the Nuzi *ḫalṣu* may be raised. The horizon of the Nuzi texts clearly includes three topographical units having administrative significance: *dimtu*, *ālu*, and *mātu*. Difficulties of definition notwithstanding, these three terms are ubiquitous in the documents. Were *ḫalṣu* a fourth such term—a unit between the *ālu* and the *mātu*—then we should expect a similar ubiquity of attestation, not the twelve texts noted above. A second peculiarity regards the nature of the names of the *ḫalṣu*'s. The problem remains unresolved as to why some *ḫalṣu*'s bear town names (e.g., Ulamme, Ṣilliya, Azuḫinni[28])

[24]This is clearly not the case in *HSS* 9 1 where the *ḫalṣuḫlu* is apparently empowered by the king of Mittanni himself to determine real estate boundaries.

[25]*JEN* 551, *HSS* 9 66, *HSS* 13 690 (=*AASOR* 16 48; the reference to, and restoration of, line 26 are made by Zaccagnini, *Assur* 2/1 [1979], 23, n. 109), *HSS* 14 103, *HSS* 15 41, 44, *HSS* 16 387, 388, 395, 397, 398, 401.

[26]Zaccagnini, *Rural Landscape*, pp. 15-20. H. Lewy, *Or.*, 11 (1942), 11-12, had already defined, in a brief discussion, the Nuzi *ḫalṣu* as a district administered by a *ḫalṣuḫlu*.

[27]See already, Hildegard Lewy, "A Contribution to the Historical Geography of the Nuzi Texts," *JAOS*, 88 (1968), 160, n. 77.

[28]*HSS* 16 397:8-9; 9 66:12-13; 14 103:9.

while others do not (e.g. *pakkante*, *kanari*, *ikeni*[29]). The latter category is doubly distressing for, included in such obscure *ḫalṣu*'s are major towns of the Nuzi region. Thus, the well-known town of Turša is located in the otherwise unattested *ḫalṣi kanata*[30] and the important town of Apena is included in the but twice attested *halṣi pakkante*.[31]

Even the constituent elements of the several *ḫalṣu*'s represent a somewhat confused and confusing picture. Twice a "*ḫalṣi* URU *Azuḫinni*" is mentioned.[32] Yet the town of Azuḫinni is elsewhere mentioned in contexts dealing explicitly with the *ḫalṣi pakkante*.[33] Almost as disturbing, a "*ḫalṣi Ulamme*," including the town of Ulamme, is attested.[34] Yet elsewhere, in lists of GN's where *ḫalṣu*'s appear, Ulamme appears as an URU/*ālu*, not as a *ḫalṣu*.[35] The town of Apena, as noted above, is linked to the *ḫalṣi pakkante*.[36] Yet, in a list in which *ḫalsu*'s appear, Apena also appears, not as part of a *ḫalṣu*, but as a discrete town.[37] Such seemingly careless employment of the term *ḫalṣu* is difficult to fathom if

[29] *HSS* 13 690:26 and 16 388:19 (cf. perhaps, N. B. Jankowska, "Legal Documents from Arrapḫa in the Collections of the U.S.S.R.," in *Peredneaziatskiy Sbornik: Voprosy Hettologii i Churritologii*, 1961, 12:3); 16 395:6; 15 41:11. It is uncertain whether this latter class of names represents PN's or some other kind of terminology. In a directive (*JEN* 551) addressed to one Tarmi-tilla (1. 1), a "district" is merely designated "*ḫalṣika*" (1. 4) without any further specification. Cf. H. Lewy, *Or.*, 11 (1942), 11 with n. 5.

[30] *HSS* 15 41:66, 67.

[31] *HSS* 13 690:18, 26. Cf. *HSS* 16 388:19 for the *ḫalṣi pakkante*.

[32] *HSS* 14 103:9; 16 387:8.

[33] *HSS* 13 690:22, 26. Cf. *HSS* 16 388:23, 19.

Zaccagnini, *Assur*, 2/1 (1979), 23 n. 109, notes the close association of the towns of Apena and Azuḫinni. In addition to other connections, both, as also noted above, are located in *ḫalṣi pakkante*. Why, then, is Apena never located in the *ḫalṣi* URU *Azuḫinni*? See also below, note 37.

[34] *HSS* 16 397:8-9, 3.

[35] *HSS* 14 103:10 (cf. 11. 8, 9); 15 41:24 (cf. 11. 11, 19, 67). Cf. *HSS* 16 401:24, 16.

[36] See above, n. 31.

[37] *HSS* 14 103:4 (cf. 11. 8, 9). Line 9 mentions the *ḫalṣi* URU *Azuḫinni*, and so, the presence of Apena is even more disconcerting: not only might *ḫalṣi pakkante* be expected to appear but, even in its absence, the *ḫalṣi* URU *Azuḫinni* could have included Apena. See above, n. 33.

The inclusion of the town of Kurruḫanni in a *ḫalṣu* in one text (*HSS* 15 44:10, 20) and its discrete appearance as a town in another text which nevertheless also mentions *ḫalṣu*'s (*HSS* 15 41:49? cf. 11. 11, 19, 67) is yet a fourth example of inconsistent usage of *ḫalṣu*.

Dr. Aharon Kempinski, private communication, 9 September 1979, informs me of close terminological, and apparently administrative, parallels between *HSS* 15 44 and a Hittite text which he intends to publish. His comparison of the two texts should aid in our understanding of the related Nuzi material.

ḫalṣu bore precise administrative significance. Many, if not all, of the problems plaguing the use of this term would, however, vanish, if the term were substantially interchangeable with *ālu* or if it bore a general, topographical meaning rather than a specific administrative one.[38] In fact, one of the texts mentioning *ḫalṣu*'s may, if I understand it correctly, testify to the vague usage of *ḫalṣu* and, therefore, sometimes to its general equation with *ālu*. The text is *HSS* 14 103. The argument I propose is somewhat lengthy and so I offer the following transliteration in partial mitigation of the resulting complexity.

HSS 14 103 (=*SMN* 3019)
(Room C19; 59 x 68 x 21)

Obv.

(1) 16 MÍ.MEŠ *ša* URU DINGIR.MEŠ
(2) 12 MÍ *ša* URU *Nu-zi*
(3) 5 MÍ *ša* UR⌜U⌝ *An-zu-gal-lì*
(4) 7 MÍ *ša* U⌜R⌝U *A-pè-na*
(5) 5 MÍ *ša* ⌜m*Š*⌝*e-el-lu-ni*
(6) 6 MÍ *ša* m*Tu-ra-ri-ya*
(7) 11 MÍ *ša* m*Ni-ki-ir-te-šup*
(8) 8 MÍ *ša ḫal-ṣí* KÁ?!.MEŠ
(9) 5 MÍ *ša ḫal-ṣí* URU *A-zu-ḫi-in-ni*
(10) 3 MÍ *ša* URU *Ú-lam-me*
(11) 7 MÍ *ša* URU *Zi-iz-za* URU *Pa-la-a*

Rev.

(12) ⌜AŠ × 2 MÍ⌝
(13) ŠU.NIGIN$_2$ 87 MÍ! (=AŠ).MEŠ *ša aš-bu*
(14) 14 MÍ.MEŠ *ša* DUMU.MEŠ LUGAL
(15) ⌜3⌝ MÍ.MEŠ *ša* URU DINGIR.MEŠ
(16) 1 MÍ *ša* URU *An-zu-gal-lì*
(17) 1 MÍ *ša* m*Še*!-⌜*el*⌝-*lu-ni*
(18) 2 MÍ *ša* URU *A-su-ḫi-ni*
(19) ⌜1 MÍ⌝[*ša* URU *Ú-lam-m*]⌜*e*⌝?
(20) ⌜1 MÍ *ša*⌝[URU]⌜*Zi*?⌝-[*iz*]-⌜*za*?⌝
(21) ⌜1 MÍ⌝[*ša* URU *Pa-la*]-⌜*a*⌝?
(22) ⌜1 MÍ *ša* x x x⌝
(23) ⌜1⌝[MÍ *ša*]

Edge

(24) 28 MÍ.MEŠ
(25) ŠU.NIGIN$_2$ 1 ME 3 MÍ.MEŠ

[38]The problem of how *ḫalṣu*'s were named would, of course, remain.

NOTES:

Ll. 11-12 Line 11 is the only line of this text to contain two GN's. The second GN, URU *Pa-la-a*, by its curve and its overlap onto the reverse, is perhaps to be dissociated from the rest of line 11. Line 12, the first on the reverse of the tablet, is almost entirely effaced. There seems to be no room for a GN. The "2 MÍ" seems clear enough, in light of both the previous entries and the appropriate total thus obtained, i.e. 85 (11. 1-11)+2 (1. 12)=87 (1.13). Though "URU *Pa-la-a*" overlaps onto the edge of the tablet, given the considerations enunciated above, it is difficult to divorce "URU *Pa-la-a*" from the "2 MÍ." Therefore, I consider them a single entry.

l. 19 The restoration [*Ú-lam-m*]⌜*e*⌝, though based on a partially effaced single horizontal wedge, seems justified for the following reason. The group of entries represented in 11. 15-23, wherever it is preserved sufficiently to be read, always recalls the group of entries represented in 11. 1-11/12. Thus 1. 15's GN is that of 1. 1; 1. 16 parallels 1. 3; 1. 17 matches 1. 5; and 1. 18's *A-su-ḫi-ni* recalls the *A-zu-ḫi-in-ni* of 1. 9. This correspondence seems to obtain even as far as the relative order of the entries is concerned. Therefore, it seems possible to restore [*Ú-lam-m*]⌜*e*⌝ in 1. 19 following the GN of 1. 10. By the same token, lines 20 and 21 are conjecturally restored on the basis of 11. 11/12. As for 11. 22 and 23, I have no suggestion unless the principle of relative ordering be here abandoned. If so, then 11. 22-23 might reflect two entries from 11. 2, 4, 6-8.

ll. 20-23 See note on 1. 19.

HSS 14 103 is an inventory of women from various towns (11. 1-4, 10-11/12), individuals (11. 5-7), and *ḫalṣu*'s (11. 8-9). An obvious difficulty with this account is the arithmetic involved. Lines 1-12 add up to 87, the total given in line 13. The operations of lines 13-24, however, are not clear, given the explicit total of 103 recorded in 1. 25. Adding the figures of 11. 13-24 yields 141 while the sum of 11. 14-24 is 54. Both 141 and 54, the two most plausible induced totals, are sufficiently distant from the total of 103 so that the possibility of a scribal error becomes remote.

The precise significance of this text is obscure but, working with the numbers first, some meaning may be forthcoming. In fact, the figures can be made to work and therein lies the key to a partial interpretation of this tablet. The operations are as follows: 87 (11. 1-12=1. 13) - 12 (11. 15-23)+28 (1. 24)=103 (1. 25). The text is, therefore, to be divided into five parts: 11. 1-12 and its total in 1. 13; 1. 14; 11. 15-23; 1. 24; 1. 25, the grand total. One possible interpretation of *HSS* 14 103, based on this schema, would run as follows. A total of 87 women are newly reported as income (1. 13). Of this number, 14 are to be allotted to the sons of the king (1. 14). This subsequent expenditure would not bear on the current total inventory of women and so, for arithmetic purposes, may be ignored. Of the 87 women, 12 are reckoned inadequate (for unknown reasons) and are therefore deducted (11. 15-23).[39] The remaining 75 women are then added to stock on hand of 28 women (1. 24), thus yielding a total current supply of 103 (1. 25).

The hypothetical and tentative character of this interpretation hardly needs to be stressed. Yet, if the arithmetic processes be correct, specifically, the subtraction of 11. 15-23 from 11. 1-12, then an interesting datum emerges—a datum which justifies this excursus. Though 5 women are listed from "*ḫalṣi āl Azuḫinni*" (1. 9), 2 women of "*āl Azuḫinni*" (1. 18) are deducted from the total. Since the second roster presumably mirrors the first one—and if the omission of "*ḫalṣi*" in 1. 18 is not accidental—then there is no significant difference between "*ḫalṣi āl Azuḫinni*" and "*āl Azuḫinni.*" In short, *ḫalṣu* has no independent technical weight as a geographical/administrative description.

We may conclude, then, that the textual evidence at our disposal suggests that *ḫalṣu* is *not* a technical term but, rather, a somewhat loose designation for a geographical area of indeterminate type; in short, "territory" or "land."[40]

Conclusions

In summing up our discussion of *ḫalṣuḫlu* above, it was asserted that he was a minor royal official whose duty was the measurement of and assignment of title to real estate. Our subsequent survey of the term *ḫalṣu* at Nuzi does not require any modification of this definition of *ḫalṣuḫlu.* In the unlikely event that the meaning of *ḫalṣu* at Nuzi turns out to be a district of some sort, there is no evidence that any such district was governed by a *ḫalṣuḫlu* or that *ḫalṣuḫlu*'s had anything to do with *ḫalṣu*'s. No person connected with a *ḫalṣu* appears in any text mentioning a *ḫalṣuḫlu.* No name of a *ḫalṣu* is ever directly linked to the home base of a *ḫalṣuḫlu.*[41] Indeed, with one doubtful exception, "*Sauš-satti ḫalṣuḫlu ša āl Atilu*^{KI}",[42] no *ḫalṣuḫlu* is ever defined or qualified

[39]This deduction is broken down into the same categories (towns, individuals, *ḫalṣu*'s) as the initial sum (11. 1-12). See above, note to 1. 19 for detailed correspondences. Note further that in each pair of entries, the second figure is less than the first, i.e., the second may be reckoned as part of the first and may be deducted from it.

[40]Such "territory," of course, could surround a city, Azuḫinni or Ulamme for example, and be identified with it.

[41]There is one indirect link. *HSS* 9 66:12-13 establishes a *ḫalṣi ša āl Ṣilliyawe*. *HSS* 13 261:18 points to [*āl*]*Ṣilliyawe* as a place to which barley possibly was sent by a *ḫalṣuḫlu*.

[42]*HSS* 9 1:7-8.

with respect to *any* GN.[43] Finally, as the foregoing remarks imply, not once do the terms *ḫalṣuḫlu* and *ḫalṣu* ever appear in the same text, much less the same context.[44]

There is no evidence at present to support the thesis that the Nuzi *ḫalṣuḫlu* was a major official, linked with the governance of the *ḫalṣu*. It is questionable if the Nuzi *ḫalṣu* was indeed anything governable. Thus, reconstructions of the Nuzi social or economic order based on either of these theses should, in light of the extant evidence, be modified accordingly.[45]

Nuzi is not the only site where *ḫalṣuḫlu*'s are mentioned. Alalaḫ, Aššur, and Amarna have all yielded texts mentioning this official.[46] However, Middle Assyrian Tell Billa, especially, attests repeatedly to the *ḫalṣuḫlu* and even connects this official with an area of jurisdiction called *ḫalṣu*.[47] Billa's *ḫalṣuḫlu*, therefore, may well be something akin to a "district commander." The divergence between that usage and Nuzi's apparently far more modest one is a problem whose solution remains to be worked out.[48]

[43]In the case of Sauš-satti, he is said, I believe, merely to hail from the town of Atilu, otherwise unattested.

[44]This situation contrasts with that attested in the Billa texts. See below, n. 47.

[45]Cf. the studies cited above, n. 7. In addition, Julius Lewy, "Ḫābīru and Hebrews," *HUCA*, 14 (1939), 601, asserts that the king of Mittanni himself appointed Teḫip-tilla *ḫalṣuḫlu*, "district officer" and "entrusted [him] with the administration and supervision of vast royal feudal estates."

One is compelled, once again, to reject the thesis that Teḫip-tilla, as a *ḫalṣuḫlu*, was a governor or other high official. The "*ḫalṣuḫlu*" texts and other Teḫip-tilla texts as well fail to support this assertion.

[46]For these references and some of those from Billa, see *CAD*, Ḫ, p. 57b. To the Billa texts there listed may be added Nos. 11:4, 16:6; 17:4; 25:3; 29:6; 31:3; 32:3; 37:5?

[47]Finkelstein, *JCS*, 7 (1953), 150, No. 6:7-8: ᴸᵁ́*ḫassuḫli ša ḫalṣi āl Bīt-Zamani*. A *ḫalṣu* URU *Ekallātu* is also attested (No. 48:2), the only other mention of a *ḫalṣu* in the Billa texts. There, there is no connection with *ḫalṣuḫlu*.

Where elsewhere identified with a toponym, the Billa *ḫalṣuḫlu* appears in the following combination: ᴸᵁ́*ḫassuḫli ša āl Šibanibe* (No. 11:4-5. Cf. Nos. 17:4-5; 25:3 [both without *ša*]). The association at Billa of *ḫalṣuḫlu* with *ḫalṣu*, on the one hand, and the *ḫalṣuḫlu* with *ālu*, on the other, strongly suggests that here, unlike Nuzi, a town could itself constitute a *ḫalṣu*. We have already seen above that, at Nuzi, there appears to be a certain amount of confusion between *ḫalṣi* GN and *āl* GN. That confusion would be but partially eliminated were we to posit a Billa-like town-*ḫalṣu* there. (The Azuḫinni conundrum, for example, still resists resolution: this town is part of the *ḫalṣi āl Azuḫinni* and of the *ḫalṣi pakkante*; the mention in *HSS* 14 103 of *ḫalṣi āl Azuḫinni* and *āl Azuḫinni* as the same thing remains striking.) Furthermore, the denial of a Nuzi administrative district called *ḫalṣu* rests, not only on the *ḫalṣu*/*ālu* confusion but on other points as well. Finally, as already stated, Nuzi contrasts with Billa in failing to link *ḫalṣuḫlu* with *ḫalṣu* at all.

[48]The dilemma was clearly recognized by Finkelstein, *JCS*, 7 (1953), 116, n. 30.

Thus, the limited data at hand point to one meaning of *ḫalṣuḫlu* at Nuzi and at least one other meaning elsewhere. We have here, then, yet another, albeit small, example of the complexities of cultural interaction in the Near Eastern Late Bronze Age.

Beiträge zum ḫurro-akkadischen Lexikon II

Walter Mayer
Münster

Das Morphem *-tḫu*

In den ḫurro-akkadischen Texten von Alalaḫ, Nuzi and Ugarit aus der zweiten Hälfte des 2. Jahrtausends v. Chr. sind viele Appellativa eindeutig ḫurrischen Ursprunges zu belegen. Einige der auch über den engeren Bereich der Nuzi-Texte hinaus produktiven ḫurrischen Wortbildungs-suffixe, die sich in diesen Appellativa nachweisen lassen, sollen in der vorliegenden und in weiteren Arbeiten näher untersucht werden.

Zu den von I. M. Djakonov[1] in "Hurrisch und Urartäisch" S. 70 aufgeführten wortbildenden Suffixen gehört das in seiner Bedeutung unklare *-tḫi* — in der akkadisierten Form *-tḫu.* Im folgenden soll dieses Morphem zunächst dokumentiert werden. Gleichzeitig sollen ausgehend vom jeweiligen Kontext Deutungen oder zumindest Eingrenzungen der Bedeutung versucht werden. Nicht mit in die Untersuchung einbezogen werden Zeugnisse aus den Boğazköy-Texten und dem Mitanni-Brief[2] wie *ḫašulatḫi*, *paššitḫi* "Gesandter" und *zalmatḫi.*[3] Im akkadischen Lexikon lassen sich bisher insgesamt zwölf Nomina mit dem Suffix *-tḫu* nachweisen.

1. *araratḫu*[4]

^{giš}*a-ra-rat-ḫu* = ŠU MSL 5, 113, 249.

Beide Wörterbücher deuten dieses Wort, das bisher nur in Hh III belegt ist, übereinstimmend als "ein Baum." Eine nähere Bestimmung dieses Baumes ist derzeit nicht möglich. Denkbar wäre vielleicht eine Verbindung von *-tḫu* mit dem ebenfalls nicht näher zu bestimmenden Pflanzennamen *ararû* I, *arāru* III.[5]

[1] I. M. Djakonov, Hurrisch und Urartäisch (= Münchener Studien zur Sprachwissenschaft, Beiheft 6, Neue Folge), München, 1971; im folgenden abgekürzt: HuU.

[2] Vgl. dazu E. Laroche, Glossaire de la langue Hourrite, RHA 34/5 (1976/7).

[3] Zu *ḫašulatḫi* s. RHA 34 (1976) 97; *paššitḫi* s. RHA 37 (1977) 198; *zalmatḫi* s. ebd. 301.

[4] AHw. 65a; CAD A_2 232b.

[5] AHw. 66a; CAD A_2 234a.

2. *arathu*[6]

^{giš}*a-rat-hu* = ŠU MSL 5, 113, 248.

Auch hier handelt es sich um einen nicht näher bestimmbaren Baum, der bisher ebenfalls nur in Hh III bezeugt ist. Sollte man an eine Verbindung des Suffixes *-thu* mit *aru*(*m*) I, *eru*(*m*), das auch "Palmwedel" bedeuten kann,[7] denken dürfen, so könnte *arathu* eine hurrische Bezeichnung für eine Palmenart sein.

3. *aruthu*[8]

⌊*x*⌋ *ka-nu-nu* AN.BAR *né-se-pé* AN.BAR *na-as-re* AN.BAR *a-ru-ut-he* AN.BAR É *bu-ṣi-ni* AN.BAR Sg. 8, 365.
6-*šú a-ru-ut-he* AN.BAR CTN 2, 155 IV 17.
1 *a-ru-ut-he* AN.BAR *né-se-pé* AN.BAR Iraq 23 (1961) 33b 40.

Alle Belege, aus denen deutlich hervorgeht, dass *aruthu* ein Gerät aus Eisen bezeichnet, stammen aus neuassyrischen Texten. In Sg. 8, 365 ist die Gesamtzahl der Geräte nicht erhalten. Es werden neben Leuchter (É *buṣīni*) Ofen (*kanūnu*), Kratzer (*nēsepu*) und (Schür-)Haken (*nasru*) aufgezählt. Folglich gehört *aruthu* zu den für den Betrieb eines Ofens nötigen Geräten. Dies wird durch den Inventartext Iraq 23 (1961) 33b 40 bestätigt, wo *aruthu* neben *nēsepu* "Kratzer" steht. Auch in dem Inventar CTN 2, 155 IV 17 erscheint *aruthu* zwischen Eisengeräten, die wohl wenigstens teilweise zum Umgang mit Feuer benötigt wurden. Der Kontext von Sg. 8, 365 legt die Vermutung nahe, dass *aruthu* eine Bezeichnung für eine Schaufel ist, da dieses Gerät, das auf jeden Fall zum Zubehör eines Ofens gehört,[9] als einziges nicht genannt wird. Denkbar ist m. E eine Ableitung des Wortes von der hurrisch-urartäischen Wurzel *ar*(*u*)-"geben"[10] — *aruthu* wäre dann wohl ein "Gerät zum Geben (der Holzkohle)."

4. *haburathu*[11]

^{giš}*ha-bu-rat-hu* = [ŠU] MSL 5, 114, 263.

Das bisher nur in Hh III belegte Wort wird von beiden Wörterbüchern als ein nicht näher zu bestimmender Baum gedeutet.

[6] AHw. 66a; CAD A_2 238b.
[7] AHw. 71b; CAD A_2 311f.
[8] AHw. 72b; CAD A_2 324a; vgl. auch AHw. 1437a s.v. *uruthu*.
[9] Vgl. auch mA *missipu* in AfO 18 (1957/8) 308, 23; AHw. 678a und CAD M_2 235b.
[10] RHA 34 (1976) 52/3.
[11] AHw. 306b; CAD H 22a.

5. *kannulatḫu*[12]

ŠU.NIGÍN 90 ^{giš}BANŠUR.MEŠ 18 ^{giš}*ka*$_4$*-an-nu-la-at-ḫu-ú* 4 *ú-ru-ú ša* GIŠ [......] HSS 14, 247, 92 (L 27).
il-te-nu-tu$_4$ *ka*$_4$*-an-nu-la-at-ḫu ša* GIŠ ..... HSS 15, 130, 17 (L 27).
2 *ta-pa-lu ka*$_4$*-an-nu-la-at-ḫu ša* GIŠ ebd. 46.
3 *ka*$_4$*-an-nu-la-at-ḫu ša* GIŠ ..... ebd. 47.
10 *ka*$_4$*-an-nu-la-at-ḫu ša* ZA[BAR] HSS 15, 134, 55 (M 79).

In den drei genannten Texten werden in erster Linie Hausgeräte aufgeführt. Somit darf wohl auch *kannulatḫu* mit einiger Berechtigung als Hausgerät, das überwiegend aus Holz aber auch aus Bronze gefertigt war, gedeutet werden.

HSS 14, 247, 92 steht am Ende eines Abschnittes, in dem Möbel wie Tische, Stühle, Schemel und dergleichen aufgezählt werden. Es könnte daher die Vermutung naheliegen, dass *kannulatḫu* eine Sammelbezeichnung für die neben den Tischen genannten Möbel ist. Da sich aber die in der Aufzählung genannten Zahlen mit denen von Z. 92 in keiner Weise in Übereinstimmung bringen lassen, wird diese Vermutung unwahrscheinlich. ŠU.NIGÍN 90 ^{giš}BANŠUR.MEŠ soll wohl besagen, dass insgesamt 90 weitere, verschiedene und nicht näher beschriebene Tische als Bestandteil der Aufzählung hinzukommen. Mit *kannulatḫu* wird die Liste dann fortgesetzt. Das darauf folgende *urû* wird als Schüssel gedeutet.[13]

Der fragmentarische Erhaltungszustand von HSS 15, 134 lässt kaum Rückschlüsse aus dem Kontext von Z. 55 zu. Etwas ergiebiger ist in dieser Beziehung HSS 15, 130. Hier erscheint *kannulatḫu* neben Schalen (*agannu* Z. 44; *pursītu* Z. 47) und Gefässen (*matqānu* Z. 15/6). Vielleicht darf man daraus folgern, dass *kannulatḫu* die Bezeichnung für ein Gefäss oder einen Behälter aus Holz oder Bronze ist. Dieses Gefäss konnte anscheinend auch als Set (*iltenūtu* HSS 15, 130, 7) oder paarweise (*tapālu* ebd. Z. 46) verwendet verwendet werden.

6. *kas/zulatḫu*[14]

2 ka$_4$*-zu-la-at-ḫu ša* ZABAR HSS 14, 263(=608), 3 (M 79).

Dieses Wort ist bisher nur einmal in einer Liste von zusammen 22 Bronze- und Kupfergeräten aus dem Besitz des Palastes belegt. Es erscheint nach Aufzählung von insgesamt vier mit Gazellen und Lämmern dekorierten Kesseln (*ruqqu*). Es folgen danach 8 *apellu*[15] aus Bronze, 1 Kassette (*quppu*) aus

[12]AHw. 438b; CAD K 157b.
[13]AHw. 1435b f.
[14]AHw. 456a; CAD K 311a; RHA 34 (1976) 140.
[15]AHw. 57a; CAD A_2 169a.

Kupfer, 1 Waschschale und 2 Becher aus Bronze, sowie 2 Pflöcke (*sikkatu*) aus Kupfer. Die Liste enthält also in erster Linie Behältnisse, die offensichtlich nach ihrer Grösse angeordnet sind. Aufgrund der Position innerhalb der Aufzählung darf man wohl annehmen, das *kas/zulatḫu* ein grösseres Bronzegefäss bezeichnet. Eine Verbindung mit akk. *kāsu* "Becher" wäre wohl möglich, sofern man das Element *-l-* zwischen der Wurzel und dem Suffix *-tḫu* als Komparativsuffix *-ol-* deutet.[16]

7. *niranitḫu*[17]

HSS 15, 131 (Palast):

8) 1 ^{gi}[^{š}G]U.ZA *ša* ^{giš}TÚG.[MEŠ *n*]*i-ra-ni-it-ḫu i'-lu ù*° [..........]
9) *š*[*a n*]*i-ra-ni-it-ḫé-e* GUŠKIN *uḫ-ḫu-zu ù* [..........]
10) *š*[*a k*]*i-na-aḫ-ḫe ù* ....
14) [1 ^{gi}]^{š}GU.ZA *ša* ^{giš}TÚG.MEŠ *n*[*i-r*]*a-ni-it-ḫu i'-l*[*u ù* ....]
15) [*ša*] *ta-ki-il-ti* ....
20) [1 ^{giš}GU].ZA *ša* ^{giš}TÚG.MEŠ *ša e-be-ri ni-ra-n*[*i-it-ḫu* ....]
21) [........]*-šu ša ta-ki*° *-il-ti* ....

HSS 15, 134 (M 79):

6) [..........] *ra-ma-ni-šu-nu ša* ^{giš}*ni-ra-ni-it-ḫé* [............]
11) [..........] *i'-lu* SAG-*sú-nu ša* ^{giš}*ni-ra-ni-*[*it*]*-ḫé* [..........]

HSS 15, 168 D:

5) [.......... *ni-r*]*a-ni-it-ḫu-šu* ..[..........]
6) [...............] *ša t*[*a-b*]*ar-ri*
7) [....... *ni-ra-n*]*i-it-ḫu i*['*-l*]*u ra-*[..........]

HSS 15, 316 R:

2) [1 ^{giš}GU.ZA] *ša* ^{giš}TÚG *ni-ra-*[*ni-it-ḫu* .....]
6) 1 ^{giš}GU.ZA *ša* ^{giš}*ša-a*[*k-ku-ul-li*(?) ....]
7) *ni-ra-ni-it-ḫu-šua-*[.......................]

Die Belege lassen trotz ihrer teilweise sehr fragmentarischen Erhaltung deutlich erkennen, dass *niranitḫu* ein Teil eines kostbaren Stuhles oder Sessels ist. Es wird angebunden (*iʾlu*: HSS 15, 131, 8.14; 168 D, 7); Teile des *niranitḫu*—wohl Kanten oder die Oberfläche—können mit Gold beschlagen sein (HSS 15, 131, 9). Auffallend ist, dass blauer (*takiltu*) und roter (*kinaḫḫu*) Purpur, sowie rote Wolle (*tabarru*) in Verbindung mit dem *niranitḫu* genannt werden. Diese Verbindung von Determinativ GIŠ (HSS 15, 134, 6.11), Goldbeschlägen (HSS 15, 131, 9) und Applikationen mit Purpurwolle lässt auf

[16]HuU 65.
[17]AHw. 793b, RHA 35 (1977) 184.

einen gepolsterten Teil des Stuhles schliessen; *niranitḫu* könnte also die Bezeichnung für das Sitz-oder Rückenpolster sein.

8. *šuanatḫu*[18]

PN *šu-a-na-at-ḫu* HSS 19, 9, 16 (P 357); LDN 130 b 15; JEN 243, 27.
PN LÚ *šu-a-na-at-ḫu* JEN 462, 21.
[*x*+]3 *ḫul-la-an-nu-ú ba-aš-lu-tu*₄ *ša* LÚ.MEŠ *šu-a-na-at-ḫé-e* HSS 14, 247, 41 (L 27).
2 Widder ..... *a-na* ᵐ*Ul-lu-ia šu-a-na-at-ḫe* / *at-ta-din ù a-na* É.GAL.LIM *it-ta-bal-šu* AASOR 16, 7, 9-10 (C 2/L 2).

Aus dēn Belegen wird deutlich, dass *šuanatḫu* eine Berufsbezeichnung ist. Viermal erscheint der *šuanatḫu* als Zeuge — seine Tätigkeit lässt sich jedoch aus diesen Stellen nicht ermitteln. Der Inventartext HSS 14, 247 führt Kleider, Geräte und Möbel für die königlichen Bankette auf. Da hierbei speziell gefärbte Decken für die *šuanatḫu*-Leute genannt werden, ist es sehr wahrscheinlich, dass der *šuanatḫu* ein fest Bediensteter des Palastes ist. Dies wird auch durch AASOR 16, 7, 9-10 bestätigt.

Man kann *šuanatḫu* in eine Wurzel *šua-*, das in seiner Bedeutung ungeklärte Suffix *-(a)na-*[19] und das Suffix *-tḫu* zerlegen. *Šua-* könnte das Partizip einer bisher im Ḫurrischen nicht belegten Verbalwurzel **šu-* sein. Ein Verbum *šu-* ist aber urartäisch bezeugt mit den Bedeutungen "einrichten, ordnen u.ä."[20] und "voll aufschütten(?)."[21] Sollte zwischen dem ḫurro-akkadischen Wort und der bisher nur urartäisch bezeugten Verbalwurzel *šu-* ein Zusammenhang bestehen, so könnte der *šuanatḫu* eine Tätigkeit als "Diener" oder "Schenk" bei königlichen Festmählern ausgeübt haben.

9. *šumkalatḫu*[22]

10 *šu-um-ka*₄-[*la*(?)]-*at-ḫu ša* ZABAR HSS 15, 130, 37 (L 27).

Die bisher nur einmal bezeugte Bezeichnung für einen Bronzegegenstand erscheint in einem grossen Inventarverzeichnis von Möbeln und Hausgeräten zwischen *ḫidduḫḫu* "Teil des Schlosses?"[23] und *kāsu* "Becher."

[18]AHw. 1255b; RHA 35 (1977) 238.
[19]HuU 66.
[20]I. I. Meščaninov, Annotirovannyj slovar' urartskogo (biajnskogo) jazyka, Leningrad 1978, 283; G. A. Melikišvili, Urartskie klinobraznye nadpisi, Moskau 1960, 407a.
[21]I. M. Djakonov, Urartskie pis'ma i dokumenty, Leningrad 1963, 91a.
[22]AHw. 1272a, RHA 35 (1977) 244.
[23]AHw. 320a s.v. *ḫandūḫu*, *ḫin/dduḫḫu*; CAD Ḫ 183a.

10. *šuraṭḫu*[24]

^{giš}*šu-rat-ḫu* = ŠU   MSL 5, 113, 247.
^{giš}*dul-bu* ^{giš}*su-rat-ḫu bal-ti* É.GAL.LIM-[*šu* ....] *ki-ma* ^{giš}TIR UGU *ta-mer-ti-šú ta-ra-nu ú-šá-áš-ši* Sg. 8, 206.
šu-ra-at-ḫu   CT 51, 12, 12; HSS 13, 34, 1 (L 44); 15, 220, 27.34 (L 27);
221, 7 (R 76); JEN 314, 7.
šu-ra-at-ḫi   JEN 108, 13.
šu-ra-at-ḫa   HSS 15, 220, 3.9.15.22 (L 27).

In MSL 5, 113, 247 und Sg. 8, 206 bezeichnet ^{giš}*šuraṭḫu* eindeutig eine Baumart. In allen anderen Fällen ist *šuraṭḫu* die Bezeichnung einer Farbe—genauer: der mit einen aus diesem Baum gewonnenen Farbstoff gefärbten Wolle. Diese gefärbte Wolle wird zusammen mit rotem und blauen Purpur (*kinaḫḫu* — *takiltu*), roter (*tabarru*) und *tamkarḫu*-farbener Wolle für Verzierungen an Gewändern (*kusītu*), Lendenschurzen (*ša-burki*) und Decken (*ḫullannu*; *nušābu*), für Teppiche (*mardatu*) und Borten (*birmu*) verwendet.[25] In CT 51, 12, 13 wird die Qualität der *šuraṭḫu*-farbenen Wolle als SIG$_5$-*qú nam-ru* "gut (und) leuchtend" bezeichnet.
Sg. 8, 206 zeigt m. E. deutlich, dass ^{giš}*šuraṭḫū* grosse Bäume sein müssen, da sie neben Platanen (*dulbū*), die 30-40 m hoch werden können, genannt werden. Unter den zahlreichen Pflanzen aus denen Farben gewonnen werden können, finden sich nur zwei grosse Bäume. Es sind dies der Walnussbaum und die Galleiche (*quercus infectoria*). Aus junger Nussbaumrinde, den grünen Schalen und Blättern können braune Farbtöne gewonnen werden. Die Gallen der in Syrien und Kleinasien beheimateten Galleiche liefern ebenfalls Brauntöne.[26] Wenngleich sich nicht entscheiden lässt, ob ^{giš}*šuraṭḫu* Walnuss oder Galleiche bedeutet, so lässt sich doch mit einiger Bestimmtheit feststellen, dass *šuraṭḫu* die Bezeichnung für braun gefärbte Wolle ist.

11. *takulatḫu*[27]

HSS 13, 174 (R 76):
    8) 1 *ta-ku-la-at-ḫu ša* ZABAR
HSS 13, 435 (R 81):
    10) 7 ^{giš}*ta-ku-la-at-ḫ*[*u* ....]
    40) 13[+*x* ^{g}]^{iš}*pí-it-nu la-*[*b*]*e-r*[*u*] 2 *ta-ku-la-at-ḫ*[*u* .....]
    41) 10[+*x*] *ta-ku-la-at-ḫé* ^{giš}[TÚG *š*]*a* SAG-*sú*(?)-*nu* [.....]
    48) 3 *tá-ku-la-at-ḫu š*[*a*] URUDU *ša i-ga$_5$-ri* [..........]
    52) [*x*] *t*[*a-ku-la-at-ḫu ša* ..... *ša*] *i-ga$_5$-ri* [..........]

[24]AHw. 1283a.
[25]Vgl. Verf., UF 9 (1977) 178ff.
[26]Vgl. K. Zipper, Orientteppiche—Das Lexikon, Braunschweig 1970, 24a f.
[27]AHw. 1309a.

HSS 13, 470 (A 23):
5) 1-*en ta-ku-la-at-ḫu*
HSS 14, 235(=529) (R 76):
12) 3 *ta-ku-la-at-ḫu ša* [.....]
23) 1 ^{giš}*ta-ku-la-at-ḫu*
HSS 14, 245(=562) (R 76):
21) 4 ^{giš}*ta-ku-la-at-ḫu ša* ^{giš}[.....]
HSS 14, 247 (L 27):
70) 7 *ta-ku-la-at-ḫu-ú* ZABAR 8 *ta-ku-*[*la*]*-at-ḫu-ú* ZABAR *š*[*a i*]*-ga*$_5$*-ri*
72) 3 *dú-dú-ú*^{MEŠ} 3 *ta-ku-la-at-ḫu-ú* URUDU *ù* 3 KI.MIN *ša* URUDU *ša i-ga*$_5$*-ri*
97) .... 9 ^{giš}*ta-ku-la-at-ḫu-ú ša* [..........]
98) [*x*] *ta-ku-la-at-ḫu-ú ša i-ga*$_5$*-ri* 13 *ta-ku-la-at-ḫu-*[*ú* ....]
HSS 15, 81 (A 26):
7) 3 *ta-ku-la-at-ḫu ša* ZABAR
HSS 15, 129 (L 27):
2) 4 *ta-ku-la-at-ḫu-ú ša i-ga*$_5$*-ri*
3) *ša* ZABAR *ša ḫa-al-qú*
24) 3 ^{giš}*ta-ku-la-at-ḫu-ú*^{meš}
HSS 15, 130 (L 27):
21) 2[+*x* ^{gi}]^{š}BANŠUR *ša* TUR.TUR 9 ^{giš}*ta-ku-la-at-ḫu ša a-šu-ḫe*
22) 9 ^{giš}*ta-ku-la-at-ḫu ku-lu-lu*(!)*-tù*
33) 5 ^{giš}*ta-ku-la-at-ḫu ša* ^{giš}TÚ[G]
34) *ša* KÙ.BABBAR *ù* SAG(?)*-sú-nu ša* KÙ.BABBAR .....
39) 2 *ta-pa-lu sí-sí-nu ša* KÙ.BABBAR 7 *ta-ku-la-at-ḫu ša* ZABAR
40) 4 *ta-ku-la-at-ḫu ša i-ga*$_5$*-ri* 2 *i-ri-pu ša* ZABAR
41) 2 *uš-pu ša* Ì(!) 4 *ku-ku-bu ša* ZABAR
42) 3 *ta-ku-la-at-ḫu* ≪URUDU≫ *ša* URUDU
44) 1 *a-ga-a-nu ša* ZABAR 3 *ta-ku-la-at-ḫu*
48) 6 *ta-ku-la-at-ḫu ša ta-ni-we ša* GIŠ
61) .... 5 *ta-ku-la-at-ḫu ša* URUDU
HSS 15, 132 (L 27):
27) 4 *ta-ku-la-at-ḫu ša* KÙ.BABBAR
30) 7 *ta-ku-la-at-ḫu ša* ZABAR
31) 2 *ta-ku-la-at-ḫu ša* URUDU
32) 1 *ta-ku-la-at-ḫu š*[*a* ...]*-le-e*
34) 8 *ta-ku-la-at-ḫu ša* ZABAR
35) *ša i-ga*$_5$*-ri*
HSS 15, 154 (R 81):
5) 3 *ta-ku-la-a*[*t-ḫu ša* .....]
HSS 15, 156 (L 27)
5) 4 *ta-ku-la-at-ḫu ša* URU[DU]
HSS 15, 302:
5) [*x ta-ku*]*-la-at-ḫu ša* URUDU

TCL 9, 1:

17) 8 *ta-ku-la-at-ḫu ša* ZABAR
22) 2 *ta-ku-la-at-ḫu ša* [*š*]*u*(?)-*uḫ*-[.....]
23) 1 ^{giš}*ta-ku-la-at-ḫu ša sí-i-ḫu*

Alle Belege für *takulatḫu* erscheinen in Texten, in denen Hausgeräte aufgezählt werden. Deutlich zu unterscheiden sind ein "gewöhnliches" *takulatḫu* und eines "für die Mauer (*ša igāri*)." Daneben kommen einige weitere zumeist unklare Zweck- oder Materialangaben vor: *ša ta-ni-we* (HSS 15, 130, 48), *ša* [*š*]*u*(?)-*uḫ*-[.....] (TCL 9, 1, 22), *ša sí-i-ḫu* "für Wermut(?)"[28] (ebd. 23) und *š*[*a* ...]-*le-e* (HSS 15, 132, 32). Als Materialien, aus denen das *takulatḫu* gefertigt werden kann, erscheinen Kupfer, Bronze, Silber und Holz, wobei Föhrenholz (*ša a-šu-ḫe* HSS 15, 130, 21) und Buchsbaumholz (*ša* ^{giš}TÚ[G] ebd. 33) ausdrücklich genannt werden. Sofern beim *takulatḫu ša igāri* das Material angegeben wird, handelt es sich immer um Kupfer oder Bronze.

In einigen der oben genannten Texte — z. B. HSS 14, 235; 245; 247; 15, 130 — erscheint *takulatḫu* zwischen oder zumindest neben Gefässen, Behältern oder Kästen. Es ist daher wohl durchaus möglich, dass mit *takulatḫu* ein Behälter bezeichnet wird, wenngleich Art und Grösse sich trotz der guten Bezeugung nicht näher bestimmen lassen.

12. *urutḫu*[29]

3 *ú-ru*(?)-*ut-ḫé* ZABAR Al.T. 400, 1.
2-*šu ú-ru-ut-ḫu* KAJ 303, 8.
5 *ú-ru-ut-ḫu* ZABAR KI.LAL 6 *me-at* PRU 3, 186, 36.

Die drei Belege zeigen, dass *urutḫu* ein aus Bronze hergestelltes Hausgerät ist.[30] Somit entfällt wohl die Ableitung von sum. u r u d u und damit auch die Bedeutung "Kupfer".[31] In Al.T. 400, 2 folgt ein Bronzegefäss. In dem Inventartext RS 16.146+161 (PRU 3, 182-86) mit der "Aussteurer" der Königin ^{f}*Aḫāt-milki* erscheint *urutḫu* am Ende einer Reihe von Bronzegefässen. Das Gewicht des einzelnen Stückes hätte nach diesem Text 120 Sekel (~1 kg) betragen. Auch in KAJ 303 steht *urutḫu* zwischen verschiedenen Gefässen und Schüsseln aus Bronze. Somit ist wohl aufgrund des Kontextes auch *urutḫu* in die Kategorie der Bronzegefässe einzuordnen.

Der Versuch die Nominalkomponenten der besprochenen Wörter näher zu bestimmen gestaltet sich überaus schwierig. Das Morphem -*tḫu* gehört nach

[28] AHw. 1040b.

[29] AHw. 1437a; RHA 35 (1977) 286. Ein weiterer mA Beleg wurde mir erst nach Abschluss des Manuskriptes zugänglich: Assur 2 (1979) 100, 7′-8′.

[30] Dies gilt auch für KAJ 303. Die Zusammenfassung in Z. 11 lautet [Z]ABAR *an-nu-tu*$_4$ . . . .

[31] So HuU 79 und RHA 35 (1977) 286f.

I. M. Djakonow zu den Wortbildungssuffixen der zweiten Gruppe.[32] Bei *ara-tḫu, arara-tḫu, aru-tḫu, ḫabura-tḫu, šura-tḫu* und *uru-tḫu* — also bei genau der Hälfte der oben besprochenen Wörter — tritt *-tḫu* offensichtlich direkt an die Wurzel. Bei *kannu-la-tḫu, kas/zu-la-tḫu, šumka-la-tḫu* und *taku-la-tḫu* erscheint zwischen der Wurzel und dem Suffix *-tḫu* wohl ein in seiner Bedeutung nicht näher zu bestimmendes Wortbildungssuffix der ersten Gruppe.[33] In einigen Fällen wird es sich dabei wohl um das Komparativsuffix *-ol-*[34] handeln, aber auch *-ala-*[35] scheint möglich zu sein. Im Falle von *nira-ni-tḫu* und von *šua-na-tḫu* scheint die Wurzel um das ebenfalls noch ungedeutete Suffix der ersten Gruppe *-(a)na/e-*[36] erweitert zu sein. Es liegt nahe, für *kannulatḫu* und *kas/zulatḫu* akkadische Wurzeln anzunehmen: *kannu* "ein grosses Gefäss"[37] und *kāsu* "Becher"[38] — eindeutig beweisen lässt sich dies nicht. Die übrigen Nominalkomponenten sind wohl ḫurrischen Ursprungs—sicherlich jedoch nicht akkadisch.

Sieben der behandelten Nomina sind Gegenstandsbezeichnungen für Hausgeräte—überwiegend aus Metall; vier sind Baumnamen und eines bezeichnet einen Beruf. Diese Analyse der Bedeutungsspäre ergibt für den Gebrauch des Morphems *-tḫu* einen reichlich heterogenen Befund.

Von den zwölf besprochenen Wörtern sind sieben in den Nuzi-Texten belegt, eines (*urutḫu*) in Alalaḫ, Ugarit und mittelassyrisch, zwei (*arutḫu, šuratḫu*) neuassyrisch und drei (*aratḫu, araratḫu, ḫaburatḫu*) aus schliesslich in Hh.

So wird nicht zuletzt auch durch die Nomina mit dem Wortbildungssuffix *-tḫu* das Bild von der kulturellen Bedeutung der Ḫurriter als Vermittler weiter ergänzt.

[32] HuU 68ff.
[33] HuU 65ff.
[34] HuU 65.
[35] HuU 66.
[36] HuU 66.
[37] AHw. 437bf.; CAD K 154ff.
[38] AHw. 454bf.; CAD K 253bff.

Evidence for Herdsmen and Animal Husbandry in the Nuzi Documents

Martha A. Morrison
Brandeis University

Professor Ernest R. Lacheman's dedication to the publication of the tablets from Nuzi has made available a wealth of material that illustrates the social and economic structure of that mid-Second Millennium community. Of particular interest are the numerous documents relating to livestock and herding. Although many genres are represented among these documents, the vast majority are administrative texts, consignment texts and *muddû* statements. Individually many of these texts might be called "lowly,"[1] but when studied as a corpus, they provide copious documentation of the activities of the herdsmen, the composition of the flocks and herds, and the management of livestock at a settled agricultural community.[2] The following study of these issues is presented respectfully to a beloved teacher by one of his deeply grateful students.*

A. The Herdsmen

The names of over ninety herdsmen who were active at Nuzi can be recovered from the livestock texts and other sources.[3] A few are designated by

* I would like to express my appreciation to Mrs. Sylvia J. Littlefield of Milestone Farm, Newbury, Massachusetts, for sharing her knowledge of livestock with me. Her assistance has, in large part, made this study possible. I would also like to thank Mr. Joel L. Uchenick of Harbridge House, Boston, Massachusetts, for his important suggestions relating to the statistical portions of this study and Professors Tsvi Abusch and Eliezer Oren for their helpful comments and observations.

[1]See Prof. Lacheman's modest remarks in *HSS* 16, p. v.

[2]It should be noted that a substantial portion of the documents derive from the archives of Šilwa-tešub *mār šarri* and of the palace. Thus, the herding practices that they describe are those of the large-scale livestock operations at Nuzi. However, the social, legal, and economic matters that the herding documents elucidate are significant for the broader range of participants in livestock activities and for the community at large.

[3]See Appendix III for the names of the herdsmen at Nuzi. Previous works on this topic include A. Leo Oppenheim, "Métiers et Professions a Nuzi," *RÉS* 1939, 2ff. and

an occupational title: ^{LÚ}SIPA,[4] ^{LÚ}SIPA.UDU^{MEŠ},[5] ^{LÚ}SIPA.GU$_4$^{MEŠ},[6] ^{LÚ}*kuzallu*,[7] or ^{LÚ}*utullu*.[8] Such designations are employed primarily in legal, military and other texts in which the individual's profession is significant but not apparent through context.[9] Most of the herdsmen, however, are known through their regular appearance in the administrative texts, consignment texts and *muddû* statements in which such titles are hardly ever employed. Through their patronymics and seals such herdsmen can be located outside these texts.[10]

1. *The Herdsmen and the Community*

Some of the herdsmen who appear in the Nuzi texts or worked for Nuzi livestock owners appear to have lived elsewhere. For instance, Kelke *mār* Ḫulukka is described as one of 16 LÚ^{MEŠ} *an-nu-tu*$_4$ *ša* ^{URU}*zi-iz-za*,[11] and Tae *mār* Kawinni and Akip-tilla *mār* Eḫel-tešub may have come from Tašeni and

---

W. Mayer, *Nuzi Studien I: Die Archive des Palastes und die Prosopographie der Berufe*, *AOAT* 205/1 (1978), 190-96.

[4]SIPA = *re*ʾ*u* (*AHw* 977). In the plural $^{\text{LÚ.MEŠ}}$SIPA-*ya-ti* (*HSS* 13 451:12 and 14 637:36) and ^{LÚ}SIPA.MEŠ-*ti* (*HSS* 13 339:23) along with $^{\text{LÚ.MEŠ}}$SIPA (*HSS* 16 282:7).

[5]Normally, ^{LÚ}SIPA, alone, serves to designate the shepherd. Other herdsmen are identified by the names of the animals that they tend.

[6]The second most common herdsman's designation, the oxherd.

[7]Apparently, a chief shepherd. *CAD* K 613 s.v.

[8]*AHw* 1445 s.v., "Oberhirt," "nicht rēʾi alpī." This view may be supported if the Niḫriya involved with the *mullû ša* $^{\text{LÚ.MEŠ}}$SIPA (*HSS* 16 314) is the Niḫriya who is identified elsewhere as ^{LÚ}*utullu* (*HSS* 15 12 and 18).

[9]Bēliya *mār* Kelum-atal ^{LÚ}*utullu* in the contract *HSS* 16 452; Šukr-apu ^{LÚ}SIPA in the military listing *RA* 28 (1931), Text 4; Taya *mār* Ward-aḫḫēšu SIPA.GU$_4$ in the law suit *JEN* 341; Teḫiya ^{LÚ}SIPA in the grain ration text *HSS* 13 451; Ḫanaya *mār* Arip-apu ^{LÚ}*kuzallu* as a witness in *JEN* 196, *inter alia*.

[10]Comparison of seal impressions to identify herdsmen can be most helpful. However, this technique must be approached with care because the herdsmen frequently use more than one seal during their careers. Akip-tilla *mār* Eḫel-tesup uses the same seal on *HSS* 14 567 and 631 but a different one on *HSS* 16 280; Kelke *mār* Ḫulukka uses different seals on *HSS* 14 614 and 16 298; the seals of Kuppatiya *mār* Ariḫ-ḫamanna on *HSS* 13 280 and 16 258 are different; Pilmašše *mār* Ḫutip-tilla uses the same seal on *HSS* 13 437 and 14 504, a different one on 14 506 and 16 290 and yet another on 14 526. In the case of Ḫanirra *mār* Šatu-kewi his seal on *HSS* 13 210 is different from the one that appears on *HSS* 9 59 and 16 246. The second seal may be that of his father in that the seal on *HSS* 16 246 is called the seal of Šatu-kewi. In *HSS* 9 59 this same seal is attributed to Ḫanirra but *za*(!)-*tù-uḫ-li* Šatu-kewi is written below Ḫanirra's name. It is possible that inexpensive materials that wore out easily were used for these herdsmen's seals and they had to be replaced. Thus, different seal impressions need not represent different people. Instead, the same seal impression would identify the same person or a family connection.

[11]*HSS* 13 363:68, 72. Kelke *mār* Ḫulukka was one of Šilwa-tešub's herdsmen.

Zuia, respectively.[12] Reference is made to three herdsmen of ᵁᴿᵁKabla and one of ᵁᴿᵁPaqqanupḫe.[13] In addition, the nature of the herding profession required that the herdsmen's primary sphere of operation be outside urban areas.[14] Nonetheless, a substantial amount of information concerning the herdsmen's participation in the social and economic lives of their community can be recovered.

A number of herdsmen can be identified in non-herding contexts that illustrate some of the herdsmen's extra-professional activities. Although some of these individuals are distinguished by an occupational title that indicates an elevated status within the herding profession,[15] others seem to have been average herdsmen. Witnesses to contracts and declarations in court include: Šatu-kewi *mār* Interta,[16] Kelke *mār* Ḫulukka,[17] Ḫutip-tilla *mār* Tauka,[18] Eḫlip-apu *mār* Arta,[19] Aštar-tilla *mār* Turari[20] and Turari *mār* Wantiya,[21] all shepherds of Šilwa-tešub; Taya *mār* Ward-aḫḫēšu,[22] the oxherd of Teḫip-tilla *mār* Puḫi-šenni; Kipiya *mār* Abeya;[23] and Hanaya *mār* Arip-apu ᴸᵁ́*kuzallu.*[24] In certain cases a connection existed between the herdsmen and one of the principle parties of the document,[25] but generally, these texts refer to a broad range of transactions and issues with which the herdsmen had no direct involvement.

[12] *HSS* 13 497, a grain loan text that is a "tablet of Tašeni" and *EN* 9 300, in which the grain is of the city of Zuya.

[13] From Kabla, *Šar-tešub* ᴸᵁ́SIPA.GU$_4$.ᴹᴱŠ *ša Tetip-tešub*, *Kelteya* ᴸᵁ́SIPA.GU$_4$ᴹᴱŠ *ša Ḫut-tešub* and *Gimillu* ᴸᵁ́SIPA (*HSS* 16 436). The herdsman from Paqqanupḫe appears in *HSS* 13 243:10.

[14] The pasturing of the flocks and herds took the herdsmen away from settled areas. Moreover, other activities such as the counting, shearing, plucking and slaughter of livestock probably occurred in agricultural areas surrounding the cities. One has only to remember the shepherd's hut in Gilgamesh to envision the herdsmen's normal environment.

[15] ᴸᵁ́*utullu* and ᴸᵁ́*kuzallu.*

[16] *HSS* 9 14 and 31, both contracts involving others associated with the estates of Šilwa-tešub.

[17] *HSS* 13 363, a transfer of property to Šilwa-tešub.

[18] *HSS* 9 13, a *titennūtu* of Šilwa-tešub.

[19] *HSS* 13 372, an exchange of real estate.

[20] *HSS* 19 146.

[21] *HSS* 13 263, a marriage document.

[22] *JEN* 6, an adoption text; 464, a servitude text; and 596, a *marūtu u kallūtu* text.

[23] *JEN* 134, a declaration in court regarding real estate.

[24] *JEN* 211 and 591, adoption texts; 228, 231 and 259, exchanges of real estate; 451, the sale of a slave; 155 and 196, declarations in court regarding real estate. In *JEN* 228, Ḫanaya is one of the surveyors.

[25] The principle party may have been another herdsman or the livestock owner for whom the herdsman worked. See *HSS* 9 13, 14, 31; 13 363; *JEN* 6, 464, 596.

Among other non-herding activities, the references to the house of Enniki[26] and the real estate adoption involving Turari *mār* Wantiya,[27] one of Šilwa-tešub's shepherds, suggest that herdsmen owned real estate. Business agreements include the contract between Bēliya *mār* Kelum-atal ^{LÚ}*utullu* and Ennamati ^{LÚ}*ḫalṣuḫlu* regarding sheep and oxen,[28] and the exchange of grain between Šekaya *mār* Urḫiya and Šušip-šamaš the *wardu* of Šilwa-tešub.[29] Fiscal and military obligations are demonstrated by the payment of a sort of tax by three herdsmen[30] and the appearance of others in military contexts: Tuḫmiya ^{LÚ}SIPA is a *maṣṣar abulli*;[31] Šukr-apu ^{LÚ}SIPA[32] and Tieš-šimika *mār* Tarmi-tilla ^{LÚ}SIPA.GU$_4$ are listed as *nakkuššu*;[33] Niḫriya ^{LÚ}*utullu* appears in two armament listings.[34]

The most significant information concerning the herdsmen's interaction with the community arises from the texts that document the herdsmen's professional activities. The existence of such titles as ^{LÚ}*utullu* and ^{LÚ}*kuzallu* suggest that there was a hierarchy among the herdsmen. The herdsmen's function was, of course, to provide herding services to livestock owners who did not tend their own livestock. Consignment texts and *muddû* documents indicate that the herdsmen contracted with livestock owners to care for the flocks and herds and to repay any deficits that occurred.[35] Furthermore, at least one herdsman contracted with another to pasture his livestock.[36] This arrangement led to a lawsuit[37] as did some agreements between livestock owners and herdsmen. Šilwa-tešub *mār šarri* took both Bēl-aḫḫēšu *mār* Arn-apu the oxherd and Šekar-zizza *mār* Ḫanakka the shepherd to court concerning missing livestock,[38] Teḫip-tilla *mār* Puḫi-šenni sued both Taya *mār* Ward-aḫḫēšu and his son Bēliya the oxherds,[39] and Ennamati *mār* Teḫip-tilla

[26] *HSS* 14 554.

[27] *JEN* 413.

[28] *HSS* 16 452.

[29] *HSS* 9 14.

[30] Eḫlip-apu *mār* Arta (*HSS* 16 253), Sin-dayyān and Šenni (*HSS* 14 514) pay sheep as *liqtu*, "designating persons given into royal service and the payments made in lieu of such service" (cf. *CAD* L 206 s.v.).

[31] *HSS* 15 284.

[32] *RA* 28 (1931), Text 4 (AO.10890).

[33] *JEN* 665.

[34] *HSS* 15 12 and 18.

[35] See below, p. 269ff.

[36] Kuppatiya *mār* Ariḫ-ḫamanna and Ḫutiya *mār* Ar-tirwi: *HSS* 9 31.

[37] *HSS* 13 321.

[38] Bēl-aḫḫēšu *mār* Arn-apu: *HSS* 9 11 and 9 148+*IM* 50805; Šekar-zizza *mār* Ḫanakka: *HSS* 13 441.

[39] Taya *mār* Ward-aḫḫēšu: *JEN* 341; Bēliya *mār* Taya: *JEN* 326 and 353.

prosecuted Pula-ḫali the shepherd.[40] It appears, then, that livestock owners had to bring suit against herdsmen in order to recoup disputed losses from the flocks or herds.

The herdsmen of Nuzi were a mobile group whose profession took them away from settled areas. However, they participated in the social and economic life of their communities, and evidence relating to both their extra-professional and their professional activities provides insight into the status of the herdsmen. Their primary means of identification was their patronymic and they owned and used seals in the course of their business. They appear as witnesses and parties to contracts and as real estate owners, and they perform certain fiscal and military obligations. Although some of these characteristics may be applied to members of the *wardu* group,[41] the facts that they are identified by patronymic, that they contract for their work, that they settle disputes with their employers in court, and that they provide specialized services distinguish them as free skilled professionals who worked willingly.[42]

2. *The Herdsmen and the Livestock Owners*

An examination of the archives in which the herdsmen are found shows that individual herdsmen are found only in one archive or in association with a specific livestock owner.[43] For example, Zikaru *mār* Šalliya is associated only with Puḫi-šenni *mār* Muš-apu;[44] Šilaḫi, Namḫiya, Niḫriya and Šiḫaš-šenni are involved only with the palace;[45] Bēliya *mār* Taya, the oxherd, is found with Teḫip-tilla *mār* Puḫi-šenni;[46] and the many herdsmen of Šilwa-tešub *mār šarri* are related only to him and to his family.[47] Additionally, in legal texts and certain administrative documents, the herdsmen frequently are identified first by profession and further by the name of the livestock owner

[40]*JEN* 350.

[41]That is, ownership of real estate, use of seals, participating in contracts and the like.

[42]See the comments of G. Wilhelm, "Zur Rolle des Grossgrundbesitzes in der Hurritischen Gesellschaft," *RHA* 36 (1978), 209.

[43]Exceptions are Aštar-tilla and Kaniya the sons of Turari, for which see below, n. 64.

[44]*HSS* 16 311 and 449 refer to the same herding arrangement between Zikaru *mār* Šalliya the herdsman and Puḫi-šenni *mār* Muš-apu. For a discussion of these texts, see T. Abusch, above, pp. 1-9.

[45]Šilaḫi: *HSS* 13 156; 14 593; 16 316, the first two from Rooms C76 and R76. Namḫiya: *HSS* 14 593 (Room R76). Niḫriya: *HSS* 15 12, 18 (Room N120); 16 314 (P400). Šiḫaš-šenni: *HSS* 14 593 (Room R76). For a description of the distribution of the Nuzi tablets, see E. R. Lacheman, *op. cit.*, pp. v-viii.

[46]In the law suits *JEN* 326 and 353.

[47]See Appendix III for their names.

for whom they worked: *Bēl-ahhēšu mār Arn-apu* SIPA.GU$_4^{\text{MEŠ}}$ *ša Šilwa-Tešub mār šarri*,[48] *Kipaya* ^{LÚ}SIPA *ša Keliya*,[49] $^{\text{LÚ.MEŠ}}$SIPA *ša Wirziyae*, [50] *Ḫuziri* ^{LÚ}SIPA *ša* É.GAL-*lim*,[51] and in the first person, ^{LÚ}SIPA-*ya*[52] and ^{LÚ}SIPA *yâši*.[53] These forms of reference are used not only when a livestock owner brings suit against his herdsman[54] or testifies concerning injury done to his herdsman[55] but also when a third party seeks to identify the herdsman's affiliation when providing testimony or information.[56] Thus, the relationship between the herdsman and the livestock owner appears to be an exclusive one. Moreover, this relationship seems to be important with reference to the herdsman's identity in the community.

The affiliation between herdsman and livestock owner is not always limited to individual herdsmen. The herding profession was hereditary,[57] and in a number of cases families of herdsmen can be found working for the same livestock owner or his family. From the archives of Teḫip-tilla *mār* Puḫi-šenni come the well known examples of Taya and his son Bēliya the oxherds.[58] The archives of Šilwa-tešub *mār šarri* provide the names of many herdsmen, of whom some are brothers and others have the same names as the fathers of herdsmen.[59] Through their personal names and certain other criteria, these

[48] *HSS* 9 11:4-6.

[49] *AASOR* 16 6:6-7.

[50] *JEN* 525:1. See also l. 19 2 $^{\text{LÚ.MEŠ}}$SIPA *ša* ^{m}*pa-ak-la-bi-ti*.

[51] *JEN* 525:34 and 670:40.

[52] *AASOR* 16 3:43 in which Warrateya refers to Kipiya *mār* Abeya.

[53] *JEN* 350:6 in which Ennamati refers to Pula-ḫali.

[54] *HSS* 9 11 and 148+*IM* 50805; *JEN* 341 and 350.

[55] *AASOR* 16 3.

[56] *JEN* 525, 670; *AASOR* 16 6; *HSS* 9 11; 13 451; 14 554.

[57] A. L. Oppenheim, *op. cit.*, pp. 50-51; D. Cross, *Movable Property in the Nuzi Documents*, *AOS* 10 (New Haven, 1937), p. 20, n. 18.

[58] See n. 57.

[59] Brothers include Kanipa and Šimika-atal the sons of Tae (*HSS* 13 297; 14 515; 16 251); Nullu and Utḫap-tae the sons of Akip-tilla (*HSS* 9 63; 13 260; 16 307); Turari and Warate the sons of Wantiya (*HSS* 9 56; 13 253). Among oxherds, Bēl-aḫḫēšu, Akkulenni and Arip-iššuḫri sons of Arn-apu (*HSS* 13 331, 333; 16 425, 430). In a few cases a herdsman appears with another whose relationship to him is not known: Ṣill-kūbi is discussed below; Ulluya (*HSS* 9 61), Taika (*HSS* 16 453) and Turariya (*HSS* 14 519, 637) are not known by patronymic. Herdsmen who have the same names as fathers of herdsmen include Tae the son of Kawinni and Akip-tilla the son of Eḫel-tešub as compared with the patronymics of the first pair of brothers above, Eḫlip-apu son of Arta and Ḫutip-apu son of Eḫlip-apu; Arilluya son of Šum-ili and Šešwiya son of Arilluya; Ḫutip-tilla son of Taukka and Pilmašše son of Ḫutip-tilla; Teḫip-tilla and Kai-tilla son of Teḫip-tilla; Sin-dayyān and Tuntuya son of Sin-dayyān; Itḫišta and Tauli son of Itḫišta; Apaya and Ḫanaya son of Apaya; Turari son of Wantiya and Aštar-tilla and Kaniya sons of Turari.

herdsmen can be organized into family groups.[60] For example, the brothers Šimika-atal and Kanipa the sons of Tae may be linked to the herdsman Tae *mār* Kawinni by means of Ṣill-kūbi *mār* Puḫi-šenni who receives sheep jointly with Šimika-atal in *HSS* 9 62 and with Tae in *HSS* 13 427. In the latter text his seal is identified as that of Ṣill-kūbi *mār* Puḫi-šenni but he is listed with Tae as the son of Kawinni in the text.[61] Ṣill-kūbi must have had a special relationship to both Šimika-atal and Tae as the scribe of *HSS* 13 427 refers to him as Tae's brother and he appears with both shepherds in the manner of a brother. He may have been a relative of the two men, or he may have joined the family of Kawinni as an apprentice in the herding profession.[62] Thus, for the family of Kawinni (Family I) two active generations of herdsmen can be reconstructed:

[60] Identification of herdsmen in the archives is fairly simple. The contracts identify the herdsmen by patronymic and establish their profession. These same herdsmen can be identified in the administrative and legal texts through their patronymics and, if the patronymic does not appear as is usual in the administrative texts, by profession. For instance, the shepherd Šešwiya *mār* Arilluya is found on eleven contracts. No other Šešwiya is known from the contracts. In that the administrative texts relate to the herding contracts, a herdsman named Šešwiya who appears in the more abbreviated administrative texts is with little doubt the same man. Some of the administrative texts record the names without patronymics of herdsmen who do not appear in the contracts. However, the infrequency of their appearance and their regular repetition in groups of herdsmen suggest that all of the references to a Sin-dayyān or an Itḫišta are to single individuals named Sin-dayyān and Itḫišta.

Once the herdsmen are isolated in the archive, personal names and involvement in the same profession are important factors in reconstructing families. However, in at least one case, two herdsmen have the same name but different patronymics (see below, n. 64). Herdsmen included in the families below are those who are clearly the only ones of their names.

Other criteria relate to the appearance of herdsmen's names on administrative texts and the degree of activity of individual herdsmen. For all of the families below members of two generations of the immediate family do not appear on the same administrative text. On this basis, a possible family composed of Šekaya son of Urḫiya and Urḫiya son of Ikkianni is rejected; Šekaya and Urḫiya appear together on *HSS* 9 48; 13 388; 14 637. In addition, one generation of each family, normally the third, is better attested by contracts. This phenomenon relates to practices of archive-keeping, a topic beyond the scope of this study.

[61] *HSS* 13 427:3-5: *Tae u Ṣill-kūbi* DUMU^{MEŠ} *Kawinni*; 10-12: NA$_4$ *Tae* NA$_4$ *Ṣill-kūbi* DUMU *Puḫi-šenni.*

[62] The use of the family pattern by the scribal schools at Nuzi is well known (G. Wilhelm, *AOAT* 9, pp. 8-11). Elsewhere at Nuzi, the weaver Tirwiya adopts Naniya the son of Ḫui-tilla as an apprentice (*JEN* 572). Outside of Nuzi, the practice of a craftsman's (*mār ummānim*) adopting a child to teach him his craft is attested in *CH* §§188-89. For discussion, see G. R. Driver and J. C. Miles, *The Babylonian Laws*, Vol. I, (Oxford, 1960), pp. 392-95.

I.

Kawinni — Puḫi-šenni
Tae — — — — — — — Ṣill-kūbi
Šimika-atal, Kanipa

Other families include:

II.[63]
Arta
Eḫlip apu
Ḫutip-apu

III.
Eḫel-tešub
Akip-tilla
Nullu, Utḫap-tae

IV.
Šum-ili
Arilluya
Šešwiya

V.
Taukka
Ḫutip-tilla
Pilmašše

VI.
?
Teḫip-tilla
Kai-tilla

VII.
?
Sin-dayyān
Tuntuya

VIII.
?
Itḫišta
Tauli

IX.
?
Apaya
Ḫanaya

X.
Interta
Šatu-kewi
Ḫanirra

XI.[64]
Wantiya
Turari, Waratteya
Aštar-tilla, Kaniya/Kanie, [Kip-tilla]

[63]W. Mayer, *op. cit.*, p. 192 identifies this family with reference to G. Wilhelm, *Privater Grossgrundbesitz im Königreich Arrapha* (Unpublished doctoral dissertation, University of the Saarlandes, 1975).

[64]The last generation of this family is late in the archive. Aštar-tilla *mār* Turari appears with Šamaš-nāṣir *mār* Akiya, the latest of the scribes to work for Šilwa-tešub *mār šarri*. Moreover, Aštar-tilla and Kaniya appear on a livestock text from Room D6. It is possible that these herdsmen left the service of Šilwa-tešub near the end of the archive to work elsewhere. In addition, two active herdsmen named Wantiya are attested: Wantiya *mār* Unkura and Wantiya *mār* Wirriš-tanni. However, both appear in connection with later individuals in the archive. Wantiya *mār* Unkura is cited in connection with Tatip-tilla the son of Šilwa-tešub in *HSS* 16 292. Wantiya *mār* Wirriš-tanni occurs in *HSS* 14 650 with Ḫanirra *mār* Šatu-kewi, Pilmašše *mār* Ḫutip-tilla, Tauli *mār* Itḫišta, and Kai-tilla *mār* Teḫip-tilla, all third generation of their respective families. Although it is possible that this family presents three active generations, the identity of Wantiya's father remains in doubt. Note, also, that Kaniya may be the

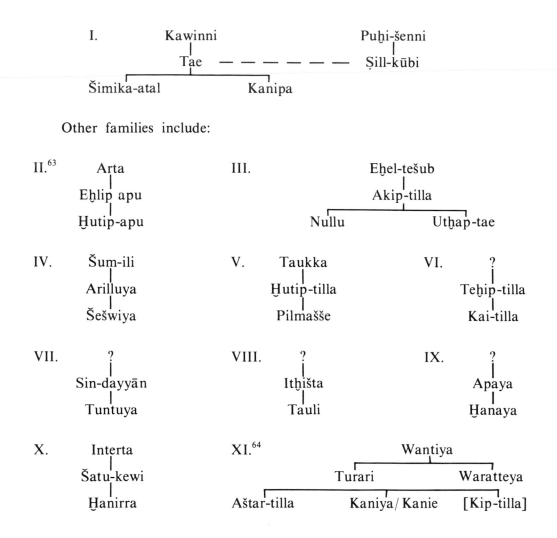

In all of these families the first generation either is not active in the archive or is not named. Members of this generation probably did not work for Šilwa-tešub. Although some generational overlap can be observed, correlations can be drawn among members of different families.[65] The resulting

same herdsman as Kanie. Both are identified as *mār* Turari (*HSS* 13 23 and 16 254). Furthermore, *HSS* 13 249 lists sheep of Kanie and of Waratteya as *ša Wantiya*. This text would then link these herdsmen quite securely.

[65]The following chart presents the distribution of herdsmen on the administrative texts in which members of the families appear. The second generation is indicated by X and the third by ●. Note that members of the second generation frequently appear together as do members of the third generation; second and third generations of the same families do not overlap, while those of different families may.

Family	Herdsman	9 48	13 221	13 224	13 248	13 268	13 311	13 358	13 388	13 389	13 451	13 457	14 519	14 590	14 596	14 637	14 650	16 240	16 249	16 272	16 304
I	Tae									X					X	X					
	Ṣill-kūbi									X											
	Kanipa	●																			
II	Eḫlip-apu		X		X			X		X				X		X			X		
	Ḫutip-apu	●																●			
III	Akip-tilla		X		X						X										
	Nullu	●				●			●	●				●						●	●
IV	Šešwiya	●			●	●			●	●				●		●		●		●	
V	Ḫutip-tilla		X																		
	Pil-mašše	●						●								●	●				
VI	Kai-tilla	●		●						●		●		●			●	●			
VII	Sin-dayyān				X					X			X				X		X	X	
	Tuntuya	●				●			●												
VIII	Itḫišta				X																
	Tauli	●		●						●		●	●	●			●			●	●
X	Šatu-kewi						X				X			X				X			
	Ḫanirra	●															●				

pattern of herdsmen in the archive corresponds well with that of the scribes attested in the archives.[66]

Not all of the herdsmen who worked for Šilwa-tešub belong to the families that have been presented. A number of others appear frequently in the livestock texts.[67] Among all of the herdsmen, some can be found in the ration texts as recipients of grain as fodder for the livestock[68] or in quantities that suggest food rations.[69] Furthermore, at least three of Šilwa-tešub's herdsmen borrowed grain from him.[70]

Šilwa-tešub's herdsmen were not unique. The archives of Teḫip-tilla *mār* Puḫi-šenni yield the names of two generations of an oxherding family.[71] At the house of Katiri, Ilī-ma-aḫī *mār* Ilānu contracts for the care of livestock.[72] From the archives of Puḫi-šenni *mār* Muš-apu come the herding contract *HSS* 16 311 and the famous "egg-shaped" tablet that contained counting stones.[73] Herdsmen of the palace are described not only as SIPA É.GAL-*lim* but also as *āšib* É.GAL-*lim* and ERÌ É.GAL-*lim*.[74] These individuals receive grain

[66]Scribes of the third, fourth and fifth generation of the family of Apil-sin write for Šilwa-tešub or members of his household. Third generation: Turari and Nērāri sons of Taya (*HSS* 9 17 and 29); fourth generation: Šar-tilla son of Iluya (*HSS* 9 35 and 13 161), Abī-ila and Simanni (-adad) sons of Nabû-ila (*HSS* 9 19 and 20), Amumi-tešub son of Sin-nādin-šumi (*HSS* 9 8) and Ar-tešub son of Turari (*HSS* 9 18 and 13 363). One fifth generation scribe appears: Šamaš-nāṣir *mār* Akiya, for which, see above, n. 64. For the families of the scribes, E. R. Lacheman, "The word *šudutu* in the Nuzi Tablets," *Proceedings of the 25th International Congress of Orientalists* (Moscow, 1960), pp. 233-38, and G. Wilhelm, *AOAT* 9, pp. 8-11.

[67]Among them, Ḫašip-tilla *mār* Eḫlip-ukur, Kelke *mār* Ḫulukka, Kuppatiya *mār* Ariḫ-ḫamanna Šar-tilla *mār* En-šukru, Šekaya *mār* Urḫiya, Šešwiya *mār* Arilliya, Urḫiya *mār* Ikkianni, and Wantiya *mār* Unkura.

[68]*Ziriqa ana* UDU^{MEŠ}/*ana ziriqa ana* UDU^{MEŠ}: Eḫlip-apu, Pilmašše and Wantiya (*HSS* 13 358:65-67); Šar-tilla (*HSS* 13 362:54); Urḫiya (*HSS* 13 414:5); Šekar-zizza (*HSS* 16 11:11); also, 5 herdsmen in *HSS* 14 641. For others, see n. 90-91 below. For the phrases *ziriqa ana* UDU^{MEŠ} and *ana ziriqa ana* UDU^{MEŠ}, see *CAD* Z 135 s.v., "Feed (scattered for animals, Nuzi only)," and D. Cross, *op. cit.*, pp. 27, 32 and 34.

[69]See n. 93 below. Bēl-ahhēšu the oxherd receives grain specifically designated as ŠE.BA in *HSS* 16 11:8-9.

[70]Šatu-kewi *mār* Interta: *HSS* 13 21; Tae *mār* Kawinni: *HSS* 13 497; Akip-tilla *mār* Eḫel-tešub: *HSS* 13 132, *EN* 9 300; Kanie *mār* Turari: *HSS* 13 23.

[71]Taya *mār* Ward-aḫḫēšu and his son Bēliya. See above, n. 57 and 58.

[72]*HSS* 5 9 and 15. See G. Wilhelm below, p. 345.

[73]See above, n. 44.

[74]^{LÚ}SIPA É.GAL-lim in *JEN* 525 and 670; *HSS* 14 554. *āšib* É.GAL-*lim* in *HSS* 15 18. ERÌ É.GAL-*lim* in *HSS* 14 593. The last is a departure from the normal pattern as the herdsmen are not generally considered *wardu*'s. Perhaps the term should be understood in this context as "dependent" or "worker."

rations, amounts of bronze, and one of them is attested on a *muddû* statement.[75]

Whereas the herdsmen were free workers, their affiliation with the livestock owners for whom they worked was both enduring and significant with respect to their identity in the community. At the root of this relationship were certain economic factors. While the livestock owner needed the herdsmen's services, the herdsmen were dependent on the livestock owner not only for the source of their livelihoods but also for support in the form of fodder, possibly rations, and, in some cases, loans of grain. In the herding process itself both the herdsmen and the livestock owners benefited from the success of the herdsmen's endeavors, because they shared in the produce of the flocks or herds,[76] and both suffered from failures. However, for the herdsmen, failures led to the accumulation of deficits which had to be repaid.[77] Considering that a sheep valued at 1.33 shekels of silver equalled approximately 3 months of average grain rations,[78] deficits could be very costly to the herdsmen, hence difficult to repay. If these deficits were carried over long periods of time, the bond between herdsmen and livestock owners could be strengthened through debt. A closer examination of the herding process helps to bring perspective to these economic factors.

B. SMALL CATTLE

1. *The* buqūnu

The brief memoranda that record total numbers of sheep and goats counted and plucked or shorn[79] and the ledgers that provide the names of herdsmen associated with total numbers of livestock[80] are the administrative

[75] *HSS* 16 316, the *muddû* of Šilaḫi. Grain rations to Šilaḫi, Šiḫaš-šenni and Namḫiya, $^{\text{LÚ.MEŠ}}$SIPA and Puḫi-šenni ^{LÚ}SIPA.GU$_4$^{MEŠ} in *HSS* 14 593:30-31, 52. Namḫiya and Šiḫaš-šenni receive bronze in *HSS* 13 493.

[76] See below, p. 284.

[77] See below, p. 284.

[78] For relative values, see B. Eichler, *Indenture at Nuzi: The Personal* Tidennūtu *Contract and its Mesopotamian Analogues* (New Haven, 1973), p. 15 with reference to D. Cross, *op. cit.*, p. 28. 1 ANŠE of barley = 1.5 shekels of silver; 1 sheep = 1.33 shekels of silver. 3 BÁN of barley equalled a normal food ration for an adult male.

[79] For example, *HSS* 9 153; 16 260, 287 (records of livestock counted); *HSS* 13 487; 16 244, 247 (records of plucking). Sheep were plucked and goats shorn. See D. Cross, *op. cit.*, p. 27; *CAD* B 97, *baqāmu* and 100, *baqmu*; *CAD* G 59, *gazāzu* and 60, *gazzu*.

[80] For example, *HSS* 9 48; 14 505 (counting); *HSS* 13 244, 249 (plucking); *HSS* 13 248, 389; 14 519, 590, 596, 637; 16 240, 304 (livestock owed); *HSS* 16 242+282 (livestock consigned). (The join of *HSS* 16 242+282 was made by G. Wilhelm at the Harvard Semitic Museum).

texts[81] that outline a part of the herding process. These texts reflect the activities conducted at the *buqūnu* or "plucking time"[82] which was the focal point of the annual herding cycle.[83] At that time supervisory personnel associated with the households of the livestock owners[84] counted the livestock, plucked and sheared them, tallied the herdsmen's accounts, including debts owed and repaid,[85] and consigned livestock to the herdsmen for another year.[86]

The administrative texts are not dated, but the *buqūnu* probably occurred in the spring[87] before the flocks were taken to pasture. Some information concerning the times when herdsmen and their flocks were in the vicinity of distribution centers derives from dated grain disbursement texts. Herdsmen received fodder for the sheep or rations for themselves in the months *Kinūnu ša al ilāni* (Nov.-Dec.),[88] *Ḫuru* (Dec.-Jan.),[89] *Mitirunnu* (Jan.-Feb.),[90] *Ḫutalši*

[81]Comprehensive administrative texts like those of Larsa are not found at Nuzi. See F. R. Kraus, *Staatliche Viehhaltung im altbabylonischen Lande Larsa* (Mededeelingen der Koninklijke Nederlandse Akademie van Wetenschappen, Afd. Letterkunde. Nieuwe Reeks, Deel 29. No. 5) (Amsterdam, 1966). However, the information that they record is similar. Only one of the texts makes reference to more than one category of information. *HSS* 16 260 notes the total of livestock counted alive, the debt of the herdsmen and numbers of sheep and goat skins. It should be noted that frequent reference will be made to three important studies of livestock and herding during other periods: F. R. Kraus, *op. cit.*; J. N. Postgate (with a contribution by S. Payne), "Some Old Babylonian Shepherds and Their Flocks," *JSS* 20/1 (1975); and S. Payne, "Kill-off Patterns in Sheep and Goats: The Mandibles from Aşvan Kale," in "Aşvan 1968-1972: An Interim Report," *AS* 23 (1973).

[82]*Buqūnu* is in the Nuzi form of the more common *buqūmu*. See *CAD* B 325 s.v.

[83]An annual *buqūmu* is quite normal. See J. N. Postgate, *op. cit.*, 4. That the accounting of the sheep was conducted annually at Nuzi is indicated by such texts as *HSS* 13 311, a ledger: 13) *ṭup-pu ša* MU-*ti an-ni-*[*ti*] 14) *ša ḫu-ti-ia iš-ṭù-ru*. See also *HSS* 13 478, 14 556 and 16 289 in which debts of livestock *i-na bu-qú-ni ú-še-ra-bá*.

[84]From Šilwa-tešub's archives: Urḫa-tarmi (*HSS* 13 400; 14 505; 16 241, 242+282, 249, and 287) and Zike (*HSS* 9 153 and 13 298). From the palace: Eḫlip-tilla *šakin bīti ša* ^{URU}*Nuzi* (*HSS* 13 156).

[85]See above, n. 80 for administrative texts recording livestock owed, and n. 83 for texts in which debts of livestock are to be repaid at the *buqūnu*. Corresponding to these statements are the ledgers recording repayments, for example, *HSS* 14 596.

[86]For example, *HSS* 16 242+282 in which a number of unrelated herdsmen receive sheep.

[87]See J. N. Postgate, *op. cit.*, 4 and n. 3. The wool and hair were removed before the heat of the summer and in time for a new growth to develop before the winter.

[88]*HSS* 13 358: Eḫlip-apu, Pilmašše and Wantiya, known to be herdsmen of Šilwa-tešub, receive *ziriqu* for the sheep.

[89]*HSS* 13 221: Akip-tilla ^{LÚ}SIPA, Eḫlip-apu ^{LÚ}SIPA, Ḫutip-tilla ^{LÚ}SIPA receive

(Feb.-March),[91] *Impurtannu* (March-April),[92] and *Ḫiaru* (April-May).[93] They seem not to appear in the ration texts for the remaining six months of the year. Thus, it is likely that the Nuzi herdsmen took the flocks to pasture in the spring, moved into the hills during the hot summer months, and returned for the fall and winter when local pastures and supplemental fodder would support the flocks.[94]

2. *Consignment Texts*

In addition to the administrative texts, two types of documents describe herding activities: the consignment texts and the *muddû* texts. Both list numbers and types of small or large cattle and the name and patronymic of one or more herdsmen, and both are sealed by the herdsmen involved. A typical example of the consignment texts is *HSS* 9 51:

1	30 UDU.NITA^{MEŠ} GAL	30 wethers[95]
2	11 UDU.MUNUS^{MEŠ} Ù.TU	11 bearing ewes[96]

undesignated quantities of grain.

[90]*HSS* 14 650: Pentammu *mār* Ninkiya, Wantiya, Kai-tilla, Karrate, Wantiya *mār* Wirriš-tanni, Sin-dayyān and others receive *ziriqu* for sheep.

[91]*HSS* 13 362; Šar-tilla, known to be a herdsman of Šilwa-tešub, receives *ziriqu* for sheep for the months Ḫutalšc to Ḫiaru.

[92]*HSS* 13 401: Ḫašip-tilla, Šar-tilla, Taule, Urḫiya, Kelke, Wantiya, and Pai-tilla receive ŠE.BA.

[93]*HSS* 13 339: 10 ^{LÚ}SIPA^{MEŠ}-*ti* receive 3 ANŠE of grain *HSS* 13 451: Kanie, Šatukewi, Šekaya, Karrate, Izkan-abi, Wara-abi, Teḫiya, Kuppatiya, Akip-tilla, Abu-rabi: 10 ^{LÚ}SIPA^{MEŠ}-*ti ša Šilwa-tešub* receive 3 ANŠE of grain. 3 BÁN of grain was the normal ration for an adult man (see M. Morrison, "The Family of Šilwa-Tešub *mār šarri*," *JCS* 30 (1979), 13, n. 82), so 3 ANŠE of grain for 10 men would equal a normal food ration for these herdsmen.

[94]April-May is somewhat later in the year for the *buqūnu* than the times attested for Southern Mesopotamia, but note Postgate's observations, *op. cit.*, 4 and n. 2. Moreover, Nuzi is farther north than the Babylonian sites and is located in the northern highlands where temperatures, rainfall, and seasonal change are different from those of the south. See. H. H. Smith, *et al.*, *Area Handbook for Iraq*, DAPam 550-31 (Washington, D.C., 1971), pp. 15-18, and *Iraq and the Persian Gulf*, B.R. 524, Geographical Handbook Series, September 1944, pp. 166-81. Interestingly, R. F. S. Starr, in *Nuzi I*, pp. 31-32 notes that in the 1920s the Turkomans would take the flocks "for a month or two in the spring . . . to graze on the fresh grass of the desert," and that the flocks were kept in the courtyards of houses "except in the worst weather . . . at night." See W. Mayer, *op. cit.*, pp. 190-91, referring to G. Wilhelm, *Privater Grossgrundbesitz im Königreich Arrapha* for observations on Nuzi practices.

[95]See below, n. 111.

[96]See below, n. 109.

3	2 *ka₄-lu-mu* MUNUS^{MEŠ} 1-*nu* *bá-aq-nu*	2 ewe-lambs once plucked
4	2 *ka₄-lu-mu* NITA^{MEŠ} KI.MIN	2 male lambs "ditto"
5	1 MÁŠ GAL ŠU.NÍGIN 52 UDU$^{\text{HÁ.MEŠ}}$	1 buck: a total of 52 small cattle
6	*ša* ^{I}*Ši-il-wa-te-šub*	which Šilwa-tešub
7	*a-na* ŠU ^{I}*Še-ka-a-a*	to Šekaya
8	DUMU *Ur-ḫi-ia na-ad-nu*	son of Urḫiya entrusted.
9	NA₄ *Še-ka-a-a* DUMU *Ur-ḫi-ia*	Seal of Šekaya son of Urḫiya

The format of the consignment texts is similar to that of the herding contracts of the Old Babylonian period.[97] As in the Old Babylonian texts, the sealing of the tablets by the herdsmen serves as their legal acknowledgment of receipt of the livestock.[98] However, the Nuzi texts differ from their earlier counterparts in three ways: the phrase *ana* ŠU PN *ša nadnū*[99] is commonly used in place of the Old Babylonian *paqdū*; the Nuzi texts are undated;[100] and the Nuzi texts do not include the terms of the contract.

Information gleaned from other sources shows that practices governing the contractual relationship between the herdsmen and the livestock owners at Nuzi were similar to those of the Old Babylonian period. Herdsmen were expected to return the livestock to their owner at the *buqūnu*.[101] Livestock that died or were lost while in the herdsman's care were to be repaid.[102] The

[97]A typical cattle consignment text is *HSS* 13 331 (transliteration only): 1) 21 bearing cows, 2) 7 4-year-old oxen, 3) 4 3-year-old cows, 4) [1] 3-year-old ox, 5) [1] 2-year-old ox, 6) X yearling oxen, 7) X yearling cows: 8) [A total] of 40 ca[ttle] 9) which Šilw[a-tešub] 10) to the hand of Ar[p-iššuḫri] 11) to the hand of Bēl-ah-[hēšu] 12) and to the hand of 13) Akkulenni 14) son of Arn-apu 15) entrusted. 16) Seal of Arp-iššuḫri. 17) Seal of Akkulenni son of "ditto." 18) Seal of Bēl-aḫḫēšu son of Ar[n-apu].

For Old Babylonian examples, see the texts cited by Postgate, *op. cit.*, 3, particularly *YOS* 13 97 (cattle), and *YOS* 13 346, 378, 426, and 434 (small cattle).

[98]See discussion of this matter in Postgate, *op. cit.*, 2, and n. 2.

[99]*HSS* 9 49, 50, 51, 52, 53, 54, 57, 59, 60, 62, 63, 64, 65, 137, 138; 13 89, 253, 260, 330, 331, 425; 14 632; 16 300 and 310. A common variant form is *ana* ŠU PN *nadnū* in *HSS* 9 58, 61; 13 495; 14 506, 557; 16 248, 266, 311 and 453.

[100]With the exception of *HSS* 13 371 in which Ḫutip-tilla the son of Tauka receives sheep *ana kuruštaena*^{MEŠ} in the month of Arkapinnu (Aug.-Sept.). Perhaps the date was added in this case because it was not the usual time for receipt of livestock.

[101]*HSS* 13 441: Šeqar-zizza ^{LÚ}SIPA was taken to court because he did not return the livestock entrusted to him.

[102]*HSS* 9 11 and 148+*IM* 50805, both lawsuits involving Bēl-aḫḫēšu son of Arn-apu. Akin to practices governing herding are those governing other uses of livestock. Compare the laws governing death or injury to a hired ox (*CH*§§224-49) and those for death or injury to livestock committed to a herdsman (*CH*§§262-67). At Nuzi, the

defenses raised in court by herdsmen indicate that the herdsmen might be excused from repaying the loss if the livestock were killed by another animal,[103] or if the herdsman could show that he had not been negligent.[104] Further, the practice of producing the skins of dead animals to prove losses seems to have been followed.[105]

One purpose of these herding contracts was, of course, to protect the livestock owner and the herdsman. The sealed record served as proof of the numbers and types of livestock that the herdsman had received, and, therefore, what he should return. Neither the owner nor the herdsman could alter the numbers of livestock involved. A second purpose, however, is suggested by the nature of the terms used to describe the livestock. Although they differ from those of the Old Babylonian period,[106] the descriptive terms used at Nuzi are no less specific, and they reveal a similar concern for the productivity of the flocks with regard to both young stock and wool and hair. Thus, the contracts might serve as a means of calculating the expected yield of the flocks and also the herdsman's share in the flock's productivity.[107]

The terms standardly used in the Nuzi herding contracts are:[108]

UDU.MUNUS; UDU.MUNUS GAL; UDU.MUNUS Ù.TU—ewe, adult ewe, bearing or pregnant ewe.[109]

---

contracts relating to cattle given out for plowing include such phrases as: *miṭūtišu* PN *umallâ* (*HSS* 13 448) and *miṭūtišu iānu u miṭūtišu* PN *umallâ* (*HSS* 16 428) (PN = the plowman), paralleled by the lengthier *ša* BA.[UGₓ(BE)] *u ša iḫalliqu iānu šumma* [*iba*]*šši ištu bītišu umallâ*. (*CAD* I/J 323 s. *iānu*). Both indicate that cattle that die or are lost while in the plowman's care are to be repaid.

103 *JEN* 341 in which Taya claims that an ox died because of injury by another ox. See W. W. Hallo, "Review of Reallexikon der Assyriologie by Erich Ebeling and Ernst Weidner (eds.) Vol. 3. fasc. 1," *JAOS* 87 (1967), 64, fn. 1.

104 *HSS* 9 11, in which Bēl-aḫḫēšu claims that he was removed forcibly from the oxen for which he was responsible. *AASOR* 16 7, in which the shepherd claims that the sheep that died while in his care were sick when they were given to him.

105 *HSS* 16 260 and 432. Perhaps also the sheep and goat hides listed in *HSS* 15 196 as *ša me-du-ti* (= *miṭūti*? vs. *CAD* M/2, 3, 5, *medutu*, "unknown meaning").

106 For standard Old Babylonian terms, see Postgate, *op. cit.*, 15-17.

107 As they did in the Old Babylonian period, Postgate, *op. cit.*, 5. Also, J. J. Finklestein, "An Old Babylonian Herding Contract and Genesis 31:38f.," *JAOS* 88 (1968), 30-36.

108 D. Cross, *op. cit.*, p. 25, calls the Nuzi sheep and goat designations a "specifically local terminology." For a discussion of these terms, see D. Cross, *op. cit.*, pp. 24-32.

109 *CAD* I/J 128 s.v. *CAD* A/1 340 s. *ālidu*, Ù.TU = *ālittu*. In general the term means "bearing" or "pregnant." The suggestion that for animals the term means "that have given birth" is problematic. The Akkadian equivalent for the term seems to be *ša*

puḫallu—ram.[110]

UDU.NITA; UDU.NITA GAL—wether,[111] ram;[112] adult wether or ram.

kalūmu MUNUS; *kalūmu* MUNUS *ḫurapu*; *kalūmu* MUNUS 1-*en baqnu*—ewe lamb,[113] spring ewe-lamb,[114] once-plucked ewe-lamb.

kalūmu NITA; *kalūmu* NITA *ḫurapu*; *kalūmu* NITA 1-*en baqnu*—ram lamb,[115] spring ram-lamb,[116] once-plucked ram-lamb.

enzu MUNUS; *enzu* MUNUS Ù.TU; MÁŠ MUNUS GAL—doe,[117] bearing or pregnant doe, adult doe.

MÁŠ GAL—adult buck.[118]

MÁŠ.TUR MUNUS; *lali*ʾ*u* MUNUS; MÁŠ.TUR MUNUS 1-*en gazzu*; MÁŠ.TUR MUNUS Ù.TU—doe-kid,[119] once-shorn doe-kid, bearing or pregnant doe-kid.

MÁŠ.TUR.NITA; *lali*ʾ*u* NITA; MÁŠ.TUR.NITA 1-*en gazzu*; MÁŠ.TUR.NITA Ù.TU(!)—buck-kid,[120] once-shorn buck-kid, bearing (!) buck-kid.

The adult stock are described with respect to gender, hence to their reproductive capabilities.[121] However, questions arise concerning the precise significance of the term Ù.TU (*ālittu*) as applied to ewes and does, the two terms *puḫallu* and UDU.NITA used for male sheep. In the first instance, the ewes and does might be either "bearing," that is capable of bearing young, or pregnant when they are given to the herdsman. In the second, although *puḫallu* is the specific designation for a ram and UDU.NITA generally designates

---

ullad, not *ša ūlid* (*HSS* 16 248). In addition, the ewes of these texts are not associated with lambs (see Table I).

[110] D. Cross, *op. cit.*, p. 24 and n. 29 with reference to B. Landsberger, "Studien zu den Urkunden aus der Zeit des Ninurta-tukul-Aššur," *AfO* 10 (1935-36), 154.

[111] D. Cross, *op. cit.*, p. 24.

[112] *CAD* I/J 129 s.v. The numbers of UDU.NITA^{MEŠ} that occur in the contracts suggest that they were commonly herded together, a practice that is not desirable for rams, so the majority of these animals were probably wethers.

[113] *CAD* K 106-7 s.v.

[114] *CAD* H 245 s.v. A spring lamb is one that is a young lamb at the beginning of the agricultural season, that is one that is born just before or during the spring.

[115] See n. 113.

[116] See n. 114.

[117] *CAD* E 180 s.v.

[118] *AHw* 1430 s. *uriṣu*(*m*), *CAD* D 120 s. *daššu*. As in the case of sheep (see n. 112), the majority of these were probably castrated males.

[119] *CAD* L 51 s.v.

[120] See n. 119.

[121] References to wool or hair yields were unnecessary because adult animals could be expected to produce a fixed amount per year. See C. Zaccagnini, below, p. 349ff. and notes.

wethers, it is possible that UDU.NITA might be used for all of the male sheep of a flock as MÁŠ GAL seems to be for male goats.[122]

Lambs and kids, on the other hand, are described with respect to both gender and age. The *ḫurapu*, spring lambs, were the more recently born young stock. Those lambs and kids described as 1-*en baqnu* or *gazzu* would be between six months of age and the time when they could be classified as adults, i.e., about a year old.[123] The rest may have been those too young to pluck or shear, but too old to be termed *ḫurapu*, approximately three to six months of age. This system for describing lambs and kids recalls that of the Larsa administrative texts.[124]

3. *The Composition of the Flocks*

The contracts that have survived surely represent only a small portion of those that were written, and individual flocks of sheep and goats vary considerably.[125] However, it can be expected that in the aggregate the

[122] *Puḫallu* is used in only two contracts, both of the same herdsman (*HSS* 9 53, 61), and the entries seem to refer to the same 3 animals. Note that in *HSS* 9 61, *puḫallu* is designated by the term UDU.NITA. There is no specific term for the uncastrated goat, however. It was not necessary to distinguish between rams and wethers and bucks and castrated goats in the contracts. All of the male sheep would produce the same amount of wool and goats hair; numbers of expected young would be figured on the basis of the female stock.

[123] As a rule, lambs and kids do not produce enough wool or hair to pluck or shear until they are about six months of age.

[124] See F. R. Kraus, *op. cit.*, pp. 22-29, where kir_x/$sila_4$.UR_4(?) describes plucked ewe- and ram-lambs and kir_x/$sila_4$.bar.gál describes unplucked ewe- and ram-lambs, as opposed to the Old Babylonian contracts in which the young are described with reference to their sexual maturity (Postgate, *op. cit.*, 11). At Larsa, such descriptions were used for the calculation of wool production. The Nuzi system suggests that the emphasis is also on wool production. Once plucked or shorn lambs and kids would have a year's growth of wool and hair at the next *buqūnu*. Those that had not been plucked or shorn would have 1 year + *x* months growth. This system is doubly efficient in that it also accounts for the age of the animal. Elsewhere at Nuzi, the numbers of pluckings an adult sheep has undergone are indicative of its age (D. Cross, *op. cit.*, p. 27. As for sexual maturity, some small cattle become sexually mature by the time they are a year old. Perhaps the MÁŠ.TUR MUNUS Ù.TU and MÁŠ.TUR.NITA Ù.TU(!) are references to livestock that developed early. In general, however, the age of the animal would be sufficient indication as to their reproductive capabilities.

[125] See Appendix I for the breakdown of the herding contracts. Some of these flocks were clearly breeding flocks (*HSS* 9 53, 60, 61, 62; 13 495; 14 506, 557; 16 248 and 311, for example). Others seem to focus on wool and hair production (*HSS* 9 51, 54, 63, 65; 13 89 and 253, for example), or meat production, depending on the ultimate use of UDU.NITA^{MEŠ}. See below, p. 275. Note *HSS* 9 51, that includes 51 sheep and

differences should level out and the figures should present an approximation of the actual composition of the flocks at Nuzi. Table I provides data[126] from which a number of observations regarding flock composition and herd management may be drawn.

- The flocks are divided between sheep and goats by a ratio of about two to one.[127]

TABLE I: Aggregate Composition of the Flocks

	Number			% Flock	% Sheep			% Adult Sheep			% Ewes		
Total Flocks	971			100									
Sheep	651			67			100.0						
Ewes	283				43.5			50.2					100.0
Wethers	275				42.2			48.8					
Rams	6				.9			1.0					
Total Adults			564				86.6			100.0			
Once-plucked ewe-lambs	9				1.4			1.6			3.2		
Ewe-lambs	22				3.4			3.9			7.8		
Ewe-lambs *ḫurapu*	8				1.2			1.4			2.8		
Total ewe-lambs		39				6.0			6.9			13.8	
Once-plucked ram-lambs	11				1.7			2.0			3.9		
Ram-lambs	27				4.1			4.8			9.5		
Ram-lambs *ḫurapu*	7				1.1			1.2			2.5		
Total ram-lambs		45				6.9			8.0			15.9	
Ḫurapu	3				.5			.5			1.1		
Total Lambs			87				13.4			15.4			30.7

1 goat. This text may reflect the common practice of using goats, browsing animals, to keep the sheep, grazing animals, moving in the pastures.

[126]These data are drawn from all of the complete herding contracts in Appendix I. Texts in which one or more category of livestock is missing have been omitted.

[127]Note that H. H. Smith. *et al.*, *op. cit.*, comments that sheep make up nearly two-thirds of the livestock of present-day Iraq (p. 252). See also S. Payne's remarks concerning Aşvan Kale, *AS* 23, pp. 299-301. Climatic conditions impact heavily on flock composition. For example, in the western Negev of the Late Bronze Age goats predominate over sheep. (Private communication, Prof. Eliezer Oren.)

	Number			% Flock	% Goats			% Adult Goats			% Does		
Goats	320			33			100.0						
Does	156				48.8			55.5					100.0
Bucks	125				38.1			44.5					
Total Adults			281				87.8			100.0			
Once-shorn doe-kids	6				1.9			2.1			3.8		
Doe-kids	17				5.3			6.0			10.9		
Total doe-kids		23				7.2			8.1			14.7	
Once-shorn buck-kids	3				.9			1.1			1.9		
Buck-kids	13				4.1			4.6			8.3		
Total buck-kids		16				5.0			5.7			10.2	
Total kids			39				12.2			13.9			25.0

- Among the sheep, bearing ewes and wethers are found in approximately the same proportions. Among the goats the proportions are similar, though does occur in higher proportions than do bucks. There are far more males than were necessary for breeding purposes. Thus, the high numbers of adult male stock suggest that these animals were kept primarily for wool- and hair-production.[128] The lower percentages for adult males probably reflects some slaughter of such animals with a preference for goats.[129]

[128]Flocks are not kept for only a single purpose. The emphasis on the production of wool and hair, dairy products and meat will vary according to numerous circumstances. These figures suggest a wool-production model. See S. Payne, *AS* 23, p. 281-84.

[129]These animals were at least a year old when they were given to the herdsmen, presumably for part or all of another year. Thus, they could be 2+ years old at the time of slaughter. This figure coincides with the optimum time for slaughtering adults, that is 18 to 30 months of age. See S. Payne, *AS* 23, p. 282. D. Cross, *op. cit.*, pp. 26-27, suggests that grain given for *kuruštae(na)* was used to fatten male animals for slaughter. However, both male and female animals are associated with the term (*HSS* 9 50; 13 57, 371), and grain was given out as supplemental fodder. It is interesting that at least one text (*HSS* 16 234) may point to special feeding of ewes so as to improve the young stock they would bear or were nursing. Note, too, that lambs and kids may have been slaughtered. See below, n. 131. Concerning the preference for goats, see the

• Lambs are also divided about equally between males and females. As in the case of adult goats, the doe-kids occur in slightly higher proportions than do buck-kids. 23% each of the lambs and kids are described as once-plucked or once-shorn, or 6+ months of age, and 18% of the lambs are designated *ḫurapu*. These figures suggest that breeding occurred randomly and that lambing and kidding extended over a number of months. The lamb/ewe percentage and the kid/doe percentage are too low to reflect birth rates. These were the lambs and kids returned to the herdsman for another season. Others either were lost[130] or were slaughtered.[131]

• The similarity between the ewe/wether ratio and the ewe-lamb/ram-lamb ratio suggests that the lambs returned to pasture were for replacement purposes. If so, the lamb/adult sheep proportion allows for a 6.5 year turn-over in the flocks.[132] A similar situation exists for goats, but the turn-over rate for goats would be about 7 years.[133]

4. *Herding Practices*

The aggregate data from the contracts and the information presented by the descriptive terms for the livestock illustrate the purpose of herding at Nuzi and Nuzi breeding and herding practices. The composition of the flocks suggests that mixed-purpose herding was conducted at Nuzi. The herds were kept at a steady size while maximizing wool and hair production. Females were kept for breeding purposes, females and males for wool-, hair- and some meat-production and young stock were retained for replacement purposes. Two possible interpretations of breeding and herding practices can be formulated:

a) The term UDU.NITA includes both rams and wethers and the term Ù.TU implies simply that the ewes were capable of bearing young. Breeding occurred randomly while the flocks were in the pastures. The main lambing season began about five months after the *buqūnu* and extended through the fall and early winter months.[134] Thus, some lambs and kids

brief analysis of bone remains from Nuzi, R. F. Starr, *op. cit.*, pp. 492-93. Goat bones are said to be "common," while sheep bones are "uncommon."

[130]See below, p. 278ff.

[131]Some lambs and kids were probably slaughtered during their first year. The preference for slaughter appears to be for goats. A higher slaughter rate for young goats would explain the adult goat statistics.

[132]Sheep have an average life span of 7-10 years (see Payne, *AS*, p. 283), so this figure allows some margin for loss.

[133]Goats tend to be hardier than sheep, so this figure is not surprising.

[134]The average gestation period is about 5 months. If breeding began in May-June, then lambing would begin in October-November. This agrees with S. Payne's

would be old enough to pluck or shear at the *buqūnu* while others, born later, were not.

b) The terms UDU.NITA and *puḫallu* are mutually exclusive and the term Ù.TU indicates that the ewes and does were pregnant. In this case, the ewes and does were bred at the time of the *buqūnu* by rams and bucks that were normally kept separate from the main flocks.[135] The main lambing season would then occur five months after the *buqūnu*, or in the early fall. At the *buqūnu* these lambs and kids would be old enough to pluck or shear.

While the second possibility suggests a degree of sophistication in herd management, the fact that the majority of the lambs recorded on the contracts are not called once-plucked might indicate that the main lambing season came later than five months after the *buqūnu*.[136] In addition, the percentages of lambs of different ages are such that it appears that lambs were born over a period of months, not at about the same time. Thus, the first possibility seems more likely. It is important to note that the contracts record those animals sent out to pasture for the season. These animals may not represent the total produce of the flocks. For instance, livestock removed from the flocks for slaughter and for other purposes would not appear on the contracts. Without further information regarding such practices it is difficult to ascertain conclusively when the main lambing season occurred.

5. *The* muddû *texts*

Whereas the contracts record the receipt of livestock by the herdsmen, the more numerous *muddû* texts refer to that stage of the herding process when the accounts of the herdsmen were tallied. The standard *muddû* text is a brief statement sealed by the herdsman, for example *HSS* 13 385:[137]

> 3 bearing ewes, 5 lambs, 2 wethers, 4 kids: Total of 15 small cattle, the *muddû* of Ḫutip-apu son of Eḫlip-apu. Seal of (Ḫutip-apu) son of (Eḫlip-apu).

Some of the texts contain additional information that indicates that the livestock described as the *muddû* were owed by the herdsman to the livestock owner.[138] The *muddû*, then, may be considered the "outstanding balance" or

---

remarks in Postgate, *op. cit.*, p. 19, keeping in mind that at Nuzi, the whole process might be advanced by as much as a month.

[135]The ram/ewe ratio would allow for this interpretation; one ram can service 50-60 ewes. See Payne, *AS* 23, p. 301.

[136]As in the Old Babylonian texts. See Payne in Postgate, *op. cit.*, 19.

[137]Transliteration only.

[138]Most of the *muddû* texts include only the phrases: *muddûšu ša* PN (*AASOR* 16 92; *HSS* 9 56; *HSS* 13 269, 271, 297, 333, 335, 385, 386; 14 515, 524, 530, 567, 573,

"deficit" of the herdsman[139] and these texts are the herdsmen's legal acknowledgments to repay their deficits.[140] These deficits would arise out of losses that occurred during the time that the herdsman was responsible for the flocks.

The manner in which the livestock are described in the *muddû* texts and the composition of the *muddû*'s shed some light on the nature of losses to the flocks and how the herdsman's deficit was calculated. The terms used to describe the adult sheep and goats are the same as those of the contracts.[141] A small percentage of young stock are described as they are in the contracts. However, 90% of the young stock are described only as "lamb" or "kid" without gender and age designations. The composition of the livestock in the *muddû* texts (see Table II)[142] reflects that of the contracts for adults. Sheep and goats occur in roughly a two to one ratio. Adult females and males occur in approximately the same proportions, though the difference between does

---

582, 584, 613, 631; 16 245, 246, 250, 254, 255, 256, 257, 259, 261, 262, 269, 271, 275, 280, 284, 285, 286, 290, 293, 296, 298, 303, 305, 307, 425, and 430. The phrases that suggest that livestock described as the *muddû* were owed by the herdsman to the livestock owner include:

muddûšu ša PN (herdsman) *ina muḫḫišu ša ašbu* (*HSS* 13 295).

muddûšu ša PN (herdsman) *ina muḫḫišu ašbu u ana* PN_2 (livestock owner) *umalla* (*HSS* 9 45; 13 317; 14 513).

muddûšu ša PN (herdsman) *u ana* PN_2 (livestock owner) *umalla* (*HSS* 9 46; 14 552)

muddûšu ša PN (herdsman) *u ana* PN_2 (livestock owner) *inandin* (*HSS* 13 475; 16 319)

muddûšu ša PN (herdsman) *ina muḫḫišu ša* PN PN_2 (representative of livestock owner) *iltakanšunūti* (*HSS* 13 295).

muddûšu ša PN (herdsman) *ina muḫḫišu šaknu* (*HSS* 13 280).

[139] *CAD* M/2 161 s.v. "outstanding balance, delivery due, deficit, leftover." See also, G. Wilhelm, *Untersuchungen zum Hurro-Akkadischen von Nuzi*, *AOAT* 9 (1970), p. 46, n. 2. In addition, in *HSS* 9 26 the herdsman specifies that he will return his *muddû* in the next year. Some others state that the herdsman will cause them to enter the *buqūnu* (*HSS* 13 478; 16 289). Earlier interpretations of the *muddû* as "share" or "distribution" (E. A. Speiser, *AASOR* 16, p. 127 *et al.*) are superseded on the basis of the lengthier texts. The kinds of descriptive terms used and the composition of the *muddû*'s reinforce the view that the *muddû* was a deficit.

[140] The sealing of these texts by the herdsmen serves the same purpose as in the contracts. These texts are, in effect, contracts whereby the herdsman agrees to repay his debt.

[141] In two cases the descriptions are even more specific. *HSS* 13 306 and 475 make reference to the number of pluckings the sheep have undergone.

[142] See Appendix II for the breakdown of the *muddû* texts. The data in Table II are drawn from all of the complete *muddû* texts in Appendix II. As in the data from the contracts, texts in which one or more categories are missing have been omitted from the calculations.

and bucks is greater than that between ewes and wethers. For young stock, however, a major difference arises. Lambs comprise 57.1% of the total sheep and kids comprise 61.4% of the total goats as opposed to the 13.4% and 12.2% for the same ratios in the contracts.

The deficits were figured at the end of the herding year,[143] undoubtedly by comparing the livestock returned to those recorded on contracts.[144] Thus, the adult and young stock that are described accurately probably refer to animals lost from the flock that the herdsman received a year earlier. Some of these deficits are distributed more or less evenly according to the composition of the flocks.[145] Generally, normal patterns of loss may be suggested.[146] The remaining young stock deficits which do not seem to refer to livestock listed on the contracts probably reflect losses of young stock born during the year. The death rate for lambs and kids is far higher during their first year of life than that for older stock.[147] Moreover, the gender and age of the young stock born during the year would not be known to the supervisory personnel who tallied the accounts.[148] Deficits in young born during the year might have been figured on the basis of the skins returned by the herdsmen, but such a system would not have the control of a contract, as it did when applied to older stock.[149] Instead, deficits in young stock might have been calculated on the

[143]See above, p. 267ff.

[144]See above, p. 271.

[145]51.9% vs. 50.2% for ewes; 48.1% vs. 48.8% for wethers; 9.1% vs. 15.4% for lambs; 41.1% vs. 55.5% for does; 58.9% vs. 44.5% for bucks; 13.7% vs. 13.9% for kids.

[146]After the first year of life, age is the most significant factor. Bearing ewes might be expected to have a higher loss rate than wethers because of birthing problems. Does are hardier. The more aggressive male goats might have a higher loss rate than does. Otherwise, these animals might have been the logical choices for unauthorized slaughter in the pastures because they were less valuable: .95 shekels of silver (Eichler, *op. cit.*, p. 15).

[147]See Payne in Postgate, *op. cit.*, 20. The birthing process, diseases, weather conditions, predators and the like take a greater toll of the young stock that are weaker and more vulnerable than adult stock. For Larsa lamb losses, see Kraus, *op. cit.*, pp. 58ff. and n. 156 below.

[148]Age designations, expressed in terms of pluckings or shearings, clearly would not be possible. Note the single mention of "14 *kalūmu ḫurapu*" without gender in *HSS* 14 504. Because they are not identified by gender, they are considered here part of the newborn lambs, not previously recorded on contracts.

[149]The returning of skins is an efficient means of protecting the livestock owner only if the number of animals that were consigned is known. Questions could be raised about animals that were not returned and for which there was no evidence of their deaths. Counting debt in young stock not recorded on a contract by means of skins would leave herdsmen the opportunity of selling or using lambs or kids before their accounts were tallied.

basis of the expected yield of the numbers of UDU.MUNUS Ù.TU and *enzu* MUNUS Ù.TU included in the contracts.[150]

TABLE II: Aggregate Composition of the *Muddû* Texts.

	Number		% Number	% Sheep		% Adult Sheep	
Total *muddû*'s	625		100.0				
Sheep	436		69.8	100.0			
Ewes	97			22.2		51.9	
Wethers	90			20.6		48.1	
Total Adults		187			42.9		100.0
Ewe-lambs	1			.2			
Ram-lambs	16			3.7			
Total Described Lambs		17			3.9	9.1	
Lambs	218			50.0			
Lambs *ḫurapu*	14			3.2			
Total Other Lambs		232			53.2		
				% Goats		% Adult Goats	
Goats	189		30.2	100.0			
Does	30			15.9		41.1	
Bucks	43			22.8		58.9	
Total Adults		73			38.6		100.0
Doe-kids	5			2.6			
Buck-kids	5			2.6			
Total Described Kids		10			5.2		13.7
Kids	106			56.1			

[150]Such as the system of the Larsa accounts where the expected birth rate was 80 lambs to 100 ewes. See Kraus, *op. cit.*, pp. 9, 12-13, 18 (with reference to the Neo-Babylonian rate of 66 2/3 lambs to 100 ewes), 24-26, 50-51.

6. *The Herding Cycle*

A comparison of an average flock to an average deficit brings some perspective to the annual cycle of the flocks at Nuzi (see Table III).[151]

TABLE III: Average Flock and Average *Muddû*

	Average Flock		Average *Muddû*	
Total Number of Livestock	37.35		13.89	
Total Sheep	25.04		9.69	
Ewes	10.88		2.16	
Wethers	10.58		2.00	
Rams	.23		-	
Total Adults		21.69		4.16
Once-plucked ewe-lambs	.35		-	
Ewe-lambs	.85		.02	
Ewe-lambs *ḫurapu*	.31		-	
Once-plucked ram-lambs	.42		-	
Ram-lambs	1.04		.36	
Ram-lambs *ḫurapu*	.27		-	
Total Described Lambs		3.24		.38
Ḫurapu	.12		.31	
Lambs	-		4.84	
Total Other Lambs	-	.12		5.15
Total Goats	12.31		4.20	
Does	6.00		.67	
Bucks	4.81		.96	
Total Adults		10.81		1.62
Once-shorn doe-kids	.23		-	
Doe-kids	.65		.11	
Once-shorn buck-kids	.12		-	
Buck-kids	.50		.11	
Total Described Kids		1.50		.22
Kids	-		2.36	

[151]The data of Table III are calculated on the basis of the total figures of the twenty-six complete contracts and forty-five complete *muddû* texts.

Out of an average flock of 37.35 sheep and goats 6.38 animals or 17.1% are known to have been lost.[152] Of this number 5.78 or 90% are adults. The question remains as to whether the *muddû* texts include all losses from the flocks or the losses in excess of some allowable loss rate.[153] It might be expected that the herdsmen would not be held responsible for deaths due to old age and the like. As seen above, the herdsmen might be excused from repaying certain losses.[154] Further, in the two texts that include figures for both deaths and amounts owed the *muddû* figure is less than that for actual deaths.[155] Thus, the actual loss rate for the Nuzi herds could be higher, by as much as 15+%[156] than the amounts indicated by the *muddû* texts. The *muddû*'s or deficits, however, were to be repaid by the herdsmen, so theoretically, these losses would be made up when the debts were settled.[157] Expected losses due to natural and other causes would have to be met through the flocks' productivity. Perhaps, then, the percentages of young stock on the contracts, considered replacement stock above, allow for the expected loss rate: 15.4% for sheep and 13.9% for goats.

Aside from loss rates, the contracts and the *muddû* texts help in an approximation of expected birth rates as well. If the proportions of the average flock are held constant, the ratio of lambs that appear on the contracts, that is, those kept for replacement purposes, plus the number of lambs on the *muddû* texts, that is, those lost, to ewes yields a minimum birth

[152]That is, Total Adult Sheep + Total Described Lambs + Total Adult Goats + Total Described Kids.

[153]Such as the allowed 15 per 100 sheep of the Larsa texts, Kraus, *op. cit.*, pp. 9, 18 (with reference to the Neo-Babylonian rate of 10 per 100 sheep), 36-38, 58ff.

[154]See above, p. 270ff.

[155]*HSS* 16 260: 481 skins of sheep and goats as compared to 313 as the *muddû* figure. *AASOR* 16 92: a *muddû* of 24 sheep and goats, as opposed to 50 sheep that were lost.

[156]The Larsa loss rate plus losses for which herdsmen could not be held responsible. (Note the lower allowable rate for the Neo-Babylonian period.) High loss rates were not unusual in the ancient Near East. The Larsa texts, for example, show total flock losses ranging from 11.2% to 28.8% ($\frac{\textit{Fall + Fehlbetrag}}{\textit{Anfangsbestand}}$) and losses among lambs ranging from 25.9% to 79% ($\frac{\textit{Lamb Fehlbetrag}}{\textit{Lamb Anfangsbestand}}$). See Kraus, *op. cit.*, pp. 58ff. and data from Tables 5, 9 and 10.

[157]The few texts that clearly refer to the repayment of deficits by herdsmen include repayments that fall short of the average *muddû* figure. The available information is minimal, hence inconclusive. However, the herdsmen may not have been able to repay

rate of 78%.[158] The same calculation for kids yields a minimum 64.3% birth rate.[159] If the lambs are compared to ewes plus some of the ewe-lambs of the contracts, the birth rate drops to 70.3%.[160] For kids, treated similarly, the birth rate becomes 56.1%.[161]

The figures for both loss rates and expected birth rates are based on the average available data for flock and deficit size and composition. The figures do not take into consideration the years in which herdsmen did not have deficits or any young stock that were removed before the flocks were returned

---

their deficits at one time. The outstanding balance was probably carried over a period of years, hence such phrases as: *ina muḫḫi* PN PN_2 *iltakanšunūti*, "PN_2 placed them on PN's account."

Muddû*'s returned*

Text	Total	Total Sheep	Total Goats	ewe	wether	ewe-lamb	ram-lamb	lamb	bearing doe	doe	adult buck	doe-kid	buck-kid	kid
13 400	15	10	5	4	3	1	2		2			1	2	
14 509	7	3	4	1	1	1				1	1			2
14 596	3	0	3									1	2	
	2	0	2									1	1	
	5	2	3			1	1		1			1	1	

158 $\frac{3.35 + 4.84 + .31}{10.88} = 78.1\%$ Only those lambs born during the year are included from the *muddû* texts.

159 $\frac{1.50 + 2.36}{6.00} = 64.3\%$ Only those kids born during the year are included from the *muddû* texts.

160 $\frac{3.35 + 4.84 + .31}{10.88 \text{ (ewes)} + .35 \text{ (once-plucked ewe-lambs)} + .85 \text{ (ewe-lambs)}} = 70.3\%$

The once-plucked ewe-lambs would be 6+ months old at the beginning of the year and 18+ months old at the end; at this age the animals could have borne young. Also, some of the ewe-lambs under 6 months of age at the beginning of the year could have borne young, if they were 1 year and 5 months of age at the end of the year.

161 $\frac{1.5 + 2.36}{6.0 \text{ (does)} + .23 \text{ (once-shorn doe-kids)} + .65 \text{ (doe-kids)}} = 56.1\%$ The same conditions apply as for sheep. See n. 160.

to the herdsmen.[162] As a result, the loss rate calculated above is probably higher and the birth rate lower than those that occurred normally.

The annual cycle of the flocks had an important impact on the herdsman's economic situation. As mentioned above, the Nuzi contracts are similar to those of the Old Babylonian period, particularly with respect to the specificity of terms used to describe the livestock. Such contracts were used to calculate the expected yield of the flocks. In general, herdsmen were responsible for returning to the livestock owner a certain fixed portion of the produce of the flocks, including young stock, wool and hair. Deficits in these amounts had to be made up by the herdsman, and the surplus was retained by the herdsman. However, there is evidence that the proportions shared by the livestock owner and the herdsman varied and that other goods might comprise part of the herdsman's recompense.[163]

The contracts and *muddû* texts suggest that this kind of system was followed at Nuzi. An examination of individual consignment texts shows that the size and composition of the flocks vary considerably. Thus, the herdsmen's share in the produce of the flocks would include varying amounts and proportions of young stock, wool and hair, depending on the nature of the flocks for which they were responsible. In good years, the herdsmen would be able to build flocks of their own or accumulate other resources with which they could support themselves and their families. The *muddû* texts, on the other hand, reflect the years in which the herdsmen could not meet their obligations to the livestock owners. The size and composition of deficits would vary in accordance with both the nature of the original flock and the fortunes of the year. These debts would have to be paid out of the herdsmen's own resources or carried until the herdsmen could repay them.[164]

In addition to a share of the produce of the flocks, the herdsmen of Nuzi may have received other recompense for their work. Surplus dairy products produced while the herdsmen were away from settled areas could, of course, be consumed by the herdsmen. The receipt of grain as fodder for the livestock suggests that livestock owners contributed to the maintenance of the flocks. However, those quantities of grain received by the herdsmen, themselves, may have been part of their payment.

[162]The birth rate for lambs is close to that expected in the Larsa texts, that is 80%. Young stock removed for slaughter, as payment for the herdsmen, or for other purposes would not appear in either the consignment texts or the *muddû* texts. The lower figure for kids may reflect slaughter of these animals as suggested above, p. 276 and n. 131.

[163]Postgate, *op. cit.*, 5-6, 9-10, and Finkelstein, *op. cit.*, 32ff.

[164]Kraus, *op. cit.*, p. 61-63, and above, n. 157.

TABLE IV: Cattle Consignment and *Muddû* Texts.[171]

Text	Total	Females	Males	GU_4 *zilluena*	GU_4.ÁB Ù.TU	GU_4.NITA	GU_4.ÁB 1-year	GU_4.NITA 1-year	GU_4.ÁB 2-years	GU_4.NITA 2-years	GU_4.ÁB 3-years	GU_4.NITA 3-years	GU_4.NITA 4-years	GU_4.ÁB *ša waldū*	GU_4.NITA *ša waldū*
Consignment Texts:															
13 330	52	43	9	2	24				10	4		4		5	3
	9				9										
13 331	40	28	12		21		?	?		1	4	1	7		
16 429	45?	32?	13?	1	22	?	7?	8	3	3			1		
16 453	58	40	18	3	29		5	7			6	8			
Totals	204?	143?	52?	6	105?		12?	15?	13	8	10	13	8	5	3
Muddû Texts:															
13 333	16?	8	7	?	7	?			1+2	2+3					
13 378	4	3	1		1				2			1			
	17	11	6		5				6	3		3			
16 425	9	1	8			8			1						
16 430	2	2	0		2										
Totals	48	25	22	?	15	8			10	4		4			

C. CATTLE

Although law suits involving cattle are considerably more frequent than those involving sheep and goats, there are far fewer texts relating to the herding of cattle. Those that exist, however, show that contracts of the same sort as those used for small cattle were employed in the consignment of large cattle to oxherds.[165] As shown above, the oxherd was responsible for repaying livestock that died or were lost while in his care, barring cases where the oxherd could show that he had not been negligent.[166] *Muddû* texts like those of the shepherds record the deficits of the oxherds.[167]

[171]See D. Cross, *op. cit.*, pp. 16-22 for discussion of terms used for cattle at Nuzi. In addition, *CAD* A/1 364 s. *alpu* and L 217 s. *littu* provide more recent data, including the note that the cow is represented at Nuzi by both GU_4.ÁB and GU_4.SAL.

[165]See above, p. 270 and n. 97.

[166]See above, p. 270f. and notes 102-4.

[167]A typical cattle *muddû* text is *HSS* 16 430:

1) 2 bearing cows, 2) the *muddû* 3) of Bēl-aḫḫēšu, 4) of Akkulenni, 5) and of Arp-iššuhri 6) sons of Arn-apu. 7) Seal of Arp-iššuhri 8) son of Arn-apu. 9) Seal of Bēl-aḫḫēšu son of Arn-apu. 10) Seal of Akkulenni 11) son of Arn-apu.

Information on herd composition is sparse. In addition, the four herds that are documented were consigned to the same family of oxherds.[168] As a result, the perspective provided by these materials may not be a balanced one. Females comprise 70% of the total herds and relatively equal proportions of yearlings, 2-year olds and 3-year olds appear, though in varying ratios of males and females. The male stock comprises only 30% of the herds. Most of these animals were probably oxen, i.e. castrated males, given the problems of managing more than one adult bull in a herd.[169] The absence of calves in both the contracts and the *muddû* texts is surprising[170] (see Table IV).

Cattle appear not only in the herding texts, but also in those related to plowing, one of the principal uses for cattle. Two texts record the receipt of cattle *ašar sugulli ana ikkarūti*, "from the herd for plowing,"[172] one in the month of *Sabutu*[173] and the other in *Ḫiaru.*[174] *HSS* 16 427 lists GU$_4^{MEŠ}$ *ikkarātu* given to 8 men.[175] Some of these men reappear as receiving oxen[176] or as owning an ox.[177] These texts recording the consignment of cattle to plowmen and the deficits of plowmen are similar to the oxherds' contracts and *muddû* statements.[178]

It is interesting that the cattle given to these men include both males and females of varying ages and descriptions:

> 1 GU$_4$.MUNUS Ù.TU *itti mūrišu* NITA; 4 GU$_4$.NITA *šulušiu* and 1 GU$_4$.MUNUS *šulušiu*[179]

[168]*HSS* 13 330, 331; 16 429 and 453. With the exception of the reference to 9 bearing cows given to Wirriš-tanni in *HSS* 13 330 and the appearance of Taika with Bēl-aḫḫēšu in 16 453, all of these refer to the sons of Arn-apu: Bēl-aḫḫēšu, Akkulenni and Arp-iššuḫri.

[169]It is conceivable that the three oxherds involved in these contracts could split the herd so as to retain more bulls. However, one would expect only one bull to be kept with a herd aside from bull-calves and a possible young bull for replacement purposes.

[170]With the possible exception of *HSS* 13 330 in which 5 GU$_4$.ÁB *ša waldū* and GU$_4$.NITA *ša waldū* are mentioned.

[172]Note *HSS* 16 428, "*ana* ^{LÚ}*ikkarūti*(!)," most likely a confusion with $^{LÚ.MEŠ}$ *ikkarātū.*

[173]*HSS* 13 448.

[174]*HSS* 16 428.

[175]Arip-papni, Šušip-šamaš, Teḫiya, Wirriš-tanni, Turariya, Turari, Pentammu and Warim-mušni.

[176]Teḫiya, Turari, Turariya, Wirriš-tanni: *HSS* 16 426. Turariya and Šušip-šamaš: *HSS* 13 425.

[177]Warim-mušni: *HSS* 13 386. Šušip-šamaš and Teḫiya: *HSS* 13 423.

[178]See above, n. 102.

[179]"One bearing cow with her bull-calf; 4 3-year-old oxen and 1 3-year-old cow." *HSS* 13 425.

2 GU$_4$.MUNUS and 1 GU$_4$.NITA[180]
x+1 GU$_4$.NITA[181]
2 to 8 GU$_4$ *ikkarātu*[182]
1 GU$_4$.ÁB[183]

The data from the contracts indicates that the herds were primarily breeding herds. The younger female stock and a portion of the male stock would be kept for replacement purposes. However, the materials referring to plow-oxen suggest that the cattle in the contracts include not only breeding stock but also those animals that were not being used for plowing. The yearlings and possibly the two-year olds might not have been old enough to train and use.[184] The male stock in excess of the number necessary for breeding were either "out to pasture" for a rest from their plowing functions or kept in reserve to replace plow oxen.

An interesting issue arises in relation to the texts that record the receipt of oxen for plowing. A number of the men who seem to be engaged in plowing have the same names as men who are either described as ^{LÚ}SIPA or appear in small cattle contexts.[185] Additionally, the same men receive fodder for the cattle, and grain for other purposes.[186] In some of these grain texts herdsmen or individuals with the same names as herdsmen also appear.[187] These occurrences may point to a close association between herding and planting, complementary seasonal activities. It would be possible for individuals to put in a crop and then take livestock to pasturelands while family members cared for the tilled fields. When the flocks returned, they could graze on the harvested fields close to home. Supervisory personnel in agricultural districts could also be involved in herding activities in conjunction with individuals living within their areas of responsibility. The nature and extent of the relationship between herdsmen and agricultural personnel requires further examination. Exhaustive

[180] "Two cows and 1 ox." *HSS* 13 448.
[181] "*x*+1 oxen." *HSS* 16 426.
[182] In a number of consignments, two to eight "plow-oxen" are given. *HSS* 16 427.
[183] "1 cow." *HSS* 16 428.
[184] The age at which training of oxen began is not known. By modern standards yearlings would be too young, but training could begin by the age of two.
[185] Šušip-šamaš, Teḫiya, Wirriš-tanni, Turariya, Turari, Pentammu.
[186] Fodder for oxen, presumably the plow owen: *HSS* 16 11 (Teḫiya; Pentammu also appears); *HSS* 13 202 (Wirriš-tanni, Arip-papni). Grain on loan for plowing: *HSS* 13 243 (Arip-papni, Turari). ŠE^{MEŠ} *ša* GU$_4^{\text{MEŠ}}$, NUMUN^{MEŠ}: *HSS* 14 598 (Šušip-šamaš, Turariya, Pentammu). Grain as ŠE.BA for others: *HSS* 13 247 (Arip-papni).
[187] *HSS* 13 243 (Ḫašip-tilla; ^{LÚ}SIPA *ša* ^{URU}*paqqanupḫe*; Ḫutip-tilla; ^{LÚ}SIPA.ÁB.GUD). *HSS* 16 11 (Bēl-aḫḫēšu ^{LÚ}SIPA.GU$_4^{\text{MEŠ}}$ - ŠE.BA; Šekar-zizza - *ziriqa ana* UDU^{MEŠ}). *HSS* 16 227 includes names that are the same as those of many herdsmen and plowmen,

analysis of both the archives in which these individuals appear and the glyptic materials may clarify these matters.[188]

Conclusion

The cumulative evidence from livestock texts and related materials provides insight into the social and economic position of the herdsmen and an outline of both the herding process and the annual cycle of the herds at Nuzi. The resulting view of these aspects of the social organization and the economy of Nuzi is consistent in part with what is known of other Mesopotamian sites but diverges in certain specific areas of consideration. In particular, the contract-deficit procedure and related practices reflect those of the Old Babylonian period. Differences in terminology and calendar are attributable to regional variations in language and climate. At any site, the factors that affect the herdsmen's position and the composition of the flocks must be sought in other sectors of the society and the economy. The herdsmen's relationship to the community is a function of the nature of the profession and the broader structure of their society. The purpose of herding and the size of the flocks are dictated by such aspects of the economy as the textile industry and the leather industry and such environmental factors as available pasture, surplus grain for fodder and housing for the animals. The free Nuzi herdsman who was engaged in mixed-purpose herding with emphasis on wool and hair production represents one of many possible variations on this most familiar ancient Near Eastern theme.

APPENDIX I

Shepherds and Oxherds in the Nuzi Texts

(Š=Archives of Šilwa-tešub; T=Archives of Teḫip-tilla *mār* Puḫi-šenni; P=Puḫi-šenni *mār* Muš-apu; E=Palace; I=Ilā-ma-aḫī *mār* Ilānu)

Akaia (Š)
HSS 16 242
Akip-tilla (Š)
HSS 13 221, 248, 451.
Akip-tilla *mār* Eḫel-tešub (Š)
HSS 13 132; 14 567, 631; 16 274, 280; *EN* 9 300.
Akiya
HSS 16 305
Akkulenni *mār* Arn-apu (Š)
HSS 13 331, 333; 16 425, 429, 430.
Alpuya (Š)
HSS 16 288.
Apaya (Š)
HSS 13 191.
Abu-rabi (Š)
HSS 13 451.

[188] We look forward to the publication of G. Wilhelm's volumes on the archives of Šilwa-tešub for whom these herdsmen and agricultural personnel worked, and to Ms. Diana Stein's doctoral dissertation on the seal impressions of Nuzi.

Arilliya *mār* Šum-ili (Š)
  HSS 16 267.
Arp-iššuḫri *mār* Arn-apu (Š)
  HSS 13 331, 333; 16 425, 430.
Ar-zizza (Š)
  HSS 14 637
Aštar-tilla *mār* Turari (Š)
  HSS 9 26; 16 324(?); 19 146.
Bēl-aḫḫēšu (Š)
  HSS 16 11; 453=*AASOR* 16 86
Bēl-aḫḫēšu *mār* Arn-apu (Š)
  HSS 9 11; 148+IM 50805; 13 330, 331, 333; 16 425, 429, 430.
Bēliya *mār* Kelum-atal
  HSS 16 452.
Bēliya *mār* Taya (T)
  JEN 326, 353.
Eḫlip-apu (Š)
  HSS 13 221, 248, 358, 389; 14 590, 637; 16 249.
Eḫlip-apu *mār* Arta (Š)
  HSS 13 57, 372; 14 530; 16 245, 253, 255, 296, 303.
Elḫip-tilla *mār* Ḫanaya
  HSS 16 384.
Ḫal-šenni *mār* Hanaya
  HSS 16 384.
Ḫanaya *mār* Apaya (Š)
  HSS 9 53, 61; 13 478.
Ḫanaya *mār* Arip-apu
  JEN 155, 196, 211, 228, 231, 259, 451, 591.
Ḫanaya *mār* Ṣilli-marta (Š)
  HSS 16 248.
Ḫanirra (Š)
  HSS 9 48.
Ḫanirra *mār* Šatu-kewi (Š)
  HSS 9 59; 13 210; 16 242+282, 246.
Ḫašip-apu (Š)
  HSS 16 241.
Ḫašip-tešub *mār* Palteya (I)
  HSS 5 9, 15.
Ḫašip-tilla (Š)
  HSS 9 48; 13 224, 248, 390, 401, 457; 14 519, 583, 590, 596, 637; 16 234, 249, 282, 304.
Ḫašip-tilla *mār* Eḫlip-ukur (Š)
  HSS 9 58; 13 329, 437; 14 572; 16 257.
Ḫašip-tilla *mār* Kelip-ukur
  HSS 13 308; *YBC* 11275.
Ḫulukka
  RA 23 (1926), Text 77.
Ḫutip-apu (Š)
  HSS 9 48.
Ḫutip-apu *mār* Eḫlip-apu (Š)
  HSS 9 60; 13 385, 495; 16 240(?), 242+282, 300.
Ḫutip-tilla *mār* Nikriya (I)
  HSS 5 9, 15.
Ḫutip-tilla (Š)
  HSS 13 221.
Ḫutip-tilla *mār* Tauka (Š)
  HSS 9 13; 13 371.
Ḫutiya *mār* Ar-tirwi (Š)
  HSS 9 31; 13 321.
Ḫuziri (E)
  JEN 525, 670.
Inniki (E)
  HSS 14 554.
Itḫišta (Š)
  HSS 13 248; 14 505.
Itḫiya
  HSS 14 236.
Izkanabi (Š)
  HSS 13 451.
Kai-tilla (Š)
  HSS 9 48; 13 224, 389, 457; 14 590, 650; 16 234, 281.
Kai-tilla *mār* Teḫip-tilla (Š)
  HSS 9 46; 14 582; 16 240, 275, 285.
Kanie (Š)
  HSS 13 249, 311, 388, 451.
Kanie *mār* Turari
  HSS 13 23.
Kanipa (Š)
  HSS 9 48.
Kanipa *mār* Tae (Š)
  HSS 13 297; 14 515; 16 251.
Kaniya (E)
  HSS 16 324, 325.

Kaniya *mār* Turari (Š)
HSS 16 254.
Karrate (Š)
HSS 13 451(?); 14 650.
Kelke (Š)
HSS 9 48; 13 389, 401; 14 596, 637; 16 304.
Kelke *mār* Ḫulukka (Š)
HSS 9 137; 13 363; 14 614; 16 298.
Kel-teya (Ḫut-tešub) (of Kabla)
HSS 16 436.
Gimillu (of Kabla)
HSS 16 436.
Qîšt-amurri (Š)
HSS 14 596, 637; 16 304.
Kipaya (Shepherd of Keliya)
AASOR 16 6.
Kipiya *mār* Abeya (Shepherd of Warrateya)
AASOR 16 3; *JEN* 134.
Kip-tilla (E)
HSS 16 325.
Kip-tilla *mār* Turari (E)
HSS 16 324, 325.
Kuppatiya (Š)
HSS 13 247, 451.
Kuppatiya *mār* Ariḫ-ḫamanna (Š)
HSS 9 31; 13 280, 321; 16 258.
Namḫeya (E)
HSS 13 493; 14 593.
Niḫriya (E)
HSS 15 12, 18; 16 314.
Nukra (Š)
HSS 13 224.
Nullu (Š)
HSS 9 48; 13 268, 388, 389; 14 590; 641; 16 242+282, 272, 304.
Nullu *mār* Akip-tilla (Š)
HSS 9 63; 13 260; 14 590; 16 262, 307.
Pai-tilla (Š)
HSS 13 401.
Pentammu *mār* Ninkiya (Š)
HSS 14 650.
Pilmašše (Š)
HSS 9 48; 13 358, 437, 447; 14 637; 16 234.
Pilmašše *mār* Ḫutip-tilla (Š)
HSS 13 437; 14 504, 506, 526; 16 242+282, 290.
Puḫi-Šenni
HSS 13 362; 14 593.
Pula-ḫali (T)
JEN 350
Sin-dayyān (Š)
HSS 13 248, 389; 14 514, 519, 650; 16 234, 249, 272.
Šar-tešub (Tetip-tešub) (of Kabla)
HSS 16 436.
Šar-tilla (Š)
HSS 9 48; 13 224, 362, 388, 401, 457; 16 234, 272.
Šar-tilla *mār* En-šukru (Š)
HSS 9 50, 54, 65; 13 271, 335.
Šatu-kewi (Š)
HSS 13 311, 451; 14 590.
Šatu-kewi *mār* Interta
HSS 9 14, 31; 13 21; 16 240.
Šekar-zizza (Š)
HSS 13 298, 389, 475; 14 519, 590, 637; 16 11.
Šekar-zizza *mār* Ḫanakka (Š)
AASOR 16 92; *HSS* 13 441; 16 240, 250.
Šekaya (Š)
HSS 9 48; 13 311, 388, 400, 451; 14 637; 16 272, 304.
Šekaya *mār* Urḫiya (Š)
HSS 9 14, 49, 51, 138; 13 317, 379; 14 613.
Šennaya (Š)
HSS 13 389; 14 519.
Šennaya *mār* Abu-bīti (Š)
HSS 13 453; 16 240(?).
Šenni (Š)
HSS 13 389; 14 514, 519, 590, 596.
Šenni *mār* Ḫuziri (Š)
HSS 9 45; 14 573.
Šeš-tae (Š)
HSS 14 519.
Šešwiya (Š)
HSS 9 48; 13 248, 268, 388, 389; 14 590, 637, 272.

Šešwiya *mār* Arilliya (Š)
HSS 13 295, 306; 14 557, 632; 16 240, 242+282, 259, 261, 271, 277, 284.
Šiḫaš-šenni (E)
HSS 13 493; 14 593.
Šilaḫi (E)
HSS 13 156; 14 593.
Šilaḫi *mār* Ip[ ]
HSS 16 316.
Šimika-atal *mār* Tae (Š)
HSS 9 62; 13 297; 14 515; 16 251.
Šukr-apu
RA 28 (1931) Text 4 (AO.10890).
Šukriya (Š)
HSS 13 191; 16 315.
Šur-tešub (Š) (?)
HSS 13 378.
Šušip-šamaš (Š)
HSS 13 248; 14 505; 519.
Tae (Š)
HSS 13 389; 14 596, 637.
Tae *mār* Kawinni (Š)
HSS 13 427, 497; 14 513.
Taika (Š)
HSS 16 453=*AASOR* 16 86.
Taika
HSS 14 37.
Taule (Š)
HSS 9 48; 13 224, 389, 401, 457; 14 519, 590, 596; 16 234, 272, 304.
Taule *mār* Itḫišta (Š)
HSS 13 89.
Taya
HSS 16 266.
Taya *mār* Ward-aḫḫēšu (T)
JEN 6, 341, 464, 596.
Teḫip-tilla (Š)
HSS 16 269.
Teḫiya (Š)
HSS 13 451.
Tieš-šimika *mār* Tarmi-tilla
JEN 665.
Tuḫmiya
HSS 15 284.
Tuntuya (Š)
HSS 9 48; 13 268, 388.
Tuntuya *mār* Sin-dayyān (Š)
HSS 13 258, 296; 14 584.
Tupkiya
URSS 60.
Turari (Š)
HSS 16 243.
Turari *mār* Wantiya (Š)
HSS 9 56; 13 253, 263, 393; *JEN* 413.
Turariya (Š)
HSS 13 248; 14 519.
Ulluya (Š)
HSS 9 61.
Unap-tešub
HSS 16 266.
Urḫi-tešub *mār* Ḫut-tešub (Š) (?)
HSS 13 378.
Urḫiya (Š)
HSS 9 48; 13 388, 401, 414; 14 590, 596, 637; 16 234.
Urḫiya *mār* Ikkianni (Š)
HSS 9 64; 14 524; 16 240, 242+282, 293, 297.
Utḫap-tae *mār* Akip-tilla (Š)
HSS 9 63; 13 260; 16 307, 242+282.
Wantiya (Š)
HSS 9 48; 13 249, 358, 389, 401; 14 590, 596, 637, 650; 16 234, 272.
Wantiya *mār* Unkura (Š)
HSS 13 255, 269; 14 508, 509; 16 240, 256, 292.
Wantiya *mār* Wirriš-tanni (Š)
HSS 13 56; 14 650.
Wara-abi (Š)
HSS 13 451.
Waratteya (Š)
HSS 9 48; 13 249, 388, 451(?); 16 249.
Waratteya *mār* Wantiya (Š)
HSS 9 56, 57; 13 253; 16 242+282.
Wirriš-tanni (Š)
HSS 13 248 (Sheep); 13 330 (Cattle).
Ṣill-kūbi (Š)
HSS 13 389.
Ṣill-kūbi *mār* Puḫi-šenni
HSS 9 62; 13 427.
Zikaru *mār* Šalliya (P)
HSS 311, 449.

APPENDIX II

The Herding Contracts

Text	Ewes	Wethers	Rams	Ewe-lambs	Ram-lambs	Total Sheep	Does	Bucks	Doe-kids	Buck-kids	Total Goats	Miscellaneous	Total Flock
HSS													
9 49	3	9*		1	1	13	5		3	1	9	1 *ḫurapu*	22
50**	5	1		2	4	12	3	2	4	4	13		25
51	11	36		2*	2*	51		1			1		52
52**		2				2	1			1*	2		4
53	28	2	3	5*	6*	44					0		44
54	4	16				20	4	8			12		32
57							9	3	1	3	16	15 UDU [ ]	31
58	12	34		3	?	49+	3	7			10		59+
59						0	6	20			26		26
60	16	9				25	8	3			11		36
61	35	1	3	8	7	54					0		54
62		4				4	26	22	5*	2*	55		59
63	6	18		1	2	27	3	5	1	1	10		37
64	2	7			1	10	11	7	1	2	21		31
65	2	18				20	1	7			8		28
137	?	?		?	?	?	?	?	?	1	?		87
138	4	11				17	4	4			8	2 *ḫirapu*	25
13 57**	13	1				14					0		14
89	14	49		1	6	70	3	14	1*		18		88
253	3	20				23	9	6			15		38
258	10	6			2	18		5			5		23
260	?	24		?	?	24+	10	?	?	?	10+		44
371**	13	2		2*	3*	20					0		20
379	5	7		7		19	7			3	11	1 MÁŠ	30
495	13	6		2	2	23	8	2	3	1	14		37
14 506	22	6		3	6	37	5	3			9	1 [MÁŠ.TUR]	46
557	21	6		3	3	33	10	4	2	1	17		52(!)
614	?	26		2	1	29+	16	16	?	?	32+		76
14 632	12	10				22	8	2	2		12		34
16 248	26	17				43	29	9			38		81

Text	Ewes	Wethers	Rams	Ewe-lambs	Ram-lambs	Total Sheep	Does	Bucks	Doe-kids	Buck-kids	Total Goats	Miscellaneous	Total Flock
266	20	?				20+	20	10			30		50+
300	15	9				24	9	3			12		36
310	?	?		?	?	?	2	?	?	?	2+		31+
311	21	8		6	4	39	6	1	3		10		49

*once-plucked or shorn
***ana kuruštaena*

ewes - UDU.MUNUS Ù.TU^{MEŠ}: 9 49, 50, 53, 54, 58, 60, 61, 63, 64, 65, 138; 13 57 (10 *baqnūtu*, 3 *ša ti-ši bu-qu-ni*), 89, 253, 495; 14 632, 16 300. UDU.MUNUS^{MEŠ} Ù.TU: 9 51; 13 371. UDU^{MEŠ}MUNUS: 13 258. UDU.MUNUS: 16 248. UDU.MUNUS GAL: 16 266. UDU^{MEŠ}MUNUS Ù.TU: 16 311. UDU^{MEŠ}MUNUS^{MEŠ} *ša* Ù.TU: 14 557. UDU.MUNUS *ša* Ù.TU: 13 379; 14 506.
wethers - UDU.NITA^{MEŠ} GAL: 9 49, 50, 51, 52, 53, 54, 60, 62, 63, 64 138; 13 253, 260, 371, 495; 14 506, 557, 614, 632; 16 300. UDU.NITA GAL^{MEŠ}: 9 58, 61, 65; 13 57; 16 266. UDU.NITA^{MEŠ}: 13 89, 258; 16 248. UDU.NITA GAL^{MEŠ}-*ti*: 13 379. UDU^{MEŠ}NITA.MUNUS(!) 16 311.
rams - *puḫallu*; 9 53. UDU.NITA *puḫallu*: 9 61.
ewe-lambs - *kalūmu* MUNUS^{MEŠ}; 9 50, 51, 53, 58, 63; 13 89, 371, 495; 14 506, 557, 614; 16 311. *kalūmu* MUNUS *ḫurapu*: 9 61. UDU *kalūmu* MUNUS: 13 379.
ram-lambs - *kalūmu* NITA^{MEŠ}: 9 50, 51, 53, 58, 63, 64; 13 89, 258, 371, 495; 14 506, 557, 614; 16 311. *kalūmu* NITA *ḫurapu*: 9 61.
does - *enzu* MUNUS Ù.TU^{MEŠ}: 9 49, 50, 54, 58, 59, 60, 62, 63, 64, 65, 138; 13 89, 253, 260, 495; 14 506, 614; 16 300. *enzu* MUNUS: 14 632; 16 248. *enzu* MUNUS GAL: 16 266. *enzu* MUNUS *ša* Ù.TU: 9 52; 13 379; 14 557. *enzu ša* Ù.TU: 16 311. *enzu* MUNUS [ ]: 9 57. MÁŠ MUNUS GAL: 13 260.
bucks - MÁŠ^{MEŠ} GAL; 9 50, 54, 57, 59, 60, 62, 63, 64, 65, 138; 13 253, 258, 495; 14 506, 632; 16 300. MÁŠ^{MEŠ} GAL.GAL.: 14 557. MÁŠ GAL: 9 51; 13 89; 14 614; 16 266, 311. MÁŠ: 16 248.
doe-kids - MÁŠ.TUR MUNUS^{MEŠ} 9 49, 50, 57, 62, 64; 13 89, 495; 14 557, 614. *laliʾu* MUNUS^{MEŠ}: 16 311. MÁŠ.TUR MUNUS Ù.TU^{MEŠ}: 9 63. MÁŠ^{MEŠ}TUR MUNUS: 14 632.
buck-kids - MÁŠ.TUR.NITA^{MEŠ}: 9 49, 50, 57, 62, 64, 137; 13 495; 14 557, 614. *laliʾu* NITA: 9 52. MÁŠ.TUR.NITA Ù.TU^{MEŠ}: 9 63.

APPENDIX III

The *Muddû* Texts

Text	Ewes	Wethers	Ewe-lambs	Ram-lambs	Lambs	Total Sheep	Does	Bucks	Doe-kids	Buck-kids	Kids	Total Goats	Miscellaneous	Total Deficit
HSS														
9 45						0			1	2		3		3
46					9	9					2	2		11
56	10	17	1			38						0		38
13 210						0	3	3			3	9		9
269					7	7	1				8	9		16
271						2	2				2	2		6
280					3	3					2	2		5
295					13	13						0		13
297						0	?	5	?	?	?	8		8
298	?	?			17	17+	?	?				?		30+
306	1	3			8	12	3	9			5	17		29
317						0	2				1	3		3
335	1	4			1	6					1	1		7
385	3	2			5	10					4	4		15(!)
400	4	3	1	2		10	2		1	2		5		15
453	10				10	20						0		20
475	5*	7*			7	19						0		19
478	4	1			6	11						0		11
14 504					14	14	1*				14	15		29
508	?	?	1		13	?	7	3				10		23
509	1	1*	1			3	1*	1			2	4		7
513						0		1	4			5		5
515		1				1	15	14				29		30
524	1*				2	3					9	9		12
530					3	3						0		3
567	1				6	7						0		7
572	1*				4	5						0		5
573					1	1					7	7		8
582	9	8			16	33		2			8	10		43
584					1	1						0		1
613		1			?	1+		1				1+		2+
631	1				14	15						0		15

Text	Ewes	Wethers	Ewe-lambs	Ram-lambs	Lambs	Total Sheep	Does	Bucks	Doe-kids	Buck-kids	Kids	Total Goats	Miscellaneous	Total Deficit
16 243					2	2	15	2			6	23	3 *ḫirapu*, 3 *azatu*	31
245	1				?	1+	?				2	2+		11
246						0		14				14		14
250		1			1	2						0		2
254					4	4						0		4
255							2			3	2*	7		7
256	17	3			21	41						9		50
257					5	5						0		5
258	?	?				?	?	?			?	?	1 *azatu*	33
259					5	5		?			?	18		23
261							20	?	?	?	?	40		40
262					1	1					7	7		8
263		16		6		22						0		22
267		3			6	9					2	2		11
269						0			?	?	?	1		1
271						?					?	?		17
274					9	9						0		9
275		?*			?						3	3		3+
280					21	21						0		21
284	3				4?	7?		1			1	2		9?
285	5	1			3	9	1				7	8		17
286	?	?			4	4+	1+	4			6	11+		15+
289					?	?					1	1		
290					6	6						4		10
293	?	?			?	?					8	8		8+
296					?	?					?	?		?
297	1*				2	3					9	9		12
298		1			?	1+					2	2		3+
301	6	5			6	17						0		17
303					3	3						0		3
316	?	12	?	?		25						0		25
319		2				2						0		2
AASOR														
16 92	10	4			10	24						0		24

* once plucked or shorn

ewes - UDU.MUNUS Ù.TU^{MEŠ}: 9 56; 13 298, 306, 385, 400; 14 509, 567, 582, 631; 16 245, 256, 284, 285, 293, 301; *AASOR* 16 92. UDU.MUNUS^{MEŠ}Ù.TU: 13 475. UDU.MUNUS^{MEŠ} *ša* Ù.TU: 13 453; 14 508. UDU *ša* Ù.TU: 16 316. UDU.MUNUS Ù.TU^{MEŠ}GAL: 13 478; 16 258. UDU.MUNUS *ša* Ù.TU *ša la bá-aq-nu*: 13 335. UDU.MUNUS^{MEŠ}: 13 475; 14 524, 572; 16 297.

wethers - UDU.NITA^{MEŠ}GAL: 9 56; 13 385, 400; 14 582; 16 267, 293; *AASOR* 16 92. UDU.NITA GAL^{MEŠ}: 13 298, 306; 14 513, 613; 16 256, 285, 316. UDU.NITA^{MEŠ}: 13 475; 14 509; 16 250, 275, 301. UDU.NITA GAL^{MEŠ} *ša la bá-aq-nu*: 13 335. UDU^{MEŠ} *la bá-aq-nu*: 16 319. UDU.NITA 2-*ni-šu*(*nu*) *bá-aq-nu*: 13 478; 16 258, 263. UDU: 13 306.

ewe-lambs - *kalūmu* MUNUS: 9 56; 13 400; 14 508, 509. *kalūmu* Ù.TU: 16 250.

ram-lambs - *kalūmu* NITA^{MEŠ}: 9 56; 13 400; 16 263.

lambs - *kalūmu*^{MEŠ}; 9 46; 13 269, 271, 280, 295, 298, 306, 335, 385, 453, 475, 478; 14 524, 530, 567, 572, 573, 582, 584, 613, 631; 16 243, 245, 254, 256, 257, 259, 262, 267, 274, 275, 280, 285, 286, 293, 296, 297, 301, 303; *AASOR* 16 92. *kalūmu*^{MEŠ} *ḫurapu*: 14 504; 16 258, 271, 289. *kalūmu ḫurapena*: 16 284.

does - *enzu* MUNUS Ù.TU^{MEŠ}: 13 210, 271, 298, 306, 400; 14 515; 16 243, 245, 255, 258, 261, 285. *enzu* MUNUS^{MEŠ} *ša* Ù.TU: 14 508. *enzu* MUNUS^{MEŠ}: 13 317; 14 504, 509. *enzu* UDU.MUNUS Ù.TU: 13 269. MÁŠ MUNUS^{MEŠ} 14 515.

bucks - MÁŠ GAL^{MEŠ} 13 298; 14 509, 513, 515, 613; 16 284. MÁŠ^{MEŠ}GAL: 13 210, 306; 14 582; 16 243, 246. MÁS^{MEŠ}: 13 297; 14 508.

doe-kids - MÁŠ.TUR MUNUS: 9 45; 13 400. MÁŠ.TUR MUNUS^{MEŠ} Ù.TU: 14 513. *laliʾu* Ù-*dì-ú*:14 504.

buck-kids - MÁŠ.TUR.NITA^{MEŠ}: 9 45; 13 317, 335, 400; 16 255.

kids - MÁŠ.TUR^{MEŠ}: 9 46; 13 210, 269, 271, 280, 306, 385; 14 509, 524, 573, 582; 16 243, 255, 256, 262, 267, 275, 284, 285, 289, 296, 297, 298. MÁŠ^{MEŠ} TUR^{MEŠ}: 16 243, 258, 293. MÁŠ.TUR.TUR: 13 271.

Gasur
nella Documentazione Epigrafica Di Ebla

G. Pettinato
Roma

Nel mio libro *Ebla. Un impero inciso nell'argilla*, Milano 1979, parlando dell'area geografica di espansione dell'impero commerciale di Ebla, ho scritto testualmente che essa comprendeva anche Gasur, la Nuzi dei periodi posteriori: "A oriente, si ha la massima espansione dell'impero di Ebla: essa controllava innanzitutto le zone dell'Eufrate con le città di Karkemiš, Emar e Mari e tutta la zona retrostante dell'attuale Gezira e Mesopotamia settentrionale. Possiamo racchiudere quest'area, che nel III millennio doveva essere popolata al massimo, nel triangolo Ḫarran-Assur-Gasur o Erbilum."[1]

Con ciò ho voluto affermare che nei testi cuneiformi rinvenuti a Tell Mardikh-Ebla, databili all'incirca alla metà dell III millennio av. Cr., si ha la menzione pure della città di Gasur[2] che, quindi, si dimostra più antica di quanto si pensasse finora: le attestazioni di Gasur risalivano, infatti, al periodo paleoaccadico e precisamente al tempo di Naram-Sin,[3] mentre adesso, con le nuove attestazioni di Ebla, la città doveva esistere già 250 anni prima.

In questo contributo presentato dietro invito dell'amico e collega D. I. Owen per il volume in onore del grande nuzologo prof. E. R. Lacheman sarà presentata e discussa brevemente la documentazione di Ebla concernente la città di Gasur e sarà esaminato il problema della sua identificazione e del suo ruolo al tempo di Ebla. Pur non disponendo di tutta la documentazione epigrafica rinvenuta ad Ebla, le dieci attestazioni in mio possesso sono

[1]Pag. 206.

[2]Per i testi cuneiformi rinvenuti ad Ebla nelle campagne di scavo 1974-76 si veda da ultimo G. Pettinato, *Catalogo dei testi cuneiformi di Tell Mardikh-Ebla* (= *Materiali Epigrafici di Ebla, 1*, abbreviato: *MEE* 1), Napoli 1979; *Ebla. Un impero inciso nell'argilla*, Milano 1979, pp. 31-57.

[3]Per la documentazione e la datazione dei testi di Gasur si veda T. J. Meek, *Old Akkadian, Sumerian and Cappadocian Texts from Nuzi*, Excavations at Nuzi, Vol. III, (= *HSS* X), Cambridge 1935, specialmente p. IX sg.; E. Weidner, *RlA* III, p. 151, s.v.; D. O. Edzard - G. Farber - E. Sollberger, *Répertoire Géographique des Textes Cunéiformes*, Band 1, Wiesbaden 1977, p. 54.

sufficienti a farci tracciare un quadro di Gasur, come una città importante non soltanto economicamente, ma anche e sopratto politicamente.[4]

Tale duplice ruolo di Gasur è d'altra parte già comprensibile, se si pensa che essa, per la sua collocazione geografica, costituiva un punto obbligato di passaggio delle vie carovaniere provenienti dall'Oriente, nella fattispecie Ḫamazi, dirette e verso la Siria e verso la Mesopotamia tutta. Da qui la sua menzione e nei testi economici e nei testi storici di Ebla.

a) Scrittura e localizzazione di Gasur:

Nei testi di Ebla si hanno due scritture diverse di resa della città di Gasur: la prima e più comune è *ga-sur*$_{x}^{ki}$ che noi riscontriamo nei testi [1]-[5], [7]-[8] e [10];[5] la seconda è invece *ga-su-lu*^{ki} documentata nei testi [6] e [9].[6]

Circa la sua identificazione con la Gasur della Mesopotamia settentrionale è rilevante innanzitutto il testo [10], dal quale si evince pure un ruolo politico molto importante di tale città al tempo di Ebla per quanto concerne l'area geografica compresa tra il Tigri e i due Zab. Non meno importanti a tale riguardo sono il testo [6], ove Gasur è menzionata in contesto con Kiš e Nagar, come pure i testi economici che richiedono una localizzazione al di là della città di Mari (si veda ad esempio il testo [5]).

La presenza poi negli stessi testi di Ebla di *er-bí-ì-lum*^{ki}, la famosa Erbīl della documentazione mesopotamica ancora oggi abitata,[7] e di Ḫamazi[8] rendono plausibile la proposta di identificazione della Gasur di Ebla con la Gasur della Mesopotamia settentrionale.

b) Documentazione epigrafica di Gasur negli Archivi di Ebla:

La dieci attestazioni di Gasur da me riconosciute nei testi in mio possesso sono tratte, come accennavo più sopra, dai testi economici ([1]-[5], [8]-[9]) e dai testi storici 6[6]-[7] e [10]. Esse saranno presentate qui di seguito secondo un ordine logico e discusse brevemente.

[4]E' sorprendente che A. Archi nel suo studio "Notes on eblaite Geography," *Studi Eblaiti* II (1980), pp. 1-16 non faccia riferimento alcuno alla presenza di Gasur nei testi di Ebla. Forse lo studioso avrebbe fatto bene a non criticare identificazioni da me mai proposte (si veda p. 5 sgg.) e invece a tentare di leggersi accuratamente i testi eblaiti.

[5]Per la lettura *sur*$_{x}$ del segno composito ŠÁRxMAŠ si veda G. Pettinato, *MEE* 2, p. 10 ad r. I 4. Per *ga-sur*$_{x}^{ki}$ e la prima proposta di identificazione con Gasur si veda G. Pettinato, *MEE* 2, p. 182 ad v. II 1.

[6]La consonante *l* in *ga-su-lu*^{ki} sta per la consonante *r*, quindi *ga-su-ru*$_{y}^{ki}$: per lo scambio *l*/*r* nei testi di Ebla si veda G. Pettinato, *Ebla. Un impero inciso nell'argilla*, p. 68.

[7]Il toponimo è attestato in *MEE* 1, n. 1867 r. XXIV 3:, n. 1868 r. XIII 26, v. XVIII 1.

[8]Si veda G. Pettinato, *MEE* 1, n. 1781 r. V 2.5 (= *Ebla. Un impero inciso nell'argilla*, p. 121; cfr. pure quanto detto a pag. 112).

[1]	=	1 *ma-na kù:babbar*	"1 mina d'argento
		ip-qì-dum	consegna[9]
		má-ḫu ga-sur$_x^{ki}$	al mercante di Gasur:
		ABxÁŠ.ABxÁŠ *è*	gli Anziani hanno elargito"[10]
	=	3 *ma-na ša-pi kù:babbar*	"3 mine e 40 sicli d'argento
		ip-qì-dum igi-dar	(dietro) consegna di .....[11]
		má-ḫu ga-sur$_x^{⸢ki⸣}$	al mercante di Gasur
		6 *kaskal-kaskal*	per 6 viaggi"[12]
	=	⸢3⸣ *ma-na ša-pi kù:babbar*	"⸢3⸣ mine e 40 sicli d'argento
		nì-ba ga-sur$_x^{ki}$	dono per Gasur"[13]
	=	10 *gín-dilmun kù:babbar*	"10 sicli dilmuniti d'argento
		( )	( )[14]
		ga-sur$_x^{ki}$	per / di Gasur"[15]

I primi due passi sottolineano il ruolo economico-commerciale di Gasur al tempo di Ebla, ruolo non certo irrilevante se suoi 'mercanti'[16] si spingevano fino ad Ebla e ricevevano da essa delle commesse. Il terzo passo menziona doni per Gasur, senza che ne venga specificato il peculiare motivo, anche se da esso è lecito concludere uno stretto rapporto tra Ebla e Gasur.

[9]Sia in *MEE* 1, p. 271 sia in *MEE* 2, p. 375 ho considerato il termine *ip-qì-dum* come nome di persona, ma a tale interpretazione si oppone chiaramente *MEE* 1, n. 1674 v. II 3 (si veda nota 11), sicchè almeno in alcuni casi ritengo che esso sia un termine amministrativo. La traduzione si fonda sull'ipotesi che *ipqidum* sia un derivato dalla radice verbale *paqādu* "consegnare, affidare," sicchè qua si avrebbe il termine eblaita che traduce l'espressione sumerica *šu mu-dúb*, per cui si veda *MEE* 2, p. 368 sub *su-dúb*.

[10]*MEE* 1, n. 1674 v. I 9 - II 1.

[11]Per *ip-qì-dum* si veda già la nota 9. *igi-dar* non so tradurlo, anche se si deve trattare di un nome d'oggetto, sempre che sia esatta l'ipotesi che *ipqidum* sia un termine amministrativo; ovviamente, qualora *ipqidum* fosse invece un nome di persona, allora *igi-dar* potrebbe essere il nome di una professione a me però sconosciuta. Le traduzioni sia accadica (*šit'āru* = *igi-gùn-nu*: *AHw*, p. 1251) sia eblaita (*igi-dar* = *ri-da-bù-um a-na-a*: *MEE* 1, n. 1438 v. VII 19-20; *igi-dar* = *ri-da-bù* 2-*igi*: *MEE* 1, n. 1439 r. XII 23′-24′) non mi sono di alcun aiuto a comprendere l'espressione.

[12]*MEE* 1, n. 1674 v. II 2-5.

[13]*MEE* 1, n. 1674 v. II 9-10.

[14]Le parentesi tonde ( ) stanno a significare che l'eventuale riga qui presente non è leggibile sulla fotografia a mia disposizione: per questo problema si veda quanto scritto in *MEE* 2, p. VII e XVIII.

[15]*MEE* 1, n. 1674 v. II 11 - III 1.

[16]Per *ma-ḫu* "commerciante" si veda G. Pettinato, *MEE* 2, p. 34 ad v. VIII 17.

[2]	1 *giš-šú kù:babbar*	"1 'corazza' d'argento[17]
	5 *ma-na kù:babbar*	di 5 mine d'argento
	2 *ḫa-bù kù:babbar*	2 picconi d'argento,
	1 *aktum-túg* 1 *íbx3(-tùg-dar)*	1 stoffa-A., 1 (gonna variopinta),
	1 *nì-lá-sag*	1 turbante,
	1 *gír-mar-tu-zú*	1 pugnale amorreo appuntito
	al-ma	ad Alma
	nì-mul	come ex-voto
	ga-sur$_x^{ki}$	per Gasur
	til	etc..."[18]

Questo passo che contiene un elenco di oggetti di metallo preziosi e di stoffe destinati come 'ex-voto' per divinità di Gasur, ci permette di concludere che lo stretto rapporto esistente tra Ebla e Gasur si estendeva pure alla religione: gli eblaiti, infatti, venerano anche divinità di Gasur.

[3]	....	" ....
	ga-sur$_x^{ki}$	per Gasur
	nidba$_x$	come offerta"[19]

La presenza di *nidba*$_x$ "offerta" conferma quanto detto sub [2] sul ruolo religioso di Gasur, anche se lo stato di conservazione della tavoletta non ci consente di individuare il tipo di offerta destinato alle divinità di Gasur.

[4]	1 *ìbx3-túg ga-sur*$_x^{ki}$	"1 gonna di Gasur
	en-na-il	per Enna-Il,
	lú-ḫu-nu	il 'messaggero'
	da-núm	di Dannum
	da-bí-na-at^{ki}	di Dabinat"[20]

Mentre i passi precedenti menzionavano beni di Ebla destinati a vario titolo per Gasur, la presente attestazione rivela che il commercio non si svolgeva a senso unico, in quanto anche Gasur aveva dei prodotti da esportare ad Ebla: *1 gonna di Gasur* è infatti da spiegare o come provenienza o come tipo specifico di lavorazione della stoffa stessa.[21]

[17]*giš-šú* è stato tradotto con 'corazza' molto ipoteticamente, in base al contesto immediato; per altre ipotesti interpretative si veda *MEE* 2, p. 114 ad r. I 12 (si corregga 12 in 2!).

[18]*MEE* 1, n. 997 v. III 9 - IV 6.

[19]*MEE* 1, n. 6403 r. II 1-2.

[20]*MEE* 1, n. 774 = *MEE* 2, 25 v. II 1-5. Si veda Ibidem, p. 182 ad v. II 3-4 per il commentario al passo.

[21]Si veda al riguardo *MEE* 2, p. 9 ad r. I 2.

[5]	[ ]	"[ ]
	1 *gaba guškin*	1 'pettorale' d'oro
	2 *ma-na* ku_5 *guškin*	di 2 mine e 30 sicli d'oro,
	1 *nì-sagšu*	1 elmo
	1 *ma-na* ku_5 *guškin*	di 1 mina e 30 sicli d'oro,
	1 *giš-šú*	1 'corazza'
	3 *ma-na guškin*	di 3 mine d'oro,
	1 *íb-lá ší-dì-tum gír-kun guškin*	1 cintura con pendaglio e pugnale ricurvo d'oro
	1 *ma-na guškin*	di 1 mina d'oro,
	[ ]	[ ]
	[ ] 50 *gín-dilmun kù:babbar*	[ ] e 50 sicli dilmuniti d'argento,
	1 *šilig guškin*	1 'bastone' d'oro
	ì-giš-sag	per l'unzione del capo
	lugal	del re,
	in ud	nel giorno, in cui
	til-til	etc..., etc...
	ga-sur$_x^{ki}$	a Gasur"[22]

I beni elencati in questo passo sono destinati al re di Mari per la cerimonia dell'unzione del capo avvenuta in un'occasione particolare riguardante tra l'altro la città di Gasur. Purtroppo l'annotazione scribale *til-til* "etc..., etc..."[23] non ci consente di conoscere la natura dell'avvenimento, anche se la ricchezza dei doni eblaiti fa pensare a qualcosa di veramente importante.

[6]	*ma-na*	"alcuni
	ší-in	per
	ga-su-lu^{ki}	Gasur,
	ma-na	alcuni
	ší-in	per
	eb-la^{ki}	Ebla
	AB	'sono disponibili'[24]

Quando avrò compreso l'intero testo, da cui è tratto il passo precedente, si potranno fare delle ipotesi concrete sui reali rapporti di forza delle varie potenze nel III millennio av. Cr. Il testo è, infatti, una relazione di Ibbi-Sipiš al sovrano di Ebla, molto probabilmente suo padre Ebrium, circa una campagna militare, in cui sembrano coinvolte Ebla, da una parte, e Kiš

[22] *MEE* 1, n. 1095 r. V 1 - VI 8.

[23] Per il valore di "*etc.*" dell'espressione *til* risp. *til-til* si veda *MEE* 2, p. 368 sub voce.

[24] *MEE* 1, n. 6411 v. II 5-11.

dall'altra. Se interpreto bene, il passo precedente, sembra che Ibbi-Sipiš stia descrivendo, come l'esercito di Kiš proceda: una parte marcia verso Ebla, l'altra verso Gasur. Se così è, si comprende quanto ho scritto in *Ebla. Un impero inciso nell'argilla*, p. 112 a proposito di un conflitto che vedeva impegnate le forze di Kiš contro i due alleati Ebla e Ḫamazi. Gasur quindi non era l'obiettivo ultimo dell'esercito di Kiš, bensí la tappa obbligata in direzione di Ḫamazi.

[7]	*wa*	"E
	e$_{11}$	la partenza
	ší-in	per
	ga-sur$_{x}^{ki}$	Gasur
	tá-mu-rù	hai controllato
	wa	e
	kú	il cibo
	kam$_{x}$	......
	uru^{ki}	della città
	[*m*]*u*$^{?}$*-ti*	hai$^{?}$ ricevuto"[25]

Anche il presente passo, così come il precedente, è tratto da un testo storico, ma mi sfugge il contesto che permetterebbe di interpretare le informazioni che lo scriba ci da.

[8]	10 *na-si*$_{11}$	"10 persone[26]
	( )	( )
	tuš	residenti
	ga-sur$_{x}^{ki}$	a Gasur"[27]

Ho voluto citare il presente passo subito dopo quelli tratti da testi storici, perchè sono convinto di un rapporto abbastanza stretto con essi. Il presente testo, infatti, è un elenco di coscritti stranieri a servizio di Ebla, verosimilmente per scopi militari, sicchè la menzione di gente residente a Gasur viene ad assumere un significato importante, anche alla luce di quanto detto sub [6].

[9]	4 *udu*	"4 ovini
	kú	come cibo
	ga-su-lu^{ki}	di (persone di) Gasur"[28]

Anche se la menzione di cibo per gente di Gasur può benissimo riferirsi al commercio, in quanto si tratterebbe di provvisione, non si può escludere a

[25] *MEE* 1, n. 6516 v. II 2 - III 4.
[26] Per il valore di *na-si*$_{11}$ nei testi di Ebla si veda *MEE* 2, p. 127 ad v. IX 12.
[27] *MEE* 1, n. 1451 r. V 7 - VI 2.
[28] *MEE* 1, n. 1676 v. V 24 - VI 2 = *OA*, 18, 1979, p. 171.

priori che il contingente di Gasur fosse presente per altri scopi. Da qui la sua citazione assieme e subito dopo i testi storici; la presenza poi di Nagar e Kiš, immediatamente dopo Gasur, ci riporta inevitabilmente nello stesso contesto del documento [6].

[10]	*ib-lul-il*	"Iblul-Il,
	lugal	re
	ma-rí^{ki}	di Mari,
	ù	e
	na-ḫal^{ki}	Naḫal
	[*ù*]	[e]
	nu-ba-at^{ki}	Nubat
	ù	e
	ša-da$_5$^{ki}	Šada
	kalam^{tim}- *kalam*^{tim}	dello Stato
	ga-sur$_x$^{ki}	di Gasur
	tùn-šè	ho sconfitto
	in	a
	kà-na-ne	Kanane
	ù	e
	7 *du*$_6$*-sar*	7 cumuli di macerie
	gar	ho eretto"[29]

Questo passo importantissimo per la localizzazione di Gasur è tratto dal documento da me identificato come 'bollettino militare' della campagna di Ebla contro Mari sotto il condottiero Enna-Dagan. Il fatto che Gasur non venga implicata direttamente nella guerra contro Mari, ma soltanto alcune città del suo Stato, assieme all'altro che Gasur è citata dopo Emar, Ḫaššum e Mane, rende plausibile la proposta di identificazione della Gasur dei testi di Ebla con quella della Mesopotamia settentrionale.

Dal punto di vista storico sembra comunque che la coalizione capeggiata da Mari contro Ebla non abbia trovato del tutto indifferente Gasur ed il suo Stato, tanto che il generale eblaita fu costretto a combattere anche nel suo territorio, sconfiggendo tre sue città. Né quanto detto finora può essere considerato un'esagerazione, soprattutto se si considera che Assur è in questo periodo strettamente legata a Mari,[30] sicchè è ben possibile che l'esercito eblaita abbia raggiunto almeno le provincie di confine dello Stato di Gasur. La menzione poi dello Stato di Gasur nel nostro testo ci rivela che la città doveva svolgere un ruolo molto importante nella compagine storica del III millennio av. Cr. La sua posizione geografica, infatti, ne faceva un naturale Stato

[29] *MEE* 1, n. 1806 v. I 9 - II 11 = *Ebla. Un impero inciso nell'argilla*, p. 107 = *OA*, 19, 1980, pp. 231-45.

[30] Si veda al riguardo G. Pettinato, *Ebla. Un impero inciso nell'argilla*, p. 106.

cuscinetto dapprima tra Ḫamazi e Mari, ed una volta sottomessa definitivamente quest'ultima, tra Ḫamazi ed Ebla. Se precedentemente Gasur, almeno fino alla caduta di Mari, era stata piuttosto ostile ad Ebla, dopo la disfatta della coalizione mariana essa entra nell'orbita commerciale del colosso eblaita.

c) Conclusione:

Dalla documentazione presentata sotto b) è lecito concludere che Gasur, la Nuzi dei tempi posteriori, è presente nei testi degli Archivi Reali di Ebla; la città quindi viene per la prima volta documentata attorno al 2500 av. Cr.

Gasur era al tempo degli Archivi di Ebla un centro economico e politico di notevole importanza: essa era infatti capitale di uno Stato omonimo e commerciava con lo Stato di Ebla. Sebbene dapprima ostile alla politica espansionistica di Ebla, a partire dal regno di Ar-Ennum ruota nell'orbita commerciale ed anche politica della città siriana.

Non è certo un caso poi che negli archivi di Gasur del periodo paleo-accadico sia in uso per la datazione dei documenti economici un calendario semitico che noi troviamo attestato per la prima volta 250 anni prima ad Ebla,[31] sicchè possiamo dedurre che i contatti con Ebla non furono certo effimeri e contingenti, ma più duraturi e pregnanti di quanto si fosse autorizzati a pensare: l'introduzione di un calendario va considerata come un elemento caratterizzante di una civiltà e come una riforma condizionante.[32]

[31] Si veda il mio contributo "Il calendario semitico del 3. millennio ricostruito sulla base dei testi di Ebla," *OA*, 16, 1977, pp. 257-85; per il calendario di Gasur si veda Ibidem, p. 283.

[32] Alla luce di quanto esposto finora e sulla base delle conoscenze acquisite grazie alla scoperta degli Archivi Reali di Ebla v'è da chiedersi se *maškān dūr Ebla* attestata nei testi di Gasur non sia da metter in relazione con la grande Ebla siriana, per cui si veda N. Freedman, "The Nuzi Ebla," in *BA*, 40, 1977, pp. 32-33, cosa questa da me precedentemente negata: *MAIS 67-68*, Roma 1972, p. 30 [Estratto anticipato].

Qualche dato di Confronto fra Nomi di Persona Hurriti

C. Saporetti
Roma

Nel lavoro di aggiornamento dei nomi di persona medio-assiri[1] sono compresi anche i nomi riporta ti in VAT 18087, un interessante elenco di persone ḫurrite deportate, e provenienti dalla zona Kašijāri-Ḫabūr.[2] Qui diamo qualche breve dato di confronto fra questa onomastica ḫurrita e l'onomastica nuziana.

Nomi maschili

1. Su 38 nomi maschili leggibili interamente, di cui però 6 incerti se ḫurriti,[3] solo 6 (di cui 3 fanno parte dei nomi non sicuramente hurriti) sono attestati in altri documenti assiri contemporanei; 16 trovano invece attestazioni, o forme molto simili, nei documenti di Nuzi[4] (2 di questi 16 fanno parte dei nomi non sicuramente hurriti). I nomi che non trovano paralleli nell'onomastica nuziana sono dunque 22: Agit-tarmija; Aram-kalzali (cf. i nomi femminili); Arip-šunatḫi; Eḫli-Ḫabūr; Eḫli-MAŠdi; Ḫabūr-di; Ḫâ-Tešup; Ippilina; Ketti-Ḫabūr; Kipusi; Kulmi-šarri; Mazi-itte; Mematar-šenni; Ninuali; Nuberi; Puššа (confrontabile però con Puššaja, OMA I, 371, *bēl pāḫete* di Nār-zuḫini, città della zona nuziana); Qatini; Sinani; Šapli-Tešup; Šatti-ani; Ubḫa (legg. Ár-ḫa? In tal caso, cf. Arḫu a Nuzi); Uḫura. Come si vede, se i nomi non sono attestati a Nuzi, alcuni però sono formati da elementi che si trovano anche a Nuzi come

[1]H. Freydank-C. Saporetti, *Nuove attestazioni dell'onomastica medio-assira* (Roma 1979).

[2]*Nuove attestazioni*. . . , "Presentazione." Il testo sarà prossimamente pubblicato da H. Freydank in MARV II, 6.

[3]Ippilina (cf. NPN, 220*a* : *ippil* Perhaps Lullian); Irregi (cf. NPN, 220*b* : H.?); Ninuali (= Ninua-alī o Ninu-alli? cf. a Nuzi Ninu-atal); Puḫi (cf. OMA I, 370); Qatini (cf. AHw, 908*b* o a Nuzi Qataja); Ketti-Ḫabūr (accad.?).

[4]Arip-šuriḫa cf. Arip-šuriḫe; Ḫutip-Tešup; Irregi; Kalli cf. Kalija; Kapuli; Kipukka; Pîa cf. Pae, Paja NPN, 109 e Bija, Cassin-Glassner, AAN, 109*a*; Puḫi cf. AAN, 110*a*; Purra cf. AAN, 112*b*; Sigi cf. Zike; Šanda cf. Šandaja; Šarišše; Šebaiš-šarri cf. Šipiš-šarri; Taggura cf. Takkaraja; Tagi cf. Takku; Tammi cf. Tamaja e Tame, Tammi . . . in AAN, 138*b*. Per Ubḫa ved. oltre.

formativi di altri nomi (es. Agit-tarmija cf. a Nuzi Akit-tirwi e Urḫa-tarmi; Eḫli-Ḫabūr cf. Eḫli-Tešup, ecc.). Tuttavia ci sono nomi che hanno un solo elemento noto a Nuzi (es. Mematar-šenni), quando non sono poi del tutto nuovi (Mazi-itte cf. nomi accadici a Nuzi Maṣīja, Maṣi-ilu?; Nuberi = Nup-eri, cf. Nupanani, Ari-pera?; Sinani cf. Zinaja, Zinapu, forse accad.?; Uḫura).

2. Altri 13 nomi maschili non sono interamente leggibili, avendo un elemento scomparso o di lettura incerta. Alcuni forse non sono ḫurriti.[5] Almeno due potrebbero trovare intera corrispondenza con l'onomastica nuziana, se la loro lettura fosse sicura;[6] 7 hanno invece almeno un elemento uguale o simile;[7] due hanno corrispondenze con gli elementi nuziani, attestati però in nomi differenti.[8]

3. Un'altra ventina e più di nomi sono troppo rovinati per permettere raffronti.

Nomi femminili

1. Su 45 nomi femminili leggibili interamente,[9] di cui 3 incerti se hurriti,[10] solo 4 sono attestati in altri documenti assiri contemporanei; 12 trovano invece attestazioni, o forme molto simili, nei documenti di Nuzi.[11] I nomi che non trovano paralleli nell'onomastica nuziana sono dunque 33: ^{f}Alla-nusi; ^{f}Aram-kalzuli (cf. i nomi maschili); ^{f}Asu-meše; ^{f}Ašnisi; ^{f}Ella-šari; ^{f}Eri-naja; ^{f}Ḫabūr-elli; ^{f}Ḫabūr-tamari; ^{f}Ḫammeja (cf. il maschile Ḫamie, AAN, 50*a* ?); ^{f}Ḫašim-allai; ^{f}Ḫišuli (cf. il maschile Ḫišalla, NPN, 60*b* ?); ^{f}Kašijāri-elli; ^{f}Kelda-naje; ^{f}Kilu-lisi; ^{f}Kumuḫuri; ^{f}Maladi-elli; ^{f}Mali-naje; ^{f}Meriḫti-gili; ^{f}Mutturi; ^{f}Napar-ešše; ^{f}Napni-elli; ^{f}Nili-paḫ; ^{f}Pinannaḫili; ^{f}Pingi-naje; ^{f}Pirat-tupzi; ^{f}Saua; ^{f}Sinunitu; ^{f}Šadna-meli; ^{f}Šarri-beli; ^{f}Šilusi; ^{f}Šina-tupzi; ^{f}Tešub-elli; ^{f}Unammeni= Unap-menni. Anche per i nomi femminili si deve dire però che molti sono formati da elementi noti a Nuzi (es. ^{f}Ḫašim-allai cf. a Nuzi ^{f}Ḫašim-matka e ^{f}Imšar-allai ecc.), e che ci sono tuttavia anche esempi di nomi con un solo elemento noto a Nuzi (es. ^{f}Pingi-naje; ^{f}Šina-tupzi), oltre a quelli che non

[5] Eḫ$^{?}$li-/ Ḫita$^{?}$-/ Kili$^{?}$-/]ri-beru, cf. NPN, 245, *per*, *pir*, *birija*; Nûla(, cf. NPN, 240*b*, *nul*, *nula*, *null*).

[6] A$^{?}$tal-Tešup; An$^{?}$nitte (cf. Anita a Nuzi).

[7] Es. Kusuḫ-ki[;]li-šarri; Pendi[.

[8] I già citati Eḫ$^{?}$li-beru e Kili$^{?}$-beru; cf. *nota* 5.

[9] Non vi comprendiamo ^{f}Ḫebat-taramni, che all'elemento divino ḫurrico accosta un elemento verbale accadico.

[10] ^{f}Jaruttu, cf. NPN, 219*b*, accad. *jāruttu*? ^{f}Šadna-meli cf. l'elemento formativo *meli*, cassita; ^{f}Šilusi cf. NPN, 257*a*: *šilu* H.?

[11] ^{f}Akap-elli; ^{f}Akap-kiaše; ^{f}Aštue cf. ^{f}Ašteja e ^{f}Aštu; ^{f}Aza cf. ^{f}Azaja; ^{f}Azue; ^{f}Eburta cf. Ipurta, maschile!; ^{f}Ḫamaš-šar, maschile a Nuzi!; ^{f}Ḫiḫḫi cf. Ḫiḫi, maschile!; ^{f}Jaruttu, ^{f}Ṣilli-naje cf. ^{f}Zilim-naja; ^{f}Šarrum-elli cf. ^{f}Šarum-elli; ^{f}Šinen-naje cf. ^{f}Šinen-naja.

trovano paralleli nemmeno parziali (^{f}Kumuḫuri, ^{f}Napareššе, cf. i nomi in *-šše* NPN, 258*a*; ^{f}Sinunitu).

2. Altri 22 nomi femminili non sono interamente leggibili, avendo un elemento scomparso o di lettura incerta. Di questi, una diecina hanno almeno un elemento uguale o simile a quelli dell'onomastica nuziana;[12] 5 hanno corrispondenze con gli elementi nuziani, attestati però in nomi differenti.[13]

3. Una diecina e più di nomi sono troppo rovinati per permettere raffronti.

In conclusione, si può dire che dal confronto dell'onomastica hurrita occidentale (Kašijāri-Ḫabūr) di VAT 18087 con quella nuziana risulta che quasi al 34% i nomi sono corrispondenti, mentre al 66% circa i nomi sono differenti, anche se spesso sono formati dai medesimi elementi; i nomi totalmente diversi sono circa l'8,50%.

Può essere interessante notare che la maggior parte dei nomi attestati nelle due onomastiche non è presente con grande frequenza a Nuzi; ciò potrebbe significare (ma è necessario affermarlo con grande prudenza) che non facevano propriamente parte dell'area nuziana, ma piuttosto di un'area occidentale, di cui ora abbiamo appunto esempi corrispondenti.

[12] Es. ^{f}Punnu$^{?}$-sagi; ^{f}Attu[; ^{f}]-elli.
[13] ^{f}Ḫabūr$^{?}$naje; ^{f}Ḫabūr-taje$^{?}$; ^{f}Pendu$^{?}$-naja; ^{f}Šarru$^{?}$-elli$^{?}$; ^{f}Šurba[cf. Šurpaja.

On Idrimi and Šarruwa, the Scribe

Jack M. Sasson
University of North Carolina
Chapel Hill

Ever since its publication by Sidney Smith in 1949, the inscription of Idrimi, engraved on a human statue, has attracted the attention of scholars who sought to extract from it information on the history of a large segment of the Levant during the early second half of the second millennium B.C.[1] The following remarks, dedicated to Ernest Lacheman, arise from a reading of a 1977 University of Pennsylvania doctoral dissertation by Gary Oller, *The Autobiography of Idrimi. A New Text edition, with Philological and Historical Commentary.*[2] Proceeding from a collation of the original, Oller's work is not only the most complete and updated assessment since Smith's pioneering effort, but is also a repository for the philological contributions, literary interpretations, and historical reconstructions of recent scholarship.[3] Therefore, to lighten the burden of footnoting, this paper will cite Oller's work unless materials came in too late for inclusion within his thesis or previous opinions and approaches have either been slighted or ignored.

Of interest to this paper is Oller's third chapter on "The Literary Nature of the Text: The Correct Procedure for its Use as a Piece of Historical Evidence." There, Oller expands on the remarks made by previous cuneiformists, who saw Idrimi's work as belonging to a literary tradition, markedly different from that of the Mesopotamian royal inscriptions, but which is known to the coastal Mediterranean world.[4]

The narrative about Idrimi and his career is sandwiched between a brief section (lines 1-2), which introduces Idrimi to his readers, and another (lines 92-98a) which, in view of Ancient Near Eastern concern for the sanctity of

[1]Most easily accessible translation is that of Oppenheim in *ANET*³, 557-58.

[2]Ann Arbor, Michigan: University Microfilms International. Order # 78-6628.

[3]See, in particular, his rich bibliography of pp. 250-66. Among the more noteworthy items which could not be adequately considered by Oller is the treatment of E. L. Greenstein and D. Marcus: "The Akkadian Inscription of Idrimi," *JANES* 8 (1976), pp. 59-96. A partial translation of the text is presented by M.-J. Seux in *Textes du proche-orient ancien et histoire d'Israël*, 1977, pp. 42-43.

[4]In addition to Oller's remarks of pp. 192-93 and 193 n. 1, cf. Greenstein and Marcus, article cited in n. 3, pp. 75-77, who compare with Jephtah and David.

human representation and for the posthumous word, contains powerful invocations against those who desecrate the finished product. As has been noted by a number of exegetes, lines 1-63 of the inscription build upon themes and motifs well-known to Near Eastern folklore: the successful younger/youngest brother and the questing hero.[5] Lines 64-91, which detail moments in Idrimi's rise, dwell upon his military and domestic achievements. These moments are easily paralleled by Phoenician and Aramaic (royal) inscriptions.[6] The inscription continues with two unusual items: an expanded colophon (lines 98b-101), and Idrimi's personal exhortation to his audience (lines 102-104).

In developing our arguments, we shall first consider these two items. By subjecting the events of Idrimi's life to content and folkloristic analyses, we hope next to justify the use of a different generic label than the one heretofore attached to the inscription: "autobiography." Finally, by rehearsing the archaeological evidence associated with the statue, we shall offer new hypotheses on the purpose of the inscription and the context in which it was fabricated.

Lines 98b-101 bristle with difficulties in deciphering specific cuneiform signs, in ascertaining the meaning of individual words, and in properly evaluating the morphology and syntax of specific phrases. For our purpose, however, we adopt Oller's reconstruction of the section, a reconstruction which is itself dependent on previous suggestions (cf. pp. 129-43), and present the following translation:

> . . . Šarruwa (is) the scribe, a worshipper [? LÚ!ÌR?] of Tešub [X], Šimiga [XX], Kušuh [XXX], and AN.ŠUR [Šauška?].[99] Since Šarruwa, the scribe, was the one who inscribed this statue, may the gods of the Universe [DINGIR.MEŠ *ša* AN u KI][100] keep him alive, protect, and favor him. May Šamaš, lord of the living[101] and dead, lord of spirits, take care of him.

The "colophon" of this inscription is restricted to l. 98b. It begins with the mention of the scribe's name. Rare, such an appendage to a statue is not unknown.[7] In determining the vocabulary behind the cryptogram of line 98b,

[5]Oller, p. 194 n. 1.

[6]Oller, pp. 195-200, gives two instances where literary considerations render suspect the historical worth of Idrimi's statements: In Idrimi's use of numbers and in his detailing of conquered territories. M. Miller, "The Moabite Stone as a Memorial Stela," *PEQ* 104 (1974), pp. 9-18, compares the structures of first millennium inscriptions: those of Barrakib, Azitawadda, and Mesha. Of interest is his passing reference to the Idrimi statue as a "statue-memorial" (p. 9 n. 3).

[7]Cf. the colophon to the copper tablet of Atal-šen of Urkiš and Nawar, *IRSA* #IIH1a (p. 128), which gives the name of the scribe, Šaum-šen. Regarding its appearance, the editors remark: "Cette signature est tout à fait étrangère aux traditions

Oller (pp. 132-40) advances his own reasons for espousing Dietrich and Loretz's suggestion, offered in *OLZ* 61(1966), 557, over Nougayrol's reading, lastly followed by Greenstein and Marcus, which would convert the cryptogram into a supposed GE_{14} MAN BÀ ("written, copied, and inspected"). Not only is the translation of these symbols into such sumerograms too exotic and partially unattested elsewhere, but it would convey the impression that the inscription at least, if not the statue also, was a copy of an earlier prototype. No scholar has ever suggested this, or is likely to. Therefore, the second part of l. 98b merely imparts Šarruwa's attachments to a series of gods.

Lines 99-101 are not colophonic, but contain elaborate blessings for Šarruwa. Since scholarship has generally regarded these as unusual extensions of the colophon, explanations have been promoted to account for their inclusions. Kempinski and Na'aman think that Šarruwa, taking advantage of widespread illiteracy, placed his own name where Idrimi's ought to have been.[8] That this unique example of scribal *chutzpah* is highly unlikely need not be emphasized. Oller (pp. 140-41) does not offer anything more plausible: as friend, servant, or author, Šarruwa was singularly honored by being permitted to share his master's monument. But when it is noted that lines 99-101 do not repeat or supplement the passage which, at the conclusion of Idrimi's narrative (92-98a), invokes the god's curses against desecrators of Idrimi's monument, then the string of blessings for Šarruwa can only be equated to similar invocations written in behalf of patrons of votive texts.[9] Such an observation forces a radical change in our assessment of the nature of Idrimi's text. No longer can it be regarded as an 'autobiography' written at the behest of its author; it can now be better ranged among memorials, written to remember the activities of a past leader. In a sense, our inscription becomes a 'biography' cast by Šarruwa in the first person narrative mode. A less exotic terminology might be invoked, however, allowing us to place Idrimi's text firmly within the category of "simulated autobiographies" or, as has been more commonly employed in recent Ancient Near Eastern scholarship, within the genre of "pseudo-autobiographies." We shall turn to this topic as a potentially fruitful way to analyse the manner in which Šarruwa organized his materials concerning Idrimi's life.

---

babyloniennes." The text is set within the Agade dynasty period, and is purely dedicatory.

[8]A. Kempinski and N. Na'aman, "The Idrimi Inscription Reconsidered [in Hebrew]," *Excavations and Studies: Essays in Honor of Prof. S. Yeivin*, 1973, p. 217.

[9]On the debate concerning the use and abuse of this terminology, see lastly, J. A. Brinkman, *Materials and Studies for Kassite History, I*, 1976, p. 56, n. 179: " 'Votive' means not only dedicated in consequence of a (prior) vow, but also dedicated in the sense of expressing a (present) vow, desire, or wish (for future benefits)."

A. Kirk Grayson's recent monograph, *Babylonian Historical-Literary Texts*[10] and B. Lewis's new edition of *The Sargon Legend*[11] treated a genre of literature, labelled *narû* by earlier cuneiform scholarship and "pseudo-autobiography" by more recent one, which share many characteristics. Lewis, pp. 87-88, arranges these under nine headings: #3-7, descriptive; #1-2, 8-9, interpretive:

1. The texts concern the figure of a great king and record either significant events or unusual experiences during his rule.
2. They are pseudepigraphical and purport to be genuine royal inscriptions.
3. They are written in the first person in the style of an autobiography.
4. Following the pattern of the royal inscription, they are constructed with a prologue, narrative, and epilogue.
5. The prologue begins with a self-presentation and may include information concerning the king's origin or the cause of the predicament he faces in the narrative section.
6. The narrative is devoted to a specific episode in the life of the king.
7. The narrative contains a message for future kings expressed in the form of a blessing oracle or curse formula.
8. The texts are didactic in nature; there is a moral to be learned from the personal experiences of the king that can be acquired by reading his "stela."
9. They are written in a poetic or semipoetic narrative style.

Proceeding backwards, we first take up the last point:

[Point #9.] Unless one stretches to the breaking point the definition of "poetry" or even that of "semipoetry," it is difficult to regard Idrimi's inscription as poetic in style. We might, however, note that Akkadian, or whatever one would label the language of the inscription, was but an acquired taste for a citizen of Alalah. And, although there is no way of proving it, the narrative may have been originally conceived in another language using a much more poetic idiom than is displayed in its translated form.

[Point #8.] As is the case of the Mesopotamian pseudo-autobiographies, the "didactic" dimension of the text is not easily identified. Lines 102-4 of our inscription read as follows: "For 30 years, I have been ruling. Having written my accomplishments upon my statue, let him (who cares to) inspect them thoroughly, and (thus) let (all of them) constantly bless me." These lines ought not to be regarded as an "epilogue" since such a statement had been made in

[10] Toronto, 1975. Note E. Reiner's remarks on this genre and her reservations regarding Grayson's typology in *Altorientalische Literaturen* (*NHLW*, 1), 1978, pp. 177-81.

[11] (*ASOR*, Dissertation Series, 4), 1980.

lines 92-98a (see below, point #7). Furthermore, they are carved out of line with the rest of the inscription. Etched on the right cheek of Idrimi, and running down his beard to perpendicularly meet lines 1-23, these lines are made to issue from Idrimi's own mouth and therefore convey the impression that the lessons for posterity will reach those who hearken to Idrimi's exhortation, learn from his accomplishments, and pay homage to him. Functionally, these lines are comparable to the legends that are placed close to the bodies of protagonists, legends that are occasionally found in the ANE, become plentiful in Hellenistic mosaics, in medieval paintings, and even in contemporary cartoons.[12]

[Point #7.] The *narrative* message, as distinguished from the *didactic* one discussed in the preceding point, is to be found in the fragmentary section which warns of dire punishment to be meted out to desecrators (lines 92-98a).

[Points #5-6.] It should not be necessary to rehearse the manner in which lines 1-6 of our inscription fulfill the requirements of these two points. The hero is introduced ("I am Idrimi"), his paternal connection stated ("the son of Ilimilimma"), and, to use a Proppian function,[13] the "initial situation" is detailed in a manner that is left (purposely?) vague: "[Because] in Halab, my paternal home, there were ill-feelings, we fled and came to settle in Emar, whose citizens were my mother's relatives."

Two interesting moments can be discussed here. *a*. Idrimi does not claim actual relationship to Halab's rulers, and it may be that we are too easily accepting that Ilimilimma was actually dethroned from Aleppo's throne, a notion which is only slightly bolstered by *inūma mār bēlišunu anāku* of line 25, a line which occurs in connection with escapees and refugees from Halab, Mukiš, Niya, and Amae. As it is, the text never calls Halab Idrimi's city, and Ilimilimma's fate is not of much concern. A solution, no less conjectural, is that Ilimilimma may have failed in an attempt to usurp Halab's throne. *b*. Alalah, which should have been at this stage of the narrative but a twinkle in Idrimi's eye, is nevertheless paraded in line 2. Such an anticipation, while naturally jolting to our chronologically oriented perception, is nevertheless of literary importance. Together with lines 88-90, which likewise speak of the gods of Alalah, line 2 blocks out the narrative of Idrimi's rise, and permits the

[12]Egyptian tomb paintings, of course, are filled with such examples. The most striking item form the Levant is Barrakib's orthostat relief from Sam'al. Barrakib is seated on a throne, his hand raised almost to meet an Aramaic inscription which, moving toward his head, reads: "I am Barrakib, son of Panammu[wa]." A divine symbol, to the right of the inscription, is met by another legend: "My lord is Baal Harran." A scribe stands at the edge of the slab and faces the enthroned king. Orthostat: E. Akurgal, *The Art of the Hittites*, 1962, pl. 131; Text, *KAI*, #218; Gibson, *TSSI*, #17. Fuller citations and more on this king below.

[13]V. Propp, *Morphology of the Folktale*, 2nd revised English edition, 1968, pp. 25-26.

attention to focus on the episodes framed within. It may be that line 1 and 91, which speak to father-son relationships, are meant to further accentuate the parameters of the narrative.

This narrative is indeed, to restate Lewis's vocabulary for point #6, "devoted to a specific episode in the king's life." It opens with Idrimi as a young man, having made a decision to strike out on his own. We need not speculate on the relationship which obtained among the brothers, nor on that between the Emar community and Idrimi's family. Idrimi's account is very miserly with details since its only points are that the youngest son thought it useless to remain with his family (10-12); that Idrimi left with a paltry patrimony ("A horse, chariot, and groom"—line 13); that he took steps which irrevocably separated him, both spatially and psychologically, from his relatives ("and having crossed into the desert, and mixed with Sutū-nomads, I spent the night with him [groom?; the Sutu as one group?] in a [?]"—lines 14-17); that having entered Canaan, he established a compact with Hapirū-refugees (17-29); that in his seventh year since he began biding his time, the opportunity came for him to take over Niya, Amae, Mukiš, and, of course, Alalah (29-42); that no sooner was his legitimacy established that a mighty king, Barrattarna, stopped his hostilities and accepted him as vassal (43-58); that kings from all regions made peace with him (59-63).[14] It is most important to note that lines 29-42 and 43-58 report synchronous events. This observation, already made by Sidney Smith (p. 59), has been disregarded by many scholars. It implies that while Idrimi was with the Hapirū, he was opposed by Barrattarna. But in his seventh year, when he triumphed, Barrattarna accepted his legitimacy. We are encouraged to think of these passages as synchronous by the fact that the name "Alalah" blocks out the Barrattarna portion in lines 38 and 58 [". . . Alalah, my city, turned to me/ And I became king of Alalah."] If this opinion is accepted, we can see how the narrative fulfills Lewis's 6th point: the rise of Idrimi occupied no more than a seven year span, a span which, as likely as not, was chosen for its symbolic implications.

By contrast, however, the next few lines, recounting Idrimi's military successes while ruling at Alalah (64-72), his efforts to confirm his dynastic claims (73-84), his domestic resettlement program (84-87), and his cultic activities (88-91) are not secured within a chronological texture. Rather, they are charted programmatically, with one set of activities providing the context, and making it possible, for the next group of actions: spoils from victory permit Idrimi to build his palace and throne; these practical embodiments of legitimacy excuse his reshuffle of Alalah's population and his allotments of privileged spaces for members of his family; the influx of Halabite/Emarite

[14]Whether one is to consider this obscure passage as reflecting on Idrimi's military or political prowesse, remains to be ascertained. Bibliography and assessments are available in Oller, pp. 83-85 and Greenstein and Marcus, pp. 85-87.

population allows him to introduce foreign worship into Alalah's temples, and to have his son, Adad-nirāri, supervise the cult.[15]

Because of their programmatic structure, it is likely, therefore, that, whatever their historical merits, lines 64-91 of Idrimi's narrative are shaped by literary considerations no less than the previous passages which are manifestly folkloristic in inspiration. In consonance with Near Eastern literary tenets, considerations which guide any narrative concerned with the establishment of legitimacy—be they applied to mythological texts regarding the triumphs of the gods, to epical sagas regarding the heroes of dim pasts, or to so-called pseudo-(auto)biographies—such narratives rarely fail to inject historicizing features. They may include mention of authentic rulers, allusions to geographical features and foreign locales, and involvement of foreign armies drawn from the repertoire of traditional national enemies. It should not be surprising therefore that scholarship has been hard put to insert Idrimi into the known list of rulers at Halab or Alalah (Oller, pp. 148-55), to establish a convincing explanation for the involvement of Barrattarna in Alalah's affairs (Oller, pp. 165-67; 205-11), to fix the boundaries of Idrimi's kingdom (Oller, pp. 174-87), or to locate the places that were raided in his Hittite sortie (Oller, pp. 187-90). Even when our lack of information on North Syria of the XVIth and XVth centuries is taken into consideration, it is remarkable how preciously fragile are almost all the historical reconstructions that proceed from Idrimi's narrative.

This is not to say that an appreciation of the literary nature of the inscription should make us question the historicity of Idrimi himself or to doubt the authenticity of his rise from humbler beginnings to kingship over Alalah. We have far too many documents from Alalah IV to testify to the truth of the first proposition and to assert the likelihood of the second (cf. Oller, pp. 150-54). Rather it is to suggest that because of its contents—that is because of its selection of materials: folkloristic, legitimizing, and historicizing —because of its structure—that is because of its scheme of presentation—we are encouraged to regard Idrimi's inscription as a "simulated autobiography." This assessment, drawn from an investigation of its content, confirms and supplements the conclusion which we presented above after analysing the "colophon" of the text.

This conclusion, however, forces us to shift our focus from the subject of the "simulated autobiography," Idrimi, to the author of the narrative, Šarruwa. An inspection of his achievement allows us to understand the method he pursued in organizing his story. Even as we observe that he presented his audience with a product which collapsed the few historical events into a barely defined stretch of time, which selected but a few years in the life of its subject,

[15] I side with those who do not regard Adad-nirāri as a royal successor to Idrimi; discussion of the problem in Oller, pp. 154-55.

which appropriated folkloristic motifs with proven verisimular hold, and which filled its canvas with touches authentically mimicking reality, we can also note that Šarruwa's final product was nevertheless a major literary achievement. For whatever were the losses experienced by a narrative which does not abide by the rules of historical exactitude, these were easily outweighed by the benefits gained by an imaginatively reshaped sequence of events which successfully infused the whole with a vivid aura of factuality. Despite the fact that Šarruwa's work is horribly abusive of language and script it employs, despite the irritating ignorance displayed by the carver of the inscription (Šarruwa himself?), the narrative succeeds, as do few of its contemporaries, in focusing the attention of the reader on the plight and success of its hero, Idrimi. And this, after all, must have been primary as a goal for its author.

But in turning our attention to Šarruwa, we are also impelled to devote some energy to establishing a context for him. If we ever hope not only to speculate on the purpose of the statue and its inscription, but also to understand the vision which inspired the work, we need to be better informed about the time in which Šarruwa lived and the circumstances that saw him accomplishing his task. To do so, we shall pursue two distinct avenues, one which depends primarily on textual evidence, the other on artistic and archaeological ones. Even as we do so, however, we are under no illusions that what is about to unfold can be anything but conjectures and hypothetical reconstructions.

A. Since Niqmepa, a well-documented king of level IV, calls himself "son of Idrimi" (*AT* 15:2), and uses his father's seal (D. Collon, *The Seal Impressions from Tell Atchana/Alalakh*, 1975, pp. 169-90), and since that level has furnished us mention of a scribe named Šarruwa, it is not surprising that scholarship has sought to locate the inscription during the reign of the early kings of Alalah IV. Two variations were advanced. The earliest, promoted by Sidney Smith and championed by Woolley, regards Šarruwa to have worked during the reign of Ilimilimma, son of Niqmepa, to have survived a palace revolt together with the latter's son, Idrimi, and to have written the account in the inscription which we are studying.[16] Present day scholarship, exemplified by the reconstruction in Oller's IVth chapter, however, has sided with another interpretation which, depending on the fact that Niqmepa was Idrimi's son, advanced the hypothesis that the narrative carved on the statue recounts the saga of a king who established the dynasty ruling throughout Alalah IV.

The name 'Šarruwa' is of Hurrian origin (cf. E. Laroche's *Glossaire de la langue Hourrite* [*RHA*, 35(1977) 217]. Level VII attestations include a LÚ.ZAG.HA (*AT* *387 [= *JCS* 8, 28: #*381]:4), a DUMU SANGA (*AT* *274:19), and an archer (?, *AT* *203:12) (last 2 references courtesy N. Na'aman). From

[16] L. Woolley, *A Forgotten Kingdom*, 1953, pp. 119-29; *Alalakh: An Account of the Excavations at Tell Atchana*, 1955, pp. 391-95.

level IV, we learn of a 'Šarruwa,' a carpenter who lived in Uniga (*AT* 220:7), of another who was an owner of a chariot (*AT* 422:8; 425:12), and of a scribe of the same name. The last occurs in a number of references: *AT* 15:20 (Niqmepa grants PN and his descendants *mariyannu*-status; cf. *CAD* M/1, 281-82); 17:23 (Abrogation of a marriage agreement; cf. *ANET*,[3] 546); 47:20 (Antichretic pledge transaction; cf. B. Eichler, *Indenture at Nuzi*, 1973, pp. 75-77); 72:16 (Purchase of an ox); 104:7 (fragment of a contract). In these texts, the last one of which is dated to Niqmepa's successor Ilimilimma, Šarruwa the scribe was acting as witness among well known Alalahian worthies. In *AT* 159, a list which records the dispensation of material goods [not clear which] to the high and lowly in the palace, a Šarruwa the scribe (line 5) receives twice the amount allotted to anyone else, but equal to the amount offered to the king's *šatammu* (line 16). Finally a possible reference to a Šarruwa of level II/I will be mentioned below.

These citations make it clear that, whatever his merits as a scribe, Šarruwa of level IV was certainly well established in the higher echelons of the palace bureaucracy. Indeed, it is not impossible that all of the references collected above may have referred to our scribe. If this Šarruwa, a dignitary in the courts of Niqmepa and Ilimilimma—"an older statesman" as Woolley, *Forgotten Kingdom*, p. 119, calls him—was indeed responsible for authoring and sponsoring our inscription, then we can offer the following scenario.

Šarruwa was a successful member of Alalah IV's community. Whether he or his parents were native to Alalah or whether they all belonged to the group Idrimi relocated when he came to power can never be ascertained. Apparently during his last years, Šarruwa decided to invoke the god's blessings and protection beyond his earthly life. To do so, he devised an approach which, as far as I can gather from current information, was totally original with him. He (has someone) fabricate(s) a statue which displays "a deliberate lack of interest in the details and (represents) an effort at schematisation (sic) which reaches the very limits where it barely preserves any relation to reality."[17] He then inscribes upon it his account of Idrimi's life, using the first person as subject throughout the narrative, but shifting dramatically to the third person when his own plea is attached. To make sure that the Idrimi segment is regarded as a true autobiography, Šarruwa, again rather uniquely, carves a three line exhortation as if emanating from Idrimi himself.

If the steps taken by Šarruwa in achieving his goals can be plausibly recreated, and the immediate benefits to Šarruwa can be conjectured, it is nevertheless not clear how the whole functioned as a monument for the kings of the level IV dynasty. If it can be shown that Šarruwa began his career during the last days of Idrimi's life—and our evidence on this is totally lacking—then we might think of an analogy in the *Life of Charlemagne*,

[17]M. Vieyra, *Hittite Art, 2300-750 B.C.*, 1955, p. 84. Cf. Woolley in Smith, *Statue of Idri-mi*, 9.

written by his chamberlain Einhart during the reign of Louis the Pious. Feeling ill at ease with this son and successor of Charlemagne, Einhart wrote his "biography," preserving much historical truth in a narrative steeped in folkloristic and anecdotal idioms, in order to enhance his own reputation as a confidant of the great emperor. But such a conjecture would not fit well with what we know of Levantine courts of the second millennium and of the relative anonymity and limited visibility of court officials. If, on the other hand, we can be certain that Šarruwa was bidding Niqmepa's order to eternalize his own father, or that of Ilimilimma, who might have delighted in remembering the activity of his namesake's son (Idrimi), it becomes very difficult to explain the absence of any allusion to these reigning monarchs. Surely such a product, especially in view of the elaborate temple setting it ultimately received, could not be undertaken without palace's approval. Rejecting the opinions of Kempinski, Na'aman, and Oller, alluded to above, we are left with no adequate explanation for the statue's existence. We might, therefore, turn to our second avenue of inquiry, an avenue which, despite its heavy dependence on non-epigraphical evidence, could yield beneficial results.

B. Despite its heavy reliance on archaeological and artistic evidence, the second avenue, I believe, offers better grounds for responding to the queries posed above. This approach depends on reconstructing a context for a Šarruwa who lived during the last days of Alalah, at the tail end of a long period in which Alalah of level III-I was under Hittite domination. Of the few documents from this period (e.g., *AT* 105, 124, 125, 440), one (*AT* 124) is a level II/I letter written in Hittite, and exchanged between two private individuals.[19] One of the correspondents may have been named *Šar*[*-ru-wa*].[20]

But our second proposal, although it could be invigorated by the restoration of the personal name in *AT* 124, proceeds from the suspicion that the statue and its setting—and hence the inscription itself—need not have been heirlooms handed down for generations until their final resting spot in a temple of Alalah IB. Rather, these might be regarded as much more deeply attached to the archaeological context in which they are found. Having asked Dr. Marie-Henriette C. Gates, who has recently studied *Alalakh-Tell Atchana, Levels VI-V* [Ph.D. Dissertation, Yale, 1976], to investigate this proposal, she was kind enough to permit me to include the following report.

> The statue of Idri-mi was found broken in several pieces in the bottom of a pit dug into the floor of the Level I temple's latest phase. It was clearly intended to sit on the broken basalt base uncovered in its original position on the floor of

[18] On this period, see H. Klengel *Geschichte Syriens im 2. Jahrtausend v. u.Z., I*, 1965, 250-57.

[19] H. Otten, review of Wiseman's *Alalakh Tablets*, *ZDMG* 106 (1956), pp. 213-14.

[20] Klengel, book cited in n. 18, reads this same *Šar*-[*ru-up-ši*?] (p. 251).

the same room as the pit. According to Woolley's lively reconstruction of the events surrounding the statue base and pit, the looters who destroyed level I—and brought the Bronze Age at Alalakh to an end—wrenched the statue from its base, and abandoned it among the temple ruins. Later, a pious individual returned to bury the statue under the temple floor, thereby protecting the relic from further depradations (C. L. Woolley in S. Smith, *The Statue of Idri-mi*, (London, 1949, p. 2).

The Idri-mi statue has become a standard handbook illustration for the supposedly clumsy provincial style of mid-second millennium Syria. The king wears a shapeless garment with the typical Syrian rolled border and a high domed cap. The statue does not, however, bear any stylistic features which characterize it chronologically, and has always been dated on the strength of its inscription to the beginning of the Late Bronze Age. Woolley noted that the only other sculptural item of dolomite—a ram's head—at Alalakh came from the Level IV palace, thus roughly contemporary with the historical Idri-mi, but admitted that dolomite is a very common stone (Woolley in Smith, p. 3). The statue is very poorly modelled, in striking contrast with the "Yarimlim" head and assorted pieces from Alalakh VII, or the very fine cylinder seal carving common in Middle and Late Bronze Age Syria.

The statue base, however, can be examined somewhat more profitably. It is a rectangular basalt block with sides carved in low relief to represent a throne, of which only the lion's paw feet are preserved (see Smith, Pl. I). Woolley completed the remainder of the throne with a standing lion on either side, the bodies in shallow relief, the heads projecting as protomes. Since the paws are stylistically similar to those on the crude stone lions which flanked the inner doorway of the Level I temple, Woolley patterned his reconstruction on them (Woolley in Smith, p. 7: fig. 2). Before the Syro-Hittite period, however, when lions occur regularly on the statue bases of kings (see the statue of a king from Zincirli, in Akurgal, *The Art of the Hittites*, 1962, pp. 96ff.), there exist no parallels for thrones such as Woolley's. Royalty and dignitaries throughout the Bronze Age in Mesopotamia sit on simple stools or chairs. This practice extends to Syria, if one can judge from a few apparently standard illustrations (see an ivory plaque from Mardikh— P. Matthiae, "Two Princely Tombs at Tell Mardikh-Ebla," *Archaeology* 33 (1980) 14; and a sculpted ritual basin from the same site—P. Matthiae, *MANE* 1, 6 ("Ebla in the time of the Amorite Dynasties") 1979 pl. IX). Only at the very end of the Late Bronze Age are dignitaries shown on elaborate thrones of the sort envisaged by Woolley. A famous ivory from Megiddo VII b (as in *ANEP* n. 332 and p. 228) shows a procession leading up to a king seated on a throne flanked by spinxes. An identical throne on the Ahiram sarcophagus—if it is indeed pre-first millennium (as in *ANEP*, n. 456 and p. 302)—and an actual stone throne from Byblos suggest that the spinx, not the lion, was the fashion in the thirteenth and twelfth centuries B.C. The inspiration was certainly Egyptian, with the finest example (albeit with lions) from Tuthankhamon's tomb (as in *ANEP*, n. 416). There is also, however, the possibility that the Idri-mi throne was not decorated beyond the lion's paws. This type with animal feet, again no doubt Egyptian, is illustrated in Syria on Late Bronze Age seals (E. Porada, *CANES* no. 937, with bull's hooves?) and by the statuette of a seated figure from a Hazor I temple (thirteenth century B.C.) (Y. Yadin et al., *Hazor III-IV*, Jerusalem 1961, pl. 326:2). The Hazor statuette had also been buried in a pit below the last temple floor, but is not inscribed.

On the strength of the parallels for Idrimi's throne, therefore, it is more likely that the statue dates to the very end of the Late Bronze Age. It was not a relic treasured in the temple over the course of several centuries, but a piece contemporary with the temple in which it was recovered.

The report of Dr. Gates, printed above, can be supplemented by the following considerations:

1. *On the sculpted style of the statue of Idrimi.* The rarity of a rounded sculpture of a throne-seated ruler, indeed, the rarity of this manifestation in relief and painted artifacts even into the Neo-Hittite period has been demonstrated by W. Orthmann (*Untersuchungen zur späthetithischen Kunst* [*SBA*, 8], 1971, pp. 364-66). On the matter of Idrimi's garb, Vieyra, *Hittite Art*, p. 84, finds striking affinity with the heavy rolled edgings of the Late Bronze Age statues of Mishrife (H. Th. Bossert, *Altsyrien. Kunst und Handwerk . . .* [1951], #585-87, plate #180; H. Frankfort, *The Art and Architecture of the Ancient Orient*, 5th paperback ed., 1970, p. 258). This type of clothing, however, is known as early as Alalah VII (Collon, *Seal Impressions*, pl. XXIX) and into Late Bronze Ugarit (Frankfort, *Art*, #298, pp. 258-59). The treatment of facial features finds closest correspondences in the Neo-Hittite art of Carchemish (Vieyra, #58), and Zinjirli (Vieyra, #76; E. Akurgal, *The Art of the Hittites*, 1962, pl. #126-27 [cf. Frankfort, *Art*, p. 300—Kilamuwa?]).

2. *On generic correspondence and parallels: (auto)biography with sculpted figure of the subject.* A diligent, but probably not exhaustive inspection of first-person narratives and life-accounts which are linked to representations of the subject of the inscriptions, indicates that most comparable extant examples come from the first millennium B.C.

a. Semitic inscriptions. A biographical sketch inscribed in Aramaic on the subject's (?) statue is known to me only in Barrakib's presentation for/of his father, Panamuwa II (Statue: Orthmann, *Untersuchungen*, p. 354 [*sub.*: Tahtali Pinar; pl. 52,c]; Text: H. Donner and W. Röllig, *Kanaanäische und Aramäische Inschriften*, II: Kommentar, 1964, #215; J. C. L. Gibson, *Textbook of Syrian Semitic Inscriptions*, II, 1975, #14. Second half of the 8th century B.C.). To be noted, however, is that the retelling of Panamuwa's life is but a rehearsal of Barrakib's own legitimacy. An autobiographical torso of Barrakib is sculpted on an orthostat, with the narrator's own relief sculpted alongside (Orthostat: Bossert, *Altsyrien*, #886; *ANEP*, #281; text: *KAI* #216-17; Gibson, *TSSI*, #15 I-II; *ANET*[3], 655 [i]). The famous Hamath stela of Zakkur, slightly earlier in date than the last text, may also be ranged in the last category, for on the reverse it presents a human figure (for reading of the king's name, cf. J. Greenfield, *JNES* 37 [1978], p. 93, n. 9; A. R. Millard, *PEQ* 110 [1978],

p. 23. Text: *KAI*, #202; Gibson, *TSSI*, #5; *ANET*[3], 655-56). Because of the arrangement and lack of direct attachment to a sculpted figure of a king, we avoid ranging here the famous "bilingual" inscriptions of Azitawadda of Adana (Karatepe) in this category. Only text C is inscribed on a statue, and this is labelled in the text as a "divine figure." Written in Phoenician and carved dwarfing the figure of the king on its left side, is the autobiographical sketch of Kilamuwa of Sam'al (Orthostat: Bossert, *Altsyrien*, #887; Text: *KAI* #24; *ANET*[3], pp. 654-55; -9th cent.).

b. Non-Semitic inscriptions. The Carchemish inscriptions written in Luwian Hieroglyphics and placed alongside the figures of kings should be classified within our category. This is especially the case of the elaborate frieze of the usurper Araras (Reliefs: Akurgal *Art of the Hittites*, pl. 120-23; Text: cf. P. Meriggi, *Manuale di Eteo-Geroglifico* II/I [= *Incunabula Graeca*, 14], 1967, #9-11). We have evidence, however, that this genre of materials may have begun during the last days of the Hittite Empire, i.e., *N.B.*, around the time of Alalah I. A text of Suppiluliumas II, brought to my attention by J. Van Seters, contains the following: ". . . This image, [my father] Tudhaliya did not [(make it)]; I Suppiluliuma, . . . made it. And just as my father, the great King Tudhaliya, was a true king, in the same way I inscribed (his) true manly deeds thereon . . . I built an Everlasting Peak. I made the image and carried it into the (building called) Everlasting Peak; I installed and [consecrated (?)] it" (*KBO* XII:38:ii:4-21 as treated by H. G. Güterbock, "The Hittite Conquest of Cyprus Reconsidered," *JNES* 26 (1967), pp. 37-81). This text, it might also be noted, introduces the subject by means of a formula, "I am . . .", better attested in Idrimi and in West Semitic inscription of the first millennium B.C.

Egyptian autobiographics inscribed on statues—as contrasted with those found in tomb inscriptions from the Vth dynasty on—become well known from the 22nd dynasty on (10th century). But these barely go beyond the conventional platitudes assigned to a dearly departed who praises his own virtues, and glories in the deserved esteem showered upon him. A sampling of these are to be found in M. Lichtheim's *Ancient Egyptian Literature*, III: *The Late Period*, 1980, pp. 13-41. A fuller study is available in E. Otto, *Die Biographischen Inschriften der Ägyptischen Spätzeit*, 1954. More worthy of bringing into comparison is the second of two stelae recounting Kamoses's war against the Hyksos (Text: Habachi, *ASAE* 53 [1956], 195-202; Translation: *ANET*[3], 554-55). Carved by the chief courtier Neshi who, exceptionally, had his own figure represented on the stone, the narrative is full of grandiloquent claims, highly colorful scenery, and implausible achievements (cf. James, *CAH*[3] II/1, 291-94). It is not possible to establish the time lapse occurring between Kamoses's alleged command to have this stela erected and its completion by Neshi.

The famous Sumerian statues of Gudea cannot be placed in this category since the inscriptions are dedicatory rather than autobiographical.

3. *On literary parallels to the Idrimi statue.* As far as I can gather, (simulated) autobiographies which are either inscribed on the subject's statue or in proximity to his relief, and which display literary affinities with the form and structure of the Idrimi inscription are rather rare. The monuments of Zakkur of Hamath and Kilamuwa of Sam'al are among the few which sequence the segments of their narratives in a similar manner: Presentation of the subject; difficulty of the speakers against foreign elements; successes in stabilizing the home population; curses and/or blessings. The folkloristic elements in these examples, however, are at a minimum, but their function is taken to some extent by the involvement of deities (Zakkur) or of the uncanny (the ineffectiveness of Kilamuwa's predecessors).[21]

With Gates' suggestion as well as our own statements in mind, we might fulfill our promise and promote the thesis that the fabrication of Idrimi's statue occurred during the last days of Alalah.

At the end of Alalah IV, the city fell under Hittite hegemony. Itūr-addu, the last king of Idrimi's dynasty, was defeated by Suppiluliumas I, and his kingdom distributed between Ugarit and Aleppo, the last being a kingdom assigned to a Hittite prince. The city of Alalah was allotted to Aleppo, but, beginning with the reign of Mursilis, its orders came from Carchemish, where the Hittite viceroy resided.[22] We know very little of Alalah after this moment, but we can presume that it fared no better, and no worse than many of the city-states whose fortunes depended on the Hittite's ebb and flow of power. Woolley, whose reconstruction of events in the eighth chapter of his *Forgotten Kingdom* is marred by lack of distinctions among the kingdoms of Mukiš, Niya, and to a lesser extent Nuhašše, proposes, p. 141, that Alalah of level II was under a "milder regime" than the one which obtained in Alalah III. According to the archaeological evidence assembled in the ninth chapter of the same book, two separate periods distinguish Alalah I. Alalah IA, vaguely datable to the first half of the 13th century, saw a shift in social disposition: cremation becomes more common and a new pottery is introduced. But our focus is on Alalah IB, a level which began around 1250 B.C. and ended with the havoc wrought by the Sea Peoples, half a century later. A new temple, built upon the ruins of its predecessor, was established in IB, one which, however, differed in style from its predecessor. A slab with the relief of Tudhaliyas, in this case probably a prince, son of Mursilis II,[23] was used to tread the steps' masonry. This, as well as other details, have led Woolley to present the following assessment:

[21]See the analysis of Miller, cited in n. 6, and that of F. M. Fales, "Kilamuwa and the Foreign Kings: Propaganda vs. Power," *WdO* 10 (1979), pp. 6-22.

[22]On the historical setting, see M. Astour, "The Partition of the Confederacy of Mukiš. . . ." *Orientalia* 38 (1969), pp. 381-414; Klengel, *Gesch. Syr. I*, pp. 252-57.

[23]H. G. Güterbock, "Carchemish," *JNES* 13 (1954), p. 105 n. 15.

> The mere burning of the temple of Alalakh [IA] might have been regarded as an accident, but when we find that it is rebuilt on different lines recalling the national buildings of a glorious past [Alalah IV palaces] and Tudkhalia's monument bearing the royal image is dishonoured and set to be trampled under foot, then we cannot but recognize the evidence of yet one more revolt against the Hittite suzerainty. The signal of revolt may well have been the fall of Babylon which was captured by the Assyrians about 1241 B.C., and by that time the Hittites were too exhausted to make any real effort to recover their position . . . (*Forgotten Kingdom*, pp. 162-63).

This picture of a weakened Hatti is clear from other archival materials concerned with the affairs of state under Arnuwandas IV and Suppiluliumas II.[24] It is during this period, we would like to suggest, that nascent "nationalistic" feelings at Alalah led a certain Šarruwa to sponsor the making of a statue and to inscribe it with his own version of the deeds of Idrimi, founder of the last independent dynasty to rule the city-state. In doing so, Šarruwa was at the vanguard of a literary style, probably originating somewhere in Northern Syria near Carchemish, which was apparently cultivated even in Hattusas of Suppiluliumas II's time. This style was to become much more commonly followed in that area during the Iron Age before, to judge from present evidence, finding appreciation in Mesopotamia. Šarruwa's simulated autobiography of Idrimi suffused the activities of the dynast with much partisan sentiment and embellished them with folkloristic details that were certain to please an audience. Set within a historical period, which might have been made familiar to Šarruwa by the monuments and archives of the fourth level, the result was a historiographical masterpiece which promoted an awareness of Alalah's glorious past even as it offered solace in detailing the manner in which that past was itself built upon inauspicious beginnings. It spoke of days when Alalah's leaders were able to muster control of territories, Amae and Niya, which— as far as can be gathered by inspection of the epigraphic evidence concerning Niya at least—never fell under the domination of Mukiš/Alalah. But more understandable in view of the strong anti-Hittite sentiments which must have festered during thc long centuries of subjugation, Idrimi was made to gloat over successful forays into Hittite territory.

The inscribed statue was fashioned so as to sit upon a throne, and the whole was placed in the temple IB annex, a multichambered building attached to the main structure by means of a narrow causeway. The presence of an altar in the vicinity of the seated statue may indicate that Idrimi was venerated, if not worshipped. That this occurred in the annex rather than the temple proper may further suggest that the veneration may have been private in nature, perhaps on the part of Šarruwa and the city's leaders, rather than priestly and

[24] A. Goetze, "The Hittites and Syria (1300-1200 B.C.)," *CAH*^{3}, 1965, II/2, pp. 291-94.

cultically official. There is evidence, however, that the statue and its throne were to be transported outside the temple, probably during important ceremonies.[25]

Idrimi's saga, with its recall of a past worthy of emulation by the present, did not end with the destruction of Alalah at the uncouth hands of the Sea Peoples. Even as the city was being razed, there were some who believed that Alalah would rise again. At some risks, it must have been, an Alalahian returned to the scene of devastation, piously collected the fragments of Idrimi's statue, and buried them not far from where the throne stood. He hoped, no doubt, that future generations of citizens would one day reestablish Idrimi on his proper stand, read his story, and be inspired to duplicate his valiant deeds. In doing so, we might note, these generations would not only heed Idrimi's command that his accomplishments be thoroughly inspected and his memory constantly blessed (lines 103-4), but they would surely not fail to intercede with the gods and to ask that Šarruwa, the scribe, be granted eternal life in the beyond.[26]

[25] Woolley in S. Smith, *Statue of Idri-mi*, p. 7.

[26] I am beholden to E. Reiner for her reading of this paper. She informs me that the *CAD* reads DUB.SAR TUR ARAD in line 98b.

[Two articles by N. Na'aman have appeared after I submitted this paper. The first concerns "The Ishtar Temple at Alalakh," *JNES* 39 (1980), pp. 209-14, and only passingly refers to our subject. The second, "A Royal Scribe and His Scribal Products in the Alalakh IV Court," *Or Ant.* 19 (1980), pp. 107-16 presumes that the mention of Šarruwa in level IV documents necessarily implies that he was their author. Na'aman, after collation, adds 91:22 (*not* followed by DUB.SAR!) as another occurrence of Šarruwa's name among witnesses. Note however that his transcriptions of the PN in pp. 108 and 111 do not match; the second of which seemingly confirms Wiseman's copy where the *wa* sign is not recorded. His analysis of these documents reveals a strong Hurrian influence in the matter of vocabulary and syntax. "These Hurrian traits," he adds (p. 109), "are somewhat in contrast to the text of Idrimi, where only a minor Hurrian influence can be shown."

H. Otten's "Zum Ende des Hethiterreiches aufgrund der Bogazköy-Texte," *Jahresbericht des Instituts für Vorgeschichte der Universität Frankfurt A.M.*, 1976 (pp. 23-35) came to my attention (courtesy G. Beckman) too late for profitable use.]

Alcune Osservazioni sui Testi HSS XIX 113 e HSS XIX 114*

Paola Negri Scafa
Roma

I due testi HSS XIX 113 e HSS XIX 114, pubblicati in copia da Lacheman nel 1962,[1] seppur di facile lettura, presentano tuttavia alcuni punti che meritano una qualche attenzione.

HSS XIX 113 (SMN 2105)

R.	1	EME-*šu ša* ^{I}*Tuḫ-mi-ja* ⌜DUMU⌝ [*A*]-⌜*ri*⌝-*im-ma-at-qa*
	2	*a-na pa-ni* LÚ^{MEŠ} *ši-bu-ti*
	3	*an-nu-ti ki-am iq-ta-bi*
	4	^{MÍ}*Me-ra-al-lu* GÉME-*ja*
	5	*it-ti* DUMU-*šu-ma a-na ši-mi*
	6	*a-na* ⌜2⌝ ⌜AN⌝ŠE 4 BÁN ŠE
	7	*a-na* ⌜I⌝[*Ut-ḫap*]-*ta-e* DUMU *Ar-tu-ra*
	8	*at*-⌜*ta*⌝-*din-mi ù* ⌜*a-na*⌝-*ku*
	9	2 ANŠE 4 BÁN ŠE *ši-im-šu-nu*
	10	*ša* [GÉ]ME *ù ša* DUMU-*šu*
	11	*a-šar* ^{I}*Ut-ḫap-ta-e el-te-qè*
	12	*ù* ⌜*ap*⌝-*la-ku-mi*
	13	*ù* ^{I}*Ut-ḫap-ta-e*
	14	*qa-an*-⌜*na*⌝-*šu a-na pa-ni*
L.in.	15	LÚ^{MEŠ} *ši-bu-ti an-nu*-⌜*ti*⌝
	16	*im-ta-šar*
V.	17	IGI *Ar*-[*z*]*i-iz-za* DUMU *En-šúk-rù*
	18	IGI *Na*-⌜*ni*⌝-*ja* DUMU *Ki-pu-gur*

*Ho avuto occasione di redigere questa breve nota durante un mio soggiorno ad Heidelberg presso il prof. K. Deller, che qui ringrazio di cuore per le fruttuose discussioni sull'argomento.

[1] E. R. Lacheman, *Excavations at Nuzi. VIII. Family Law Documents*, Harvard Semitic Series XIX, 1962.

19 IGI *Šúk-ri-te-šup*
20 DUMU ⸢*Ar*⸣*-ru-um-ti*
21 IGI ⸢*Qar*⸣*-ra-te* DUMU *Pu-i-ta-e*
22 IGI *Ši-ma-an-ni* DUB.SAR
23 DUMU ^{d}AK.DINGIR.RA
24 NA$_4$ ^{I}*Tuḫ-mi-ja*
25 ⸢NA$_4$⸣ $^{[I]}$*Qar-ra-*<*te*>
26 NA$_4$ ^{I}*Šúk-ri-te-šup*
27 NA$_4$ ^{I}*Ar-*⸢*zi*⸣*-iz-za*
L.si. 28 NA$_4$ ^{I}*Na-ni-ja* NA$_4$ DUB.SAR

HSS XIX 114 (SMN 2159)[2]

R. 1 EME-*šu ša* ^{I}*Tuḫ*^{úḫ}*-mi-ja*
2 DUMU *A-ri-im-ma-*⸢*at*⸣*-qa*
3 *a-na pa-ni* LÚ^{MEŠ} IGI$^{⸢MEŠ}$*-ti*⸣
4 *an-nu-ti ki-am-ma iq-*[*ta-bi*]
5 ^{MÍ}*Mi-ra-al-lu* GÉME-[*ja*]
6 *it-ti* DUMU-*šu a-na ši-*⸢*mi*⸣
7 *a-na* 2 ANŠE 4 BÁN ŠE^{MEŠ}
8 *a-na* ^{I}*Ut-ḫap-ta-e* DUMU *Ar-*[*tu*]*-ra*
9 *at-ta-din-*⸢*mi*⸣ *ù*
10 ^{I}*Ut-ḫap-ta-e* 2 [ANŠE] ⸢4 BÁN⸣ ŠE^{MEŠ}
11 *ši-im-*[*šu*] ⸢*ša*⸣ GÉ[ME] *ù ša na-a-ri-*[*šu*]
12 *a-na* ^{I}⸢*Tuḫ*⸣*-mi-ja i+na-an-din*
13 *šum-ma* GÉME *ù na-a-ru*
14 *bi-ir-qa ir-ta-ši*
15 ^{I}*Tuḫ-mi-ja ú-za-ak-ka*$_4$
16 *a-na* ^{I}*Ut-ḫap-ta-e i+na-an-din*
17 EME-*šu* <*ša*> ^{MÍ}*Mi-ra-al-lu*
18 *a-na pa-ni* LÚ^{MEŠ} *ši-bu* (su Rasura)*-ti*
L.in. 19 *ki-am-ma iq-ta-bi*
20 *a-na-ku ra-ma-ni-ja-*⸢*ma*⸣
21 *it-ti* DUMU-*ja-ma*
V. 22 *a-na* ^{I}*Ut-ḫap-ta-e*
23 *it-ta-din-ni-in-ni-mi*
24 *ma-an-nu ša i+na be-ri-šu-nu*

[2] Da quanto si può inferire da E. Cassin, *Anthroponymie et Anthropologie de Nuzi*, I, Malibu, 1977, pp. 14a, 27b, 67a, 70a, l'autrice legge differentemente la lista dei testimoni. Per quanto mi è dato di conoscere, finora non è stata mai pubblicata una trascrizione di questi due testi.

	25	KI.BAL-*at* 1 GÊME SIG$_5$-*qá*		
	26	*ú-ma-al-la* (Rasura)		

	27	*ṭup-pu i+na* EGIR-*ki šu-du-ti*		
	28	*eš-ši i+na* ⌜*lìb*⌝-*bi* URU *Nu-zi*		
	29	*i+na* KÁ $^{d!}$[NÈ.IRI$_{11}$].GAL *šá*-ṭì-ir		
	30	NA$_4$ ^{I}ŠEŠ^{hu}-*na*-[*din*/*ṣir*]		
	31	(Sigillo)	II.	NA$_4$ ^{I}*A-ri-ik*-⌜*ku*⌝-*šu*
	32	DUMU *Ip-šá-ḫ*[*a-lu*]		(Sigillo)
	33	NA$_4$ ^{I}*I-ri-ja*		DUMU *Zi-in-na-ap-š*[*i-ir*]
	34	(Sigillo)		NA$_4$ ^{I}DINGIR-*ha*-⌜*bi*⌝-*il*
	35	DUMU *Ḫa-ni-ú*	II.	DUMU *A-kip-til-la*
	36	NA$_4$ ^{I}*Ki-ir-ru-ge* SANGA		
L.su.	37	DUMU *A-kip-til-la*		
L.si.	38	(Sigillo)		NA$_4$ ^{I}*Be-la-a+a* DUB.SAR
	39	NA$_4$ ^{I}*Tuḫ-mi-ja*		DUMU *Ḫa-nu-qa*

E' evidente che i due testi, entrambi provenienti dalla Stanza S 110, che ha restituito i documenti dell'archivio di Utḫap-tae f. Ar-tura, sono strettamente collegati fra di loro, in quanto redazioni diverse di uno stesso contratto. Quel che colpisce a prima vista è il fatto che sia la lista dei testimoni sia gli scribi sono completamente diversi. Una spiegazione di questa differenza può essere che il contratto di vendita in oggetto sia stato stipulato e perfezionato in tempi diversi, e di conseguenza di fronte a testimoni diversi e con scribi differenti; e questo sembra essere confermato anche dal contesto.

Infatti in HSS XIX 114, che è stata certamente la tavoletta stilata per prima, Tuḫmija f. Arim-matka ha dato (l. 9: *attadinmi*) la sua schiava Merallu con il figlio ad Utḫap-tae f. Ar-tura, ma deve ancora riceverne il prezzo (ll. 10-12: *Utḫap-tae . . . ana Tuḫmija inandin*), che tuttavia viene fissato e stabilito esplicitamente in 2 imēru e 4 sāti d'orzo. Inoltre Merallu conferma con una propria dichiarazione di essere stata data ad Utḫap-tae insieme al proprio figlio.[3] Concludono il testo la formula della penalità prevista in caso di rottura del contratto e le formule *šaṭir* e di datazione (*ina arki šudūti eššì*).

Ad un momento successivo, e precisamente all'atto del pagamento convenuto, fa riferimento HSS XIX 113: Tuḫmija afferma di aver ricevuto (*elteqe*) il prezzo della schiava e del di lei figlio e di essere stato pagato; a sua volta Utḫap-tae imprime l'orlo del mantello (nell'argilla) in presenza dei testimoni. Mancano la formula di datazione e quella relativa alla sanzione prevista per la rottura del contratto, che del resto sarebbero pleonastiche, dato

[3]Si noti la forma verbale *it-ta-din-ni-in-ni-mi* (l. 23).

che tutto era già stato stabilito in precedenza e che questo documento altro non sembra essere se non la ricevuta del pagamento del prezzo pattuito. Manca altresì la dichiarazione di Merallu, inutile anch'essa, giacché la donna aveva già espresso il suo consenso alla vendita.

Ma è proprio la dichiarazione di Merallu il secondo punto di HSS XIX 114 su cui si fissa la nostra attenzione.

I documenti relativi alla vendita di schiavi all'interno del *corpus* dei testi di Nuzi non sono numerosi[4] e sono spesso redatti sotto forma di dichiarazione:[5] in genere il dichiarante è il venditore che afferma di aver ricevuto[6] una certa quantità di beni[7] *ana šīmi* di uno schiavo, o di aver dato[8] uno schiavo in cambio di un dato ammontare di beni, *šīmi* dello schiavo. Seguono le formule *rašû* (relativa ad un'eventuale rivendicazione) e *nabalkutu* (riguardante la penale prevista in caso di rottura del contratto) —che non mancano nemmeno nei casi di vendita espressa in forma diversa dalla dichiarazione—ed inoltre, talvolta, la formula di datazione e l'atto di imprimere l'orlo del mantello.

Ciò che manca sempre è una dichiarazione da parte dello schiavo o della schiava che accettano di essere fatti oggetto di compravendita. Perciò il fatto che Merallu in HSS XIX 114 dichiari il suo consenso alla vendita è in qualche modo singolare e merita di essere preso in esame.

I soli casi in cui uno "schiavo" dichiara la propria accettazione alla "schiavitù" sono i testi relativi ai *ḫabirū*,[9] che sono quindi ben altra cosa dai documenti di compravendita di schiavi, così come i *ḫabirū* non possono essere considerati alla stregua degli altri schiavi, giacché la loro situazione è chiaramente differente.

Non sembra perciò azzardato inferire che anche Merallu costituisca un caso a sé rispetto agli altri schiavi di cui è registrata la vendita. Certamente non è una *ḫabiru*, giacché i documenti a questi ultimi sono del tutto differenti sia da HSS XIX 113 sia da HSS XIX 114; ma del resto, i testi che la riguardano differiscono anch'essi, sia pur per il solo particolare della dichiarazione della donna, dalla casistica sin qui nota della compravendita degli schiavi.

[4]Come già notava A. Saarisalo, *New Kirkuk Documents Relating to Slaves*, "Studia Orientalia" V/3 (1933-1934).

[5]Cfr. *e.g.* JEN 115, 119, 179, 192; HSS XIX 122. Non hanno forma di dichiarazione, p. es., JEN 451 e HSS V 100.

[6]Cfr. JEN 115.

[7]Che possono essere argento, o bestiame, o altro.

[8]Cfr. JEN 119 e 179. JEN 192 citato alla n. 5 fa riferimento ad situazione leggermente diversa.

[9]Cfr. E. Cassin-J. Bottéro, *Le problème des* Ḫabiru à la 4e *Rencontre Assyriologique Internationale. VI. Les textes de Nuzi*, C.S.A. 12 (1954) pp. 43-70.

Una spiegazione potrebbe essere fornita da HSS XIX 122, in cui un *warad ekalli* di nome Tuḫmija insieme alla moglie Merallu vende ad Ḫutija f. Arip-šarri uno schiavo di nome Tuntuki. La coincidenza dei nomi fra HSS XIX 113-14 e HSS XIX 122 è impressionante; tuttavia il fatto che in HSS XIX 122 il nome di Tuḫmija non è seguito dal patronimico, bensì solo da una qualificazione professionale, induce a più attenta verifica prima di poter affermare che si tratta della stessa persona; purtroppo la documentazione non è particolarmente ricca né per Tuḫmija f. Arim-matka né per il *warad ekalli* Tuḫmija: tuttavia, se sarà possibile in qualche modo riconoscere sufficienti e significativi punti di contatto fra le sfere di attività dei due soggetti, non sarà fuor di luogo concludere che siamo di fronte all'identica persona.

Tuḫmija f. Arim-matka è noto solo dai testi in esame. L'altro contraente del contratto è, come abbiamo visto, Utḫap-tae f. Ar-tura, mentre i testimoni sono Ar-zizza f. En-šukru, Šukri-tešup f. Aril-lumti, Karrate f. Pui-tae (HSS XIX 113), e Aḫu-na[din/ṣir] f. Ipša-ḫalu, Arik-kušuḫ f. Sîn-napšir, Irija f. Ḫaniu, Ilu-ḫabil e Kirruke *šangû* ff. Akip-tilla (HSS XIX 114).

A parte Ar-zizza f. En-šukru, che è noto solo da una ricevuta relativa ad orzo (HSS XV 244), e Aḫu-na[din/ṣir] f. Ipša-ḫalu ed Irija f. Ḫaniu, che sono *hapax*, gli altri testimoni mostrano di avere una serie di legami reciproci abbastanza estesi:

1) il *šangû* Kirruke e suo fratello Ilu-ḫabil in HSS XVI 457 sono in lista con un [ ]-tešup f. Ar-tura[10] e con un certo Tarmija f. Ḫuja.
2) Tarmija f. Ḫuja ritorna in una lista di HSS XVI 83 insieme ad un altro testimone di questo contratto: Arik-kušuḫ f. Sîn-napšir. Sempre in questa lista compaiono altre persone, quali Eḫli-tešup f. Waqar-bēlī, Tarmi-tilla f. Šurki-tilla e Šennaja *warad bīt ḫurizāti*, che anzi è compagno (*šutapû*) di Tarmija f. Ḫuja (a proposito del quale si osservi che in HSS XVI 232 è in lista con Ar-tura f. Kuššija padre di Utḫap-tae).
3) Con Tarmi-tilla f. Šurki-tilla siamo in pieno ambiente di *rākib narkabti*, un ambiente che ci riguarda da vicino, visto che un altro testimonio di questo contratto, Šukri-tešup f. Aril-lumti (HSS XIX 113) ricorre nella lista di *rākib narkabti* di HSS XIII 6,[11] dove sono enumerati anche Waqar-bēlī f. Taja e AK.DINGIR.RA f. Sîn-napšir.
4) Di nuovo Tarmi-tilla f. Šurki-tilla ha a che fare con uno dei testimoni di HSS XIX 113, e precisamente con Nanija f. Kip-ukur, che in JEN 108 e JEN 151 si occupa dei problemi relativi all'acquisto di cavalli per Tarmi-tilla, il che non stupisce, visto che quest'ultimo è un *rākib narkabti*. Inoltre il nome di

[10]La Cassin integra [Šeḫal]-tešup. E' un fratello di Utḫap-tae?

[11]Cfr. G. Dosch, *Die Texte aus Room A 34 des Archivs von Nuzi*, Magisterarbeit, Un. Heidelberg, 1976, p. 262 N. 188.

Nanija f. Kip-ukur ricorre in HSS XIII 65 insieme a quello dello scriba Arip-šarri e a quello dello *šakin bīti* Erwi-šarri (che sappiamo, grazie a HSS XV 187, avere responsabilità verso una *bīt ḫurizāti*).

Quindi, anche se Tuḫmija f. Arim-matka è praticamente un *hapax*, tuttavia è possibile inferire che l'ambiente in cui si muove e le persone con cui ha a che fare appartengono al mondo dei *rākib narkabti*, degli alti funzionari del palazzo e dei loro collaboratori.

Analoga è la situazione del *warad ekalli* Tuḫmija, che oltre a HSS XIX 122, è noto anche da HSS XIV 593, una lista di razioni per *warad ekalli*. I nomi di questi *warad ekalli* (83 in tutto) sono seguiti per lo più dalle loro professioni. Tra queste, oltre a quelle di tessitore, fullone, fornaio, pastore, fabbro, mercante, giardiniere, sarto, pentolaio, bovaro, cuoco, ed altre non identificate, sono citate quelle di aiutante dello *šakin bīti* e di scriba.

Uno degli scribi in questione è Arip-šarri, padre di quel Ḫutija a cui il *warad ekalli* Tuḫmija vende in HSS XIX 122 uno schiavo; ed è lo stesso Arip-šarri che in HSS XIII 65 ricorre in elenco con Nanija f. Kip-ukur e con lo *šakin bīti* Erwi-šarri.

Si delinea così, nonostante la scarsità dei dati, anche l'ambiente di Tuḫmija *warad ekalli*: un ambiente di artigiani del palazzo, scribi, collaboratori di alti funzionari, che richiama molto da vicino quello di Tuḫmija f. Arim-matka, ed ha anzi precisi punti di contatto con esso, rappresentati soprattutto dallo scriba Arip-šarri e dai suoi collegamenti con Nanija f. Kip-ukur ed i suoi legami, più indiretti, con gli altri testimoni di Tuḫmija f. Arim-matka.

Non sembra perciò fuor di luogo affermare che Tuḫmija *warad ekalli* e Tuḫmija f. Arim-matka sono la stessa persona.

Le conseguenze che discendono da questa affermazione sono duplici. In primo luogo diventa chiaro il motivo di una dichiarazione di assenso da parte di Merallu in HSS XIX 114: il fatto di essere (o essere stata) una moglie di Tuḫmija la rendeva certamente diversa dagli altri schiavi, conferendole forse più diritti, o una maggiore personalità giuridica; di qui la necessità di una sua dichiarazione.

Inoltre questi tre testi forniscono una qualche nuova informazione, sia pure indiretta, sulla posizione della donna a Nuzi: se numerosi aspetti della situazione della donna, specie nell'ambito familiare, sono già stati messi ben in luce,[12] tuttavia molto rimane ancora da fare, ed ogni più piccolo elemento od indizio, quindi, sono benvenuti. La constatazione che una stessa persona possa essere sia moglie sia schiava, sebbene forse in tempi diversi, permette di aprire un piccolo spiraglio sulla situazione delle "mogli" secondarie a Nuzi, sulla loro collocazione nell'ambito della famiglia, sia sotto il profilo giuridico sia sotto quello economico. L'esistenza delle "mogli" secondarie a Nuzi è certa, anche se

[12]E. Cassin, *Pouvoirs de la femme et structures familiales*, RA 63 (1969) pp. 121-48.

la documentazione al loro riguardo è piuttosto elusiva, indiretta e sfuggente, giacché solo raramente alcuni documenti, come per esempio i testamenti, lasciano intuire la loro esistenza. Mai, quindi, attestazioni dirette: solo indizi od aporie, come nel caso presentemente in esame della dichiarazione di assenso della schiava/moglie venduta.

Inoltre si ripropone con nuova forza il problema dell'esatta interpretazione del significato (o dei significati) dei segni GÉME (e conseguentemente Ì R) e DAM, che, come già da tempo è emerso, sottintendono più di una sfumatura di significato, spesso assai in contrasto.

Überlegungen zu einigen Demonstrativa und Partikeln des Hurritischen

H. J. Thiel
Freie Universität
Berlin

Im folgenden werden einige hurritische Demonstrativa und Partikeln auf die Möglichkeit hin untersucht, in zwei Gruppen zusammengefasst zu werden. Die phonologischen Beziehungen, in der die Mitglieder der beiden Gruppen zueinander stehen, werden dabei als solche von Stärkeabstufungen aufgefasst, die als überwiegend durch verschieden starke Grade von Druckakzenten bewirkt erklärt werden. Dabei wird eine neue Deutung der Partikel *au* vorgeschlagen, und für *ai* 'wenn' eine andere mögliche etymologische Beziehung als die bislang angesetzte erörtert, die vielleicht auch zur weiteren Klärung der Endung *-ai*, *-ae* dienlich sein könnte.

1. *Die zweigliedrigen Gruppen der Demonstrativa.*

11. *Die* aku-*Gruppe.*

Bekannt ist das Formenpaar der 'particularizing demonstratives' *akku* 'dieser (von zweien)' und *aku* 'jener (von zweien).'[1] Auffällig ist, dass das Vokalmuster in beiden Formen identisch ist (*a . . . u*) und die konsonantischen Mittelstücke der Formen dieses Paares in einer Beziehung zueinander stehen, die sich als eine der (phonologischen) 'Stärke' beschreiben lässt: *kk* (/k:/) ist als geminiert (bzw. fortis)[2] als 'stärker,' *k* (/k/) dagegen als simplex (bzw. lenis) als 'schwächer' anzusehen.

[1]F. W. Bush, A Grammar of the Hurrian Language (Ann Arbor, 1964) (hinfort: GHL) 107; E. Speiser, Introduction to Hurrian (New Haven, 1941) (hinfort: IH) 77; I. Diakonoff, Hurrisch und Urartäisch (München, 1971) (hinfort: HuUr), 112.

[2]Die Entscheidung zwischen den phonologischen Deutungen als 'geminiert' (/C_1/ + /C_2/) oder 'fortis' (/C:/) des phonetisch wohl als [C:] anzusetzenden graphischen C_1C_2 ist nicht einfach und kann—wie dem Phonologen bekannt ist—für die verschiedenen Tiefenebenen der phonologischen Struktur unterschiedlich ausfallen. In denjenigen Fällen, in denen sich dem Teil [:] eine morphologische Deutung geben lässt, ist der Ansatz von /C:/ vorzuziehen, da sie eine Segmentierung /C/ + /:/ erlaubt. Ein solcher Fall wird unten gegeben werden. Zu weiteren Fällen s. V. Haas und H. J. Thiel, Das hurritologische Archiv (Berlin, 1974) (hinfort: Archiv) 117 und

Es ist anzunehmen, dass das stärkere /k:/ in *akku* als das phonologisch einen höheren Grad an Markiertheit aufweisende Segment auch im Bedeutungsinhalt und in morphologischer Hinsicht als markiert anzusehen ist. Wir extrahieren so aus dieser Form ein Morphem der Gestalt /-:-/ ('Fortis' bzw. 'Geminierung') und erteilen ihm die Bedeutung 'Hinweis auf Nähe zum Sprecher' zu. Diese Form mit /-:-/ kontrastiert so mit der—morphologisch nicht markierten—Ausgangsform der Bedeutung '(allgemeiner) Hinweis.'

Wir wollen das eben behandelte Formenpaar hinfort als *aku*-Gruppe bezeichnen, da ihnen—wie gezeigt werden soll—noch weitere Elemente anzuschliessen sind.

12. *Die* anni-*Gruppe.*

Betrachten wir weiter das Formenpaar der 'general demonstratives' *anti* 'dieses' und *anni* 'jenes.'[3] Auch hier finden wir Identität im Vokalschema. Weiterhin sind sich auch die Mittelstücke *-nt-* und *-nn-* ähnlich genug—Anwesenheit eines dentalen Nasals—dass man nach Analogie von /-k-:-/ vs. /-k-/ auch in /-nt-/ vs. /-nn-/ einen Kontrast im Stärkegrad sehen möchte.

Da sich auch in *anti* 'dieses' ein Hinweis auf 'Nähe zum Sprecher' findet, wird man diese Form in Analogie zu *akku* als /a-*X*-:-i/ segmentieren, die Form *anni* 'jenes' entsprechend als /a-*X*-i/ ohne /-:-/. Durch *X* bezeichnet ist hier der als phonologisch basishaft bzw. als historisch ursprünglich anzusetzende Wert der im belegten Hurritischen als *nt* bzw. *nn* erscheinenden Segmente. Er wird so vorerst unbestimmt gelassen, um weiter unten auf seinen mutmasslichen Wert hin untersucht zu werden.

Wie wir oben den Begriff der '*aku*-Gruppe' eingeführt haben, soll auch hier das eben behandelte Formenpaar hinfort als die—ebenfalls noch um weitere Elemente zu erweiternde—*anni*-Gruppe bezeichnet werden.

2. *Zur Dreigliedrigkeit der Gruppen.*

21. *Erweiterung der* anni-*Gruppe durch* ati *'so'.*

Bei der Betrachtung von *anti* und *anni* wird man an die adverbiale Partikel *ati* 'so'[4] erinnert: das Vokalmuster ist ebenfalls *a . . . i*, das Mittelstück enthält einen Dental—wenngleich auch ein Nasal fehlt—und die Bedeutung ist ebenfalls hinweisenden Charakters: 'so' i.e. 'in dieser/jener Weise.'

182ff.—Die Deutung als 'simplex' vs. 'geminiert' geht auf F. Bush zurück (GHL 82ff.); bei anderen wird allgemein ein Kontrast nach 'stimmlos' vs. 'stimmhaft' angesetzt.

[3]GHL 106f., IH 76, 109.—Das dem /anti/ entsprechende alte *adi* aus Urkiš (RA 42,12 [1948]) wird hier nicht in die Betrachtung einbezogen. Doch mag diese Form für das /(n)d/—Problem (s. Abschnitt 332) bedeutsam sein.

[4]GHL 241 'thus, so (result),' IH 92 'thus,' HuUr 147 '"also, nun, somit," o.ä.'

Vergleicht man das einfache /t/ mit der Konsonantenverbindung /nt/ und der Geminata /nn/, so zeigt sich, dass es unter diesen den geringsten phonologischen Komplexitätsgrad aufweist. Man möchte daher /t/ einen noch schwächeren phonologischen Grad als /nn/ (gegenüber /nt/) zuerteilen.

Es soll mithin die oben gegebene zweigliedrige Unterscheidung von /nt/ 'stark' vs. /nn/ 'schwach' durch die folgende dreigliedrige ersetzt werden: /nt/ 'stark,' /nn/ 'normal' und /t/ 'schwach.'

Diese Schwachheit gerade von *ati* 'so' dürfte darin begründet sein, dass es als eine im Satz weniger betonte Partikel aufzufassen ist.

22. *Erweiterung der* aku-*Gruppe durch* au.

Lässt sich als Parallelfall zu *ati* auch zu dem Paar *akku* vs. *aku* eine Form mit *a . . . u* finden, die als geschwächte Form angesehen und somit in eine Reihe mit diesem Paar gestellt werden könnte? Tatsächlich bietet sich hier die Form *au* an, die bislang gemeinhin als Interjektion gedeutet wird.[5] Sie erscheint alleinstehend KUB XXVII 38 iv 8ff. im 'Weltkönigstext,'[6] aber auch mit Assoziativen verbunden in der Form Mit. III 121 *a-ú-un-ni-ma-a-an*, die—im Rahmen der Deutung als Interjektion—als 'not clear' bezeichnet worden ist.[7] Tatsächlich sprechen die Belege nicht dagegen— die Verbindung mit Assoziativen hingegen eher dafür—in *au* ebenfalls ein Demonstrativum bzw. Adverbium schwach hinweisenden Charakters zu sehen: 'dieser/jener (unter den anderen)' bzw. 'und so auch (unter den anderen).'

Auch die *aku*-Gruppe ist somit dreigliedrig: *akku* 'stark,' *aku* 'normal' und *au* 'schwach.'

Es ist jetzt am Platze, Überlegungen zur phonetischen und phonologischen Gestalt der bisher gegebenen Formen in ihrer historischen Entwicklung anzustellen.

3. *Zur Phonologie der behandelten Gruppen.*

31. *Die phonologischen Bedingungen der Schwächungen.*

Die Formen *akku* und *aku* haben wir—in Analogie zu *anti* und *anni* in ihrem Verhältnis zu *ati*—als phonologisch stärker betont als die schwächere Form *au* angesetzt. Wir wollen diesen Kontrast durch die Ansetzung von (vorerst nur) zwei Stärken des Druckakzentes (1) /'.../ (stärker) und (2) /^.../ (schwächer) beschreiben. Es soll angenommen werden, dass diese Unterschiede in der Druckstärke phonologische Realität hatten und zur Erklärung der 'Schwächungen' dienen können.

[5] E. Forrer BoTU 2.25*[1] 'siehe!'; IH 90f.; HuUr 147 'wohlan!, siehe da!'.

[6] Ausserdem erscheint *au* auch KUB XXVII 31,4 (*a-a-u*).

[7] IH 91 n. 66.

32. *Phonologie der* aku-*Gruppe.*

321. *Zum Wert von* au *im belegten Hurritischen.*

Als phonetische Werte sind im belegten Hurritischen anzusetzen: für *kk* die Werte 'lang' und 'stimmlos' [k:], für *k* 'kurz' und 'stimmhaft' [g] wenn zwischen zwei stimmhaften Segmenten stehend (i.e. zwischen Vokalen und nach Nasal etc.), sonst stimmlos [k].

Als Lautwert des geschwächten velaren Konsonanten in einer anzusetzenden geschwächten Form von /aku/ [agu] könnten daher nur 'stimmhaft' und 'frikativisch' erwartet werden, i.e. phonetisches [γ]. Dieses Phon wäre jedoch nach unserer Kenntnis der Schreibgewohnheiten durch *-ḫ-* wiedergegeben worden; ihm entspräche phonemisches /x/, der velare Frikativ. Nun liegt aber in *au* diese Schreibung nicht vor, mithin auch kein [γ]. Vielmehr können wir hinter der Schreibung *au* nichts anderes als entweder ein [a.u]—wobei [.] die Silbengrenze bezeichnet—oder ein [ahu] oder aber ein [awu] sehen. Es scheint der letztere Ansatz der plausibelste zu sein; ungeklärt soll bleiben, ob wir [w] als subphonemischen Gleitlaut oder als phonemisches /w/ zu interpretieren haben, eine Unentschiedenheit, die durch die Schreibung [a(w)u] bzw. /a(w)u/ zum Ausdruck gebracht werden soll.

322. *Zum Wert von* [(w)] *in einer vor-hurritischen Sprachstufe.*

Dieses [(w)] ist für die belegte und uns bekannte Sprachstufe des Hurritischen anzusetzen. Es ist jedoch als Reflex eines vor-hurritischen (oder früh-hurritischen) *[γ] anzusehen, das sich zu [(w)]—vielleicht über die Zwischenstufen [h] und Ø entwickelt hat. Es ist dies eben das *[γ], das wir als schwachstufige Entsprechung zu /k/ [g] in einer füheren Sprachstufe des Hurritischen erwarten.[8] Diese Sprachstufe soll hinfort als Sprachstufe I bezeichnet werden.

Wir gewinnen somit folgendes Bild von den Verhältnissen auf der Sprachstufe I:

Stark	normal	schwach
/'.:./	/'.../	/ˆ.../
/[k:]/	[γ]	[γ]
	/k/	

[8]Auch im Tamil hat /k/ ein Allophon [γ]. Wie für eine frühere Sprachstufe der Kontrast dieses *[γ] mit dem später durch *-ḫ-* wiedergegebenen Frikativ phonologisch zu beschreiben wäre, muss hier unerörtert bleiben. Vielleicht sind die in den Schreibungen *ḫ* und *ḫḫ* vorliegenden Frikative eher als Uvulare statt als Velare aufzufassen, so HuUr 51.

In einer noch früheren Sprachstufe II können wir weiter von einer velaren Reihe ausgehen, in der */ g, k, k′/ (stimmhaft, stimmlos, glottalisiert) (desgleichen lang */ gg, kk, k′k′/) kontrastieren. Es ist dies das System, das von I. Diakonoff für das Proto-Hurritisch-Urartäische erschlossen worden ist.[9] Innerhalb dieses Systems lässt sich eine Entstehung von [γ] aus einem Phonem */g/, nicht aus einem [g] als Allophon von */k/, annehmen. Die Schwächung hätte mithin ursprünglich nur in der Veränderung von */k/ zu */g/, i.e. nur im Wandel von stimmlos zu stimmhaft bestanden.

Es folgert aus dem, dass in diesem System der Sprachstufe II für */k/ kein Allophon [g] anzusetzen ist. Erst in der jüngeren Sprachstufe I fallen intervokalisches */k/ und */g/ [g] (dieses Allophon nur in stärker akzentuierter Position) in einem [g] als Allophon eines */k/ zusammen. Gleichzeitig wird in dieser späteren Sprachstufe ein [g] in schwächer akzentuierter Position zu [γ]. Dieses [γ] entwickelt sich dann weiter zu dem oben behandelten [(w)].

Wir gewinnen so folgendes vorläufiges Bild von der Verhältnissen auf Sprachstufe II:

stark	normal	schwach
/′.:./	/′.../	/˄.../
/ [k:] /	/ [k] /	/ [g] /

Die Entwicklung von Sprachstufe II über Sprachstufe I zum belegten Hurritischen stellt sich wie folgt dar:

II: / [k] / / [g] /

I: /([k ~ g] ~ [γ] /

/ [k ~ g] / / (w)/

33. *Phonologie der* anni-*Gruppe.*

331. *Zum Stand von* /nt/ *und* /nn/ *im Vor-Hurritischen.*

Auch bei der Suche nach einer Erklärung für die Entstehung des Kontrastes /nt/ vs. /nn/ wie er uns in den belegten Formen *anti* und *anni* vorliegt, ist von der früheren Sprachstufe II auszugehen.

Die Ausgangsform bildet ein */′anti/, die Starkform wäre so mit */nt/+ /-:-/ anzusetzen. Da wir auch in der dentalen Reihe von einem Kontrast /d, t,

[9]HuUr 45. Im Hurritischen wird der Kontrast nach ‘stimmhaft’ vs. ‘stimmlos’ vs. ‘glottalisiert’ aufgehoben, während der Kontrast nach ‘simplex’ vs. ‘geminiert’ erhaltem bleibt. Für das Urartäische gilt das Gegenteil.

t′, (dd, tt, t′t′)/ auszugehen haben, ist für */nt/ der phonetische Wert [nt], für */nt/ + /-:-/ ein Wert [n:t] mit Längung des */n/ statt des */t/ anzusetzen. Nach dem Zusammenfall von */d/ und */t/ im /t/ der Sprachstufe I entwickelt /t/ nach Nasal das stimmhafte Allophon [d]. Weiter muss von einer Tendenz zur Vereinfachung des [n:d] ausgegangen werden, die eine Schwächung von [n:d] zu [nd] bewirkt. Um den Kontrast der Formen mit und ohne ursprüngliche Länge zu wahren, wurde der gleichzeitige Wandel von [nd] zu [n:] (Assimilation des [d]) erforderlich. Es entstehen so aus *[an:ti] die Form /anti/ [andi], aus */anti/ die Form /anni/ [an:i].

332. *Die Form* ati *im Vor-Hurritischen.*

Die der Normalform /′anti/ entsprechende Schwachform, aus der die Form /ati/ [adi] des belegten Hurritischen abzuleiten ist, muss im Rahmen des ursprünglichen Systems mit den Kontrasten */ d, t, .../ als*/ˆandi/ angesetzt werden. Sie zeigt—entsprechend der Schwächung von */k/ zu */g/—die Schwächung von */t/ zu */d/. Jedoch muss wohl auch mit einer durch die Schwächung bedingten Aufgabe des nasalen Elementes gerechnet werden. Es soll diese Form mithin als /ˆa(n)di/ geschrieben werden.

4. *Unregelmässigkeiten in der phonologischen Realisierung der Schwächungen.*

Wir hatten bislang die Formen *ati* und *a(w)u* als Schwachformen bezeichnet. Sind diese beiden Formen aber tatsächlich in identischer Weise geschwächt? Offenbar nicht, denn das alte */d/ erscheint weiterhin als Okklusiv, während das alte */g/ als Halbvokal bzw. als Ø erscheint. Wohl ist nicht auszuschliessen, dass ein allgemeiner Vorgang der Schwächung einen Velar stärker erfasst als einen Dental,[10] doch ist zunächst nach einer hurritischen Form Ausschau zu halten, die nicht nur ebenfalls geschwächt ist, sondern die Form /a(w)u/ im Detail parallelisiert. Eine solche Form wäre /a(y)i/, mit einem /(y)/, das vor /i/ auf demselben Wege wie /(w)/ vor /u/ entstanden wäre.

5. *Viergliedrigkeit der* anni-*Gruppe*: ai ‘*wenn.*’

Nun liegt eine solche Form tatsächlich vor, und zwar in der Partikel *ai* ‘wenn,’ wohl /a(y)i/.[11] Diese Partikel könnte durchaus als eine weitere— und zwar als die schwächste—Form der *anni*-Gruppe zugeteilt werden. Sie stünde dann unmittelbar neben *ati* ‘so’ und wäre als deren Schwächung aufzufassen.

[10]Zu Literaturhinweisen s. J. B. Hooper, An Introduction to Natural Generative Phonology (New York 1976) 202, 211 n. 3.

[11]F. Bush, GHL 246, entscheidet sich für den Ansatz dieser Partikel als *ay*-, schliesst jedoch *ayi*- als Möglichkeit nicht aus.

Zu der semantischen Nachbarschaft von 'so' und 'wenn' (bzw. einer Entwicklung von 'so' zu 'wenn') vergleiche man im (älteren) Deutschen 'so' im Gebrauch von 'wenn' ('So Gott will, . . .').

Bei dieser noch stärker als *ati* geschwächten Partikel *a(y)i* findet die hochgradige Schwächung eine Erklärung in dem satzeinleitenden Charakter dieser Partikel gegenüber dem adverbialen Charakter von *ati*.

Es muss hier erwähnt werden, dass diese Partikel von F. Bush mit E. Speiser als 'probably related to nominal *ay-* used prepositionally with the force of "presence"' angesehen wird. Er bemerkt jedoch: 'The semantic relation is not clear.'[12] Eher dürfte wohl dies nominale *ayi* zu *awi* 'Gesicht, Vorderseite' zu stellen sein. Das /y/ wäre dabei über eine durch benachbartes /i/ bewirkte Palatalisierung des als ursprünglich anzusehenden [w] zu [ẅ] (halbvokalisches [ü]) mit anschliessender Entrundung zu [y] entstanden.[13]

Es ist sogar weiter zu erwägen, ob nicht in dem *-ai* (*-ae*) der Endung eines 'adverbialen Kasus,' die auch in Verbindung mit Verbstämmen erscheint, eine weiter zur Endung geschwächte Form der *anni*-Gruppe zu sehen ist. Eine Bedeutung 'so'—dem *ati* entsprechend—scheint hier in vielen Fällen noch nachvollziehbar zu sein.[14]

Parallel zu der angesetzten Entwicklung *[g] >*[γ] >*[h] > [(w)] (vor /u/) können wir zur Erklärung des *ai* /a(y)i/ eine Entwicklung *[(n)d], *[d] >*[δ] (Frikativ) >*[h]>[(y)] (vor /i/) annehmen.

6. *Zum Ansatz zweier Schwachformen.*

Die Einbeziehung der Form /a(y)i/ in die *anni*-Gruppe zwingt uns zum Ansatz von zwei statt bisher einer Schwachform. Es sind anzusetzen:

(1) Eine in geringerem Masse geschwächte Form bei einem mässig starken Druckakzent /ˆ. . ./.

(2) Eine stärker geschwächte Form bei sehr schwachem Druckakzent, der durch /°. . ./ bezeichnet werden soll.

Unter dem Einfluss von /ˆ. . ./ wird in der Sprachstufe II ein stimmloser Konsonant stimmhaft (*/k/, */t/ > */g/, */d/) und unter dem Einfluss von /°. . ./ stimmhaft und frikativ, wobei die so entstandenen *[γ] und *[δ] zunächst nur als Allophone von */g/ und */d/ mit /°. . ./ aufzufassen sind.[15] Diese Frikative *[γ] und *[δ] entwickeln sich in späteren Sprachstufen in der Weise, dass an ihrer Stelle /(w)/ und /(y)/ (vor /u/ bzw. /i/) erscheinen.

[12]GHL 246f.

[13]V. Haas und H. J. Thiel, Die Beschwörungsrituale der Allaituraḫ(ḫ)i (Neukirchen-Vluyn, 1978) 115f., auch 110, 116, 175, 263; Archiv 146f.

[14]GHL 166f. mit der dort angegebenen Literatur; HuUr 141, 71ff., 130ff.; Archiv 225ff.

[15]Zum Ansatz von frikativischen Allophonen von basishaften Okklusiven im belegten Hurritischen vgl. GHG 56f.

7. *Ergebnisse.*

Wir sind zu dem Ansatz zweier Gruppen von Demonstrativa/Partikeln gelangt: der *aku*-Gruppe und der *anni*-Gruppe. Die Mitglieder dieser Gruppen sind Abwandlungen eines Basismorphems in verschiedenen phonologischen Stärkegraden oder Stufen.[16] Diese Stufen repräsentieren:

(1) Die Einführung eines morphemischen /-:-/ (Längung des Konsonanten) mit der Bedeutung 'Hinweis auf Nähe zum Sprecher' in die Basisform mit dem starken Druckakzent /'. . ./.
(2) Die unveränderte Basisform mit /'. . ./.
(3) Eine in geringerem Masse unter dem Einfluss eines mässig schwachen Druckakzentes /^. . ./ geschwächte Form.
(4) Eine in stärkerem Masse unter dem Einfluss eines ausgeprägt schwachen Druckakzentes /°. . ./ geschwächte Form.

Es liegen so folgende Glieder der *aku*- und der *anni*-Gruppe in der belegten Sprachform des Hurritischen in den folgenden Abstufungen vor:

akku	*aku*		*a(w)u*	
anti	*anni*	*ati*	*a(y)i*	(*-ai, -ae* ?)

Das Fehlen einer der Form *ati* entsprechenden Form in der *aku*-Gruppe ist weniger störend, als auf den ersten Blick erscheinen mag. Die Vorformen */'aku/ und */^agu/ können bei dem später erfolgenden Zusammenfall von */k/ und */g/ nicht anders als hurritisches /k/ [k ~ g] erscheinen. Es könnte somit durchaus noch mit zwei verschiedenen—in ihrer phonologischen Gestalt jedoch zusammengefallenen—Formen auch im belegten Hurritischen zu rechnen sein:

akku	aku_1	(aku_2)	*a(w)u*	
anti	*anni*	*ati*	*a(y)i*	(*-ai, -ae* ?)

Diesen oben gegebenen Formen des belegten Hurrisch entsprächen in einem Früh- oder Vor-Hurritisch die folgenden Formen, in denen die Abstufung nach phonologischem Stärkegrad hervortreten:

*ak-:-u	*aku	*agu	*aγu
*ant-:-i	*anti	*a(n)di	*aδi

[16]Vergleichbar, wenn auch nicht zu parallelisieren mit den Verhältnissen beim 'Stufenwechsel' des Finnischen.

Zusammenschlüsse von Nuzi-Texten

Gernot Wilhelm
Saarbrücken

E. R. Lacheman hat alle, die am Studium der Nuzi-Tafeln mitwirken, durch seine unermüdliche Publikationstätigkeit zu Dank verpflichtet. So seien auch die im folgenden mit freundlicher Genehmigung des Semitic Museum der Harvard University mitgeteilten Textzusammenschlüsse, die sich eher zufällig neben der Arbeit am Archiv des Šilwa-teššup ergaben, als Ausdruck des Dankes verstanden, der sich mit dem Wunsch verbindet, dem Jubilar mögen noch viele Jahre fruchtbaren Schaffens beschieden sein.

I

HSS XIX 42 (SMN 2492) + 1 Frg. aus NTF M 25 A

Rs. 25 [*ṭup-pí/u i+na* EGI]R-*ki šu-du-ti*
26 [*eš-ši š*]*a* É.GAL-*lì i+na ba-ab* KÁ.[GAL *ša*]
27 [URU DUB.S]AR-*ri-we ša-ṭì-ir*
28 [IGI *U*]*t-ḫáp-ta-e* DUMU *Zi-g*[*e*]
29 [IG]I *A-mur-ra-bi* DUM[U] *Ḫu-*[*ti-i*]*a*
30 IGI *A-ki-ia* DUMU [Ì]R-DINGIR.MEŠ-*l*[*i-š*]*u*
31 [IGI *W*]*u-ur-še-e*[*n*]*-ni* DUMU ÌR-[DINGIR.MEŠ]-*li-šu*
32 IGI *Zi-i*[*l-la-p*]*u* DUMU *I*[*t*]*-ḫi-pu-gur*
33 IGI *A-ri-*[*ip-pa-ap-n*]*i* DUMU x (x)-*bi-ia*
34 IGI *Be-l*[*a-am?-mu?-šal?-lim?* DUB.S]AR-*rù*
35 NA$_4$ *Ut-ḫáp-ta-*⸢*e*⸣ NA$_4$ ⸢*A*⸣*-mur-ra-bi*

HSS XIX 42+ ist ein Vertrag zwischen Ḫanaja, Sohn des Šešwe, und seinem Sklaven Ullû über die Manumission des letzteren und seiner Familie gegen eine hohe Auslösungssumme (ein Sklave, eine Sklavin sowie Güter im Wert von ungefähr 2 Minen Silber) nebst der Verpflichtung zur Alimentierung des früheren Herrn und—im Falle von dessen Tod—seiner Kinder.

Durch das Anschlussfragment, das den grössten Teil der Lücke auf der Rückseite der Tafel ausfüllt und damit die *šaṭir*-Formel und die Zeugenliste ergänzt, erweist sich die Urkunde nun als (ebenso wie HSS XIX 97, 99, 126,

SIL 316[1] und 1 Frg. aus, NTF N 1 C) in Tupšarri(ni)we geschrieben, einem Ort in der Nähe von Kurruḫanni (Tell al-Faḫḫār). A. Fadhil, Rechtsurkunden und administrative Texte aus Kurruḫanni, Magister-Arbeit Heidelberg 1972, hat die Prosopographie von Tupšarri(ni)we eingehend untersucht, davon ausgehend einige Urkunden ohne *šaṭir*-Angaben demselben Ort zugewiesen (HSS XVI 231, AASOR XVI 97, SMN 2379, 2381, 2383, 2384 sowie fünf Tafeln aus Kurruḫanni) und aus dem Kurruḫanni-Material eine weitere Tafel (IM 70882) mit der *šaṭir*-Angabe Tupšarriniwe publiziert. Eine weitere Tafel mit demselben Vermerk hat F. N. H. al-Rawi in seiner Dissertation "Studies in the Commercial Life of an Administrative Area of Eastern Assyria in the Fifteenth Century B.C., Based on Published and Unpublished Cuneiform Texts," University of Wales, Cardiff 1977, behandelt (IM 70956).

Die in Nuzi gefundenen, in Tupšarri(ni)we ausgefertigten Tafeln gehören zu dem Archiv der Söhne des Pula-ḫali, Paššia/Pašši-tilla und Kipal-enni, die in Tupšarri(ni)we Grundbesitz hatten (HSS XIX 97) und öfter als Darlehensgeber auftreten (HSS XVI 231, XIX 126, AASOR XVI 97; das unveröffentlichte Fragment [aus NTF P 51] eines Darlehensvertrages über 20 Minen Bronze, rückzahlbar mit Zinsen im Monat *kurillu*, ist mit K. Deller [mdl.] gleichfalls dem Archiv der Söhne des Pula-ḫali zuzuweisen).

Mit HSS XIX 42+ erschliesst sich nun ein zweiter Tafelkomplex mit Bezug auf Tupšarri(ni)we, dessen prosopographischer Horizont von dem des Archivs der Pula-ḫali-Söhne gänzlich verschieden ist, da Ḫanaja den Pula-ḫali-Söhnen um zwei Generationen vorausgeht. Die Tafel des Ḫanaja war zwar—nach dem Fundort (S 151) zu schliessen—im Archiv der Pula-ḫali-Söhne abgelegt, doch ist eine Rechtsbeziehung zwischen diesen und Ḫanaja noch nicht zu erkennen.

Die Person des Ḫanaja ist nicht unbekannt. In der Liste von *rākib narkabti* und *ālik ilki* HSS XIII 6 (aus Raum A 34, nicht jünger als die III. Generation) erscheint er l. 40 unter den *ālik ilki*; dass die Namensgleichheit kein Zufall ist, zeigen die Einträge Amurr(u)-rabi, Sohn des Ḫutia, und Utḫap-tae, Sohn des Zike, unter den *rākib narkabti* (ll. 23-24), die beide als Zeugen nunmehr in HSS XIX 42+ belegt sind. Daraus ergibt sich nun auch die wichtige Information, dass HSS XIII 6 nicht etwa nur *rākib narkabti* und *ālik ilki* aus Nuzi nennt.

Ḫanaja, Sohn des Šešwe, erscheint ferner in dem Gerichtsurteil HSS V 52 unter den Zeugen eines Streits um die unrechtmässige Abweidung eines Feldes (l. 12). Dass der Fall als solcher jetzt nach Tupšarri(ni)we zurückverfolgt werden kann, unterliegt keinem Zweifel, da der Bruder des Feldbesitzers und Klägers, Utḫap-tae, Sohn des Zike, nun auch in der Zeugenliste von HSS XIX 42+ erscheint.

[1]Cf. die Bearbeitung dieser Urkunde von M. Müller, Ein Prozess um einen Kreditkauf in Nuzi, in dieser Festschrift.

Weniger klar ist, ob der Prozess in Nuzi oder in Tupšarri(ni)we stattfand, d. h. ob die Parteien von Tupšarri(ni)we nach Nuzi vor Gericht zogen, oder ob das Richterkollegium an verschiedenen Orten und so eben auch in Tupšarri(ni)we Gerichtstag hielt. Die Richter sind wohlbekannt und vornehmlich in Nuzi attestiert, doch ist es auffällig, dass die Tafel von dem Schreiber Bēlam-mušallim geschrieben wurde, der zwar nicht selten in Nuzi (JEN 13, wahrscheinlich auch HSS V 68, IX 93, 95, XIII 467), doch auch in Tupšarri(ni)we (RA XXIII 64, möglicherweise HSS XIX 42+; dazu sofort) geschrieben hat.

Die Ergänzung desselben Schreibernamens in HSS XIX 42+ scheint naheliegend zu sein. Hier wie in allen anderen Fällen ist kein Patronym angegeben, was darauf zurückgeht, dass dieser Schreiber Sklave ist (HSS V 68:34 sq.; die merkwürdige Schreibung des Namens ist—die Richtigkeit der Kopie unterstellt—als UMUN^{be}-<*lam*->*mu-šá-lim* zu lesen). Die Zuschreibung sämtlicher genannter Tafeln an nur einen Bēlam-mušallim wird ausser durch die prosopographisch ermittelte Datierung aller Texte in die Zeit der späten II. und der III. Generation noch durch eine ganz auffällige Schreibgewohnheit bestätigt, nämlich die fast[2] ausschliessliche Verwendung des Zeichens DA für *da*/*ta*/*ṭa*, während von anderen Schreibern eindeutig TA bevorzugt wird. Dies ist aber nun gerade der Ausgangspunkt eines Zweifels an der Richtigkeit der Zuschreibung von HSS XIX 42+ an Bēlam-mušallim, da auf dieser Tafel durchgehend das Zeichen TA verwendet wird (l. 14, 28, 35).

II

HSS XIX 19 (SMN 1700 + 2817) + 1 Frg. aus NTF N 18

Vs. 1 *ṭup-pí ši-im-ti ša* ^{m}*T*[*ar-mi-ia* DUMU x x (x)]-*ia*
2 *ši-im-ta a-na* DUMU.M[EŠ]x-*šu a*
3 ⸢^{f}⸣*Ti-e-eš-na-*[*a+a* DAM-*ti-šu i-ši-im-šu-nu*]?-*ti*
4 [*u*]*m-ma* ^{m}*Tar-mi-i*[*a-ma mi-nu-um-me-e* A.ŠÀ.MEŠ]?
5 *ù* 2 É.MEŠ [
6 (Spuren)
....
o.Rd. 57 [*š*]*a* KA *ṭup-pí a-na* DAM-*i*[*a ù*] *še-er-ri-šu ad-din-nu*

Das Anschlussstück liefert keine neuen Informationen über die Identität des Erblassers und die Namen seiner Söhne. So bleibt es leider weiterhin offen, ob die Gattin des Tarmia identisch ist mit der gleichnamigen Tochter des Teḫip-tilla (MAH 16026). Problematisch ist nun die Lücke in l. 2, da nicht genügend Raum für die Ergänzung der Namen der Söhne bleibt—schon gar nicht, wenn man den l. 11 genannten *A-r*[*i-ip*]-*t*[*e-šu*]*p* als einen der ihren

[2] Ausnahmen: HSS V 52:17, XIII 467:3.

ansieht. Eine Lesung **ù a-na* DA]M-*šu a-<na>* entspricht weder den Raumverhältnissen in l. 2 noch denen in l. 3.

Die beiden Fragmente, die in der Edition in der Mitte der Vorderseite eingefügt sind und in ihrem erkennbaren Inhalt so wenig zu dem Zusammenhang passen (ll. 5-6: *i+na* E[GIR? ...] *la i-ša-*[*as-si*?], haben zwar eine ähnliche Schrift wie XIX 19+, bilden aber mit der Rückseite dieser Tafel keinen sandwich-join und sind deshalb auszuscheiden.

III

HSS XVI 279 (SMN 1186) + XVI 299 (SMN 1578)

Masse der vollständigen Tafel: 48 x 36 x 20 mm.

Vs.	1	3 MÁŠ GAL.MEŠ
	2	25 UDU NITA GAL
	3	13 UDU SAL.MEŠ *ša* Ù.TU
	4	7 *ka*$_4$*-lu-mu* NITA
	5	6 *ka*$_4$*-lu-mu* SAL
u.Rd.	6	ŠU.NÍGIN 54 UDU.ḪI.A.MEŠ
	7	*ša* ^{m}*Ḫé-el-ti-ip-te-šup*
Rs.	8	*a-na* ŠU ^{m}*I-la-nu*
	9	DUMU *Ta-i-ú-ki*
	10	*na-ad-nu*
		(Siegelabrollung)
	11	NA$_4$ ^{m}*I-la-nu*

Die Urkunde ist eine Empfangsbestätigung über Kleinvieh. Ähnliche Texte gibt es in grosser Zahl, und zwar insbesondere im Archiv des Šilwa-teššup.[3] Allerdings ist der Empfänger dabei stets ein Hirte, der die Schafe zur Hütung übernimmt. Dies ist bei dem vorliegenden Text jedoch ausgeschlossen. Ilānu, Sohn des Tajuki, ist ein wohlbekannter Grundbesitzer der Zeit der III. Generation, von dem ein Archiv im Zusammenhang der heterogenen Tafelfunde im Raum 34 des Hauskomplexes A (sog. "Haus des Zigi") erhalten ist. Von seinem Sohn Ilī-ma-aḫī ist mit dem gleichen Kontrahenten ein ganz ähnlicher Vertrag geschlossen worden (HSS IX 112 = SMN 88):

Vs.	1	5 MÁŠ GAL
	2	2 UDU NITA GAL
	3	9 UDU SAL *ša* Ù.TU
	4	2 *ka*$_4$*-lu-mu* SAL
u.Rd.	5	2 *ka*$_4$*-lu-mu* NITA
	6	ŠU.NÍGIN 20 UDU.ḪI.A.MEŠ
Rs.	7	*ša* ^{m}*Ḫé-el-ti-ip-te-šup*

[3] Cf. demnächst G. Wilhelm, Das Archiv des Šilwa-teššup, Heft 5.

8 *a-na* ŠU ᵐDINGIR-*ma-ḫi*
9 DUMU DINGIR-*a-nu*
10 *na-ad-nu*
o.Rd. 11 NA₄ ᵐDINGIR-*ma-ḫi*

Ilī-ma-aḫī hat seinerseits Hirten beschäftigt (HSS V 9, 15), so dass man in ihm einen weiteren Vertreter jenes Typus von Grundbesitzer sehen darf, der neben der Getreideproduktion die Kleinviehzucht zur Wollgewinnung und Textilproduktion betreibt, wie dies in grossem Massstab Šilwa-teššup tut. Es handelt sich also nicht um den üblichen Hütevertrag zwischen Herdenbesitzer und Hirt, sondern wahrscheinlich um ein Kommissionsgeschäft. Die Möglichkeit eines Kaufvertrags ist ausgeschlossen durch die Formulierung "*ana qāt* PN *nadnū*," die nie im Falle einer Eigentumsübertragung verwendet wird.

Der Eigentümer des Kleinviehs ist in beiden Fällen Ḫeltip-teššup, der ohne Patronym erscheint. Dies könnte auf den Status eines Sklaven deuten, oder aber, nach Analogie der gleichartig formulierten Hüteverträge des Šilwa-teššup, in denen dieser nur selten ausdrücklich DUMU LUGAL genannt wird, auf prinzlichen Status. Ein Ḫeltip-teššup mit dem Titel DUMU LUGAL ist zwar nicht bezeugt, doch erscheint in einer Gruppe von Rationenlisten des Palastes,[4] die alle der Zeit der V. Generation angehören, ein Ḫeltip-teššup an der Spitze einer Personengruppe, zu der auch nachweisbar Prinzen gehören.[5] Die naheliegende Identifizierung des Ḫeltip-teššup von XVI 279+ und IX 112 mit dem der Rationenlisten des Palastes wird allerdings durch chronologische Erwägungen kompliziert, indem Ḫeltipteššup wegen seines Vertrages mit Ilānu bereits zur Zeit der III. Generation geschäftsfähig gewesen sein, aber aufgrund seiner Attestation in den Palastlisten auch noch die Zeit der V. Generation erlebt, also ein hohes Alter erreicht haben müsste.

Der Fundort von XVI 279 ist als "R 50" angegeben, ein Raum des Palastes, in dem sonst keine Tafeln gefunden wurden. Eine Fundortangabe für das Anschlussstück fehlt. IX 112 ist angeblich in Raum "36" des Hauses des Šilwa-teššup gefunden worden. Dieselbe Herkunft wird sonst nur noch für HSS XVI 20 angegeben, ein Text aus dem Komplex der *rākib narkabti*-Listen der II./III. Generation, wie sie in grosser Zahl in Raum A 34 gefunden wurden. Diese Herkunftsangabe darf somit unbedenklich zu "A 34" korrigiert werden. Da IX 112 keinerlei Beziehung zum Archiv des Šilwa-teššup, wohl

[4]HSS XIV 46, 48, 49, 52, 53, XV 239, etc. Der Fundort dieser ganz eng zusammengehörigen Tafeln ist grösstenteils unbekannt, bei einer Tafel ist Raum K 32 des Palastes angegeben (HSS XIV 110 = 604), bei einer anderen Raum D 3 der Norddependence (XV 239). Allein aus dieser Situation wird deutlich, dass eine systematische Rekonstruktion der Palastarchive sich nicht ausschliesslich auf den vielfach zufälligen, gar nicht oder unkorrekt dokumentierten Fundort der Tafeln stützen kann.

[5]Wirraḫḫe nach XIII 418, Tatip-teššup nach XVI 332, beide IV./V. Generation

aber zu Ilī-ma-aḫī, Sohn des Ilānu, hat, dessen Archiv in A 34 gefunden wurde, möchte man auch die Herkunftsangabe dieser Tafel zu "A 34" verändern. Dem steht jedoch das Bedenken entgegen, dass die Tafel von Ilī-ma-aḫī gesiegelt ist und damit dem Ḫeltip-teššup einen Rechtstitel gibt, also zu dessen Archiv gehören muss. Es ist deshalb wahrscheinlicher, dass sie ebenso wie HSS XVI 279 aus dem Palast stammt.

IV

HSS XV 138 (SMN 1439) + ein als "HSS XV 319" abgelegtes unidentifiziertes Fragment.

1 ⸢1⸣ ⌊*ma-a*]*t* 30 GIŠ.GU.ZA.M[EŠ] *zi-ku-li-i*[*t-tu*$_4$ *ša* GIŠ *ša-aš-šu*]-*gi*$_5$[a]
2 42[+4[b]] GIŠ.GU.ZA.M[EŠ *ša* GIŠ *ša-a*]*k-ku-ul-li* *š*[*a*] *p*[*u-ra-ki*[c]] *še-e-tu*$_4$
3 70 GI[Š.G]U.ZA.MEŠ *ša* [GIŠ *š*]*a*-[*aš-š*]*u-gi*$_5$ *uz-zu-li-g*[*a-ru*?[d]] *p*[*u-r*]*a-ka*$_4$ *še-e-tu*$_4$
4 ⸢30⸣ GIŠ *pí-it-nu*.MEŠ [*ša* GIŠ.TASKARIN?[e] *ù*] GIŠ *ṣú-ul-ma* *u*[*ḫ*]-*ḫu-zu*
5 [2+] ⸢6⸣ [G]IŠ *pí-it-nu*.[MEŠ *ša*] GIŠ *ṣú-ul-mi* *ù* GIŠ *ša-ak-ku*-[*li*].MEŠ *u*[*ḫ*]-*ḫu-zu*
6 6 [G]IŠ *pí-it-nu*.MEŠ [*ša* x]x *i-šu-ú* *ša* *ši-i*[*n-ni-p*]*í*-[*ri* *ge-la*]-*mu-tù*[f] 1 GIŠ *pí-it-nu* *ša*? x x [2 GIŠ *ú-ru-un*]?-*za-an-na*[g] ZI-*i-ḫa*
7 1 GIŠ *pí-it-nu* *ša* x[(x)] *š*[*a*] x x x x x x [x x x *u*]*ḫ-ḫu-uz* 1 GIŠ *pí-it-nu* *ša* GÌR?.[R]A?[x GIŠ] ⸢*zu*⸣-[*u*]*z-zu-ul-ki*
8 1 GIŠ *zu*-⸢*uz*⸣-*zu-u*[*l-ki*] *ša* G[IŠ ... GI]Š *ša-ak-ku-li* [*u*]*ḫ-ḫu-uz*
9 19 GIŠ *zu-u*[*z-zu-ul-ki*.M]EŠ [x x x x] x x [
10 5 GIŠ *pí-it-n*[*u*
11 1 GIŠ *pí-it-nu* [ ] x x x [x x *uḫ*]-*ḫu-zu*
12 10 GIŠ BANŠUR [ ]x x[
13 *ša* GIŠ ⸢*ša*⸣-[
14 x[

---

[a]Erg. nach HSS XV 130:5, 132:1. [b]Erg. nach HSS XIII 435:2. [c]Erg. nach HSS XV 130:3. [d]Erg. nach HSS XV 132:5. [e]Erg. nach HSS XV 130:6. [f]Erg. nach HSS XV 134:9. [g]Erg. nach HSS XIII 435:9, XV 132:13.

Die Tafel gehört zu einer Gruppe von Möbelinventaren des Palastes, die aus der Zeit der späten II. und der III. Generation stammen.[6] Durch das neue Anschlussstück ergibt sich, dass HSS XV 138+ teilweise Duplikat ist zu SMN 435 (Nuziana II p. 157 = HSS XIII 435).

[6]Eine Bearbeitung dieser Textgruppe wird von Michael Klein vorbereitet.

V

HSS IX 156 (SMN 328) +? 1 Frg. aus NTF M 8 B.

Vs. 12 [*a-na ti-te-en-nu-ti a*]-*na* 3 MU-*ti*
13 [*a-na* ^{m}*I-la-a-nu* DUMU *Ta-ú-ki* SUM-*nu*][a]
14 [*ù* ^{m}*I-la-a-nu* 10 ANŠE ŠE *ù* 5[b] ...]
15 [*a-n*]*a* ⸢*ti*⸣-[*te-en-nu-ti-ma*]
16 [*a*]-*na* ^{m}*Tup*-⸢*ki-še*⸣-*e*[*n-ni* SUM-*nu*]
17 ⸢*e*⸣-*nu-ma* 3 MU-*ti*.M[EŠ *im-ta-lu-ú*]
18 [KÙ].BABBAR.MEŠ *ša* KA *ṭup-p*[*í* ^{m}*Tup-ki-še-en-ni*]
19 [*a-na* ^{m}*I*]-*la-a-nu* GUR-[*ru*
20 [ ] *ù mi-i*[*m-ma*

[a]Erg. nach HSS IX 98:13-15.
[b]Erg. nach Rs. 2.

Der Anschluss konnte nicht vollzogen und damit bestätigt werden, da SMN 328 sich in Baghdad befindet. Eine zusätzliche Unsicherheit ergibt sich daraus, dass die Tafel nur in Transliteration veröffentlicht ist.

Die Tafel gehört zum Archiv des Ilānu, Sohnes des Tajuki, und zwar zum Komplex der *tidennūtu*-Verträge mit den Nachkommen des Iriri-tilla (HSS IX 104, 107). Sie stammt mit G. Dosch, Die Texte aus Room A 34 des Archivs von Nuzi, Magister-Arbeit Heidelberg 1976, 6, aus der Zeit der III.-IV. Generation (IV. Schreibergeneration).

HSS IX 156 ist von Turar-teššup, Sohn des Itḫ-apiḫe, geschrieben, was weitere Indizien zugunsten des Joins liefert: Formulierung und Schreibweise der Phrase KÙ.BABBAR.MEŠ *ša* KA *ṭup-pí* sind recht selten belegt, finden sich aber genauso in der *tidennūtu*-Urkunde HSS IX 98 wieder, die gleichfalls von Turar-teššup geschrieben wurde. *enūma* statt des weit häufigeren *immatimē* in der Lösungsklausel von *tidennūtu*-Verträgen wird von verschiedenen Schreibern gewählt (z. B. Ḫašia IX 28, Šimanni, Sohn des AG.DINGIR.RA, IX 101, JEN 490, AG.DINGIR.RA, Sohn des Sîn-napšer, V 84, Urad-šerua RA XXIII 2, Pai-tilla, Sohn des Elḫip-tilla, RA XXIII 3, TCL IX 16), so dass diese Formulierung nicht dezisiv ist. Immerhin ist festzustellen, dass auch Turar-teššup *enūma* schreibt (IX 98).

A Note on Nuzi Textiles

CARLO ZACCAGNINI
University of Bologna

Forty years ago it was observed that the (wool-)cloths manufactured at Nuzi—and described simply as TÚG—appear to be of standard dimensions and weight.[1] However, this fact may now be stated with greater assurance. The data from the Nuzi texts regarding cloth represent a unique corpus within the body of ancient Near Eastern epigraphic evidence and these data are extremely homogeneous. Consequently, a fresh and exhaustive analysis of the Nuzi textual material pertaining to cloth (TÚG) is warranted. The following study on this topic is offered as a very modest token of gratitude to a scholar whose entire life has been generously devoted to the study of Nuzi civilization.

The texts that contain passages pertinent to the dimensions and/or the weight of the wool cloths may be divided into three categories:

I. *Texts that state dimensions and weight of TÚG.*

1. HSS 5, 95:8-10:
   8. 1 TÚG *sà-sú-lu* SIG$_5$-*tu*$_4$ *ša* 6 MA.NA *šu-qú-ul-ta-šu*
   9. 15 *i+na am-ma-ti mu-ra-ak-šu*
   10. 5 *i+na am-ma-ti ru-pu-us*$^{!}$(PU)-*sú*[2]

[1]D. Cross, MPND, pp. 50-51. The author, however, maintains that "the comparatively low weight shows that the material in question could not have been wool, but cloth" (ibid., p. 51). I fail to understand the grounds for such a statement, especially in the light of HSS 5, 95 (=Text 1) and HSS 13, 455 (=Text 19). As for the weight of hand woven woollen fabrics, see the remarks of K. R. Veenhof, AOATT, p. 93 with fn. 151. Besides D. Cross, see also A. L. Oppenheim, ArOr 8 (1936), p. 299 fn. 4; id., JA 230 (1938), p. 658; H. Lewy, RSO 39 (1964), p. 183 with fn. 6.

[2]Line 8: *sa*(*s*)*sullu*: cf. AHw, p. 1032*b*. HSS 5, 95 clearly shows that wool (SÍG) was employed to manufacture these textiles. The text runs as follows: [1]6$^{?!}$(text: 14) MA.NA SÍG^{MEŠ} [2]*ša* [1]*I-la-an-nu* DUMU *Ta-i-ú-ki* [3]*ù* [1]*Pu-ḫi-še-en-ni* [4]DUMU *En-šúk-rù* [5]*a-na ar-ta-ar-te-en*<*-nu*>*-ti* [6]*il-qè ina* EGIR-*ki* [7]EBUR-*ri ina* ITU *Ki-ri-il-li* / *ina na-pa-ḫi* [8-10](see main text) [11][1]*Pu-ḫi-še-en-ni* [12]*a-na* [1]*I-la-an-nu* [13]*ú-ta-ar šum-ma* [14][TÚ]G *i+na* ITU *Ku-ri-il-li* [15]*la ú-ta-ar* [16]1-*nu-tù na-aḫ*[-*la*-]*ap-tù* [17]*ša* 2 MA.NA [18]*šu-qú-ul-ta-šu-nu* [19]*i+na muḫ-ḫi* ⌜TÚG⌝ [20]*i-sa-ka*$_4$*-an* (Seals). "PN$_2$ has taken 6$^{?!}$ minas of wool belonging to PN (Ilānu son of Taluki gives wool also in HSS 5, 97 [=Text 23] and HSS 5, 98 [=Text

2. IM 73413: 8-10:[3]
   8. TÚG *a-na* 6 MA.NA *ša-qal-⌜šu⌝*
   9. 15 *i+na* [*am*]*-ma-ti mu-ra-ak-šu*
   10. 5 *i+na am-ma-ti ru-pu-us-sú*

3. HSS 9, 98:16-19:
   16. . . . 1 TÚG *eš-šu ša* ŠI MI SIG₅*-qú*
   17. 15 *ina am-ma-ti mu-ra-ak-šu*
   18. 5 *ina am-ma-ti ru-pu-us-sú*
   19. *šu-qú-ul-ta-šu* 5 MA.NA 55 SU[4]

4. HSS 9, 152: 3-6:[5]
   3. [1 TÚG] *ša*! 4 [*ku-ud-ge-te*]
   4. SIG₅?!*-qú*?! *eš-šu ša* [0]
   5. 15 *i+na am-ma-ti mu-ra-*[*ak-šu*]
   6. 5 *i+na am-ma-ti ru-pu-us-sú*[6]

5. HSS 9, 103:10-13:
   10. . . . 1 TÚG SIG₅*-qú* 14 *i+na am-ma-ti* *ù ma-la ki-in-ṣí*

24]) for . . . After the harvest, at the end of the month of Kurillu, PN₂ shall give back to PN one quality *sa*(*s*)*sullu*-cloth weighing 6 minas, 15 *ammatu* its length, 5 *ammatu* its width. If he does not give back the cloth in the month of Kurillu, one *naḫlaptu* weighing 2 minas shall be debited in addition to the cloth." The emendation in line 1 raises no particular difficulties from a paleographical viewpoint and seems necessary in order to assign a plausible meaning to the transaction recorded in this text. For the weight of the *naḫlaptu*, see HSS 5, 36:13-16 (cf. fn. 9); in HSS 9, 152:7-8 (=Text 4), the weight of one *naḫlaptu* is given at 2 *kuduktu*, for which see below.

[3]The present quotation reproduces that offered by K. Deller in WdO 9 (1978), p. 299. The text comes from Tell el-Fakhar=Kurruḫanni.

[4]Line 16: *ša šīmi* "Kaufgut, Ware" (AHw, p. 1240*a*) ? or: *ša* MÍ?! GE₆ "for women('s dresses) black" ??

[5]Transliteration only (by R. H. Pfeiffer). A new treatment of the text is offered by K. Deller, WdO 9 (1978), pp. 298-99.

[6]Lines 3-4: Pfeiffer's transliteration runs as follows: ³. . . ᵃˡᵘ*za-* . . . ⁴*ù eš-šu ša* . . . K. Deller (l.cit.) emends in the following way: ³[1 TÚG *a-*]*na*! 5! [MA.NA] ⁴*ù* 30! GÍN! *ša-*[*qal-šu*]. Pfeiffer's *za* in line 3 clearly stands for "4"; hence my restoration. Another, though less likely possibility, is: 4[+2 MA.NA (*šaqālšu*/*šuqultašu*)]. Deller's emendation *eš-šu* in 30! GÍN! is not convincing: there is no parallel evidence for such a weight for Nuzi cloths measuring 15 x 5 *ammatu*. Also, the qualification *eššu* for TÚG is quite frequent (see, e.g., HSS 5, 20:6; 82:11; 87:12; HSS 9, 98:16-19; Gadd 31:24′-25′; 32:5; ZA 48 [1944], p. 183, n. 3: 16′) and exactly parallels the wording of lines 7-8 of the same text: ⁷*ù il-te-en-nu-tu₄ na-aḫ-la-pa-tu₄* ⁸*ša* 2 *ku-ud-ge-te eš-šu*. The unusual sequence of lines 7-8 (i.e. textile + weight [expressed in *kuduktu* and without *šaqālšu*/*šuqultašu*] + qualification of the textile) most probably parallels that of lines 3-4. A similar, but not identical sequence is that of HSS 5, 87:12-14 (=Text 6).

11. *mu-ra-ak-šu* 4 *i+na am-ma-ti*
ù ma-la ki-in-ṣí
12. *ru-pu-us-sà ša* TÚG 5 MA.NA 50 SU
13. *šu-qú-ul-ta-šu* . . .[7]

6. HSS 5, 87:12-14:[8]
12. . . . 1 TÚG *eš-šu šu-qú-ul-ta-šu* 5 (/6$^{?!}$) MA.NA SIG$_5$-*qú*
13. 15 *i+na am-ma-ti mu-ra-ak-šu*
14. 5 *i+na am-ma-ti ru-pu-us-sú*

7. HSS 5, 36:5, 8-10:
5. . . . 1 TÚG SIG$_5$-*qú*
8. 6 MA.NA *šu-qú-ul-ta-šu ša* TÚG
9. 15 *ina am-ma-ti mu-ra-ak-šu*
10. 10(sic!) *i+na am-ma-ti ru-pu-us*$^{!}$*-sú ša* TÚG[9]

8. HSS 13, 489:1-4, 13-16:[10]
1. 1 TÚG^{M}[^{EŠ} 14$^{?}$ *i+na am-ma-ti ù ma-la ki-in-ṣí*]
2. *mu-ra-ak-š*[*u* 4$^{?}$ *i+na am-ma-ti ù ma-la ki-in-ṣí*]
3. *ru-pu-us-*[*sú*]
4. *ù šu-qú-ul-t*[*a-šu* 5$^{?}$ MA.NA SÍG (*ša* TÚG^{MEŠ})]
13. . . . 1 TÚG^{MEŠ} 12$^{?!}$[+2$^{?}$ *i+na am-ma-ti ù ma-la*] *ki-in-ṣí*
14. *mu-ra-ak-šu* [4$^{?}$ *i+na am-ma-ti ù ma-la ki*]-⸢*in-ṣí*⸣
15. *ru-pu-u*[*s-sú ù š*]*u-qú-ul-ta-šu*
16. ⸢5$^{?}$/6$^{?}$⸣ MA.N[A SÍ]G *ša* TÚG^{MEŠ} [11]

[7]For *kimṣu* (=a fraction of the *ammatu*), see CAD K, p. 375*b* and AHw, p. 479*a*, with quotation of previous literature.

[8]Cf. E. A. Speiser, JAOS 53 (1933), pp. 28-29.

[9]HSS 5, 36 offers a very close parallel to HSS 5, 95 (=Text 1 and see fn. 2). The text runs as follows: ^{1}*um-ma* ^{Id}*Uta-an-dul*<*-ma*> ^{2}DUMU *Ḫa-ma-an-na* 1 TÚG$^{ḪI.A}$ ^{3}*ša* ^{I}*I-li-ma-*ŠEŠ DUMU *Ila-nu* ^{4}*a-na ar-ta-ar-te*$_9$*-en*$_6$*-nu-ti* ^{5}*il-te-qè-mi ù* 1 TÚG SIG$_5$-*qú* ^{6}*i+na na-pá-aḫ* ITU-*ḫi Ḫi-in-zu-ri-we* ^{7}*a-na* ^{I}*Ili-ma-*ŠEŠ *a-na-an-din-mi* $^{8-10}$(see main text) ^{11}*ina* ITU *ša qà-bu-ú a-na-an-din* ^{12}*šum-ma ina* ITU *qa-bu-ú* TÚG *a-na* <^{I}>*Ili-ma-ḫi* ^{13}*la a-na-an-din ù* 1*-nu-tu*$_4$ ^{14}*na-aḫ-la-ap-tu*$_4$ SIG$_5$(-[*qú*/*tu*$_4$]) ^{15}2 MA.NA *šu-qú-ul-ta-šu* ^{16}*ša na-aḫ-la-ap-ti* ^{17}*i+na muḫ-ḫi* TÚG$^{ḪI.A}$ *a-š*[*a-ka*$_4$*-an*] ^{18}*ṭup-pu ina* KÁ.GAL *Ti*$_4$-[*iš-ša*]*-e* ^{18}*ša* URU *Nu-zi ša-ṭì-ir* (Seals). "Thus (declares) PN: I took one cloth belonging to PN$_2$ for . . . At the end of the month of Ḫinzuri I shall give (back) to PN$_2$ one quality cloth weighing 6 minas, 15 *ammatu* its length, 5 *ammatu* its width. In the (above) said month I shall give (it back). If in the (above) said month I do not give (back) to PN$_2$ the cloth, one quality *naḫlaptu* weighing 2 minas shall be debited in addition to the cloth. The tablet was written at the city-gate Tiššae in Nuzi."

[10]Transliteration only.

[11]My restorations, that are different from those given in HSS 13, have been suggested on the basis of text HSS 9, 103 (=Text 5), which seems to be very similar.

9. SMN 3587:8-10, cf. 14-16:[12]
   8. 1 TÚG^{MEŠ} [*šu*]-*qú-ul-ti* 4 *ku-duk-ti še-eḫ-tù-ni*
   9. 15 *i+na*[*a*] *am-ma-ti mu-ra-ak-šu*
   10. 5 *i+na am-ma-ti ru-pu-us-sú*[13]

10. JEN 311:2-4:
   2. 1 TÚG 4 *ku-duk-ti ša šu-qú-ul-ti*
   3. 14(/15$^{?!}$) *i+na am-ma-ti mu-ra*$^{!}$(ŠA)-*ak-šu*
   4. 5 *i+na am-ma-ti ru-pu-us-sú*

11. ZA, 48 (1944), p. 183, n. 3: Obv. 15′-18′:[14]
   15′. 1 TÚG *eš-*⸢*šu*⸣ 11[+4$^{?}$] *i+na am-ma-ti*
   16′. *mu-*⸢*ra*⸣*-ak-šu ù* 5 *i+na am-ma-ti*
   17′. ⸢*ru*⸣*-pu-us-*⸢*sú*⸣ *ù šu-qú-ul-tu*
   18′. [3$^{?}$+]1 *ku-dú-uk-tu*$_4$ ⸢SÍG⸣^{MEŠ} . . .

II. *Texts that state only the weight of* TÚG.

12. HSS 5, 20:6-7:
   6. . . . 1 TÚG *eš-šu*
   7. 6 MA.NA *šu-qú-ul-ta-šu*

13. HSS 5, 82:11:
   11. 1 TÚG *eš-šu* 6 MA.NA *šu-qú-ul-ta-šu*

14. HSS 13, 8:2-8:[15]
   2. 1 TÚG SIG$_5$ [*ku-la-a-e*]
   3. 6 MA.NA [*šu-qú-ul-tù*]
   4. *ša* É.GAL-*lì* [*i+na*]
   5. *muḫ-ḫi-ya a-*[*ši-ib*]
   6. *ù i+na-an-na* 1 TÚG
   7. *ku-la-a-e* 6 MA.NA
   8. *šu-qú-ul-tù* . . .

[12]The text is given in transliteration, translation and commentary by B. L. Eichler, Nuzi Personal ditennūtu Transactions and their Mesopotamian Analogues, Ph.D. diss., University of Pennsylvania 1967, pp. 87-89. In id., Indenture at Nuzi: The Personal tidennūtu Contract and its Mesopotamian Analogues, New Haven-London 1973, p. 110, only the translation and commentary of SMN 3587 are given.

[13]The term *kuduktu* will be discussed below. Lines 8 and 14 are also quoted by CAD K, p. 494*a*, which has *3 kuduktu* (line 8) and *2 kuduktu* (line 14).

[14]Cf. P. Koschaker, ibid., pp. 180-87.

[15]Transliteration only.

15. SMN 3719:8-9:[16]
    8. . . . 1 TÚG 4 *ku-duk-*tu_4
    9. *ina šu-qú-ul-ti*[17]

16. Gadd 32:5-6:
    5. 2 TÚG^{MEŠ} *eš-šu ša* ⸢2⸣[+6?]
    6. *ku-duk*$^{!}$*-*tu_4 *šu-*⸢*qú*⸣*-ul*$^{!}$*-ti*[*-šu-nu*]

17. HSS 15, 216:
    1. NA_4? ^{MÍ}*Aš-ta-*[ ]
    2. 1* GUN S[ÍG?! MEŠ]
    3. *ša* É.GAL-*lì*
    4. *a-na* 10 TÚG^{MEŠ} *š*[*i*?!*-na-ḫi-lu* (?)]
    5. *a-na* MÍ^{MEŠ} *du-ša-*[*a-na*]
    6. *e-pè-ši*
    7. *a-na* ^{I}E-WA[-]
    8. *ša* URU *Pu*[*-ru-ul-li-we* (?)]
    9. [ ]⸢x⸣[ ]

Each TÚG would thus weigh 6 minas of wool.[18]

III. *Texts that state only the dimensions of* TÚG.

18. TCL 9, 29:6′-7′:
    6′. . . . 1 TÚG *ša* 15 *i+na am-m*[*a-ti*]
    7′. [*mu-ra-ak-šu*] 5 *i+na am-ma-ti ru-pu-*[*us-sú*]

The evidence quoted above supports the hypothesis that the Nuzi wool cloths were of standard sizes (i.e. 15 x 5 *ammatu*) and weight (i.e. 6 minas). Interestingly enough, at least one document shows that TÚG of exactly half weight (i.e. 3 minas) were woven occasionally and presumably joined later in pairs.

19. HSS 13, 455:[19]
Obv. 1. 12 MA.NA SÍG^{MEŠ} *ša* É.GAL-*lì*
    2. *a-na* 4 *ta-pa-lu* TÚG^{MEŠ}
    3. *ša* LÚ^{MEŠ} *ta-lu-uḫ-le-e*

[16]Transliteration, translation and commentary: B. L. Eichler, Nuzi Personal ditennūtu, cit., pp. 95-96; cf. id., Indenture, cit., p. 115.

[17]Eichler's transliteration *šu-qul-ti* seems to be a typographical error.

[18]The restoration in line 8 is suggested by comparison with HSS 13, 455:32 (=Text 19) and HSS 13, 288:18 (=Text 21).

[19]Transliteration only.

4. ^{I}*Ir-wi-ḫu-ta ša* URU *A-šu-ḫi-iš*
5. *il-qè ù* 4 *ta-pa-lu* TÚG^{MEŠ}
6. *i-ip-pu-uš*

---

7. 12 MA.NA SÍG^{MEŠ} *a-na*
8. 4 *ta-pa-lu* TÚG^{MEŠ} *a-na*
9. ^{I}*Mu-ut-ta na-ad-nu*
10. *ù* ^{I}*Ú-lu-li-ya ša*
11. URU GEŠTIN-*na il-qè*

---

12. 6 MA.NA SÍG^{MEŠ} *a-na*
13. 2 *ta-pa-lu* <TÚG^{MEŠ}> *a-na* ^{I}*Wa-aḫ-ri-še-en-ni*
14. *ša* URU GEŠTIN-*na na-ad-nu*
15. SÍG^{MEŠ} ^{I}*Ú-lu-li-ya* [*il-qè*]

---

16. 30 MA.NA SÍG^{MEŠ}
Lo.e. 17. *a-na* 10 *ta-pa-lu* TÚG^{MEŠ} [*a-na*]
18. *e-pè-ši a-na*
19. ^{I}*Ú-na-ap-še-en-*[*ni*]
Rev. 20. *ša* URU *Kum-ri na-ad-nu*

---

21. 24 MA.NA SÍG^{MEŠ}
22. *a-na* 8 *ta-pa-lu*
23. TÚG^{MEŠ}(<*a-na*>) *e-pè-ši a-na*
24. ^{I}*Ar-ta-ḫu-bi*
25. *ša* URU *Ṣíl-lí-ya-we*
26. *na-ad-nu ù* SÍG^{MEŠ}
27. *šá-a-šu* ^{I}*Ú-na-ap-še-en-ni*
28. *il-te-qè*

---

29. 6 MA.NA SÍG^{MEŠ}
30. *a-na* 2 *ta-pa-lu* TÚG^{MEŠ} (<*a-na*>)
31. *e-pè-ši a-na* ^{I}*Ir-wi-ḫu-ta*
32. *ša* URU *Pu-ru-ul-li-we*
33. *na-ad-nu*

Le.e. 34. NA$_4$ ^{I}*Ú-na-ap-še-en-ni* NA$_4$ ^{I}*Ú-lu-li-ya*
Up.e. 35. NA$_4$ ^{I}*Ir-wi-ḫu-ta*

The constant ratio 3 minas of wool to 1 cloth occurs throughout this text.

* * *

In connection with the weight of Nuzi TÚG the delicate problem of the value of the *kuduktu* (Texts 4(?), 9, 10, 11, 15, 16) arises. D. Cross maintained that the term indicated "the amount of wool obtained from the plucking or shearing of a single animal."[20] A. L. Oppenheim rejected this assumption, which was "dépourvue de toute preuve."[21] Evidence available now supports Oppenheim's assertion:

20. HSS 13, 312:[22]
    1. 32 UDU^{MEŠ} *ina* ŠÀ-*šu-nu*
    2. 8 UDU *ša bá-aq-nu*
    3. *ù* 16 *ku-du-uk-ti* SÍG^{MEŠ}
    4. *ša* ^{I}*Ili*-SUM-*na* DUMU *Na-ig-gi*
    5. *ša maḫ-rù ša* 8 UDU^{MEŠ}
    6. SÍG-*šu-nu i-na ṭup-pa-ti*
    7. *ša mu-ul-li-i ša*-[ ]
    8. [ ] *ša*
    9. [ ]

"32 sheep, among which 8 sheep have been plucked, and PN received 16 *kuduktu* of wool. The wool of (these) 8 sheep is [ ] in the tablets (recording) the fine of [ ]."[23]

From the plucking of one sheep 2 *kuduktu* of wool were obtained. This datum supports A. L. Oppenheim's suggestion that 1 *kuduktu* = 1 mina[24] and finds significant parallels in other groups of ancient Near Eastern textual material, i.e., the average yield of wool from one sheep was ca. 2 minas.[25]

The same conclusion could be drawn from a comparison of HSS 5, 95:16-18 and HSS 5, 36:13-16 (where the weight of one *naḫlaptu* is 2 minas) with HSS 9, 152:7-8 (where the weight of one *naḫlaptu* is 2 *kuduktu*). This would show that 1 *kuduktu* = 1 mina. Note, however, that HSS 13, 288:5 lists 5 *naḫlaptu* each weighing 1 *kuduktu*. Further information is required regarding the comparative weight in minas for these smaller *naḫlaptu*.

The question of how many shekels equalled a *kuduktu* is also complex. The textual evidence is intriguing and suggests that the whole problem of the Nuzi measures of weight employed for reckoning wool and hair deserves a separate treatment. Thus, the following observations are limited to some preliminary remarks.

[20]D. Cross, MPND, p. 48 and p. 15.

[21]A. L. Oppenheim, JA 230 (1938), p. 653.

[22]Transliteration only.

[23]Cf. CAD M II, p. 190*a*.

[24]A. L. Oppenheim, JA 230 (1938), p. 653; id., AfO 11 (1936-37), p. 238 fn. 4.

[25]See most recently the data collected by M. Liverani, Economia delle fattorie palatine ugaritiche, Dialoghi di Archeologia 1/2 (1979), p. 70 with fn. 69.

Besides talents, minas and shekels, wool (and hair) was reckoned in *nariu*, *kuduktu* and *šeḫtunnu.*[26] It is possible that 1 *nariu* = 6 minas (= 360 shekels), i.e. 1/10 of one talent. This hypothesis is favored by texts like HSS 13, 246 and HSS 13, 288:1, 2, 4, both of which list several TÚG each weighing one *nariu*. Quantities of *nariu* seem not to be expressed in terms of talents. *Nariu* appears to be an independent weight unit. For example, in HSS 13, 288 the sub-total is 18 *nariu* +..... and the grand total is 32 *nariu* +....., and in HSS 14, 251, 107 + 84 + 19 = 210 *nariu* of wool are listed.

Šeḫtunnu[27] appears to be a fraction of the *kuduktu*, possibly half of it, whatever the value of the *kuduktu*.

The relationship between *kuduktu* and *nariu* is not at all clear and the evidence provided by the texts is both inconclusive and contradictory. On the one hand, texts such as HSS 19, 102 and 13, 288, in which both *nariu* and *kuduktu* occur together, might suggest that 4 *kuduktu* (HSS 19, 102:4) or 5 *kuduktu* (HSS 13, 288:5) were *less* than one *nariu* or represented a quantity *different* from one *nariu*. Note, however, that in the latter case 5 *kuduktu* are the weight of 5 *naḫlaptu*; this may be an itemized sum of the single pieces. On the other hand, HSS 15, 206 lists 5 *kuduktu* of wool to be used for the manufacture of one *siyānātu* three times (11. 1, 4, [8]). The weight of these garments is reckoned at 3 *kuduktu* and 2 *kuduktu* of hair in HSS 15, 218:9-11 and HSS 15, 331:4-5, respectively. HSS 13, 2:1-2 records 24 *nariu* of wool given for the manufacture of 20 *siyānātu*, i.e. one *siyānātu* requires 1.2 *nariu* of wool. A comparison of this datum with that provided by HSS 15, 206 (where the wool for one *siyānātu* is 5 *kuduktu*) suggests that 1 *nariu* = ca. 4.2 *kuduktu*.

It appears that no relationship between *nariu* and *kuduktu* can be established from the above-mentioned HSS 13, 288, the only text in which the two units of weight are totaled.

21. HSS 13, 288:[28]

Obv. 1. 1 TÚG *ši-la-an-nu* 1 *na-r*[*i-i* SÍG^{MEŠ}]
2. 1 TÚG *nu-uḫ-pu-ru* 1 *na*-[*ri-i*] SÍG^{MEŠ}
3. 1 TÚG *ša* MÍ 1 *na-ri-i* 1 *ku*-[*duk-ti* SÍG$^{(MEŠ)}$]
4. 10 TÚG^{MEŠ} *šina*(II)-*ḫi-lu* 10 *na-ri*-[*i* SÍG$^{(MEŠ)}$]
5. 5 TÚG.GÚ.È 5 *ku-duk-ti* SÍG-*šu*
6. 2 *iš-ku-uš-ḫu-ra* ^{GIŠ}GIGIR^{MEŠ} 1 *na-ri-i* SÍG
7. 3 *iš-ku-uš-ḫu-ra* ŠU-*ti*
8. 1 *ku-duk-ti še-eḫ-tu-un-nu*
9. 1 *na-ri-i* SÍG *a-na mé-re-eš-ti*
10. 18 *na-ri-i* 2 *ku-duk-ti ù* [*še-eḫ-tu-un-nu*]

[26]Contra AHw, p. 1209*b*: "eine Art Wolle?"
[27]SMN 3587:8, 14 (=Text 9); HSS 13, 288:8, [10], 17.
[28]Transliteration only.

11. SÍG *a-na iš-ka-ri-*[*šu*]
Lo.e. 12. ^{I}*Zi-ge il-*[*qè*]
Rev. 13. 4 MÍ^{MEŠ} *es-r*[*e*]*-tu*$_4$ 6 *na-ri-*[*i* SÍG]
14. 4 MÍ^{MEŠ} *uz-zu-li-ka-ru*
15. 4 *na-ri-i* SÍG *il-qú-ú*
16. 3 DUMU^{MEŠ} É.GAL 4 *na-ri-i* [SÍG]
17. ŠU.NIGÍN 32 *na-ri-i* 2 *ku-duk-ti še-e*[*ḫ-tu-un-nu*]
18. SÍG ^{I}*Zi-ge ša* URU *Pu-ru-u*[*l-li-we* SÍG$^{?}$ *ša*]
19. *šar-ra-tì*

The total in line 17 equals the sub-total in line 10 plus the entries in lines 13, 15, 16. The sub-total in line 10 seems to be wrong,[29] but this does not offer clues for establishing the relationship between *nariu* and *kuduktu*.

As will be seen presently, the standard weight for cloths measuring 15 x 5 *ammatu* is reckoned at 6 minas or at 4 *kuduktu* / 4 *kuduktu* 1/2$^{?}$. This fact possibly supports the tentative proposal of equating 1 *nariu* (=6 minas) with (4 to) 4.5 *kuduktu*.

Concerning the relationship between *kuduktu* and mina, an analysis of HSS 13, 387 and HSS 5, 97 and 98 yields some interesting pieces of information. These texts concern the moulding of bricks and state the amount of wool given to the persons in charge of the work (cf. W. Mayer, *Zur Ziegelherstellung in* Nuzi *und* Arrapḫe, UF 9 [1977], pp. 191-204).

22. HSS 13, 387:1-9:[30]
1. 2 MA.[NA] SÍG^{MEŠ} ⸢*ša*⸣ ^{I}*Túr-še-en-ni*
2. *a-na* ⸢SIG$_4$⸣^{MEŠ} *a-na* (<*e-pè-ši*>?)
3. ^{I}*Ig-g*[*e*]*-en-nu* DUMU *Al-*[*ki*]*-ya il-qè*
4. *ù* 1 *li-im* 2 *ma-*[*ti*] SIG$_4$^{MEŠ}
5. *i-la-ab-bi-nu*

---

[29]The text needs to be collated. On the basis of the available transliteration, the only tentative explanation that I am able to offer for the 18 *nariu* 2 *kuduktu* 1 *šeḫtunnu* in line 10 is the following one:

	13 *nariu*	1 *kuduktu*	(lines 1-4)
		{5 *kuduktu*}	(line 5: omitted in the sum)
+	1 *nariu*		(line 6)
+	3 *nariu*!		(line 7: "3" *iškušḫura* taken as *nariu* and included in the sum)
+		1 *kuduktu*	1 *šeḫtunnu* (line 8)
+	1 *nariu*		(line 9)
=	18 *nariu*	2 *kuduktu*	1 *šeḫtunnu* (total in line 10)

[30]Transliteration only.

6. 3 MA.[NA] SÍG^{MEŠ} *a-na* (sic!) ^{I}⌈*Pu-ḫi*⌉*-še-en-ni*
7. DUMU *Ú-ku-*[*y*]*a il-qè*
8. *ù* 1 *li-im* 8 *ma-ti* SIG$_4^{\text{MEŠ}}$
9. *i-la-ab-bi-nu*

This means a ratio of one mina (=60 shekels) of wool per 600 bricks, i.e. 1 shekel of wool = 10 bricks.

23. HSS 5, 97:1-7:
   1. *ku-duk-ti*!(QA) 30 SU SÍG *eš-še-tu*! *ša*!
   2. ^{I}*Ila-a-nu* DUMU *Ta-ú-ki*
   3. *ù* ^{I}*Tu ra ri* DUMU *Ši-il-wa-a+a*
   4. *ù* ^{I}*A-ri-ḫa-a+a* DUMU *A-ta*
   5. *a-na* ŠÁM$^{?!}$*-mi il-qè*
   6. 2 *li-im* SIG$_4^{\text{MEŠ}}$ *i+na* URU *Nuzi*
   7. *i-la-bi-in*!(IT) . . .[31]

24. HSS 5, 98:1-10:
   1. *ma-la ku-du-uk-tù* SÍG^{MEŠ}
   2. 1 BÁN 4 SÌLA ŠE^{MEŠ} *ša* <I>*I-la-an-nu*
   3. DUMU *Ta-i-ú-ki ù*
   4. ^{I}*Pá-i-te-šup* DUMU *Be-li-ya*
   5. *ig-ra ù ma-ka*$_4$*-la*
   6. *a-na* 1 *li-im* SIG$_4^{\text{MEŠ}}$ *il-qè*
   7. *ù* 1 *li-im* SIG$_4^{\text{MEŠ}}$ *ina* EGIR-*ki*
   8. EBUR-*ri ina* ITU *Ú-lu-li*
   9. *ina* URU *Nu-zi* ^{I}*Pá-i-te-šup*
   10. *a-na* ^{I}*I-la-an-nu i-la-ab-bi-in*!(IT)

One might surmise that 1 mina (= 60 shekels) of wool : 600 bricks = 1 *kuduktu* : 1000 bricks, and consequently hypothesize that 1 *kuduktu* = 100 shekels. But in HSS 5, 97 the amount of wool actually is 2 *kuduktu* + 30 shekels, while in HSS 5, 98 a certain amount of barley is added to the wool. As a consequence, it must be inferred that one *kuduktu* comprised *less* than 100 shekels, assuming that the wool:bricks ratio is constant in the three texts. One *kuduktu* thus comprised either 80 or 90 shekels:

(80 x 2 =)160 + 30 = 190 shekels of wool for 2,000 bricks i.e. 10 bricks = 1.05 shekels of wool

[31]Line 1: Mayer's rendering (l.cit., p. 196): *30* (*qa*) ŠE seems hardly tenable. Line 5 is not clear to me: cf. HSS 9, 98:16 (=Text 3)? Mayer (*ibid.*) reads *a-na-tum-mi* "dies."

(90 x 2 =)180 + 30 = 210 shekels of wool for 2,000 bricks i.e. 10 bricks = 9.5 shekels of wool.[32]

A comparison of weights of TÚG of similar dimensions but reckoned either in minas or in *kuduktu* may elucidate the problem further. CAD K, p. 494*a* suggests on the basis of the parallel between JEN 311 (= Text 10) and HSS 9, 103 (= Text 5) that one *kuduktu* represents one mina of 100 shekels. However, in the former the weight would be 400 shekels (= 4 *kuduktu*), and in the latter the weight would be 350 shekels (= 4 minas 50 shekels). This difference in weight does not quite reproduce the "similarity in size" of the two cloths.

Thus, it seems that only two possibilities remain. The first one is to assume that a standard wool cloth measuring 15 x 5 *ammatu* weighed 6 minas or 4 *kuduktu*, in which case 1 *kuduktu* = 90 shekels (6 x 60 = 4 x 90 = 360 shekels). Otherwise, the normal 15 x 5 *ammatu* textiles (weighing 6 minas) and the evidence provided by SMN 3587 (= Text 9) and JEN 311 (= Text 10) should be compared.

	15 x 5 *ammatu* = 75 *ammatu*^{2} = 6 minas	= 360 shekels
SMN 3587:	15 x 5 *ammatu* = 75 *ammatu*^{2} = 4 *kuduktu* 1/2?	= 360 shekels
	→ 1 *kuduktu* = 80 shekels	
JEN 311:	14 x 5 *ammatu* = 70 *ammatu*^{2} = 4 *kuduktu*	= 320 shekels
	→ 1 *kuduktu* = 80 shekels	

360 shekels for a surface of 75 square *ammatu* correspond to a weight of 4.8 shekels per square *ammatu*. Accordingly, the weight of the TÚG in JEN 311 ought to be 336 shekels (4.8 x 70): 16 shekels more than the 320 shekels gained from operating with a 80 shekel-unit. This difference raises no serious problems, because deviations from the standard weight of 6 minas for cloths measuring 15 x 5 *ammatu* are attested (see Text 3, i.e., -5 shekels).

On the other hand, no TÚG measuring 15 x 5 *ammatu* and weighing more than 6 minas (i.e. 360 shekels) is known. If one *kuduktu* = 100 shekels, then there would be TÚG weighing 400 shekels or *even more* (Text 9). This seems very suspect.

Thus, it might be concluded that 1 *kuduktu* = 90, or, more likely, 80 shekels. As for the *nariu*, a tentative suggestion is that it corresponded to 6 minas of 60 shekels and to 4.5 *kuduktu*. Should this be the case, it would seem that the *nariu* was connected with the mina instead of being sequentially related to the *kuduktu*.

[32]The datum of KAJ 111:1-8 is of no comparative help; there we have a ratio of 1 mina of wool per 100 bricks. Mayer's reckonings and conclusions (l.cit., pp. 202-3) diverge from those offered here.

What is the meaning of a unit of 80 shekels in the framework of ancient Near Eastern metrology? Such a unit might represent the double of the subdivision of the "Hittite" mina that is reckoned at 40 shekels.[33] This would mean that at Nuzi the "Babylonian" mina (=60 shekels), the (double-) "Syrian" mina (=50 x 2 = 100 shekels)[34] and the (double-) "Hittite" mina (= 40 x 2 = 80 shekels) existed contemporaneously. The relationship among these metrological systems and the actual standards of weight (i.e. shekels of ca. 8.4, 9.4 and 11.75 gr., respectively) must be left open for the time being. The same holds true for the relationship of the latter two systems with a possible larger standard, i.e. the talent of 3,600 (the "Babylonian" talent), 3,000 (the "Syrian" talent), or 2,400 (the "Hittite" talent) shekels.

* * *

TÚG in Nuzi thus represented a commodity of standard dimensions and weight. It was employed often as a means of payment.[35] It seems that only once the value of a TÚG (presumably of standard weight) is provided. JEN 297:20 lists 1 TÚG *ki-i-mu* ⌜5⌝ SU KÙ.BABBAR among a list of commodities given as a pledge in a *tidennūtu* transaction (11. 17-24). This aspect of the Nuzi wool cloth does not require lengthy comments.

In conclusion, some interesting similarities may be shown between this class of Nuzi textiles and the cloths attested in other groups of ancient Near Eastern documents. By no means are the following remarks intended to be exhaustive. On the contrary, additional comparative evidence would be most welcome.

The average weight of Old Assyrian textiles has been reckoned at 6 minas,[36] or possibly a little bit less.[37] This is in perfect agreement with the Nuzi evidence. Also the data pertaining to the weight of larger textiles in Ur III texts (reckoned at ca. 5 minas) fits the Nuzi evidence as well.[38]

The dimensions of the textiles, however, seem to be different. As shown above, the standard measures of Nuzi cloths are 15 x 5 *ammatu*. The unique OA reference TC 3/1, 17:33-37 gives for a "finished textile" the following dimensions: 9 *ammatu* in length and 8 *ammatu* in width.[39] This is 72 square *ammatu*, only a little bit less than the 75 square *ammatu* for the Nuzi TÚG. Assuming that the dimensions provided by TC 3/1, 17 were the normal ones

[33]Cf. H. Otten, AfO 17 (1954-56), pp. 128-31; N. F. Parise, Dialoghi di Archeolgia 4-5/1 (1970-71), pp. 18, 22.

[34]A. L. Oppenheim, OLZ 1938, cols. 485-86.

[35]See the texts quoted by D. Cross, MPND, p. 51.

[36]H. Lewy, RSO 39 (1964), pp. 182-83.

[37]K. R. Veenhof, AOATT, pp. 89-91; cf. M. T. Larsen, Old Assyrian Caravan Procedures, Istanbul 1967, p. 148.

[38]Cf. K. R. Veenhof, AOATT, p. 91.

[39]Ibid., p. 92; CAD Ṣ, p. 222*b*; A. L. Oppenheim, Or 7 (1938), p. 133.

for OA textiles,[40] the weight of which was ca. 6 minas, the parallel with the Nuzi cloths becomes even more striking. In fact, both types of textiles would have very close, if not identical, weight and almost identical surface area. Only the shape would be different.

The dimensions of Ur III textiles are fairly wide-ranged,[41] but maximum sizes normally do not surpass 7 x 8 *ammatu.*[42] Such a figure agrees well with the shape and sizes of OA textiles. For comparative purposes, the most interesting piece of information is provided by ITT 5, 9996: Obv. III 8-Rev. I 2,[43] which gives the sizes of one textile and the weight of its warp and weft. The cloth measures 7 x 7 *ammatu*, its total weight is 4 minas (2/3 + 3 1/3 minas). Thus, 49 square *ammatu* weighed 240 shekels, i.e. one square *ammatu* weighed 4.9 shekels—almost exactly the weight of Nuzi (and OA) textiles, which amounted to 4.8 shekels per square *ammatu*.

Abbreviations employed in the present article:

D. Cross, MPND = D. Cross, Movable Property in the Nuzi Documents, New Haven, 1937.

K. R. Veenhof, AOATT = K. R. Veenhof, Aspects of Old Assyrian Trade and its Terminology, Leiden 1972.

Gadd = C. J. Gadd, Tablets from Kirkuk, RA 23 (1926), pp. 49-161: the number corresponds to that of the tablets.

[40] K. R. Veenhof, AOATT, p. 93.

[41] Cf. H. Waetzoldt, Untersuchungen zur neusumerischen Textilindustrie, Roma 1972, pp. 144-48.

[42] Ibid., p. 148.

[43] Ibid., pp. 232-33; cf. pp. 144, 145 with fn. 564.

PART TWO

CUNEIFORM TEXTS FROM ARRAPḪA, KURRUḪANNI, AND NUZI

Ein frühes *ṭuppi mārūti* aus Tell al-Faḫḫār/Kurruḫanni

ABDULILLAH FADHIL
Baghdad

Die Frage "Was ist das *ṭuppi mārūti*" beantwortet M. P. Maidman,[1] nach sorgfältiger Analyse aller bislang vorgebrachten Theorien, mit den Worten: "Real estate adoption was a device whereby the adoptee obtained clear title to land and other immovables. This acquisition involved immediate transfer of legal title and at least eventual physical possession as well. Such real estate was inheritable by the family of the adoptee. Not all such transactions were simple sales but included debt foreclosures and variations on that theme." Allerdings, so hob P. Koschaker[2] hervor, "durfte das Veräusserungsgeschäft nicht sich selbst Kauf nennen." Obwohl es mehr als ein Dutzend Belege für die Verwendung des Terminus *šīmu* in Verbindung mit Grundstückstransaktionen gibt, findet sich "unter den vielen Hunderten von arrapchäischen Urkunden keine einzige, die sich terminologisch als Grundstückskauf bekennte,"[3] d.h. in einem *ṭuppi mārūti* ist *šīmu* niemals bezeugt.

Zu den grossen Überraschungen, welche die Tontafelfunde der iraqischen Grabungen in Tell al-Faḫḫār, dem antiken Kurruḫanni, 1967-1969, bereithielten, gehört auch ein frühes *ṭuppi mārūti*, in dem *šīmu* zweimal vorkommt.

Die Tafel TF_1 40/ḫ = IM 70764 hat die Dimensionen 70 x 55 mm; der rechte Rand ist weggebrochen. Neben archaischen Zeichenformen (besonders für ŠÁM, das als GAZ-A-AN statt NÍNDAxŠE-A-AN erscheint) und fast durchgängiger Defektivschreibung (nur die Präposition *it-ti* Z.2 ist plene geschrieben) fällt auf, dass die Urkunde nicht gesiegelt ist. Nach den letzten beiden Zeilen der Rückseite (Angabe des Schreibers und seiner Filiation) sind vier dicht beieinander liegende waagerechte Linien gezogen. Die verbleibende letzte Zeile der Rückseite und der obere Rand sind unbeschriftet. Auch der

[1] A Socio-Economic Analysis of a Nuzi Family Archive. Dissertation, University of Pennsylvania, Philadelphia, Pa., 1976. University Microfilms 77-861, S.122-23.

[2] ZA 48 (1944), S.202.

[3] P. Koschaker, ebd.

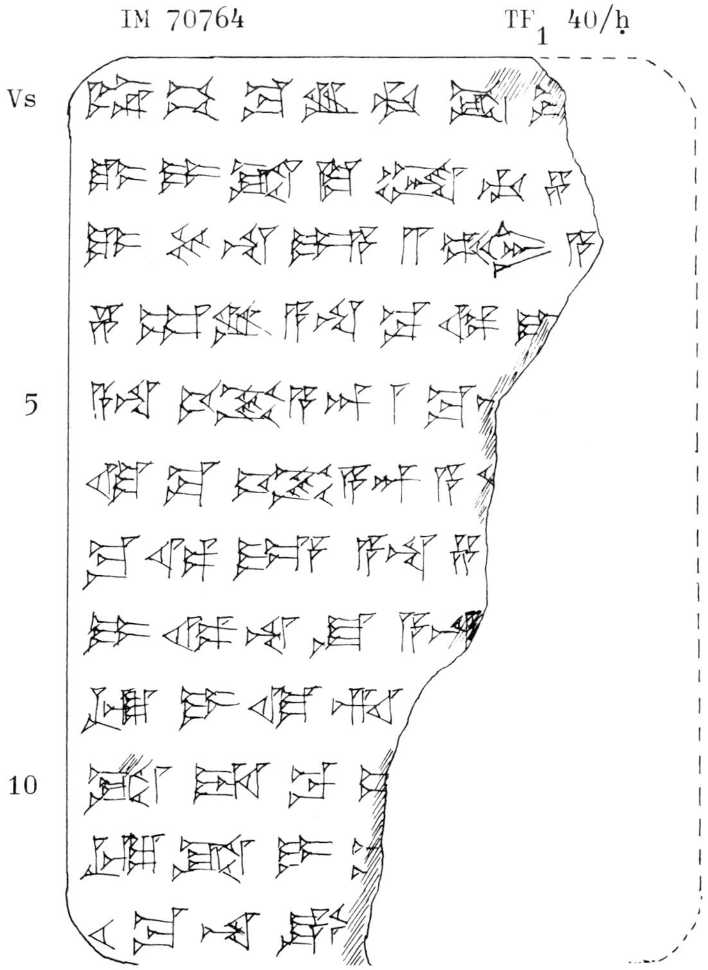
IM 70764
TF_1 40/ḫ
Vs
5
10

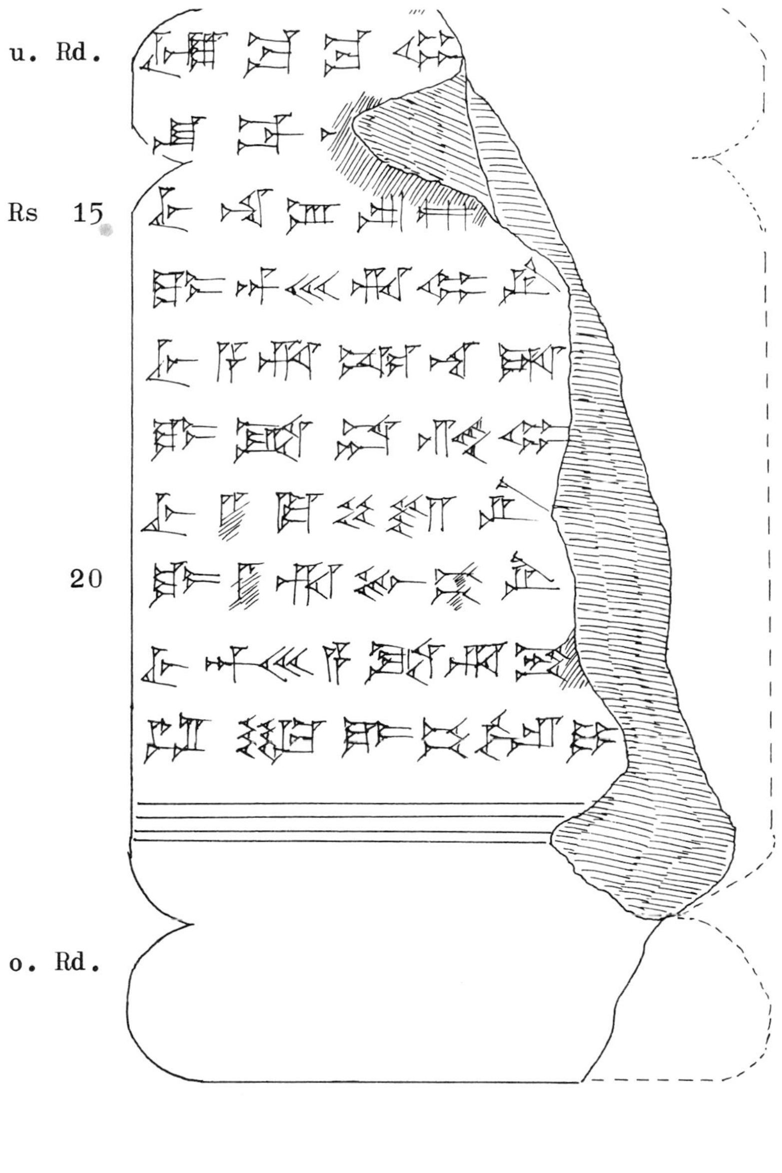
u. Rd.
Rs 15
20
o. Rd.

linke Rand weist weder Beschriftung noch Siegelabrollungen auf. Der Text lautet in Umschrift:[4]

Vs 1 *ṭup-pí ma-ru-ti ša M*[*a-di-ja*]
2 DUMU *Ì-ša-ku it-ti Ṣa*-[*ab-ru*]
3 DUMU *Še-na-ja* 2 ANŠE A.[ŠÀ(^{MEŠ})]
4 *Ṣa-ab-ru a-na Ma-di-j*[*a i-di-na-šu*]
5 *a-na* GAZ-A-AN 1 MA.N[A KÙ.BABBAR]
6 *ki-ma* GAZ-A-AN A.Š[À(^{MEŠ})]
7 *Ma-di-ja a-na Ṣa*-[*ab-ru*]
8 *i-di-na-šu* A.Š[À?]
9 *ù Ì-ki-ri* [ ]
10 *ša da-ba-b*[*i*]
11 *ù ša i-b*[*a-*]
12 10 MA.NA KÙ.BABBAR [Ì.LÁ.E]

——————————— – – –

Rd 13 *ù ma-ma mi*-[ ]
14 ŠU.BA.A[N.TI]
Rs 15 IGI *Na-ú*-⌜ṣú?-ur⌝?[ ]
16 DUMU ^{d}30-*re-mé-ni*
17 IGI *A-ri-ka-na-da* [ ]
18 DUMU *Ša-du-ge-mi*
19 IGI ⌜A⌝-*ku*-≪ŠE≫-*le-ni*
20 DUMU *A-ri-pu*-⌜*bi*⌝-*ni*
21 IGI ^{d}30-*a-ša-re-e*[*d*]
22 DUB.SAR DUMU *Bé-el-i*-[ ]

"Adoptionsurkunde des Matija, Sohn des Iššakku, mit Ṣabru, Sohn des Šennaja. Zwei Imēru Feld [hat] Ṣabru dem Matija zum Kauf [gegeben]. Eine Mine [Silber] als Kaufpreis des Feldes hat Matija dem Ṣabru gegeben. Das Fe[ld ist rechtskräftig verkauft(?)], und Ikkiri [ist der Vermesser des Feldes(?)]. Wer Prozesse [anstrengt] und wer ver[tragsbrüchig wird], [bezahlt] 10 Minen Silber. Und jeder(?) hat das [ihm Zustehende(?)] erhal[ten].

Vor Na-uṣur(?), Sohn des Sîn-rēmēni. Vor Arik-kanata [ ], Sohn des Šatu-kewi. Vor Akkulenni, Sohn des Arip-uppinni. Vor Sîn-ašarēd, dem Schreiber, Sohn des Bēl-i[ddina(?)]."

Z.1: Für das Formular eines *ṭuppi mārūti* vgl. Elena Cassin, L'Adoption à Nuzi (Paris 1938), S.8ff. Von den sechs konstitutiven Elementen findet sich

[4]Autographie s. Fig. 1.—Ich danke dem Direktorat des Iraq Museums, Baghdad, The State Organization of Antiquities, Republic of Iraq, für die mir freundlichst erteilte Publikationserlaubnis.

hier nur die Überschrift und die *nabalkutu*-Klausel. Es fehlen: *ana mārūti īpuš, kīma zitti, kīma qīšti,* die *birqu/bāqirānu-* und die *ilku*-Klauseln. Das Formular von IM 70764 ist somit (bis jetzt) ohne Parallelen, wodurch die Ergänzung, speziell der Zeilen 8-10 und 13-14, sehr erschwert wird. - Die Setzung bzw. Nicht-Setzung des Personenkeils ist sicherlich ein Kriterium zur Altersbestimmung von Nuzi-Texten. Gänzliches Fehlen von Personenkeilen hat IM 70764 gemeinsam mit den Urkunden des Schreibers Šumu-libši JEN 563, eventuell auch JEN 442 und 544, während er etwa in JEN 567 im Corpus (bereits) vereinzelt DIŠ setzt. Auch Ṭāb-milki-abi ist noch sehr sparsam in der Setzung des Personenkeils (z.B. JEN 568 nur bei ^{I}*Ḫa-ši-ja* Z.1). Genauere Statistiken wird Frau Paola Negri Scafa in ihrer Arbeit über die Schreiber von Nuzi vorlegen. - Das Graphem *Ma-di-ja* (Z.[1].4.7) ist hapax; wegen der defektiven Orthographie des Schreibers Sîn-ašarēd ist eine Entscheidung darüber unmöglich, ob Mat-teja (das Hypochoristikon zu Mat-Tešup) oder Matija (Hypochoristikon zu Namen des Typs Enna-mati) vorliegt.

Z.2: Das Graphem *I-ša-ku* liegt bisher (mit unsicherem *-ša-*) nur HSS 5,65:18 vor, einem der ältesten Texte aus dem Archiv Akkuja S. Katiri. Man wird den Namen wohl zu den von NPN 47a und AAN 45a unter En-šaku registrierten Graphemen zu stellen haben. Ob er als *iššakku,* wie in der Umschrift der Übersetzung angedeutet, aufzufassen ist, bedarf noch näherer Untersuchung, bei der besonders danach zu fragen ist, wann die Geminatendissimilation einsetzt.

Der Name Ṣabru ("Zwinkerer," vgl. AHw 1071b und CAD Ṣ 44b) ist neu im Nuzi-Onomastikon, jedoch aB und mB gut bezeugt. In Z.2 und 7 sind auch die (flektierten) Ergänzungen *Ṣa-*[*ab-ri*] möglich. - Die Verwendung der Präposition *itti* "mit" in der Einleitung eines *ṭuppi mārūti* ist ganz ungewöhnlich. Die Zeichenform des *it* in Z.2 ist zwar durch zwei vorgeschaltete Keile (im Vergleich mit *e*[*d*] Z.21) verformt; dennoch ist an der Lesung *it-ti* nicht zu zweifeln.

Z.3: Auch das Graphem *Še-na-ja* ist neu (vgl. NPN 130b/131a und AAN 125a/b), findet aber ein Analogon in Schreibungen wie *E-en-na-ja* HSS 13,179 = 14,109:15.

Z.4: Da sicher der Ausdruck *ana šīmi nadānu* "verkaufen" (Belege AHw 1240b,5b) vorliegt, ist *i-di-na-šu* am Ende der Z.4 zu ergänzen oder in Z.5 vor 1 MA.N[A zu interpolieren.

Z.5-6: Das Zeichen ŠÁM hat hier eine Form, die nicht bei R. Borger, ABZ, Nr.187, S.106, registriert ist: das Zeichen NÍNDAxŠE hat am Ende noch zwei zusätzliche Winkelhaken, so dass es praktisch mit dem Zeichen GAZ identisch ist—daher die tentative Umschrift GAZ-A-AN. Es kann jedoch kein vernünftiger Zweifel bestehen, dass es sich um das Zeichen ŠÁM handelt.

Z.8: Es ist nicht ganz eindeutig festzustellen, ob *a-n*[*a* oder A.Š[À an der Bruchstelle zu lesen ist. Die obige Übersetzung (und Ergänzung) ist daher mit Vorbehalt aufzunehmen. Liegt *ana* vor, müsste natürlich *a-n*[*a* PN_3] ^{9}*ù I-ki-ri* [ergänzt werden.

Z.9: *I-ki-ri* ist sicher Personenname, vgl. die Grapheme *Ik-ki-ri* NPN 67b und *Ik-ki-ri*!(ḪU) HSS 19, 95:17 sowie die Toponyme URU *I-ki-ru/rù* HSS 9, 144:16.23.28 und URU *I-ki-[ru/rù]* HSS 16, 205:1. Falls mit Z.9 ein neuer Satz beginnt, könnte [*mušelwû/mušelmû*] zu ergänzen sein.

Z.10: Die Verwendung von *dabābu* ist in Nuzi-Texten ganz selten, vgl. [16]*ù da-ba-bu* [17]*ja-a-nu* [18]*ša da-ba-ba an-na-am* [19]*uš-ba-la-ka-tu* [20]*i+na* A.ŠÀ-*šu ù* É-*šu* [21][*uš-te-e*]*l-le* JEN 570:16-21. Hier scheint auch eine transitive Verwendung vorzuliegen mit *šubalkutu* oder *bu"û* als Prädikat. Z.11 ist sicher *u ša ibbalakkatu* zu ergänzen.

Z.12: Die Verbalform ist nach JEN 414:19, JEN 566 und 567 passim, am ehesten als [Ì.LÁ.E] anzusetzen, wenn auch [*umalla*] nicht ganz auszuschliessen ist. Bei der ebenfalls möglichen Verwendung von *nadānu* müsste die Form (ohne Nasalierung) [*inaddin*] lauten.

Z.13-14 ist innerhalb der Nuzi-Texte ganz ohne Parallele. Am ehesten lässt sich *mi-*[zu *mi-*[*ma šu-un-šu*] ergänzen. Das dritte Zeichen der Z.14 könnte gut A[N sein, was an ŠU.BA.A[N.TI denken liesse, das freilich in Nuzi sonst nicht bezeugt ist. Syntaktisch schwierig ist bei der vorgeschlagenen Übersetzung jedoch die Verwendungsweise von *ma-ma* (=*mamma*) i.d.B. "jeder (von beiden)."

Z.15: *Na-ú-*⌈ZU-UR⌉ entspräche den Spuren einigermassen. Der Name begegnet HSS 19, 76:23 und 118:32. Ob er wirklich akkadisch zu deuten ist (so Elena Cassin, AAN 99a), muss wegen des unerklärten *Na-* dahingestellt bleiben.

Z.16: Sîn-rēmēni ist im Nuzi-Onomastikon gut bezeugt, vgl. NPN 122a und AAN 116a.

Z.17: Der Name *A-ri-ka-na-da* ist neu; möglicherweise folgt auf *-da* noch eine Silbe oder eine Berufsbezeichnung. Das Element *-ka-na-da* ist zu vergleichen mit dem Namen Kanatu (Grapheme *Qa-na-tu*$_4$/*du*, s. NPN 79b).

Z.18: Für Šatu-kewi vgl. NPN 127a und AAN 122a; das Graphem *Ša-du-ge-mi* ist nur noch aus JEN 173:2 (*Ša-du-*[*ge*]*-mi*) nachzuweisen. Es ist ein Charakteristikum der ältesten Nuzi-Texte, in ḫurritischen Namen statt *wa*, *we*, *wi*, *wu* die Zeichen *ma*, *me*, *mi*, *mu* zu verwenden, ganz im Kontrast der Entwicklung *w* > *m*, der beim Übergang vom aB zum mB zu beobachten ist. Erst die jüngeren Nuzi-Texte schreiben *wa*, *we*, *wi*, *wu*.

Z.19: Der Name Akkul-enni kann nur durch Annahme eines Schreibfehlers (des sonst sehr sorgfältigen Schreibers) rekonstruiert werden. Die defektive Schreibung **A-ku-le-ni* ist sonst nicht nachweisbar (vgl. NPN 17b/18a und AAN 20b/21a).

Z.20: Auch der Name *A-ri-pu-*⌈*bi*⌉*-ni* ist neu; das zweite Element dürfte identisch sein mit dem selbständigen PN Umpinne (Grapheme *Um-bi-in-né-e*, *Um-bi-né-e*, *Um-bi-in-né*, s. NPN 163b und AAN 156b), allerdings—der Phonetik von IM 70764 entsprechend—ohne Geminatendissimilation.

Z.21: Der Name Sîn-ašarēd ist aus Nuzi-Texten weder *per se* noch als Schreiber nachzuweisen; der Typus ist aber aB/mB gut bezeugt (vgl. CAD A/2, 417b).

Z.22: Die wahrscheinlichste Ergänzung des Patronyms ist *Bé-*⌜*el*⌝*-i-*[*di-na*].

Nicht gesiegelte Urkunden sind z.B. JEN 563, 566, 568, 569 und 570. Sie zählen durchwegs zu den ältesten in Nuzi gefundenen Tafeln.

Nach Analogie der späteren, "kanonischen" Form des *ṭuppi mārūti*, ist Adoptant = "Verkäufer" und Adoptierter = "Käufer"; in IM 70764 wäre demnach Ṣabru S. Šennaja Adoptant und Matija S. Iššakku Adoptierter; die Urkunde wäre weiterhin Bestandteil des Archivs des letzteren, wahrscheinlich des ältesten Archivs von Kurruḫanni, zumindest kontemporär mit den Archiven des Puḫi-šenni S. Turi-šenni und seiner Ehefrau ᶠW/Minnirke. Warum diese Grundstückstransaktion (schon zu so früher Zeit) als Adoption stilisiert wurde, bleibt uns verborgen. Wegen der textuellen Unsicherheit Z.8-9 können leider keine Aussagen darüber gemacht werden, in welchem Verhältnis *I-ki-ri* zu den beiden Vertragsparteien stand; dieses aber könnte für die Wahl des Formulars bestimmend gewesen sein.

Die These, dass Grund und Boden im Königreich Arrapḫa schlechthin unveräusserlich war (weil alles anbaufähige Land aus *ilku*-Feldern bestand), wurde zuletzt von M. P. Maidman erschüttert, der die Puḫi-šenni-Urkunde JEN 552 folgendermassen interpretiert: "The exact nature of this real estate transaction is uncertain. The text contains no superscription of telltale formulary. Puḫi-šenni "gives" gold to three individuals for a plot of land. That land he gives to the youngsters of Winnirke. On the face of it, the simplicity of the transaction suggests an outright purchase" (A Socio-Economic Analysis of a Nuzi Family Archive, 1976, S.359-60, Anm.366). Dennoch wird auch in diesem Dokument die Verwendung des Terminus ŠÁM oder *šīmu* vermieden.

Bedeutet aber die Absenz des akkadischen Terminus *šīmu* in JEN 552 auch, dass der *Begriff* "Kauf" in dieser Urkunde nicht zum Ausdruck kommt? Lesen wir Z.1-8:

¹ ᴵ*Pu-ḫi-še-ni* DUMU *Tu-ri-še-ni* ² 1 GÍN KÙ.GI *i-ra-na* ³*a+na Ú-na-ap-ta-e* ⁴*a+na Al-pu-ja* ⁵*a+na A-ri-ma-at-qa* ⁶3 DUMU^MEŠ *Ḫa-nu-ja it-ta-ad-na-šu-nu-ti-ma* ⁷1 *ma-a-at* ANŠE A.ŠÀ^ḪI.A. ⁸[*a-š*]*ar* D[UMU^MEŠ] *Ḫa-nu-ja il-te-qé*

Falls in diesen Zeilen von "Kauf" die Rede sein soll, käme für diesen Begriff nur *i-ra-na* (Z.2) in Frage. Nach CAD I/J 173b (JEN 551 Druckfehler für JEN 552) ist *irana* "either a qualification of gold or referring to its provenience"; AHw 386a emendiert fragend zu *ḫ*(*urāṣa*) *i-*<*pí*>*-ra-na* "Staubgold," mit Verweis auf eperu. Nun ist das Nebeneinander von *ḫurāṣu* und *irana* in JEN 552:2 rein akzidentell, wie vier neue Belege für dieses Lexem deutlich machen.

> ^{8}*um-ma* ^{I}*Ku-uš-ši-ḫar-be* ^{9}2 UDU^{MEŠ} ^{I}*Ḫu-ti-ja* ^{10}*a-na ja-ši ka-am-ma* ^{11}*id-dì-i-na* ^{12}*šum-ma a-na i-ra-na* ^{13}*ša* A.ŠÀ^{MEŠ} *ša* ^{14} ^{I}*Za-ba-ki a-na-ku él-qú-*[*ú*]: SMN 855:8-14 (zitiert R. E. Hayden, Court Procedure at Nuzu, Waltham, Mass. 1962, S.176).

"Folgendermassen gab Kušši-ḫarpe zu Protokoll: 'Die zwei Schafe hat mir Ḫutija als *kamma* gegeben. (Ich schwöre, dass) ich sie nicht als *irana* für die Felder des Zabaki erhalten habe."

Da wegen des ergangenen *huršān*-Urteils die Aussage des Ḫutija kontradiktorisch sein muss, ist die Aussage des Ḫutija wie folgt zu rekonstruieren:

> [*um-ma* ^{I}*Ḫu-ti-ja-ma šum-ma* 2 UDU^{MEŠ}] *a-na* ^{2}[*i-ra*]*-ni a-na* ^{I}*Ku-uš-ši-ḫar-be* ^{3}*la ad-dì-nu-ma* . . . SMN 855:1-3.

"Folgendermassen gab Ḫutija zu Protokoll: (Ich schwöre, dass) ich zwei Schafe dem Kušši-ḫarpe als *irana* gegeben habe."

Die Ergänzung [*i-ra*]*-ni* (mit *-ni* statt *-na*) stützt sich auf einen unpublizierten Text, auf den R. E. Hayden, Court Procedure, S.210, Anm.245, hinweist: "This word also occurs in HM (Harvard Museum Text) 8400 in the phrase *ina irani* as a description of the place of houses." Ohne Kenntnis des genauen Kontexts ist dieser Beleg jedoch hier nicht verwertbar. (S. jetzt Addendum und Postscriptum.)

Den folgenden Beleg verdanke ich der Freundlichkeit von Herrn Dr. Fārūq ar-Rāwī, Baghdad. Er stammt, wie IM 70764, aus der ersten Grabungskampagne in Tell al-Faḫḫār und trägt die Fundnummer TF_1 K/40. Die ersten fünf Zeilen des Textes lauten:

> ^{1}1 GÉME *Nu-*[*ul-l*]*u-a+a-ú* ^{2}1 GU$_4$ 1 ANŠE *an-nu-ti* ^{3} ^{I}*Ḫa-na-tu*$_4$ DUMU *Ḫi-in-nu-ja* ^{4}*a-na i-ra-na a-na* ^{I}*Eḫ-li-pa-pu* DUMU *Te-ḫi-pa-pu it-ta-din*

"Eine nulluäische Sklavin, ein Rind, einen Esel hat Ḫanatu S. Ḫinnuja dem Eḫlipapu S. Teḫip-apu, *ana irana* gegeben."

Aus SMN 855 ist zu entnehmen, dass *ana irani nadānu* und *ana irani leqû* korrespondierende Begriffe sind, analog *ana šīmi nadānu* und *ana šīmi leqû*. Man könnte daraus unmittelbar schliessen, dass *irana* ein nicht-akkadisches Wort mit der Bedeutung von *šīmu* sei, wenn nicht Gold, zwei Schafe, eine Sklavin, ein Rind, ein Esel Zahlungsmittel wäre. Mit einem Silberbetrag ist *irana* bislang noch nicht attestiert. So könnte in der Tat *irana* "an Zahlungsstatt" bedeuten.

Die zweite Unsicherheit bei der Bedeutungsbestimmung von *irana* besteht darin, dass, ebenfalls in SM 855, als weiteres Korrelat zu *irana* der Terminus *ka-am-ma* erscheint, der wenigstens in zwei weiteren Texten bezeugt ist:

^{5}*um-ma* ^{I}*Wa-an-ti-ja ù um-ma* [^{I}*Ša-aš-ta-e-ma*] ^{6} ^{I}*Nu-i-še-ri a-bu-ni* ^{I}*Wa-*[*ar-ḫi-še-en-ni*] *a-na* DUMU^{MEŠ} DÙ^{MEŠ}-*šú* ^{7}*ù* 1 ANŠE A.ŠÀ^{MEŠ} *i+na mi-in-dá-ti* [*ša* É.GAL-*lì*] ^{8}*ka_4-am-ma a-na* ^{I}*Nu-i-še-ri* [*it-ta-ad-nu*] ^{9}*ù ṭup-pu iš-ṭú-ur* JEN 383:6-9

und

^{5}12 ANŠE A.ŠÀ^{MEŠ} *i+na a-aḫ a-ta-ap-*[*p*]*í ša Sa-a-ra* ^{6}*a+na* <^{I}>*Te-ḫi-ip-til-la ki-ma* ḪA.LA-*šu* SUM-*šu* ^{7}*ka-am-ma i+na ḫa-de_4-e-em*$^{!}$(ḪI)-*ma* ^{8}*a-na ma-ru-ti i-pu-sú-ma* A.ŠÀ^{MEŠ} *an-na-ti* [SUM-*šu*] JEN 69:5-8.

Die beiden letzteren Belege werden von den Wbb. als kontrahierte Form von *kīam-ma* "so" verstanden (AHw 432b, nur JEN 69:7; CAD K 328a, JEN 69:7 u. 383:8). Doch zeigt ein analytischer Vergleich von SMN 855:10 und JEN 383:8, dass diese Deutung nicht zutreffen kann, dass vielmehr *kamma* als eigenes Lexem nicht akkadischer Herkunft zu verstehen und zu verbuchen ist. Dass *ka-am-ma* und *a-na i-ra-na* in SMN 855 in relativer Opposition zueinanderstehen (und sich darum gegenseitig ausschliessen) darf als evident vorausgesetzt werden. In JEN 383, einer Prozessurkunde aus dem Archiv des Enna-mati S. Teḫip-tilla, Dossier Zizza, ist nicht strittig, dass Warḫi-šenni den Nui-šeri adoptiert hat und ihm ein Imēru Feld nach dem Palast-Standard veräussert hat, sondern vielmehr der Umstand, dass Warḫi-šenni behauptet, Nui-šeri hätte ihm als Kaufpreis des Feldes (*a-na ši-im* A.ŠÀ^{MEŠ}, Z.16) 1 Imēru Gerste versprochen (*iq-bi a-na na-dá-ni*, Z.17), aber niemals übergeben. Damit ist ganz klar, dass die relative Opposition in JEN 383 *ka_4-am-ma* und 1 ANŠE ŠE *a-na ši-im* A.ŠÀ^{MEŠ} lautet. Damit erhalten wir zwei Gleichungen mit zwei Unbekannten:

ka-am-ma : *a-na i-ra-na ša* A.ŠÀ^{MEŠ} (SMN 855)
ka_4-am-ma : *a-na ši-im* A.ŠÀ^{MEŠ} (JEN 383)

Lösung Nr.1 lautet: *a-na i-ra-na* = *a-na ši-im*. Lösung Nr.2 kann dann nur lauten: *ka*/*ka_4-am-ma* ist nicht *a-na ši-im*, sondern "gratis," "unentgeltlich," "als Geschenk." Wir können diese Mathematikaufgabe sogar noch weiterspielen und die "Probe" machen. Wenn also das *ṭuppi mārūti* eine verkappte Verkaufsurkunde ist, in welcher der Kaufpreis der Immobilien als *qīštu*, "Geschenk" verschlüsselt ist (in Prozessurkunden besteht offenbar kein Anlass zu solcher Verschlüsselung), dann dürfte die dem Prozess JEN 383 zugrundeliegende Adoptionsurkunde auch keine Angabe über die *qīštu* enthalten.

Die dem Prozess JEN 383 zugrundeliegende Adoptionsurkunde ist JEN 60. Als Adoptierter figuriert ^{I}*Nu-i-še-*[*ri* DUMU]x-⌜ ⌝-*ú-ki* (Z.3), der Vater des Wantija und Šaš-tae aus JEN 383. Die Adoptanten sind die Brüder ^{I}*Še-en-ni* und ^{I}*Wa-*[*aḫ-ri-še-e*]*n-ni* DU[MU]^{M}[^{EŠ}] ^{I}*Še-ga-rù* (Z.2-3), die als Adoptanten des Teḫip-tilla wieder in JEN 201 bzw. JEN 215 begegnen. Die Feldfläche von 1 Imēru ist identisch in JEN 60 und JEN 383. Sieben der zwölf Zeugen des *ṭuppi mārūti* JEN 60 erscheinen als Zeugen der Nui-šeri-Söhne in dem Prozess JEN 383:21-27. Die entscheidenste und beweiskräftigste Übereinstimmung von

JEN 60 und 383 besteht darin, dass sie die einzigen Texte sind, in denen *ina mindati ša ekalli* bei einem anderen Adoptierten als Teḫip-tilla S. Puḫišenni verwendet wird.[5] Dass im Prozess JEN 383 nur Waḫri-šenni und nicht auch sein Bruder Šenni erscheint, mag verschiedene Gründe haben, die wir nicht kennen: war Šenni bereits gestorben oder vertritt Waḫri-šenni auch die Interessen seines Bruders? Schwierigkeiten, die die Kombination von JEN 60 und 383 beeinträchtigen, sind der zerstörte Zustand des Namens ᴵ*Wa*-[*aḫ-ri-še*]-⌜*en*⌝-*ni* oder ᴵ*Wa*-[*ar-ḫi-š*]*e-en-ni* in JEN 60:2 und die offensichtliche Diskrepanz seiner Filiation: nach JEN 60 ist er Sohn des *Še-ga-rù*, nach JEN 383:3 DUMU *p*/*Pa-ta-li*. Nun wäre *p*/*Pa-ta-li* als Personennamen hapax; es darf sicher nicht getrennt werden von [20]⌜EME⌝-*šu ša* [21] ᴵ*Tar-mi-til-la* [22] ᴵ⌜*A-ri*⌝-*iḫ-ḫa-a+a* [23]*a-na pa-ta*-(Rasur)-*al-lì* DÙ-*uš* JEN 540:20-23.[6] Wenn nicht alles täuscht, bezeichnet *pa-ta*-(*al*)-*li*/*lì* einen Titel oder Status.

Nun ist JEN 60 dadurch gekennzeichnet, dass die Angabe der *qīštu* fehlt. Damit stimmt die Aussage der Zeugen von JEN 60 in JEN 383:36-38 exakt überein: [36]*ù* ŠE^MEŠ *ša ši-im* A.ŠÀ^MEŠ [37]*i+na pí-i* ᴵ*Nu-i-še-ri a-na* ᴵ*Wa-ar-ḫi-še-ni* [38]*na-dá-ni la ni-iš-mé-mi*. Der Rechtsvorgang des *ṭuppi mārūti* JEN 60 ist also kein Feld*kauf*, sondern eine Feld*schenkung*.

Auch in JEN 69 fehlt die Angabe einer *qīštu*. Zum Verständnis der Z.7 ist die Feststellung wichtig, dass in Z.4 *a+na ma-ru-ti i-pu-uš-ma* steht (was dem Formular entspricht), in Z.8 aber nochmals *a+na ma-ru-ti i-pu-sú-ma* erscheint (was ganz aus dem Rahmen fällt). So steht zu vermuten, dass mit Z.7 *ka-am-ma i+na ḫa-de*$_4$*-e-em*!(ḪI)-*ma* die spezifische Form dieser Adoption charakterisiert werden soll. Sowohl AHw (336a *ḫatēḫi*) als auch CAD (Ḫ 149b *ḫatēḫi*) gehen davon aus, dass ein ḫurritisches Wort vorliegt. Ich lese hingegen *ina ḫadêm-ma* (Inf. **ḫdū*, vgl. AHw 307b G 2) "belieben"; CAD Ḫ 27a/b "to be agreeable, to do voluntarily, to be willing"); zwar konnte ich die Stelle nicht kollationieren lassen, berufe mich aber auf die Parallele *ki-ma* [ḪA].LA-*šu-ma* [10][SUM-*šu ka-am-ma i+na ḫa*]-*de*$_4$*-e-em*-[*m*]*a* [11][*a+na ma-ru-ti*] ⌜*i*⌝-*pu-šu-uš* JEN 576:9-11. Dazu berechtigt die Erkenntnis, dass sowohl JEN 69 als auch JEN 576 von dem Schreiber Kiannipu abgefasst sind. JEN 69:25 lässt sich unschwer zu IGI ⌜*Ki*⌝-[*an-ni-pu*] DUB.SAR-*rù* ergänzen; JEN 69 weist so viele graphematische und prosopographische Gemeinsamkeiten mit JEN 66, 205, 410 und 576 auf, dass jeder vernünftige Zweifel an der Autorschaft des Kiannipu verstummt. Die Einzelnachweise hierfür wird Frau Paola Negri Scafa in ihrem Buch über die Schreiber von Nuzi liefern. JEN 69:7-8 kann also unbedenklich wie folgt übersetzt werden: "Unentgeltlich (und) freiwillig hat er ihn adoptiert und [ihm] diese Felder [übergeben]."

[5]Hinsichtlich JEN 60:5-6 ist diese Feststellung bereits von Frau Hildegard Lewy, Or NS 11 (1942), S.24, Anm.5, getroffen worden.

[6]Frau Martha T. Roth hat JEN 540:20-23 kollationiert und die Korrektheit der Kopie bestätigt. Ihr gebührt dafür mein aufrichtiger Dank.

Abschliessend ist zu fragen, welcher Sprache nun *ka*/*ka*$_4$-*am-ma* und *i-ra-na*/*ni* angehören. Man ist in der Nuzologie nur allzu leicht geneigt, jedes nicht-akkadische Wort als ḫurritisch einzustufen. Die neueren Erkenntnisse der Heidelberger Schule geben der Einsicht Raum, dass so wie im Onomastikon kassitisches Namengut neben ḫurritischem steht, auch im Lexikon beide Sprachen in den Nuzi-Texten repräsentiert sind. Zusammen hören wir die Wörter *ka-am-ma* und *i-ra-na* nur aus dem Munde des Kušši-ḫarpe (SMN 855:10.12), der einen kassitischen Namen trägt. Was läge also näher, in *ka-am-ma* und *i-ra-na* kassitische Lexeme zu vermuten? Doch hätte eine solche linguistische Festlegung möglicherweise weitreichende Folgen. Man muss ja nach den tieferen Ursachen fragen, die dazu führten, ein Rechtsgeschäft wie den Immobilienkauf als Adoption zu kaschieren. Irgendwie sieht das doch nach einem Kompromiss zwischen zwei sich gegenseitig aufhebenden sozio-ökonomischen Systemen aus. Diese Systeme könnten sehr wohl verschiedenen ethnischen Ursprungs sein.

Nicht weniger entscheidend dürfte aber auch der chronologische Faktor sein. Das hohe Alter der beiden Feldkaufurkunden IM 70764 und JEN 552 ist unbestritten, sie gehören zum ältesten Bestand der Nuzi-Texte überhaupt. JEN 60 stammt zweifellos aus einer Phase der Besiedelungsgeschichte von Zizza, die den Aktivitäten des Teḫip-tilla S. Puḫi-šenni in dieser Stadt vorausging, und die prosopographisch durch ^{I}*Nu-i-še-ri* und ^{I}*A-ni-ta-i-il*, dem Eponym der teils Anitail, teils Anitani geschreibenen *dimtu* von Zizza, charakterisiert ist. Für letzteren Namen wurde anatolischer Ursprung angenommen (NPN 200b), seine kassitologische Überprüfung wäre jedoch dringend erwünscht. Auch JEN 69 scheint recht alt und unter die frühesten Teḫip-tilla-Urkunden einzuordnen zu sein: dafür spricht das Graphem Ì.LÁ.E (Z.10) und der Zeuge Sîn-napšir, Sohn des Schreibers Apil-Sîn, (Z.11). Der Schluss liegt nahe: Urkunden, die den Grundstückskauf beim Namen nennen, sind älter als die *ṭuppi mārūti*, die *šīmu* bzw. *irana* durch *qīštu* kaschieren. Die *ṭuppi mārūti* mit *qīštu* sind ein Produkt der ḫurritischen sozio-ökonomischen Systems, während die sich zum Immobilienkauf bekennenden Urkunden möglicherweise das kassitische System repräsentieren, das zwei Modi des Erwerbs von Besitztiteln an Grundstücken kannte, *kamma* und *irana*. Dabei erscheint es sogar möglich, dass das *kamma*-Modell die *qīštu*-Konstruktion beeinflusst hat.

Der Jubilar, zu dessen Ehrung ich die Veröffentlichung eines kleinen, aber wichtigen Dokuments beitragen möchte, möge einem *newcomer* nachsehen, dass er sich zu einem der Zentralprobleme der Nuzologie in unkonventionellen Gedankengängen äussert. Die Einzigartigkeit von IM 70764 bietet dazu jedoch hinreichend Anlass.

Addendum (D. I. Owen)

In view of the significance of the only other known reference to *irani* I am including, with the permission of Prof. Lacheman, a complete transliteration of HM 8400 which will appear as EN 9 122.

HM 8400 = EN 9, 122

1 *um-ma* ^{I}*Ik-ki-ri-ma*
2 DUMU *Šar-ru-ug-ge*
3 É$^{\text{ḪI.A}}$ *i+na i-ra-ni*
4 *a-bu-ja* ^{I}*Šar-ru-ug-ge*
5 *a-šar* ^{I}*Ar-te-ja* DUMU *Ta-ku-ur-ra-am*
6 *i+na* AN.ZA.KÀR *ša* ^{I}*Ta-kùr-ra-am*
7 *ša šu-pa-la il-te-qè*
8 *ù i-na-an-na a-na-ku*
9 *a+na be-li-šu-nu-*[*m*]*a a+na*
10 DUMU^{MEŠ} ^{I}*Ar-te-j*[*a u*]*n-te-eš-ši-ir*
11 A.ŠÀ *ša-šu-nu* [*at-t*]*a-din* (A.ŠÀ scribal error for É$^{\text{ḪI.A}}$)
12 *ù i+na ar-*[*ki* É^{ḪI}]$^{\text{.A}}$ *ša-šu-nu*
13 *ù-ul a-ša-a*[*s-sí*] *šum-ma*
14 *i+na ar-ki* DUMU[^{MEŠ} ^{I}*A*]*r-te-ja*
15 *aš-šum* É$^{\text{ḪI.A}}$ *an-*[*na*]*-ti*
16 *a-ša-as-sí* 1 MA.NA KÙ.BABBAR
17 1 MA.NA KÙ.GI *a+na* DUMU^{MEŠ}
18 ^{I}*Ar-te-ja ú-ma-al-la*
19 *a-na-an-din ù*
20 *ṭup-pu an-nu-um*
21 *ša a+na* É$^{\text{ḪI.A}}$ *an-na-ti*
22 *ša-aṭ-ru*
23 *ḫal-qa-at*
24 *šum-ma* ŠEŠ^{MEŠ}*-šu š*[*a*]
25 ^{I}*Ik-ki-ri i+na a*[*r-ki*]
26 É$^{\text{ḪI.A}}$ *i-ša-*[*as*]*-sú*
27 *ù pì-ḫa-*[*at* É]$^{\text{ḪI.A}}$
28 ^{I}*Ik-k*[*i-ri na*]*-ši*
29 IGI [ ]
30 DUMU [ ]
31 IGI [ ]
32 IGI [ ]
33 IGI [ ]
34 I[GI]x-*el-te-šup*
35 [*Ḫa*]*-ši-ge-mar*
36 [IGI $^{\text{(I)}}$*Tu-ra-ri*] DUB.SAR-*ri*
37 [NA$_4$] *Ip-ša-a*<+*a*>
38 NA$_4$ KIŠIB
39 ^{I}*Ip-ša-ḫa-lu*
40 NA$_4$ KIŠIB ^{I}*Ar-te-eš-še*

41 NA₄ KIŠIB ^I*Zi-il-te*
42 [N]A KIŠIB ^I*Tu-ra-ri* DUB.SAR

Postscriptum (A. Fadhil)

Den Herren Proff. Lacheman und Owen für ihre Liebenswürdigkeit dankend, erlaube ich mir, aus dem mitgeteilten Text zu folgern: er bestätigt sowohl die kassitische Etymologie von *irana* als auch den Bedeutungsansatz "Kauf, Kaufpreis."

HS 8400 kommt aus einem kassitischen Milieu; dies ergibt sich klar aus der Zusammengehörigkeit mit SMN 20 = HSS 13, 20. Darin übereignet Arteja S. Takurram ein (in Bauland umgewidmetes) Feld in der *dimtu ša* Ar-teja dem *Ša-ru-ug-ge* DUMU *Mi-li-sa-aḫ* und erhält dafür ein Rind als 'Geschenk' (*qí*^!*-il-ta*, Z.6). Der Grossvater des Ikkiri trägt also einen kassitischen Namen, Meli-Saḫ (s. K. Balkan, Kassitenstudien I, S. 70), Die *dimtu* Takurram (auch dieser Name dürfte kassitisch sein) liegt nach IM 6818:12 (E. R. Lacheman, Sumer 32, S. 133-34) im Gebiet der Städte Ansukalli, Unsuri, Matiḫa (und Akmašar), die (nach Ausweis der *šaṭir*-Formel von HSS 5, 69) in unmittelbarer Nähe der Kassitenstadt Temtenaš zu lokalisieren sind. Das Dossier der genannten Städte ist besonders reich an kassitischen Namen. HSS 13, 20 weist ferner in Z. 18 die Pönalklausel *ù sí-ik-ka-tu ša* URUDU *i+na pí-šu i-ma-ḫa-ṣú* auf, der M. Müller, WdO 9, S. 25-26 und AoF 6, S. 263-67 Studien gewidmet hat, dic auf drei mB Belegen aus Ur (UET 7, 21.22.25) und sieben Nuzi-Belegen (VS 1, 108.109; TCL 9, 14; JEN 79; HSS 13, 20.366; IM 70726) basieren. Letztere kann ich um zwei (IM 70731 und SMN 2647) vermehren. Von diesen neun Belegen stammen wenigstens sechs aus kassitischem Milieu (bei dreien, TCL 9, 14; JEN 79; IM 70726, ist es zumindest nicht auszuschliessen): VS 1, 108 und 109 gehören zum Archiv des Zilija S. Ipša-ḫalu, Dossier Apenaš; Ipša-ḫalu ist ein kassitischer Name (K. Balkan, S. 56). Von HSS 13, 20 war bereits oben die Rede. HSS 13, 366 ist (Z. 37-39) gesiegelt von den drei Brüdern Kilikše, Ar(iḫ)-ḫamanna und Šati-kintar, S.e Turi-kintar aus der Kassitenfamilie Kizzuk (vgl. den Beitrag von K. Deller und G. Dosch in diesem Band). Die Kenntnis des Belegs ^G[^IŠGAG URU]DU *a-na* K[A-*šú*] *i-ma-aḫ-ḫa-*⸢*ṣú*⸣ IM 70731:16 (TF₁ 113) verdanke ich wiederum der Freundlichkeit von Herrn Dr. Fārūq ar-Rāwī, seine Lesung Gudrun Dosch. Er stammt aus dem Testament des Šeršija S. Ašar[-ili^?], in welchem über Ländereien in Temtenaš verfügt wird. Der Beleg SMN 2647:27 (vgl. CAD M/I 76b) entstammt einem *ṭuppi tamgurti* zwischen Ḫampizi S. Ar-šatuja und Ḫurazzi S. Alkija, dessen Residenz die Stadt Dūr-zanzi ist und der HSS 13, 337 zusammen mit dem kassitischen Kaufmann Kuš-kipa erwähnt wird; der Name Ḫurazzi (S. Ennaja) begegnet häufig in kassitischem Kontext in den Dossiers Ansukalli und Matiḫa. Von den drei weniger gesicherten Texten scheint zumindest JEN 79 kassitischen Bezug zu haben, weil seine Zeugenliste u.a. den Namen des Kassiten *Tu-uš-ma-na* DUMU *Tu-ri-ki-tar*!, wiederum aus der Familie Kizzuk, enthält. [Korrekturzusatz: Zwei weitere Belege für die *sikkatu*- Klausel enthalten die von A. R. Millard in diesem Band veröffentlichten Urkunden BM 85311:13-14 und BM 85355:12-13, Archiv Zilija S.Ipša-ḫalu, Dossier Tarkulli].

YBC 5130:	*ù i+na-an-na*	9*a-na-ku* (Feld)	10*a-na be-li-šu-ma*	11*a-na* Adoptant	*um-te-eš-ši-ir-*⌜*mi*⌝
HM 8400:	*ù i-na-an-na*	*a-na-ku* (Häuser)	9*a+na be-li-šu-nu-*[*m*]*a*	*a+na* 10DUMUMEŠ des Adoptanten	[*u*]*n-te-eš-ši-ir*

Damit zeigt sich deutlich, dass die *mārūtu*-Transaktion mit *qīštu* und die *irana*-Transaktion dasselbe meinen, nämlich den Immobilienkauf. So bestätigt HM 8400:3, die oben entwickelte These, dass *irana* das kassitische Äquivalent von babylonisch *šīmu* ist.

Texts from Arrapḫa and from Nuzi in the Yale Babylonian Collection

In loving memory of
Ernest R. Lacheman, Jr.
February 28, 1938 - February 2, 1980

Ernest R. Lacheman
Wellesley, Massachusetts
and
David I. Owen
Cornell University, Ithaca, New York

The publication of the following group of texts from the Yale Babylonian Collection would not have been possible without the help and encouragement of our honored colleague and teacher, Professor Lacheman. For some years he had been preparing a substantial study of these texts and had accumulated numerous notes and references which were to form the basis of his publication. However, due to his preoccupation with the preparation of the publication of *EN* 9 and *JEN* 7 and with his recently completed *Personal Names from Arrapḫa* he turned over his copies and notes to me with the request that I prepare them for publication in a suitable format. It was my decision to include the texts in this volume both as an additional tribute to Professor Lacheman and to fulfill his wish that the publication of these important tablets not be delayed any longer.

Professor Deller and his staff at the University of Heidelberg facilitated the preparation of this publication by providing exhaustive indexes and by offering numerous important suggestions and references many of which have been incorporated into the comments and transliterations. During a brief visit to Heidelberg I had the opportunity to discuss these texts with Deller in greater detail and the results of these discussions have also been incorporated where possible.

The great importance of these texts to the Nuzi/Arrapḫa corpus in general and to the Wullu archive in particular is self evident. But the elaboration of these new materials will have to await another occasion. With the impending publication by Lacheman of the remaining Nuzi tablets in the Harvard Semitic Museum and in the Oriental Institute coupled with the promised publication of the related texts from Kurruḫanni, we appear to be entering a renaissance of Nuzi studies. It is our sincere hope that the publication in this jubilee volume of an important group of new texts from Arrapḫa, Kurruḫanni and Nuzi will represent the onset of this renewal.

CATALOGUE*

TEXT NUMBERS		DIMENSIONS (cms.)	TYPE OF TEXT
1	*YBC* 5141	6.3 × 10.3	*ṭuppi mārūti*
2	*YBC* 5138	6.6 × 5.9	*ṭuppi mārūti*
3	*YBC* 5143	5.6 × 7.5	receipt for purchase of slave
4	*YBC* 5131	5.9 × 6.7	*ṭuppi šupeʾulti*
5	*YBC* 5135	6.0 × 5.5	sale of wooden beams
6	*YBC* 5142	7.5 × 7.5	*ṭuppi šīmti*
7	*YBC* 5137	6.7 × 9.1	*lišānu*
8	*YBC* 9113	5.2 × 7.1	deposition
9	*YBC* 5139	8.5 × 6.8	inventory
10	*YBC* 5125	3.7 × 6.5	court case
11	*YBC* 5126	4.6 × 5.2	*ṭuppi tamgurti*
12	*YBC* 9112	6.8 × 7.1	*lišānu*
13	*YBC* 5132	4.8 × 5.2	receipt for animals
14	*YBC* 5127	4.8 × 4.1	deposition
15	*NCBT* 1933	5.5 × 8.4 (est.)	*ṭuppi mārūti*
16	*NCBT* 1934	6.9 × 10.7	*ṭuppi šupeʾulti*
17	*YBC* 5130	7.5 × 11.6	*ṭuppi tamgurti*
18	*YBC* 5136	5.7 × 5.6	*ṭuppi mārūti*
19	*YBC* 5133	5.8 × 6.7	*ṭuppi mārūti*
20	*YBC* 5140	6.5 × 8.6	*ṭuppi tidennūti*
21	*YBC* 5129	7.2 × 9.7	*ṭuppi tamgurti*
22	*YBC* 5134	5.5 × 4.9	*ṭuppi mārūti*
23	*YBC* 11275	3.8 × 2.6	*muddû*
24	*NBC* 6500	3.9 × 4.1	receipt for barley
25	*YBC* 5145	3.0 × 2.4	receipt for sheepskins
26	*YBC* 5128	5.4 × 4.5	*lišānu*
27	*YBC* 5144	3.4 × 6.9	legal text

* I would like to thank Prof. Gary Beckman of Yale University for clarifying a number of questions on the collection numbers and for providing the measurements of the tablets. The texts were acquired for the Yale Babylonian Collection by Prof. A. Clay.

CONCORDANCE

NBC 6500	No. 24
NCBT 1933	No. 15
NCBT 1934	No. 16
YBC 5125	No. 10
YBC 5126	No. 11
YBC 5127	No. 14
YBC 5128	No. 26
YBC 5129	No. 21
YBC 5130	No. 17
YBC 5131	No. 4
YBC 5132	No. 13
YBC 5133	No. 19
YBC 5134	No. 22
YBC 5135	No. 5
YBC 5136	No. 18
YBC 5137	No. 7
YBC 5138	No. 2
YBC 5139	No. 9
YBC 5140	No. 20
YBC 5141	No. 1
YBC 5142	No. 6
YBC 5143	No. 3
YBC 5144	No. 27
YBC 5145	No. 25
YBC 9112	No. 12
YBC 9113	No. 8
YBC 11275	No. 23

1 *YBC* 5141

obv. 1 *ṭup-pí ma-*⸢*ru*⸣*-ti ša*
2 ^{I}*Mu-uš-te-ja* DUMU ⸢*Ge-en*⸣*-né-en-na*
3 *ù* ^{I}*Wu-ul-lu* DUMU *Pu-ḫi-še-en-ni*
4 *la-lu-šu-nu it-ta-la-ak*[*-ku*?]
5 *a-na ma-ru-ti i-pu-*⸢*šu*⸣
6 *mi-nu-um-me-*⸢*e*⸣ [A.ŠÀ]^{MEŠ} *a-šar* AN.⸢ZA⸣.K[À]R *Ḫu-ul-ma-ti-ja*
7 EDIN-*ti* É^{ḪI}[$^{\text{.A}}$ *i+n*]*a lìb-bi*
8 ⸢*ša*⸣ ^{URU}⸢*Ar*⸣*-r*[*a-ap*]*-ḫe* GÌR-*šu ú-še-el-li a-na*
9 [^{I}*Wu-ul-lu*] *la-lu-šu i-din*
10 [*ù* ^{I}]*Wu-ul-lu* 47 MA.NA URUDU
11 [x ANŠE Š]E 2 UDU *a-na* NÌ.BA-*šu*
12 [*a-na*] ^{I}*Mu-uš-*⸢*te-ja i*⸣*-din*

13 [*um-m*]*a* ^{I}[*Mu-uš-te-j*]*a*-<*ma*>
14 [ ]x[ ]x *a-šar*
15 [*Šu-a-n*]*i* ⸢*ù*⸣⸢*a*⸣-*š*[*ar Še-eḫ-le-en-ni*]
16 [A.ŠÀ] *ṭe*$_4$-*eḫ-ḫe pá-i-*[*ḫu*]
17 [-*t*]*ar-ra ša* URU DINGIR[^{MEŠ}]
18 [*a-n*]*a* DUMU-*ja a-na* ^{I}*Ak-ku*-⸢*le-en-ni*⸣
19 ⸢*i*⸣-*din il-ka-šu ša*
20 [^{I}*M*]*u-uš-te-ja ù*
21 [^{I}*A*]*k-ku-le-en-ni na-š*[*i*]
l.e.22 [*ù* ^{I}*Wu*]-*ul-lu ul na-ši*
23 [*ma-an-n*]*u i*-BAL-*tu*
24 [1 MA.NA KÙ.BABB]AR 1 MA.NA KÙ.GI ⸢*ú*⸣-[*ma-al*]-*la*
rev.25 [*um-ma* ^{I}*M*]*u-uš-te-ja*-<*ma*>
26 [ ]x-*ja*^{MEŠ} A.ŠÀ *pá*-⸢*i*⸣-[*ḫu*]
27 [*a-šar Pa-a*]*k-ka-an-ti ù*
28 [ ]-*li-im* 2-*šu*
29 [^{I}*Ak-ku-le-e*]*n-ni it-ti*
30 [*a-ḫa-mi-iš i*]-*zu-zu*
31 [*ù* ^{I}*Mu-uš*]-*te-ja* KÙ.BABBAR
32 [*ma-la i+na ṭu*]*p-pí š*[*a*] *ša-aṭ*-[*ṭi*]-*ir*
33 [*il-t*]*e*-⸢*qú-ú*⸣ *ù* ^{I}*Wu*-⸢*ul*⸣-*lu*
34 [*a-n*]*a pa-ni* ^{LÚ}IGI-*šu qà-an-na-šu*
35 [*i*]*m-ta-šar*

---

36 [IGI *N*]*i-iḫ-ri-ja* DUMU *Ta-be-li*
37 [IGI *E*]*r-ra-zi* DUMU *En-na-a+a*
38 [IGI *Mil-ku-ja*] DUMU *A-ri-ma-at-ka*
39 [IGI *A-kap-dug-g*]*e* DUMU *It-ḫi-pu-gur*
40 [IG]I ⸢*Šur*⸣-*kum-a*-⸢*tal*⸣ DUMU *Ar-ta-še-en-ni*
41 IGI *Ar-téš-še* DU[MU] ⸢KI⸣.MIN
42 IGI *Ḫa-ši-ja* DUMU [*T*]*a-a+a*
43 ŠU ^{I}*E-ḫé-el-te-šup* ⸢DUB⸣.SAR
44 NA$_4$ ^{I}*Mil-ku-ja*
u.e.45 NA$_4$ *Ḫa-ši-ja*
le.e.46 [NA$_4$ $^{(I)}$*Er-r*]*a-zi*

Comments

Tablet of adoption wherein Muš-teja son of Kennenna adopts Wullu son of Puḫi-šenni. From the archive of Wullu son of Puḫi-šenni, dossier Arrapḫa, *dimtu* Ḫulmatija. To be compared with Jankowska 29. It is probably this adoption contract which established the relationship between the two families that later soured and resulted in the two court cases recorded in Gadd 28 and 35.

line 2. The name Kennenna/i should be added to both *NPN* and *AAN* 1. Read also in Gadd 38:22 *mu-uš-te-ja* DUMU *ge-*[*en-né-en-ni*] and Gadd 39:20 *mu-uš-te-ja* DUMU *ge-en-né*(over erasure)*-en-ni*, both restorations based on collations by Lacheman.

line 4. The phrase *lalûšunu ittalak* occurs here for the first time in a *ṭuppi mārūti* between men. It regularly occurs in *aḫātu*-marriage documents such as text 12:4 below. Cf. also *CAD* L 49 sub *lalû*. It appears to correspond to the phrase *ina migrātišu* (*JEN* 569:2) and *ina migrātišunu* (*JEN* 404:2) in earlier Nuzi texts. Cf. *CAD* M/2 48 sub *migru*. The restoration of [-ku] at the end of the verb is based on Lacheman's analysis of the phrase.

lines 6-8. The location of the properties corresponds to Jankowska 29:6-11.

line 9. Deller would restore here [^{I}*Wu-ul-lu ki-ma* ḪA].LA-<<LU>>-*šu i-din* but notes that the space appears to be too small to accommodate the seven signs. Furthermore since the *šēpu šūlû* clause is so far not attested in a *ṭuppi mārūti* there is no way of knowing if the *zittu* clause is to be expected here.

lines 13-17. Restorations based on the comparisons with Jankowska 29 by Deller.

line 27. Restoration based on the suggestion of Deller who compares this with Jankowska 12:3, *i+na Pa-ak-ka-ti.*

2 *YBC* 5138

obv.	1	*ṭup-pí ma-r*[*u-ti ša*]	
	2	^{I}*Ni-ir-bi-j*[*a* DUMU *Še-en-na-a+a*]	or ^{I}*Ni-ir-bi-j*[*a*]
	3	*ù ša* ^{I}*Pu-ḫi-š*[*e-en-ni* DUMU *Ú-zu-ge*]	or *ù ša* ^{I}*Pu-ḫi-š*[*e-en-ni*]
	4	2 ŠEŠ^{MEŠ} *an-nu-*⌜*tu*$_4$⌝? x[ ]	or 2 ŠEŠ^{MEŠ} *an-nu-tu*$_4$ DU[MU^{MEŠ} xxx]
	5	^{I}*Wu-ul-lu* DUMU *Pu-ḫi-*[*še-en-ni*]	
	6	*a-na ma-ru-ti i-pu-*[*u*]*s-s*[*ú-ma*]	
	7	*ù* AN.ZA.KÀR *i+na* AN.ZA.KÀR *š*[*a Uk-ni-ip-pa*]	
	8	*it-ti na-ak-ka-ti-šu* [*x i+na am-ma-ti*]	
	9	*li-wi-is-sú ša na-ak-k*[*a-ti*]	
	10	*ù bu-ur-tu*$_4$ *ki-ma* Ḫ[A.LA-*šu*]	
	11	*a-na* ^{I}*Wu-ul-lu it-ta-ad-*[*nu*]	
	12	*ù* ^{I}*Wu-ul-lu* 1 TÚG 4 *ku-*[*duk-tù*]	
	13	*i+na šu-qú-ul-ti* 1 GÚ.⌜È⌝ [x *ku-duk-tù*]	
	14	⌜*i+na*⌝ *šu-qú-ul-ti ù* 2 ANŠ[E]	
	15	[*ki-ma* ḪA.LA-*šu-nu a-na*]	
	16	[^{I}*Ni-ir-bi-ja ù a-na*]	
	17	[^{I}*Pu-ḫi-še-en-ni* ^{I}*Wu-ul-lu it-ta-din*]	

rest of obverse and beginning of reverse destroyed

18 IGI *M*[*il-k*]*u-ja* DUMU *A-ri-*[*ma-at-qa*]
19 IGI [*Er-r*]*a*$^{!}$*-zi* DUMU *En-na-*[*a+a*]
20 [IGI *Ar*]*-šu-li-ḫé*
21 [DUMU *Pu*]*-ja*
22 [IGI *Šur-k*]*um-a-tal* DUMU *Ar-t*[*a-še-en-ni*]
23 IGI *A-kap-dug-ge* DUMU *It-ḫi-i*[*p-ú-gur*]
24 LÚ^{MEŠ} *mu-še-el-wu ša* AN.ZA.K[ÀR *ša*]
25 A.ŠÀ *na-aq-qa-ti ša* A.ŠÀ *ḫa-*[*wa-al-ḫi*]
26 *ù ša bu-ur-ti ù na-*[*dì-na-nu ša*]
27 KÙ.BABBAR^{MEŠ}*-šu-nu-ma*
28 IGI *Ḫu-ti-ja* DUB.SAR DUMU ⌈d⌉[UTU-MA.AN.SUM]
29 NA$_4$ KIŠIB ^{I}*Er-*[*ra-zi*]
u.e.30 NA$_4$ KIŠIB ^{I}*Mil-ku-ja* NA$_4$ KIŠIB ^{I}*Ar-*[*šu-li-ḫé*]
31 NA$_4$ KIŠIB ^{I}*Šur-kum-a-t*[*al*]
le.e.32 NA$_4$ KIŠIB ^{I}*Ḫu-ti-ja* DUB.SAR

Comments

Tablet of adoption wherein Nirpija and Puḫi-šenni adopt Wullu son of Puḫi-šenni. From the Wullu archive, dossier Āl Ilāni. Two possible restorations for lines 2-4 are offered. The first was suggested by Deller, the second by Lacheman.

line 2. This restoration is based on *TCL* 9 44:1-2 where Wullu is adopted by Nirpija son of Šennaja alone. It is further supported by *YBC* 9113 where Šar-teja claims that Wullu had promised 1 TÚG *a-na ši-mi* ^{7}*a-na* A.ŠÀ^{MEŠ}. This may be the same 1 TÚG in line 12 of our text. This Šar-teja is probably the son of Nirpija to judge from Bachmann no. 2 (*ZA* 48 [1944] 172 2,2) and from Kelsey 89522 + *AO* 6029:2 edited elsewhere in this volume.

line 3. The restoration of the patronymic of Nirpija's companion (ŠEŠ) is only a suggestion based on the witness list of *TCL* 9 44:21 and 28 (courtesy of K. Deller).

line 4. Deller offers no restoration for this line. Lacheman's restoration appears to conform to the traces copied. However, the latter reading would exclude Deller's restorations of lines 2-3.

line 7. For the double meaning of AN.ZA.KÀR see *CAD* D 144 s.v. The restoration of the *dimtu* name follows a suggestion of K. Deller.

line 13. G. Wilhelm suggests we read here 1 ÍB.[LÁ^{MEŠ} (= *nēbeḫu*, "belt")].

lines 28, 32. Dr. Paola Negri Scafa has traced nineteen tablets written by Ḫutija s.Utu-mansum so far (*AASOR* 16 3, 6, 7, 8, 10; *HSS* 5 47; *HSS* 13 93 [= 14 2], 215, 325, 326, 430; *JEN* 140, 327, 347, 380, 622; *JENu* 485, 648; *TCL* 9 10); none of these belongs to Wullu's archive.

3 *YBC* 5143

obv. 1 30 SU KÙ.BABBAR^{MEŠ} *ša* ^{I}*Wu-ul-*[*lu* DUMU *Pu*]*-ḫi-*⌈*še-en*⌉*-ni*
2 *ù* ^{I}*El-ḫi-ip-til-la* DUMU ⌈*Ḫa-ši-pu*⌉*-gur* ^{LÚ}DAM.GÀR *il-te-qè*
3 *ù lu-ú ṣú-ḫa-ru ù lu-ú ṣú-ḫa-ar-tu*$_4$
4 2 *am-ma-ti ú-uṭ-ṭá ù* 4 *ú-ba-ni*
5 *i+na am-ma-at* ^{I}*Wu-ul-lu ù*
6 ^{I}*El-ḫi-ip-til-la i+na ga-ma-ar* ITU-*ḫi Ge-nu-ni*
7 *a-na* ^{I}*Wu-ul-lu i+na-an-din*

8 IGI *Ar-šu-li-ḫé* DUMU *Pu-ú-ja*
9 IGI *Ú-ba-a+a* DUMU *En-te-ja*
10 IGI *A-ki-i-we* DUMU *Šu-ri*
11 IGI *Ge-el-še-er-wi ša* NIN.DINGIR.RA
12 IGI *Še-en-na-a+a* DUMU *Pu-ḫi-še-en-ni*
13 IGI *Ku-un-ni-ja* DUMU *Ḫa-ši-ja*
14 IGI *El-ḫi-ip-til-la* DUB.SAR
15 NA$_4$ KIŠIB ^{I}*Ar-šu-li-ḫé*
l.e.16 NA$_4$ KIŠIB ^{I}*A-ki-i-we*
rev.17 NA$_4$ KIŠIB ^{I}*Ú-ba-a+a*
18 NA$_4$ KIŠIB ^{I}*Ge-el-še-er-wi*
19 NA$_4$ KIŠIB ^{I}*Ku-un-ni-ja*
20 NA$_4$ KIŠIB ^{I}*Še-en-na-a+a*
21 NA$_4$ KIŠIB ^{I}*El-ḫi-ip-til-la* ^{LÚ}DAM.<GÀR>
le.e.22 NA$_4$ KIŠIB ^{I}*El-ḫi-ip-til-la* DUB.SAR

Comments

Receipt of thirty shekels of silver belonging to Wullu son of Puḫi-šenni by Elḫip-tilla son of Ḫašip-ukur. The latter agreed to deliver either a male or a female slave at least two and one half forearms (=cubit) and four fingers tall, according to the forearm (=cubit) of Wullu. Elḫip-tilla agreed to deliver the slave by the end of the month of Kinuni.

line 4. *Ú-uṭ-ṭá* is presumed to be an unconventional spelling for *ūṭu*, "half cubit" (*AHw* 1447 s.v.).

line 5. The phrase, *ina ammat* PN, does not occur elsewhere in the Nuzi texts. It is interesting to note that Wullu insists that the "cubit" be according to his own forearm. Does this imply that there was no "official" standard in effect at Nuzi?

line 11. For NIN.DINGIR.RA cf. the study of Deller and Fadhil, *Mesopotamia* 7(1972), 193-213.

line 14, 22. The scribe who wrote this text is probably Elḫip-tilla son of Wurru-kunni who is known from a number of texts from Āl Ilāni (*HSS* 9 15;

13 114; 14 568; Gadd 22 and 30). He is to be distinguished from Elḫip-tilla son of Kel-tešup known from Unapšewe (references courtesy of K. Deller).

4 *YBC* 5131

obv. destroyed. Preserved signs from rev.

1′ [AN.ZA.KÀR (*ša*) *Uk-n*]*i-ip-pa*
2′ [*i-na Za-ta-ru-u*]*š-še*
3′ [G]U$_4^{\text{MEŠ}}$
4′ [*šum-ma* A.ŠÀ *ša ma-an-ni*]*-im-mé-e*

gap of undetermined length

l.e. 1 IGI x[ ]
2 IGI *Er-*⌈*ra-zi* DUMU⌉ *En-na-a+a*
rev. 3 IGI *It-ḫi-ge-wa-ar* DUMU *En-na-a*[*a+a*]
4 IGI $^{\text{d(upon erasure)}}$UTU-NI(upon erasure).DU DUB.SAR-*rù*
5 *an-nu-ú* LÚ^{MEŠ} *mu-šel*$_4$*-wu-ú š*[*a* A.ŠÀ]
6 *na-dì*$^{!}$*-na-nu ša* KÙ.BABBAR<M>EŠ
7 *qa-an-na-šu* ^{I}*Wu-ul-lu im-ta-*⌈*šar*⌉
8 NA$_4$ ^{I}⌈*Er*⌉*-ra-z*[*i*]
9 NA$_4$ ^{I}*Šur-kum-a-tal*
10 NA$_4$ ^{I}*Ar-šá-li-ḫe*
11 NA$_4$ ^{I}*Mil-ku-ja*
12 ⌈NA$_4$ ^{I}*Ni*⌉*-ir-bi-*[*ja*]
rest of reverse destroyed

Comments

Only reverse of the tablet is preserved. But from the overrun of some of the lines from the obverse onto the reverse it was possible to establish the nature of the text (so according to Deller who provided the restorations). The text is a *ṭuppi šupeʾulti* from the archive of Wullu son of Puḫi-šenni, dossier Āl Ilāni, *dimtu* (*ša*) Ukinippa. The text should be compared to Gadd 38 where our obv. 1′ corresponds to Gadd 38:6; obv. 2′ to Gadd 38:8; obv. 3′ to Gadd 38:11; obv. 4′ to Gadd 38:13. Zatarušše also occurs in Gadd 29:22,27,32 (references courtesy of Deller).

On the basis of our witness list Gadd 38:21 should be emended to read IGI *it-ḫi-ge-wa-*<*ar*>$^{!}$ DUMU *En-*[*na+a*]; the restoration DUMU *En-na-*[*a+a*] in line 3 of *YBC* 5131 is likely since he follows *Er-ra-zi* DUMU *En-na-a+a*.

line 4. The scribe ^{d}UTU-NI.DU is otherwise known only from Gadd 38. The reading of his name as ^{d}*Šamaš-ukîn* (*NPN* 124) is hardly certain.

line 9. Son of Arta-šenni.

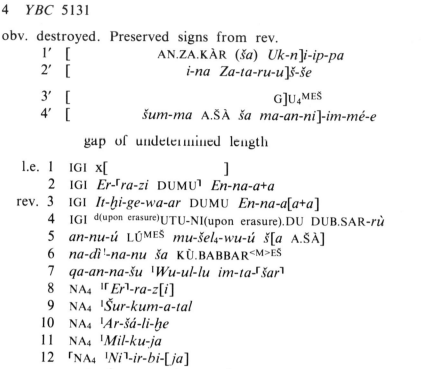

line 10. Son of Puja. The spelling of his name with *šá* rather than *šu* is an idiosyncracy of the scribe ^{d}UTU-NI.DU and occurs also in Gadd 38:23 and 26 (courtesy of K. Deller).

line 11. Son of Arim-matka.

line 12. Son of Šennaja. That Nirpija is the son of Šennaja is clear from his *ṭuppi mārūti*, *TCL* 9 44.

5 *YBC* 5135

obv.	beginning of obverse destroyed
1	[^{I}]⸢*Wu-ul-lu*⸣ [ ]
2	6 ⸢MA⸣.NA 100 SÍG^{MEŠ}
3	*ú* 20 MA.NA URUDU^{MEŠ}
4	*a-na ši-im* GIŠ.ÙR^{MEŠ}
5	*a-na* ^{I}*Ḫa-ma-an-na* SUM
6	[*m*]*i-nu-um-me-e* ^{GIŠ}ÙR$^{\text{!?MEŠ}}$
7	[*ri-ḫu-t*]*i*$^{?}$ *ša i+na qa-aq-qa-*⸢*ri*⸣
8	[*ú-mé-eš-ši*$^{?}$]*-ru*
9	[ ]x *la ša-aṭ-ru*
10	[ ]x
l.e.11	[ ]x
rev.12	[ ]x
13	[ ]x-ma
14	[^{I}]*Wu-ul-lu*
15	[*i-l*]*eq-qè-šu-nu*
16	[IGI *Er-ra-zi* DUMU] *E-en-na-a+a*
17	[IGI *Mil-ku-ja* DUMU *A*]*-ri-im-ma-at-qa*
18	[IGI *Q*]*a-bi-in-ni* or: *Ar-q*]*a-bi-in-ni*
19	[IGI *Ar-šu-li-ḫé* DUMU *Pu*]-⸢*ú*⸣*-a*
20	[IGI *A-kap-dug-ge* DUMU *It-ḫ*]*i-pu-gur*
21	[ ]x
	rest of reverse destroyed

Comments

Fragment of a text concerning the purchase of wooden beams for wool and copper. From the Wullu archive.

line 2. Deller notes that the numerical notation 6 MA.NA 60+40 SÍG^{MEŠ} may indicate that there was a "heavier" mina used for wool than for metals. However, further study of the problem is required before any firm conclusions can be suggested.

lines 7-8. The restorations here are based on a suggestion by Deller.

6 *YBC* 5142

obv. 1 [ṭup-pí ši-im-ti ša]
2 [^{I}Pu-i-ta]-⸢e⸣ D[UMU] W[u-ul-lu]
3 [a]-na ^{MÍ}Wa-ti-la a-na ^{MÍ}[ ]
4 a-na ^{MÍ}Ú-ri-še-el-li
5 ù a-na ^{MÍ}Aš-te DUMU.MÍ x y z[ ]
6 ši-im-ta i-ši-im ⸢um-ma⸣
7 ^{I}Pu-i-ta-e-ma 3 [DUMU.MÍ^{MEŠ}-ja]
8 an-ni-tu_4 a-na ma-ru-t[i i-te-pu-u]š$^{?}$-šu
9 mi-nu-um-me-e A.ŠÀ^{MEŠ}-j[a É^{MEŠ}-ja]
10 mi-im-mu šu-un$^{\check{s}um}$-su-j[a]
11 a-na DUMU.MÍ^{MEŠ}-ja an-ni-tu_4 a[d-din]
12 um-ma ^{I}Pu-i-ta-e-ma
13 A.ŠÀ^{MEŠ} É^{MEŠ} ša ^{I}Šúk-ri-t[e-šup]
14 ša iš-tu É.GAL-lì ša a-n[a]
15 ša SUM-nu m[a-a]n-nu-um-me-⸢e⸣
16 i+na lìb-b[i]
17 ša x[ ]
rest of obverse destroyed
rev. beginning of reverse destroyed
18 x (x)[ ]
19 ú-u[ṣ-ṣí]
20 i+na lìb-b[i]
21 30 SU KÙ.BABBAR a-na ^{MÍ}Aš-t[e]
22 ma-an-nu-um-me-e i+na DUMU.MÍ[^{MEŠ}-ja]
23 i+na É-ja aš-bu ù a-na DU[MU.MÍ]
24 ^{MÍ}Aš-te i+na-an-din
25 NA_4 ^{I}Tar-mi-j[a]
26 um-ma ^{I}Pu-i-ta-e-ma šum-ma
27 [^{M}]^{Í}Aš-te im-tù-ut ù ma-an-nu-[um-me-e]
28 ⸢i+⸣na DUMU.MÍ^{MEŠ}-ja A.ŠÀ^{MEŠ} É^{MEŠ}-⸢ja⸣
29 ⸢ú⸣-ka_4-al-lu i+na É-ja aš-⸢bu⸣
30 [DIN]GIR^{MEŠ} ù e-$ṭe_4$-em-mì-ja
31 ⸢i⸣-pal-la-aḫ-šu ù
32 [m]i-nu-um-me-e A.ŠÀ^{MEŠ}-ja
33 [É]^{MEŠ}-ja ka_4-lu-ma-ni-ja
34 [ ]x x x[ ]
rest of reverse destroyed
le.e.35 [NA_4 ^{I}Ša]-ar-te-š[up] NA_4 ^{I}Ar-[ ]
36 [ ] DUMU Še-⸢ḫé⸣-el-te-š[up]
37 [r]i [N]A_4 x[ ]
38 [ ]-ge NA_4 ^{I}[DU]MU Ḫa-ši-til-la

Comments

This is almost certainly the will of Pui-tae son of W[ullu] in which he leaves his estate to his three daughters who are "adopted" as sons and to Ašte daughter of [PN], who may have been his wife (so Lacheman) or his niece (so Deller). Crucial for the understanding of the text are the restorations of the lines 1-5, 14 and 23 which have not been attempted here in view of the numerous implications and justifications required. It is clear than when this will was written Pui-tae did not have any male heirs. As a result his three daughters were given the status of male heirs by being "adopted" as sons. Ašte (wife or niece) retains the control of the fields and houses (some of which were given to Pui-tae by the palace) while she lives in his house. Furthermore, the will stipulates that after Ašte's death, "whoever among my daughters holds my fields and houses will revere my (household) gods and my spirits." This is the only case at Nuzi where the household gods are willed to women and this will obviously be associated with the Jacob and Laban story in Genesis 31.

7 *YBC* 5137

obv. 1 [E]ME-*an-šu ša* ^{I}*En-na-ma-*⸢*ti*⸣
2 [DUMU] *Ša-ar-te-a a-na pa-ni ši-bu-ti*^{MEŠ}
3 ⸢*ki*⸣*-am iq-ta-bi* 1 ANŠE A.ŠÀ *ma-a+a-ru na-ás-qú*
4 [*i+*]*na* AN.ZA.KÀR *ša Uk-ni-ib-ba-we*
5 ⸢*i+*⸣*na il-ta-an* A.ŠÀ *ša* ^{I}*Wa-an-ti-iš-še-en-ni*
6 *i+na šu-pa-al* A.ŠÀ *ša* ^{I}*A-pu-uš-qa*
7 [*ù*] *i+na e-le-en* A.ŠÀ *ša* ^{I}*Qa-ni*
8 [1 ANŠE] A.ŠÀ *an-nu-ú i+na* 2 ANŠE A.ŠÀ *i+na* 1 *aš-li*
9 [*a*]*-n*[*a-ku ak-k*]*i-is ù a-na ti-de-en-nu-ti*
10 *a-na* ^{I}[*Pu*]-⸢*i*⸣*-ta-e* DUMU *Wu-ul-lu*
11 ⸢*at*⸣*-t*[*a-din*] ⸢*ù*⸣ *a-na-ku* 8 MA.NA AN.NA
12 ⸢*a*⸣*-šar* [^{I}*Pu-i-t*]*a-e a-na ti-de-en-nu-ti-ma*
13 [*e*]*l-t*[*e-qè ù* ^{I}]⸢*Pu*⸣*-i-ta-e*
14 SAG.⸢DU-*sú*⸣ [*ša* A].ŠÀ *šá-a-šu*
15 *ú-gal-l*[*a-ma e-nu-ma* ^{I}*En-na*]-⸢*ma-ti*⸣
16 ⸢8⸣ MA.NA[AN.NA *a-na* ^{I}*Pu-i-t*]*a-e*
l.e.17 [*i-na-an-din ù* A.ŠÀ-*šu a-šar*]
[???????]
18 ^{I}*Pu-*⸢*i*⸣-[*ta-*]⸢*e*⸣ *i-leq-q*[*è*]
rev.19 [*šum*]*-ma* A.ŠÀ *ub-*[*t*]*a-qar*
20 [^{I}]*En-na-ma-*⸢*ti*⸣*-ma*
21 *ú-za-ak-ka*$_4$ ⸢*a*⸣-[*n*]*a* ^{I}*Pu-i-ta-*⸢*e*⸣
22 *i+na-an-din ṭ*[*up*]*-pu i+na* EGIR *šu-du-ti*
23 *eš-ši ša* É.[GA]L *in* URU DINGIR^{MEŠ} *a-šar*

24 KÁ.GAL *sa-[a]ṭ-rat*
25 ⸢IGI⸣ [^{I}*W*]*a-an-ti-iš-še-en-ni* DUMU *Ḫa-ši-ip-til-la*
26 [IGI ^{I}]*Ši-mi-qa-tal* DUMU *Ar-ša-du-ú-ja*
27 IGI ^{I}*Ša-la-ap-ur-ḫé* DUMU *Zi-li-ja*
28 IGI ^{I}*Ši-qa-ar-til-la* DUMU *Nu-ul-lu*
29 IGI ^{I}*Wu-ur-te-šup* DUMU *A-ki-ja*
30 ŠU ^{I}ÌR-*Še-ru-ja* DUB.SAR
31 NA$_4$ ^{I}DUB.SAR-*ri*
u.e.32 [N]A$_4$ ^{I}⸢*Ši-mi-qa-tal*⸣ NA$_4$ ^{I}*Wa-an-ti-še-en-ni*
le.e.33 [NA$_4$ ^{I}*En-n*]*a-ma-ti* NA$_4$ ^{I}*Wu*!-*u*[*r-te-šup*] NA$_4$ ^{I}*Ša-la-ap-u*[*r-ḫé*]

Comments

Declaration before witnesses by Enna-mati son of Šar-teja concerning one homer of plowed and irrigated field in the *dimtu* of Uknippawe given as *tidennūtu* to Pui-tae son of Wullu who deposited eight minas of tin as security. When Enna-mati returns the tin to Pui-tae he will get the field back. This text is from the dossier of Pui-tae son of Wullu in the city Āl Ilāni. Although the debtor is not otherwise attested Deller has noted that his father, Šar-teja son of Šeḫel-tešup, owned a field in the same *dimtu* (Gadd 47:3-10).

line 3. *Eqlu nasqu* does not occur elsewhere in Nuzi texts. But following *AHw* 754 it would mean "ausgesuchtes Feld." H. Waetzoldt, with whom Deller had discussed this text, suggests we read here *na-áš-qu*, (*našqû*) "irrigated," which we have followed here.

lines 14-15. For the phrase *qaqqad eqli gullubu* see *CAD* G 131 and K. Deller *Or* NS 27 (1958) 208. It would appear that the obligation "to shave the field" rested upon the creditor. The restoration in line 15 could also be *ú-gal-l*[*a-ab*.

8 *YBC* 9113

obv. 1 ^{I}*A-qa-wa-til* DUMU *Wu-ul-lu*
2 *ṭup-pu ša a-na* ^{I}*Wu-ul-lu*
3 *a-na ma-ru-ti i-ip-pu-šu*
4 *uš-te-li ù il-ta-sí*
5 *um-ma* ^{I}*Ša-ar-te-ja-ma*
6 ^{I}*Wu-ul-lu* 1 TÚG *a-na ši-mi*
7 *a-na* A.ŠÀ^{MEŠ} *a-na na-dá-ni*
8 *iq-ta-bi ù la i+na-an-din*
9 IGI *A-ú-ur-na-ḫu* DUMU *Ar-tèš-še*
10 IGI *Ik-ki-ja* DUMU *Ku-um-pu-uz-zu*
11 IGI *Mu-ut-ta* DUMU *Ge-li-ja*
12 IGI *Tar-mi-ja* DUMU *Na-ni-ja*
13 IGI *Pu-ḫi-še-en-ni* DUMU *A-ki-ja*
14 IGI *Eḫ-li-te-šup*

15 DUMU *Zi-ki-in-ta*
l.e.16 IGI *Tar-mi-te-šup*
17 DUMU *Wa-aḫ-ri-še-en-ni*
rev.18 IGI *A-ki-ja* DUMU MU-*líb-ši*
19 DUB.SAR-*rù*
20 IGI *A-kap-dug-ge* DUMU *A-kip-še-en-ni*
21 NA$_4$ KIŠIB ^{I}*Ik-ki-ja*
22 NA$_4$ KIŠIB ^{I}*Mu-ut-ta*
23 NA$_4$ ^{I}*Pu-ḫi-še-en-ni*
24 NA$_4$ ^{I}*Tar-mi-ja*
u.e.25 NA$_4$ KIŠIB ^{I}*Eḫ-li-te-šup*
le.e.26 NA$_4$ KIŠIB ^{I}*A-ú-ur-na-ḫu* NA$_4$ ^{I}*Tar-mi-te-šup*

Comments

Deposition from court proceedings of Akawatil son of Wullu versus Šar-teja (son of Nirpija, see comments to no. 2 above). Šar-teja appears to have maintained control over the fields that his father had ceded to Wullu claiming that Wullu had failed to hand over the full *qīštu*, the outstanding portion being one garment.

lines 9-20. Out of the eight witnesses listed here only one is attested elsewhere. Mutta son of Kelija occurs in *HSS* 19 61:27 where he is associated with Arrapḫa.

line 18. According to Dr. Paola Negri Scafa the scribe Akija son of Šumu-libši writes exclusively for Wullu, his four sons and his grandson Wantiš-šenni son of Ḫašip-tilla. She notes nine tablets written by him: Gadd 7, 15, 46, 48, 49; Jankowska 49 and 51; Kelsey 89522 + *AO* 6029 (=*TCL* 9 12); *TCL* 9 19.

9 *YBC* 5139

obv. 1 26 ^{GI}[G]AG.Ú.TAG.GA URUDU^{MEŠ}
2 ⌈2⌉^{KUŠ}*iš-pa-tù*^{MEŠ} *la-bi-ru-ti*
3 [x+]2 *né-en-*⌈*sé*⌉*-tù ša* UD.KA.BAR 1 ^{GIŠ}GAG *ša* URUDU
4 [1] *mu-še-lu-*⌈*ú*⌉ *ša* UD.KA.BAR 1 *a-pí-il-lu ša* ⌈UD⌉.KA.BAR
5 1 KUŠ.SÍG.NÁ.⌈A⌉ 3 ^{GIŠ}BANŠUR$_x$^{MEŠ} (wr. URUDU.DUB) 8 *ta-pa-lu* ^{GIŠ}NÁ^{MEŠ}
6 23 ^{GIŠ}GU.ZA^{MEŠ} 4 *nu-ša-bu* 1 *ka*$_4$*-sú ša* UD.KA.BAR
7 2 ^{GIŠ}BÁN^{MEŠ} 1 *sú-us-sú-lu*
8 1-*en-nu-tu*$_4$ ^{GIŠ}*a-sú-ú*^{MEŠ} 3 *ta-pa-lu* ^{GIŠ}*ma-mu-ul-lu*^{MEŠ}
9 2 $^{KUŠ!}$*gu*$_5$*-sà-an-na-tù re-qú-tù*^{MEŠ}
10 2 *ta-pa-lu* T[A]L *ša ṭá-ab-ti*^{MEŠ}
11 1 GÉME 1 ÌR 1 GU$_4$ 1 ANŠE 1-*nu-tu*$_4$ ^{GIŠ}MAR.GÍD.DA
12 1$^{!}$(text 2)-*nu-tu*$_4$ ^{GIŠ}*za-wa-ar-ru ša*
l.e.13 *ma-gàr-ra i-šu*

14 1-*nu-tu*$_4$ *za-wa-ar-ru*
15 *ša ma-gàr-ra la-i-šu*
rev. 16 2 $^{\text{NA}_4}$ḪAR^{MEŠ} *qa-du na-ar-ka*$_4$*-bi-šu-nu*
17 2 ^{GIŠ}*né-pé-tù*^{MEŠ} 2 ^{GIŠ}*ma-ḫal-tù*^{MEŠ}
18 1-*nu-tu*$_4$ *še-qa-ru-uḫ-ḫu ša* URUDU
19 5 ^{GIŠ}⸢ÁLAL⸣^{MEŠ} 1 *ša-a-šu ša* URUDU
20 1 ^{GIŠ}*ta-ku-l*[*a-a*]*t-ḫu* 6 KUŠ *ša en-zi*^{MEŠ}
21 2 *nam-za-qú ša* UD.KA.BAR
22 4 ^{GIŠ}*sú-us-*⸢*sú*⸣*-ul-ku*^{MEŠ} 1 $^{\text{⸢KUŠ⸣?}}$*mu-ur-ru-uš-ḫu re-qú*
23 1 Ì.DUB [*š*]*a* Ì.ŠAḪ^{MEŠ} 2 ⸢*ta*⸣*-pa-lu*
ú-nu-tù ša URUDU^{MEŠ}
24 *an-nu-tù ša* ^{I}*A-qa-wa-til*$^{!}$
25 *ša* ^{I}*Šúk-*⸢*ri-te*⸣*-šup il-ṭù-ru*
26 *a-na* ^{M}[^{Í} -*š*]*e-*⸢*en-na*⸣*-a+a na-ad-nu*
27 *ù a-na* ^{I}*Šúk-*⸢*ri-te*⸣*-šup*
u.e. 28 *ú-ta-ar*
29 *an-nu-tù* [*ú-n*]*u-tù ša* É-*šu*
30 *š*[*a* ^{I}]⸢*A*⸣*-qa-wa-til*

Comments

Inventory of items belonging to Akawatil and Šukri-tešup (sons of Wullu son of Puḫi-šenni) given to a woman whose name ends in -ennaja (line 26). Only one woman whose name ends this way is known from the Wullu archive, ^{f}Teššennaja, but we cannot be certain her name is to be restored here. A similar inventory occurs in *TCL* 9 1. Other lists of household items and tools are also found in the archives of Šilwa-tešup (see Lacheman, apud Starr *Nuzi* I 528ff.). The purpose of this inventory is not clear. This text contains a number of rare lexical entries.

line 3. *Nensētu*, "washbowl," cf. *AHw* 777 s.v. *nemsētu.*

line 4. *Apellu*, "arrowhead," cf. *CAD* A/2 169 s.v. *Mušelû*, "plow," cf. *CAD* M/2 264 s.v.

line 5. KUŠ.SÍG.NÁ.A may be a fleece bed cover.

line 6. *Nušābu*, "cover," cf. *AHw* 806 s.v.

line 8. ^{GIŠ}*asû*, "part of a loom," cf. *CAD* A/2 347. ^{GIŠ}*mamullu* is probably to be equated with ^{GIŠ}*namullu*, *AHw* 730 s.v. Its exact meaning is not known.

line 9. $^{\text{KUŠ!}}$*gusannātu*, "a leather bag and cover," cf. *CAD* G 142 s.v. *gasānu*. The entry here seems to mean 2 empty covered leather bags.

line 10. The reading TAL has been suggested by G. Dosch. The entry would mean something like "two pair of TAL-containers for salt."

line 12. ^{GIŠ}*zawarru*, "a kind of sledge/wagon that comes with or without wheels," is a hapax. Lacheman suggests that this might be a Hurrian equivalent for *narkabtu*.

line 16. $^{\text{NA}_4}$ḪAR^{MEŠ} *qadu narkabišunu*, "Millstones with their upper stones (literally, their riders)," cf. *AHw* 747 s.v. *narkabu*.

line 17. ^{GIŠ}*nēpētu*, "kneading trough(?)," cf. *AHw* 779 s.v. *nēpītu*. The meaning suggested by von Soden may be supported by the word's occurrence here between millstones and sieves, ^{GIŠ}*maḫḫaltu* for which cf. *CAD* M/1 89 s.v.

line 18. *Šekaruḫḫu*, "an implement or vessel (of copper)," cf. *AHw* 1210 s.v.

line 19. *Šāšu*, "an implement (of copper)," cf. *AHw* 1198 s.v.

line 20. *Takulatḫu*, "an implement (of wood or metal)," Hurrian loanword, cf. *AHw* 1309 s.v.

line 21. *Namzāqu*, "a key (of bronze)," cf. *AHw* 730 s.v.

line 22. ^{GIŠ}*sussulku*, "a wooden implement." Von Soden associates this word with *sussulu*. However, the latter occurs above in line 7. Thus they must be considered separate words. *Murrušḫu* does not occur elsewhere and is probably a Hurrian word.

10 *YBC* 5125

obv. beginning of obverse destroyed

1 [ ]x x[ ]
2 ⸢*e*⸣-*te-né-er*-[*ri-iš*]
3 *ù um-ma* ^{I}*A*-[*kap-dug-ge-ma*]
4 *a-šar* ^{I}*Pu-i-t*[*a-e*]
5 *e-te-né-er*-[*ri-iš*]
6 *ù a-na-ku* ⸢*i*⸣-[*na-an-na*]
7 1 *né-en-s*[*í-tù* 1-*nu-tù*]
8 *ḫul-la-an*-[*nu el-te-qè-mi*]
9 *ù* DI.KU$_5$[^{MEŠ} *a-na* ^{I}*A-kap-dug-ge iq-ta-bu-ú*]
10 *ši-bu-ti-k*[*a i-bá-aš-ši-mi*]
11 *ù bi*-⸢*lam*⸣-[*mi*]
12 [^{I}]x-*zu*-x[ ]
13 [^{I}]x-*te*-[ ]
l.e. 14 [ ]x *i-n*[*a pa-ni* DI.KU$_5$^{MEŠ}]
15 [^{I}*A*]-*kap*-[*dug-ge im-ta-nu*]
16 [*iq-ta*]-*bu-mi*
17 [ ] *ú-ub*-[*ba-lu-mi*]
rev. 18 ⸢*ù*⸣ DI.KU$_5$[^{MEŠ}]
19 [*ki*]-⸢*i*⸣ EME-*š*[*u ša* ^{I}]
20 [ ] *a-na ši-b*[*u-ti*]
21 [*ù š*]*i-bu-t*[*i*]
22 [*š*]*a-nu-t*[*i*]
23 [*a-na p*]*a-ni* D[I.KU$_5$^{MEŠ}]

24 [ ]x x[ ]
rest of reverse destroyed

Comments

Fragment of a lawsuit from the lower half of a badly broken tablet. The names of the contesting parties are only partially preserved and the restorations are tentative. Pui-tae is probably the son of Wullu and Akkap-tukke is probably the son of Itḫip-ukur, a late contemporary of Wullu. Restorations based mostly on suggestions by Lacheman.

11 *YBC* 5126

obv. beginning of obverse destroyed
1 [ ]x x[ ]
2 [*mi-nu-um*]-*me-e* ⌜É⌝Ḫ[I.A]
3 [A.ŠÀ^{M}]^{EŠ} ^{I}*En-ša-ku*
4 [*ša*] ⌜*ú*⌝-*mé-eš-ši-ru*
5 [*ù*] *i+na-an-na it-ti*
6 [^{I}*Še-g*]*a-ar-til-la*
7 [*i-z*]*u-uz-zu*
8 [ ]x *ri-ik-sú*
9 [*ša ir-k*]*u-sú-ù*
10 [*ṭup-pu la-b*]*i-ru iḫ-te-pé*
11 [ ]x x[ ]
rest of obverse destroyed
rev. reverse entirely destroyed except for one line on
le.e. 12 [N]A$_4$ ^{I}*Še-eš-w*[*i-qa*]

Comments

Fragment of a *tamgurtu* document. Both Šekar-tilla (son of Wanti-muša) and En-šaku (son of Nuzza) are known respectively from the Yale and from the Gadd tablets.

line 10. Deller remarks that one might also restore here [*ṭup-pu ša-n*]*u-ú*. The traces are ambiguous.

line 12. One might also read here [N]A$_4$ ^{I}*Še-eš-w*[*e*].

12 *NBC* 9112

obv. 1 EME-*šu ša* ^{MÍ}*Ḫi-in-zu-ri* DUMU.MÍ *Qa-qa-az-zu*
2 *a-na pa-ni ši-bu-ti iq-ta-bi*
3 ^{I}*Wa-an-ti-iš-še-en-ni* DUMU *Ḫa-ši-ip-til-la*
4 *i+na sú-qí la-lu-šu at-tal-ka$_4$-aš-šu*
5 *a-na a-ḫa-tù-ti a-na ja-ši e-*[*pu-u*]*š*
6 *ù im-ma-ti-me-e a-na* [LÚ *ša* KUR *Ar-ra-ap-ḫe*]

7 *a-na aš-šu-ti i+na-an-din-*[*an-ni*]
8 ^{I}*Wa-an-ti-iš-še-en-*⸢*ni*⸣ [ ]
9 1 GU$_4$.MÍ SIG$_5$.GA *na-*[*ás-qú*]
10 *a-šar* ^{LÚ}*mu-ti-j*[*a šu-ra-am-ba-aš-ḫe*(*-šu*)]
11 *i-leq-qè ù šu*[*m-ma* ^{I}*Wa-an-ti-iš-še-en-ni*]
12 *a-na aš-šu-ti l*[*a i+na-an-din-an-ni*]
13 *i+na* É*-šu a-*[*di ba-al-ṭá-at*]
14 *aš-b*[*u*]
15 x[ ]
rest of obverse destroyed
rev. beginning of reverse destroyed
16 N[A$_4$]
17 NA$_4$ *I-ši-*⸢*ip*⸣*-*[*ḫa-lu*]
18 NA$_4$ *Ar-ta-ḫu-bi*
19 NA$_4$ ÌR-^{d}AMAR.UTU DUB.SAR-*rù*
20 NA$_4$ *Ḫi-in-zu-ri*
le.e.21 NA$_4$ *Te-ḫu-up-še-en-ni*

Comments

Declaration of Ḫinzuri daughter of Kakkazzu before witnesses concerning the fact that she had accepted the attentions of Wantiš-šenni "in the street" and he had adopted her as his sister. Whenever he arranges for her marriage to a man from the land of Arrapḫa she agrees to give him one fine cow. However, should he not marry her off she will continue to dwell in his house. The text is similar to Gadd 31 and to *HSS* 5 26. Wantiš-šenni was the grandson of Wullu.

line 17. The restoration is based on [IGI ^{I}*I*]*-ši-ip-ḫa-lu* DUMU *Ip-šá-a*[*+a*] in *TCL* 9 16:35 from the archive of Wantiš-šenni son of Ḫašip-tilla (courtesy K. Deller).

line 19. This is the first tablet known to be written by the scribe Warad-Marduk.

13 *YBC* 5132

obv. 1 7 UDU NITA ⸢GAL⸣-*tù*
2 6 UDU MÍ^{MEŠ} *ša* Ù.TU
3 1 *ka$_4$-lu-mu* MÍ
4 1 *ka$_4$-lu-mu* NITA
5 1 MÁŠ
7 6 *en-zu* MÍ ⸢*ša*⸣ Ù.TU
8 2 MÁŠ.TUR MÍ
9 ŠU.NÍGIN 23 UDU *ù en-zu*
10 *ša* ^{I}*Wa-an-téš-še-ni*
l.e.11 *a-na* ŠU$^{«I»}$

12 ^{I}*Uz-zu-qa-a+a*
rev. 13 *na-ad-nu*
rest of reverse uninscribed

Comments

Record of transfer of various kinds of sheep and goats from Wantiš-šenni to Uzzukaja. According to Gadd 30, the two were brothers, sons of Ḫašip-tilla.

line 1. The reading GAL-*tù*, *rabûtu*, is based on a suggestion of Deller. However, no other example of this writing can be noted.

14 *YBC* 5127

obv. 1 [*um-ma* ^{I}*Mu*]-*uš-til-la-ma*
2 [DUMU *Ša-a*]*r-te-ja a*(upon erasure)-*ni-na*
3 [x ANŠE x] ^{GIŠ}APIN A.ŠÀ *ša-pát*
4 [x(?) *a-t*]*a-ap-pí i+na pa-na-nu-um-ma*
5 [A.ŠÀ *ša*]-*a-šu* ^{I}*El-ḫi-ip-til-la*
6 [DUMU]x *a-na ti-te-en-nu-ti*
7 [*a-na* ^{I}*Še-q*]*a-a+a* DUMU ⌜*Wa*⌝-*a*[*n*]-⌜*ti*⌝-*m*[*u-ša*]
8 [*id-d*]*ì-nu* ḪA.L[A -*šu*]
9 [ ]x[ ]x[ ]
rest of obverse destroyed
rev. beginning of reverse destroyed
10 [NA$_4$ ^{I}*Mu-uš*]-*til*-⌜*la*⌝
11 [NA$_4$ ^{I}*Er-w*]*i*-LUGAL NA$_4$ ^{I}*Ḫu-ti-ja*
12 [NA$_4$ ^{I}*Ḫa*]-*na-tu*$_4$
rest of reverse destroyed

Comments

Fragmentary tablet, part of an affidavit concerning the renewal of a *tidennūti* agreement. Of the contracting parties, Muš-tilla son of Šarteja is otherwise unknown. Šekaja (=Šekar-tilla) son of Wanti-muša occurs in *YBC* 5133:2 and 5136:2 as well as in other published texts from Arrapḫa and Nuzi.

15 *NCBT* 1933

obv. 1 *ṭup-pí ma-ru-ti*
2 *ša* ^{I}*Ta-ú-uḫ-ḫe* DUMU *Te-ḫi-ja*
3 ^{I}*Te-ḫi-ip-til-la* DUMU *Pu-ḫi-še-en-ni*
4 *a-na ma-ru-ti i-pu-us-sú*
5 *ù qa-aq-qa-ra pa-i-ḫa*
6 *i+na* URU *Ta-še-ni-we i+na e-le-en*

7 É$^{\text{ḪI.A}}$ *ša* ^{I}*Ma-at-te-šup*
8 24 *i+na am-ma-ti mu-ra-<ak>-šu*
9 *ù* 14 *i+na am-ma-ti ru-pu-us-sú*
10 *ša* A.ŠÀ *ki-ma* ḪA.LA-*šu*
11 *a-na* ^{I}*Te-ḫi-ip-til-la id-din*
12 *ù* ^{I}*Te-ḫi-ip-til-la* 5 UDU^{MEŠ}
13 3 ANŠE ŠE^{MEŠ} *ki-ma* NÌ.BA-*šu*
14 *a-na* ^{I}*Ta-ú-uḫ-ḫe id-dí-na-aš-šu*
15 *šum-ma* A.ŠÀ *an-nu-ú di-na*
16 *i-ra-aš-ši* ^{I}*Ta-uḫ-ḫe ú-za-ak-ka*$_4$*-ma*
17 *a-na* ^{I}*Te-ḫi-ip-til-la i+na-an-din*
18 *šum-ma* ^{I}*Ta-uḫ-ḫe* KI.BAL-*at*
19 5 MA.NA KÙ.BABBAR 5 MA.NA KÙ.GI
20 *a-na* ^{I}*Te-ḫi-ip-til-la ú-ma-al-la*
21 IGI *A-kip-ta-še-ni* DUMU *Me-li-ja*
22 IGI *Zi-il-te-šup* DUMU *Tar-mi-ja*
l.e.23 IGI *Še-eḫ-li-ja*
24 DUMU *Ar-te-šup*
25 IGI *Ak-ku-le-en-ni*
rev.26 DUMU *Ú-na-ap-ta-e*
27 IGI *Ni-iḫ-ri-te-šup* DUMU *Ge-li-ja*
28 IGI *A-ki-ja* DUMU *Mu-uš-te-šup*
29 IGI *Ip-⸢ša⸣-ḫa-lu* DUMU *Šúk-ri-ja*
30 IGI *Qa-t*[*i*]*-ri* DUMU *Ḫa-ši-ja*
31 IGI *It-ḫi-iš-ta* DUMU *Ar-ta-e*
32 IGI *Ta-a+a* DUMU IBILA-$^{\text{<d>}}$30 DUB.SAR
33 IGI *En-šúk-ru* DUMU ⸢*Zi*⸣*-im-bar*
34 NA$_4$ KIŠIB ^{I}*Ni-iḫ-ri-te-šup* DUMU *Ge-li-ja*
35 NA$_4$ KIŠIB ^{I}*A-kip-ta-še-ni* DUMU *Me-li-ja*
u.e.36 NA$_4$ KIŠIB ^{I}*Zi-il-te-šup*
37 DUMU *Tar-mi-ja*
38 NA$_4$ ^{I}*Ak-ku-le-en-ni*
le.e.39 NA$_4$ KIŠIB ^{I}*Ta-a+a* DUMU IBILA-^{d}30 DUB.SAR

Comments

Tablet of adoption wherein Tauḫḫe son of Teḫija adopts Teḫip-tilla son of Puḫi-šenni. Tauḫḫe gave Teḫip-tilla an enclosed (? *paiḫu*) piece of land in the town of Tašenniwe. As his gift to Tauḫḫe, Teḫip-tilla gave him five sheep and three homers of barley. This document is from the Tašenniwe dossier of Teḫip-tilla from which five additional texts are known: *JEN* 19, *JEN* 99, *JEN* 236, *AO* 10888 (*RA* 28 [1931] 35 no. 2), and *AO* 10889 (*RA* 28 [1931] 35 no. 3) (references courtesy of K. Deller). Tauḫḫe son of Teḫija who adopts

Teḫip-tilla in our tablet is known from three Tašenniwe texts. In *JEN* 236 he exchanges houses with Teḫip-tilla in Tašenniwe; in *AO* 10889 he adopts Teḫip-tilla along with Kelija son of Akkul-enni and they both enter into a brotherhood (*aḫḫūtu*) agreement with Teḫip-tilla in *JEN* 99. Furthermore, as Deller points out, in *JEN* 99 they seal the tablet jointly (NA$_4$ KIŠIB ^{I}*Ta-ú-uḫ-ḫe ù Kè-li-ja* ŠEŠ, line 25) and in *JEN* 19 Kelija again adopts Teḫip-tilla but this time with his real brother Aḫuja son of Akkul-enni.

16 *NCBT* 1934

obv. 1 *ṭup-pí šu-pé-ul-ti ša* ^{I}*Ḫa-na-a+a*
2 DUMU *It-ḫi-til-la it-ti* ^{I}*Te-ḫi-ip-til-la*
3 DUMU *Pu-ḫi-še-en-ni* É$^{ḪI.A}$ *uš-pé-i-lu*
4 É$^{ḪI.A}$ ḪA.LA-*šu ša* ^{I}*Ḫa-na-a+a*
5 *ina* URU *Ar-ra-ap-ḫe ina li-it* É$^{ḪI.A}$
6 *ša* ^{I}*A-ri-gur-we-e ina su-qa-ni*
7 *ša ḫu-ri-za-ti* ^{I}*Ḫa-na-a+a a-na*
8 [^{I}*T*]*e*-⌜*ḫi*⌝-*ip-til-la id-dì-in*
9 [*ù* ^{I}*Te*]-*ḫi-ip-til-la* É$^{ḪI.A}$ *i+na* ⌜x x x x⌝ (erasure)
10 [URU *Ú-l*]*am-me* ⌜*a-na* ^{I}*Ḫa*⌝-*na-a+a ki-ma* É$^{ḪI.A}$-*šu*
11 [*id-dì-in ša m*]*a-an-ni-im-me-e*
12 [É$^{ḪI.A}$-*šu di-na* TUK *ù ú*]-⌜*za-ak*!-*ka*$_4$⌝!
13 [*ša* BAL 1 MA.NA KÙ.BABBAR]
14 [1 MA.NA KÙ.GI *i+na-an-d*]*in*
rest of obverse destroyed
rev. beginning of reverse destroyed
15 [IGI DU]MU *Ar-r*[*a-*]
16 [ŠU ^{I}TI.LA-KUR DUMU *A-p*]*il*-30 DUB.S[AR]
17 [NA$_4$ ^{I}TI.L[À]-⌜KUR⌝ ^{LÚ}DUB.SAR
18 NA$_4$ ^{I}*Mu-uš-te-šup* DUMU *Zi-ir-ri*
19 NA$_4$ ^{I}*Ḫu-i-te* DUMU <*Ma-li-ja*> (sic!)
u.e. 20 NA$_4$ ^{I}*Mu-uš-te-šup*
21 DUMU *Ar-na-a-pu*

Comments

Tablet of exchange wherein Ḫanaja son of Itḫi-tilla exchanged houses in the city of Arrapḫa with Teḫip-tilla son of Puḫi-šenni who gave him in return houses in the town of Ulamme. From the archive of Teḫip-tilla son of Puḫi-šenni. K. Deller offers the following observations on this text.

As for the origin of *NCBT* 1934 it should be compared with *FLP* 1282 (*Orient and Occident. Essays presented to Cyrus H. Gordon* [Kevelaer 1973], p. 233), another exchange tablet of Teḫip-tilla concerning É$^{ḪI.A}$ ⌜*i+na*⌝ URU ⌜*Ar-ra*⌝-*ap-*[*ḫe*] (1.5). Since the dossier Arrapḫe of Teḫip-tilla is not represented among the

JEN/*JENu* texts, these two tablets might come from clandestine digs in Kirkuk itself. The exchange partner, Ḫanaja s.Itḫi-tilla, is known from two witness lists in documents from Teḫip-tilla's dossier Ulamme, *JEN* 20:22 and *JENu* 225:14. It does not become fully evident if the phrase *ina su-qa-ni* [7]*ša ḫu-ri-za-ti* contains a new lexeme **sūqānu*, or simply the (hitherto unattested) plural of *sūqu*, viz. "in the streets of the sheds."

lines 11-12. Restorations are based on *JEN* 244:9-10 and *JENu* 275:13-14 both of which were written by the same scribe as our text, Balṭu-kašid (courtesy K. Deller).

17 *YBC* 5130

obv. 1 *ṭup-pí tam-gu*$_5$*-ur-ti*
2 *ša* ^{I}*Še-qar-til-la* DUMU *Wa-an-ti-m*[*u-š*]*á*
3 *ù ša* ^{I}*Ḫa-ni-ú* DUMU *Ar-nu-*[*u*]*r-ḫ*[*é*]
4 *i+na be-ri-šu-nu it-tam-ga*$_{14}$*-ru-ma*
5 *um-ma* ^{I}*Še-qar-til-la-ma*
6 *i+na pa-na-nu-um-ma* ^{I}*Ḫa-ni-ú*
7 *a-na* 4 ^{GIŠ}APIN A.ŠÀ *a-na ma-ru-ti*
8 *i-pu-ša-an-ni-mi ù i+na-an-na*
9 *a-na-ku* 4 ^{GIŠ}APIN A.ŠÀ *ša-a-šu*
10 *e-ez-zu a-na be-li-šu-ma*
11 *a-na* ^{I}*Ḫa-ni-ú um-te-eš-ši-ir-*⸢*mi*⸣
12 *ù a-na-ku* 10 SU KÙ.BABBAR 2 ANŠE ŠE KÙ.[BABBAR]-*š*[*u*]
13 *i+na ku-tal-li-šu-ma a-šar*
14 ^{I}*Ḫa-ni-ú* ⸢*el*⸣*-te-*[*qè-mi* (*ù*)]
15 *um-ma* ^{I}*Ḫa-ni-*[*ú-ma*]
16 *ù um-ma* ^{I}*Še-*[*qar-til-la-ma*]
17 *ri-ik-sú š*[*a pí-i ṭup-pí*]
18 *la-bi-ri n*[*i-iḫ-te-pé* (*ù*)]
19 *qà-an-na-šu* ^{I}*Ḫ*[*a-ni-ú*]
20 *a-na pa-ni ši-*[*bu-ti im-ta-šar*]
21 *ma-an-nu i+n*[*a be-ri-šu-nu* (*ša*)]
22 KI.BAL-*tù* [1 MA.NA KÙ.BABBAR 1 MA.NA KÙ.GI *umalla*]
23 IGI *Zi-*[DUMU]
24 IGI *A-*x[DUMU]
25 IGI ⸢*E*⸣*-*[*ge-ge* DUMU]
rev.26 [IGI DUMU]
27 I[GI DUMU]
28 ŠU ^{I}x[ ]
29 NA$_4$ ^{I}[ ]
30 N[A$_4$ ^{I}]
31 NA$_4$ ^{I}*A-*[ ]
32 NA$_4$ ^{I}*Še-qar-til-la*

33 NA$_4$ ^{I}*E-ge-ge*
34 N[A$_4$ ^{I}*D*]*u-ra-ar-te-šup* NA$_4$ ^{I}*Šúk-ri-a*
35 [NA$_4$ ^{I}]-⌈*na-a+a*⌉ DUB.[SAR]

Comments

Tablet of agreement wherein Šekar-tilla son of Wanti-muša and Ḫaniu son of Arnurḫe agreed to the following: Šekar-tilla stated that Ḫaniu had previously adopted him in exchange for five homers of land. Now Šekar-tilla has returned that 5 homers of *ezzu*-land to Ḫaniu and received ten shekels of silver and two homers of barley from Ḫaniu. This is the only case so far known from the Nuzi texts where a field obtained by a "sale adoption" is "returned (=*ezzu*)" to the adopter. This text is of crucial importance for the understanding of the system of sales adoption at Nuzi. It should be compared with *HM* 8400 = *EN* 9 122 published above. See also the discussion by A. Fadhil in the *postscriptum* to his article in this volume.

line 10. The term *ezzu* appears to be the base form of the Hurrian adjective *ezzuššiḫe* (*AHw* 270 s.v.; *CAD* E 435 s.v.) and possibly to be associated with A.ŠÀ *i-zu-zu-uš-ši*, *JEN* 103:6 (*CAD* I/J 319 s.v. *izuzušši*. In *JEN* 513:3, a summary of real estate acquisitions, *ezzuššiḫe* fields are distinguished from *eqlēti* [*ša ana*] *mārūti epšū* and *eqlēti ša tidennūti*. Lacheman long ago concluded that the term meant something like "return" and this is supported by independent conclusions reached by Fadhil, Deller and Owen. Furthermore, the use of the phrase *ana bēlišuma* shows why the adoptant in a *ṭuppi mārūti* frequently seals it with the by-script *bēl eqli*. Deller adds that the phrase *ana bēlišu*(*nu*) *muššuru* is also found in *HM* 8400 = *EN* 9 122:9-10 where the houses were acquired not by *marūtū* but *ina irani*, i.e. by purchase (according to the interpretation by Fadhil). The latter transaction is probably an "undisguised" sale adoption in which case *YBC* 5130 and *HM* 8400 would be considered parallel transactions.

18 *YBC* 5136

obv. 1 *tup-pí ma-ru-ti ša* [^{I}]
2 DUMU *Ur-ḫi-ja ù* [^{I}*Še-qa-a+a*]
3 DUMU *Wa-an-ti-m*[*u-ša a-na ma-ru-ti*]
4 *i-te-pu-uš* [*ù* É$^{\mathrm{ḪI.A}}$]
5 *i+na lìb-bi* URU [DINGIR^{MEŠ} *i+na e-le-en* É$^{\mathrm{ḪI.A}}$]
6 *ša* ^{I}*Še-qa-a+*[*a i+na*] É^{MEŠ} *ša* ^{I}*Pu-ra-sa*
7 *šum-ma* É$^{\mathrm{ḪI.A.MEŠ}}$ [GAL *la i-na-ak-ki-is*]
8 *ù šum-ma* T[UR *la ú-ra-ad-dá*]
9 *ki-ma* Ḫ A.[LA-*šu a-na* ^{I}*Še-qa-a+a*]
10 *it-ta-*[*din ù* ^{I}*Še-qa-a+a*]
11 20 M[A.NA]
rest of obverse and beginning of reverse destroyed

rev.12 [N]A$_4$ ^{I}*Ḫa*-[ ]
13 NA$_4$ ^{I}*Ḫa-iš-te-*[*ja*/*šup*]
14 NA$_4$ ^{I}*Ir-šu-uḫ-ḫe* NA$_4$ ^{I}[ ]
15 NA$_4$ ^{I}DUMU-^{d}U-DAR
16 [NA$_4$ ^{I}]*Ḫu-ti-ip*-LUGAL/DUB.SAR-*rù*
17 [NA$_4$ ^{I} -*e*]*n-ni*

Comments

Tablet of adoption wherein [PN] son of Urḫija adopted Šekaja son of Wanti-muša. [PN] son of Urḫija gave Šekaja houses in the city of Āl Ilāni and Šekaja gave him twenty minas of [×].

Of the five tablets so far known which were written by Ḫutip-šarri (Gadd 6 and 25, *HSS* 9 36, *RI* 309 and *TCL* 9 7) all but *HSS* 9 36 were written in Āl Ilāni (references courtesy of K. Deller). It is therefore likely that the archive of Šekaja originated there, hence the restoration in line 5.

19 *YBC* 5133

obv. 1 [*ṭup-pí ma-ru-t*]*i* [*š*]*a* [^{I}]⌈*Ḫa-ni-ú*]
2 [DUMU *Zi-li-j*]*a ù* ^{I}*Še-qa-a+a*
3 [DUMU *Wa-an-t*]*i-mu-*⌈*šá*⌉ *a-*[*n*]*a* [DUMU]-⌈*ti*⌉ DÙ-*sú*
4 [x ANŠE/^{GIŠ}APIN A.]⌈ŠÀ⌉ ⌈*i+na*⌉ [ ]
5 [*Ḫ*]*u-*⌈*ti*⌉-[ ]
6 [*i+na*] URU [ ]
7 [*i+na il-t*]*a-an* A.[ŠÀ *ša* ^{I}]-*ri-ku*
8 [*ki-ma* ḪA.LA-*šu*] *a-na* ^{I}*Še-q*[*ar*]-⌈*til*⌉-*la* SUM
9 [*šum*]-⌈*ma*⌉ A.ŠÀ *u*[*b-t*]*a-aq-qar*
10 [^{I}*Ḫa-ni*]-*ú ù* ^{I}[*N*]*a-i-ip-til-*⌈*la*⌉ ⌈DUMU⌉ *Te-ḫi-ip*-LUGAL
11 [*ú*]-⌈*za*⌉-*ak-ku-ú-ma a-na* ^{I}*Še-qa-*⌈*a+a*⌉ [SUM-*n*]*u*
12 [*š*]*a* BAL-*tu*$_4$ 1 MA.NA [K]Ù.BABBAR 1 MA.NA KÙ.G[I]
13 ⌈*ú*⌉-*ma-al-la*
14 NA$_4$ ^{I}*Ḫa-ni-ú* EN A.ŠÀ
15 NA$_4$ ^{I}*Ak-ku-le-ni*
l.e.16 NA$_4$ ^{I}x[ ]
17 [NA$_4$ ^{I}]⌈x x (x⌉)[ ]
rev.18 *ṭup-pu ina* EGIR *šu-du-ti š*[*a-ṭì*]-*ir*
19 IGI ^{I}*Nu-uz-za* DUMU *Šu-ri*
20 IGI ^{I}*Ša-an-ḫa-ra-a+a* DUMU *Ḫa-ni-ku-z*[*i*]
21 IGI ^{I}*Ar-qa-bi* DUMU *Ak-ku-*⌈*ja*⌉
22 [IGI ^{I}*K*]*u*$^{?}$*-un-nu* DUMU $^{MÍ.I}$*Ḫi-in-zu-*⌈*ra-a+a*⌉
23 [IGI ^{I}*Ar-t*]*e*$^{?}$*-ku-še* DUMU *G*[*e-w*]*i-ta-*⌈*e*⌉
24 [IGI ^{I}*Pu-ḫ*]*i-še-ni* DUMU [ ]-*ja*
25 [IGI ^{I}*Ak-ku-le*]-*ni* DUMU *Pu-i-ta-e*
26 [ŠU ^{I}*Wa-qar*]-EN DUB.SAR-*rù*

27 [NA$_4$ ^{I}Na-i-ip-til-la DUMU Te-ḫi]-ip-LUGAL
28 [ ]x
u.e.29 [NA$_4$ ^{I}]Ar-qa-b[e]

Comments

Tablet of adoption wherein Ḫaniu son of [Zilij]a adopts Šekaja (= Šekar-tilla) son of Wanti-muša.

line 2. Probably the same individual known from Gadd 14:12; 43:27 and *AASOR* 16 3:15 where the full form of his name is Zilip-tilla.

lines 10 and 27. Deller notes that the name may also be restored as ^{I}[Ḫ]u-i-ip-til-la. An individual with this patronymic is otherwise unknown.

line 26. The restoration of the scribe's name is only a suggestion. Other restorations such as [IGI DI.KU$_5$]-EN are also possible.

20 *YBC* 5140

obv. 1 [ṭup-pí ti-te-en-nu-ti ša]
2 [^{I}A-kip-še-en-ni DUMU It-ḫi-iš-ta]
3 [x ANŠE A.ŠÀ]
4 [^{I}A-kip-še-en-ni DUMU It-ḫi-i]š-⸢ta⸣
5 [a-na ti-te-en-nu-ti a-n]a 5 MU^{MEŠ}-ti
6 [a-na ^{I}Mu-šu-ja DUMU T]a$^{?}$-a+a SUM-in
7 [ù ^{I}Mu-šu-j]a [x+] 3 BÁN ŠE 5 [M]A.<NA> AN.NA^{MEŠ}
8 [a-na ^{I}A]-⸢kip⸣-še-e[n-n]i ⸢id⸣-d[in]
9 [šum-ma] ⸢A.⸣ŠÀ [m]a-ad ⸢ù⸣ ^{I}M[u-šu-ja]
10 [la i+n]a-ak-ki-í[s šum-ma A.ŠÀ]
11 [TUR l]a ú-ra-a[d-dá]
12 [EME]-šu ša ^{I}A-ki[p-še-en-ni]
13 [a-na] ⸢pa⸣-ni LÚ^{MEŠ} š[i-bu-ti]
14 [ki-a]m iq-ta-bi K[Ù.BABBAR^{MEŠ}]
15 [ša p]í-i ṭup-pí an-n[i-i]
16 [a-š]ar ^{I}Mu-šu-ja el-[te-qè-mi]
17 [šum]-ma A.ŠÀ ba-qí-ra-n[a ir-ta-ši]
18 ⸢ù⸣ ^{I}A-kip-še-en-ni [?]
l.e.19 ⸢ú⸣-za-ak-ka$_4$
20 NA$_4$ ^{I}Ḫu-tar-ra-a[p-ḫe]
rev.21 [a-na ^{I}M]u-šu-ja i+na-a[n-din]
22 [šum-ma A.Š]À ma-ja-ru ù [?]
23 [^{I}A-kip]-še-en-ni i+na ŠU-[ti]
24 [^{I}Mu-šu]-ja ⸢la⸣ i-ik-ki-[im]
25 [ṭup-pu] an-nu-ú i+na EGIR [šu-du-ti]
26 [i+na UR]U DINGIR^{MEŠ} i+na KÁ.GAL [ša-ṭì-ir]
27 [im-ma-t]i-me-e 5 MU^{MEŠ} [im-ta]-lu ù
28 [KÙ.BABBA]R ša ^{I}Mu-šu-ja ú-[ta-a]r ù A.Š[À-šu i-leq-qè]

29 [IGI *Še-q*]*a-rù* DUMU *Ḫu-*⸢*ti-ip*⸣*-pu-gur*
30 [IGI *A*]*-ki-ja* DUMU *Ip-ša-a+a*
31 [IGI *Ge*]*-el-*[*t*]*i-ja* DUMU *Ge-el-du-*⸢*x*⸣
32 [3 LÚ^{MEŠ} *a*]*n-nu-tu*$_4$ *mu-še-el-wu-ú*
33 [*ša* A.ŠÀ *na-d*]*ì-na-nu ša* ⸢KÙ⸣.BABBAR
34 [IGI DUMU *Še-q*]*a-rù*
35 [IGI DUMU *En*]*-na-ma-ti*
36 [IGI DUMU]⸢*e*⸣/*j*]*a*?
rest of reverse destroyed

Comments

Tidennūtu contract wherein Akip-šenni son of [Itḫi]šta loaned x homers of land for a period of five years to Mušuja son of [T]aja for the sum of one homer of barley and five minas of tin.

lines 1 and 4. Akip-šenni son of Itḫišta is known from *EN* 9 64:15,22 and *JEN* 540:28.

21 *YBC* 5129

obv. 1 *ṭup-pí tam-gu*$_5$*-ur-*⸢*ti*⸣ [*ša* ^{1}*Zi-ka-a+a*]
2 DUMU *Mu-ka-ru ù it-ti* ^{1}[*It-ḫi-ip*-LUGAL]
3 DUMU *Mu-lu-ja it-ta-am-*[*ga*$_5$*-ru*]
4 *ù* A.ŠÀ^{MEŠ}*-šu ša* ^{1}*I*[*t-ḫi-ip*-LUGAL]
5 *ša* ^{1}*Zi-ka-a*<*a+a*> *ú-ka-*[*al-lu*]
6 ^{1}*Zi-ka-a+a* A.ŠÀ^{MEŠ} [*a-na* ^{1}*It-ḫi-ip*-LUGAL]
7 *um-te-eš-ši-ir* ⸢*ù*⸣ [^{1}*It-ḫi-ip*-LUGAL]
8 5 ANŠE ŠE 2 ANŠE ZÍZ.AN.N[A *ù*]
9 1 UDU *ana* ^{1}*Zi-ka-a*[*+a*]
10 *ut-te-er ù* A.ŠÀ-[*šu il-te-qè*]
uninscribed space
11 *ma-an-nu-um-me-e š*[*a* KI.BAL]-⸢*tu*⸣
12 1 MA.NA KÙ.BABBAR 1 MA.NA [KÙ.GI] ⸢*ú*⸣*-ma-al-la*
13 IGI *I-ta-aḫ-ḫe* DUMU *A-ba-zu*
14 IGI *Al-ki-ja* DUMU *Ba-a+a*
15 IGI *Še-ḫé-el-te-šup* DUMU *A-ri*-WA-AḪ-*lu*
l.e.16 IGI *Ku-uz-za-ri-ja* DUMU *Ḫa-al-ta-a+a*
17 IGI *Ḫa-ma-an-na* DUMU *Ḫa-bi-ru-ku*
18 IGI *Ši-mi-qa-tal* DUMU *Wa-an-ti-a*
rev.19 IGI *Še-eš-wi-qa* DUMU *A-ki-ja*
20 IGI *Ta-a+a* DUMU *A-ri-ib-ba-ab-:-ni*
21 IGI *Še-eš-wi-qa* DUMU *Na-al-du-a*
22 IGI *Na-ni-ip-til-la* DUMU *E-pa-ta*
23 IGI *Še-ka-rù* DUMU *Šu-pa-ḫa-li*
24 IGI *Ip-ša-ḫa-lu* DUMU *En-na-a+a*

25 IGI *Šúk-ri-ja* DUMU *Wa-an-ti-a*
26 IGI ^{d}TIŠPAK-LUGAL DUMU *Ar-téš-še*
27 IGI *A-ki-ja* DUMU *Ar-ta-še-*⌜*en*⌝-[*ni*]
28 IGI *Tar-mi-ja* DUMU EN-ŠEŠ^{MEŠ} D[UB.SAR]
29 IGI *Ta-e-na* DUMU *Še-qa-ru*
30 NA$_4$ ^{I}⌜*I*⌝-*ta-aḫ-ḫ*[*e*]
31 NA$_4$ ^{I}*Tar-mi-ja* DUB.SAR
32 NA$_4$ ^{I}*Zi-qa-a+a*
33 NA$_4$ ^{I}*Al-ki-ja*
u.e.34 NA$_4$ ^{I}*Še-eš-wi-qa*
35 NA$_4$ ^{I}*Še-q*[*a-ru*]
l.e.36 NA$_4$ ^{I}*Ḫa-ma-an-na*
37 NA$_4$ ^{I}*Ku-*⌜*uz-za*⌝*-ri-a*

Comments

Tablet of agreement wherein Zikaja son of Makaru and I[tḫip-šarri] son of Muluja agree to the following: the fields belonging to I[tḫip-šarri] which Zikaja held were released and in return I[tḫip-šarri] gives Zikaja five homers of emmer and one sheep. K. Deller kindly offered the following observations.

This agreement tablet belongs to the small archive of Itḫip-šarri s.Muluja of which so far only two documents, Jank. 50 and Jank. 11 (both written by the same scribe, Kip-arrapḫe), have come to light.
Jank. 50, another *tamgurtu* between Ipḫip-šarri s.Muluja on the one hand, and his "brothers" (read *a-na* ^{I}*It-*[*ḫi-ip*]*-šarri aḫ-ḫu*$^{!}$*-ú ni-nu-mi*, 1.6) Akap-tukke s.Munate and Tauka s.Arkapinni on the other. Jank. 11 is a *ṭuppi titennūti* of Kelija s.Šešwe in favor of Itḫip-šarri (here without patronymic).
Though housed in two different museums, Jank. 50 in the Gosudarstvennyj muzej izobrazitel'nych iskusstv im.Puškina, Jank. 11 in the Gosudarstvennyj Ërmitaž, they belong closely together. In both tablets Itḫip-šarri's son Niḫrija acts as a witness.
That Itḫip-šarri is the correct restoration in ll.2.4.6.7 follows from the traces in l.4, ^{I}I[t-, and a comparison of the witness lists of these three tablets. Out of the sixteen witnesses of *YBC* 5129, Alkija s.Paja and Šešwikka s.Akija are found in Jank. ll, [IGI *Še-eš*]*-wi-iq-qa* DUMU *Na*$^{!}$*-al-tu-ja* in Jank. 50:20.
Unfortunately we are unable to locate Itḫip-šarri's habitat because the *dimtu* name in Jank. 11:4 is completely broken away.
The first witness of *YBC* 5129, Itaḫḫe s.Apazu, might help us to trace Itḫip-šarri in time and space. He also figures as the first witness (spelled IGI *I-ta-aḫ-ḫe* DUMU *A-ba-zu*) in *IM* 10856:28.44 (Abdulilah Fadhil, *Rechtsurkunden und administrative Texte aus Kurruḫanni*, Appendix, Nr.34). This tablet is a *ṭuppi mārūti* of Teḫip-tilla s.Puḫi-šenni, dossier Āl Ilāni (1.5); the scribe is Sîn-nādin-šumi s.Taja. It has not been excavated in an organized expedition, but was purchased "from Azebouni" according to the catalogue of the Iraq Museum, Baghdad.

So Itḫip-šarri is a (probably younger) contemporary of Teḫip-tilla and it is quite likely that he was a resident of Āl Ilāni.
YBC 5129 is the first known tablet written by the scribe Tarmija s.Bēl-aḫḫē. He must be the brother of Šelluni s.Bēl-aḫḫē, the scribe of *HSS* 13,15 and *HSS* 19,63. No tablets written by their father Bēl-aḫḫē are known so far.

22 *YBC* 5134

obv. 1 [*ṭup-pí ma-a*]*r-tù-*[*ti*] *ša* [I]*I*[*p-šá-ḫa-lu*]
2 [DUMU *Ḫa-ma-a*]*n-na ù ša* [MÍ]*Ku-un-d*[*u-ja*]
3 [DUMU.MÍ *Ni*]*-in-ki-ja ù* DUMU.MÍ-*su-nu*
4 [[MÍ] *Ú-lu-l*]*i-du a-na ma-ar-tù-*⸢*ti*⸣
5 [*a-na* [I]*Pu-*]⸢*i*⸣*-ta-e* DUMU *Eḫ-li-ba-tal*!(ḪU)
6 [*i-ta-din-š*]*u-nu-ù* [I]*Pu-i-ta-e*
7 [[MÍ] *Ú-lu*]*-li-du a-na* LÚ *ša* KUR *Ar-r*[*a-ap-ḫe*]
8 [*a-na aš-šu-t*]*i i+na-an-d*[*in*]x[ ]
9 [x SU KÙ.G]I *a-na* ⸢*qa*⸣*-*[*an-ni-šá*]
10 [ ]x x (x)[ ]
rest of obverse destroyed
rev. beginning of reverse destroyed
11 [NA_4 [I]]*x-šá*
12 NA_4 [I]*Tar-mi-te-šup*
13 [NA_4 [I]*Ip-šá-ḫ*]*a-lu*
rest of reverse destroyed

Comments

Tablet of “daughtership” wherein Ip[ša-ḫalu] son of [Ḫama]nna and (his wife) Kunt[uja] daughter of Ninkija give their daughter [Ulu]litu for adoption to Pui-tae son of Elḫip-atal for x shekels of gold. In return Pui-tae agrees to marry her off to a man from the land of Arrapḫa.

line 1-2. Ipša-ḫalu son of Ḫamanna is well known from the Arrapḫa texts published by Gadd (cf. *NPN* 72 for references) and from *JEN* 252:35 where his name is written Ipšaja.

The restoration of his wife’s name is only a suggestion and is not based on additional references.

lines 3, 4 and 7. The restoration of the daughter’s name was suggested by Lacheman. A woman by this name does occur at Arrapḫa in Gadd 76:9.

23 *YBC* 11275

obv. 1 1 MÁŠ TUR
2 *mu-*UD-DA-*šu*
3 *ša* [I]*Ḫa-ši-ip-til-la*
4 DUMU *Ge-li-pu-gur*

rev. 5 NA$_4$ *Ḫa-ši-ip-til-*⌜*la*⌝
6 DUMU *Ge-li-pu-gur*

Comments

Text recording the outstanding balance of one young goat owed by Ḫašip-tilla son of Kelip-ukur. The text is from the archives of prince Šilwa-tešup. According to *HSS* 13 308:6 Ḫašip-tilla was one of Šilwa-tešup's debtors in Āl Ilāni.

24 *NBC* 6500

obv. 1 3 ANŠE 6 BÁN 6 *qa* ŠE
2 *a-na* ANŠE.KUR.RA
3 *ša* GÌR^{MEŠ} LUGAL
4 *a-na* 7 *u*$_4$*-mi*
5 *a-na i-sí-ni*
6 *ša ge-nu-ni*
l.e. 7 ^{I}*Ḫa-ši-ip-til-la*
8 *il-qè*

Comments

This tablet stands out among the Yale texts. It is of the very same type found during the last two years of the Nuzi excavations conducted by the Harvard Semitic Museum and found in rooms C-19, C-28, D-3, D-6, F-24, G-29 and G-73. Nearly all of the tablets from these rooms are of the same color, yellowish-brown, in contrast with those from the houses of Teḫip-tilla and Zike either light yellow (almost white) or very dark (almost black) colored clay. Lacheman states, "I am convinced that this is one of the very few tablets (if not the only one) which was stolen from the excavations themselves. The tablets were discovered unbaked, and baked in a field oven, heated by crude native oil found in the nearby oil fields, which probably explains the uniformity in color. Therefore it does not seem possible that the tablet was obtained from native digging after the Harvard excavations were finished since they would have had to bake the tablet for no baked tablets were found at Nuzi."

Receipt by Ḫašip-tilla of barley for the horses of the royal chariot-guard. To be compared with *HSS* 14 59 (from Rm. D-6) and *HSS* 16 139 (from Rm. D-3) both from the Nuzi palace archives.

25 *YBC* 5145

obv. 1 5 KUŠ *ša* UDU^{MEŠ}
2 *a-na na-ak-bá-sà*
3 *a-na* ^{GIŠ}GIGIR
4 ^{I}*An-ti-ja*

5 *il-qè*
rev. 6 NA$_4$ ^{I}*An-ti-ja*

Comments

Receipt by Antija of five sheepskins (to be used) for a chariot mat.

26 *YBC* 5128

obv. 1 EME-*šu ša* ^{I}*Šúk-[ri-te-šup]*
2 DUMU *Wi-ir-re-eš-t[a-an-ni]*
3 *a-na pa-ni* LÚ^{MEŠ} *ši-[bu-ti]*
4 *an-nu-ti ki-am iq-[ta-bi]*
5 3 ANŠE ŠE^{MEŠ} *ša* ^{I}*P[u-i-ta-e]*
6 DUMU *Eḫ-li-pa-tal ina m[uḫ-ḫi-ja aš-bu]*
7 ⌜*ù*⌝ *i+na* ITU-*ḫi Še-ḫa-l[i ša* ^{d}IM/*Nergal*]
8 [SAG].⌜DU⌝-*ma a-na* ^{I}*Pu-i-[ta-e* SUM]
rest of obverse destroyed
rev. beginning of reverse destroyed
9 N[A$_4$ ^{I}]
10 NA$_4$ ^{I}[ ]
u.e.11 DUMU *Ḫu-ti-*[ ]
l.e.12 [NA$_4$ ^{I}*Ḫa*]-*ši-ip-ta-še-*
13 [:]-*en-ni* DUB.S[AR]

Comments

Declaration by Šukri-tešup son of Wirriš-tanni before witnesses in which he promises to return three homers of barley to Pui-tae son of Eḫlip-atal in the month of *Šeḫali* [*ša Tešup*/*Nergal*]. It is not clear whether one is to restore the beginning of line 13 as the scribe's name or to consider it as the end of the scribe's name begun on line 12. In any case a scribe by either name is not yet attested.

27 *YBC* 5144

obv. beginning of obverse destroyed
1 [*k*]*i-ma* x[ ]
2 [ ]x *id-d*[*ì-*]
3 [*um-ma* ^{I} -t]*e-šup-ma*
4 [*iš-tù* u$_4$-*mi an-n*]*i-i-im*
5 [E]N-*šu-ma*
6 [ ]x-*ma*
7 [*n*]*i-šu-mi*
8 [^{I}]*Še-qa-a+a*
9 [ ]x *el-te-qè*

10 [*ap-la-ku-m*]*i šum-ma* É$^{\text{HI.A.MEŠ}}$
11 [*bi-ir-qa i-ra-as*]-*šu-ú*
12 [^{I} -*te-šup ú-za*-[*ak-ka*$_4$-*ma*
rest of obverse destroyed
rev. beginning of reverse destroyed
13 [*ṭup-pu an-nu-ú*]
14 [*i+na* EGIR *šu-d*]*u-ti ša* [É].GAL
15 [*a-šar* K]Á.GAL
16 [*i+na* URU DINGIR^{MEŠ} *š*]*a-ṭì-ir*
17 [IGI DUMU]-*na-a+a*
18 [IGI DUMU] *Ar-nu-ur-ḫe*
19 [IGI DUMU *E*]*r-wi*-LUGAL
20 [IGI DUMU] *Ar-téš-še*
21 [IGI *n*]*i* DUMU *A-ri-iḫ-ḫar-me*
22 [IGI DUM]U *Zi-ku-ja*
23 [IGI DUMU *Š*]*i*-[*il*]-⌜*wa*⌝-*a+a*
24 [ ]x
25 [ ]x
rest of reverse destroyed

Comments

Fragment of a legal text.

TEXT COPIES

by

E. R. LACHEMAN

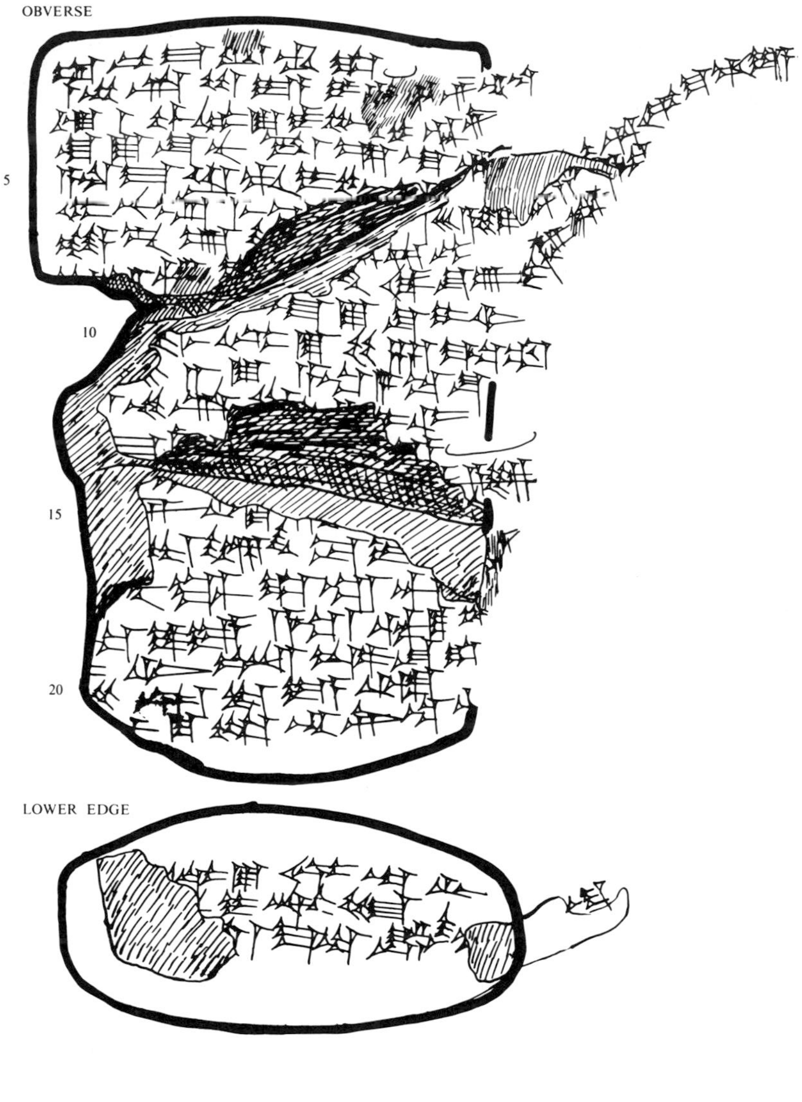
OBVERSE
5
10
15
20
LOWER EDGE

1 *YBC* 5141

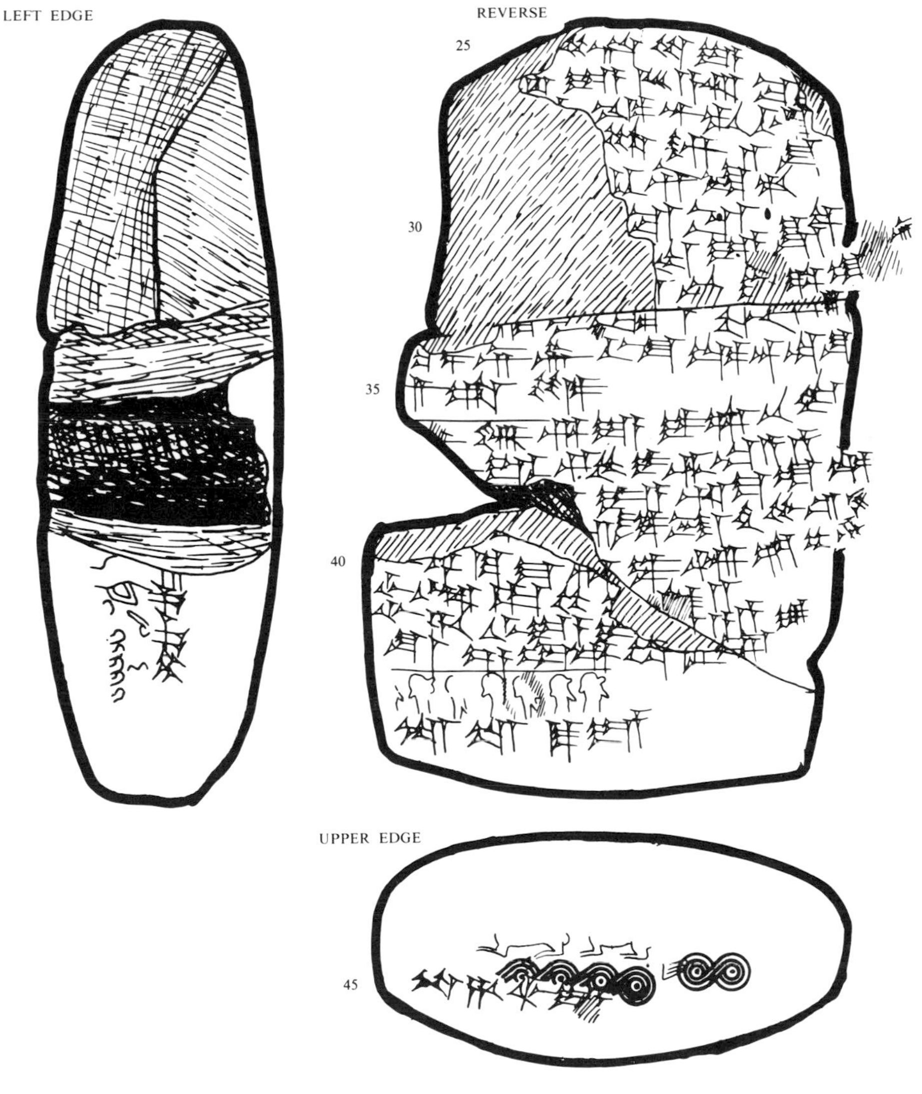

1 *YBC* 5141 (continued)

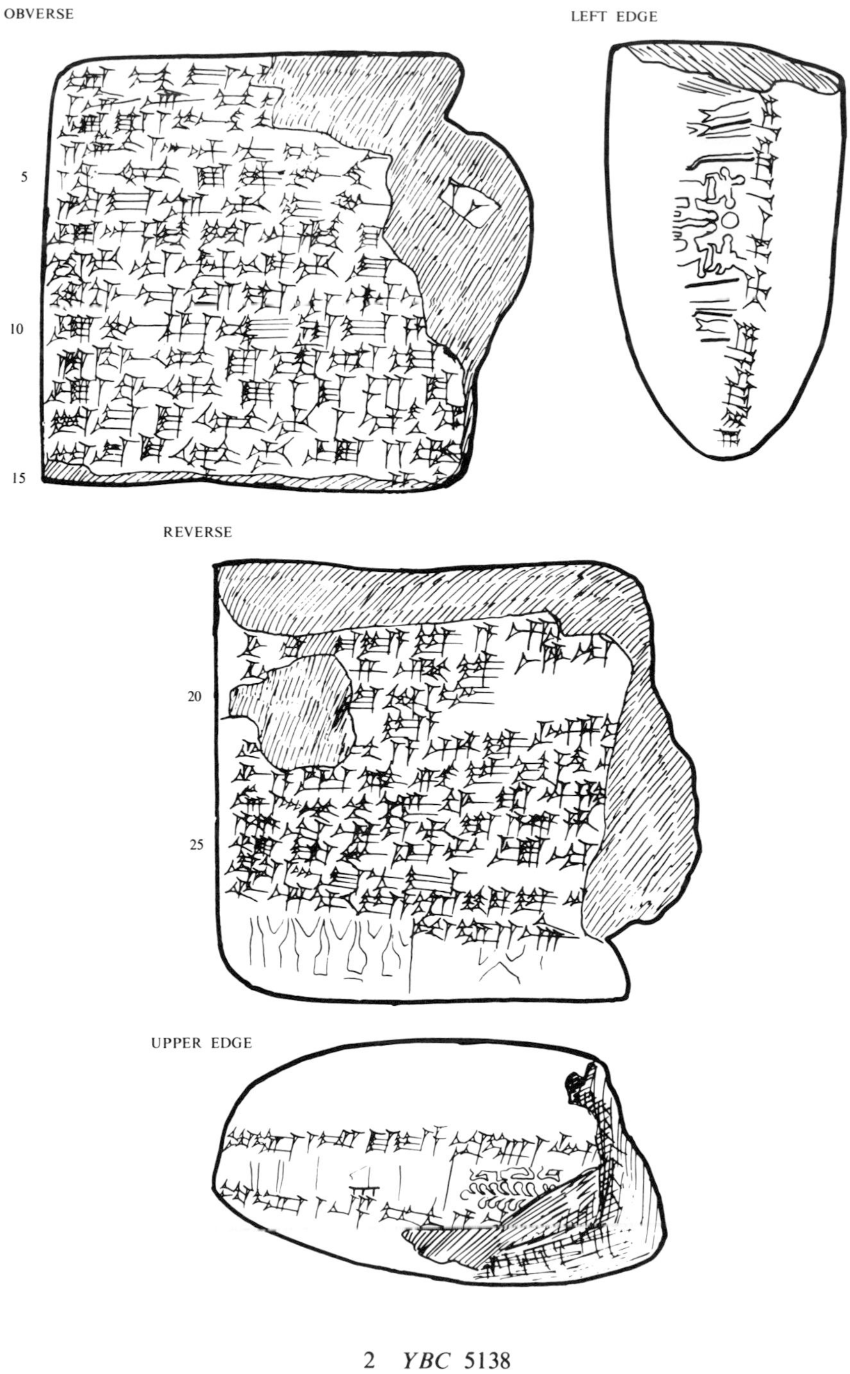
OBVERSE
LEFT EDGE
REVERSE
UPPER EDGE

2 *YBC* 5138

OBVERSE

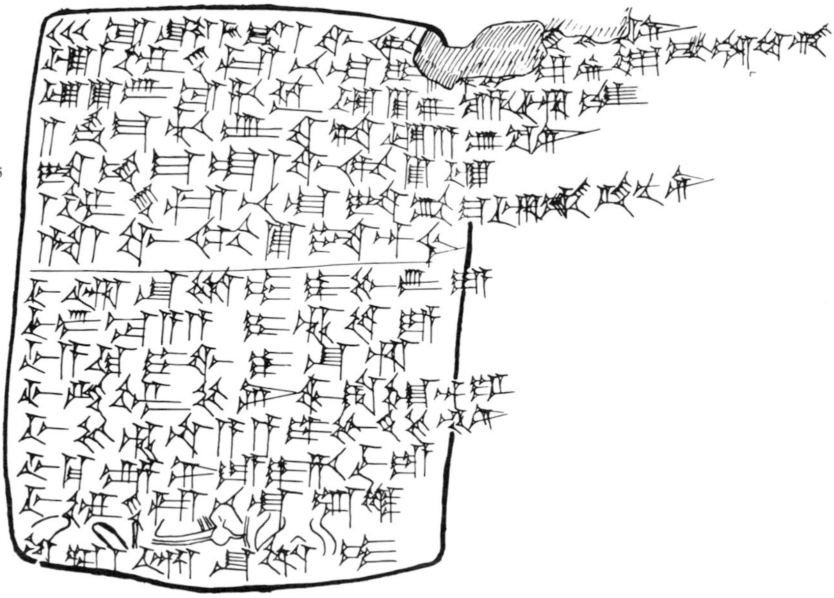

LOWER EDGE

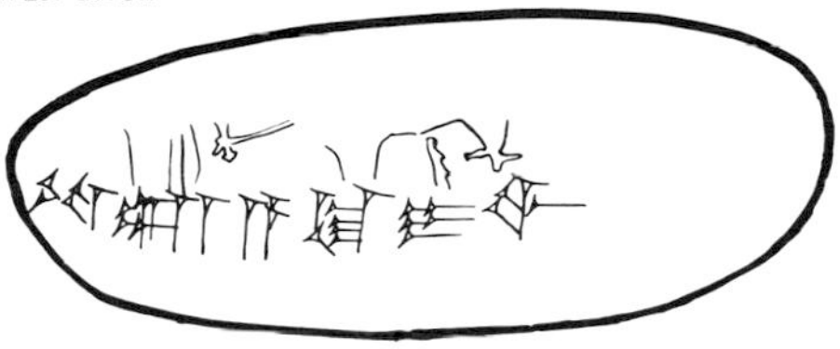

REVERSE

3 *YBC* 5143

LEFT EDGE

4 *YBC* 5131

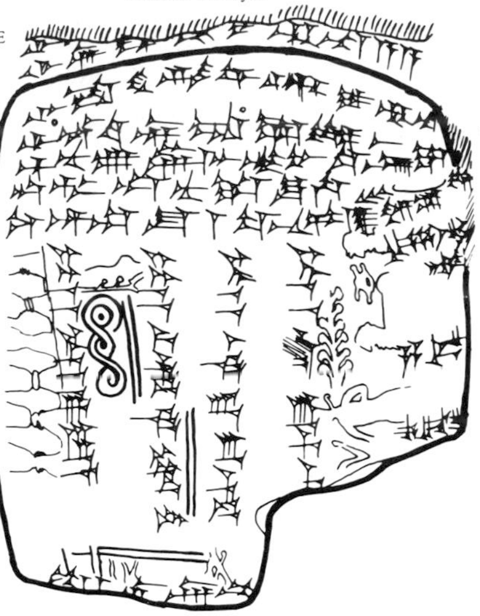

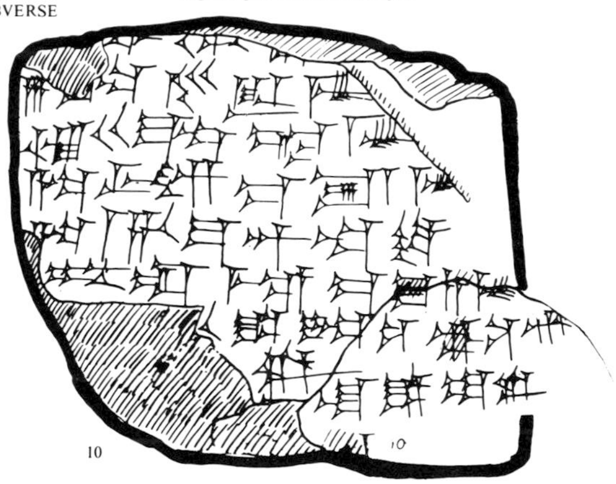

5 *YBC* 5135

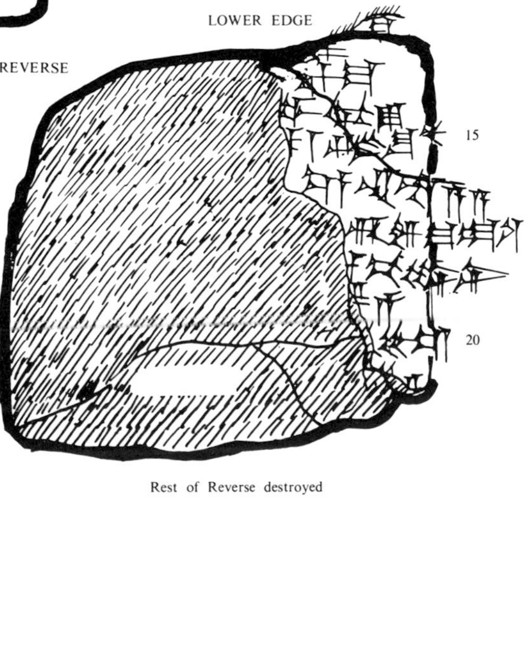

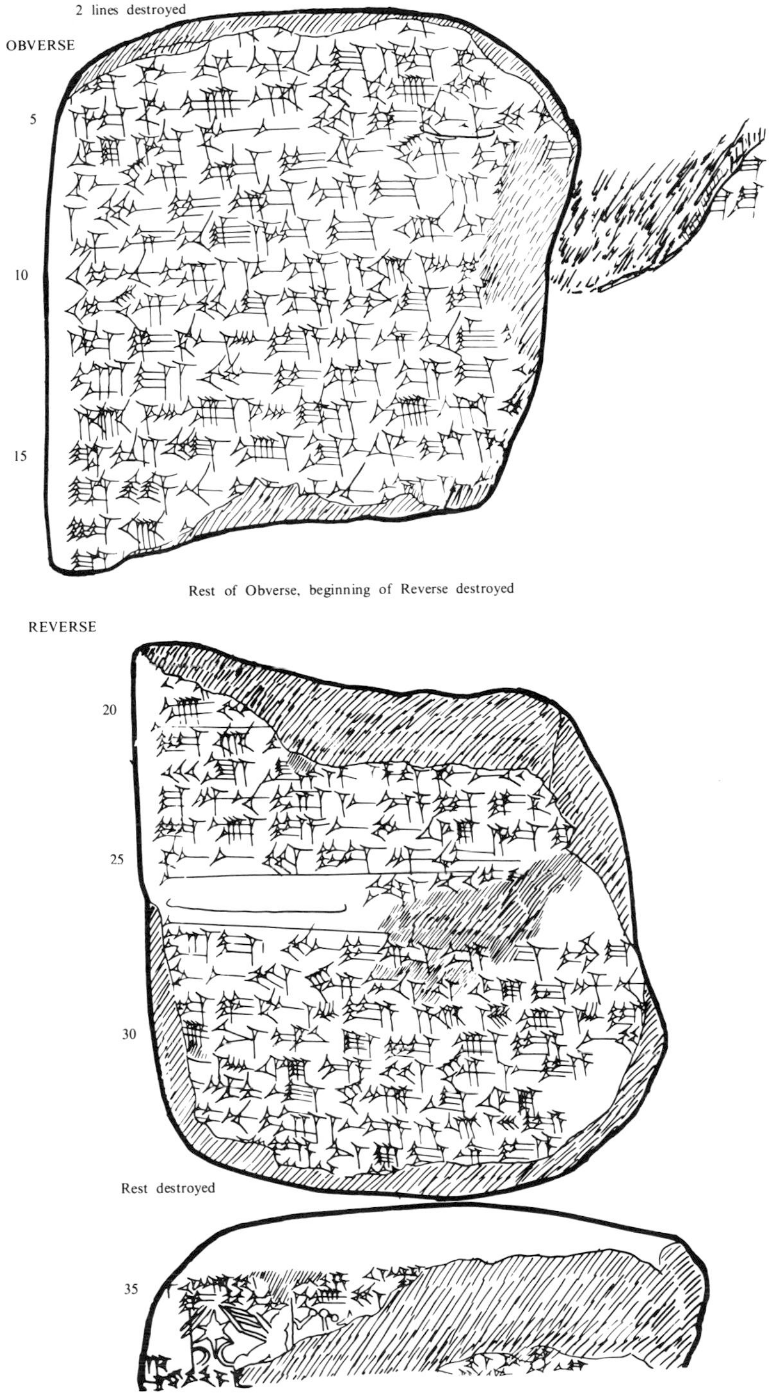
2 lines destroyed
OBVERSE
Rest of Obverse, beginning of Reverse destroyed
REVERSE
Rest destroyed

6 *YBC* 5142

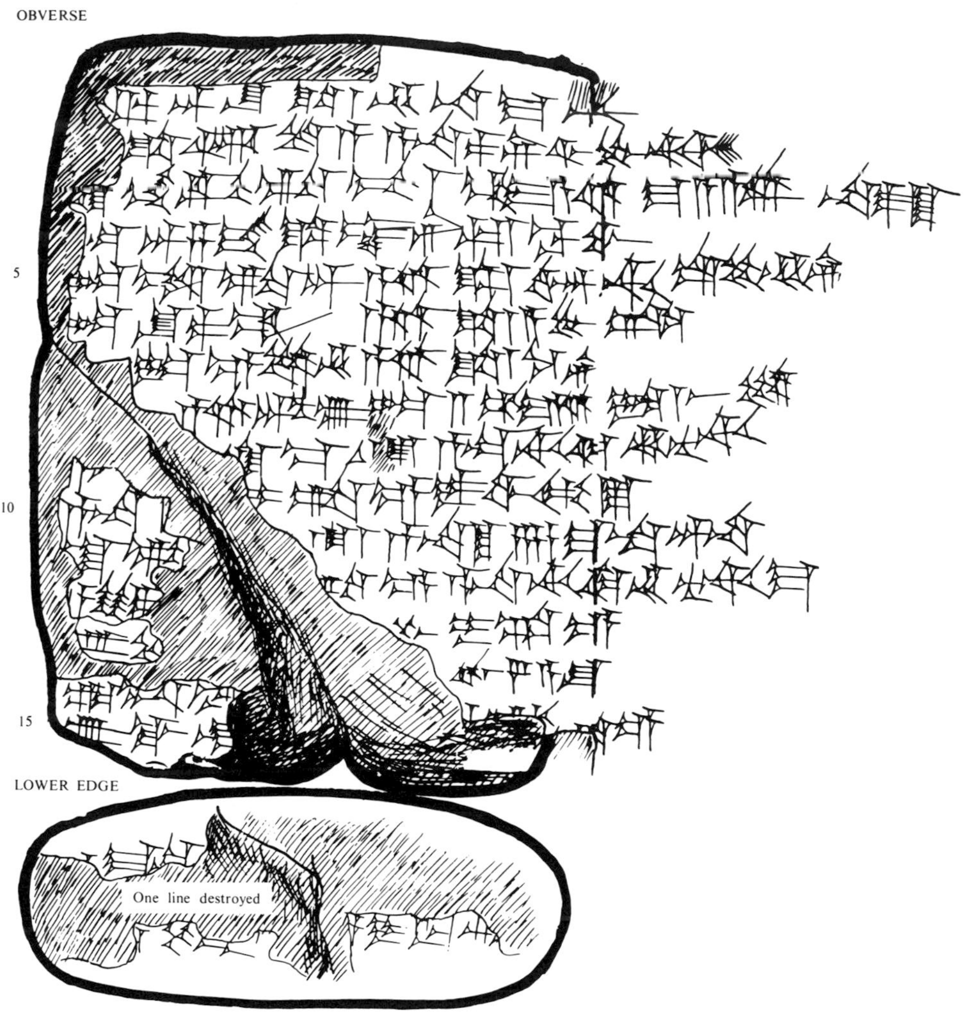
OBVERSE
5
10
15
LOWER EDGE
One line destroyed

7 *YBC* 5137

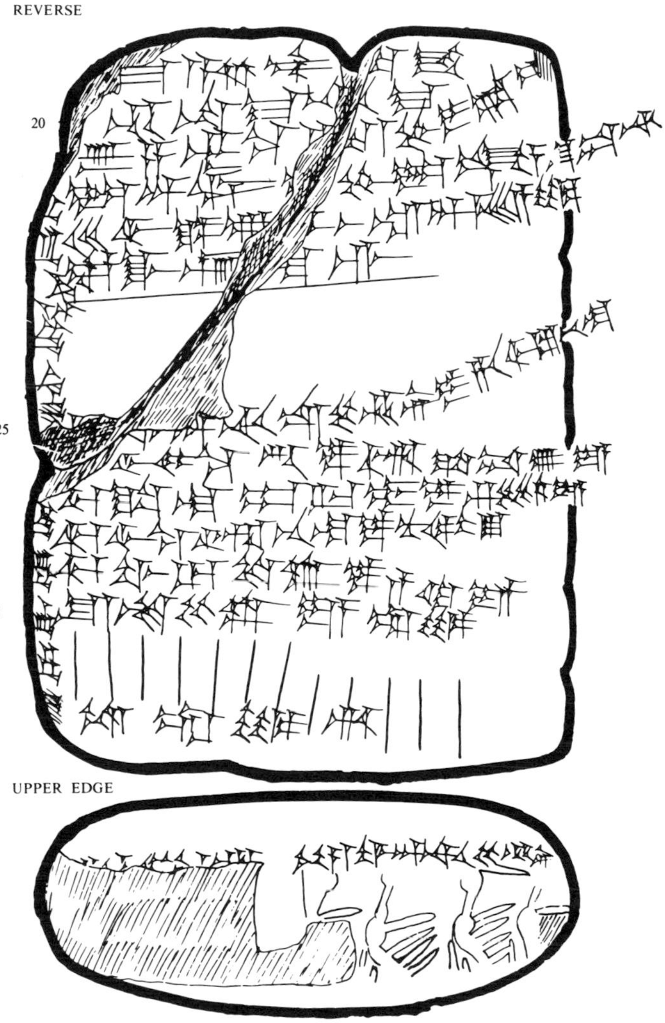

7 *YBC* 5137 (continued)

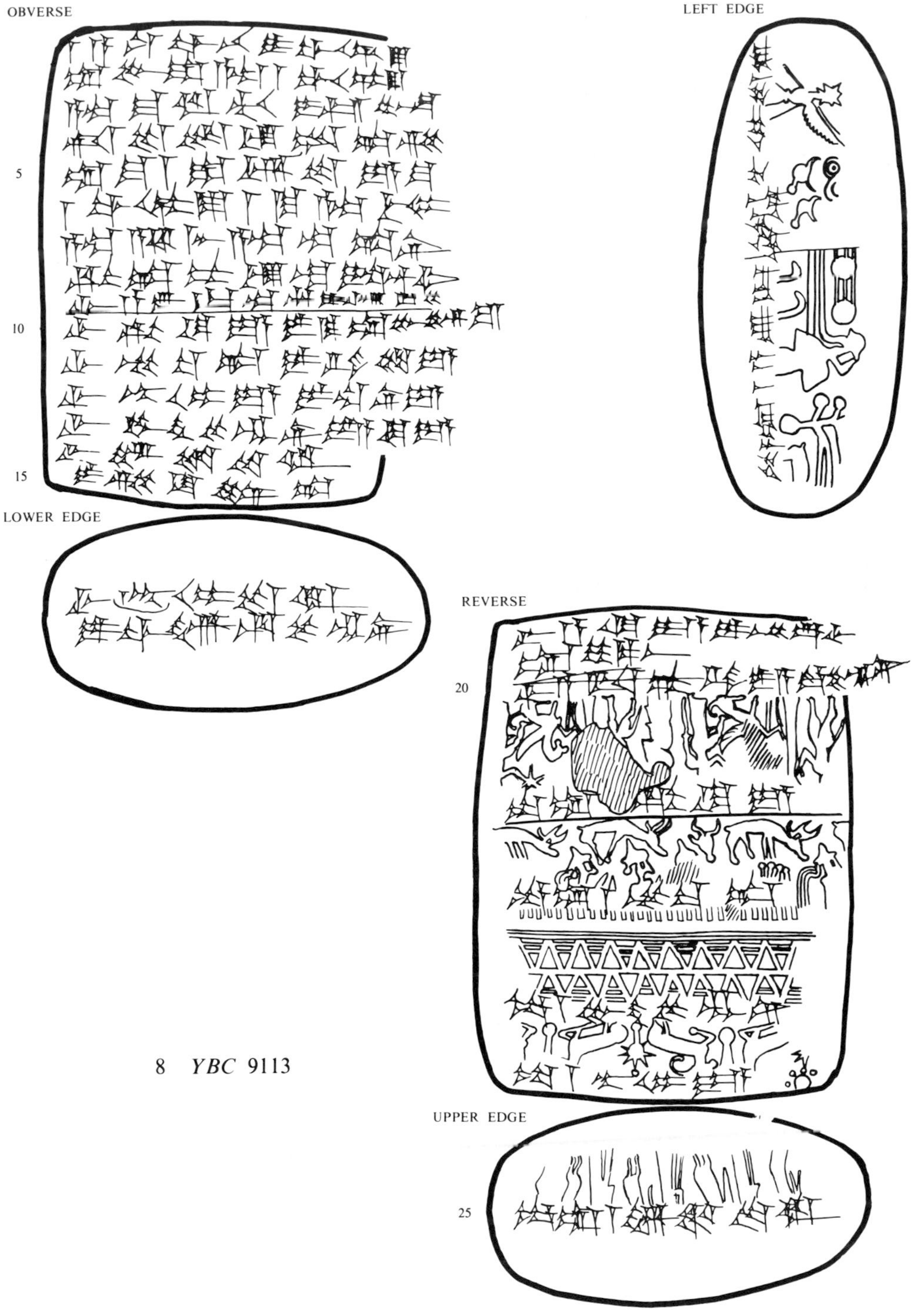
OBVERSE
LEFT EDGE
LOWER EDGE
REVERSE
UPPER EDGE

8 *YBC* 9113

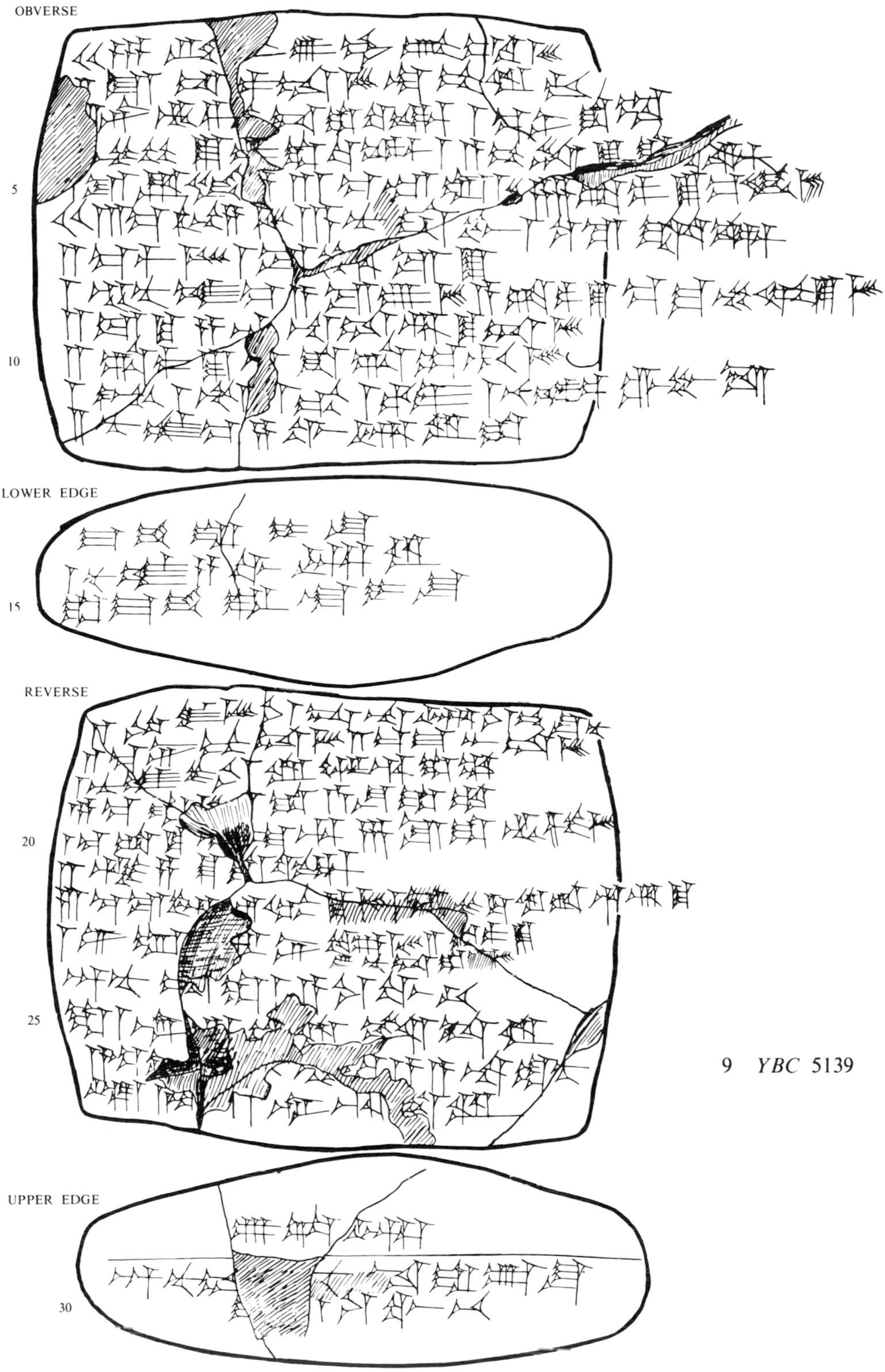

9 *YBC* 5139

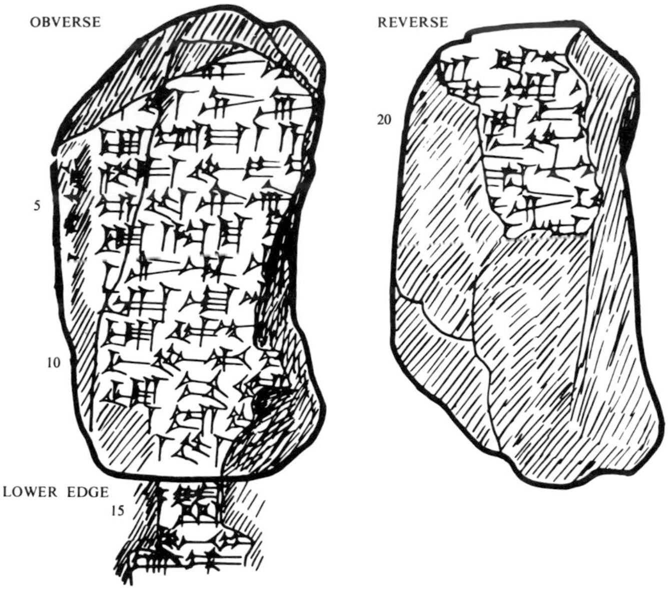

10 *YBC* 5125

11 *YBC* 5126

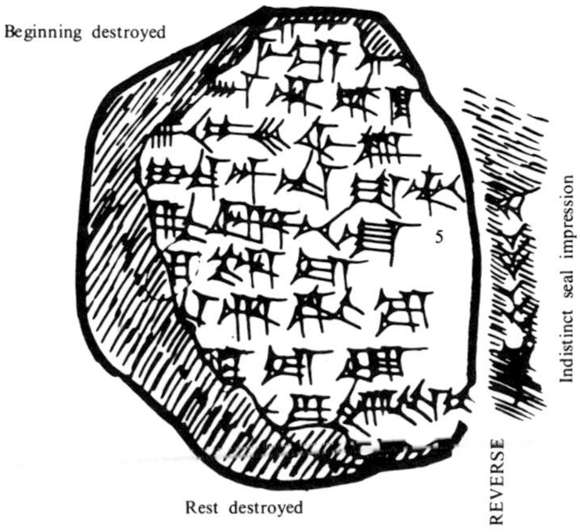

OBVERSE

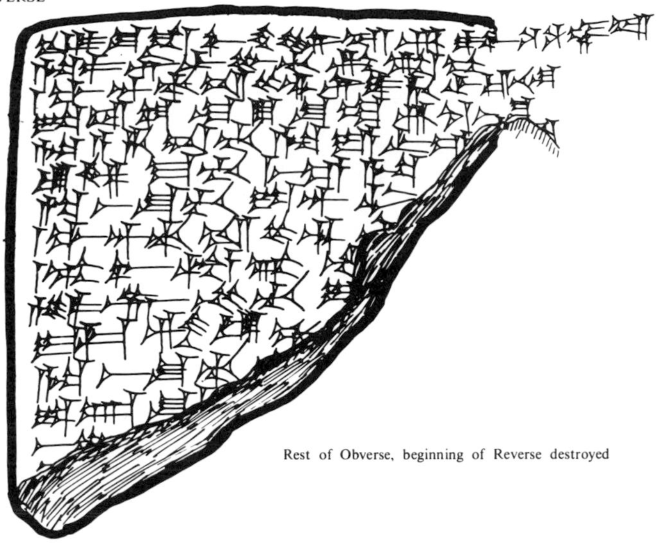

Rest of Obverse, beginning of Reverse destroyed

LEFT EDGE

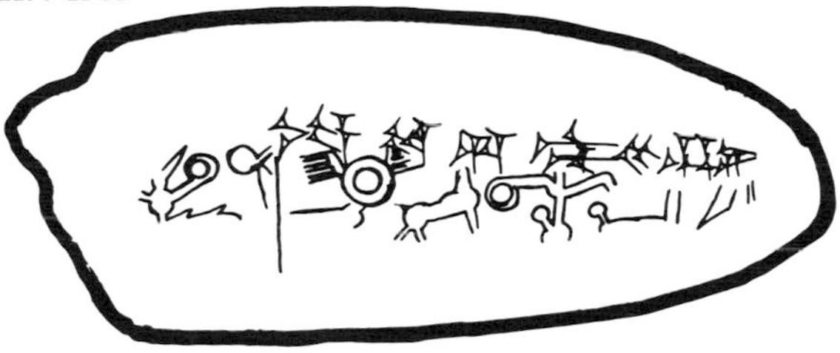

REVERSE

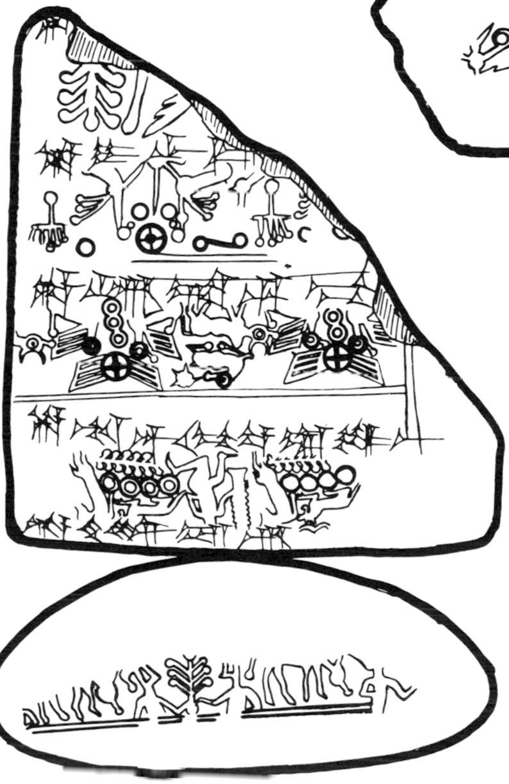

12 *NBC* 9112

13 *YBC* 5132

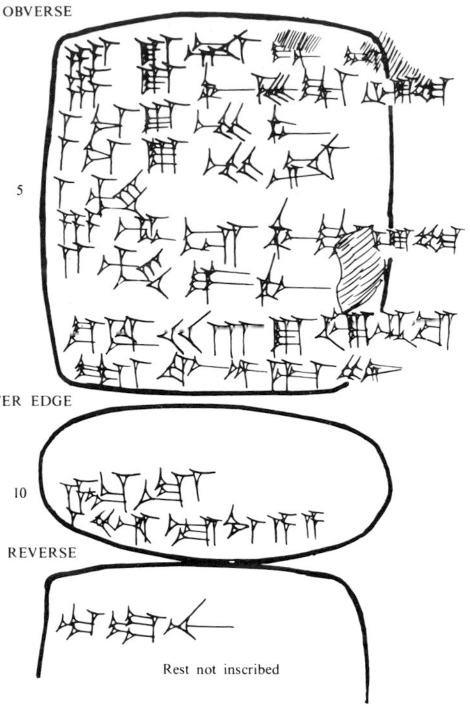

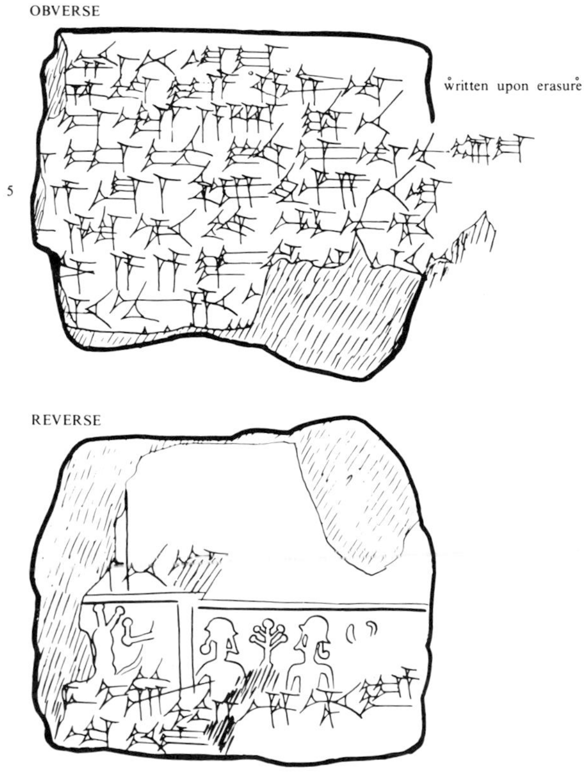

14 *YBC* 5127

OBVERSE

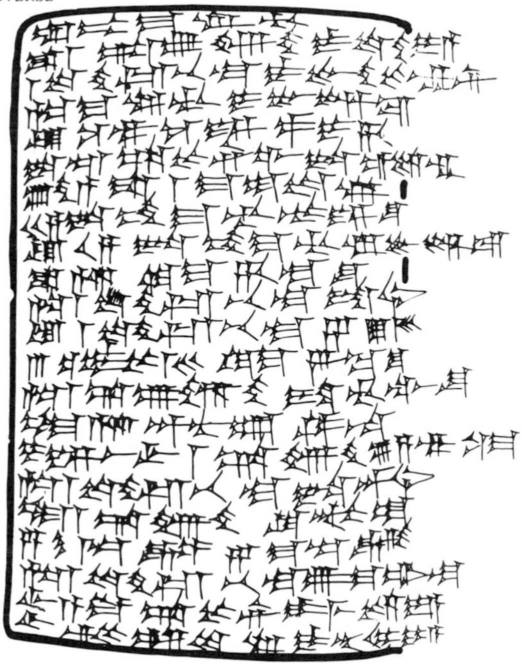

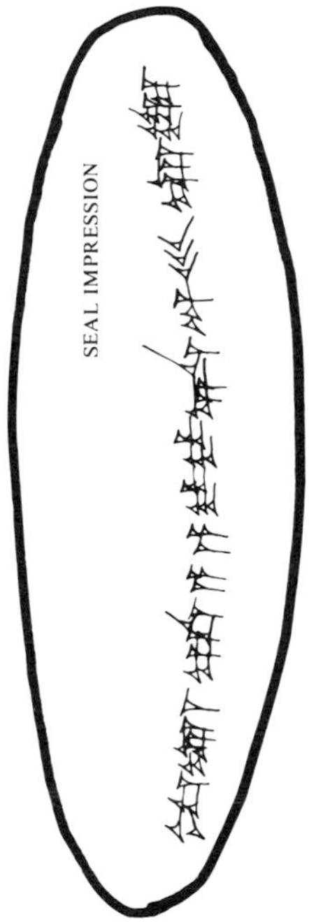

LOWER EDGE

REVERSE

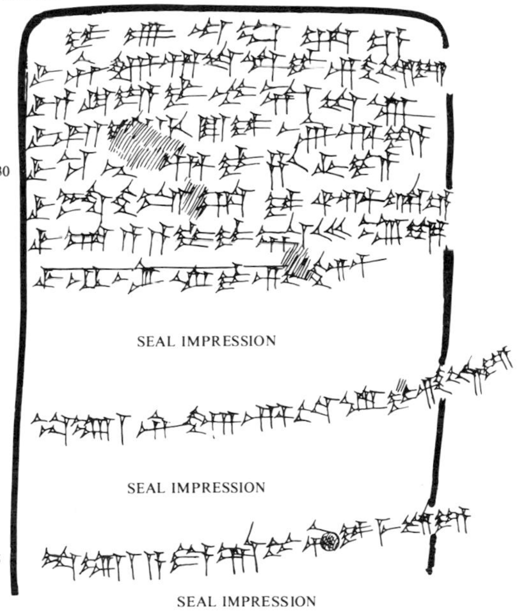

15 *NCBT* 1933

UPPER EDGE

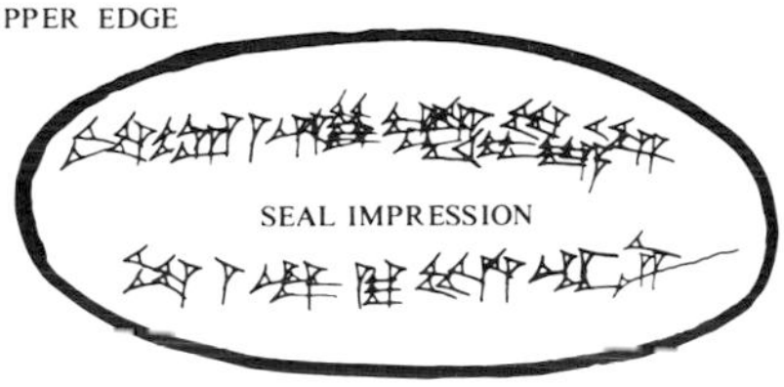

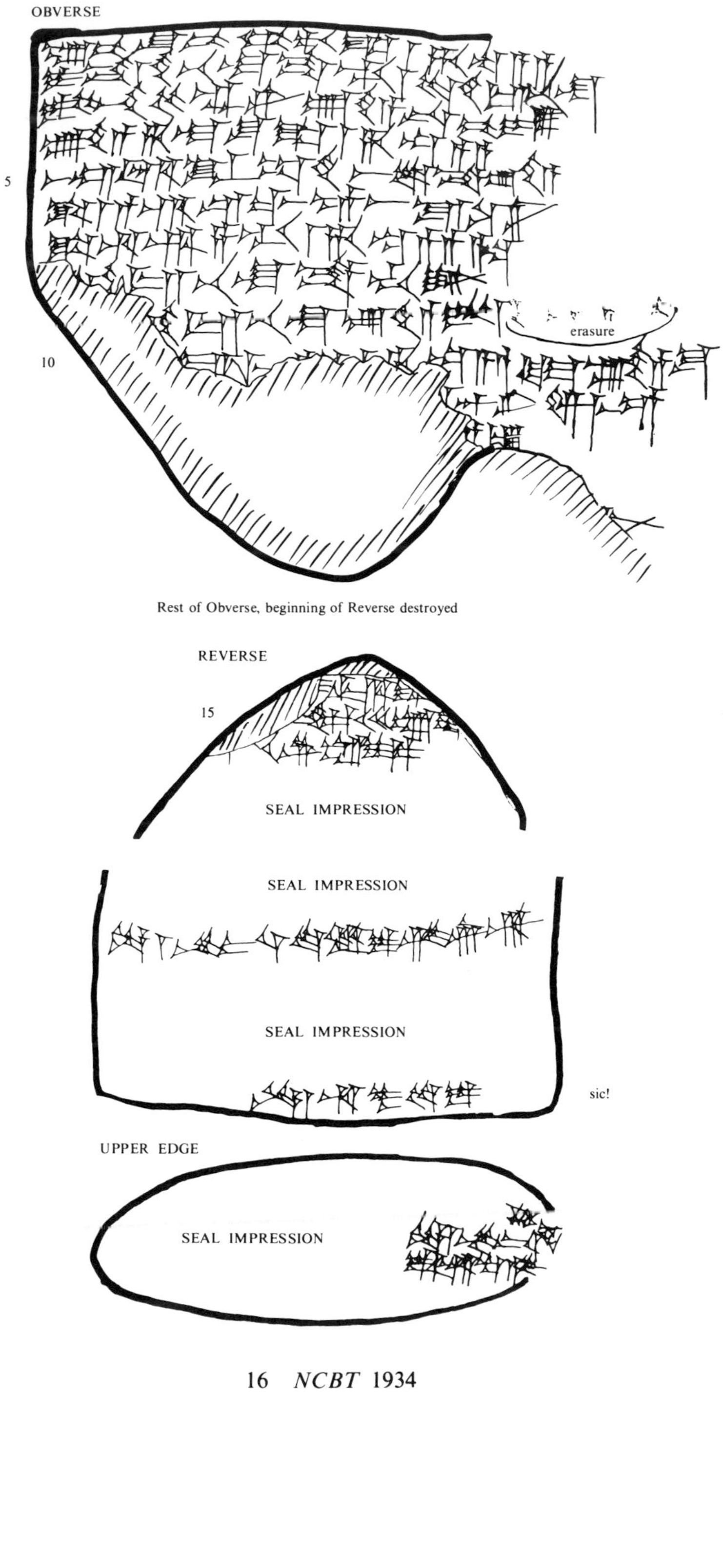
OBVERSE
5
erasure
10
Rest of Obverse, beginning of Reverse destroyed
REVERSE
15
SEAL IMPRESSION
SEAL IMPRESSION
SEAL IMPRESSION
sic!
UPPER EDGE
SEAL IMPRESSION

16 *NCBT* 1934

OBVERSE

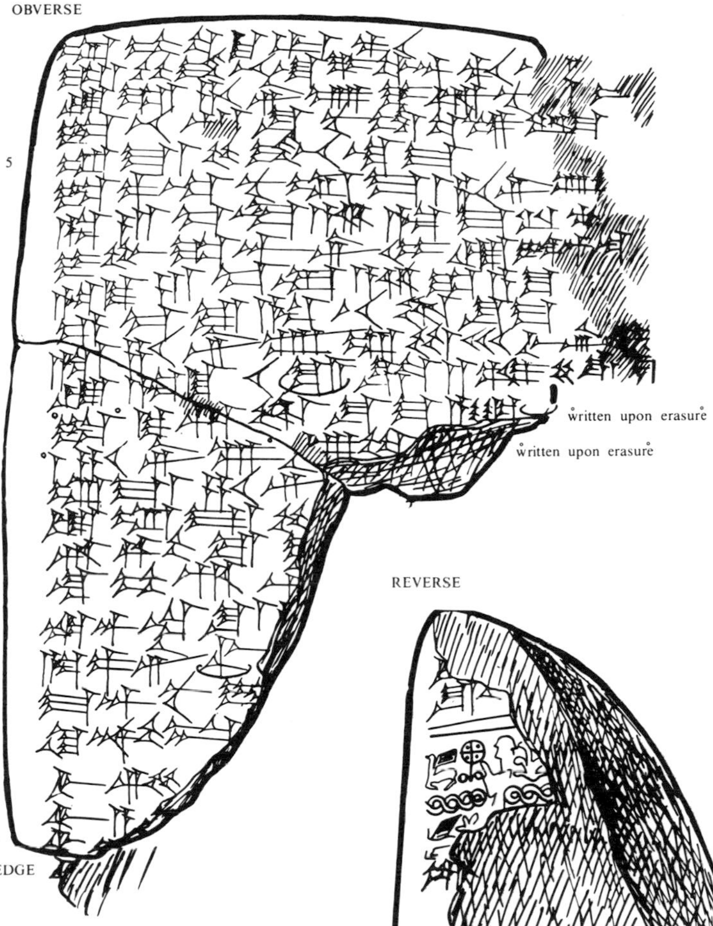

REVERSE

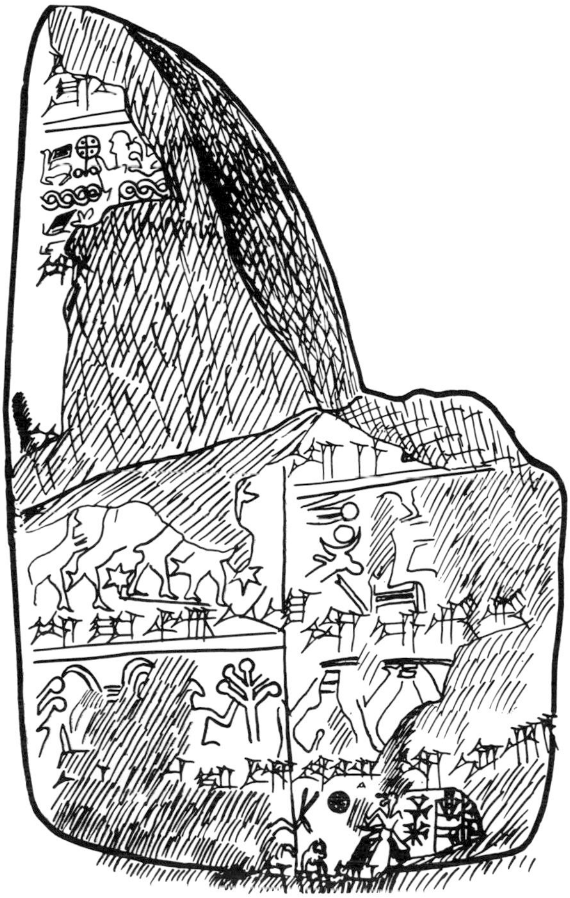

17 *YBC* 5130

OBVERSE

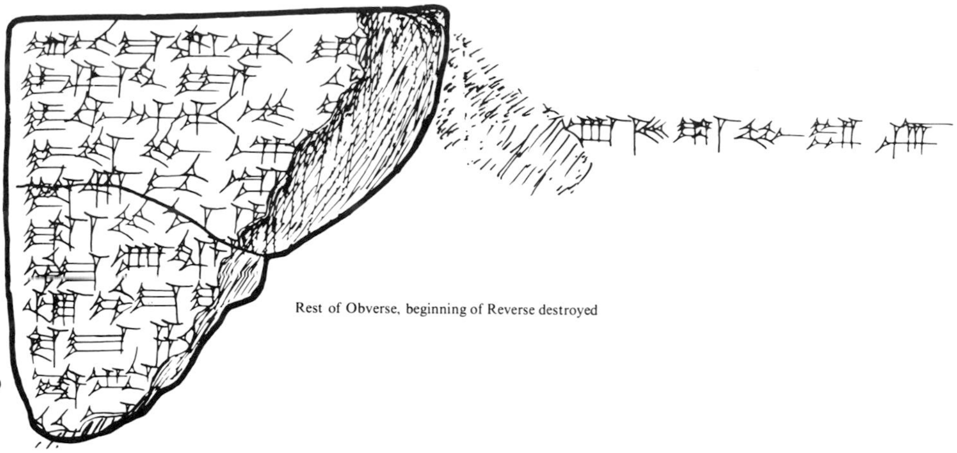

REVERSE

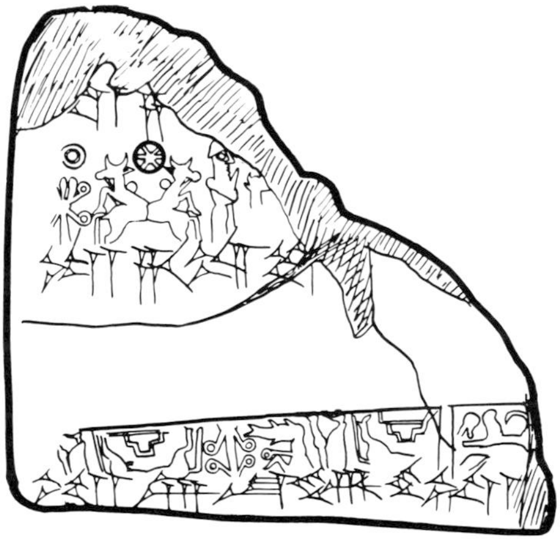

LEFT EDGE

UPPER EDGE

18 *YBC* 5136

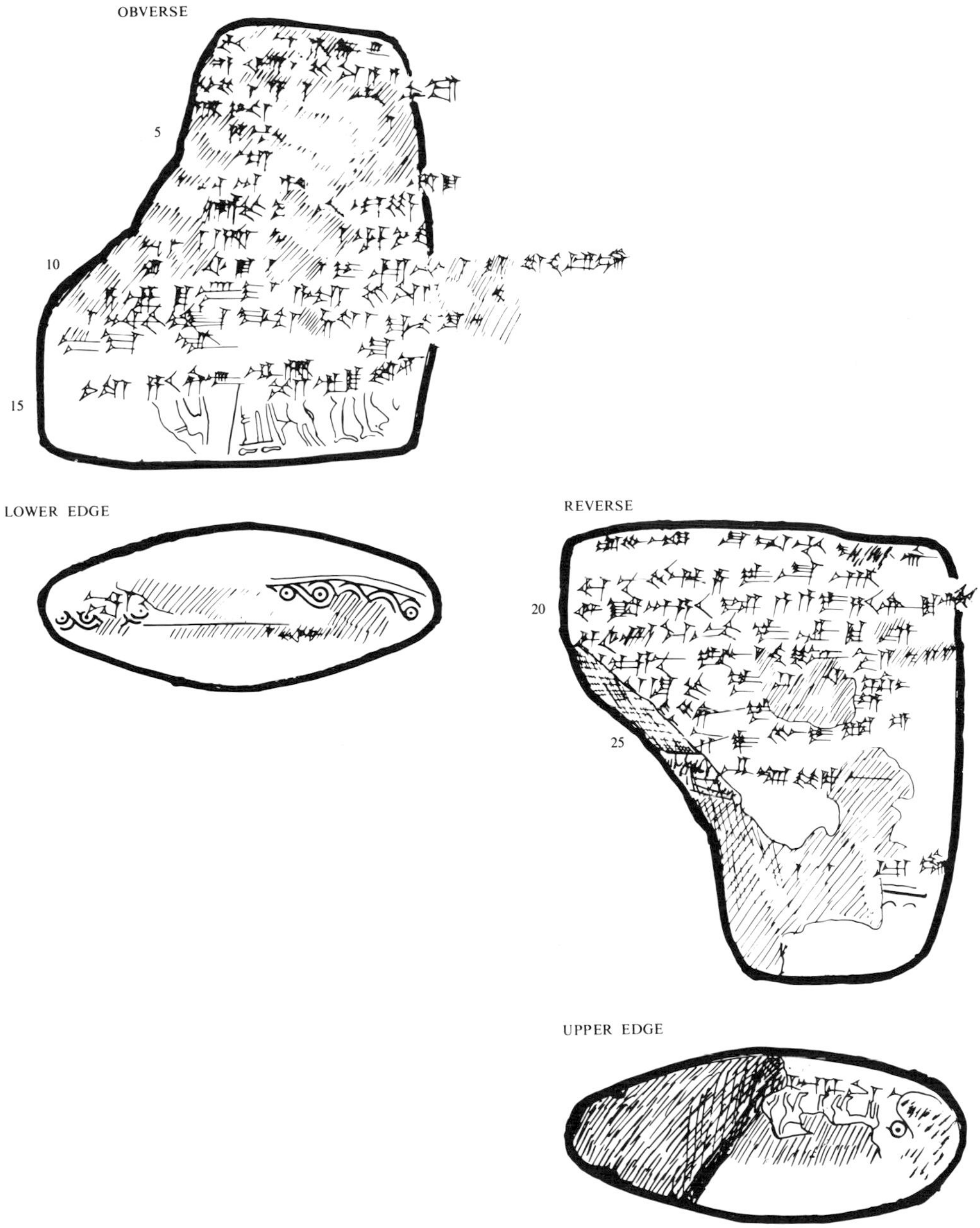

19 *YBC* 5133

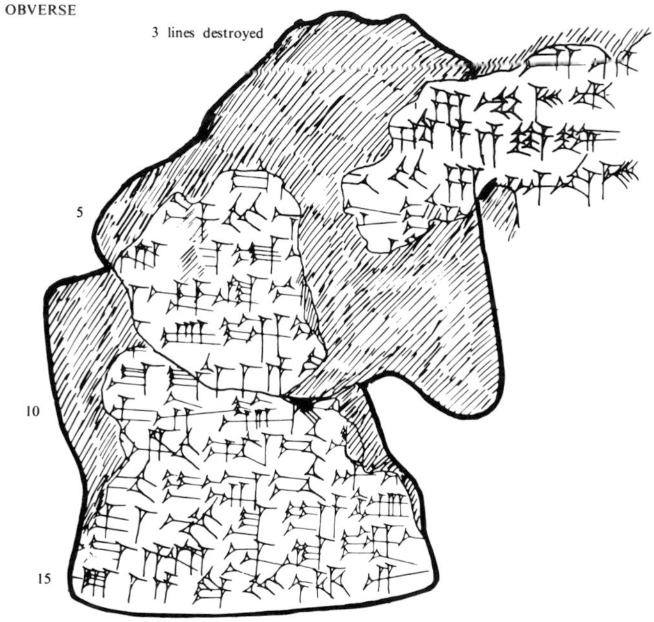

20 *YBC* 5140

LOWER EDGE

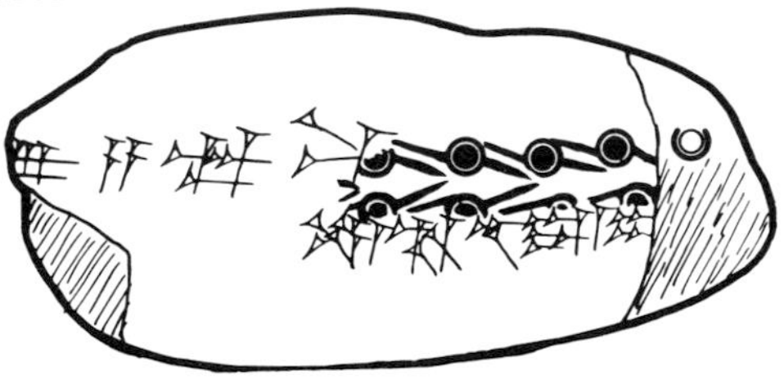

REVERSE

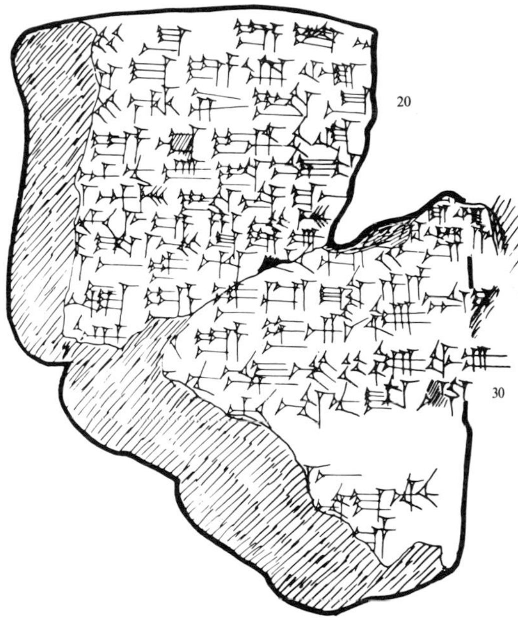

Rest destroyed

20 *YBC* 5140 (continued)

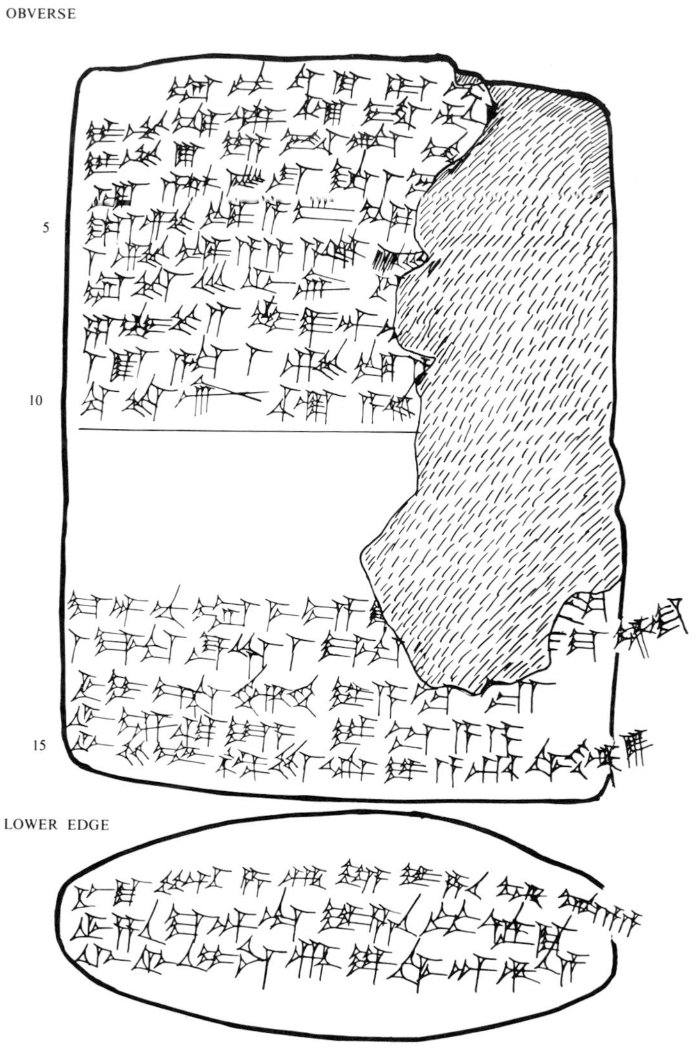

21 *YBC* 5129

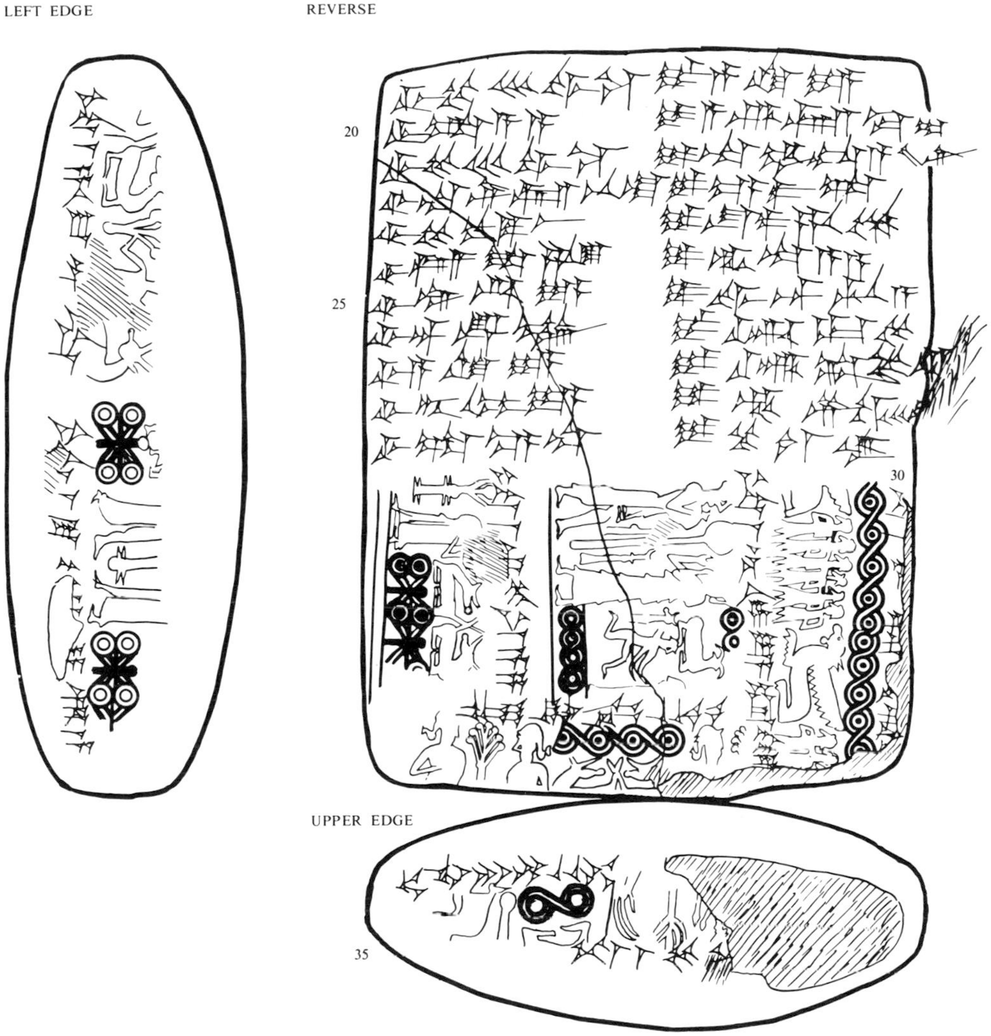

21 *YBC* 5129 (continued)

OBVERSE

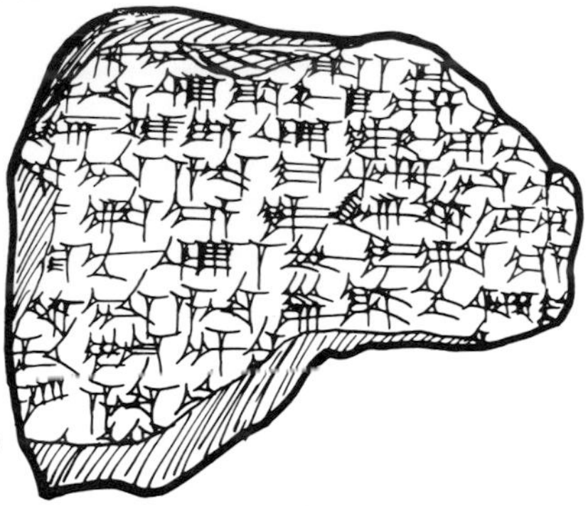

REVERSE

22 *YBC* 5134

OBVERSE

REVERSE

SEAL IMPRESSION

23 *YBC* 11275

OBVERSE

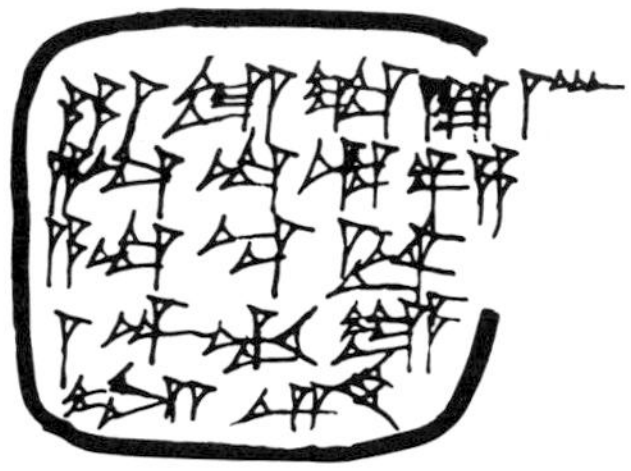

5

REVERSE

SEAL IMPRESSION

25 *YBC* 5145

OBVERSE

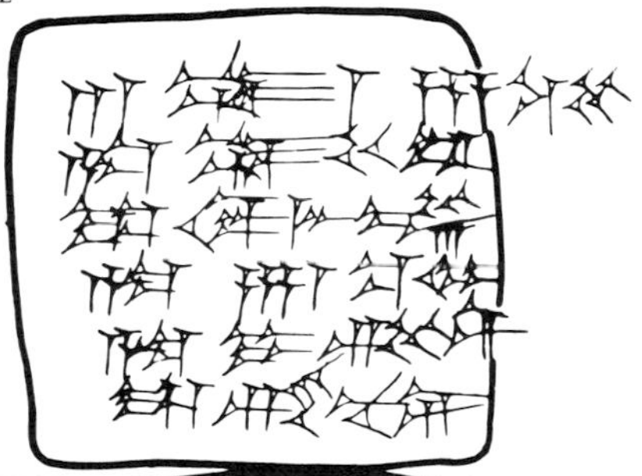

5

LOWER EDGE

24 *NBC* 6500

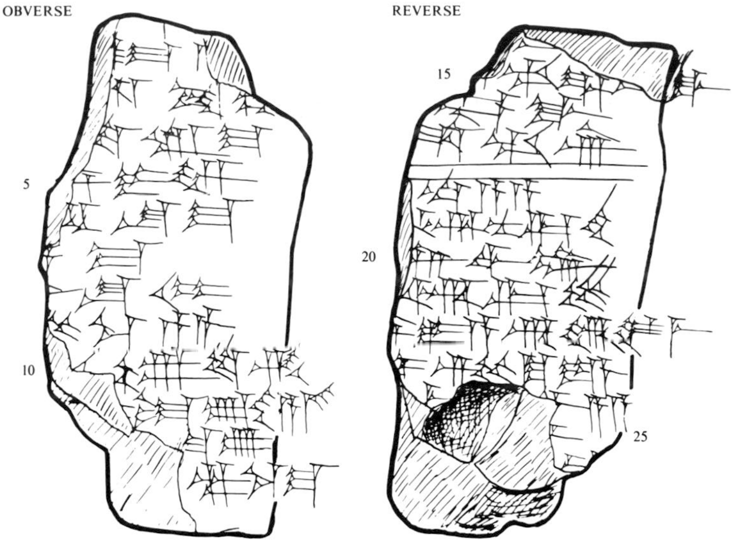

26 *YBC* 5128

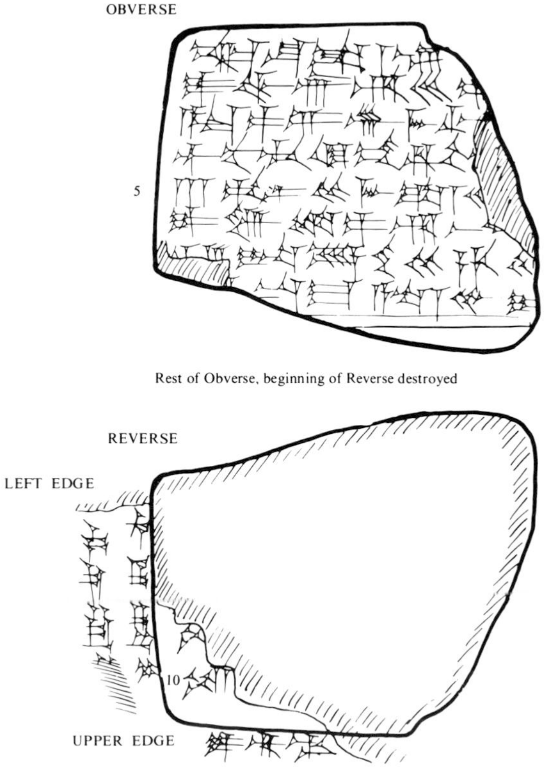

27 *YBC* 5144

Strays From a 'Nuzi' Archive

with an appendix:

Two 'Nuzi' Texts in the Wellcome Institute for the History of Medicine

A. R. MILLARD
The University of Liverpool

'Nuzi' texts first came to scholarly notice when T. G. Pinches published one example from the British Museum's collections in 1896 (*CT* 2.21). That was one of many tablets of the same sort which entered the Museum between the years 1890 and 1905. Local treasure hunters dug them from a group of mounds south-west of Kirkuk, transporting them in sacks by donkey for sale in Baghdad.[1] There the representatives of foreign museums purchased them. As he published one example, Bruno Meissner commented, in 1902, that three hundred of the tablets had been sold to London a few years before.[2] The accidental discovery of similar documents in Kirkuk itself, just before the First World War, 33 acquired by the Iraq Museum, 18 brought to the British Museum by the resident surgeon, W. Corner, resulted in C. J. Gadd's pioneer edition 'Tablets from Kirkuk'.[3] With these 51 tablets, Gadd included 28 from a group bought by the Museum in 1894, and 1 obtained in 1899. Other groups were identified by H. H. Figulla as he catalogued some of the Museum's tablets, and were brought to the writer's notice in 1960 by D. J. Wiseman, then a member of the Museum staff. Further groups of 'Nuzi' tablets were located among the uncatalogued collections during the next few years. There are now between three and four hundred identified Nuzi texts although some are but small fragments. Unfortunately other commitments have delayed the task of editing all of these, but it is a pleasure to offer three texts here in tribute to E. R. Lacheman who characteristically gave advice and encouragement when I began to examine the British Museum's Nuzi collections. Thanks are also due to the Trustees of the British Museum and to Dr. Edmond Sollberger, Keeper

[1]C. J. Gadd, *RA* 23 (1926) 50-52, and R. F. S. Starr, *Nuzi* I (1939) xxix-xxx, give accounts of the local activities that put the first Nuzi tablets on the antiquities market.

[2]*OLZ* 5 (1902) Sp. 245.

[3]*RA* 23 (1926) 49-161

of the Department of Western Asiatic Antiquities for permission to study and publish these tablets.

Two of the tablets are deeds of 'adoption' identical in every respect apart from the names and the number of the men acting as 'adoptive fathers'. The script is fairly small and neat, the tablets well shaped with square corners.

BM 85311 7.8x5.3 cms.

1. ^{I}*Na-i-še-ri* DUMU *Ta-e*
2. ^{I}*A-ri-ba-ar-ra-ap-ḫe* DUMU *Ḫa-nu*
3. ^{I}[*T*]*a-ar-mi-ja* DUMU *Ar-še-eḫ-li*
4. 3 LÚ^{MEŠ} *an-nu-tu*$_4$ ^{I}[*Zi*]*-li-ja*
5. DUMU *Ip-ša-ḫa-lu a+na ma-ru-ti*
6. *i-pu-šu-uš-ma* GIŠ.SAR *i-na* ^{URU}*Ta-ar-gu-li*
7. *ki-ma zi-ti-šu i-di-nu-ni-šu*
8. *ù* ^{I}*Zi-li-ja a+na* 3 LÚ^{MEŠ}
9. *an-nu-ti* 4 GU$_4$^{MEŠ} *ki-mu-ú*
10. *ma-*[*ru*]*-ti-šu i-di-in*
11. *ša ib-ba-la-ka-tu*$_4$
12. 1 MA.NA KÙ.BABBAR *ù* 1 MA.N[A KÙ.G]I
13. Ì.LÁ.E *ù* ^{GIŠ}GAG *ša* [URUDU]
14. *a+na pí-šu i-maḫ-ḫa-ṣú*
15. IGI *Tu-up-ki-ja* DUMU *Te-šu-*[*ja*]
16. IGI *Na-al-du-ú-ja* DUMU *Ni-nu-a-ša-al*
17. IGI *A-ga-mi* DUMU *Tu-ra*

---

rev.

18. IGI *Zu-zu-ja* DUMU *I-ri-ki*
19. IGI *I-ra-zi* DUMU *E-na-ja*
20. IGI *Šu-uk-ri-ja* DUMU *A-ar-ta-e*
21. IGI *Ta-ú-ga-an-ni* DUMU *Nu-ur-*^{d}*Adad*
22. IGI *Ḫu-di-ja* DUMU *Šu-uk-ri-ja*
23. IGI *Pu-ú-ja* DUMU *A-ar-nu-ur-ḫe ša-*[*gu-ú*]
24. IGI *Pu-di-ja* DUMU *Na-ni-ja*
nu-a-ru
25. IGI *Zi-ni-ja* DUMU *Be-el-*MA.AN.SUM
DUB.SAR

---

26. NA$_4$ KIŠIB *Šu-uk-ri-ja ḫa-za-ni*
ša $^{URU.KI}$*Ta-ar-gu-li*

BM 85355 7.2x5.4 cms.

1. ^{I}*Ka-ni-ja* DUMU *Ar-til-la*
2. ^{I}*A-mi-iš-ta-e* DUMU *Ku-ni-i*
3. 2 LÚ^{MEŠ} *an-nu-tu*$_4$ ^{I}*Zi-li-ja*
4. DUMU *Ip-ša-ḫa-lu a+na ma-ru-ti*
5. *i-pu-šu-šu-ma ù* GIŠ.SAR

6. *i-na* URU.KI*Ta-ar-gu-ul-li*
7. *ki-ma zi-ti-šu i-di-nu-ni-šu*
8. *ù* I*Zi-li-ja a+na* 2 LÚ^{MEŠ} *an-nu-*[*ti*]
9. 2 GU$_4$^{MEŠ} *ki-mu-ú ma-ru-ti-šu*[3a]
10. *i-di-in ša ib-ba-la-ka-ti*
11. 1 MA.NA KÙ.BABBAR *ù* 1 MA.NA KÙ.GI
12. Ì.LÁ.E [*ù*] GIŠGAG *ša* URUDU[3b]
13. *a+na pí-šu i-ma-ḫa-ṣú*
14. IGI *Tu-up-ki-ja* DUMU *Te-šu-ja*
15. IGI *Na-al-du-ja* DUMU *Ni-nu-a-ša-al*
16. IGI *A-ga-mi* DUMU *Tù-ra*
17. IGI *Zu-zu-ja* DUMU *I-ri-ki*

---

rev.
18. IGI *I-ra-zi* DUMU *I-na-ja*
19. IGI *Šu-uk-ri-ja* DUMU *A-ar-ta-e*
20. IGI *Ta-*[*ú*]*-ga-an-ni* DUMU *Nu-ur-*d*Adad*
21. IGI *Ḫu-di-ja* DUMU *Šu-uk-ri-ja*
22. IGI *Pu-ú-ja* DUMU *Ar-nu-ur-ḫe ša-gu-ú*
23. IGI [*Pu-di*]*-ja* DUMU *Na-ni-ja*
[*nu*]*-a-ru*
24. [IGI *Zi-ni*]*-ja* DUMU *Be-el-*MA.AN.SUM
[DU]B.SAR
25. [NA$_4$ KIŠIB *Šu-uk-ri-ja ḫa-za*]*-ni*
[*ša* URU.KI*Ta-ar-gu-ul-l*]*i*

Among the names in these two texts Ariparrapḫe, Ninuašal, and Pudiya were previously unknown. Outside of the present group of texts, the witness Irazi son of Enaya may be the Errazi son of Ennaya appearing in other tablets from the early finds (*RA* 23 34:26 etc.; *TCL* 9 44:24; see also index below) and Šukriya son of Artae could be the Šukriya son of Arteya known from a number of excavated texts (*HSS* 16 24:18 etc.). There is a Šukritešub titled *ḫazannu* in *HSS* 14 24:1, but he is a *ḫazannu* of the town of Aršalibi. The principal, Zilija, son of Ipšaḫalu, was tentatively identified with Zilip-apu son of Ipšaḫalu by Gelb, Purves, and Macrae in *NPN* 177b. Such equivalences require further study by those examining the generations and genealogies of Nuzi.

The witnesses Nalduya, Zuzuya, and Sukriya occur in the fragment *VAT* 4581 (*VS* I 107), the present texts permitting restorations there. The tablet had been written for Ziliya by the same scribe, Ziniya.

[3aThe use of *ki-mu-ú ma-ru-ti-šu* in *BM* 85311:9-10 and *BM* 85355:9 instead of NÌ.BA-*šu*/*qīštišu*/*qīltišu* is unique, eds.]

[3bFor the use of the *sikkatu* clause see the *postscriptum* to the article of Fadhil, eds.]

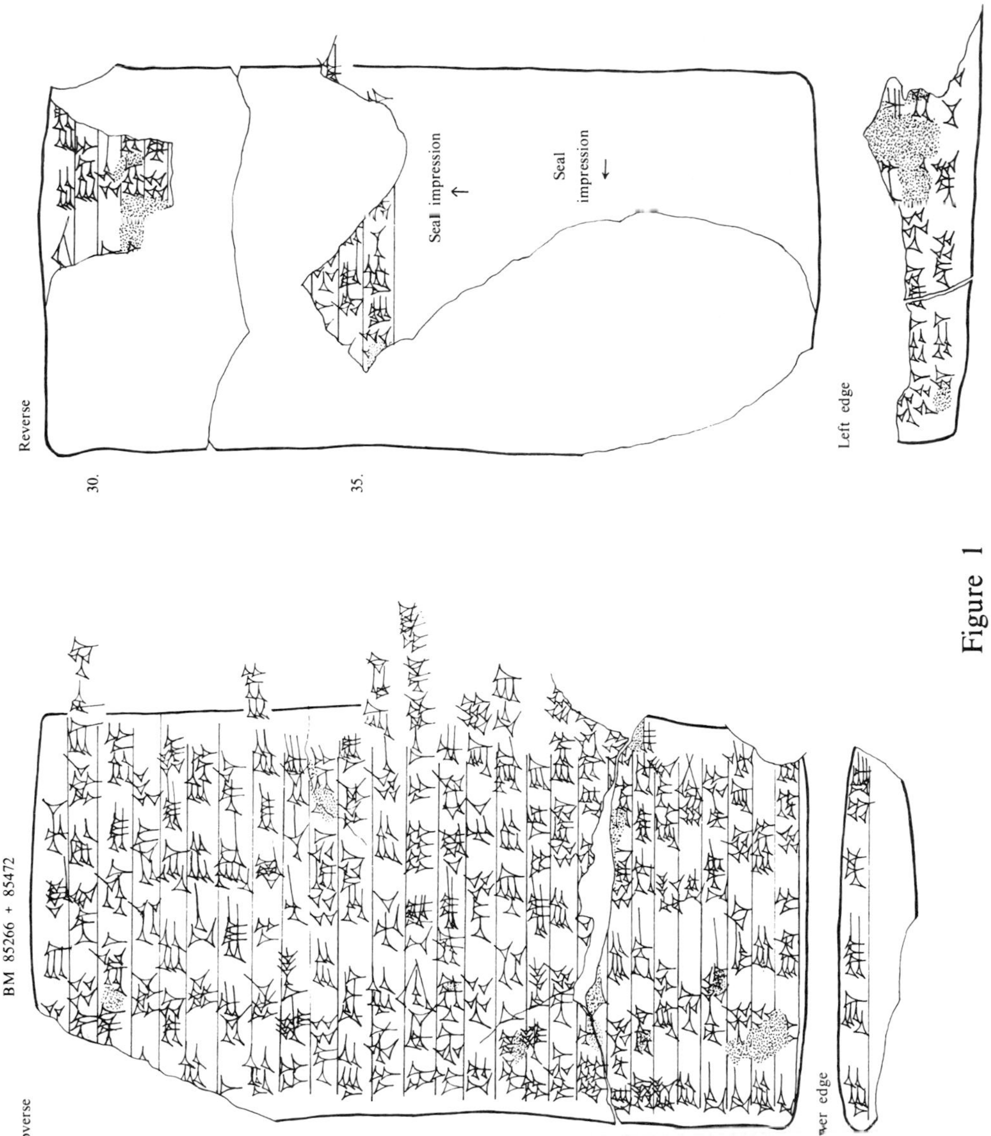
BM 85266 + 85472
Obverse
1.
5.
10.
15.
20.
25.
Lower edge
Reverse
30.
35.
Seal impression
Seal impression
Left edge

Figure 1

Tarkulli is a place named in other texts and believed to survive as the village of Tarkhalan, one and a half miles north-east of Yorghan Tepe (Nuzi).[4]

* * *

The third tablet is also an 'adoption' deed written for Ziliya, but has a rather different appearance, the signs being wider and the lines being separated by rulings, often uneven. This text varies, too, in its orthography and expression of the penalty clauses, clearly indicating a different scribe.

BM 85266 + 85472 11.5x6.1 cms. (Figure 1)

1. [*ṭup-p*]*í ma-ru-ti*
2. [*ša* ^{1}]*Zi-gi* DUMU *Ḫa-ma-an-na*
3. [^{1}*A*]*r-ša-du-ú-ja*
4. [DU]MU *Ḫa-bi-iš-še*
5. [^{1}]*Ta-i-šu-ú-uḫ*
6. DUMU *Ḫa-ši-i-ja*
7. ^{1}*Tu*$_4$*-ú-ra-ri*
8. DUMU *Ḫa-a-ru-ú-i-ja*
9. 4 LÚ^{MEŠ} *an-nu-tu*$_4$
10. *Zi-i-li-ja*
11. DUMU *Ip-ša-ḫa-lu*
12. *a-na* DUMU-*ti i-pu-šu-uš*
13. 3 ANŠE *ù* 8 *a-me-ḫa-ri* A.ŠÀ
14. *a-na* ^{URU}*Du-ú-ru-ul-pa*
15. *ki-mu zi-ti-šu* SUM
16. A.ŠÀ 1 *bi la i-ra-ši-ma*
17. 4 LÚ^{MEŠ} *ú-za-ku-ma*
18. *a-na Zi-i-li-ja* S[UM]
19. 19 AN[ŠE] Š[E *a*]*-na qí-il-*[*ti-šu-nu*]
20. *ù*$^{!}$ *Zi-i-li-ja* SUM
21. *ša da-ba-ba ú-ba-ú*
22. GÚ KÙ.BABBAR GÚ KÙ.GI
23. *i-na-di-in*
24. IGI ^{d}IM$^{!}$ *ù* ^{d}UTU
25. IGI *Mu-uš-te-šu-ub*
26. DUMU [*Z*]*i-i-ja*
27. IGI *A*$^{?}$*-ša-a-še-j*[*a*$^{?}$]

lower edge

28. DUMU *Šu-ú-ḫu-ut-tu*$_4$

[4]E. R. Lacheman, *BASOR* 81 (1941) 12, accepted by H. Lewy, *JAOS* 88 (1968) 160, n. 77.

reverse
29-33. 5 lines damaged
4-5 lines lost
34. [ ]x *m*[*u*]-*ni*
35. [IGI/ŠU *B*]*e*!-*el*-Š[EŠ! MEŠ]
36. [DUB.S]AR DUMU *Be-e*[*l*-MA.AN.SU]M
traces of three seal impressions
left edge
37. NA_4 [KIŠIB]x x[ ]
38. NA_4 KIŠIB *Ta-mu-x-x-bi*? [ ]
39. NA_4 KIŠIB *Zi-gi be-e*[l A.ŠÀ?]

None of the persons named is found in other texts, except for Ziliya and the scribe's father. Several are of uncertain reading.

The place Dur-ulpa is probably the same as Dur-ubla which H. Lewy tried to locate south-west of Nuzi, by a swamp.[5]

Ziniya son of Bel-iddina, scribe of the first two tablets edited here, also wrote the Berlin tablets *VAT* 4586 (*VS* I 106) and *VAT* 4581 (*VS* I 107) for Ziliya. On the first two British Museum tablets the scribe used a ligature for *a-na* (the head of the horizontal of *na* beginning between the legs of the *a*), which may be indicated for two more tablets, *VAT* 4580 and 4582 + 4585 (*VS* I 108, 109) by the closeness of the signs in Ungnad's copies. These two texts share with *BM* 85311 and 85355 the known but rare penalty of a copper peg

[5]H. Lewy, *JAOS* 88 (1968) 159. [This tablet has many Kassite names and Dūr-ubla is to be sought close to or even within Kassite territory. With this interesting new spelling of the toponym in l.14 it might be useful to add a list of all the attested spellings for this town:

URU	*Du-ru-ub-la*	*AASOR* 16 90:5-6; *HSS* 13 37:2; *HSS* 15 283:7; *JENu* 698:6
URU	*Du-ur-ub-la*	*JEN* 16:28
[URU]	*Du-lu-ub-ra*	*HSS* 144 99:10
URU	*Tu-ru-ub-la*	*HSS* 14 208A:2
URU	*Tu-ru-*[*ub*]-⌈*la*⌉	*HSS* 15 73:9
URU	*Tu-rù-u*[*b-la*]	*HSS* 15 286:19 (courtesy C. Zaccagnini)
URU	BÀD-*ub-la*	*HSS* 14 175:2′-3′; *HSS* 15 264:13; *SMN* 1067:46 (=*EN 9* 165, Eichler)
URU	BÀD-*u*[*b-la*]	*JEN* 497:2
URU	*Du-ú-ru-ul-pa*	*BM* 85266+85472:14 (the new reference)

Note also the use as personal name:

ᴵ*Du-ru-ub-la HSS* 16 81:7; ᴵ*D*[*u-r*]*u-ub-la-a HSS* 13 19:31; ᴵ*Tu-ru-up-li HSS* 13 417:9 [*D*]*u-ru-ub-li* DUMU *Šúk-ri-ja HSS* 19 85:35, but (same person) NA_4 ᴵ*Du-lu-ub-ri* 1.47. References courtesy of K. Deller, eds.]

hammered into the mouth of a defaulter, and with *BM* 85266 + 85472 the invocation of divine witnesses. The occurrence of ^{d}IM with ^{d}UTU in *VS* I 108.10' (cf. 109.18) shows that the sign in the third of our tablets is to be read as the Storm-god's name,[5a] presumably Tešub.[6] Both this text and *VS* I 108 prescribe an enormous fine, 1 talent of silver and 1 talent of gold, contrasting with the mina of other deeds.

No other tablets, so far as the writer can discover, record the business of Ziliya son of Ipšaḫalu (unless he be the Zilip-apu of various texts, see above). He was clearly a typical 'Nuzi' business man. Likewise, there are no other examples of the skill of Ziniya, a clerk who wrote with a neater hand than most of his local contemporaries. Whether other unusual features of these texts arise from his whim or from varying local situations cannot be determined. His writing of *zittu* syllabically but of *šaqālu* with Ì-LÁ-E set him beside the earlier scribes at Nuzi, although he employs the term *ṭuppi mārūti* as the title of the texts and the term *qīštu* for Ziliya's reciprocal gift (*BM* 85266 + 85472.19), which were not current among the earliest of the Nuzi scribes.[7] Unique in Nuzi is the phrase *dababa buʾʾû* (*BM* 85266 + 85472:21) otherwise standard in legal deeds of Middle and Late Assyrian origin. The name of his father, written with MA-AN-SUM for *iddina*, stands as the scribe's name on *AO* 6028 (*TCL* 9 14), a text which also includes the copper peg penalty, and which bears a seal impression having the owner's name engraved on the stone, an unusual practice at Nuzi. Again, whether these were father and son, or pupil, is a topic for future study.

Thus a few stray pieces from an ancient archive can be re-united, and together make their contribution to knowledge of the culture which E. R. Lacheman has laboured so devotedly to bring to light.

Appendix: Two 'Nuzi' Texts in the Wellcome Institute for the History of Medicine

The Wellcome Institute for the History of Medicine, established in London by the late Sir Henry Wellcome, housed a miscellany of cuneiform tablets acquired in the period between the two World Wars. Most of them were bought at auction sales in London. At various times the staff at the Institute have given the writer access to these texts, and thanks are due to them for their help, and for permission to publish pieces from the collection. In 1979-80 the whole collection of tablets was transferred to the Birmingham City Museum.

[[5a] For another reference to ^{d}IM *ù* ^{d}UTU *cf.* the fragmentary text *JENu* 1098b, eds.]
[6] *Cf.* E. Laroche, *Or* NS 45 (1976) 98.
[7] See E. Cassin, *JESHO* 5 (1962) 115ff.

Among the Wellcome tablets are two small 'Nuzi' texts which find an appropriate place of publication in this volume.[1]

WHM 170489 is a dark grey square tablet, 4.2 × 4.2 cms. (Figure 2). The text records the delivery of 12 sheep (11 grown rams, 1 mother ewe) by Wištanzu, wife of Zigi, to Wantiya, perhaps a shepherd. Traces of the impression of Wantiya's seal remain on the reverse, showing a standing figure with a standard. Wištanzu is known as the wife of Zigi from Gadd 61 (*BM* 17614). Wantiya, son of ŠEŠ-[xxx] is not to be confused with the shepherd Wantiya, son of Unkura known from *HSS* 14 508; 509; 590; and 637.

obv.	1	11 UDU NITA^{MEŠ} GAL
	2	1 UDU MÍ *ša* <Ù>.TU
	3	ŠU.NÍGIN 12 UDU^{MEŠ} *ša*
	4	^{MÍ}*Wi-iš-ta-an-zu*
	5	*aš-ša-*≪TA≫*-a*[*t* $^{\text{(I)}}$]*Zi-ge*
	6	*a-na* ŠU-*ti a-na*
	7	⸢^{I}⸣*Wa-an-ti-ja* DUMU ŠEŠ-[ ]
	8	[*n*]*a-ad-nu*
rev.		seal impression
	9	NA_4 *Wa-an-ti-ja* ^{L}[^{Ú}SIPA$^{?}$]
		remainder of reverse uninscribed

WHM 152335 is a fragmentary tablet, brown in colour, 5.1 × 4.5 cms. (Figure 3), bearing a list of personal names. The preserved portions of the text do not indicate the purpose for which the list of names was compiled.

obv.	1	[^{I}*Ut-ḫ*]*a*$^{!}$*-a+a* DUMU *Eḫ-li*$^{!}$*-te-*⸢*šup*⸣
	2	[^{I}*Er-w*]*i-šarri* DUMU ⸢*En*⸣$^{!}$*-šúk-rù*
	3	[^{I}*D*]*u-ra-ar-te-šup* DUMU *Ku-du*[*q-*]⸢*qa*⸣
	4	[^{I}]⸢*Ú*⸣*-ta-an-*<*til*> ^{LÚ}DUB.SAR
	5	[^{I}*N*]*a-ni-p*[*u-g*]*ur* DUMU *Ḫa-lu-ut-*⸢*ta*⸣
	6	[^{I}*T*]*a-i-*⸢*te*⸣*-šup* DUMU *Er-wi-šarri*
	7	[^{I}]x*-ni-ku-up-še-en*$^{!}$*-ni* DUMU ⸢*Er*⸣$^{!}$*-wi-šarri*
	8	[^{I}]⸢*A*⸣*-ri-iq-qa-a+a* DU[MU]
	9	[^{I}]*Šur-ki-til-la* DUMU *A-mu*[*r-*GAL]
l.e.	10	[^{I}*P*]*al*$^{!}$*-te*$^{!}$*-a* D[UM]U *A-li-*[*ib-bi-ja*]
	11	[^{I}*Šúk*]*-ri-*⸢*ja*⸣ [DUMU]x[ ]
	12	[ ] *te* x[ ]
rev.	13	[*j*]*a* [ ]
		remainder of reverse uninscribed

[1] I would like to thank the editors and Prof. K. Deller for their helpful suggestions and references.

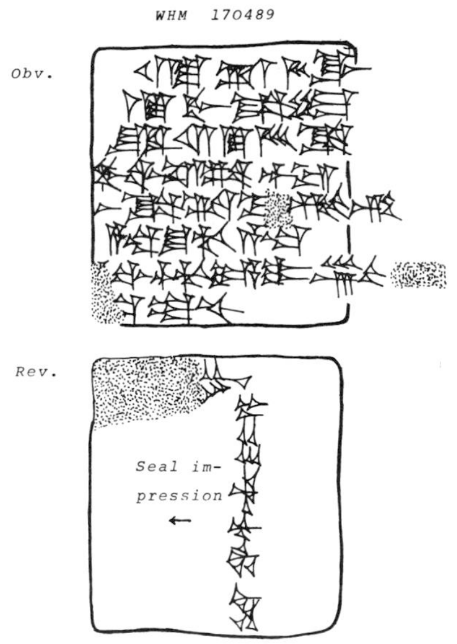

Figure 2

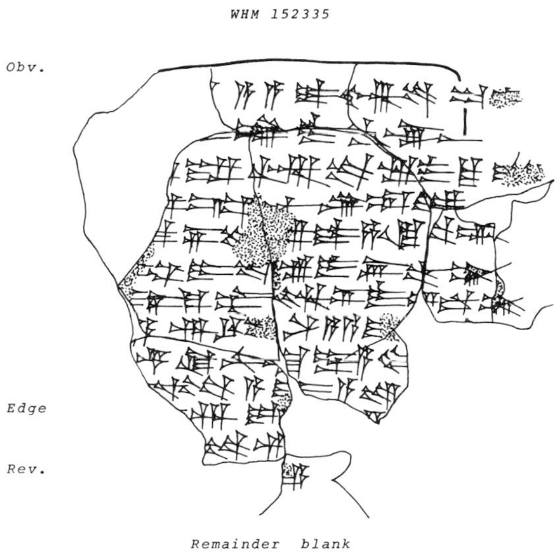

Figure 3

Ein Prozess um einen Kreditkauf in Nuzi

MANFRED MÜLLER
Karl-Marx-Universität
Leipzig, DDR

In der kleinen Tontafelsammlung an der Sektion Afrika-und Nahostwissenschaften der Karl-Marx-Universität Leipzig[1] befindet sich ein einziger, bisher unpublizierter ḫurro-akkadischer Text. Diese Tontafel, eine Prozessurkunde, die im folgenden veröffentlicht wird, trägt die Inventarnummer SIL 316.[2] Über ihre Herkunft ist leider nichts bekannt. Da jedoch der betreffende Prozess nach Aussage des Textes (Z. 3′, vgl. auch Z. 22′) in Nuzi durchgeführt wurde, ist dieser Ort vermutlich auch der Fundort der Tafel.

Die oben und an der linken unteren Ecke abgebrochene Tafel misst 7,1 (Höhe) × 6,2 (Breite) × 3,2 (Stärke) cm; sie besteht aus hellbraunem Ton, ist gebrannt und auf der Vorderseite stark geschwärzt.

Wieviele Zeilen am Anfang der Tafel fehlen, ist nicht sicher festzustellen. Nach der Wölbung der Tontafel zu urteilen, dürften etwa zwei oder drei Zeilen vollständig verloren sein. Diese Schätzung sowie die in Z. 1′ erhaltenen minimalen Zeichenreste[3] deuten sicher darauf hin, dass im abgebrochenen Teil der Urkunde ausser den Prozessparteien auch der Prozessgegenstand genannt war. Davon ausgehend ist der zu Beginn der Tafel verlorene Text auf der Grundlage des Inhalts der vorliegenden Urkunde und entsprechend dem in Nuzi üblichen Schema der Einleitung einer Prozessurkunde versuchsweise ergänzt worden.

Transliteration:

Vs. [ᴵ*ḫa-ši-ja* DUMU ...]
[*it-ti* ᴵ*šu-ru-uk-ka₄* DUMU...(?)]
[...(?) *aš-šum* 1 GÍN GUŠKIN](?)
1′ [*š*]⌜*a qa*⌝-[*at* ᴵ*šu-ru-uk-ka₄*](?)

[1]Zu dieser Sammlung vgl. die vorläufigen Bemerkungen des Verf. in seinem Beitrag zu B. Hruška und G. Komoróczy (Hrsg.), Festschrift für Lubor Matouš, Bd. II (= Assyriologia, Bd. V), Budapest, Anm. 2 (im Druck).

[2]SIL = Semitistisches Institut Leipzig.—Für einige Hinweise zu der folgenden Bearbeitung bin ich Herrn Prof. H. Petschow zu herzlichem Dank verpflichtet.

[3]Vgl. dazu die Bemerkung zu. Z. 1′.

2′ *i+na d*⌈*i*⌉*-ni* ⌈*a-na p*⌉[*a-ni* DI.KU$_5$]
3′ *i+na* URU *nu-zi i-*⌈*te-lu*⌉*-*⌈*ú*⌉-[*ma*]
4′ *um-ma* ^{1}*ḫa-ši-ja-ma*
5′ 1 GÍN GUŠKIN-*ja a-na ši-mi*
6′ *a-na* ^{1}*šu-ru-uk-ka*$_4$ *at-ta-din-m*[*i*]
7′ *ù* DI.KU$_5$ ^{1}*šu-ru-uk-ka*$_4$ ⌈*iš*⌉*-t*[*a-al-šu*]
8′ *um-ma* ^{1}*šu-ru-uk-ka*$_4$*-ma a-an-ni*[*-mi*](?)
9′ 1 GÍN GUŠKIN *ša* ^{1}*ḫa-ši-ja*
10′ *id-dì-nu* LÚ$^{<MEŠ>}$ *ša* URU *tup-šar-r*[*i*(*-ni*)*-we*]
(Fortsetzung auf der Rs. zwischen Z. 22′ und 23′:)
[*ki-na-a*]*n-na iq-ta-bu šum-ma* ŠE.BA^{MEŠ} *i-leq-q*⌈*è*⌉[4]
11′ *a-na ši-mi-ni il*$_5$*-te-qè-šu-*⌈*nu-ti-m*⌉[*a*]
12′ *ù ši*[5]*-mi*[5]*-šu ša* GUŠKIN ŠE^{MEŠ} *i+na-an-din*
13′ 3 ANŠE 5 BÁN ŠE *a-na* ^{1}*ḫa-ši-ja a-n*⌊*a ši-m*⌋*i*
14′ *ù šum-ma* AN.NA^{MEŠ} 30 MA.NA AN.NA
15′ ⌊*a-n*⌋*a-an-din ki-ma* EME*-šu*
16′ [*ša*] ^{1}*šu-ru-*⌊*u*⌋*k-ka*$_4$ ^{1}*ḫa-ši-ja*
UR 17′ [*i+na*] ⌈*di*⌉*-ni il-te-e-ma*
18′ [*ù*] DI.KU$_5$ *ki-ma* EME*-š*[*u*]
19′ [^{1}*šu-r*]*u-uk-ka*$_4$ 30 MA.[NA⌉ [AN.N][A⌉
Rs. 20′ [*a-na* ^{1}*ḫ*]*a-ši-ja*
21′ [*it-t*]*a-du-uš*
(Siegel A)[6]
22′ NA$_4$ ^{1}*šúk-ri-ja* DUMU *ar-te-e ša* URU *nu-zi*
23′ ŠU ^{1}*tu-ra-a*[*r-te-šup* DUB.SAR]
DUMU *i*⌈*t*⌉*-*[*ḫa-pí-ḫe*]
(Siegel B)[7]

Übersetzung:

[Ḫašija, der Sohn des. . . , ist mit Šurukka, dem Sohn des. . . , wegen(?) eines Sekels Gold(?), (1′-3′) de]r (sich in) ⌈der Ha⌉[nd des Šurukka](?) (befindet), zum P[r]ozess ⌈vo⌉[r dem Richter] in Nuzi er⌈schienen⌉.

(4′-6′) Folgendermassen (hat) Ḫašija (gesprochen): “Einen Sekel Gold, der mir gehört, habe ich dem Šurukka verkauft (wörtl.: für einen Kaufpreis gegeben).”

[4]Darunter ist eine Zeile gelöscht. Erkennbar ist davon:]⌈ŠE.BA⌉^{MEŠ} *l*⌊*a i+na-an-din*⌋ “[G]erste[r]ationen ⌊soll er (= Šurukka) nicht geben⌋.” Diese Zeile bildete allem Anschein nach ursprünglich die Fortsetzung von Z. 10′ auf der Rückseite. Nachdem der Schreiber sie gelöscht hatte, schrieb er den neuen Text darüber.

[5]Über Rasur geschrieben.

[6]Siehe Abb. 1.

[7]Diese Siegelabrollung ist fast vollständig abgebrochen.

SIL 316

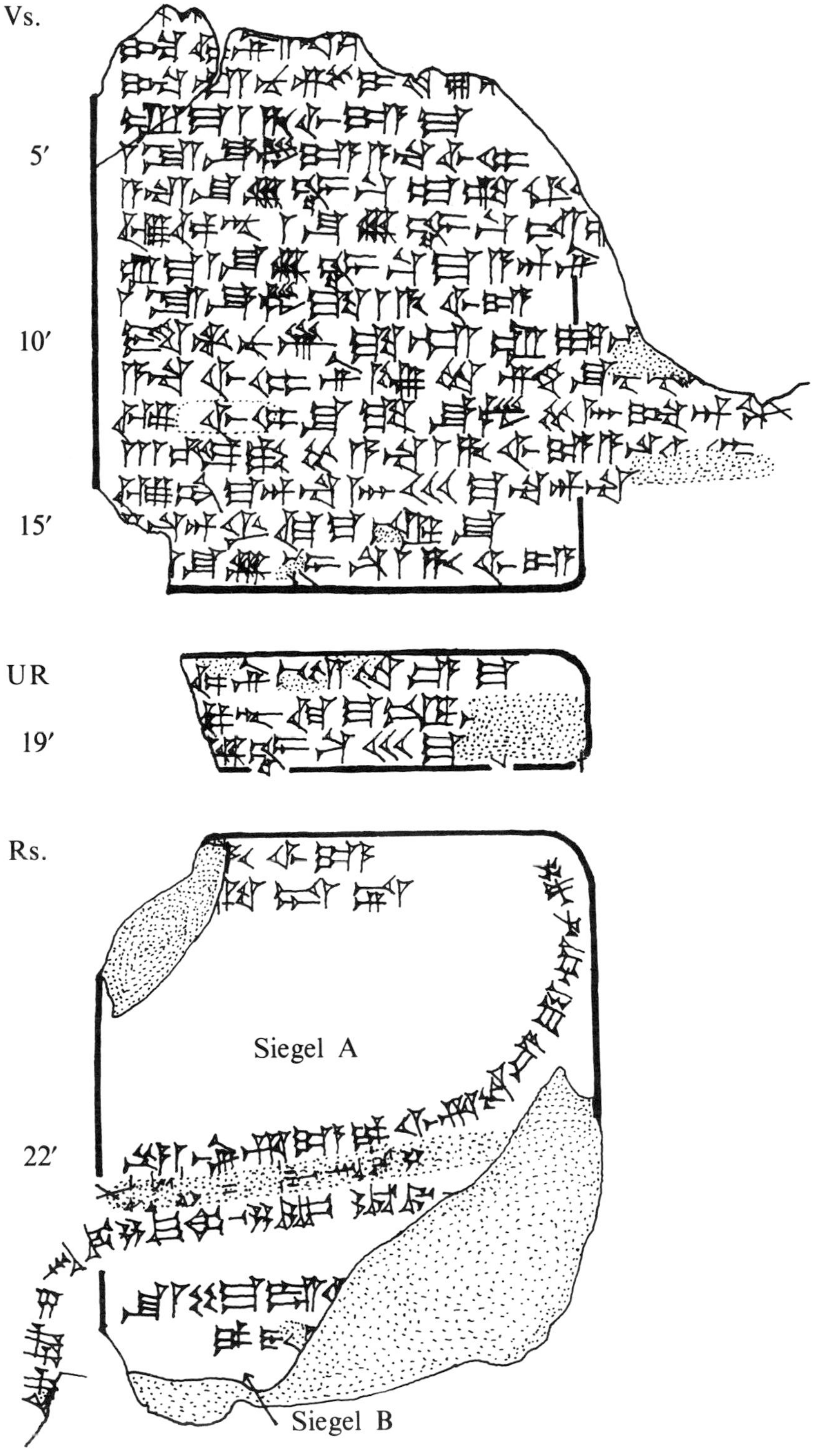

Abbildung 1. SIL 316, Siegelabrollung A: Siegel des Richters Šukrija, des Sohnes des Ar-teja.

(7′-15′) Dann verh[örte] der Richter den Šurukka. Folgendermassen (hat) Šurukka (gesprochen): "Ja, richtig, (aber) bezüglich des einen Sekels Gold, den Ḫašija (mir) gab, haben die(!) "Ältesten"(?) von Tupšarr[i(ni)we folgender] massen gesprochen: 'Wenn er(=Ḫašija) Gersterationen nehmen will, soll(!) er(=Ḫašija) s⌜ie⌝ zu unserem Preis nehmen und er(=Šurukka) möge als Kaufpreis für das Gold die (entsprechende) Gerste geben.' Ich bin bereit, dem Ḫašija als Kaufpreis 3 Homer (und) 5 Seah Gerste oder—wenn (es) Zinn (sein soll)—30 Minen Zinn zu geben."

(15′-21′) Entsprechend der Erklärung [des] Šurukka hat Ḫašija [im] Pr[o]zess gewonnen [und] der Richter [veru]rteilte(!) [den Šur]ukka entsprechend s[einer] Erklärung dazu, 30 Mi[ne]n [Zin]n [an Ḫ]ašija (zu zahlen).

(22′) Siegel des Šukrija, des Sohnes des Ar-teja, (des Richters) aus Nuzi.

(23′) Hand des [Schreibers] Tura[r-tešup], des Sohnes des I[tḫ-apiḫe].

Einzelbemerkungen:

Die Filiationen der beiden Prozessgegner Ḫašija und Šurukka, die aller Wahrscheinlichkeit nach in den abgebrochenen ersten zwei Zeilen der Tafel genannt waren, können nicht mit Sicherheit bestimmt werden. Die Urkunde selbst gibt nur für Šurukka einen richtungweisenden Anhaltspunkt: Wenn dieser, wie es der Zusammenhang nahelegt, ein Einwohner der Ortschaft Tupšarri(ni)we war (vgl. dazu im folgenden die Bem. zu Z. 10′), dann dürfte es sich nach dem bisher für diesen Ort bekannten Personen-Onomastikon wohl um Šurukka, den Sohn des Arip-urekke, handeln. Dieser ist in den Urkunden AASOR XVI 97 und SMN 2116 (= D. I. Owen, The Loan Documents from Nuzu, Diss. Brandeis Univ. 1969, S. 118f.) Schuldner der Pula-ḫali-Söhne aus Tupšarri(ni)we, in SMN 2445 (ebd. S. 116f.) Schuldner des Paššija, des Sohnes des Pula-ḫali, und in IM 70981 (= Abdulillah Fadhil, Rechtsurkunden und administrative Texte aus Kurruḫanni, Magister-Arbeit Heidelberg 1972, Nr. 13) ebenfalls Schuldner. In IM 70882 (= A. Fadhil, a.a.O. Nr. 18) ist er erster Zeuge in einer *ṭuppi tidennūti* aus Tupšarriniwe. Nach der relativen Chronologie der Urkunden aus Nuzi gehören die Pula-ḫali-Söhne—und damit auch Šurukka, der Sohn des Arip-urekke—etwa in die Zeit der Söhne und Enkel des bekannten Teḫip-tilla, des Sohnes des Puḫi-šenni, aus Nuzi, also in die 3. bis 4. der durch eigene Urkunden belegten Generationen.[8] Da die vorliegende Prozessurkunde ebenfalls etwa in die 3. bis 4. Generation datiert werden kann (s. dazu die Bem. zu Z. 22′ und 23′), erscheint die Identität des Šurukka unserer Urkunde mit dem für Tupšarri(ni)we während dieser Zeit bezeugten Šurukka, Sohn des Arip-urekke, naheliegend. Auch seine soziale Stellung, die durch die Tatsache charakterisiert wird, dass er als Vertragspartner immer der Schuldner ist, stimmt überein mit der Position des Šurukka in der vorliegenden Prozessurkunde.

Problematischer ist der Versuch, den Kläger Ḫašija zu bestimmen. Sollte es sich ebenfalls um einen Bewohner von Tupšarri(ni)we handeln, käme dafür Ḫašija, der Sohn des Ward-aḫḫē, in Frage, ein offenbar tonangebender Bürger dieses Ortes. Als ^{LÚ}*zazukku* führt er in IM 70985, lf. (s. dazu A. Fadhil, a.a.O. S.25 und unten Bem. zu Z. 10′) die Liste der "Ältesten"(?) von Tupšarri(ni)we an; ein Ward-aḫḫē, vermutlich sein Vater, besass Grundbesitz in der Flur dieses Ortes (HSS XIX 97, 6.7). Wie aus der Urkunde IM 70985 zu erschliessen ist, waren Šurukka, der Sohn des Arip-urekke, und Ḫašija, der Sohn des Ward-aḫḫē, Zeitgenossen.[9] Wenn dennoch wesentliche Zweifel an der Identität beider Ḫašija bestehen bleiben, liegt dies an der Tatsache, dass der Prozess nicht in Tupšarri(ni)we, sondern in Nuzi stattfand, obwohl nach Aussage von SMN 2372, 4f. (= R. E. Hayden, Court Procedure at Nuzu, Diss. Waltham/ Mass. 1962, S. 148f.) auch in Tupšarri(ni)we Prozessverfahren durchgeführt wurden. Ursache dafür könnte sein, dass sich der Kläger Ḫašija—eventuell in

[8]Pula-ḫali war nach SMN 2359 (= D. I. Owen, a.a.O. S. 112f.) wohl ein Zeitgenosse des Teḫip-tilla, da der Schreiber dieser Urkunde, Muš-teja (, der Sohn des Sîn-ibni), mehrfach auch als Schreiber von Urkunden des Teḫip-tilla, Sohnes des Puḫi-šenni, belegt ist (JEN 259, 287 und 587). Für die Söhne des Pula-ḫali sei hier nur darauf hingewiesen, dass der Schreiber Akkul-enni (, der Sohn des Ariḫ-ḫamanna,) einerseits die Urkunde HSS XIX 126 für Paššija, den Sohn des Pula-ḫali, andererseits die Urkunde JEN 386 über einen Prozess des Tarmi-tilla, des Sohnes des Šurki-tilla, also eines Enkels Teḫip-tillas, geschrieben hat.

[9]Vgl. dazu vor allem die Nennung von Pašši-tilla, dem Sohn des Pula-ḫali, in Z. 13.

"zweiter Instanz"— an das vermutlich höhere Gericht in Nuzi gewendet hatte oder dass Ḫašija ein Bürger von Nuzi war. In letzterem Falle ist bei der Häufigkeit dieses Namens keine Personenbestimmung möglich.

Z. 1′f.: Die entsprechend dem Wortlaut von Z. 2′f. in Übereinstimmung mit dem Formular und den Schreibgewohnheiten naheliegendste Ergänzung des Anfangs dieser Zeile zu *it-ti* oder allenfalls zu ^{I}Šurukka ist nach den erhaltenen Zeichenresten nicht möglich. Nach diesen und den Raumverhältnissen ist vielmehr zu Beginn der Zeile mit sehr hoher Wahrscheinlichkeit [*š*]⸢*a*⸣ und danach wohl ⸢*qa*⸣-[*at*](?) zu lesen, was nur zur Beschreibung des Prozessgegenstands gehören kann, der in Prozessurkunden aus Nuzi nicht selten an dieser Stelle genannt ist.

Z. 10′: Die Ergänzung von MEŠ nach LÚ wird durch die Verbalform *iqtabū* gefordert. Sachlich ist nicht eindeutig zu bestimmen, was unter den LÚ$^{\text{<MEŠ>}}$ *ša* URU *tup-šar-r*[*i*(*-ni*)*-we*] zu verstehen ist: die Einwohner allgemein oder nur die "Ältesten" dieser Ortschaft. In der Prozessurkunde IM 70985 aus Tell al-Faḫḫār (vgl. dazu vorläufig A. Fadhil, a.a.O. S. 25f.) werden 14 namentlich aufgeführte Personen als LÚ^{MEŠ} (*an-ni-i*) *ša* URU *tup-šar-ri-we* (Z. 16f. und 45) bezeichnet. Nach dem Zusammenhang zu urteilen, handelt es sich dabei offenbar um die Repräsentanten, die "Ältesten" der Ortschaft. Das Gleiche ist mit recht hoher innerer Wahrscheinlichkeit für die vorliegende Urkunde anzunehmen: Der Ältestenrat der Ortschaft Tupšarri(ni)we hatte, wie der Beklagte Šurukka zur Rechtfertigung vor Gericht aussagt (Z. 8′-12′), entschieden, dass Šurukka das auf Kredit gekaufte Gold zwar—wie wohl vom Verkäufer gefordert—in Gerste bezahlen mag, aber nur unter Zugrundelegung des in Tupšarri(ni)we gültigen (hohen!) Gerstepreises. Der Passus macht deutlich, dass Šurukka offenbar der "Jurisdiktion" dieses Ältestenrates unterstand, was ihn als Einwohner von Tupšarri(ni)we ausweisen dürfte.

Die Bedeutung von ŠE.BA^{MEŠ} = *iprū* im vorliegenden Zusammenhang ist nicht ganz klar. Denkbar wäre, dass Ḫašija für einen Sekel Gold "(Gerste für die Ausgabe von) Gersterationen" kaufen wollte oder dass mit ŠE.BA^{MEŠ} vielleicht einfach "Gerste für Nahrungszwecke"—etwa im Gegensatz zu ŠE.NUMUN "Saatgerste" —gemeint ist. Eine Illustration für die erstgenannte Möglichkeit ist die Urkunde HSS IX 43, wo zwei Personen ein Gerstedarlehen über 150 Homer Gerste abschliessen, um den *nīš bīti* des Königssohnes Šilwi-tešup Gersterationen (ŠE.BA^{MEŠ}) austeilen zu können.

Z. 10′-12′: In der zitierten wörtlichen Rede der LÚ$^{\text{<MEŠ>}}$ *ša* URU *tup-šar-r*[*i* (*-ni*)*-we*] bereiten die Bestimmung des grammatischen Subjekts der

Verbalformen am Ende von Z. 10′ und 11′ und die Perfektform in Z. 11′ Schwierigkeiten.

Bei der Deutung dieses Bedingungssatzes kann man davon ausgehen, dass die Protasis mit *ileqqe* (Z. 10′) endet und die beiden folgenden Sätze (Z. 11′-12′)—wie deren Verbindung durch *-ma ù* zeigt—die Apodosis darstellen.[10] Daraus ergibt sich bereits, dass die auffällige Perfektform in Z. 11′ ein Irrtum des Schreibers sein und als Präsens verstanden werden muss. Weiterhin steht fest, dass das Subjekt des abschliessenden Satzes (Z. 12′) nur Šurukka sein kann, denn dieser hat den Kaufpreis für das empfangene Gold zu entrichten. Als Subjekt der Protasis (Z. 10′) kommt wohl nur der Verkäufer Ḫašija in Frage. Die Protasis scheint auf sein Recht anzuspielen, zwischen Gerste und Zinn (vgl. Z. 14′) als alternativen Kaufpreisgegenständen wählen zu können, ein Recht, das durch den Kreditkaufvertrag HSS XIX 127, 8 bezeugt ist (s. dazu unten S. 451). Danach liegt zwischen Protasis und Apodosis oder zwischen dem ersten und zweiten Satz der Apodosis ein Subjektswechsel vor. Ersterenfalls lautete der Passus: "Wenn er(=Ḫašija) Gersterationen nehmen will, wird(!) er(=Šurukka) s⸢ie⸣ zu unserem Preis nehmen und dann möge er(=Šurukka) als Kaufpreis für das Gold Gerste geben." Diese Möglichkeit ist jedoch aus sachlichen Gründen wenig wahrscheinlich. Auffallend wäre schon die Tatsache, dass Šurukka, der allem Anschein nach zu den Grundbesitzern der Ortschaft Tupšarri(ni)we gehörte,[11] die Gerste, die er zur Bezahlung brauchte, erst selbst hätte kaufen müssen. Vor allem aber bliebe bei dieser Übersetzung unklar, worin für den Beklagten in dieser von ihm zitierten Stellungnahme der "Ältesten"(?) von Tupšarri(ni)we eine Entlastung bestünde. Wenn wir dagegen unter Berücksichtigung dieser Umstände den Subjektswechsel zwischen den beiden Sätzen der Apodosis annehmen—wie in der Übersetzung S. 444f. geschehen,—dann stellt der Hinweis auf die Entscheidung der "Ältesten"(?) von Tupšarri(ni)we die Begründung für das Verhalten des zahlungspflichtigen Käufers dar.

Z. 21′: [*it-t*]*a-du-uš*: Fehler für *ittadišu* bzw. *ittadiš*. Der Schreiber folgte dem üblichen Formular, da nach den bisher publizierten Prozessurkunden aus Nuzi das Urteil jeweils von einem Richterkollegium,

[10]In ḫurro-akkadischen Texten wird in Bedingungssätzen, die mit *šumma* eingeleitet werden, die Apodosis an die Protasis unverbunden oder durch die Konjunktion *ù* angeschlossen. Der Gebrauch von *-ma* (*ù*) ist auf die Verbindung von zwei Vorder- oder Nachsätzen untereinander beschränkt.

[11]Vgl. dazu die oben S. 447 zitierten Urkunden SMN 2445 und IM 70981, nach denen Šurukka, Sohn des Arip-urekke, Schuldbeträge "nach der Ernte" zurückzuzahlen hat.

nicht aber von einem Einzelrichter—wie im vorliegenden Prozess—gefällt wurde.

Z. 22′: Der Richter Šukrija, Sohn des Ar-teja, ist als Richter auch in der Prozessurkunde HSS XIX 72, oberer Rand, bezeugt. Ohne Filiationsangabe erscheint ein Richter Šukrija in JEN 650, 28. Dessen Siegelabrollung auf dieser Tafel (s. auch die Abb. in AASOR 24 (1947) Nr. 366) ist mit dem Siegel des Richters Šukrija, des Sohnes des Ar-teja, auf der vorliegenden Tafel (s. Abb. 1) allerdings nicht identisch. Es muss daher vorläufig offenbleiben, ob Personengleichheit vorliegt. Ein Šukrija ohne Berufs- und Filiationsangabe begegnet mehrfach als Siegelnder in publizierten und unpublizierten Prozessurkunden aus Nuzi (s. die Belege bei R. E. Hayden, Court Procedure at Nuzu, Diss. Waltham/Mass. 1962, S. 252). Über eine eventuelle Identität mit dem Richter Šukrija, dem Sohn des Ar-teja, könnte vor allem ein Vergleich der (unpublizierten) Siegelabrollungen entscheiden. Als einziger sicherer Ausgangspunkt für eine Bestimmung der Wirkungszeit des Richters Šukrija, des Sohnes des Ar-teja, steht damit vorläufig nur die Prozessurkunde HSS XIX 72 zur Verfügung. Der Schreiber dieser Urkunde, Nanna-adaḫ, ist für die Zeit des Enna-mati, des Sohnes des Teḫip-tilla, (JEN 618) und des Königssohnes Šilwi-tešup (HSS IX 11) belegt. Alle drei neben Šukrija in diesem Prozess urteilenden Richter—Ataja, Sohn des Muš-teja/Muš-tešup, Urḫija, Sohn des Zike, und Akap-tukke, Sohn des Kakki—wirken auch in dem JEN 662 protokollierten Prozess aus der Zeit des Zike und des Tarmi-tilla, der Enkel des Teḫip-illa, mit. Zwei der Richter—Akap-tukke, Sohn des Kakki, und Ataja, Sohn des Muš-tešup—gehören dem Richterkollegium des HSS IX 12 protokollierten Prozesses aus der Zeit des Šilwi-tešup an. Dieser Befund spricht für eine Datierung des Richters Šukrija, des Sohnes des Ar-teja, etwa in die Zeit der Söhne und Enkel des Teḫip-tilla.

Z. 23′: Der Schreiber Turar-tešup, Sohn des Itḫ-apiḫe, hat mehrfach für die Söhne und Enkel des bekannten Teḫip-tilla Urkunden ausgefertigt: JEN 130 (vgl. auch 154, 17.25) für die Söhne des Teḫip-tilla; AASOR XVI 52 und HSS XIII 55 (ohne Filiationsangabe) und vielleicht auch 267 (ohne Berufs- und Filiationsangabe) für Uzna, die Gattin des Enna-mati; HSS XIII 241 (ohne Berufsangabe) und 462 (ohne Filiationsangabe) für Takku, den Sohn des Enna-mati; JEN 535, 540, 542 (ohne Filiationsangabe), 549, 550 und 642 für Tarmi-tilla, den Sohn des Šurki-tilla. Der Schreiber Turar-tešup, Sohn des Itḫ-apiḫe, gehört damit ebenso wie der Richter der vorliegenden Urkunde zur 3. und 4. durch eigene Urkunden bezeugten Nuzi-Generation.

Kommentar:

Die vorliegende kleine Prozessurkunde SIL 316 verdient aus mehreren Gründen Beachtung:
1. Unter den zahlreichen publizierten Prozessurkunden aus Nuzi ist SIL 316 das bisher einzige Dokument über einen Prozess um den Kauf von vertretbaren Sachen. Dem Prozessverfahren liegt ein Kreditkauf von einem Sekel Gold zugrunde; um die Bezahlung des gekauften und übergebenen Goldes entwickelt sich der vorliegende Prozess.

Die betreffende Kaufurkunde ist nicht überliefert oder zumindest bisher nicht publiziert. Doch sind drei andere Urkunden aus den Ausgrabungen in Nuzi ediert, die den Kauf von Gold auf Kredit belegen und zur sicheren Deutung der vorliegenden Prozessurkunde wesentlich beizutragen vermögen. Die Texte HSS XVI 231 und XIX 126 betreffen jeweils—wie in der vorliegenden Prozessurkunde—den Kauf von einem Sekel Gold.[12] Die Bezahlung hat nach der Ernte (in den Monaten Kurillu bzw. Ulūlu) in Gerste zu erfolgen. Die jeweiligen Beträge sind exakt festgelegt (15 bzw. 19 Homer Gerste). Beide Urkunden stammen—vielleicht nicht zufällig—aus Tupšarri(ni)we und sind in die Zeit der vorliegenden Prozessurkunde zu datieren.[13] Die dritte derartige Kreditkaufurkunde, HSS XIX 127,[14] weicht von diesen beiden erstgenannten erheblich ab. Sie beurkundet den Kauf von 3 Sekel Gold, zahlbar in Zinn oder Gerste (Z. 8). Als Verrechnungsäquivalent (*ḫašaḫušennu*) werden für die 3 Sekel Gold 27 Sekel gutes Silber (Z. 6f.) genannt. Für den Fall der Bezahlung in Zinn ist zusätzlich die Zinn-Silber-Relation verbindlich festgesetzt: 3 Minen Zinn für 1 Sekel Silber (Z. 9), was leicht über dem durchschnittlichen Zinnpreis liegt.[15] Für Gerste erfolgte dagegen keine derartige Normierung. Offenbar sollte die mögliche Bezahlung in Gerste auf der Grundlage des üblichen Kurses zur Zeit der in der Urkunde angegebenen Zahlungstermine (es wurde Zahlung in zwei Raten vereinbart) erfolgen.

Die letztgenannte Urkunde trägt wesentlich dazu bei, den Sachverhalt, der dem vorliegenden Prozess zugrundeliegt, seine Ursache und seinen Verlauf zu rekonstruieren und zu deuten: Šurukka hatte von Ḫašija einen Sekel Gold auf Kredit gekauft. Die Bezahlung sollte—so war in der betreffenden Urkunde

[12]HSS XIX 126, 15, danach Z. 1 sicher zu ergänzen. Die gleiche Ergänzung ist auch HSS XVI 231, 1 naheliegend, wie ein Vergleich der Kaufsummen zeigt.

[13]Verkäufer des Goldes ist jeweils Paššija/Pašši-tilla, der Sohn des Pula-ḫali (s. dazu oben S. 447).

[14]Bearbeitet von G. Wilhelm in Baghdader Mitteilungen 7 (1974) S. 206.

[15]Das durchschnittliche Verhältnis von Zinn zu Silber beträgt 200:1 oder leicht darüber, vgl. D. Cross, Movable Property in the Nuzi Documents, New Haven 1937, S. 21 und 47 und B. L. Eichler, Indenture at Nuzi, New Haven and London 1973, S. 15 m. Anm. 26.

wohl vereinbart worden—in Gerste oder Zinn erfolgen. Dabei war, dem Prozesszusammenhang nach zu urteilen, die Gerste—analog HSS XIX 127—mengenmässig nicht festgelegt worden. Als Ḫašija später Zahlung in Gerste verlangt, als Berechnungsgrundlage aber allem Anschein nach nicht den zu dieser Zeit in Tupšarri(ni)we üblichen Preis für Gerste anerkennt, kommt es zum Prozess. Dabei beruft sich der Käufer Šurukka auf eine Stellungnahme der "Ältesten"(?) von Tupšarri(ni)we, wonach seine Schuld, falls er in Gerste zahlen soll, auf der Grundlage des ortsüblichen Gerstepreises zu begleichen sei. Dementsprechend erklärt sich Šurukka bereit, entweder—wie vom Verkäufer gewünscht—in Gerste, aber zu dem derzeit leicht erhöhten Preis (für 1 Sekel Gold nur 3 Homer und 5 Seah Gerste[16]), zu zahlen oder in Zinn zu dem üblichen Umrechnungskurs.[17] Der Richter akzeptiert offenbar die Entscheidung der "Ältesten"(?) von Tupšarri(ni)we und ordnet Bezahlung in Zinn zu den vom Käufer genannten Bedingungen an.

Um die Zahlung des Kaufpreises aus einem Kredit(?)kauf geht es auch in dem durch die unpublizierten Texte SMN 3097 und 2514 (s. dazu E. R. Hayden, Court Procedure at Nuzu, Diss. Waltham/Mass. 1962, S. 147f.) bezeugten Prozess. Danach hatte ein gewisser Ḫutija ein Pferd für 30 Sekel Silber (auf Kredit?) gekauft und empfangen, den Kaufpreis aber nicht bezahlt. Der Verkäufer klagt nun auf Zahlung des Kaufpreises, wozu der Käufer "entsprechend seiner Erklärung" (vgl. dieselbe Formulierung in SIL 316, 18′f.) auch verurteilt wird.

2. Die vom Beklagten alternativ vorgeschlagene Bezahlung des einen Sekels Gold durch 30 Minen Zinn, die vom Richter akzeptiert und zur Grundlage seines Urteils gemacht wurde, entspricht der bisher nur durch SMN 2615 = HSS XIX 127 für Nuzi bezeugten Gold-Silber-Relation von 1:9[18] bei einer Silber-Zinn-Relation von 1:200.[19] Die Urkunde bietet damit eine erwünschte Bestätigung für dieses Verhältnis.

Allerdings hat G. Wilhelm[20] die Überzeugung ausgesprochen, dass die in Nuzi übliche Gold-Silber-Relation auf Grund des Textes HSS XIX 127 nicht zu bestimmen sei, da in der kreditierten Kaufsumme Zinsen enthalten seien. Das ist möglich, doch bietet die betreffende Urkunde dafür keinen sicheren Anhaltspunkt. Die ausdrückliche Bezeichnung des äquivalenten Silberbetrags als "Kaufpreis des Goldes" (*ši-im-šu ša* GUŠKIN, Z.7) spricht a priori eher

[16]Nach dem durchschnittlichen Preis von 1 1/2 Sekel Silber für 1 Homer Gerste (s. Cross, a.a.O. S. 35f. und Eichler, a.a.O. S. 15 m. Anm. 29) und einer zugrundegelegten Gold-Silber-Relation von 1:6 (vgl. dazu oben unter Punkt 2) entspricht 1 Sekel Gold 4 Homer Gerste.

[17]Vgl. oben Anm. 15 und im folgenden unter Punkt 2.

[18]Erster Hinweis darauf durch E. R. Lacheman bei D. Cross, a.a.O. S. 39.

[19]Vgl. dazu Anm. 15.

[20]Baghdader Mitteilungen 7 (1974) S. 207.

gegen eine Berücksichtigung von Zinsen in dieser Summe. Auch andere Kredit- und Lieferungskaufurkunden aus Nuzi scheinen keinen Beweis für die zumindest gelegentliche Berechnung von Zinsen zu enthalten. Bei den Urkunden HSS XVI 231 und XIX 126, wonach jeweils 1 Sekel Gold im Anschluss an die Ernte mit 15 bzw. 19 Homer Gerste zu bezahlen ist,[21] liegt dies allerdings sehr nahe. Der ausserordentlich niedrige Gerstepreis ist jedoch kein absolut sicherer Beweis dafür, dass in die kreditierte Kaufsumme Zinsen eingerechnet sind, da in beiden Fällen offensichtlich bewusst der niedrige Gerstepreis nach einer guten Ernte in Rechnung gestellt ist. Das mag allerdings ergänzend zur Berechnung von Kreditzinsen geschehen sein.

Auf einen niedrigeren Goldwert weisen drei Urkunden, die in den bisherigen Diskussionen um die Gold-Silber-Relation in Nuzi keine Rolle gespielt haben: JEN 86, HSS IX 17 und XIX 129. In JEN 86 ist der Kaufpreis eines Feldes von 1 Homer Fläche folgendermassen beschrieben (Z.7f.): 5 UDU^{MEŠ} 50 GÍN *a-na-ku* 1 GÍN GUŠKIN *an-nu-ti*. Wenn dabei der eine Sekel Gold als Summation der vorgenannten 5 Schafe und 50 Sekel Zinn (so C. Zaccagnini, JESHO 22 (1979) S.5) und nicht als Teil der Kaufsumme (so E. Cassin, L'adoption à Nuzi, Paris 1938, S. 138) zu verstehen ist, widerspiegelt diese Berechnung ein Gold-Silber-Verhältnis von 1:6,9. In der Urkunde HSS IX 17 wird alternativ zur Lieferung "einer tüchtigen, auserlesenen Sklavin" (1 MUNUS SIG$_5$.GA *na-sí-iq-tu*$_4$, Z. 6 und 8) die Möglichkeit der Zahlung von 10 Sekeln guten Goldes eingeräumt. Das Verhältnis von 1:9 erscheint hier, falls in der genannten Summe von 10 Sekeln Gold nicht etwa ein Strafbetrag für Nichtlieferung der geschuldeten Sklavin enthalten sein sollte, zu hoch. Für die Beschaffung einer Sklavin gleicher Qualitätsbezeichnung wird in dem Kaufauftrag AASOR 16, 95 (vgl. 96) der Betrag von 60 Sekeln Silber gezahlt. Das spräche für einen Umrechnungskurs von etwa 1:6. Die dritte Urkunde, HSS XIX 129, legt fest, dass ein—ebenso wie in den vorerwähnten Texten HSS XVI 231 und XIX 126—auf Kredit gekaufter Sekel Gold zu einem festgesetzten späteren Termin mit vier nach Geschlecht und z.T. Alter bestimmten Schafen zu bezahlen sei. Diese Schafe entsprechen—ausgehend von dem in Arrapḫe üblichen Standardwert—etwa 5,33 Sekel Silber. Möglicherweise ist dieser Betrag jedoch deshalb etwas höher anzusetzen, weil Tiere bestimmter Qualität gefordert werden. Ein Kreditzins ist bei diesem Geschäft zweifellos nicht berücksichtigt.

Während die Texte HSS XIX 127 und SIL 316 eine Umrechnung von Gold in Silber im Verhältnis 1:9 bezeugen, liegt den drei letztgenannten Urkunden offenbar ein Umrechnungskurs von etwa 1:6 zugrunde. Zur Erklärung dieser Divergenz bieten sich zwei Deutungen an:

1. Es gab keine konstante Gold-Silber-Relation im Land Arrapḫe. Der Goldpreis war vielmehr erheblichen Schwankungen unterworfen—ähnlich wie

[21]Vgl. oben S. 451 m. Anm. 12.

etwa im altbabylonischen Larsa und in Kappadokien während der altassyrischen Zeit[22]—, die von der unterschiedlichen Qualität des Goldes und/oder Preisentwicklungen abhingen.
2. Die Gold-Silber-Relation im Land Arrapḫe lag bei 1:6. In diesem Fall entspräche das Verhältnis von 1:9 in den durch HSS XIX 127 und SIL 316 bezeugten Kreditkäufen dem durchschnittlichen Umrechnungskurs von 1:6 plus 50% Zins.[23] Das setzt voraus, dass es bei Kreditkäufen—ähnlich wie bei den *ḫubullu*-Darlehen—solche mit und ohne Zinsberechnung gab, wobei die Berechnung von Zins—dies im Unterschied zu den *ḫubullu*-Urkunden—offenbar niemals ausdrücklich genannt und damit aus den Urkunden selbst ablesbar ist.

Für die zweite Möglichkeit spricht nicht nur die schlüssige Erklärung der beiden unterschiedlichen "Wechselkurse," sondern auch die Tatsache, dass ein Gold-Silber-Verhältnis von 1:6 den wirtschaftlichen Verhältnissen im Vorderen Orient zur Zeit des hurritischen Staates von Arrapḫe besser zu entsprechen scheint als die archaische Relation von 1:9.[24]

3. Der vorliegende Prozess wurde im Unterschied zu allen anderen bisher aus Nuzi und Umgebung bezeugten Gerichtsverfahren nicht von einem Richterkollegium, sondern von einem Einzelrichter durchgeführt und entschieden. Die Ursache dafür ist nicht sicher festzustellen. Die auffällige Tatsache mag jedoch dadurch ermöglicht worden sein, dass der Fall auf der Grundlage des zweiten Vorschlags des Beklagten, der—wenn unsere Annahme zutrifft—der im zugrundeliegenden Kaufvertrag enthaltenen Alternativregelung für die Bezahlung entspricht, leicht und vor allem eindeutig zu entscheiden war.
4. Vorausgesetzt, dass die Deutung von LÚ<MEŠ> *ša* URU *tup-šar-r*[*i*(-*ni*)-*we*] als " 'Älteste' von Tupšarr[i(ni)we]"[25] korrekt ist und die zitierte Stellungnahme dieser "Ältesten" inhaltlich richtig erfasst wurde,[26] bietet die vorliegende Urkunde ein interessantes Zeugnis für die Wirksamkeit des Ältestenrates einer Dorfgemeinde im Staat Arrapḫe im sozialen Bereich: Der "Spruch" der "Ältesten" bezweckte danach den Schutz eines Mitglieds der Dorfgemeinschaft vor materieller Übervorteilung.

[22] Vgl. W. F. Leemans, RLA 3, S. 512.

[23] Vgl. die Zusammenstellung von Belegen für die Erhebung von 50% Zinsen in Nuzi bei D. I. Owen, The Loan Documents from Nuzu, Diss. Brandeis Univ. 1969, S. 38-40.

[24] Vgl. W. F. Leemans, RLA 3, S. 512f. und G. Wilhelm, Baghdader Mitteilungen 7 (1974) S. 205.

[25] Vgl. dazu die Bemerkung zu Z. 10′.

[26] Vgl. die Bemerkung zu. Z. 10′-12′.

Text Fragments from Arrapḫa in the Kelsey Museum of Art and Archaeology, The University of Michigan

DAVID I. OWEN
Cornell University
Ithaca, New York

The three fragments published below were brought to my attention by Professor Matthew Stolper during my visit to the Kelsey Museum in the spring of 1978.[1] They are published with the kind permission of Professor John Pedley, Director of the Kelsey Museum. The texts had been identified as "Nuzi" by Professor Albrecht Goetze many years ago and his identification remained in his notes to the collection which are on file in the museum. The three texts clearly stem from the early clandestine finds at Kirkuk a number of which have found their way into various museums and collections and most of which are now published. Indeed the join of Kelsey 89522 (no. 2, below) with *AO* 6029 (=*TCL* 9 12) by Professor G. Wilhelm, demonstrates that these fragments are part of the same batch of texts which probably also includes the Yale tablets published by Professor Lacheman and this writer above. In spite of their fragmentary nature they nevertheless add a surprising number of new names, family relationships, and other bits of information to the materials so far known from Arrapḫa.[2]

1. Kelsey Museum 89393 (photo, plate 1). Deposition before witnesses by Pui-tae (son of Wullu?) concerning some (silver?) he claims to have paid/weighed out to Wullu. The restorations of the personal names are based on *YBC* 5143 published above.

[1]I wish to thank the Cornell University Humanities Faculty Research Grant Committee for the funding which allowed for my visit to the Kelsey Museum. Prof. Matthew Stolper was a most gracious host during that visit and he facilitated the taking of the excellent set of photographs reproduced below.

[2]Professors Lacheman and Deller both provided important observations and references for these texts. It was through Deller's interest in these fragments that Prof. G. Wilhelm became aware of them and was able to make the long distance join between our no. 2 and *TCL* 9 12. I am most grateful to all of them for their interest and for their generous cooperation.

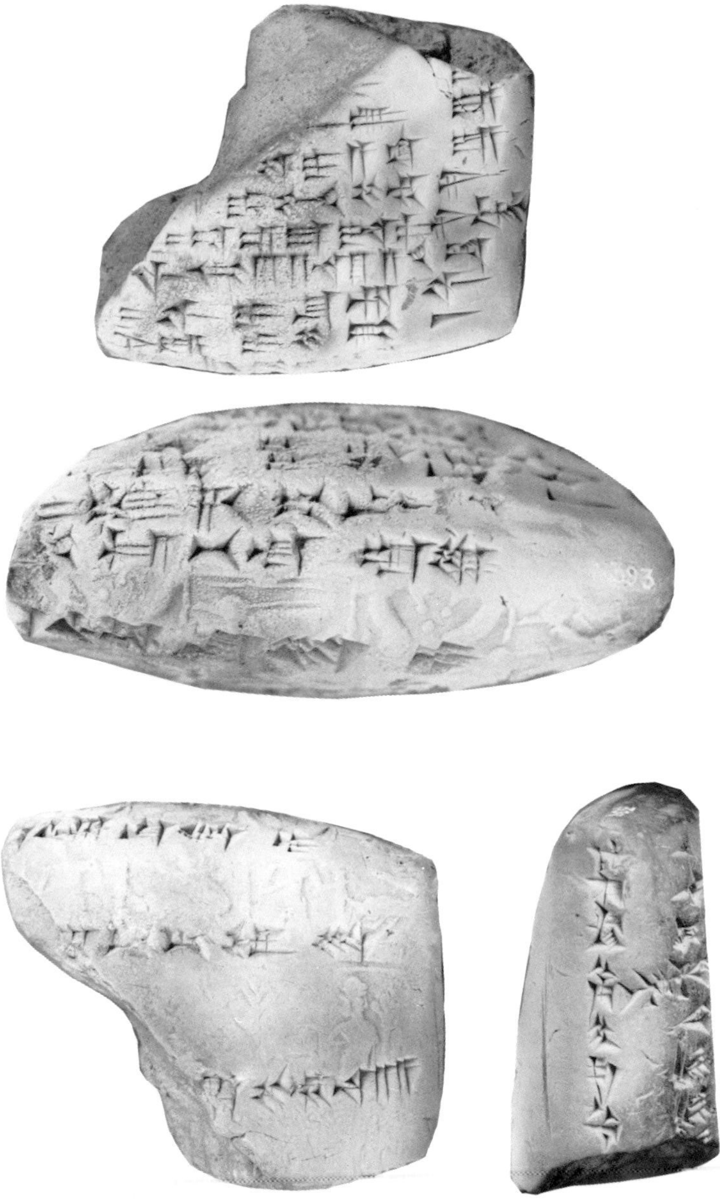

N.B. Edges not to scale.

PLATE 1. Kel. 89393

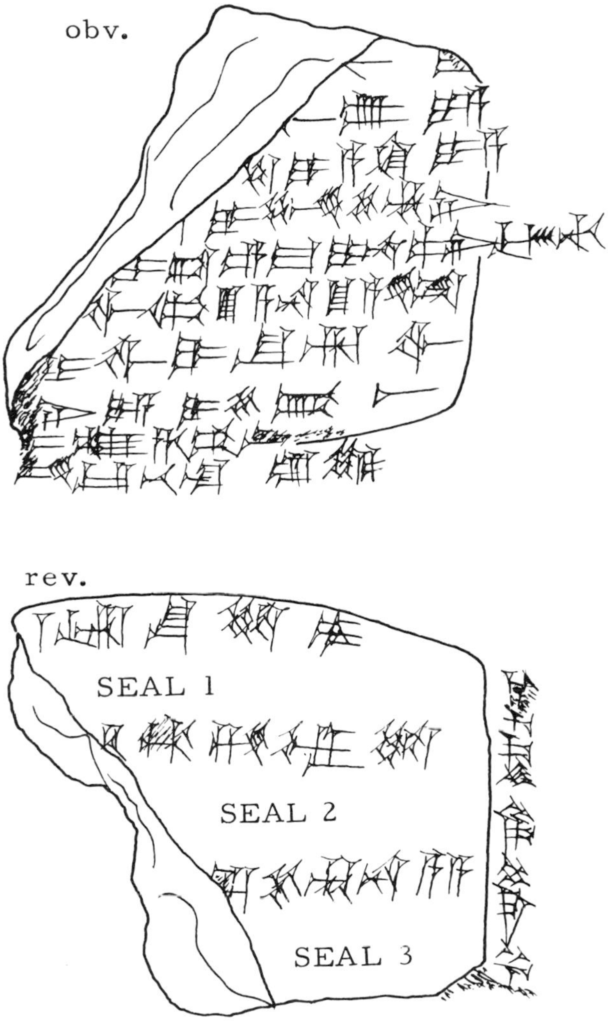

FIGURE 1. Kel. 89393

Left edge, beginning of obverse and end of reverse destroyed.

(1) [IGI ^{I}.... DUMU ....]-*j*[*a*?]
(2) [IGI ^{I}*Ar-šu-li-ḫé* DUMU *P*]*u-ú-ja*
(3) [IGI ^{I}...]-*te* DUMU *A-ki-ja*
(4) [IGI ^{I}*Še-en-na-a+*]⸢*a*⸣ DUMU *Pu-ḫi-še-en-ni*
(5) [*um-ma* ^{I}*Pu*]-⸢*i*⸣-*ta-e-ma i+na pa-ni* IGI^{MEŠ}-*ti*
(6) [..*ša* ^{I}]*Wu-ul-lu a-na-ku a-ḫi-iṭ*
(7) [IGI ^{I}*A-ki*]-⸢*i*⸣-*we* DUMU *Šu-ri-we*
(8) [IGI ^{I}...-*n*]*i-ja* DUMU *Še-kar-rù*
(9) [IGI ^{I}...]-*x-tu*$_4$ *ḫa-bi-r*[*u*]
(10) [IGI ^{I}*El*]-*ḫi-ip-til-la* DUB.SAR
Seal 1
(11) [NA$_4$.KIŠIB] ^{I}*Ar-šu-li-ḫé*
Seal 2
(12) [NA$_4$.KIŠIB ^{I}*A-r*]*i-ik-ké-el-li*(=*te*!?)
Seal 3
(13) [NA$_4$.KIŠ]IB ^{I}*Še-en-na-a+a*
(14) NA$_4$(?) ^{I}*Ké-el-še-er-wi*

Comments

Line 2. For Ar-šuliḫe son of Puja cf. *NPN* 33 s.v. He is known from a number of texts from Arrapḫa.

4. Šennaja son of Puḫi-šenni is known only from Arrapḫa texts. Cf. *NPN* 130 s.v.

5. It is not certain if this Pui-tae is, in fact, the son of Wullu or another individual. The name is quite common at Nuzi and Arrapḫa.

6. As far as can be ascertained at this time there is only one person by the name of Wullu (son of Puḫi-šenni) known from the archives of Arrapḫa and Nuzi. The Wullu family archives have been studied by Lacheman (unpublished) and by C. Schmidt-Colinet (unpublished) and additional texts from that archive are published above among the Yale tablets. The use of the verb *ḫâṭu*, "to weigh (out), to pay," is known to me from only one other Nuzi text, *HSS* 9 95, 21 (*CAD* Ḫ 159 sub meaning 4). Unfortunately the object of the verb is not preserved.

7. For this restoration see *YBC* 5143:10 above.

10. The scribe Elḫip-tilla is, as Deller suggests, probably the son of Wurru-kunni known from Gadd 22, 30 and 45 as well as *HSS* 9 15.

14. The sign before the name Kelšerwi is probably a poorly written NA$_4$ perhaps overwritten with a KIŠIB. The name Kelšerwi is otherwise unknown and may be compared with Kelšeḫwa(?) of *NPN* 83 s.v. (=Gadd 31, 38) which I would read as *ké-el-še-er*!-*wi* (copy is closer to *er* than to *eḫ*) and assume to be the same individual. Probably to be analyzed as Kelš-erwi.

2. Kelsey Museum 89522 (photo, plate 2). Fragment of a legal deposition given by Pui-tae son of Eḫlip-atal before the judges. On the basis of my photos and copy sent to Prof. K. Deller, Prof. G. Wilhelm was able to join this fragment to the Louvre fragment *AO* 6029 which was published by Contenau as *TCL* 9 12 and discussed by Koschaker in *ZA* 48 (1944) 170ff. The tablet relates to a breach of agreement whose details are known from Bachmann 2, published by Koschaker, ibid. 172. A complete transliteration is presented here.

(1) ^{1}*Pu-i-ta-e* DUMU *Eḫ-l*[*i-pa-ṯal*]
(2) *it-ti* ^{1}*Ša-ar-te-j*[*a* DUMU *Ni-ir-pí-ja*]
(3) *it-ti* ^{1}*Eḫ-li-te-š*[*up* DUMU *Zi-ki-in-ta*]
(4) *ù it-ti* ^{1}*Wa-an-t*[*i-iš-še-en-ni*]
(5) DUMU *Ḫa-ši-ip-til-la i+n*[*a di-ni*]
(6) *a-na pa-ni* DI.KU$_5^{MEŠ}$ *i-te-l*[*u-ú-ma*]
(7) *um-ma* ^{1}*Pu-i-ta-e-*[*ma*]
(8) A.ŠÀ-*ja tup-pa-aḫ-ḫu-*[*ra-ti i+na* AN.ZA.KÀR]
(9) *Uk-ni-ip-pa-we* L[Ú^{MEŠ} *an-n*]*u-ú*
(10) *i-re-ú-šu-nu-ti ù* [*aš-šum*]
(11) A.ŠÀ^{MEŠ}-*ja ša-a-šu* LÚ[^{MEŠ} *ša-a-šu-nu*]
(12) *it-ti-ja it-tam-ga*$_5$-[*ru*]
(13) *ù ṭup-pa il*$^!$-*ta-ṭar*$^!$ [*ù*$^?$]
(14) *ma-an-nu i+na be-ri-šu-nu*
(15) *ša* KI.BAL-*tu*$_4$ 1 GU$_4$.ÁB SA$_5$-*la*
(16) *ù i+na-an-na* LÚ^{MEŠ} *ša-a-š*[*u*]-*nu*
(17) A.ŠÀ^{MEŠ}-*ja ḫa-al-*<*wu-*>*um-ma la* DÙ$^!$-*šú*
(18) *ù i-re-ú-šu-nu-ti*
(19) *ù* DI.KU$_5^{MEŠ}$ LÚ^{MEŠ} *ša-a-šu-*<*nu*>
(20) *iš-ta-al-šu-nu-ti*
(21) *ù um-ma šu-nu-ma*$^!$ *a-an-ni-mi*
(22) A.ŠÀ^{MEŠ}-*šu ša* ^{1}*Pu-i-ta-e*
(23) *e-re-ú-šu-nu-ti*
(24) *ù ni-i-nu aš-šum* A.ŠÀ^{MEŠ}
(25) *ša-a-šu it-ti* ^{1}*Pu-i-ta-e*
(26) *ni-it-tam*$^!$-*ga*$_5$-*ru-mi*
(27) A.ŠÀ^{MEŠ} *ša-a-šu a-na ḫa-*<*al-*>*wu-me* DÙ$^!$
(28) *ni-iq-ta-bi ù ḫa-*<*al-*>*wu-um-ma*
(29) *la ni-ip-pu-uš ù* DI.KU$_5^{MEŠ}$
(30) *ṭup-pu ša tam-gu*$_5$-*ur-ti*
(31) *iš-te-mu-ú ša* KI.BAL-*tu*$_4$
(32) 1 GU$_4$.ÁB SA$_5$-*la i+na di-ni*
(33) ^{1}*Pu-i-ta-e il-te-e-ma*
(34) *ù* DI.KU$_5^{MEŠ}$ ^{1}*Ša-ar-te-ja*
(35) ^{1}*Eḫ-li-te-šup ù* ^{1}*Wa-an-ti-*[*iš-še*]-*en-ni*

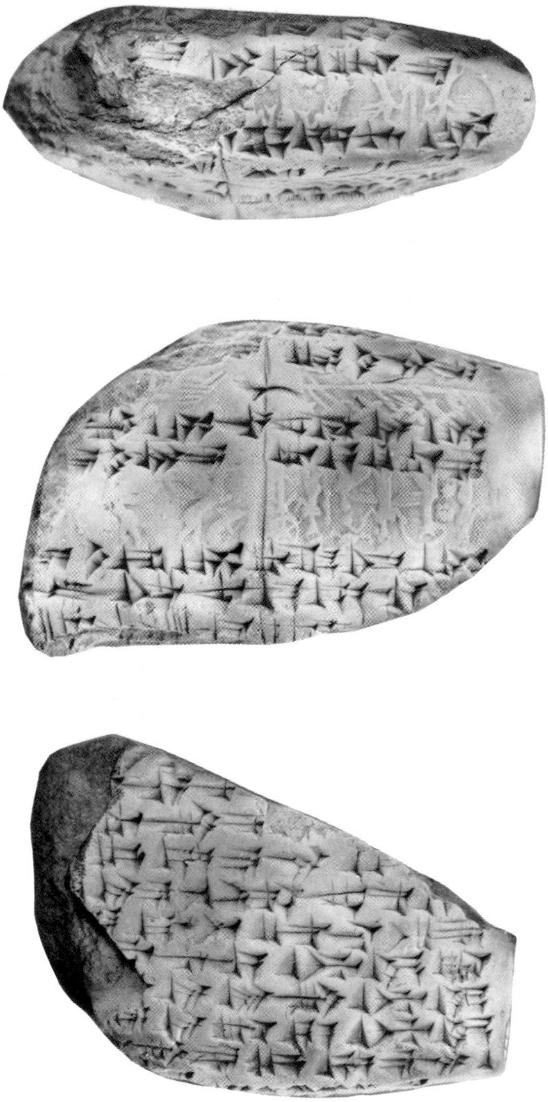

Plate 2. Kel. 89522

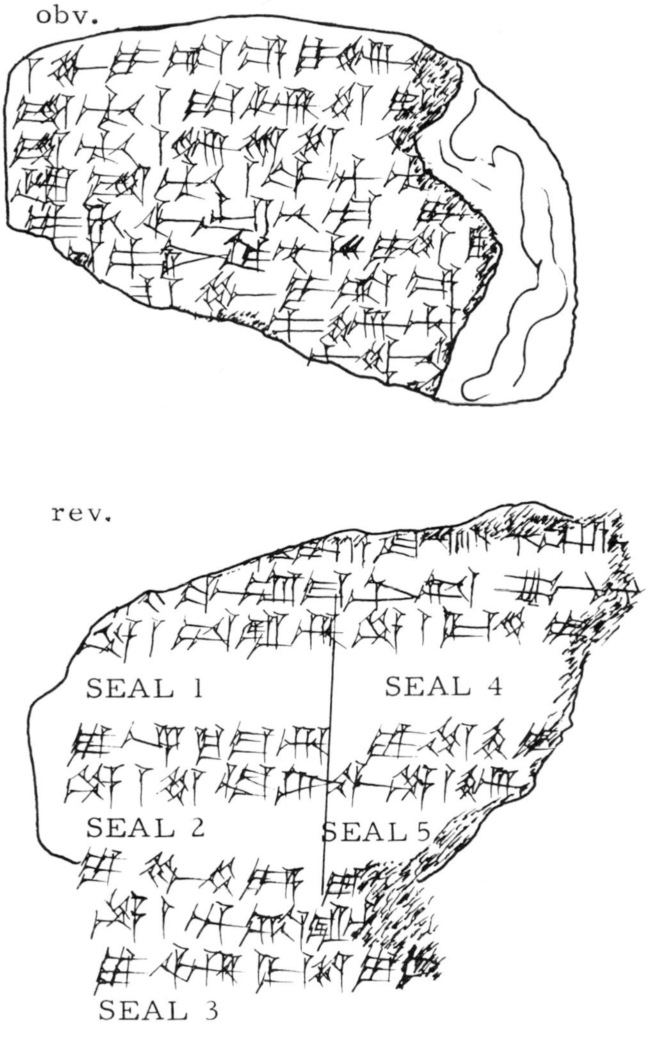

FIGURE 2. Kel. 89522

(36) *a-na* 1 GU$_4$.ÁB *ru-bu-ú a-na*
(37) ^{I}*Pu-i-ta-e it-ta-du-š*[*u-nu-ti*]
(38) *ù* LÚ^{MEŠ} *ša-a-šu-nu* A.ŠÀ^{MEŠ} *ša-a-š*[*u-nu*]
(39) [*ḫa-a*]*l-wu-um-ma* DÙ-*uš*

(40)	NA$_4$ ^{I}*Tù-ra-ri*	NA$_4$ ^{I}*Ur-ḫi-j*[*a*]
	Seal 1	Seal 4
(41)	DUMU *Šur-ku-ma-tal*	DUMU *Te-ḫi-j*[*a*]
(42)	NA$_4$ ^{I}*Te-šup-er-wi*	NA$_4$ ^{I}*Eḫ*-[*li-te-šup*]
	Seal 2	Seal 5
(43)	DUMU *Pu-ḫi-ja*	DUMU [*Zi-ki-in-ta*]
(44)	NA$_4$ ^{I}*An-ta-ra-r*[*i*]	[NA$_4$ ^{I}*Ar-ta-še-en-ni*]
	Seal 3	[Seal 6]
(45)	DUMU *Ar-téš-še*	DUMU *N*[*i-iḫ-ri-ja*]

(46) ŠU ^{I}*A-ki-ja* DUMU MU-*líb-ši*

Translation

Pui-tae son of Eḫlip-atal together with Šar-teja son of Nirpija, together with Eḫli-tešup son of Zi[kinta] and together with Wantiš-šenni son of Ḫašip-tilla for a judgment went up before the judges. Thus (said) Pui-tae, "My *tuppaḫurati*-field [in the district of] Uknipa those men were (supposed) to pasture (their sheep on). Concerning that field of mine [these] men made an agreement with me and they[!] wrote a tablet (which stated) whoever breaks the agreement one cow he shall pay. Now these men do not enclose my fields (with a wall) but let (the sheep) pasture on them."

And the judges questioned these men and they (replied) that they (indeed) pastured on Pui-tae's field (stating), "We said that we made an agreement with Pui-tae concerning those fields to enclose (them) with a wall (for pasturing). But we did not do it."

And the judges heard the tablet of agreement (which stated that) whoever breaks the agreement shall pay one cow. (Thus) Pui-tae prevailed in the judgment. And the judges made Šar-teja, Eḫli-tešup and Wantiš-šenni give to Pui-tae one four year old cow. Furthermore, these men were made to enclose these fields (with a wall). Sealed by six judges and the scribe.

Comments

This text has been partially restored and extensively discussed by Koschaker (*ZA* 48 [1944], 170ff.). Curiously, the *ṭuppi tamgurti* mentioned in line 30 here and upon which the legal decision recorded in this text is based, is identical in most every way with Bachmann 2 (*ZA* 48 [1944], 172) except for one important detail. In Bachmann 2, 7 the agreement is made with Pui-tae son of Wullu whereas in our text the complainant is Pui-tae son of Eḫlip-atal. I am at a loss to reconcile this difference except to suggest that the traces copied in Bachmann 2, 7 are not, in fact, accurate.[3] The Louvre fragment *AO* 6029 was collated by D. Arnaud and the results published in *RA* 68 (1974), 176. The transliteration here and the translation is a composite of all these sources and comments.

Lines 13-14. Collated by D. Arnaud, loc. cit.

17. So according to *CAD* H 57 s.v. *ḫalwu*, "border wall." However *CAD* reads DÙ$^{!}$-úš$^{!}$.

27-29. For these lines cf. *CAD* H 57 s.v. *ḫalwu.*

40. For a drawing of this seal and references to other texts see the comments of D. Stein apud the article of C. Gavin published in this volume.

46. There are eight other texts which are known to have been written by the scribe Akija son of Šumu-libši. They are Gadd 7, 15, 46, 48, 49 and Jankowska 49, 40 (ŠU ^{I}*A-k*[*i-ja* DUMU MU-*líb-ši*]). References and suggested restoration courtesy of P. Negri Scafa apud K. Deller, letter of 7/xi/80.

3. Kelsey Museum 89548 (photo, plate 3). Fragment of *ṭuppi mārūti* document from the Wullu archive. The text contains an unusual number of individuals who are adopting Wullu. Furthermore, the ductus is particularly distinct in form and is otherwise unknown from published texts.

(1) *ṭup-p*[*í*] *ma-ru-ti ša* $^{<I>}$*Ku-a-ri*
(2) *ša* ^{I}*Nu-*[*u*]*z-za ša* ^{I}*A-ki-ip-pu-ú*
(3) [*š*]*a* ^{I}*Š*[*u*$^{?}$]*-ú-ri ša* ^{I}*A-ki-ja*
(4) *ù*$^{?}$ *ša* ^{I}*Še-en-na-pè ù* $^{<I>}$*A-ka*$_{4}$*-wa-til*
(5) ⌈DUMU$^{?M}$]^{EŠ} ^{I}*Ú-*[*na*]*p*$^{?}$*-še ù* ^{I}*Wu-ul-lu* DUMU *Pu-ḫi-še-en-ni*
(6) [*a-na ma-r*]*u-ti i-pu-us-sú*
(7) [x ANŠE x ^{G}]^{IŠ}APIN [A.Š]À^{MEŠ} *ša Nu-pu*$^{?}$-[*u*]*l*$^{?}$*-wa-til*
(8) [.... *Nu-u*]*z-za* x x *ša*$^{?}$ *A-*[*k*]*i*$^{?}$*-ti-an-*[*n*]*u*$^{?}$
(9) [.... ^{ME}]^{Š} ŠEŠ^{MEŠ} [....]
Remainder of obverse and beginning of reverse destroyed.
(10) [NA$_{4}$ ^{I}.... N]A$_{4}$ ^{I}*A-k*[*i-ip-pu-ú*]
(11) [NA$_{4}$ ^{I}*Šu-ú-r*]*i*
Seal 1 Seal 2

[3]However, Deller now informs me that the Bachmann tablets published in *ZA* 48 are in the possession of W. von Soden who has collated this passage at Deller's request. Von Soden comments as follows, "*Wu* ist 100%-ig, *ul* so gut wie sicher, es gibt jedenfalls keine Alternative. *Lu* ist grössenteils ergänst, aber glaubwürdig" (letter to Deller, 16/iii/81). This would mean that in spite of the amazing similarity between the documents we must consider them to be independent of one another.

PLATE 3. Kel. 89548

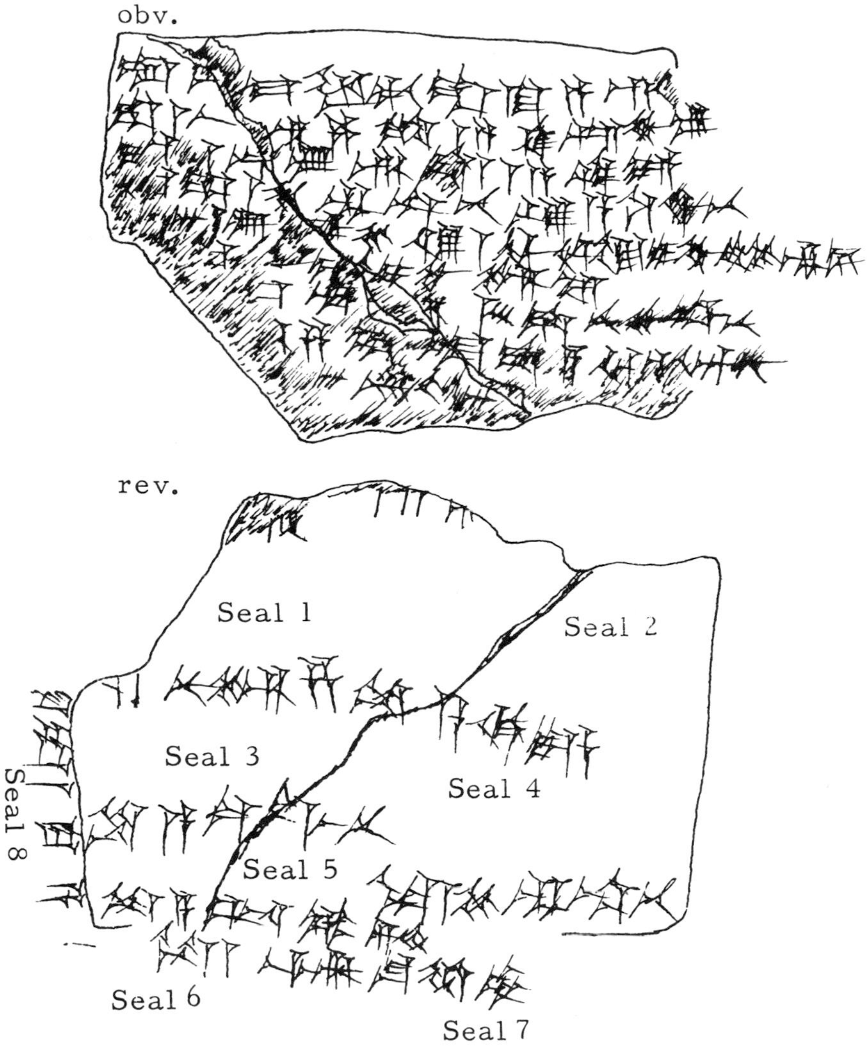

FIGURE 3. Kel. 89548

(12) [N]A$_4$ ^{I}*Nu-uz-za* NA$_4$ $^{<\mathrm{I}>}$*A-ki-ja*
Seal 3 Seal 4
(13) NA$_4$ $^{<\mathrm{I}>}$*A-ka*$_4$*-wa-til*
Seal 5
(14) NA$_4$ ^{I}*Še-en-na-pè*
(15) NA$_4$ $^{<\mathrm{I}>}$*A-kap-tùk-ké*
(16) NA$_4$ ^{I}*Ar-šu-li-ḫé*
Seal 6 Seal 7
(17) [NA$_4$ ^{I}.... N]A$_4$ ^{I}*Ku-a*<*-ri*>
Seal 8

Comments

The script on this tablet is particularly difficult to decipher and even more difficult to copy accurately. Furthermore, the surface of the tablet is badly damaged which makes the readings and particularly the restorations sometimes very tenuous. Photos have been provided of all the sides and edges except for the left edge which was inadvertently left out. I believe that the photos clearly show how unusual the ductus of this unknown scribe is.

Line 2. One might have expected the personal name to be *a-ki-ip-pu-kùr*$^{!}$ (i.e. Akip-ukur, otherwise not attested but a perfectly acceptable name) but the last sign has three verticals. However, note that the *ú* in the partially restored name in line three has four verticals as does the *ú* in line four.
3. Deller, letter of 8/xi/80, suggests a reading *a-ri-ip*-LUGAL-*ri* for the name that I would read as *š*[*u*$^{?}$]-*ú-ri*. In favor of his reading is the long space between the *ša* and what I take to be the DIŠ followed by *šu*. Perhaps collation might solve the problem.
7-8. The restorations of the personal names at the ends of both of these lines are very tenuous at best. Neither suggested reconstruction is known from Arrapḫa or Nuzi.

A Note on the Kelsey Seal Impressions

Ms. Diana Stein of the Harvard Semitic Museum is currently working on a study of the Nuzi seals and kindly contributed the material for the following notes and references. Her observations on the seals were made on the basis of my photographs and not from an examination of the original tablets.[4]

[4] I wish to thank Ms. Stein for her help and cooperation in the preparation of these notes. She is not responsible for the organization or the form of their presentation here.

Seal User	Text No.	Seal No.	Comparisons
Akap-tukke	3	6	No comparisons.
Akawatil	3	5	Same seal used by Akija. *AASOR* 24 group VII.
Akija	3	2	Same seal used by Akawatil. *AASOR* 24 group VII.
Akipu	3	-	Not preserved.
Antar-atal son of Ar-tešše	2	3	*AASOR* 16 62:E (Rm. C-112); *AASOR* 24 820's group XXIV; *EN* 9 117:F (Rm. C-28); *HSS* 14 504:A (Rm. A-23); *HSS* 15 300:A; *HSS* 16 107 (Rm. C-19).
Arik-elli	1	2	No comparisons.
Ar-šuliḫe	1	1	*AASOR* 24 456 group X (not close comparison); *HSS* 5 9:C (Rm. A-34); *HSS* 14 35:A (Rm. C-19) (similar style but different composition); *HSS* 19 127:C (Rm. P-401).
Ar-šuliḫe	3	7	No comparisons.
Artašenni son of Niḫrija	2	6	No comparisons.
Eḫli-tešup	2	5	No comparisons.
Kelš-erwi	1	4	No comparisons.
Kuari	3	8	No comparisons.
Nuzza	3	1	No comparisons.
Šennaja	1	3	*AASOR* 24 272 group V, 292 group VI; *HSS* 5 2:C (Rm. A-34) and 16:A (Rm. A-34); *HSS* 15 192:A (Rm. A-23); *HSS* 19 93:A (Rm. S-112) and 132:A-C (Rm. A-30).
Šennape	3	4	*AASOR* 16 24:A (Rm. C-120) and 30:A (Rm. C-120); *AASOR* 24 102-112 group III; *HSS* 19 70:G (Rm. C-28) and 119:F (Rm. C-28).
Šuari	3	1	No comparisons.
Tešup-erwi son of Puḫija	2	2	This is the same seal used by Akip-šenni son of Alpuja on *HSS* 13 161 (Rm. A-26); *HSS* 13 30:F (Rm. C-76); *HSS* 19 42:A (Rm. S-151), 64:B (Rm. P-465) and 87:C (Rm. P-382).
Turari son of Šurkum-atal	2	1	*AASOR* 16 95 (Rm. C-465); *AASOR* 24 711-715 group XX; *HSS* 13 114, same seal, *ḫazannu* (Rm. A-26) and 161, same seal (Rm. A-26); *HSS* 14 9:A (Rm. G-29) and 595:B (Rm. A-14); *HSS* 15 194:A (Rm. D-3) and 294:B (Rm. S-113); *HSS* 16 95 (Rm. C-465).
Urḫija son of Teḫija	2	4	*AASOR* 24 820's group XXIV; *HSS* 9 29 (Rm. A-23).

In view of the above comparisons but primarily with the *JEN* impressions in mind, the following tentative conclusions may be suggested.

Text 1. The seals on this tablet reflect Cappadocian and Syro-Cappadocian influence and date to Teḫip-tilla's generation.
Text 2. Three seal impressions on this tablet belong to the latter part of the Nuzi period by which time the Mitannian style had evolved as an independent glyptic style.
Text 3. Seals on this tablet reflect Syrian influence and probably also date to the time of Teḫip-tilla.

INDEXES TO PART II*

Compiled by

KARLHEINZ DELLER
Universität Heidelberg

*Materials that arrived after K. Deller completed the reading of the first proofs were inserted by the editors. We regret any inconsistencies that may have resulted.

INDEX OF PERSONAL NAMES

[1]References without museum siglae all refer to the Yale tablets.

Amur-rabī f.Šurki-tilla:
[ᴵ]*Šur-ki-til-la* DUMU *A-mu*[*r*-GAL] WHM 152335:9
Antarari s.Ar-teššе:
NA₄ ᴵ*An-ta-ra-r*[*i*] [45]DUMU *Ar-téš-še* Kel 89522 + AO 6027:44-45, judge
Antija:
ᴵ*An-ti-ja* 25:4.6
Apazu f.Itaḫḫe:
IGI *I-ta-aḫ-ḫe* DUMU *A-ba-zu* 21:13
Apil-Sîn f.Balṭu-kašid:
[IGI TI.LA-KUR DUMU *A-p*]*il*-30 DUB.S[AR] 16:16
Apil-Sîn f.Taja:
IGI *Ta-a+a* DUMU IBILA-30 DUB.SAR 15:32
NA₄ KIŠIB ᴵ*Ta-a+a* DUMU IBILA-ᵈ30 DUB.SAR 15:39
Apuška:
ᴵ*A-pu-uš-qa* 7:6, field neighbor of Enna-mati s.Šar-teja
Arra[ ] f.[ ]:
[IGI DU]MU *Ar-r*[*a-*] 16:15
Ariḫ-ḫarpa f.[n]i:
[IGI *n*]*i* DUMU *A-ri-iḫ-ḫar-me* 27:21
Arik-kaja f.[ ]:
[ᴵ] *A-ri-iq-qa-a+a* DU[MU] WHM 152335:8
Arik-kanata s.Šatu-kewi:
IGI *A-ri-ka-na-da* [ ] [18]DUMU *Ša-du-ge-mi* IM 70764:17-18
Arik-kelte:
[NA₄ ᴵ*A-r*]*i*-⌜*ig*⌝-*ge-el-li*(=*te*!?) Kel 89393:12
Arik-kurwe
ᴵ*A-ri-gur-we-e* 16:6, house neighbor of Ḫanaja s.Itḫi-tilla
Arim-matka f.Milkuja:
[IGI *Mil-ku-ja*] DUMU *A-ri-ma-at-ka* 1:38
IGI *M*[*il-k*]*u-ja* DUMU *A-ri-*[*ma-at-qa*] 2:16
[IGI *Mil-ku-ja* DUMU *A*]*-ri-im-ma-at-qa* 5:17
Arip-arrapḫe s.Ḫanu:
ᴵ*A-ri-ba-ar-ra-ap-ḫe* DUMU *Ḫa-nu* BM 85311:2
Arip-papni f.Taja:
IGI *Ta-a+a* DUMU *A-ri-ib-ba-ab-:-ni* 21:20
Arip-uppinni f.Akkul-enni:
IGI ⌜*A*⌝-*ku*-≪ŠE≫-*le-ni* [20]DUMU *A-ri-bu-bi-ni* IM 70764:19-20
Ariw-WAḫlu f.Šeḫel-tešup:
IGI *Še-ḫé-el-te-šup* DUMU *A-ri*-WA-AḪ-*lu* 21:15
Ar-kapi s.Akkuja:
IGI ᴵ*Ar-qa-bi* DUMU *Ak-ku-*⌜*ja*⌝ 19:21
[NA₄ ᴵ]*Ar-qa-b*[*e*] 19:29
Ar-kapinni f.[ ]:
[IGI DUMU *Ar-q*]*a-bi-in-ni* 5:18

Ekeke:

NA$_4$ ^{I}*E-ge-ge* 17:33, witness

possibly IGI ⸢*E*⸣-[*ge-ge* DUMU] 17:25

Elḫip-tilla s.Ḫašip-ukur, merchant:

^{I}*El-ḫi-ip-til-la* DUMU *Ḫa-ši-pu-gur* ^{LÚ}DAM.GÀR 3:2, debtor of Wullu s.Puḫi-šenni

^{I}*El-ḫi-ip-til-la* 3:6

NA$_4$ KIŠIB ^{I}*El-ḫi-ip-til-la* ^{LÚ}DAM.<GÀR> 3:21

Elḫip-tilla s.[ ]x:

^{I}*El-ḫi-ip-til-la* ^{6}[DUMU]x 14:5-6

Elḫip-tilla, scribe:

IGI *El-ḫi-ip-til-la* DUB.SAR 3:14

NA$_4$ KIŠIB ^{I}*El-ḫi-ip-til-la* DUB.SAR 3:22

[IGI *E*]*l-ḫi-ip-til-la* DUB.SAR Kel 89393:10

Ennaja f.Errazi:

[IGI *E*]*r-ra-zi* DUMU *En-na-a+a* 1:37

IGI [*Er-r*]*a*$^{!}$*-zi* DUMU *En-na-*[*a+a*] 2:17

IGI *Er-*⸢*ra-zi* DUMU⸣ *En-na-a+a* 4:2

[IGI *Er-ra-zi* DUMU] *E-en-na-a+a* 5:16

IGI *I-ra-zi* DUMU *E-na-ja* BM 85311:19

IGI *I-ra-zi* DUMU *I-na-ja* BM 85355:18

Ennaja f.Ipša-ḫalu:

IGI *Ip-ša-ḫa-lu* DUMU *En-na-a+a* 21:24

Enna[ja] f.Itḫi-kewar (restoration based on *En-na-a+a* 4:2, but not quite certain):

IGI *It-ḫi-ge-wa-ar* DUMU *En-na-*[*a+a*] 4:3

Enna-mati s.Šar-teja:

^{I}*En-na-ma-*⸢*ti*⸣ ^{2}[DUMU] *Ša-ar-te-a* 7:1-2, debtor (*titennūtu*) of Pui-tae s.Wullu

^{I}*En-na-ma-*⸢*ti*⸣*-ma* 7:20

[NA$_4$ ^{I}*En-n*]*a-ma-ti* 7:33

Enna-mati f.[ ]:

[IGI DUMU *En*]*-na-ma-ti* 20:35

En-šaku:

^{I}*En-ša-ku* 11:3

En-šukru s.Zimpar:

IGI *En-šúk-ru* DUMU ⸢*Zi*⸣*-im-bar* 15:33

En-šukru f.Erwi-šarri

[^{I}*Er-w*]*i-šarri* DUMU ⸢*En*⸣$^{!}$*-šúk-rù* WHM 152335:2

En-teja f.Upaja:

IGI *Ú-ba-a+a* DUMU *En-te-ja* 3:9

Epata f.Nanip-tilla:

IGI *Na-ni-ip-til-la* DUMU *E-pa-ta* 21:22

Errazi s.Ennaja:
[IGI *E*]*r-ra-zi* DUMU *En-na-a+a* 1:37
[NA$_4$ $^{(I)}$*Er-r*]*a-zi* 1:46
IGI [*Er-r*]*a*$^{!}$*-zi* DUMU *En-na-*[*a+a*] 2:17
NA$_4$ KIŠIB ^{I}*Er-*[*ra-zi*] 2:27
IGI *Er-*⸢*ra-zi* DUMU⸣ *En-na-a+a* 4:2
NA$_4$ ^{I}⸢*Er*⸣*-ra-z*[*i*] 4:8
[IGI *Er-ra-zi* DUMU] *E-en-na-a+a* 5:16
IGI *I-ra-zi* DUMU *E-na-ja* BM 85311:19
IGI *I-ra-zi* DUMU *I-na-ja* BM 85355:18

Erwi-šarri s.En-šukru:
[^{I}*Er-w*]*i-šarri* DUMU ⸢*En*⸣$^{!}$*-šúk-rù* WHM 152335:2

Erwi-šarri:
[NA$_4$ ^{I}*Er-w*]*i-šarri* 14:11, witness

Erwi-šarri f.Tai-tešup:
[^{I}*T*]*a-i-te-šup* DUMU *Er-wi-šarri*

Erwi-šarri f.[X]nikup-šenni:
[^{I}]x*-ni-ku-up-še-en*$^{!}$*-ni* DUMU ⸢*Er*⸣$^{!}$*-wi-šarri* WHM 152335:7
]x*-ni-ku-up-še-en*$^{!}$*-ni* DUMU ⸢*Er*⸣*-wi-šarri* WHM 152335:7

Erwi-šarri f.[ ]:
[IGI DUMU *E*]*r-wi-šarri* 27:19

Ḫaiš-te[ ]:
NA$_4$ ^{I}*Ḫa-iš-te-*[*ja*/*šup*/*0*] 18:13, witness

Ḫaltaja f.Kuzzarija:
IGI *Ku-uz-za-ri-ja* DUMU *Ḫa-al-ta-a+a* 21:16

Ḫalutta f.Nanip-ukur
[^{I}*N*]*a-ni-p*[*u-g*]*ur* DUMU *Ḫa-lu-ut-*⸢*ta*⸣ WHM 152335:5

Ḫamanna s.Ḫapiruku:
IGI *Ḫa-ma-an-na* DUMU *Ḫa-bi-ru-ku* 21:17
NA$_4$ ^{I}*Ḫa-ma-an-na* 21:36

Ḫamanna:
^{I}*Ḫa-ma-an-na* 5:5, seller

Ḫamanna f.Ipša-ḫalu:
^{I}*I*[*p-šá-ḫa-lu*] ^{2}[DUMU *Ḫa-ma-a*]*n-na* 22:1-2

Ḫamanna f.Zike:
^{I}*Zi-gi* DUMU *Ḫa-ma-an-na* BM 85266 + 85472:2

Ḫanaja s.Itḫi-tilla:
^{I}*Ḫa-na-a+a* ^{2}DUMU *It-ḫi-til-la* 16:1-2, exchange partner of Teḫip-tilla s.Puḫi-šenni
^{I}*Ḫa-na-a+a* 16:4.7.10

Ḫanatu s.Ḫinnuja:
^{I}*Ḫa-na-tu*$_4$ Ḫanatu:
[NA$_4$ ^{I}*Ḫa*]*-na-tu*$_4$ 14:12 (restoration uncertain)

Ḫanikuzzi f.Šanḫaraja:
  IGI [1]*Ša-an-ḫa-ra-a+a* DUMU *Ḫa-ni-ku-z*[*i*] 19:20
Ḫaniu s.Arn-urḫe:
  [1]*Ḫa-ni-ú* DUMU *Ar-nu-u*[*u*]*r-ḫ*[*é*] 17:3, ex-adoptant
  [1]*Ḫa-ni-ú* 17:6.11.14
  [1]*Ḫa-ni-*[*ú-ma*] 17:15
  [1]*Ḫ*[*a-ni-ú*] 17:19
  [IGI *Ḫa-ni-ú* DUMU] *Ar-nu-ur-ḫe* 27:18 (restoration uncertain)
Haniu s.[Zilija]:
  [[1]]⌜*Ḫa-ni-ú*⌝ [2][DUMU *Zi-li-j*]*a* 19:1-2, adoptant
  [[1]*Ḫa-ni*]*-ú* 19:10
  NA4 [1]*Ḫa-ni-ú* EN.A.ŠÀ 19:14
Ḫanu f.Arip-arrapḫe:
  [1]*A-ri-ba-ar-ra-ap-ḫe* DUMU *Ḫa-nu* BM 85311:2
Ḫapiruku f.Ḫamanna:
  IGI *Ḫa-ma-an-na* DUMU *Ḫa-bi-ru-ku* 21:17
Ḫapišše f.Ar-šatuja:
  [[1]*A*]*r-ša-du-ú-ja* [4][DU]MU *Ḫa-bi-iš-še* BM 85266 + 85472:3-4
Ḫaruja f.Turari:
  [1]*Tu4-ú-ra-ri* DUMU *Ḫa-a-ru-ú-i-ja* BM 85266 + 85472:7-8
Ḫašija s.Taja:
  IGI *Ḫa-ši-ja* DUMU [*T*]*a-a+a* 1:42
  NA4 *Ḫa-ši-ja* 1:45
Ḫašija s.[ ]:
  [[1]*Ḫa-ši-ja* DUMU] (restored in break at the beginning of SIL 316), litigant
  [1]*Ḫa-ši-ja* SIL 316:4′.9′.13′.16′
  [[1]*Ḫ*]*a-ši-ja* SIL 316.20′
Ḫašija f.Katiri:
  IGI *Qa-t*[*i*]*-ri* DUMU *Ḫa-ši-ja* 15:30
Ḫašija f.Kunnija:
  IGI *Ku-un-ni-ja* DUMU *Ḫa-ši-ja* 3:13
Ḫašija f.Tain-šuḫ:
  [1]*Ta-i-šu-ú-uḫ* DUMU *Ḫa-ši-i-ja* BM 85266 + 85472:5-6
Ḫašik-kewar:
  [*Ḫa*]*-ši-ge-mar* HM 8400 = EN 9,122:35, probably patronymic
Ḫašip-tašenni, scribe:
  [NA4 [1]*Ḫa*]*-ši-ip-ta-še-*[13][:]*-en-ni* DUB.S[AR] 26:12-13 (restoration not quite certain)
Ḫašip-tilla s.Kelip-ukur:
  ša [1]*Ḫa-ši-ip-til-la* [4]DUMU *Ge-li-pu-gur* 23:3-4
  NA4 *Ḫa-ši-ip-til-la* [6]DUMU *Ge-li-pu-gur* 23:5-6
Ḫašip-tilla:
  [1]*Ḫa-ši-ip-til-la* 24:7

Ḫašip-tilla f.Wantiš-šenni:
　⸢IGI⸣ [^{I}*W*]*a-an-ti-iš-še-en-ni* DUMU *Ḫa-ši-ip-til-la* 7:25
　^{I}*Wa-an-ti-iš-še-en-ni* DUMU *Ḫa-ši-ip-til-la* 12:3
　^{I}*Wa-an-t*[*i-iš-še-en-ni*] ^{5}DUMU *Ḫa-ši-ip-til-la* Kel 89522 + AO 6029:4-5
Ḫašip-ukur f.Elḫip-tilla:
　^{I}*El-ḫi-ip-til-la* DUMU ⸢*Ḫa-ši-pu*⸣*-gur* ^{LÚ}DAM.GÀR 3:2
Ḫaši-tilla f.[ ]:
　NA_4 ^{I}[DU]MU *Ḫa-ši-til-la* 6:38
Ḫinnuja f.Ḫanatu:
　^{I}*Ḫa-na-tu*$_4$ DUMU *Ḫi-in-nu-ja* TF$_1$ K/40:3
^{f}Ḫinzuraja m. [K]$^{?}$unnu:
　[IGI^{I}*K*]*u*$^{?}$*-un-nu* DUMU $^{MÍ.I}$*Ḫi-in-zu-*⸢*ra-a+a*⸣ 19:22
^{f}Ḫinzuri d.Kakazzu:
　^{MÍ}*Ḫi-in-zu-ri* DUMU.MÍ *Qa-qa-az-zu* 12:1, enters *ana aḫātūti* to Wantiš-šenni s.Ḫašip-tilla
　NA_4 *Ḫi-in-zu-ri* 12:20
Ḫui-te s.<Malija>:
　NA_4 ^{I}*Ḫu-i-te* DUMU <*Ma-li-ja*> 16:19, witness
Ḫut-arrapḫe:
　NA_4 ^{I}*Ḫu-tar-ra-a*[*p-ḫe*] 20:20, witness
Ḫuti[ ] f. [ ]:
　NA_4 ^{I}[ ] ^{11}DUMU *Ḫu-ti-*[ ] 26:10-11
Ḫutija s.Šukrija:
　IGI *Ḫu-di-ja* DUMU *Šu-uk-ri-ja* BM 85311:22; BM 85355:21
Ḫutija s.Utu-mansum, scribe:
　IGI *Ḫu-ti-ja* DUB.SAR DUMU $^{⸢d⸣}$[UTU-MA.AN.SUM] 2:26
　NA_4 KIŠIB ^{I}*Ḫu-ti-ja* DUB.SAR 2:30
Ḫutija:
　NA_4 ^{I}*Ḫu-ti-ja* 14:10, witness
　[^{I}*Ḫu-ti-ja-ma*] SMN 855:1, litigant
　^{I}*Ḫu-ti-ja* SMN 855:9
Ḫutip-šarri, scribe:
　[NA_4 ^{I}[*Ḫu-ti-ip-šarri* ^{17}DUB.SAR-*rù* 18:16-17
Ḫutip-ukur f.Šekaru:
　[IGI *Še-q*]*a-rù* DUMU *Ḫu-*⸢*ti-ip*⸣*-pu-gur* 20:29
Ikkija s.Kumpuzzu:
　IGI *Ik-ki-ja* DUMU *Ku-um-pu-uz-zu* 8:10
　NA_4 KIŠIB ^{I}*Ik-ki-ja* 8:21
Ikkiri s.Šarrukke (for this reading see below, Šarrukke):
　^{I}*Ik-ki-ri-ma* ^{2}DUMU *Šar-ru-ug-ge* HM 8400 = EN 9,122:1-2, buyer of houses
　^{I}*Ik-ki-ri* HM 8400 = EN 9,122:25
　^{I}*Ik-k*[*i-ri*] HM 8400 = EN 9,122:28

Ikkiri:
I-ki-ri IM 70764:9
Ipša-ḫalu s.Ennaja:
IGI *Ip-ša-ḫa-lu* DUMU *En-na-a+a* 21:24
Ipša-ḫalu s.Ḫamanna, husband of ^{f}Kuntu[ja] d.[N]inkija, f.[^{f}Ulu]litu:
^{I}*I*[*p-šá-ḫ*]*a-lu* ^{2}[DUMU *Ḫa-ma-a*]*n-na* 22:1-2, gives his daughter *ana mārtūti* to Pui-tae s.Eḫlip-atal [NA₄ ^{I}*Ip-šá-ḫ*]*a-lu* 22:13
Ipša-ḫalu s.Šukrija:
IGI *Ip-*⸢*ša*⸣*-ḫa-lu* DUMU *Šúk-ri-ja* 15:29
Ipša-ḫalu:
NA₄ KIŠIB ^{39} ^{I}*Ip-ša-ḫa-lu* HM 8400 = EN 9,122:38-39, witness
Ipša-ḫalu f.Zilija:
^{I}[*Zi*]*-li-ja* ^{5}DUMU *Ip-ša-ḫa-lu* BM 85311:4-5; BM 85355:3-4.8
Zi-i-li-ja ^{11}DUMU *Ip-ša-ḫa-lu* BM 85266 + 85472:10-11.18.20
Ipšaja:
NA₄ (KIŠIB) ^{I}]*Ip-ša-a*<*+a*> HM 8400 = EN 9,122:37, witness
Ipšaja f.Akija:
[IGI *A*]*-ki-ja* DUMU *Ip-ša-a+a* 20:30
Iriki f.Zuzuja:
IGI *Zu-zu-ja* DUMU *I-ri-ki* BM 85311:18; BM 85355:17
Ir-šuḫḫe:
NA₄ ^{I}*Ir-šu-uḫ-ḫe* 18:14, witness
Išip-ḫalu; possibly identical with Išip-ḫalu s.Ipšaja (TCL 9,16:35):
NA₄ *I-ši-*⸢*ip*⸣*-*[*ḫa-lu*] 12:17, witness
Iššakku f.Matija (derivation uncertain; the spelling *I-ša-ku* could, in view of the writing *E-ša-ku* JEN 177:4 and 510:16, also be connected with the name En-šaku):
M[*a-di-ja*] ^{2}DUMU *I-ša-ku* IM 70764:1-2
Itaḫḫe s.Apazu:
IGI *I-ta-aḫ-ḫe* DUMU *A-ba-zu* 21:13
NA₄ ^{I}⸢*I*⸣*-ta-aḫ-ḫ*[*e*] 21:30
Itḫ-apiḫe f.Turar-tešup:
ŠU ^{I}*Tu-ra-a*[*r-te-šup* DUB.SAR] DUMU *I*⸢*t*⸣*-*[*ḫa-bi-ḫe*] SIL 316:23′
Itḫi-kewar s.Enna[ja] (reading of patronymic not quite certain):
IGI *It-ḫi-ge-wa-ar* DUMU *En-na-*[*a+a*] 4:3
Itḫip-šarri s.Muluja:
^{I}[*It-ḫi-ip-šarri*] ^{3}DUMU *Mu-lu-ja* 21:2-3, litigant in *ṭuppi tamgurti*
^{I}*I*[*t-ḫi-ip-šarri*] 21:4
[^{I}*It-ḫi-ip-šarri*] 21:6.7
Itḫip-ukur f.Akap-tukke:
[IGI *A-kap-dug-g*]*e* DUMU *It-ḫi-pu-gur* 1:30
IGI *A-kap-dug-ge* DUMU *It-ḫi-i*[*p-pu*/*ú-gur*] 2:21
[IGI *A-kap-dug-ge* DUMU *It-ḫ*]*i-pu-gur* 5:20

Itḫišta s.Ar-tae:
IGI *It-ḫi-iš-ta* DUMU *Ar-ta-e* 15:31
Itḫišta f.Akip-šenni:
[^{I}*A-kip-še-en-ni* DUMU *It-ḫi-iš-ta*] 20:2
[^{I}*A-kip-še-en-ni* DUMU *It-ḫi*]-⸢*iš-ta*⸣ 20:4
Itḫi-tilla f.Ḫanaja:
^{I}*Ḫa-na-a+a* ^{2}DUMU *It-ḫi-til-la* 16:1-2
Kakazzu f. ^{f}Ḫinzuri (possibly to be interpreted as Qaqqassu):
^{MÍ}*Ḫi-in-zu-ri* DUMU.MÍ *Qa-qa-az-zu* 12:1
Kani:
^{I}*Qa-ni* 7:7, field neighbor of Enna-mati s.Šar-teja
Kanija s.Ar-tilla:
^{I}*Ka-ni-ja* DUMU *Ar-til-la* BM 85355:1
Katiri s.Ḫašija:
IGI *Qa-t*[*i*]-*ri* DUMU *Ḫa-ši-ja* 15:30
Kelija f.Mutta:
IGI *Mu-ut-ta* DUMU *Ge-li-ja* 8:11
Kelija f.Niḫri-tešup:
IGI *Ni-iḫ-ri-te-šup* DUMU *Ge-li-ja* 15:27
NA$_{4}$ KIŠIB ^{I}*Ni-iḫ-ri-te-šup* DUMU *Ge-li-ja* 15:34
Kelip-ukur f.Ḫašip-tilla:
ša ^{I}*Ḫa-ši-ip-til-la* ^{4}DUMU *Ge-li-pu-gur* 23:3-4
NA$_{4}$ *Ḫa-ši-ip-til-la* ^{6}DUMU *Ge-li-pu-gur* 23:5-6
Kelš-erwi:
IGI *Ge-el-še-er-wi ša* NIN.DINGIR.RA 3:11
NA$_{4}$ KIŠ.IB ^{I}*Ge-el-še-er-wi* 3:18
NA$_{4}$ ^{I}*Ge-el-še-er-wi* Kel 89393:14 (identification with 3:11.18 virtually certain)
Keltija s.Keltu[ ]:
[IGI *Ge*?]-*el*-[*t*]*i-ja* DUMU *Ge-el-du*-⸢x⸣ 20:31
Keltu[ ] f. [G]eltija:
[IGI *Ge*?]-*el*-[*t*]*i-ja* DUMU *Ge-el-du*-⸢*x*⸣ 20:31
Kennenna f.Muš-teja (previous references to Kennenna/i are wrongly entered under the heading Kenni NPN 83b and Kinnanni AAN I 82a):
^{I}*Mu-uš-te-ja* DUMU ⸢*Ge-en*⸣-*né-en-na* 1:2
Kewi-tae f.Arte-kušše:
[IGI ^{I}*Ar*?-*t*]*e*?-*ku-še* DUMU *G*[*e-w*]*i-ta*-⸢*e*⸣ 19:23
Kuari s.Unapše, br.Nuzza, Akippu, Šuri, Akija, Šennatil, Akawatil:
<I>*Ku-a-ri* $^{2-4}$. . . ^{5}[DUMU]^{MEŠ} ^{I}*Ú*-⸢*nap*⸣-*še* Kel 89548:1-5, adoptant
[N]A$_{4}$ ^{I}*Ku-a-ri* Kel 89548:17 (*-ri* not visible on photo)
Kumpuzzu f.Ikkija; possibly to be interpreted as *Kubbussu (see AHw 497b, *kubbutu*):
IGI *Ik-ki-ja* DUMU *Ku-um-pu-uz-zu* 8:10

Kuni f.Amiš-tae:

^{I}*A-mi-iš-ta-e* DUMU *Ku-ni-i* BM 85355:2

Kunnija s.Ḫašija:

IGI *Ku-un-ni-ja* DUMU *Ḫa-ši-ja* 3:13

NA₄ KIŠIB ^{I}*Ku-un-ni-ja* 3:19

Kunnu s.^{f}Ḫinzuraja:

[IGI ^{I}K]*u*?-*un-nu* DUMU $^{MÍ.I}$*Ḫi-in-zu-*⌜*ra-a+a*⌝ 19:22

^{f}Kuntu[ja] d. [N]inkija, wife of Ipša-ḫalu s.Ḫamanna, m.[^{f}Ulu]litu:

^{MÍ}*Ku-un-d*[*u-ja*] ^{3}[DUMU.MÍ *Ni*]-*in-ki-ja* 22:2-3, gives her daughter *ana mārtūti* to Pui-tae s.Eḫlip-atal

Kušši-ḫarpe:

^{I}*Ku-uš-ši-ḫarbe* SMN 855:2.8, litigant

Kutukka f.Turar-tešup:

[^{I}*D*]*u-ra-ar-te-šup* DUMU *Ku-du*[*q*]-⌜*qa*⌝ WHM 152335:3

Kuzzarija s.Ḫaltaja:

IGI *Ku-uz-za-ri-ja* DUMU *Ḫa-al-ta-a+a* 21:16

NA₄ ^{I}*Ku-*⌜*uz-za*⌝*-ri-a* 21:37

Malija f.Ḫui-te:

NA₄ ^{I}*Ḫu-i-te* DUMU <*Ma-li-ja*> 16:19

Mār-Ištar:

NA₄ ^{I}DUMU-^{d}U-DAR 18:15, witness

Matija s.Iššakku:

M[*a-di-ja*] ^{2}DUMU *I-ša-ku* IM 70764:1-2, "adoptee"

Ma-di-j[*a*] IM 70764:4

Ma-di-ja IM 70764:7

Mat-tešup:

^{I}*Ma-at-te-šup* 15:7, house neighbor of Tauḫḫe s.Teḫija in Tašenniwe

Melija f.Akip-tašenni:

IGI *A-kip-ta-še-ni* DUMU *Me-li-ja* 15:21

NA₄ KIŠIB ^{I}*A-kip-ta-še-ni* DUMU *Me-li-ja* 15:35

Milkuja s.Arim-matka:

[IGI *Mil-ku-ja*] DUMU *A-ri-ma-at-ka* 1:38

NA₄ ^{I}*Mil-ku-ja* 1:44

IGI *M*[*il-k*]*u-ja* DUMU *A-ri-*[*ma-at-qa*] 2:16

NA₄ KIŠIB ^{I}*Mil-ku-ja* 2:28

NA₄ ^{I}*Mil-ku-ja* 4:11

[IGI *Mil-ku-ja* DUMU *A*]*-ri-im-ma-at-qa* 5:17

Mukaru f.Zikaja:

[^{I}*Zi-ka-a+a*] ^{2}DUMU *Mu-ka-ru* 21:1-2

Muluja f.Itḫip-šarri:

^{I}[*It-ḫi-ip-šarri*] ^{3}DUMU *Mu-lu-ja* 21:2-3

Muš-teja s.Kennenna:

^{I}*Mu-uš-te-ja* DUMU *Ge-en-né-en-na* 1:2, adoptant

Bēl-iddina f.Bēl-aḫḫē:
[IGI/ŠU *B*]*e*$^{!}$-*el*-Š[EŠ$^{!MEŠ}$] ^{36}[DUB.S]AR DUMU *Be-e*[*l*-MA.AN.SU]M BM 85266 + 85472:35-36
Bēl-iddina f.Zinija:
IGI *Zi-ni-ja* DUMU *Be-el*-MA.AN.SUM DUB.SAR BM 85311:25
[IGI *Zi-ni*]-*ja* DUMU *Be-el*-MA.AN.SUM [DU]B.SAR BM 85355:24
Bēl-i[ ] f.Sîn-ašarēd:
IGI ^{d}30-*a-ša-re-e*[*d*] ^{22}DUB.SAR DUMU *Bé-el-i*-[ ] IM 70764:21-22
Puḫija f.Tešup-erwi:
NA$_4$ ^{I}*Te-šup-er-wi* ^{43}DUMU *Pu-ḫi-ja* Kel 89522 + AO 6029:42-43
Puḫi-šenni s.Akija:
IGI *Pu-ḫi-še-en-ni* DUMU *A-ki-ja* 8:13
NA$_4$ ^{I}*Pu-ḫi-še-en-ni* 8:23
[IGI ^{I}*Pu-ḫ*]*i-še-ni* DUMU [*A-ki*]-*ja* 19:24 (restoration uncertain)
Puḫi-šenni [s.Uzzuke] (restoration uncertain):
^{I}*Pu-ḫi-š*[*e-en-ni* DUMU *Ú-zu-ge*] 2:3, adoptant
Puḫi-šenni f.Šennaja:
IGI *Še-en-na-a+a* DUMU *Pu-ḫi-še-en-ni* 3:12
[IGI *Še-en-na-a+*]⸢*a*⸣ DUMU *Pu-ḫi-še-en-ni* Kel 89393:4
Puḫi-šenni f.Teḫip-tilla:
^{I}*Te-ḫi-ip-til-la* DUMU *Pu-ḫi-še-en-ni* 15:3
^{I}*Te-ḫi-ip-til-la* ^{3}DUMU *Pu-ḫi-še-en-ni* 16:2-3
Puḫi-šenni f.Wullu:
^{I}*Wu-ul-lu* DUMU *Pu-ḫi-še-en-ni* 1:3
^{I}*Wu-ul-lu* DUMU *Pu-ḫi-*[*še-en-ni*] 2:5
^{I}*Wu-ul-*[*lu* DUMU *Pu*]-*ḫi*-⸢*še-en-ni*⸣ 3:1
^{I}*Wu-ul-lu* DUMU *Pu-ḫi-še-en-ni* Kel 89548:5
Pui-tae s.Eḫlip-atal (correct fils d'Eḫli-papu, AAN I 111a):
[^{I}*Pu*]-⸢*i*⸣-*ta-e* DUMU *Eḫ-li-ba-tal*$^{!}$(ḪU) 22:5
^{I}*Pu-i-ta-e* 22:6
^{I}*P*[*u-i-ta-e*] ^{6}DUMU *Eḫ-li-pa-tal* 26:5-6
^{I}*Pu-i-*[*ta-e*] 26:8
^{I}*Pu-i-ta-e* DUMU *Eḫ-l*[*i-pa-tal*] Kel 89522 + AO 6029:1
^{I}*Pu-i-ta-e* Kel 89522 + AO 6029:7.22.25.33.37
Pui-tae s.Wullu; f.^{f}WAtila and ^{f}Uriš-elli; br. Ḫašip-tilla, Akawatil, Šukri-tešup and ^{f}Akap-šušše:
[^{I}*Pu-i-ta*]⸢*e*⸣ D[UMU] *W*[*u-ul-lu*] ^{3}[*a*]-*na* ^{MÍ}*WA-ti-la a-na* ^{MÍ}[ ] ^{4}*a-na* ^{MÍ}*Ú-ri-še-el-li* 6:2-4 (*ṭuppi šīmti*)
^{I}*Pu-i-ta-e-ma* 6:7.12.26
^{I}[*Pu*]-⸢*i*⸣-*ta-e* DUMU *Wu-ul-lu* 7:10, creditor (*titennūtu*)
[^{I}*Pu-i-t*]*a-e* 7:12
[^{I}]⸢*Pu*⸣-*i-ta-e* 7:13
[^{I}*Pu-i*]-⸢*ta*⸣-*e* 7:16
^{I}*Pu*-⸢*i*⸣-[*ta*]-⸢*e*⸣ 7:18

^{I}*Pu-i-ta-*⌜*e*⌝ 7:21
^{I}*Pu-i-t*[*a-e*] 10:4
[^{I}*Pu*]-⌜*i*⌝-*ta-e-ma* Kel 89393:5

Pui-tae f.Akkul-enni:
[IGI ^{I}*Ak-ku-le*]-*ni* DUMU *Pu-i-ta-e* 19:25

Puja s.Arn-urḫe:
IGI *Pu-ú-ja* DUMU *A-ar-nu-ur-ḫe ša-*[*gu-ú*] BM 85311:23
IGI *Pu-ú-ja* DUMU *Ar-nu-ur-ḫe ša-gu-ú* BM 85355:22

Puja f.Ar-šuliḫe:
[IGI *Ar*]-*šu-li-ḫé* ^{19}[DUMU *Pu*]-*ja* 2:18-19
IGI *Ar-šu-li-ḫé* DUMU *Pu-ú-ja* 3:8
[IGI *Ar-šu-li-ḫé* DUMU *P*]*u-ú-ja* Kel 89393:2

Purasa:
^{I}*Pu-ra-sa* 18:6 (houses adjoining the houses of P.)

Putija s.Nanija:
IGI *Pu-di-ja* DUMU *Na-ni-ja nu-a-ru* BM 85311:24
IGI [*Pu-di*]-*ja* DUMU *Na-ni-ja* [*nu*]-*a-ru* BM 85355:23

Sîn-ašarēd s.Bēl-i[ ], scribe:
IGI ^{d}30-*a-ša-re-e*[*d*] ^{22}DUB.SAR DUMU *Bé-el-i-*[ ] IM 70764:21-22

Sîn-rēmēni f.Nauṣur:
IGI *Na-ú-*⌜*ṣú*?*-ur*⌝?[ ] ^{16}DUMU ^{d}30-*re-mé-ni* IM 70764:15-16

Šalap-urḫe s.Zilija:
IGI ^{I}*Ša-la-ap-ur-ḫé* DUMU *Zi-li-ja* 7:27
NA4 ^{I}*Ša-la-ap-u*[*r-ḫé*] 7:33

Šamaš-NI.DU (NPN 124a suggests reading Šamaš-ukîn), scribe:
IGI ^{d}UTU-NI.DU DUB.SAR-*rù* 4:4

Šanḫaraja s.Ḫanikuzzi:
IGI ^{I}*Ša-an-ḫa-ra-a+a* DUMU *Ḫa-ni-ku-z*[*i*] 19:20

Šarrija s.Šekaru:
[IGI LU]GAL?-*ja* DUMU *Še-ga-rù* Kel 89393:8

Šar-teja s.Nirpija, f.Enna-mati:
^{I}*Ša-ar-te-*⌜*ja*⌝ [DUMU *Ni-ir-bi-ja*] Kel 89522 + AO 6029:2, litigant
^{I}*Ša-ar-te-ja* Kel 89522 + AO 6029:34
^{I}*En-na-ma-*⌜*ti*⌝ ^{2}[DUMU] *Ša-ar-te-a* 7:1-2
^{I}*Ša-ar-te-ja-ma* 8:5

Šar-tešup s.Šeḫel-tešup:
[NA4 ^{I}*Ša*]-*ar-te-š*[*up*] ^{36}DUMU *Še-*⌜*ḫé*⌝*-el-te-š*[*up*] 6:35-36, witness

Šar-tilla:
NA4 ^{I}*Ša-ar-til-la* 17:30, witness

Šarrukke (s.Meli-saḫ HSS 13,20:4.15.33), f.Ikkiri (reading Šarrukke follows AAN I 120a; the final GI, however, most likely stands for a form of **kūn* D):
^{I}*Ik-ki-ri-ma* ^{2}DUMU *Šar-ru-ug-ge* HM 8400 = EN 9,122:1-2
a-bu-ja ^{I}*Šar-ru-ug-ge* HM 8400 = EN 9,122:4

Šatu-kewi f.Arik-kanata:
IGI *A-ri-ka-na-da* [ ] ^{18}DUMU *Ša-du-ge-mi* IM 70764:17-18
Šeḫel-tešup s.Ariw-WAḪlu:
IGI *Še-ḫé-el-te-šup* DUMU *A-ri*-WA-AḪ-*lu* 21:15
Šeḫel-tešup f.Šar-tešup:
[NA$_4$ ^{I}*Ša*]-*ar-te-š*[*up*] ^{36}DUMU *Še-*⸢*ḫé*⸣*-el-te-š*[*up*] 6:35-36
Šeḫlija s.Ar-tešup:
IGI *Še-eḫ-li-ja* ^{24}DUMU *Ar-te-šup* 15:23-24
Šekaja s.Wanti-muša see Šekar-tilla s.Wanti-muša
Šekar-tilla s.Nullu:
IGI ^{I}*Ši-qa-ar-til-la* DUMU *Nu-ul-lu* 7:29
Šekar-tilla/Šekaja s.Wanti-muša:
[^{I}*Še-g*]*a-ar-til-la* 11:6
[^{I}*Še-q*]*a-a+a* DUMU *Wa-a*[*n*]*-ti-m*[*u-ša*] 14:7, creditor (*titennūtu*)
^{I}*Še-qar-til-la* DUMU *Wa-an-ti-m*[*u-š*]*á* 17:2, ex-adoptee
^{I}*Še-qar-til-la-ma* 17:5
^{I}*Še-*[*qar-til-la-ma*] 17:16
[^{I}*Še-qa-a+a*] ^{3}DUMU *Wa-an-ti-mu-š*[*a*] 18:2-3, adoptee
^{I}*Še-qa-a*[*+a*] 18:6
[^{I}*Še-qa-a+a*] 18:9.10
^{I}*Še-qa-a+a* ^{3}[DUMU *Wa-an-t*]*i-mu-*⸢*šá*⸣ 19:2-3, adoptee
^{I}*Še-q*[*ar*]*-til-la* 19:8
^{I}*Še-qa-*⸢*a+a*⸣ 19:11
[^{I}]*Še-qa-a+a* 27:8
Šekaru s.Ḫutip-ukur:
[IGI *Še-q*]*a-rù* DUMU *Ḫu-ti-ip-pu-gur* 20:29
Šekaru s.Šupa-ḫali:
IGI *Še-ka-rù* DUMU *Šu-pa-ḫa-li* 21:23
NA$_4$ ^{I}*Še-q*[*a-ru*] 21:35
Šekaru f.Šarrija:
[IGI LU]GAL$^{?}$*-ja* DUMU *Še-ga-rù* Kel 89393:8
Šekaru f.Taena:
IGI *Ta-e-na* DUMU *Še-qa-ru* 21:29
Šekaru f.[ ]nija:
[IGI ... *-n*]*i-ja* DUMU *Še-kar-rù* Kel 89393:8
Šekaru f.[ ]:
[IGI DUMU *Še-q*]*a-rù* 20:34
Šennaja s.Puḫi-šenni:
IGI *Še-en-na-a+a* DUMU *Pu-ḫi-še-en-ni* 3:12
NA$_4$ KIŠIB ^{I}*Še-en-na-a+a* 3:20
[IGI *Še-en-na-a+*]⸢*a*⸣ DUMU *Pu-ḫi-še-en-ni* Kel 89393:4
[NA$_4$ KIŠI]B ^{I}*Še-en-na-a+a* Kel 89393:13
Šennaja f.Ṣabru:
Ṣa-[*ab-ru*] ^{3}DUMU *Še-na-ja* IM 70764:2-3

Šennape: (See under Šennatil)
Šennatil s.Unap-še; br.Kuari, Nuzza, Akippu, Šuri, Akija, Akawatil:
  ^{I}*Še-en-na-til* ... ^{5}[DUMU]^{MEŠ} ^{I}*Ú-nap-še* Kel 89548:4-5, adoptant
  NA$_4$ ^{I}*Še-en-na-til* Kel 89548:15
Šešwikka s.Akija:
  IGI *Še-eš-wi-qa* DUMU *A-ki-ja* 21:19
  NA$_4$ ^{I}*Še-eš-wi-qa* 21:34 (or seal of Šešwikka s.Nal-tuja ?)
Šešwikka s.Nal-tuja:
  IGI *Še-eš-wi-qa* DUMU *Na-al-du-a* 21:21
  NA$_4$ ^{I}*Še-eš-wi-qa* 21:34 (or seal of Šešwikka s.Akija ?)
Šešwikka:
  [N]A$_4$ ^{I}*Še-eš-w*[*i-qa*] 11:12 (restoration uncertain)
Šilwaja f.[ ]:
  [IGI DUMU *Š*]*i*-[*il*]-⸢*wa*⸣-*a+a* 27:23
Šimika-atal s.Ar-šatuja:
  [IGI ^{I}]*Ši-mi-qa-tal* DUMU *Ar-ša-du-ú-ja* 7:26
  [N]A$_4$ ^{I}⸢*Ši-mi-qa-tal*⸣ 7:32
Šimika-atal s.Wantija:
  IGI *Ši-mi-qa-tal* DUMU *Wa-an-ti-a* 21:18
Šuḫuttu f.Aša-šeja:
  IGI ⸢*A*⸣$^{!}$-*ša-a-še-j*[*a*$^{!}$] ^{28}DUMU *Šu-ú-ḫu-ut-tu*$_4$ BM 85266 + 85472:27-28
Šukrija s.[ ]:
  [^{I}*Šúk*]-*ri*-⸢*ja*⸣ [DUMU] WHM 152335:11
Šukrija s.Arteja:
  NA$_4$ ^{I}*Šúk-ri-ja* DUMU *Ar-te-e* SIL 316:22′, witness
  IGI *Šu-uk-ri-ja* DUMU *A-ar-ta-e* BM 85311:20; BM 85355:19
Šukrija s.Wantija:
  IGI *Šúk-ri-ja* DUMU *Wa-an-ti-a* 21:25
Šukrija:
  NA$_4$ ^{I}*Šúk-ri-a* 17:34, witness
  NA$_4$ KIŠIB *Šu-uk-ri-ja ḫa-za-ni ša* $^{\text{URU.KI}}$*Ta-ar-gu-li* BM 85311:26
  [NA$_4$ KIŠIB *Šu-uk-ri-ja ḫa-za*]-*ni* [*ša* $^{\text{URU.KI}}$*Ta-ar-gu-l*]*i* BM 85355:25
Šukrija f.Ḫutija:
  IGI *Ḫu-di-ja* DUMU *Šu-uk-ri-ja* BM 85311:22; BM 85355:21
Šukrija f.Ipša-ḫalu:
  IGI *Ip*-⸢*ša*⸣-*ḫa-lu* DUMU *Šúk-ri-ja* 15:29
Šukri-tešup s.Wirriš-tanni:
  ^{I}*Šúk*-[*ri-te-šup*] ^{2}DUMU *Wi-ir-re-eš-t*[*a-an-ni*] 26:1-2, debtor of Pui-tae (s.Eḫlip-atal)
Šukri-tešup s.Wullu; br.Ḫašip-tilla, Pui-tae, Akawatil, ^{f}Akap-šušše:
  ^{I}*Šúk-ri-t*[*e-šup*] 6:13
  ^{I}*Šúk*-⸢*ri-te*⸣-*šup* 9:25.27
Šumu-libši f.Akija:
  IGI *A-ki-ja* DUMU MU-*líb-ši* ^{19}DUB.SAR-*rù* 8:18-19
  ŠU ^{I}*A-ki-ja* DUMU MU-*líb-ši* Kel 89522 + AO 6029:46

Šupa-ḫali f.Šekaru:
  IGI *Še-ka-rù* DUMU *Šu-pa-ḫa-li* 21:23
Šuri s.Unap-še, br.Kuari, Nuzza, Akippu, Akija, Šennatil, Akawatil:
  ^{I}*Šu-ú-ri* . . . ^{4}. . . ^{5}[DUMU]^{MEŠ} ^{I}*Ú-nap-še* Kel 89548:3-5, adoptant
  [NA4 ^{I}*Šu-ú-r*]*i* Kel 89548:11
Šuri f.Akiwe:
  IGI *A-ki-i-we* DUMU *Šu-ri* 3:10
  [IGI *A-ki*]-⌜*i*⌝-*we* DUMU *Šu-ri-we* Kel 89393:7
Šuri f.Nuzza:
  IGI ^{I}*Nu-uz-za* DUMU *Šu-ri* 19:19
Šurki-tilla s.Amur-rabī:
  [^{I}]*Šur-ki-til-la* DUMU *A-mu*[*r*-GAL]
Šurkum-atal s.Arta-šenni; br.Ar-tešše; f.Turari:
  [IG]I ⌜*Šur*⌝-*kum-a*-⌜*tal*⌝ DUMU *Ar-ta-še-en-ni* ^{41}IGI *Ar-téš-še* DU[MU] ⌜KI⌝.
  MIN 1:40-41
  [IGI *Šur-k*]*um-a-tal* DUMU *Ar-t*[*a-še-en-ni*] 2:20
  NA4 KIŠIB ^{I}*Šur-kum-a-t*[*al*] 2:29
  NA4 ^{I}*Šur-kum-a-tal* 4:9, witness
  NA4 ^{I}*Du-ra-ri* ^{41}DUMU *Šur-ku-ma-tal* Kel 89522 + AO 6029:40-41, judge
Šurukka s.[ ]:
  [^{I}*Šu-ru-uk-ka*4 DUMU] (restored in break at the beginning of SIL 316), litigant
  [^{I}*Šu-ru-uk-ka*4](?) SIL 316:1′
  ^{I}*Šu-ru-uk-ka*4 SIL 316:6′.7′.8′
  ^{I}*Šu-ru*-⌞*u*⌟*k-ka*4 SIL 316.16′
  [^{I}*Šu-r*]*u-uk-ka*4 SIL 316.19′
Tae f.Nai-šeri:
  ^{I}*Na-i-še-ri* DUMU *Ta-e* BM 85311:1
Taena s.Šekaru:
  IGI *Ta-e-na* DUMU *Še-qa-ru* 21:29
Tain-šuḫ s.Ḫašija:
  ^{I}*Ta-i-šu-ú-uḫ* ^{6}DUMU Ḫa-ši-i-ja BM 85266 + 85472:5-6
Tai-tešup s.Erwi-šarri:
  [^{I}*T*]*a-i-te-šup* DUMU *Er-wi-šarri* WHM 152335:6
Taja s.Apil-Sîn, scribe:
  IGI *Ta-a+a* DUMU IBILA-30 DUB.SAR 15:32
  NA4 KIŠIB ^{I}*Ta-a+a* DUMU IBILA-^{d}30 DUB.SAR 15:39
Taja s.Arip-papni:
  IGI *Ta-a+a* DUMU *A-ri-ib-ba-ab-:-ni* 21:20
Taja f.Ḫašija:
  IGI *Ḫa-ši-ja* DUMU [*T*]*a-a+a* 1:42
Taja f.Mušuja:
  [^{I}*Mu-šu-ja* DUMU *T*]*a*$^{?}$-*a+a* 20:6 (restoration not quite certain)
Takurram f.Ar-teja:
  ^{I}*Ar-te-ja* DUMU *Ta-ku-ur-ra-am* HM 8400 = EN 9,122:5

^{f}Uriš-elli d.Pui-tae, sister of ^{f}WAtila:
  ^{MÍ}*Ú-ri-še-el-li* 6:4
Uta-andul, scribe:
  [^{I}] ⌜*Ú*⌝*-ta-an-*<til> ^{LÚ}DUB.SAR WHM 152335:4
Utḫaja s.Eḫli-tešup:
  [^{I}*Ut-ḫ*]*a*$^{!}$*-a+a* DUMU *Eḫ-li*$^{!}$*-te-*⌜*šup*⌝ WHM 152335:1
Utu-mansum f.Ḫutija:
  IGI *Ḫu-ti-ja* DUB.SAR DUMU ⌜^{d}⌝[UTU-MA.AN.SUM] 2:26
Uzzukaja s.Ḫašip-tilla, br.Wantiš-šenni:
  ^{I}*Uz-zu-qa-a+a* 13:11
Uzzuke f.Puḫi-šenni:
  ^{I}*Pu-ḫi-š*[*e-en-ni* DUMU *Uz-zu-ge*] 2:3, adoptant (restoration uncertain)
Waḫri-šenni f.Tarmi-tešup:
  IGI *Tar-mi-te-šup* ^{17}DUMU *Wa-aḫ-ri-še-en-ni* 8:16-17
Waqar-bēlī s.Taja, scribe:
  [ŠU ^{I}*Wa-qar*]-EN DUB.SAR-*rù* 19:26 (restoration uncertain)
Wantija s.ŠEŠ[ ], shepherd:
  ^{I}*Wa-an-ti-ja* DUMU ŠEŠ-[ ] WHM 170489:7
  NA_4 *Wa-an-ti-ja* ^{L}[^{Ú}SIPA$^{?}$] WHM 170489:9
Wantija f.Šimika-atal:
  IGI *Ši-mi-qa-tal* DUMU *Wa-an-ti-a* 21:18
Wantija f.Šukrija:
  IGI *Šúk-ri-ja* DUMU *Wa-an-ti-a* 21:25
Wanti-muša f.Šekar-tilla/Šekaja:
  [^{I}*Še-q*]*a-a+a* DUMU *Wa-a*[*n*]*-ti-m*[*u-ša*] 14:7
  ^{I}*Še-qar-til-la* DUMU *Wa-an-ti-m*[*u-š*]*á* 17:2
  [^{I}*Še-qa-a+a*] ^{3}DUMU *Wa-an-ti-mu-š*[*a*] 18:2-3
  ^{I}*Še-qa-a+a* ^{3}[DUMU *Wa-an-t*]*i-mu-*⌜*šá*⌝ 19:2-3
Wantiš-šenni s.Ḫašip-tilla, br.Uzzukaja:
  ⌜IGI⌝ [^{I}*W*]*a-an-ti-iš-še-en-ni* DUMU *Ḫa-ši-ip-til-la* 7:25
  NA_4 ^{I}*Wa-an-ti-še-en-ni* 7:32
  ^{I}*Wa-an-ti-iš-še-en-ni* 7:5, field neighbor of Enna-mati s.Šar-teja
  ^{I}*Wa-an-ti-iš-še-en-ni* DUMU *Ḫa-ši-ip-til-la* 12:3, accepts ^{f}Ḫinzuri *ana aḫātūti*
  ^{I}*Wa-an-ti-iš-še-en-*⌜*ni*⌝ 12:8
  [^{I}*Wa-an-ti-iš-še-en-ni*] 12:11
  ^{I}*Wa-an-téš-še-ni* 13:10, gives 23 sheep and goats to his brother Uzzukaja
  ^{I}*Wa-an-t*[*i-iš-še-en-ni*] ^{5}DUMU *Ḫa-ši-ip-til-la* Kel 89522 + AO 6029:4-5, litigant
  ^{I}*Wa-an-ti-*[*iš-še*]*-en-ni* Kel 89522 + AO 6029:35
Warad-Marduk, scribe:
  NA_4 ÌR-^{d}AMAR.UTU DUB.SAR-*rù* 12:19
^{f}WAtila, d.Pui-tae, sister of ^{f}Uriš-elli:
  ^{MÍ}WA-*ti-la* 6:3

Zike:
NA$_4$ KIŠIB *Zi-gi be-e*[*l* A.ŠÀ?] BM 85266 + 85472:39
Zike h.Wištanzu:
^{MÍ}*Wi-iš-ta-an-zu* ^{5}*aš-ša*-«TA»-*a*[*t* $^{(I)}$]*Zi-ge* WHM 170489:4-5
Zikinta f.Eḫli-tešup:
IGI *Eḫ-li-te-šup* ^{15}DUMU *Zi-ki-in-ta* 8:14-15
^{I}*Eḫ-li-te-š*[*up* DUMU *Zi-ki-in-ta*] Kel 89522 + AO 6029:3
NA$_4$ ^{I}*Eḫ-li-te-šup* DUMU [*Zi-ki-in-ta*] Kel 89522 + AO 6029:42-43
Zikuja f.[ ]
[IGI DUM]U *Zi-ku-ja* 27:22
Zilija s.Ipša-ḫalu:
^{I}[*Zi*]-*li-ja* ^{3}DUMU *Ip-ša-ḫa-lu* BM 85311:4-5; BM 85355:3-4.8
Zi-i-li-ja ^{11}DUMU *Ip-ša-ḫa-lu* BM 85266 + 85472:10-11.18.20
Zilija f.Ḫaniu:
^{I}*Ḫa-ni-ú* [DUMU *Zi-li-j*]*a* 19:1-2
Zilija f.Šalap-urḫe:
IGI ^{I}*Ša-la-ap-ur-ḫé* DUMU *Zi-li-ja* 7:27
Zil-te:
NA$_4$ KIŠIB ^{I}*Zi-il-te* HM 8400 = EN 9,122:41, witness
Zil-tešup s.Tarmija:
IGI *Zi-il-te-šup* DUMU *Tar-mi-ja* 15:22
NA$_4$ KIŠIB ^{I}*Zi-il-te-šup* DUMU *Tar-mi-ja* 15:36
Zimpar f.En-šukru:
IGI *En-šúk-ru* DUMU ⸢*Zi*⸣-*im-bar* 15:33 (restore JEN 235:19 accordingly)
Zinija s.Bēl-iddina, scribe:
IGI *Zi-ni-ja* DUMU *Be-el*-MA.AN.SUM DUB.SAR BM 85311:25
[IGI *Zi-ni*]-*ja* DUMU *Be-el*-MA.AN.SUM [DU]B.SAR BM 85355:24
Zirri f.Muš-tešup:
NA$_4$ ^{I}*Mu-uš-te-šup* DUMU *Zi-ir-ri* 16:18, witness
Zuzuja s.Iriki:
IGI *Zu-zu-ja* DUMU *I-ri-ki* BM 85311:18; BM 85355:17

]x-*el-te-šup* HM 8400 = EN 9,122:34 (presumably patronymic of a witness)
]-⸢*na-a+a*⸣ DUB.[SAR] 17:35
]-*na-a+a* 27:17 (patronymic of a witness)
-*n*]*i-ja* DUMU *Še-kar-rù* Kel 89383:8, witness
^{M}[^{Í} *š*]*e*-⸢*en-na*⸣-*a+a* 9:26
]-*te* DUMU *A-ki-ja* Kel 89393:3, witness
-*t*]*e-šup-ma* 27:3
]*x-tu*$_4$ *ḫa-bi-ru* Kel 89393:9, witness

INDEX OF GEOGRAPHICAL NAMES

INDEX OF PROFESSIONS AND TITLES

INDEX OF MONTH NAMES AND FESTIVALS: